Getting the Story

An Advanced Reporting Guide to Beats, Records and Sources

About the Authors

Henry H. Schulte is a former editor with the *St. Petersburg Times* in Florida, *The Louisville Times* in Kentucky, *The Nashville Tennessean* and *The Chicago Daily News*. He directed the Kiplinger Program in Public Affairs Reporting at The Ohio State University, a midcareer program for professional journalists. He was also the first Frank E. Gannett Professor at Marshall University, and taught the senior semester at the University of South Carolina. He wrote the journalism textbook *Reporting Public Affairs* (Macmillan, 1981), and teaches professional workshops at the University of South Carolina since retiring from OSU as a tenured faculty member.

Marcel P. Dufresne is an assistant professor of journalism at the University of Connecticut. He is a former reporter and editor for *The Day* in New London, Conn., and *The Narragansett Times* in Rhode Island, where he covered environmental affairs, science, medicine and the defense industry. In 1986, he won first place in enterprise reporting from the New England Associated Press Managing Editors Association for an investigation of defense contractors. He earned a master's degree in journalism from the Kiplinger Program at The Ohio State University, and writes for *Columbia Journalism Review* and *American Journalism Review*.

HENRY H. SCHULTE • MARCEL P. DUFRESNE

Getting the Story

An Advanced Reporting Guide to Beats, Records and Sources

Macmillan College Publishing Company
New York

Maxwell Macmillan Canada
Toronto

Maxwell Macmillan International
New York   Oxford   Singapore   Sydney

Editor: Kevin M. Davis
Production Editor: Colleen Brosnan
Art Coordinator: Peter A. Robison
Cover Designer: Robert Vega
Production Buyer: Patricia A. Tonneman
Electronic Text Management: Matthew Williams,
    Marilyn Wilson Phelps
Illustrations: Jessel Design Company

This book was set in Bitstream Dutch 801 and Swiss 721 by
Macmillan College Publishing Company and was printed and
bound by R. R. Donnelley & Sons Company. The cover was
printed by Phoenix Color Corp.

MacMillan Publishing Company
160 Gould Street,
Needham Heights, MA 02194-2310.

Library of Congress Cataloging-in-Publication Data
Schulte, Henry H.
    Getting the story : an advanced reporting guide to beats,
records, and sources / Henry H. Schulte, Marcel P. Dufresne.
        p.   cm.
    Includes bibliographical references and index.
    ISBN 0-02-408042-X : $26.25
    1. Reporters and reporting.   I. Dufresne, Marcel P.
II. Title.
PN4781.S387   1994
070.4'3—dc20   93-30543
                                               CIP

Printing: 2 3 4 5 6 7 8 9   Year: 4 5 6 7

About the Book

In selecting a title for this text, the authors considered no fewer than a dozen alternatives. Several possible titles included the phrase "public affairs reporting" or a variation, but each version seemed overused, dating back to *Public Affairs Reporting* by Victor J. Danilov, published in 1955.

But journalism teachers and students should make no mistake about this book's intent and focus. *Getting the Story: An Advanced Reporting Guide to Beats, Records and Sources* is about reporting in all its modern forms, and its goal is to teach young reporters what the title suggests: how to find and present news about issues and events important to the public.

This textbook grew from the authors' long involvement as journalists and journalism teachers and their belief that of all journalistic pursuits, public affairs reporting plays a crucial role in helping a democratic nation to govern itself.

As never before, the news media needs reporters who understand how public and private institutions work, who can identify and report news of public import so citizens can make sense of their communities and their lives.

Old challenges remain as new ones emerge. Increasingly, quasi-public special district governments veil the public's business in secrecy, while public relations practitioners and "spin doctors" try to shape news on every beat. The reporter's job has never been more difficult, nor more important.

With this in mind, the authors have tried to remain faithful to time-honored reporting beats and traditions, while exploring the changing nature of news and innovative tools such as computer-assisted reporting that will take public affairs reporting into the 21st century.

General college courses can teach the theories and current issues in business, politics, sociology and other fields, but journalism courses teach students *how* to report on these subjects. It is with this purpose that *Getting the Story* was conceived—to present a practical handbook for covering the various forms of government and private sector institutions that shape and define public issues. The text is designed as a guide for the advanced journalism student as well as a handbook for the young professional. Throughout, the goal is to provide an understanding of public affairs beats, along with detailed advice for "getting the story."

Although the authors devote considerable attention to explaining the operations of government and private institutions, the primary emphasis is teaching students how to successfully navigate through these organizations. Students will learn how reporters become part of the scene; how they identify important issues and key players on each beat; and how they develop story ideas and reliable sources, locate public records, follow up on breaking stories, and localize national ones.

This book emphasizes the traditional legwork necessary to produce solid news reports, along with the need to explain those stories to readers and viewers in clear, understandable language.

Part One, *The Reporter at Work*, sets the stage, providing a detailed review of new and traditional reporting skills, including beat coverage, interviewing, observation and public records research. Considerable attention is given to modern reporting techniques such as on-line database research, polling and journalism's most exciting frontier, computer-assisted reporting.

Parts Two through Four provide background and explanation about key institutions and organizations across the spectrum of public affairs. Each chapter presents a practical strategy for covering a specific public affairs beat, from local and state governments, police and the courts, to specialized areas such as politics, business and the workplace, education, the environment, science and medicine. The dynamics of each beat are examined: who holds power, how they exercise it, and how they interact with the press, the public, special interest groups and other government agencies. Pitfalls, obstacles and special problems reporters face on these beats are discussed, and important public records are identified.

Part Five explores the relationships between reporters and their frequent sources—politicians, government officials, public relations professionals and private citizens. How a reporter handles these complex relationships often determines whether he or she will get the "real" story. Problems of manipulation, favoritism and invasion of privacy are discussed, with practical guidelines for the student.

A word about the composition of the book: The authors have written brief news story extracts, based on information culled from many sources, to advance the student's knowledge of issues and develop familiarity with documents and other sources.

News leads and other story examples are based on information from stories in newspapers around the United States, their supplemental news services, and wire services such as the Associated Press and United Press International. Information was also taken from news releases, actual budgets and other pertinent documents. The authors acknowledge the assistance of all these sources in helping students understand the complexities of public affairs reporting.

Such an ambitious undertaking could not have been completed without the assistance of many people who deserve our thanks—dozens of journalists and teachers who have been generous with valuable advice and information: in particular, journalism faculty at the University of Connecticut for their counsel and support, and reporters and editors at *The Hartford Courant; Newsday;* The Atlanta *Journal and Constitution; The Miami Herald; The Day* in New London, Conn.; *The State* in Columbia, S.C.; and *The Beaufort* (S.C.) *Gazette*.

Illustrations and photographs came from many sources, too numerous to mention. But we are particularly indebted to the photography departments at *The Hartford Courant* and *The Day* for providing us with excellent photographs on a tight deadline; in particular, Photo Editor John Long of the *Courant*, and Assistant Managing Editor Harold Hanka and photographers Andrea Hoy and William Burrows of *The Day*.

The authors also would like to thank our editors at Macmillan—Kevin Davis, Colleen Brosnan and art director Peter Robison—for their help throughout the process; copy editor Key Metts, for her careful scrutiny of the manuscript and many helpful suggestions; and graphic artist A.J. Greenwood, whose newspaper-style graphics illustrate much of this book.

Thanks also are due to the following reviewers for their helpful comments: William E. Coté, Michigan

State University; Wallace B. Eberhard, University of Georgia; Jan Johnson Elliott, University of North Carolina–Chapel Hill; James W. Johnson, University of Arizona; Marion Lewenstein, Stanford University; and Roger Simpson, University of Washington.

And finally, our deepest gratitude is reserved for our spouses, Esther Lou Schulte and Bethe Dufresne, who edited and critiqued each chapter, listened patiently to our frustrations, and offered support and encouragement when we needed it most.

Contents

Chapter 14   Politics and the Reporter   279

Chapter 15   Business and Consumerism   300

Chapter 16   Covering the Work Force   332

Contents

Part One

The Reporter at Work

Chapter 1

The Changing Face of News

The laws of the United States give reporters no special powers or privileges not enjoyed by any private citizen. Yet as a practical matter, reporters venture where the public cannot or will not go and ask questions that the public cannot or will not ask. The public affairs reporter, in particular, is asked to dig deeper.

Few people want to spend their free time sitting through long and tedious city council meetings, much less sifting through voluminous records that might point to broken promises, undue influence or disturbing trends. Few people have the opportunity to directly question candidates for public office about their political platform, or the time and training to separate real progress from slick public relations efforts after the election. Yet the public wants accountability from those in public service and private enterprise who exercise control over their lives.

The victim of an armed assault meets with journalists after his release from the hospital. Dramatic breaking stories remain a staple of daily reporting.
Photo by Andrea Hoy, courtesy of The Day, New London, Conn.

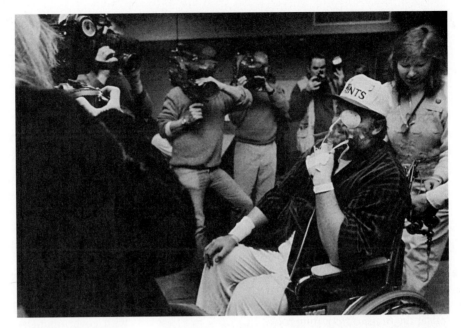

Most journalists view themselves as the public's representatives, guardians of the public interest, with the right and responsibility to report on events of consequence. But representing the public is only one of the roles public affairs reporters perform.

At times they serve as **watchdogs**, digging out abuses of power and evidence of incompetence, error and outright wrongdoing by those who serve the public. Many see their role as **ombudsmen**, assisting citizens in communicating with their government and powerful institutions. The most skilled among them may serve as **critics**, offering an independent assessment of government performance and, when necessary, dissecting official explanations. Always, they provide a **forum** for ongoing debate of public issues.

The broad freedoms enjoyed by the news media to report, investigate and comment on public issues stem from the belief that citizens in a democracy need accurate, timely and detailed information to make informed decisions about matters that affect them. Today's public affairs reporter continues to cover what some still call "hard" news, providing balanced and accurate accounts of breaking news events. The event can be a murder trial or a labor strike, the opening of school or the recall of a dangerous product. But the reporter who moves from one breaking story to the next, never digging deeper into causes and effects, never looking back to assess the effect of those stories on people's lives, neglects other significant functions that are part of the job.

Modern life continually confounds and confuses. Big-city crime has invaded the suburbs. Public schools graduate students who cannot read and write. Environmental dangers seem to lurk around every corner. Institutions created to serve and protect the public appear ineffectual or corrupt. Yet while society's problems often seem infinite and insurmountable, citizens continue asking questions that they hope will lead to answers. At its best, public affairs reporting not only informs and educates, angers and inspires, but also leads to positive change.

It is a critical, demanding and sometimes daunting responsibility that continually challenges the skills, perseverance and ingenuity of today's public affairs reporter.

CONTINUING CHANGES IN PUBLIC AFFAIRS REPORTING

Since the first beat reporters began covering police departments, courts and city halls more than 150 years ago, journalism has undergone a continual process of change and re-examination.

Technological changes have transformed the news industry. Reporters who once pounded out stories on noisy manual typewriters now tap softly on the keys of computer terminals. News stories, and even newspapers themselves, are transmitted by satellite. Newsroom computers can store and analyze vast amounts of information. Writing styles have changed; reporting beats have come and gone. Even the definition of news has expanded to reflect a broader range of issues and viewpoints.

In *The American Journalist: Paradox of the Press*, newspaper publisher Loren Ghiglione described eight broad categories of reporters involved in public events throughout U.S. history: street reporter, persuader, crusader, investigator, exploiter, entertainer, war correspondent and broadcast journalist. Yet Ghiglione acknowledges that even those categories do not fully reflect the range of reporting roles.

"The American journalist works in many different worlds and performs a multitude of functions," Ghiglione wrote. "There remains, however, one constant. The American journalist continues to enlarge the definition of news."

In each era journalists have been presented with new issues and problems, and they have responded to these new challenges in a variety of ways. When old approaches to reporting seemed inadequate to satisfy the needs of society, journalists stretched the boundaries of traditional beats, experimented with new ways of reporting and writing, expanded their network of sources, and re-examined their concept of news.

In its narrowest sense, public affairs reporting is "government" reporting, news coverage that focuses on the actions, policies and pronouncements that emerge from key officials and public agencies. This view evolved from a handful of traditional reporting beats that sprang up more than a century and a half ago, when big-city newspaper editors discovered that they could produce a steady stream of timely, often dramatic news stories by assigning reporters to city halls, police precincts and courthouses.

Today, the reporter on the beat still plays an integral part in the daily flow of news, making rounds in small towns and state capitals, interviewing public offi-cials and people on the street, gathering timely information, and writing stories on deadline.

And while city council meetings, political disputes, crimes and sensational trials remain staples of daily journalism, public affairs reporters must now look beyond old formulas and familiar sources to meet the growing challenges of their beats.

Looking Beyond Government

Leading journalists and media critics long ago recognized the need to expand public affairs reporting beyond narrow coverage of breaking news events and government actions to incorporate a fuller range of issues and institutions that interest and affect the public.

Reporting now covers diverse segments of the private sector, such as business and the workplace, industry, medicine and education, that intersect frequently with government and play an integral role in public issues. Often these interests derive much of their financial base from public money, through grants, tax breaks and government contracts.

Even at the local level, the public and private sectors are intertwined in ways that require reporters to look beyond mere actions to examine causes and effects.

The mortgage loan policies of local banks become newsworthy when they discriminate against members of minority groups or single mothers. The quality of a construction company's work is a public issue when the roof of a new school it built leaks or the roads it paved crumble. A manufacturing firm's production methods are the public's business when the company stores dangerous materials near residential areas or emits toxic fumes into the air. Each of these stories requires the reporter's attention.

New Beats, New Viewpoints

Today's news media cast an ever-widening net over such specialized topics as health risks, environmental dangers, business practices and family issues, partly because the public is interested in them, and partly because each affects the public interest. From the public's standpoint, the most visible recent changes in

---

BOX 1–1

S&L Scandal Hits Home

✳ ✳ ✳

This story about the federal government's savings and loan bailout in the late 1980s illustrates how the relations between government and private institutions often affect the public.

ARLINGTON, Texas (AP)—Jean Shoults was careful to pick a stable neighborhood with solid home values when she moved here two years ago. But a government decision to sell savings and loan properties in her neighborhood to a developer of low-cost tract homes may reduce the value of her house by 25 percent.

She's not alone. Across the country, more people are finding they, too, are being affected by the savings and loan crisis. Small businesses can't find loans. Subcontractors get stiffed on payments. Real estate markets are in ruins, and neighborhoods are tied up in government red tape.

For years, the $500 billion crisis had little effect on millions of Americans because federal deposit insurance protected their bank accounts. Now, changes made by Congress and regulators, plus a restructuring of the industry, are contributing to a credit crunch and possibly helping push a sluggish U.S. economy closer to recession, economists say. All this before the tax bite, estimated at almost $20 per family each month over the next 30 years to finance the government bailout.

---

news coverage have been the trend toward specialized reporting and increased attention to ethnic and cultural differences.

New beats and shifts in news coverage have often been a response to social, economic or technological changes in society. In the 1960s, the growth of federal and state social programs fostered a "social services" beat at many newspapers. Prison unrest led to creation of a corrections beat at some newspapers, while the deplorable condition of state mental hospitals brought an increase in mental health reporting. The emergence of the women's and civil rights movements as important political forces brought increased coverage of abortion laws, child care, discrimination in employment and housing, and other legal and social issues.

In the 1970s, the energy crisis and a growing consumer movement gave rise to reporting on business and industry, particularly the government's regulation of large public utilities such as power companies. Awareness of environmental problems sparked aggressive coverage of government's progress in controlling and correcting widespread pollution. A robust economy during most of the 1980s, fueled by booms in real estate and the stock market, resulted in expanded business coverage.

In recent years, the news media have re-examined their coverage of racial minorities, women, gays and people with disabilities to better reflect the great diversity in cultures, lifestyles and concerns in American society. The increased sensitivity to ethnic and other differences has altered reporting methods and writing styles in many newsrooms and expanded the range of issues being covered.

Among the criticisms often leveled against the press are negative stereotyping, ignorance of cultural differences, use of biased or insensitive language, a double standard in covering women and minority politicians, and failure to interview and photograph members of minorities. David Shaw, media critic for the *Los Angeles Times*, described how the news media's depiction of blacks and Latinos does not always jibe with reality:

If all one knew about real-life blacks and Latinos in particular was what one read in the newspaper or saw on television news . . . one would scarcely be aware that there is a large and growing middle class in both cultures, going to work, getting married, having children, paying taxes, going on vacation and buying books and VCRs and microwave ovens.

Only 15 percent of the poor people in the United States are black, but one would not know that from most press coverage. Nor would one know that most violent criminals, drug users, prostitutes, drunks, illiterates, high school dropouts, juvenile delinquents, jobless and poor people in this country are neither black nor Latino but white. Or that the vast majority of blacks and Latinos are none of the above.

Faced with such criticism—and declining readership—many newspapers have tried to more accurately report on diverse segments of the population and to supply them with useful, relevant information. Increasingly, journalists attempt to cover everyday life and concerns in black, Hispanic and Asian-American communities, to emphasize women's and gay issues, and to depict people with disabilities as competent, functioning citizens. Many newsrooms now give more prominence to stories about racial and sexual discrimination, health and economic concerns, and legislation and court decisions affecting minorities, women and other groups (see Figure 1–1).

Reporters and editors are more apt to recognize harmful stereotypes and make writing and editing choices that enhance tolerance and understanding of different races, lifestyles and cultures. Racial identifications in crime stories, once commonplace, are increasingly rare. Now, many editors insist that reporters expand their source lists to include the views of bankers, lawyers, doctors and other professionals of color in their stories.

In short, the daily flow of news is beginning to reflect a changing and increasingly diverse society.

LIMITATIONS OF TRADITIONAL NEWS GATHERING

The creation of new beats and realignment of old ones cannot by themselves satisfy society's changing information needs. Reporters who apply an outmoded definition of news simply perpetuate the common assumptions and reporting approaches rooted in the old police and city hall beats. Reporters too closely linked to a government body—whether it is a police department, an environmental agency or a public utilities commission—tend to rely on meetings, votes and policy statements as their primary sources of news. To be sure, more enterprising reporters seek information from nongovernment sources, but the agencies and officials themselves often remain the chief focus

FIGURE 1–1
The number of minorities working on the staffs of U.S. daily newspapers has continued to rise since the 1970s, but has remained well below the percentage of minorities in the total population. Recruiting and training minorities for journalism careers is one attempt to diversify the content of news reports and broadcasts.
Sources: American Society of Newspaper Editors and U.S. Census Bureau. Adapted from *Washington Journalism Review*, July/August 1992, p. 41. Reprinted with permission of American Journalism Review (formerly Washington Journalism Review), College Park, MD.

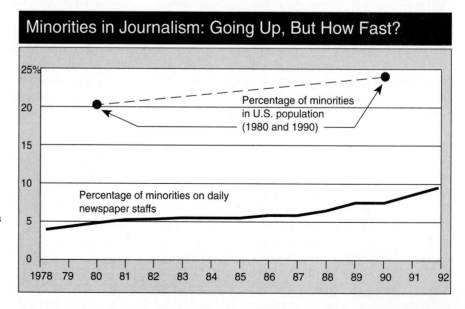

A reporter interviews the mayor in his office. Officials still provide much of a reporter's material, but interviews with nonofficial sources are needed to produce more complete stories.
Photo by Michael Kodas, courtesy of The Hartford Courant.

of coverage. This approach sometimes limits the reporter's ability to explain events in meaningful ways and makes the news vulnerable to manipulation by media-savvy officials and other newsmakers.

Early in their training, journalism students are presented with a list of values, such as timeliness, effect, proximity, conflict, prominence and uniqueness, that make something "newsworthy." Reporters are taught to be neutral, unbiased, objective. Such values are still valuable in helping young reporters develop news judgment and avoid partisan, one-sided reporting. However, application of these values can create a rigid view of reporting that is event-oriented and ignores causes and effects.

News from the Top

Too often public affairs reporting relies on official viewpoints in deciding what is news. A president, governor or police chief can create news by scheduling a press conference, issuing a news release or staging a media event. The simple identity of its source makes it newsworthy in many newsrooms. Newsmakers are thus able to set the news media's agenda, deciding what issues are worthy of coverage and often shaping a story's central theme.

Experienced reporters know these official pronouncements can be distorted, manipulative and self-serving, and they look for nonofficial, nongovernment sources against which to check official statements and versions of events.

During the Vietnam War, Associated Press reporter Seymour Hersh walked out of an unproductive Pentagon briefing, startling fellow correspondents. Hersh doubted the truth of many of the Pentagon's claims about the war and often used unofficial but credible sources to uncover important stories, including the 1968 My Lai massacre in which more than 300 Vietnamese civilians, including women and children, were murdered by U.S. troops.

The reporter whose information comes only from the top will be handcuffed into presenting only the official version. The reporter who examines issues from many viewpoints, who gathers information from many sources, stands a better chance of getting at the truth.

Consider the example of a police department's annual report showing a drop in crime in one of the city's problem neighborhoods. A police official tells a reporter that the department has received fewer calls for help in the past year and that the number of reported crimes and arrests in the neighborhood has declined. On the surface, this information, coming as it does from an official source, sounds legitimate. But a reporter may get a very different picture by visiting the neighborhood.

Residents may tell the reporter that the level of crime is higher than ever, that the reason they don't report it is that police response has been slow or nonexistent. Perhaps criminals are intimidating residents, who are afraid to report crimes. Arrests may be down because police don't follow up on crime reports or have cut patrols in those neighborhoods.

Any of these scenarios would explain the drop in crime statistics, but a reporter wouldn't get the whole story without looking beyond the official report.

On the other hand, further investigation may support the official version. Residents may praise the department's more visible presence in the neighborhood. They may express relief that the neighborhood is finally turning around. In this case, the additional sources make the story more reliable, and the residents' comments make for better reading.

Even when accurate, official versions by themselves often lack texture and dimension. If reporting is to examine and explain how news events and issues affect people's lives, reporters must venture into the world they write about—into the neighborhoods, schools, and business districts—to gather material that verifies, refutes or enlivens official versions of reality. Reporters must reach beyond officialdom and immerse themselves in their beats to get a more complete story.

The Myth of Objectivity

The ideal of objectivity in reporting, which one critic referred to as "the Eleventh Commandment for journalism's faithful," has been perhaps the most confining and yet resilient of all journalistic principles.

"Objective" reporting surfaced near the turn of the century in response to the era's highly partisan, personal style of reporting that more often resembled propaganda than what today is considered journalism. Wire services and news syndicates developed standardized newswriting styles to appeal to a broad range of clients. Waves of reporters were trained in "objectivity," to be simple conduits of information, to give equal weight to all viewpoints and let readers decide what to believe and trust. Such reporting, while valuable for eliminating overtly opinionated writing, often left out important background or the reporter's own knowledge that might illuminate or contradict what others said.

Although "objective" reporting came to dominate news reporting, it has been under almost continual assault from inside and outside the profession for half a century. Journalists and critics alike have seen how it often failed to get to the truth about public issues and problems, and thus failed to meet society's needs for information. And they saw how clever politicians and other newsmakers exploited its limitations.

The weaknesses of objective reporting were exposed in press coverage of the late U.S. Sen. Joseph McCarthy, who commanded intense press attention in the early 1950s with his accusations that the State Department had been infiltrated by Communists. From the start, McCarthy's position gave him credibility and access to news reporters. Some reporters became mere stenographers for McCarthy's charges, reporting them immediately without obtaining denials from people who were accused. Even after it became clear to journalists that McCarthy had little evidence for most of his charges, many reporters continued to report them.

McCarthy understood the competitive pressures on reporters to come up with dramatic new leads and to beat other reporters to a story. Wire services were particularly susceptible to his manipulation. One of his favorite ploys was to release information to wire service reporters on Friday, knowing his statements would get prominent play Sunday and Monday, both slow news days.

Edwin R. Bailey, a former journalism dean at the University of California, interviewed more than 40 journalists who had covered McCarthy and summarized the effect of that period on American journalism. "Newspaper people realized that it was not enough simply to tell what happened or what was said, but that they had to tell what it meant and whether or not it was true," Bailey wrote.

Newspapers and broadcast reports still use one-dimensional stories that quote this official or that, with little background or context. Faced with complex issues and conflicting ideas, some editors and reporters cling to objectivity like a life preserver, uneasy with the notion of interpretive journalism or ill-equipped to supply it.

But journalism also has learned from past mistakes. Today's news media contain numerous examples of detailed, in-depth and incisive reporting that exposes problems and offers solutions. This is not the partisan, subjective reporting of the past, but one that combines accuracy and fairness with exhaustive research that illuminates events and issues.

Many journalists now view objectivity as elusive, if not unattainable. Try as they might, reporters and editors cannot separate themselves from their feelings, cultural background, personal preferences and subconscious biases, all of which affect their choices about what to cover, who to quote and what information to use. A more realistic goal is fairness and balance, combined with a continuing commitment to reflect the broad range of opinions and concerns held by diverse segments of the population.

MODELS OF REPORTING

In the past, various models of reporting have been proposed that attempted to expand, refine or redefine the reporter's role. Journalists were urged to adapt to a complex, changing world to provide news consumers with more insightful and useful information.

More than a half-century ago, journalism educator Curtis D. MacDougall popularized the term *interpretative* reporting, an approach to news gathering that challenged reporters to push beyond stenographic reporting methods to present news that helped the public understand the meaning and effect of events. The 1960s and 1970s brought new or revitalized models: advocacy reporting, New Journalism, investigative reporting. Each found deficiencies with mainstream reporting, and each in turn attracted some measure of support and criticism within the profession.

To some, the notion of advocacy reporting—writing to advance a cause—ran counter to the role of an unbiased press and seemed like a return to the days before objectivity. New Journalism, which adopted writing devices usually associated with novels, was viewed with distrust by many editors who suspected some of it was as much fiction as fact. Even investigative reporting, with its venerable tradition of uncovering corruption and abuse, was accused of excesses in the post-Watergate era. Each left its imprint on news gathering methods and expanded, even if only for a brief period, the definition of public affairs reporting.

Today, educators and editors talk about *humanistic* reporting, which tries to make news meaningful to the public by showing how issues and events affect them, and about *explanatory* reporting, which re-examines

major news events to find out why and how they occurred.

The evolution of reporting models, both those in and out of vogue, reveals a common thread. Journalists are continually seeking, as Loren Ghiglione wrote, to enlarge the definition of news and, in the process, to improve on existing reporting methods.

Reporters will continue to cover "hard" news and significant events because their effect is immediately felt and they often signal deeper problems. A stock market crash in 1987 and widespread rioting in Los Angeles in 1992 both received saturation coverage. These dramatic events affected people across the nation. But in their aftermath, many journalists took their reporting to another level, evaluating the long-term effects of those events and examining the conditions that caused them to occur.

Call it interpretative, explanatory or in-depth reporting, serious journalists from the local government beat to the White House press corps strive to understand issues and events beyond a superficial level, so they can present them to the public in meaningful ways.

A REPORTER'S TRAINING

The ideals of modern reporting cannot be achieved by the novice who lacks skills, knowledge and experience.

The reporter who attempts to cover public affairs issues without proper preparation is like the athlete who neglects to train before a tryout with a professional team or the lawyer who attempts to try a case without reading the court file. All are likely to fail. In all professional endeavors—business, law, medicine, sports, the arts and journalism—preparation usually means the difference between success and failure.

The demands of both covering events and writing in-depth reports about those events require much of young reporters. They first must refine their basic skills to produce accurate stories on deadline about speeches, fires, meetings and other events. Only after the reporter has demonstrated maturity and mastery of skills is an editor likely to permit interpretative reporting.

BOX 1–2

What Makes Great Reporters?

✳✳✳

More than 40 years ago, the editors of a classic book called *A Treasury of Great Reporting* described the skills and abilities that have marked the best reporters throughout history.

> The reporter must have the ability to produce a rapid-fire story under conditions hardly ideal for creative writing. And to keep doing so. He must carry the burden of unrelenting and monotonous regularity, intensified by the pressure of meeting a deadline. His perceptive powers must be keyed to the fast and exciting pace he has to maintain.
>
> Like the scientist explorer, the critic of the arts, and the novelist, the great reporter must be able to see what is significant and distinctive about the event he is covering. . . . The reporter must be constantly on the alert to question, to challenge, to probe. His acute power of observation must be implemented by that X factor—the detective instinct. . . . The reporter must be prepared to take risks, to stay at his post of danger, and at times to operate on his last reserves of adrenaline.

While this description may overdramatize, and perhaps romanticize, the job of reporter, it describes the essential characteristics a reporter needs and the skills he or she must master.

Reporting is a craft that can be learned, but the student must bring to the task a combination of knowledge, curiosity, ingenuity and perseverance.

Students train for careers in journalism by taking journalism courses, working for college newspapers and radio stations, or stringing for local newspapers. But adequate preparation for a reporting job requires more. It is an accumulation of skills, knowledge and awareness that also can be amassed through other college courses, travel, extensive and varied reading, and life experiences. Most journalists have a college degree, and many have completed advanced degrees or graduate-level courses in fields such as economics, business, science or the environment.

In the past, students with strong liberal arts backgrounds were prized as reporters because of their broad education, their ability to write and communicate effectively, and their general knowledge of many disciplines such as economics, psychology, history, political science, literature and sociology. That has not changed. Such a foundation remains essential for covering today's complex issues and problems.

While some editors still tout the praises of majoring in English or political science, the most common route to an entry-level reporting job today is through a journalism degree. Most editors want graduates who can hit the ground running, who can cover a speech, a murder or a city council meeting, who can work quickly and accurately, and who don't have to be told the difference between attribution and verification.

Life experiences also contribute to a future reporter's maturity and understanding of the world. Students who volunteer at a soup kitchen or women's shelter can learn much about urban problems and family violence. The student who backpacks through the Rocky Mountains or helps clean up the local river banks will have a better appreciation of a clean environment.

Training can begin with college journalism courses, but it can't end there. The best preparation for journalism will continue to combine reporting, writing and editing skills with broad general knowledge in a range of fields.

Getting It Right

The quest for accuracy, the overriding compulsion to get things right, should guide every reporter's training.

Consider the student reporter who, while covering a speech, heard a vaguely familiar reference to the famed marble mausoleum built for the wife of an Indian shah. His story called one of the world's most beautiful buildings the "Tajama Hall." In one careless lapse, the reporter displayed both his ignorance and his complacency.

Another reporter wrote about a family that had been overcome by fumes from a chlorine gas leak, saying that the victims had been "fumigated." Still another turned euthanasia, the painless killing of someone who has an incurable disease, into "youth in Asia."

No student or professional journalist can know everything. Understanding that is part of being an educated person. Journalists take that understanding one step further, sensing when something is incorrect and finding the right answer.

A reporter should have a thorough knowledge of printed and electronic information sources and know where to find important indexes, reference books and specialized periodicals that can deliver background, explanations and technical information quickly.

Understanding the System

A familiarity with the workings of government—what high schools once taught as civics—is essential. Each level of government, from the U.S. Congress to the local zoning board of review, has unique functions, procedures and terminology. Reporters covering any beat should become familiar with these basic features before undertaking their first assignment.

The court reporter must know the difference between an arraignment and an acquittal, between an appeals court and a court of original jurisdiction, between "nolle prosequi" and "nolo contendere." He or she cannot write "probation" when a convict is granted a "parole."

The city hall reporter must know what is required before a proposed city ordinance becomes law. Does it require a public hearing and referendum? If it proves unworkable or unpopular, how can citizens repeal it? Which public official is responsible for inspecting public buildings or prosecuting environmental violations? What public documents does each government agency

maintain, and what does the law say about gaining access to them?

These and other organizational questions must be answered by the journalism student as he or she prepares to enter the ranks of reporting.

Putting Theories to Work

Reporters must see the theories of government studied in political science and history classes as more than abstractions and must recognize how these theories are manifested in daily events.

The "system of checks and balances" described in political science textbooks becomes tomorrow's headline when the governor and state legislature reach a stalemate over next year's budget. The constitutional separation of church and state is driven home when a state court bans a Nativity scene from the city hall Christmas display. The power of legislative committees is demonstrated when special-interest lobbies have an important health care bill killed in committee. Each of the principles and purposes of government are played out daily, and a reporter must understand their roots before he or she can report on their effect. At the same time, reporters must be astute and informed enough to apply their theoretical understanding to real issues and real problems.

Knowledge of the important laws, social movements and political trends that shaped this country and the world is also necessary to report on today's public issues. No reporter can adequately cover the abortion controversy without knowing the political and social antecedents of the U.S. Supreme Court's Roe vs. Wade decision. Understanding the growth of suburbs after World War II and the subsequent "white flight" from American cities is critical to writing about urban problems. The reporter trying to explain today's environmental problems must know that a century of unregulated industrial growth in this country was followed by two decades of intense, and often ineffective, government regulation.

Journalism is a continual process of judgment and selection: deciding what stories to cover, what information to use, what sources to interview and what background to include. These and other decisions facing reporters cannot be made in a vacuum if their stories are to satisfy the public's need for informed, balanced journalism.

Reporters who combine these skills and knowledge with strong academic training, the ideals and ethics of journalism, and a voracious appetite for information about current events and issues should find themselves well-prepared for the challenges of public affairs reporting.

***

SUGGESTED READINGS

Downie, Leonard Jr. *The New Muckrakers: An Inside Look at America's Investigative Reporters*. Washington: New Republic Book Co., 1976.

Examines the work of prominent investigative reporters of the 1970s, including Woodward and Bernstein, Seymour Hersh, Jack Anderson, Donald Barlett and James Steele.

Dygert, James H. *The Investigative Journalist: Folk Heroes of a New Era*. Englewood Cliffs, N.J.: Prentice Hall, 1976.

Fry, Don. *Believing the News*. St. Petersburg, Fla.: The Poynter Institute for Media Studies, 1985.

Gans, Herbert J. *Deciding What's News*. New York: Pantheon Books, 1974.

A provocative and often-cited book that examines how news is made.

Hollowell, John. *Fact and Fiction: The New Journalism and the Nonfiction Novel*. Chapel Hill: University of North Carolina Press, 1977.

Examines the use of literary techniques in contemporary journalism.

Roshco, Bernard. *Newsmaking*. Chicago: University of Chicago Press, 1975.

Useful discussion of news definitions and the way society influences news content.

Schudson, Michael. *Discovering the News*. New York: Basic Books, 1978.

Sims, Norman. *Literary Journalism in the 20th Century*. New York: Oxford University Press, 1990.

An insightful collection of essays examining the roots and evolution of literary techniques in journalism.

Weber, Ronald. *The Literature of Fact*. Athens: Ohio University Press, 1980.

Analysis of the New Journalism.

Chapter 2

The Working Journalist

Movies, novels and television shows are filled with images of reporters at work:

- A reporter, hot on the trail of a story, thumbs through yellowed clippings in the newspaper's library until she finds the one that brings recent events into perspective.

- Reporters crowd around a man accused of murder, thrusting microphones into his face and shouting questions.

- With shells exploding overhead, a war correspondent gives a gripping radio account of what he has seen and heard.

- A lone reporter sits at a computer terminal in her newsroom library, searching a government database of public files for details that will nail down her investigation.

These distinct images—sometimes heroic, sometimes inspiring, sometimes unflattering—reflect the different methods reporters use to gather information. Whatever their assignment, reporters rely on background research, interviews, direct observation and document searches to collect information about people, events and issues. Mastering each of these skills is necessary to produce complete and insightful reporting, whether the assignment is local government, the state legislature or a specialized beat.

COVERING A BEAT

Local reporters and photographers cover the full spectrum of life, from the arrest of the man lying drunk in the gutter, to the mayor's speech at city hall, from the first baby born in town this year, to the Spanish-American War veteran who died in his sleep. These journalists create the images that people have of their communities and of themselves.

This brief, unglossed description of journalists who cover local news was penned in 1990 by newspaper publisher Loren Ghiglione to describe the street reporter of the past. Although the issues and concerns covered by local reporters continue to change, the notion that local news plays an important role in shaping people's view of their communities has not. Surveys done for newspapers and television news stations confirm what editors instinctively know: People want news about local issues, problems, personalities and institutions. This demand creates opportunities for budding journalists to practice and sharpen their reporting and writing skills.

No matter a reporter's ultimate goal—managing editor, foreign correspondent, arts critic—most still begin by covering local beats, reporting on school board meetings, the local planning and zoning commission, and perhaps the police department. These first assignments provide young reporters with an opportunity to apply what they have learned and to test their abilities. They learn to find and develop stories, work with different types of people, and write quickly and often. It is common for local reporters to write five or more stories from their beat each day.

Beginning reporters are usually assigned to cover a single community, sometimes two or three at smaller newspapers. These reporters are responsible for everything from the council to the school board, from police news to business developments. If they perform well, they move to a larger beat and may be given greater latitude in what to cover and how to write their stories.

Reporters at many papers have responsibilities that span several related beats. The environmental reporter also may cover health and local hospitals. The police reporter may double on courts. At the same time, reporters frequently cross traditional beat lines in pursuit of a story. A court reporter researching how child abuse cases are prosecuted may interview police officers, social workers and psychiatrists. A police reporter writing about a truck accident that spilled dangerous chemicals near a reservoir will contact health and environmental officials, the water department and the fire chief.

Local conditions often influence reporting assignments. The business desk in a coastal area may assign someone full time to report on tourism and its effect on businesses and local residents. Agriculture may be a priority in a rural area. Communities whose economic survival depends on one or two major employers, whether a defense plant or an automobile factory, may assign a full-time reporter. In a large city with a high crime rate, two or more reporters may cover police.

The stature that is sometimes bestowed on specialized beats fails to acknowledge that every good beat reporter is a specialist. The experienced court reporter is an expert in the judicial system, the city hall reporter is a government specialist, and the veteran police reporter is a student of law enforcement and human behavior. Each knows the subject thoroughly, has a network of reliable and trusted sources, and brings a wealth of historical and contemporary background to his or her work.

Getting Started

A reporter can learn a beat's history by reading clippings from the past few years in the newspaper's library. Many newspapers now file stories in their own electronic libraries, allowing for faster and more efficient background research on specific topics. The clips will identify major news stories and ongoing issues, as well as provide the reporter with names of high-profile officials and other newsmakers.

Reporters must understand the structure and powers of agencies they cover, and past stories may answer some important questions at the outset. Who sets policy and controls the purse strings? Who is authorized to speak for the organization? What political figures, lobbyists or business interests have access to policymakers and the power to influence decisions?

The clippings also may suggest possible follow-up stories. Perhaps a study was commissioned, or a new program started, that can be updated. A school superintendent who was hired a year ago might be worth an anniversary story. Such stories, if they have legitimate news value, can bring readers up to date and provide a cordial first encounter for the new reporter.

Several key documents can give reporters a quick overview of their beats. Organizational charts of government agencies, the courts and other institutions help reporters understand the functions and responsibilities of each, as well as where they fit in a hierarchy. For public agencies, annual budgets available from finance departments show spending levels, priorities and sources of revenue. Most public agencies are required to obtain independent audits that can help reporters assess their financial condition and accounting practices. These usually are public records.

Also available are annual reports produced by police departments, municipal governments and quasi-public institutions such as hospitals and social agencies. Annual reports identify key individuals and supply important details about programs and goals.

Meetings of boards and agencies—from zoning commissions to legislative committees—are a staple of beat reporting and often provide the reporter's introduction to the beat. Important issues are discussed, votes taken and controversies aired. Reporters who are knowledgeable about their beats usually can find several good stories from a meeting. In addition, an alert reporter will hear things that may not make an immediate story but can be developed later. Public meetings are often a sounding board for people's problems and concerns, and a magnet for diverse segments of the population.

Monitoring the Beat

On most beats, the primary assignment is the same—to learn about and report every breaking news story of significance. As time allows, beat reporters also are expected to produce features, in-depth articles, investigative pieces and enterprise stories developed outside the flow of daily events.

Reporters must open lines of communication with people across the spectrum. Regular contact with top officials is essential, but reporters also should seek out and cultivate secretaries, business and civic leaders, grass-roots activists and private citizens whose activities place them in the current of public issues. Whether the assignment is a police department, a judicial district, a state agency or a municipal government, reporters need sources whom they trust and who trust them, people who will alert them to possible stories and provide background that can help guide news decisions.

New beat reporters should visit key agencies and introduce themselves to everyone from top administrators to secretaries and clerks. Each is a potential news source, and periodic visits for informal conversations

---

BOX 2–1

Preparing for a Beat

✳ ✳ ✳

- Review past news clippings.
- Identify important issues and newsmakers.
- Study organizational chart of key agencies.
- Review recent budget and audit reports.
- Examine annual reports.
- Create telephone list of key officials, interest groups.
- Visit key agencies, officials and spokespersons.
- Develop contacts across the beat.

can establish trust and respect on both sides. Reporters who show up at the police station or city hall only when a big story breaks risk getting a minimum of cooperation from busy officials. Those who are well-known and respected may get more information—and a better story.

Developing informal sources across the beat is one way to be sure important stories won't be missed. Some reporters make a habit of stopping by places where gossip is exchanged or politics discussed, such as barbershops, employee cafeterias, taverns and local diners. Being recognized in these informal settings can establish trust with citizens or government employees who are well-informed.

Follow-Ups and Local Angles

An important facet of beat reporting is following up on important stories days, weeks, or even months after they first break. Reporters should keep an ongoing list, which they revise frequently, of stories that need to be checked and those that need updating.

Reporters also take stories of national and regional importance and develop local angles. When an aspirin manufacturer has to recall millions of packages, reporters around the country find out how the recall is being implemented locally and what steps are being taken to protect consumers. When the Supreme Court hands down a controversial decision on the rights of arrested suspects, reporters call defense attorneys, prosecutors and law enforcement officials for their reactions.

The range of stories that can be given a local angle is limited only by a reporter's ingenuity. While the local angle sometimes can be taken to almost comic extremes—"Local School Children Worried About Global Warming"—such stories can hold a mirror up to a community and tell residents how national events are being felt locally.

Specific beats, including coverage areas, sources and story ideas, are discussed in Chapters 4 through 18.

USING PUBLIC RECORDS

Young reporters often concentrate their reporting efforts on interviews and events coverage and often are surprised at the range and depth of information available from public records. Even experienced reporters do not take full advantage of the wealth of detail and documentation available from documents.

Every branch of government—every federal, state and local agency—keeps extensive records of both routine and significant activities. Many of these records are public and can supply reporters with background and documentation that cannot always be obtained through interviews and first-hand observation. Government agencies also accumulate extensive files on people, private organizations and businesses with whom they deal. These records, too, are valuable in news gathering.

The Value of Records

Public documents are used in daily reporting, for in-depth stories and frequently during investigative projects. On beats where many stories may be breaking simultaneously, public records help reporters gather information quickly and efficiently. Court reporters, for example, can't personally cover the multitude of trials, arraignments and motions that pass through a courthouse each day. They rely on court records to learn what new cases have been filed and how a particular criminal case or civil lawsuit is progressing through the judicial system.

Records also allow reporters to report on events that might have escaped public attention when they occurred. Alerted to the possibility of a conflict of interest, a reporter reviewing the month-old transcript of a zoning hearing might discover that a board member voted to grant a variance to a business in which his brother has a financial interest.

Reporters often use public documents to verify tips and popular perceptions and to unearth little-known facts that cast even seemingly routine news events in a new light. Consider these examples of how public records can be used in daily reporting:

- A school system facing serious budget problems is considering laying off teachers and cutting extra-curricular activities. Parents and teachers complain that the administration is top-heavy and overpaid, but offer no evidence. By examining records at the finance department, a reporter documents that several new administrative positions have been created in recent years and that the superintendent and assistants have received substantial raises each year.

- A reporter is told that a man arrested on a rape charge has several convictions for rape. By checking court records in several counties, the reporter is able to obtain specifics.

- The county announces plans to buy a vacant building and convert it to office space. The reporter researches property transfers at the county clerk's office and discovers that the building has recently changed hands several times, being sold back and forth between two companies. Each time the sale price increased from the previous transaction. Corporation filings at the secretary of state's office show that the two companies have some of the same officers, one of them a relative of the official who negotiated the building purchase. The reporter's story discloses the connection and shows how the

owners artificially inflated the building's market value to reap a hefty profit.

In each case, an examination of public documents strengthened the reporter's story and brought to light information of obvious public interest.

Sources Point the Way

The key to using public records is knowing what is available and who has it. As in other areas of reporting, trusted sources can point the way, helping reporters find documents and alerting them to little-known ones.

A city manager quietly asks the finance department to review expense accounts for department heads to detect possible abuse. Two weeks later, a clerk mentions the review to a reporter off the record, adding that several officials have been reprimanded as a result. The reporter requests and gets a copy of the

A reporter pores over real estate records in the City Hall documents room. Public records are an essential source of documentary information on every public affairs beat.
Photo by Andrea Hoy.

report and writes a story, also interviewing the manager and the employees who were reprimanded.

Sources also can help reporters understand and interpret technical documents. A wildlife biologist may be able to explain an environmental impact statement that shows why a proposed highway project will destroy animal habitats. A cooperative accountant can help a reporter sort through financial data and prevent errors that could damage a story's credibility.

Many reports and records that would make good stories never become public because no one asks to see them. State auditors, for example, frequently review irregularities and inefficiency throughout state government, yet these reports may not be officially released to the press. State auditors will usually tell reporters who ask about them and provide a copy.

Types of Records

Reporters on all beats must be familiar with the kinds of documents kept by public agencies they cover and know how to gain access to them. Public records commonly used by reporters include:

- **Minutes and transcripts.** These are written or taped records of public meetings, hearings, court cases and other official proceedings. Minutes usually contain key votes and a summary of matters discussed. Transcripts are a verbatim record of everything that was said during the public portion of a proceeding.

- **Property records.** County and municipal governments keep extensive files showing transfers of property and the ownership history of each house, building and land parcel within its boundaries. These records usually provide a description of the property and may contain details about selling price, mortgages, liens, assessed values and tax payments.

- **Incorporation papers.** In most states, companies that become corporate entities must file the names of officers, their holdings and a statement of the company's purpose.

- **Court files.** Unless specifically sealed by a judge, most criminal and civil court records are public. Criminal case files detail indictments, arraignments,

plea bargains, motions, rulings, verdicts and appeals. Civil case files provide details about lawsuits, injunctions, liens and judgments. A wealth of financial information about individuals and businesses is available from bankruptcy files.

- **Financial records.** For public agencies, these can range from annual budgets and audit reports to expense accounts, travel vouchers, purchase orders, bid proposals and contracts involving public agencies and officials.

- **Police files.** Records of routine calls, arrests, traffic violations and motor vehicle accidents are commonly available to reporters the same day. Investigation files, however, are usually not made public until a case is closed. In most states, police departments and other law enforcement agencies have wide latitude in deciding what records will be made public.

- **Personal information.** Records are available about births, deaths, marriages, divorces, military discharges, driving records, bankruptcies and wills. These can be pieced together from the files of several agencies, such as municipal clerks, motor vehicle departments and probate courts.

- **Campaign contributions and financial disclosure statements.** In most states and counties, candidates for local, state and federal office must file reports listing contributors to their campaign by name and amount, and separate expenditure statements showing how the money was used. Many states require top elected and appointed officials— and members of their immediate family—to disclose their income sources and personal assets, including interest in real estate, stocks and bonds.

- **Licenses, permits and inspection reports.** People obtain licenses and permits to sell liquor, erect buildings, operate restaurants and to provide professional services in law, medicine, building trades and other fields. Licensing agencies keep records of complaints, violations, investigations, fines and disciplinary actions.

Specific public records that reporters use on various beats are discussed in Chapters 3 through 18.

Requesting Public Records

Some records are routinely available. Clerks and other records custodians who often deal with reporters generally know what is public and what isn't and make files available as soon as is practical. Property records and court files, for example, are easily obtained by reporters. In some police departments, police dispatchers may hand familiar reporters the daily log or a stack of arrest reports.

Sensitive or controversial material whose public nature is not so clearly defined may be more difficult to obtain. Department heads or top officials may insist on personally releasing all such material.

Agencies that funnel information through a few sources pose a problem for reporters who need the information for a deadline. Reporters should explain their specific needs to the department head and ask that the agency designate someone on duty to release material that is clearly a public document. When informal channels fail, the alternative is usually to file a written request under the appropriate open records law.

The federal Freedom of Information Act (FOIA) gives reporters access to a huge volume of information from the files of federal agencies. The law establishes categories of exceptions and, in theory at least, all other information must be made public. Most states have a statutory equivalent of the federal FOIA law, and like the federal law, these usually presume that government records and meetings of government bodies should be open to the public unless specifically exempted. However, the degree of public access varies greatly among states. Reporters should become familiar with laws in their states.

Federal and state Freedom of Information laws, categories of exempt records and appeal procedures are discussed in Chapter 19.

Proceed with Caution

Reporters should observe a few precautions as they use public records. First, data gathered from reports can make for dry reading if it is presented without context and other detail. People close to a story can often be interviewed to elaborate on information or react to it.

Reporters also should be alert to factual errors that sometimes turn up in public records and should check information that is suspected of being wrong or incomplete. Inaccuracies can range from misspelled names and incorrect ages to more serious errors that can falsely indict news subjects.

It is especially critical to confirm information that accuses someone of improper or illegal activity and to get the person's response. The city tax rolls may show that Councilman Jones hasn't paid property taxes in several years, but there might be another explanation why his name is still among delinquent taxpayers. It may be the result of a clerical error, or there may be several city residents with the same name. A reporter who confirmed the information with the tax collector might avoid an embarrassing and possibly libelous mistake.

Information taken from public records is usually granted qualified privilege in libel actions, meaning that even if the information is incorrect, reporters are protected if they copied it accurately from the document. However, that protection tends to be applied to deadline situations. Juries look less kindly on reporters who have plenty of time to check damaging material for accuracy but fail to do so.

DIRECT OBSERVATION

Whenever possible, reporters try to observe news events firsthand. With an eye on the clock, they often must gather information over the telephone, but given the choice, they should go where the news is.

Police reporters and photographers have radio scanners in their cars so they can arrive at breaking news stories as quickly as possible, sometimes even as the first police car arrives at the scene. While necessary for some types of stories, relying on second-hand accounts seldom produces the type of action, detail and vivid description that is possible when reporters see events unfold.

Details gathered through observation can enliven coverage of news events. A description of a heated exchange between city council members, for example, can speak volumes about a close vote on a new city

---

BOX 2–2
Seeing Firsthand
✳ ✳ ✳
Direct observation enables reporters to:
• Collect descriptive details about people, locations and events that are part of breaking news stories.
• Verify information or impressions provided by others.
• Obtain evidence not available through other sources.
• Re-create events for readers or viewers.
• Characterize news events as peaceful or tense, cordial or confrontational.

ordinance. Reporters look for episodes that are dramatic, unique or representative of the larger story.

Capturing the Drama

This story about the 10th day of a plant strike contains a passage describing the reaction of strikers to union members who crossed the picket lines for the first time. The story begins with a straight news lead that brings the reader up to date on the strike:

> A half-dozen members of the Amalgamated Foundry Workers broke with their union leadership yesterday, crossing picket lines at the Colsen Machine Works and putting in their first day of work since the strike began 10 days ago.
>
> Negotiators for both sides reported no progress in the talks, which are stalled over wage give-backs and pension benefits.

The story then shifts to a scene outside the plant as workers prepared to report to work:

> Minutes before the 8 a.m. shift change, a police escort ushered the strike breakers through a thick crowd of some 100 striking workers outside the plant's main gate. The strikers carried placards and chanted, "Scabs go home, scabs go home."

> Police, dressed in riot gear and carrying nightsticks, cleared a 3-foot path through the mass of strikers, most of whom stepped back but continued chanting and waving clenched fists.
>
> As the escorted workers filed toward the gate, a lone striker pushed past a police officer and confronted the lead strike breaker. "Scabs go home," the striker yelled, his face inches from the other man's.
>
> "Go to hell," the man answered, staring back. "My kids gotta eat."
>
> The striker moved closer, but a policeman shoved his nightstick between the pair and pushed the striker back into the crowd.
>
> "Stay there or go to jail," the policeman barked. The man resumed chanting but moved no closer.
>
> The escort was completed without further incident. There were no arrests and police said the workers were escorted out of the plant after their shift without disturbance.

Descriptive detail of this kind would have been impossible without the reporter being at the scene. This one incident captured the level of anger and animosity among strikers and the motivations of strike breakers.

By being there to witness the police escort, the reporter made his own decisions about what was important. In this case, he chose a few moments that crystallized the scene for the reader.

Notice the writer's use of dialogue, the spontaneous words spoken by participants. Dialogue can capture the moment and give the story a "you are there" feel.

A reporter's positioning at an event can be critical. This reporter had to be close enough to see the exchange and record the words and reactions of participants. Many reporters have a knack for sizing up a situation and anticipating where something significant might occur. It is part instinct, part preparation and part luck.

By getting there early and talking with strikers, the reporter saw their level of anger. Scanning the crowd, he might even have foreseen where a disturbance might occur. Reporters try to get as close to the action as prudence dictates.

The final statement in this story is attributed to police. Although the reporter was at the scene in the morning, he was back at the office when the shift changed and had to rely on the police account of the workers' uneventful exit.

Reporters should be aware how their presence can affect news events. Anyone who has witnessed the arrival of a TV crew at a demonstration knows how press coverage can alter people's behavior. To a lesser degree, pulling out a notebook or tape recorder also can alter behavior; sources become guarded or fearful and begin to act and speak differently. Reporters should be sure what is said and done for their benefit represents what is really going on.

Deciding What to Use

Reporters use observational techniques in a variety of situations, ranging from crime and disaster stories to protest rallies and public hearings.

An arson story, for example, might describe investigators as they pick through the rubble looking for clues. A story about a murder trial might mention the defendant's reaction as she listens to damaging testimony. A feature profile might note the subject's appearance, mannerisms and dress, even the kind of neighborhood he or she lives in.

Descriptions should always be focused and purposeful. Noting that a murder defendant taps the table with his index fingers may be pointless—unless he does it only when prosecution witnesses are testifying.

Descriptive details and scenes should be selected because they support the theme of a story. Such information should reflect, not exaggerate, reality, and reporters should not let random or inconsequential details dominate a story at the expense of newsworthy information.

In the hands of a skilled writer, carefully selected details and scenes can set a powerful tone. For a news story about a string of killings in Northern Ireland, Francis X. Clines, reporter for *The New York Times*, began with a delayed lead that focused on a young girl playing outside the funeral of a slain IRA rebel. The story combines several distinct images to set up the reader for the factual details of the recent deaths.

> BELFAST, Northern Ireland—Beyond the coffin, out in the churchyard, red-haired Kathleen Quinn was full of fun and flirting shamelessly for all her eight years of life. "Mister, I'm to be on the TV tonight," she told a stranger, squinting up happy and prim. Kathleen had taken her brother's bike and skinned her knee bloody, all while people were praying goodbye inside the church to another rebel body in another coffin.
>
> Soon the cameras were watching the coffin being carried out from the windowless fortress of a church, down the curl of the street in the simple hamlet, and on to the ever-filling graveyard patch devoted to republican rebels.
>
> As it turned out, the television ignored Kathleen and missed a classic Irish truth, a sight for sore eyes. She climbed back on the bike and headed off in a blur, oblivious to a piece of nearby graffiti that seemed about all of life's withering dangers: "I wonder each night what the monster will do to me tomorrow."

This is no typical lead, but the effect is dramatic and unmistakable. With one brief episode, Clines found a unique way to convey the daily anguish in Catholic and Protestant Northern Ireland.

The Need for Verification

One has to look no further than press coverage of the Persian Gulf War in 1991 to understand the power of on-location reporting. News coverage of every previous war involving the United States, from the Civil War to Vietnam, had delivered vivid, powerful images, both written and photographic, to the American public.

News coverage of the Vietnam War is often credited—or blamed, depending on one's perspective—for turning the majority of Americans against U.S. involvement in that conflict. Military leaders in charge of the U.S. mobilization in the Persian Gulf believed this to be true and imposed widespread censorship, strictly controlling access to locations and military personnel. Print and broadcast journalists were prevented from traveling with the ground phase of that war to report from the front lines, as correspondents had done in previous wars.

While history will judge both the correctness of that war and the military's censorship of the press, the fact that reporters were not allowed to see events firsthand meant the public never saw how the war was being conducted. The military's version of the war became the only version, until the fighting stopped.

The only reporting not controlled by the U.S. military was delivered by three correspondents for the television network CNN who were inside a hotel in Baghdad, the Iraqi capital, when the war began. Their reports were censored by the Iraqis. For 17 hours the correspondents provided live narration of the first U.S. bombing attacks. Their vivid and emotional descriptions transfixed the American public and won over the majority of viewers to CNN for the duration of the war.

CNN's lead correspondent Peter Arnett, who won a Pulitzer Prize for his reporting in Vietnam, continued to cover the war from behind Iraqi lines. Arnett offered a compelling confirmation of the power of a reporter's firsthand observations and underscored another important reason for seeing things firsthand—verifying information provided by others. "I learned in Vietnam to believe only what my eyes have seen as (opposed to) anything I hear from any official of any government or from any person," Arnett said.

Control and manipulation by news sources is not confined to war reporting. Consider these examples:

- The director of a state mental hospital accused of forcing patients to live in filthy conditions takes a reporter through selected portions of the facility—after walls have been painted, floors scrubbed and patients issued new clothing.

- Officials of a nuclear power plant cited by federal regulators for safety violations arrange a press tour of the facility to show off its new equipment and procedures.

- After parents complain of widespread violence in a local high school, the principal arranges a news conference with student council members who insist the problem is being exaggerated.

In each case, the responsible officials stand to lose public confidence, the backing of superiors, and perhaps their jobs if the negative stories continue. Administrators under fire will use various forms of "damage control" to counter adverse publicity. In these examples, the officials tried to present a version of reality far different from the truth.

For reporters, the preferred alternative to these staged situations is to have open access to facilities and individuals to verify official versions. However, that is often difficult, especially if the facilities are private.

Direct observation of sensitive situations is usually easier before they have been exposed. Later, evidence will be harder to come by. Reporters may need to rely on inside sources rather than their own observations to check the official version.

Going Undercover

Reporters sometimes use "participant observation" to gather information, posing as someone else or not identifying themselves as journalists. Reporters have taken jobs as migrant workers, nursing home aides, "temp" employees and attendants in mental hospitals to obtain facts and details they couldn't get any other way. The results can be revealing and dramatic.

Reporters working undercover have exposed deplorable working conditions and abuses in government-run institutions. In 1887, an investigative reporter named Nellie Bly (her real name was Elizabeth Cochrane) faked insanity to gain admittance to an asylum on Blackwell's Island, New York. Inside the asylum, she saw patients eating garbage and attendants bathing them with buckets of ice water. Her reporting in the *New York World* led to management and funding reforms of the asylum.

Participant observation often was employed for investigative projects during the 1960s and 1970s. However, undercover reporting has fallen from favor with many editors increasingly concerned with the ethics of reporters hiding their identity.

Another concern with this type of reporting is that what reporters see, though accurate, may not represent the broader picture. Stories that generalize about deplorable conditions in a nursing home or mental hospital based on a reporter's limited observations in a single ward may indict an entire system unfairly.

Participant observation has not disappeared from journalism, but it is generally done only after careful consideration and under the close scrutiny of top editors. The guiding principle before such reporting is attempted is, "Can the story be obtained any other way?"

Tantalized by the idea of "going undercover," young reporters may want to try this approach before exhausting more traditional newsgathering methods. There are also legal ramifications to consider. Reporters who trespass, give phony names or obtain jobs under false pretenses could face criminal charges or a civil lawsuit. Reporters always should consult with their editors before misrepresenting themselves for a story.

ASKING QUESTIONS, GETTING ANSWERS

Planning and conducting effective interviews is an essential skill for reporters and may be the most often used method of gathering information.

Whether the assignment is a breaking news story or a feature profile, reporters must be able to find the right people to interview, ask the right questions and accurately record the answers. They must be skilled in eliciting information from a variety of sources—some of them cooperative, some hostile, some apprehensive—and they must do so under a variety of circumstances. They often must do several things simultaneously—listen, observe, take notes, plan their next question—and they may need to shift directions suddenly, prompted by the interviewee's verbal and nonverbal signals.

Interviews can be brief or formal, friendly or adversarial. Most share certain characteristics, but no two are exactly alike. Reporters continually build on their interview skills and techniques and usually learn something from each new interview.

What Interviews Do

Interviews enable reporters to gather specific facts for a story or to obtain a source's insights, explanations and opinions. They also can provide vivid or colorful quotes that convey the source's values, character and feelings.

After shipments of unusually pure heroin were seized in several Northeast cities, a reporter for *The Hartford Courant* interviewed drug enforcement officials to explain what seemed to be a disturbing trend. His story outlined their theories and added succinct quotes to crystallize them for the reader.

A new, rapidly growing network of drug dealers is flooding New England cities with a highly potent grade of heroin in an effort, law enforcement officers believe, to create a large new class of addicts that can be exploited for profit.

Officials say the phenomenon is a marketing scheme likely organized by the multibillion-dollar cartels that distribute Colombian cocaine. Among other things, narcotics officers believe processors are distributing purer heroin to provide a powerful "high" to heroin sniffers and smokers who are afraid of the AIDS risk associated with injecting the drug.

Michael A. Priore of the U.S. Drug Enforcement Administration said the traffickers' strategy is painfully simple: "Put it out on the street, get people hooked immediately and they'll come back to buy it."

Reporters also use interviews to get public officials on the record, to hold them accountable for policies and actions. For breaking stories such as a bank robbery or natural disasters, on-the-scene interviews provide firsthand accounts of participants and witnesses.

In the aftermath of Hurricane Andrew in 1992, a reporter for *The Washington Post* described the devastation to a large Miami hotel where 600 people were huddled in a windowless ballroom when the storm's 160-mph winds hit. Interviews helped convey the event's drama and emotion.

"It was like something in a movie," said Tracey Martin, 18, from Port Washington, N.Y. "We were all lying on the floor, everybody quiet, even the babies. It was eerie. You could hear the smashing and crashing up above. The wind blew the door to the ballroom open. It was frightening."

"People were trying to shut one of the doors," added Eva Slodarz of Coral Gables, "and the wind was sucking them out of the room like a vacuum."

The effective interviewer assumes many roles. Sometimes he or she is a confidant, lending a sympathetic ear to a crime victim who agrees to relive the ordeal for the reporter. Sometimes the role is that of inquisitor, questioning a public official with sharply focused questions about sensitive issues.

Whatever posture interviewers take, they must not forget the purpose is to gather information. Interviews are not intended for making friends, although reporters must be able to build rapport with sources.

BOX 2–3

Interviews for All Occasions

✳ ✳ ✳

Interviews provide reporters with a variety of information to add different dimensions to a story:

- **Specific facts**. Information that answers initial questions about who, what, where, when and why.

- **Responses**. Sources can confirm, deny or explain facts, opinions or allegations obtained by the reporter.

- **Quotes**. Verbatim record of a person's words that add color and a human dimension to a story and put officials and spokespersons on the record.

- **Examples and anecdotes**. Revealing, dramatic or humorous stories that humanize public issues.

- **Context**. On-the-scene observations by participants that add perspective.

- **Background**. Early interviews with informed sources that provide an overview of an issue, policy or institution.

Reporters should not try to impress sources with their knowledge about a subject, yet they must be sufficiently prepared to establish their credibility and show they understand the subject. And the interview should never turn into an argument or debate, although at times the dogged pursuit of answers may require an aggressive, even confrontational, style.

Planning the Interview

Reporters who march up to a source and begin firing questions are likely to walk away with incomplete or inaccurate information, or worse, no interview at all.

Before each interview, reporters must consider the assignment, the type of information needed from the interview, and how receptive the source is likely to be. The office seeker will respond differently to questions about her lead in the latest public opinion polls than she would to inquiries about her private life. The police officer investigating a string of hate crimes against residents of an ethnic neighborhood may provide a factual, dispassionate account, while a citizen whose car was vandalized or whose children were threatened may give the story an emotional urgency.

Each interview requires its own type of questions and style of questioning, and reporters must evaluate each source to determine how best to elicit information.

- Is the person a public figure who fields reporters' questions daily, or a private citizen who has never faced a reporter's notebook or television camera?

- Is the source likely to be cooperative or reluctant, talkative or evasive?

- Is the source qualified or informed enough to render reliable information or opinions?

Reporters cannot always predict which response—cooperation, reticence, hostility—questions will elicit. Sensing that one approach isn't working, reporters may need to try another tack.

One Story, Four Approaches

With one hour until deadline, the newsroom police scanner blares a report of a major fire at a housing project. The city editor dispatches a reporter to gather details.

Situation No. 1—Breaking Story

The assignment is seemingly uncomplicated at the scene: The reporter finds out who was injured and how seriously, what caused the fire and how much damage occurred. She needs basic, factual information—the who, what, when, and where of the event—and the information must be obtained quickly. The reporter conducts brief interviews, moving from fire chief, to witnesses, to residents who fled the burning building.

After collecting essential details, the reporter calls the local hospital from a pay phone to check on the condition of two people who were overcome by smoke and taken away by ambulance. She is told that both appear to be unharmed.

Situation No. 2—Human Interest

After filing a story by telephone, the reporter returns to the fire scene. Her editor has suggested a follow-up story, perhaps a feature on residents left homeless by the blaze. The fire chief tells her the fire apparently was caused by faulty wiring in one of the apartments. The chief also tells her that just before firefighters arrived, a young child was rescued from a third-story apartment by an elderly man who lived downstairs, a fact that wasn't known when the reporter first interviewed the chief.

Both man and child were unhurt, the chief says, but it was a close call. The reporter decides the rescue is worth a story and seeks out the man and the parents of the rescued child.

A feature profile about the man's heroism calls for a different type of interview. No longer satisfied with simple facts, the reporter seeks information that will add details, drama, background and emotion, along with a chronology of the rescue. The hero is asked how he accomplished the rescue and what he was thinking at the time. The parents are encouraged to express their relief and gratitude for the man's heroism. Witnesses are coaxed into recalling every detail of what they saw and heard.

Situation No. 3—Tragedy and Loss

The reporter then drives to the local Red Cross shelter for a sidebar story about families displaced by the fire. The reporter questions the shelter's director about the families hardest hit who might be willing to be interviewed. The director points out one family who lost everything in the fire. The reporter introduces herself to the parents and expresses concern for their loss. Would they be willing to answer a few questions? The couple agree.

The parents talk at length about their narrow escape from the fire, their lost belongings and their future prospects. As she listens, the reporter notes their expressions, their clothing, the way they relate to their three young children huddled around them. Their answers and the additional details will become part of the story. She conducts similar interviews with two other families.

Situation No. 4—Pursuing a Tip

As the reporter is leaving, a resident pulls her aside and mentions that two smaller fires occurred at the same housing project in recent months, both caused by faulty electrical wiring. Residents have complained to the housing authority about wiring problems and broken smoke detectors but have gotten no action, the resident says. This new information suggests another follow-up story.

The next day the reporter returns to the housing project to interview residents. If the information checks out, she will produce a story about safety conditions at the housing project and the authority's slow response to residents' concerns.

Many of the residents interviewed the first day are questioned again. They remember the reporter from the day before and willingly answer questions. They confirm the tip, describing strange electrical problems and smoke detectors that don't work. Residents say they have repeatedly complained to the housing authority but have received no response. One woman even has a copy of a letter she sent the authority director two months earlier and gives it to the reporter.

The next stop is the fire marshal's office to examine inspection reports for any notice of safety violations. The fire marshal produces several reports that show violations and a letter to the authority ordering it to correct deficiencies. The reporter asks about the authority's overall record and is told about safety violations in other projects and its poor compliance record.

The final stop is the authority offices. The reporter is greeted warmly by the director, who invites her into his office and offers coffee.

"A terrible thing about the fire," the director says. "We hope to find apartments for the displaced families in one of our other projects. Then we'll try to get their apartments repaired as soon as possible."

The reporter tells the director of her conversations with residents. "What about these complaints that the authority ignores safety conditions and refuses to repair problems?" she asks.

"You know how tenants are," the director says. "They complain about every little problem. I can assure you that we take all safety problems seriously. In fact, we have a schedule of repairs we're planning. I'd be glad to give you a copy of it."

"Are you saying that the complaints are unfounded, that the agency responds promptly to all serious problems?"

"I'm saying we do the best we can. This is a big city, and we have other projects to take care of. If we consider something serious, we take care of it right away. But if you want a real story, you should write about the way these tenants treat the apartments. We're having to do repairs all the time. It costs the city a bundle."

"That may be true," the reporter interjects, "but the fire marshal's office says the authority does not repair serious problems. And he's given me a list of violations that you've failed to correct. Why is that?"

In this case, the reporter chose not to mention her interview with the fire marshal at the outset. The reason was not to ambush the director, but to see if he would answer honestly. The reporter provided the director with several opportunities to mention the violations and explain the delay. Instead, the director played down the safety problems and tried to divert the reporter from the story. Once it was clear the director did not intend to respond honestly, the reporter confronted him with the record of violations.

What the Reporter Did

These situations illustrate the variety of stories that can flow from a single news event and the types of interviews needed to gather appropriate material.

For each story, the reporter knew the purpose of the interview and the type of information needed from each. She also evaluated the different types of sources being interviewed—public officials, victims, casual bystanders—and how cooperative and reliable they were likely to be. She adjusted her questions and interviewing style to the particular story and to the person being interviewed.

For the initial story, fire officials provided basic information about the fire willingly and professionally, as they had done with other reporters for other fires. Sources for the upbeat hero's profile, from witnesses to the rescuer himself, were eager to talk. For the feature about displaced families, the reporter's sympathetic manner and low-key style helped persuade people who had just suffered a serious loss to be interviewed. And finally, for the fire safety story, the authority director's evasiveness and lack of candor prompted a more assertive and persistent line of questioning.

As she pursued the various stories, this reporter was prepared, curious, sensitive, flexible, observant and persistent, all important qualities for successful interviewing.

Deciding Whom to Interview

Selecting the right person to interview saves time in gathering information and eliminates unproductive interviews with people who can't or won't supply what the reporter needs. Reluctant sources often can be persuaded to cooperate, but unless their input is critical to a story, lengthy attempts to win them over may be wasted if the information is available from someone else.

Before deciding whom to approach for an interview, reporters ask several key questions:

- Is the information available from only one person or from many?
- Can the information be trusted or must it be verified with others?
- Is the person speaking for an organization or larger group, or expressing a personal viewpoint?
- Do the sources have firsthand knowledge, or can they supply the names and telephone numbers of people who do?

Reporters will seek sources at various levels of participation and authority. A school superintendent may be the only person authorized or knowledgeable enough to discuss official policy for a city's school system. At the same time, principals, classroom teachers and students can supply useful insights—and a reality check on official versions—about whether those policies are working.

BOX 2–4

What Makes Good Sources?

✳✳✳

In her book *Interviews that Work*, Shirley Biagi, journalism chair at California State University, describes four characteristics that make people attractive as interviewees:

- **Accessibility.**   These sources are available, cooperative and willing to be interviewed. They take time for questions, often on short notice, and are especially valuable when reporters need information for deadline stories.

- **Reliability.**   Reporters tend to return to sources who have given them accurate information, explanations or background before. These can be tipsters, established experts, beat cops or bartenders. At minimum, they will be candid about their own positions and suggest ways to verify their information.

- **Accountability.**   By interviewing policy-makers, official spokespersons and chief administrators, reporters obtain the viewpoints of larger groups and organizations. However, the "official" versions should be checked with other sources to determine if they are truly representative.

- **Quotability.**   A well-informed source who speaks clearly and colorfully can add vitality to a news report. Reporters gravitate to scientists, economists and other experts who can translate complex ideas into everyday language. However, politicians and other experienced news sources are adept at "sound-bite" journalism, producing and rehearsing quotable tidbits that are big on color but short on substance.

Source: Shirley Biagi, *Interviews That Work*, pp. 57–58. Belmont, Calif.: Wadsworth Publishing Co., 1992.

The ideal interviewee should combine several of these attributes. A quotable politician who is ill-informed, or an accessible union official who misrepresents the views of his membership usually does more harm than good to a story's accuracy and a reporter's credibility.

Getting Help

Some sources are what reporters call "pathfinders," people with extensive knowledge about a subject or a high-level insider who can help them maneuver their way through a particular system or organization. Pathfinders can summarize the situation, explain background and technical information, direct the reporter's efforts, correct misconceptions or faulty theories, and point the way to other sources.

Reporters locate pathfinders in a number of ways. They ask sources they respect for the names of authorities or knowledgeable insiders. They call professional associations or a university public relations office. Some universities produce an "experts list" of professors and researchers in specific fields. Virtually every police department, political party, school system or government agency has pathfinders who can assist reporters. As with any source, pathfinders must be evaluated for objectivity and fairness.

Arranging the Interview

Reporters who are well-known around their beat usually can get interviews just by stopping by someone's office. Longer, formal interviews often require an appointment. It is often helpful to tell the source how much time will be needed and the topics to be covered. If an interview is going well, the source will often allow additional time.

Letting interviewees know the topics allows them to prepare and may ease whatever fears they have about being interviewed. It also allows them to assemble whatever documents, reports or statistics the reporter will need. The interviewee won't be able to put off the reporter with vague answers or responses such as, "Why don't you check back with me in a few days," if he or she knows ahead of time that the reporter will be asking about a specific topic.

Reporters who plan to confront a source with damaging information need not be too specific at this time. Common sense should dictate how much to tell the source in advance and how much to hold back until the interview.

People sometimes refuse to be interviewed. This often happens when scheduling is done by a secretary or public relations office. If the interview is important enough, the reporter should not be deterred. The reporter may want to approach the person away from the office or send a request in writing to his or her home. Busy people often are impressed by persistence, and a reporter who combines that with a professional and respectful appeal may get the interview.

Some people may be put off by the word "interview," especially on sensitive stories. Instead, the reporter can ask for the person's "help" in resolving discrepancies or different versions of an event. Emphasizing that the source can help produce an accurate story can be effective in gaining his or her cooperation and confidence.

News interviews are conducted on street corners, in corporate offices, laboratories and meeting rooms, or even sitting at someone's kitchen table. It is usually best to pick a place where sources will feel relaxed enough to speak candidly. Sources may prefer a local diner, a park or their own home. A police detective investigating a string of murders may prefer to be interviewed in his office during his regular shift. That same detective may want to meet a reporter at some out-of-town location to discuss what he knows about problems in his department.

In the ideal situation, reporters are alone with the person being interviewed, but sometimes they may need to interview groups, such as a class of third-graders for a school feature or several senior citizens for a story on nursing home conditions. Sometimes reporters must compete with other reporters for a single source's attention, jostling for position to interview a lawyer on the courthouse steps or trying to be recognized at a news conference. In all situations, under a

A reporter interviews a police captain in his office. Selecting the right location for an interview can help put a source at ease.
Photo by Andrea Hoy.

variety of conditions, reporters must learn to focus their attention, to listen carefully and record the person's answers accurately.

Understanding Sources

No matter what the story, realizing how sources feel about being interviewed—whether they are nervous, intimidated, bored or flattered—helps reporters decide on an approach that will result in cooperation and candor. This is called empathy, understanding of how another person views a situation—in this case, being interviewed and the prospect of being quoted in the newspaper or news broadcast.

Barriers between reporters and sources can exist because of age, social standing, racial and ethnic differences, even the way people speak. Breaking down these barriers can best be accomplished by reporters who are sincere, honest and willing to empathize with potential sources.

Reporters should try to understand why some people don't want to be interviewed and why some almost insist on it. A reporter must recognize the fears of a woman who has just witnessed a drive-by shooting if he hopes to get her to talk about it. An executive who believes all reporters are anti-business will have to be convinced otherwise if the reporter hopes to get an interview. Reporters should stress that they want to produce a story that is fair, accurate and complete, and that the source can help achieve those goals by answering questions.

People accused of a crime or impropriety may decline to be interviewed, often on the advice of their lawyer. This does not necessarily imply guilt. The person may be distraught and fear that public comment will only hurt his or her cause. Experienced newsmakers understand that it is often in their best interest to confront accusations head on. Some even schedule news conferences or seek out particular reporters to tell their side of the story. Private individuals facing similar charges may find it easier to avoid comment. Badgering these people seldom works. But an empathetic appeal, explaining why the reporter wants the interview and what the source stands to gain by agreeing, may result in the desired interview. Such an appeal can be made through friends and family members, or by letter.

Empathy should never be feigned. Reporters must understand the possible consequences of quoting people and respect their concerns. Tenants who complain about their landlord can be out in the street after the story appears. Employees who criticize their employer or whistleblowers who report safety problems may lose their jobs. Reporters may not be able to control what happens to a source after a story appears, but they should never knowingly place the source's safety or livelihood in jeopardy for the sake of a quick quote or a more dramatic story.

Preparing for the Interview

Reporters should gather as much background as possible on the topic and people being interviewed. The newspaper's library is the logical place to start. Talking with pathfinders and other sources also can help in planning questions and selecting an approach for a specific interview. These preliminaries will suggest questions and perhaps tips about topics that should be discussed or avoided.

Whenever possible, reporters should prepare a list of questions in advance, noting important topics they want to discuss. For formal interviews, such a list will ensure key subjects aren't missed during a wide-ranging or emotional interview. A list also can help trigger a reporter's memory during lulls in the conversation.

The list of questions should be used as a guide rather than a blueprint. Interviewers who rattle off question after question from a prepared list may stifle spontaneous responses and discourage the interviewee from elaborating with colorful quotes or unexpected details.

Experienced interviewers recognize potentially interesting digressions. During an interview about local taxes, for example, the mayor mentions that a major manufacturer is negotiating for a new plant site in the region. The reporter either follows up immediately with questions about the company or makes a note to ask about it later in the interview. Either way, the mayor's tip, whether he intended to let it slip or not, is worth a story, and the reporter who blindly follows a prepared list of tax questions may miss it.

Concentration, a keen ear and accurate note-taking are essential to a successful interview.
Photo by Andrea Hoy.

Conducting the Interview

To the casual observer, an interview might seem like an informal conversation between two people. But while a conversation implies an equal exchange of information, insights or feelings, the balance of information should flow from source to reporter in an interview. For that reason, reporters must be able to control and direct interviews. Reporters who lose control or fail to follow up on evasive answers may end up with a notebook lacking specific information and filled instead with platitudes and generalities.

Some sources deliberately try to control an interview, to establish their expertise or to avoid sensitive topics. At the other extreme, some sources are so

pleased to have an attentive audience they will talk nonstop about anything and everything. Reporters must provide cues, through questions, gestures and expressions, that focus the source's responses and keep them moving in the desired direction.

A few guidelines for conducting interviews can ensure they will proceed smoothly and effectively:

- Plan the first question carefully. The right question can set an appropriate tone, relax the source and demonstrate the reporter's preparation.

- Be alert to comments or answers that suggest a follow-up question.

- Don't interrupt. If it is necessary to bring the discussion back to a specific topic, gently guide the source in that direction.

- Listen carefully for angles or points that were not anticipated.

- Ask for clarification. It is better to admit you didn't understand something than to include inaccuracies in the story.

- Use silence effectively. Avoid launching into another question as soon as an answer is completed. Silence encourages the source to elaborate, add new information or simply remember something. Sometimes a nervous source will blurt out something he or she had not intended to, simply to fill the void.

- Don't argue. A reporter may disagree with a source, but the interview should never become a debate, which serves neither party. Greet a source's provocative or outrageous statements with a comment that prompts elaboration, such as, "Why do you believe that?" or "Wouldn't your critics disagree?"

- Delay sensitive questions. Queries that may anger or put the source on the defensive are best held until late in the interview. Questions that confront or accuse the source may be necessary, but asking them too early may sour the interview or end it prematurely. If you wait, you already will have collected considerable material if the source terminates the interview in response to a sensitive question.

Telephone Interviews

Reporters often rely on the telephone to overcome time or distance constraints. With known sources, reporters may be able to launch into questions after a quick introduction. With unfamiliar sources, however, a few preliminaries can help overcome initial resistance to a faceless voice.

In all situations, reporters should identify themselves and their news organization and explain the story they are working on. This will either put the source at ease or on the defensive, but either way the person's response will suggest how to proceed.

Remember that telephone calls often interrupt a person's activity. Reporters should ask whether an interview is convenient and offer to call back later or have the person return the call.

An indirect approach can be effective with reticent sources. Rather than asking point-blank questions, reporters can solicit the person's help in checking accuracy, filling in missing facts or explaining background.

Accuracy is an important concern in telephone interviews. Words and numbers, for example, can easily be misunderstood. A few simple steps will help avoid errors:

- Check proper names and numbers by carefully reading them back to the person.
- When in doubt, rephrase questions to be sure you heard the answer correctly. Most sources will appreciate the added care.
- Speak clearly and avoid long, meandering questions that may confuse the person.
- Ask questions one at a time and allow time for complete answers.

A final note: Reporters should not use the telephone to avoid directly confronting people against whom allegations are made. An accused person deserves more than a cursory phone call seeking a routine denial. For deadline stories, fairness dictates that reporters call often, both to the person's home and office, to provide every opportunity for a response. Reporters should leave a detailed message with a secretary or family member, explaining the purpose of the call. If a story will contain accusations, the message should say so.

Investigative stories often culminate in what reporters call a "confrontational" interview, where specific allegations are presented to a source for a response. Unless distance is a genuine deterrent, such interviews should always be done in person.

To Tape or Not to Tape?

Should print reporters use tape recorders? There are several negatives:

- A tape recorder can become a crutch that keeps a reporter from developing note-taking skills.
- Taped interviews must be transcribed, a time-consuming and often unnecessary step.
- Some people are intimidated by tape recorders.
- The tape recorder can jam or batteries can run out, leaving the reporter with no record of the interview.

On the plus side, tape recorders are useful for in-depth profiles where long, expressive quotes are needed or for controversial stories where a taped record can protect the reporter from claims of inaccuracy. Taped interviews with scientists and other experts can be replayed to ensure technical subjects are understood.

In all cases, a tape recorder should complement rather than replace note-taking, and sources should be told when an interview is being taped.

Taping telephone interviews raises legal questions. State laws on the subject vary greatly, and many are being reviewed because of the availability of telephone answering machines that can tape a conversation at the push of a button. Some states require that the person being interviewed agree to the taping, while other states specify only that one party must be aware of it, a protection against illegal wiretaps. Reporters should be aware of laws in their states and as a rule should inform interviewees when an interview is being taped.

Going Off the Record

Sooner or later, every reporter is faced with a source who wants to go "off the record." The reporter's response may determine whether the source keeps talking and under what terms, if any, the information can appear in a story. It is best to stop taking notes and clarify what the source means by "off the record."

"Off the record" means the information cannot be used under any circumstances, even if it can be verified on the record from someone else. People unaccustomed to dealing with reporters often want to go off the record when they really mean they don't want their name linked to the information. They want a reporter to know something—a tip worth checking, another source worth pursuing—but they don't want to be quoted as supplying the information. They really mean, "Don't use my name," or "Don't tell anyone where you heard this."

Defining Terms

Experienced journalists have adopted working definitions of key terms that can guide both reporter and source.

- **On the record.** The reporter may use any and all information and may quote the source as providing it.

- **Not for attribution.** The reporter may use the information but cannot disclose the source. The reporter is free to verify the information elsewhere.

- **On background.** The reporter may use the information but supply only general attribution such as "a source close to the investigation" or "a source in the mayor's office."

- **Off the record.** The reporter cannot use the information under any circumstances. The information is provided only for the reporter's background. Other sources cannot be used to confirm the statement, and it cannot appear in print.

Reporters should avoid accepting off-the-record information; doing so ties their hands and prevents them from using material that may be critical to a story. Granting sources off-the-record status may be necessary to obtain background and context, but it can hinder reporters who need specific facts or a source's reaction for the record. Sometimes sources can be persuaded to supply information off the record with the

understanding that the reporter will be able to use it in the future.

Reporters who use information after accepting it off the record damage their credibility and may lose the future cooperation of sources.

Negotiating Attribution

Each request to go off the record should be evaluated individually. The reporter may be able to negotiate with a reluctant source to release the information "on background," allowing a general attribution that links the information to a credible, but unidentified source. This strengthens the story without jeopardizing the person's identity.

Specific sources often do not need to be identified at all; their information is the critical element, not their identity. Identifying an official who tells the reporter where to find an important document is unnecessary since the document itself will provide the critical facts.

When accepting information "on background," reporters should press sources for the most specific attribution possible. It is better to report that "a reliable source in the mayor's office" said auditors found problems with the city's accounting procedures than it is to attribute it to "a source who requested anonymity." In the first attribution, the word "reliable" tells the reader that the reporter has reason to believe the source and that the source is close to the situation. The latter is overly vague and lends little credibility to the information.

Sometimes people say something they would rather not see quoted or aired and may ask a reporter not to use the statement. In theory, the reporter is not bound to honor the request since the statement came while the source was on the record. But some reporters agree to ignore the quote if it is not critical to the story or if the person is unaccustomed to being interviewed. It is usually better to leave out marginal information than to lose a valuable news source.

Uses and Abuses of Anonymous Sources

Anonymous sources are an essential pipeline for public affairs reporters. They provide background that helps reporters understand complex events. They supply valuable tips that direct reporters to a story or to critical documents that will nail down an investigation. Without anonymous sources, valuable avenues of information would be cut off, and reporters' ability to report on the inner workings of their beat would be impaired.

However, abuses by some journalists have prompted many editors to place tight restrictions on anonymous sources. *USA Today*, for example, does not permit the use of unidentified sources in news stories. Some editors believe that uncontrolled use of anonymous sources erodes the credibility of journalists and their stories.

Some reporters may grant anonymity too willingly, letting officials hide behind a cloak of secrecy when they should be held accountable for their statements. Editors especially dislike "blind" anonymous quotes that criticize a person or situation. After numerous news stories in *The Hartford Courant* used anonymous sources to comment negatively on everything from a rock concert to a college president, the newspaper's ombudsman Henry McNulty criticized the practice in a column. One story, about George Washington University President Stephen Trachtenberg, quoted an unidentified professor as saying, "Is he as big an egomaniac as he seems to be?" That prompted McNulty to write, "I'll wager that the professor wouldn't walk up to Trachtenberg, look him in the eye, and ask, 'Are you really as big an egomaniac as you seem to be?' So why do we let such an offensive question be raised anonymously?"

McNulty urged the newspaper to confine the use of anonymous sources to two situations: when the story involves an important public policy issue, and when the person being quoted offers verifiable facts, not opinion.

On his retirement in 1991, Ben Bradlee, former executive editor of *The Washington Post*, expressed similar reservations about the overuse of anonymous sources by reporters in Washington, D.C. Under Bradlee's direction, *Post* reporters Carl Bernstein and Bob Woodward skillfully used anonymous sources to break major stories in the Watergate scandal that toppled President Richard M. Nixon's administration. But Bradlee, like others, believes that anonymous sources

can be misused. "The purely explanatory anonymous source is not the great evil," Bradlee said. "The evil comes from the guy who's taking a cheap shot." Increasingly, editors are purging unattributed criticism or accusations from news stories.

Editors recognize that anonymous sources are sometimes necessary in reporting public issues and permit their use by experienced reporters. Often editors insist on knowing the identity of confidential sources before allowing their information to be printed or aired.

Reporters face another dilemma when a source says one thing publicly but something different in private. They either can use the on-the-record quote, knowing that it is untrue, or they can do what R.W. Apple, political writer for *The New York Times*, did during the 1992 presidential campaign—leave out the name but use both quotes.

> Already the (Republican) party's hard line on abortion has cost votes, although it is impossible even to estimate how many. A prominent Republican woman who favors abortion rights said all the right things in an interview Thursday, promising to vote for (George) Bush because "he is right on so many other things."
>
> When the on-the-record interview ended, she changed her tune, promising that "they'll get theirs this fall when we vote for (Bill) Clinton."

By using the contradictory quotes, Apple succeeded in showing how the abortion issue had divided the Republican Party and posed a serious obstacle for the president. Readers were enlightened rather than misled.

Granting a source anonymity is serious business. Courts have fined reporters or sent them to jail for refusing to identify confidential sources in cases that involved criminal acts. Once confidentiality has been granted, a reporter must take every precaution to protect the source's identity.

People who provide reporters with sensitive information or leak confidential documents often do so at considerable risk, both personally and professionally. Reporters who fail to protect sources soon will find others unwilling to cooperate, while the careful and trusted reporter will gain greater access and earn the trust of other potential sources.

***
SUGGESTED READINGS

Biagi, Shirley. *Interviews that Work*. Belmont, Calif.: Wadsworth, 1992.

In-depth discussions of planning, conducting and using interviews.

Kessler, Lauren, and Duncan McDonald. *The Search: Information Gathering for the Mass Media*. Belmont, Calif.: Wadsworth, 1992.

Describes range of sources and research techniques.

Killenberg, George M., and Rob Anderson. *Before the Story*. New York: St. Martin's Press, 1989.

Describes basic and advanced interview skills, complications and ethics.

Murray, Donald. *Writing for Your Readers*. Chester, Conn.: Globe Pequot Press, 1983.

Chapter 4 offers reporters valuable tips about observation, using their senses and using the information in their writing.

Ullman, John, and Jan Colbert, eds. *The Reporter's Handbook*. New York: St. Martin's Press, 1991.

Single best source for reporters on finding and using public documents of all types. Comprehensive and invaluable.

Chapter 3

New Tools
for the
Reporting Process

The mayor's late afternoon news conference had ended and a few reporters were still milling around, asking questions of the mayor and his guest.

With great fanfare but few specifics, the mayor had announced the hiring of a newly formed development company to oversee the city's plan to revitalize its downtown commercial district. New Horizons Group, headed by president Albert Jackson, was being awarded a $200,000 consulting contract ahead of several other firms. A one-page press handout outlined the mayor's announcement and briefly listed Jackson's credentials.

One reporter asked Jackson about his company's lack of a track record. Jackson confidently assured him of his experience as a private developer and said he had assembled an experienced staff from several of the state's top firms. Jackson offered no specifics but promised to make a public presentation within several weeks. With that, the news conference broke up.

Back at the *Gazette* newsroom, Reporter A looked over his notes, then looked at his watch. 4 p.m. Offices everywhere would close in 30 minutes.

He checked the *Gazette*'s clip file for articles about Jackson or New Horizons but found nothing. Then he telephoned the Builders Association in the state capital. It had no record of the company. Neither did the Chamber of Commerce nor the Better Business Bureau.

Minutes before closing for the day, a source at the secretary of state's office pulled the company's incorporation papers and gave Reporter A the names of its officers. The reporter checked the clip file again, but none of the names turned up.

Jackson's resume listed the names of several of his past projects around the state, but no other information. By now it was 4:30 and offices were closing. The reporter made a note to check on New Horizons more closely tomorrow, then wrote a 12-inch story, based mostly on the press conference.

> Mayor Arthur Jones yesterday announced that a new company, New Horizons Group, has been hired to coordinate the city's downtown revitalization.
>
> Company president Albert Jackson, who has worked in other communities as a private developer, said he has hired an experienced staff of planners and other professionals to oversee the commercial district's rejuvenation.

Across town at the *Herald*, Reporter B was busily typing at a lone computer terminal in the corner of the newsroom. The terminal, installed just a month before, was linked to several electronic databases and the county's public records files. After logging into the secretary of state's files, she searched the name of company president Albert Jackson. The search listed Jackson as a principal officer in two companies besides New Horizons—Atlas Developers and Hometown Construction, both based in Richland, a city located across the county.

Next she signed onto Vu/Text, a commercial database containing articles from more than 70 regional newspapers, searching the names of Jackson and all three companies. Jackson's name appeared in three related stories.

She called up the full text of the first article and learned that Jackson and his two Richland companies had been implicated two years earlier in a kickback scheme involving public officials in Richland. Charges were dropped when Jackson testified against the officials. Follow-up stories provided additional details.

Switching to the county's computerized file of court records, Reporter B found federal tax liens against Jackson and his two firms. The search also revealed that both companies had filed for bankruptcy just two weeks before New Horizons was incorporated.

Within minutes the reporter was on the phone to the mayor's office—with some tough questions. Her story, "Mayor Hires Developer with Checkered Past," led the *Herald's* morning edition.

> The company hired by the city to plan the downtown renewal is headed by a man implicated two years ago in a kickback scheme involving Richland city officials.
>
> In addition, state records show that Albert Jackson, president of New Horizons Group, is also listed as chief officer of two companies that have filed for bankruptcy and are being prosecuted by federal officials for unpaid taxes.

COMPUTER-ASSISTED REPORTING

Readers of the *Herald* learned a great deal more about New Horizons and its president than those of the *Gazette*, in part because Reporter B had at her disposal one of the most powerful innovations in news gathering—computer-assisted reporting.

The use of computers in the newsroom has vaulted far beyond word processing and page design, and is revolutionizing the way enterprising journalists do their jobs. Reporters are finding new ways to harness the immense storage and analytical power of computers to help them gather background for stories, search news clips and government files, and make sense of mind-numbing statistics.

Computer-assisted reporting, a broad term that encompasses a variety of journalistic computer uses, is the most recent development in a field often called "precision journalism." Precision journalism bolsters traditional reporting methods with the tools of social science research, such as surveys, polling and statistical analysis.

The explosion in computer information storage, combined with innovations in personal computers, has created new opportunities for journalists on both general and specialized beats, working on deadline stories and investigative projects.

Most computer information is stored in electronic libraries called databases. Depending on their purpose, these databases can contain entries from hundreds of major and regional newspapers, magazines and professional journals. Some databases include government records, scientific studies, business reports, trade publications, encyclopedias and even law libraries. A reporter sitting at a computer terminal can search through databases with amazing speed, to check facts or gather background information. Research that might take hours in a library can be completed in minutes.

Reporters also are using the analytical power of computers to sort through the growing mass of information in government computers, to spot trends, unearth misdeeds and report on changing social, political and economic conditions.

Here are a few examples of how reporters have used computer-assisted reporting.

- Curious about membership in the men's-only Bohemian Club, the *San Francisco Chronicle* searched the word "bohemian," in a database version of *Who's Who*. The computer stopped each time it found a name whose biographical data included the word. Among the list of members was then-Secretary of Defense Caspar Weinberger. (By one estimate, a manual search of the printed *Who's Who* would have taken a reporter eight years.)

- The *Sun-Sentinel* in Fort Lauderdale, Fla., analyzed Florida's Police Certification Board files and other records on computer to show how hundreds of police officers charged with misconduct had escaped punishment. The newspaper also reported how some officers who were fired from one police force were able to hide their records and get hired elsewhere.

- When *The Providence Journal-Bulletin* analyzed thousands of records of a state housing agency,

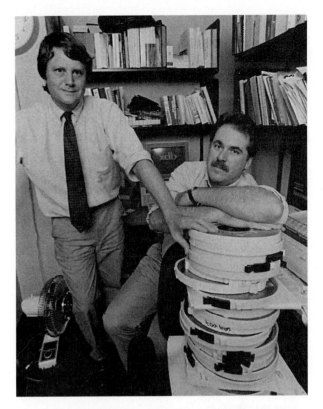

Reporters Brant Houston and Kenton Robinson of The Hartford Courant shown with the personal computers and nine-track computer tapes they use in computer-assisted reporting projects.
Photo by Victor Durao.

reporters found that low-interest mortgages intended for low- and moderate-income buyers had been diverted to the relatives of top state officials. As a result of the investigation, several agency officials resigned and were prosecuted on criminal charges.

In the early 1980s, John Ullmann, an officer of Investigative Reporters and Editors Inc., alerted journalism students and working reporters to the coming trend in database research and its potential to bring a new level of depth and authority to their work.

In *Tapping the Electronic Library*, Ullmann described the wonders of a technology that enabled reporters to rummage through computerized libraries containing hundreds of newspapers and specialized publications for information pertinent to stories they were working on.

The technology described by Ullmann promised to satisfy the journalist's recurring need to become an "instant expert" on a topic. At the same time, reporters could save time by not "reinventing the wheel"— relearning things other reporters already had written about. Ullmann warned that journalists who failed to learn this new technology soon would be overshadowed by a new generation of reporters for whom a computer background search would be as routine as checking clip files.

The Computer at Work

Reporters today are using computers for two distinct but related purposes—searching for and analyzing information contained in databases.

- **Searching.** Locating information in computerized databases is the most common form of computer-assisted journalism. Electronic libraries linked to a computer terminal by telephone lines place vast storehouses of published and unpublished information at a reporter's fingertips.

  Using a carefully constructed command—usually a word, phrase or a combination of several ideas—a reporter can search single or multiple databases. The computer scans each entry to find a match, and tells the user how many matches it has found. The reporter can see a list of entries, short summaries of each or, in the case of "full-text" services, the complete story. Each entry can be called up on the screen, printed or copied onto a computer disk. Reporters can search by name, address, topic, or combination, and usually can specify which years will be searched.

  Journalists search news databases containing articles from national and regional newspapers and magazines to learn what has been written about a topic. By combining the words "airline crash" and "de-icing," for example, a reporter could get a list of articles in newspapers and trade journals about commercial jetliners that crashed because ice was not properly removed from their wings.

Reporters also use database searching to find background or technical explanations of a topic quickly. A reporter looking for general information about Lyme disease might search it by name in a government-subsidized database of the National Library of Medicine. If more current information were needed, such as recent scientific studies about possible vaccines, the reporter might search a more research-oriented source such as Medline, which contains articles from medical and scientific journals.

Computerized databases may never replace the library altogether, but their use can cut research time dramatically and give reporters access to millions of citations from thousands of sources within minutes.

- **Analysis.** Reporters using the power of computers can sort, organize and analyze massive amounts of information from government computer files and new databases they create from paper files. Computers can help reporters find single important facts amid millions of records or identify meaningful patterns and trends that can be supported with statistical evidence.

  The *Dayton Daily News* produced a compelling indictment of workplace safety enforcement by the Occupational Safety and Health Administration by analyzing an agency database containing 1.8 million records of investigations and fines.

  The newspaper showed that companies paid average fines of $500 in connection with accidents in which workers were killed or maimed, and that many companies failed to correct serious hazards even after they were cited. It also identified the 10 U.S. companies with the most serious violations.

  The two reporters on the series also interviewed more than 200 people and examined thousands of written documents, but they credited their computer analysis for providing the statistical proof to conclude that OSHA was not doing its job.

The Information Explosion

In 1992 the Directory of Online Databases listed more than 800 available databases and on-line services, totaling nearly 5 billion citations, and that number is expected to increase. As the number of database services has grown, searching has often become easier, quicker and cheaper.

Surveys of print and broadcast newsrooms around the country show that an increasing number of journalists are making database searching a routine part of their news operations. Once the exclusive domain of projects and investigative reporters, on-line databases are increasingly being used on deadline to produce more detailed stories and to get a jump on the competition.

When a commercial airliner crashed in Detroit, a TV reporter used a database search of news and technical articles to check for prior problems with the aircraft. The reporter typed in the model number of the aircraft and got back a dozen reports showing engine problems with that model. His story went on the air the next day.

The speed advantage of database searching over traditional research methods lies in the reporter's ability to search two or more ideas at once and to locate only articles containing both ideas. For example, by combining the words "malpractice" and "military

hospitals" into a single search command, a reporter will get a list of stories that mention both concepts. Stories that mention only one of the concepts are not included in the list.

If a search is too broad, the computer warns the user that hundreds of articles are available—services such as NEXIS stop searching at 500 citations—and may suggest narrowing the search by adding another key phrase. If the word "Navy" were added to the search command mentioned earlier, only stories about malpractice in Navy hospitals would appear. Adding "obstetrics" would locate stories about shoddy medical procedures during childbirth.

In the Detroit plane crash situation, a search of "airline crash" and "de-icing" on a commercial database produced several hundred citations, too many to be examined individually. The researcher added the term "FAA" to identify stories in which investigative action by the Federal Aviation Administration was mentioned. The second search cut the list to 49. Limiting the search to the two most recent years further reduced the list. This is how a few of the promising citations appeared on the researcher's screen.

Your search request is:
AIRLINE CRASH AND DEICING AND FAA

Number of STORIES found with your search request through:
LEVEL 3...   26

1. Aviation Week and Space Technology, June 29, 1992, AIR TRANSPORT; Vol. 136, No. 26; Pg. 29, 1462 words, NTSB Seeks to Improve Odds For Takeoffs in Icy Conditions, JAMES T. MCKENNA, NEW YORK

2. Aviation Week and Space Technology, June 8, 1992, NEW DEICING PROCEDURES; The Push Is On; Vol. 136, No. 23; Pg. 20, 1660 words, Airlines Strive to Reduce Risks in Winter Operations, JAMES T. MCKENNA, RESTON, VA.

3. Airports(R), June 2, 1992, Vol. 9, No. 22; Pg. 216, 613 words, Airports, Airlines To Work on Deicing Programs Before Winter

4. Newsday, May 30, 1992, Saturday, CITY EDITION, NEWS; Pg. 3 Other Edition: Nassau and Suffolk Pg. 7, 798 words, Rules Out of Ice; FAA pledges sweeping changes in wake of LaGuardia crash, By Glenn Kessler.

In this case, the search was conducted of general news sources and trade publications. While general sources such as the Gannett News Service and *Newsday* covered the issue, the reporter found that specialized publications such as *Aviation Week and Space Technology* reported on it more often and in greater depth. Within minutes, the reporter had obtained several articles that provided extensive background on the topic plus the names of possible sources.

Communicating by Computer

Some services allow reporters to communicate with one another through "electronic mail." A user can leave notes to reporters at other publications, or transmit stories directly to their "mailbox" in much the same way files are transferred between reporters and editors in a newsroom.

A related function called electronic bulletin boards lets users post notices to other users in the system. Reporters can place a kind of classified ad on a bulletin board, seeking information or leads for stories they are working on.

One useful variation of electronic mail is an electronic clipping service that automatically searches new database entries each day and sends pertinent articles to the reporter's mailbox. A reporter might set up a search command looking for any breaking stories involving police brutality against members of minority groups. Each day, any new stories fitting the search profile would be copied directly into the reporter's mailbox.

An Expanding Resource

For purposes of news reporting, databases fall into three general categories: commercial on-line database services; government information, including a range of public records; and in-house data.

Commercial On-Line Database Services

These computerized libraries give reporters access to thousands of published sources in the general and specialized press, science and technology, social sciences, health, medicine, education, business and entertainment. They are called "on-line" because they can be accessed from a terminal in the newsroom or from a home computer via a modem.

Two commercial services commonly used by journalists are Vu/Text, which provides the complete text of articles from more than 70 newspapers, and NEXIS, a comprehensive database that supplements major newspapers and magazines with articles from wire services such as Associated Press and United Press International, hundreds of specialized publications and a range of government information.

It is important to understand the difference between a database service, a database and a gateway. Database services like NEXIS often are compared to a supermarket offering a variety of products, in this case individual databases. NEXIS has more than 350 databases, in categories such as news, government legislation, medical and drug information and others, which can be searched using common commands. Gateways bring together several database services, allowing the researcher to search each using a single command language.

Sitting at a terminal at home or in the office, a reporter linked to NEXIS can call up a corporation's latest filings with the U.S. Securities and Exchange Commission, a senator's testimony in the Congressional Record, and a list of a local company's officers filed with the secretary of state.

A companion service called LEXIS is a legal research source that contains details of millions of state and federal laws and legal cases, rulings of the Internal Revenue Service, and other legal information.

DIALOG, the oldest and the largest of the major on-line information services, contains *Facts on File*, plus access to more than 800 magazines, including the major news magazines, trade journals and newsletters. DIALOG also offers specialized information such as Dun and Bradstreet's Market Identifiers, which contains information on private businesses not found elsewhere; Donnelly Demographics, with population and income data available by state, city and zip code; and the results of surveys by major polling organizations.

Another favorite of journalists is DataTimes, which provides full texts of *USA Today* and *The Wall Street Journal*, along with many regional newspapers, including *The Orange County Register, The Seattle*

TABLE 3–1
A wealth of sources

Newsday's news librarians help reporters tap into a wide range of general and specialized databases. Here is a partial list:

NEWSPAPERS AND MAGAZINES (full-text)

DATATIMES—regional newspapers plus some large metros.
DIALOG—Full text, statistical and bibliographic information in a range of fields, including finance and demographics. Includes index of hundreds of magazines and results of major polls.
NEWSNET—Full text of specialized newsletters on topics including religion, computers, airline safety and education.
NEXIS—Newspapers, magazines, wire services, professional and trade journals, business, industry and government information. Includes *Time, Newsweek, Washington Post* and *The New York Times.*
VU/TEXT—Full text of more than 70 regional newspapers.

U.S. GOVERNMENT AND ELECTIONS

CIS—Indexes and abstracts of Congressional publications. Includes public laws, hearings, executive reports. Produced by Congressional Information Service.
FEC DATABASE—Contains Federal Elections Commission data, including filing information for presidential and congressional candidates and PACS.
WASHINGTON ALERT—Congressional action including history and status of legislation, text of bills and resolutions, and committee schedules.

LEGAL

LEXIS—Contains legal decisions in state and federal courts.

BUSINESS AND FINANCIAL

DISCLOSURE—Securities and Exchange Commission filings of publicly held companies.
DOW JONES NEWS AND RETRIEVAL—Company and industry news information and stock quotes. Includes *Barrons, Wall Street Journal* and historical stock information.
UNIFORM COMMERCIAL CODE—Filings on secured loan transactions, searchable by company and personal name.
REUTERS MEDIA SERVICES—Includes currency exchange rates, stock figures, international economics and balance of trade.
DEPARTMENT OF MOTOR VEHICLES DATABASE—Driving and registration records of persons licensed to drive in New York State.

MILITARY AND ESPIONAGE

SPYBASE—Database of more than 40,000 names and organizations connected to intelligence gathering. Emphasis on the intelligence community, right wing, Latin America, domestic surveillance and assassination theory.
PERISCOPE—Text and statistical information on worldwide military power and spending.

INTERNATIONAL

COUNTRY REPORTS—Demographics, local customs, geography and climate, energy, politics, economics and other detailed information about the world's countries.
TEXTLINE—News publications from around the world. Some full text, some abstracts.

ENTERTAINMENT

BASELINE—Entertainment industry database covering television and movies. Provides box office grosses, full credits, film history, films in production and celebrity biographies.

Source: Reprinted with permission of *Newsday.*

Times, Chicago Sun-Times, the *Star Tribune* in Minneapolis, *The Dallas Morning News* and *The Record* in Bergen County, N.J.

Government Records

Virtually every city in the United States stores some records in computers. To varying degrees, governments at the federal, state, county and municipal level also maintain an assortment of public records in computers, from an individual's driving record to a list of a candidate's campaign contributions.

As governments move toward increased computer storage of records, many government agencies are reducing their paper files or not generating any new ones. For example, the federal Securities and Exchange Commission encourages companies to submit mandatory reports directly into that agency's

computers because it saves the time and cost of having clerks type in the information.

Some city clerk's offices, court systems and other government agencies maintain both paper files and computerized versions of those records; however, many agencies are gradually computerizing all files and phasing out paper records. Reporters not accustomed to searching government records from a computer terminal increasingly may find they can't get the information any other way. Some agencies provide public terminals for searching these records in their offices, while some newspapers have negotiated with a state or county government to establish on-line access to public files from a newsroom terminal.

Newspapers in North Carolina, Florida, Ohio and Connecticut were among the first to install remote terminals that give them direct access to certain state and county records. From their offices, reporters can

A city hall clerk helps a reporter search computerized property records from a public terminal. Computer files are replacing paper records at many state and municipal agencies, and reporters must learn to access those records via computer. Photo by Andrea Hoy.

call up real estate tax records, property deeds, voter registrations, individual driving records, vehicle registrations and court records to add details to breaking stories.

Within minutes, a reporter can check the driving record of a bus driver involved in a serious accident, or the number of malpractice lawsuits pending against a physician. The possible uses of government databases are limited only by the reporter's ingenuity and persistence.

Shortly after the *Dayton Daily News* linked one of its personal computers to the county's computer, one enterprising reporter working on a single tip was able to compile a detailed and revealing financial profile of an immigration attorney who apparently had skipped town with his clients' money.

By searching various county records, the reporter learned that during the previous year the lawyer had purchased a $305,000 house with a $275,000 mortgage, and then, a week before disappearing, had obtained another mortgage for $40,000. Automobile title records showed he had purchased a Mercedes for $40,000.

Civil court files showed nearly $60,000 in federal tax liens on the man's house and business, and provided the reporter with a list of creditors who had sued the lawyer, along with their attorneys' names and telephone numbers. The research took about an hour, and convinced the reporter he was onto a good story.

NEXIS and other commercial vendors provide access to Uniform Commercial Code filings, which contain details of secured loans obtained by private companies and individuals, including a description of the borrower's collateral. UCC filings are a staple for reporters checking the financial condition of companies or their officers. These records are usually kept in the office of the secretary of state, and sometimes in the county recorder's office. Using an on-line search, either by the company name or key individuals, a reporter can check UCC filings in a few minutes.

Reporters also can research a Federal Elections Commission database that lists campaign contributions to presidential and congressional candidates, and political action committees. Using the Environmental Protection Agency's Toxic Release Inventory database, available through direct on-line dial-up, many reporters in the late 1980s began tracking major polluters in their region.

In-House Databases

Computerized news libraries found at many large newspapers are the most simple and common type of in-house database. Each day's newspaper is "filed" electronically and can be searched using single or multiple concepts. A reporter doesn't need to look through every City Council clipping to find out when it awarded a contract for rubbish removal. A carefully worded search on the computer will locate the story in seconds.

Some newspapers create in-house databases to assist day-to-day reporting. Databases are assembled using local statistics on topics such as crime, population and hospital room rates, plus directories of names and telephone numbers of public officials and organizations. Reporters at those newspapers can call up the information without leaving their desks.

The most innovative form of in-house database involves creating new databases from government records or combining existing ones and storing them in the newspaper's own computer to be analyzed later. Most often used in investigative projects, in-house databases allow reporters to spot trends by electronically "sorting" the information to their specifications. In-house databases and their uses as an investigative tool by journalists are described in more detail later in this chapter.

Forms of Information

Depending on the commercial service being used, computerized information is available in one of three forms: full-text, bibliographic and numeric.

- **Full-text.**   This provides a reporter with complete articles from newspapers, magazines and journals. A journalist's concerns for speed and timeliness make full-text capability the most desirable service, but it is also the most expensive.

Full-text articles can be printed directly from the database (which is time-consuming and costly because it accumulates computer time) or copied onto a floppy disk in the user's personal computer, a process called "downloading." Working from their own computers, reporters can then call up the articles and print them as needed, with no additional charges for computer time.

Full texts of articles can provide useful background, identify sources who can be contacted for interviews, and suggest angles for the reporter's story. In the airline example cited earlier, the reporter learned about several crashes caused by de-icing problems, industry research to develop new de-icing substances, and steps that the FAA and airports were taking to minimize icing during inclement weather. The stories also outlined the latest FAA investigations, plus the names of sources at the FAA and on the Senate Aviation subcommittee that was studying the problem.

As with any background material, information from database searches may have to be verified, and reporters must be wary when using news articles as primary sources of statistics and other factual matter.

- **Bibliographic.** In this form, the reporter's search yields a list of articles, plus an abstract or summary of each article and a complete citation of where it can be found. Many college and university libraries have Info-Trac, NewsBank or comparable computer resources that provide information only in bibliographic form.

  The main disadvantage of bibliographic searches is that to get the complete article, the researcher must manually search through microfilm or bound library volumes—assuming that the library receives the publication.

  Bibliographic entries list the author and title of the article; the newspaper or journal in which it appeared; the volume, date and page; a list of search terms; and an abstract 50 to 100 words long. Scanning the abstract may show whether the full article is worth obtaining. Some abstracts are detailed enough to give the reporter the information he or she needs. For reporters on deadline, however, getting the full text of articles is usually the

preferred option. Bibliographic services usually cost less than those providing full-text. Some services contain information in both forms.

- **Numeric.** Some databases provide raw figures for such things as stock and commodities prices, currency rates or health statistics that are updated daily. Reporters may locate the figures they need for a particular day, or download the information over a period of time and review it later to track trends.

  For example, a business reporter interested in the price of crude oil during the Persian Gulf War could quickly extract just those figures from the raw data to show fluctuations over several weeks or months. Some numeric databases provide information already assembled in this time-series form. Business writers also can use numeric stock information to chart the ups and downs of local companies and banks.

THE TECHNOLOGY SPREADS

Until recent years, computer-assisted reporting has been used mostly by larger newspapers, but that situation is changing for several reasons:

- The costs for computer time and equipment, once prohibitive for smaller news operations, have started to drop.

- Having seen what other journalists have accomplished with computers, more editors are willing to commit financial and staff resources to add database capabilities.

- The growing volume of government records on computer adds weight to the argument that reporters need to develop searching skills.

- New computer hardware and software have simplified database analysis on low-cost personal computers.

- A new generation of young reporters is entering the field after learning database research in college journalism programs.

Although the relatively high cost of newsroom searching has kept most small and medium-size newspapers from hiring a commercial database service, reporters at these publications still can find ways to conduct database searches.

If the story is important enough, an editor might authorize hiring a private "information broker" to run a single search for a fee. Public and university libraries can provide another alternative, and often have trained staff who can help the reporter plan a "pre-search strategy" to cut down on expensive computer time.

Some reporters link their home computers to a budget database service. Two popular options are Knowledge Index (offered by DIALOG) and BRS after Dark (a service of Bibliographic Research Service). Each contains more than 100 of the most popular databases provided by the full-service versions.

Reporters often find that when they can produce better stories in less time, even the most reluctant editors are willing to pay for computer time.

Advantages of Database Searching

Reporters should remember that information obtained through database research never will replace interviews with sources or the reporter's own firsthand observation of events. Quotes, color and detail gathered through more traditional methods remain essential to compelling and readable stories.

However, when it comes to collecting background and casting a wide search net over a topic, electronic libraries offer several advantages over traditional library and documents research methods.

- **Speed.**   Research time can be cut dramatically. Searches of articles and records that might take days manually can be reduced to hours or minutes on the computer. Time saved can be spent on interviews, writing or getting the story into print sooner.

- **Focus.**   A carefully constructed computer search allows a reporter to examine only those articles or statistics of specific interest. An initial search may be broad, but it can be quickly narrowed to discard information that is unrelated or too general.

- **Volume.**   A reporter has direct access to many more sources than could be found in even the best library. A single search on Vu/Text, for example, will scan more than 70 major and regional

newspapers in minutes. During a search, reporters often find sources or information they didn't know existed.

- **Timeliness.**   Most news databases and many specialized libraries are updated daily, so that articles printed yesterday are available for searching today. Information from statistical sources and government files is available as soon as it is loaded into the agency's records. Minutes after Congress passed the 1990 Civil Rights bill compromise, reporters were able to obtain copies through a specialized database called Washington Alert.

- **Proximity.**   Records or published sources that might be a county, state or even a continent away can be accessed as easily as if they were in the next room. Distances that once kept reporters from traveling to Washington, D.C., or their state capital to check records can be traversed by a telephone call.

- **Accuracy.**   Rather than relying on other news accounts, reporters can check census figures, AIDS statistics and other information with primary sources such as the U.S. Census Bureau's on-line file CEN-DATA. Amendments to laws or federal regulations usually are listed with the original language, minimizing the chance that reporters will miss important revisions.

Limiting Factors

Cost may be the single biggest factor limiting database use. Time logged onto a commercial database can cost $35 to $300 in charges for long-distance hookups and each full record accessed. New discount services are cropping up, and some vendors offer low-cost searching during off-peak hours such as evenings and weekends.

To control costs, many news operations limit search authority to newsroom librarians or a handful of senior reporters. Others must get approval and work with an experienced searcher so that correct keyboard commands are used and the best databases are searched.

Other potential disadvantages to database use include:

- **Repeating errors.**   The adage "Don't believe everything you read" applies to database information.

The feared newsroom lapse of picking up errors from news clippings can be multiplied with databases. Verifying the accuracy of computerized information can be difficult but reporters should be careful to check any information they sense might be suspect.

- **Information overload.**   The volume of available information can slow some reporters to a crawl, especially until they become proficient at narrowing their search quickly. They also may become distracted by interesting tidbits only loosely related to their stories. Serendipity has its place in research, but seldom on deadline.

- **Loss of contacts.**   Reporters enamored with the ease of obtaining background may find themselves spending more time at the computer and less time on the street or at City Hall developing sources. Reporters must strike the right balance between electronic and in-person research.

SEARCHING A DATABASE

Computer searching is more art than science, requiring a combination of planning, flexibility, creativity and practice. A poorly planned search can be frustrating and costly.

Help can come from newsroom librarians, other reporters or the on-line service's technical support staff. Many college and university libraries offer limited database services for students. These generally use the same searching principles as do the more elaborate services, and can give students a low-cost introduction to searching.

Reporters can begin with a modest search to see what turns up. From there they may expand their search and the citation list. Finally, they will come full circle with a more specific search that narrows the list to only the most useful articles.

Each commercial database service has its own *protocol*, a unique way of searching files using specified keyboard commands. Although specific commands and directions may vary among services, they usually have enough in common that a reporter who can search NEXIS can usually adapt to a new database such as Vu/Text with a little instruction.

Searching Logic

What most commercial on-line services have in common is a logical search process, known as Boolean logic, that is similar to algebra but uses words instead of numbers to establish relationships.

Major relationships among key ideas are defined by using connector words, usually **AND**, **OR** and **NOT**, that limit the search. For example, searching the word "lion" will produce a list of every article in that database in which lion appears. If the reporter is also interested in tigers, the search would be expanded to read "lions **OR** tigers." A list of every article that mentions *either* lions or tigers would appear on the screen. However, if the reporter wants only articles that mention *both* types of animals, the search would be revised to "lions **AND** tigers."

Such a broad topic undoubtedly would produce a long list. Most databases alert the user when a search has found an unwieldy number of citations, and may suggest a narrower search.

At that point, the reporter might decide to limit the search to articles about the breeding of lions or tigers. A new search might read:

(lion **OR** tiger) **AND** breeding

Notice that parentheses are placed around (lion **OR** tiger). This tells the computer to search first for articles about either lions or tigers, and then to select only those that also mention breeding. In this way, articles about taxidermy or lion hunting in Africa would be excluded.

Databases can also search for proximity, meaning that an article will be cited only when a word appears within a specified number of words of another. If the researcher is interested only in zoo breeding, the second part of the search might say "... breeding **w/10** zoo." In that case, the word "breeding" would have to appear within 10 words of "zoo" for the article to be selected. The complete search would appear as:

(lion **OR** tiger) **AND** breeding **w/10** zoo

Taking it one step further, if the reporter is only interested in zoo breeding programs outside the United States, the search could be refined by using the connector **NOT**:

(lion **OR** tiger) **AND** (breeding **w/10** zoo) **NOT** United States

A word of caution: Exclusionary commands can backfire. In the above example, an article might mention the United States but focus on foreign zoos. A better search command might be:

(lion **OR** tiger) **AND** (breeding **w/10** zoo) **AND** foreign

---

BOX 3–1

Tracking a Connection

✳✳✳

When the Mashantucket Pequot Indian tribe opened the first legalized gambling casino in New England in 1992, some local critics warned that organized crime could gain a foothold in the operation. One reporter used the NEXIS® service to find stories written about the subject across the country.

The computer turned up 18 stories, using the simple NEXIS command:

CASINO AND (INDIAN GAMBLING W/10 ORGANIZED CRIME)

First, the computer searched the command in parentheses, identifying articles in which the phrase "INDIAN GAMBLING" appeared within 10 words of the phrase "ORGANIZED CRIME." The search then narrowed the first list by selecting only those containing the word "CASINO."

This is how the first six articles appeared on the reporter's screen. (Note that each listing includes the type of bibliographic information found in printed indexes.)

LEVEL 1 - 18 STORIES
1.NPR, MORNING EDITION, May 13, 1992, Wednesday, 692 words, FORT MCDOWELL GAMING CENTER RAIDED BY FEDS. PHOENIX
2.States News Service, March 4, 1992, Wednesday, 702 words, FEDERAL STATUS WOULD MEAN MORE MONEY FOR HOUMAS, BIA SAYS, By ELLEN GAMERMAN, States News Service, WASHINGTON

3.The Washington Post, February 15, 1992, Saturday, Final Edition, STYLE; PAGE C1, 2407 words, CASINO ON SACRED GROUND; IN CONNECTICUT, THE PEQUOTS TAKE A GAMBLE ON THEIR HERITAGE, KEN RINGLE, The Washington Post Staff Writer, LEDYARD, Conn., NATIONAL NEWS
4.GANNETT NEWS SERVICE, February 5, 1992, Wednesday, 760 words, INDIAN LEADERS DENY MOB TIES TO GAMING, CHET LUNNER; Gannett News Service, WASHINGTON
5.GANNETT NEWS SERVICE, February 4, 1992, Tuesday, 819 words, U.S. WARNS THAT MOB POISED TO JUMP ON INDIAN CASINOS, KEN MILLER; Gannett News Service, WASHINGTON
6.Los Angeles Times, January 10, 1992, Friday, San Diego County Edition, Part A; Page 3; Column 2; Metro Desk, 744 words, ABSENCES MAR HEARING ON INDIAN CASINOS; GAMBLING: JUSTICE DEPARTMENT OFFICIALS FAIL TO SHOW UP BEFORE HOUSE INTERIOR COMMITTEE. By GLENN F. BUNTING, Times Staff Writer. WASHINGTON, Full Run

To account for variations in spelling or plural forms, databases also will search versions of a root word by using a wild card symbol such as an exclamation point or question mark. Wild cards must be used carefully because they often broaden the search to include unwanted citations. Searching for "tax?", the reporter would get "taxi," "taxpayer," "taxidermy" and "taxonomy."

The experienced reporter plans his or her search in advance, often by writing a sentence stating exactly what information is being sought. Sometimes just the process of writing out key ideas will suggest ways to construct the search and may help to narrow it even further.

A reporter who wrote the phrase "Any article about zoo breeding of lions or tigers outside the U.S." before sitting down at the terminal would be several steps ahead of one who began by searching "lions or tigers." The bill for computer time also would be much lower.

Database vendors usually provide written instructions or training disks to familiarize users with their search protocols. As with many new technologies, reporters who learn to use database research with skill and confidence often wonder how they ever got along without it.

Getting Help

Reporters venturing into database searching on their own, with limited resources and support from editors, often can enlist the help of reference staff at public and university libraries. Some libraries will conduct searches for reporters, charging only for computer time.

More and more newsroom librarians are training in database use, and are often the best source for help in selecting a database and constructing a search. Several major vendors now offer low-cost packages to colleges and universities, providing students free searches to complete class assignments.

Database searching is becoming an integral part of the reporting process, and new journalists would do well to learn to use one major on-line database or CD-ROM service to practice searching on their own.

The CD-ROM Option

One low-cost research alternative for journalists is CD-ROM (Compact Disc-Read Only Memory), which uses the same technology that revolutionized the quality of recorded music.

Instead of tapping into a library stored in a distant computer, a reporter using CD-ROM selects a compact disc on which information is stored and slips it into a microcomputer. Some CDs can store 80,000 pages of text, and collections cover nearly as broad a range of general and specialized topics as is found in on-line databases.

A few CD-ROM collections have proven to be invaluable to journalists. Some news organizations subscribe to a CD locator directory called Phone Disc USA that lists the names, addresses and telephone numbers of people across the country. Phone Disc is a kind of national telephone book that a reporter can search either by name or telephone number. If a reporter believes someone lives in a particular state or region of the country, the search can be narrowed by selecting certain area codes.

The main advantages to CD-ROM are low cost and availability. Many libraries subscribe to CD-ROM services in the same way they would purchase magazines or trade journals, and there is often no charge for using it. Unlike database use, reporters need not be concerned with time spent at the computer screen, since it costs nothing to operate the terminal and there are no expensive on-line charges.

However, there are a few disadvantages, including timeliness and speed. Information stored on CD-ROM is not as current as that available through on-line services. While many databases are updated daily, CD-ROM holdings can be weeks or months behind. Reporters who need up-to-date information may still need to use the CD's companion on-line service, if one exists.

While some CD-ROM collections offer full texts of articles, some are simply indexes. To obtain the full article, the researcher must look elsewhere, usually on microfiche.

The NewsBank Electronic Index, for example, contains listings of selected newspaper articles from more than 450 newspapers. Using NewsBank, reporters can obtain a list of articles by searching in much the same way they would with an on-line service. However, the articles themselves would need to be located individually on microfiche.

Despite its limitations, CD-ROM is a useful research tool for journalists, especially those on tight budgets who are not on a tight deadline.

THE ELECTRONIC TRAIL

Harnessing the power of computers to sort, organize and analyze massive amounts of information is the fastest growing area of computer-assisted reporting. It has been called the "chic investigative beat of the '90s," and its use has spread to newsrooms around the country. In 1991 eight of 10 finalists for the Pulitzer Prize used some form of computer analysis.

The accumulation of information in government computers during the past two decades has created new obstacles to public affairs reporting but also some new opportunities. Powerful personal computers and software that can analyze government files open up uncharted possibilities within the means of even small newspapers.

Public affairs reporters have always used public records to monitor the activities of government. Enterprising reporters used to spend days or weeks examining public documents, taking notes and then organizing them to spot trends or to document misdeeds. A reporter investigating the competency of fire safety inspectors, for example, might review hundreds of inspection reports and other documents to detect a pattern of lax enforcement.

Today, that same work can be accomplished in a few hours or less by a reporter using a personal computer to analyze the computer version of those files.

The Roots of Precision Journalism

Using computers to analyze data and improve reporting was pioneered in the 1960s by Philip Meyer, who coined the term *precision journalism* and wrote a book by that title.

Meyer used a large mainframe computer to study the survey responses of black residents living in Detroit neighborhoods during the 1967 civil rights riots. His analysis refuted several popular theories about the riots and led to a series of stories that helped win a Pulitzer Prize for the *Detroit Free Press* in 1968.

One such theory, according to Meyer, was that "rioters were the most frustrated and hopeless cases at the bottom of the economic ladder." But Meyer's analysis of survey results found that people who had attended college were "just as likely to participate in the riot" as those who had dropped out of high school. A second theory held that rioters tended to be immigrants from the South who had not assimilated into northern culture. But the survey showed blacks raised in the North were more than twice as likely to have rioted than southern immigrants.

Today's reporters continue to extend the boundaries of creative computer use, analyzing all manner of government computer records and creating new databases from paper files when what they need doesn't exist in computer form. While mainframe computers are still used on the biggest projects, desktop PCs costing only a few thousand dollars can handle the type of "number crunching" done by Meyer a quarter century ago.

Computers enable reporters to organize millions of computer files, find single important facts, and spot patterns and trends. They can search specific categories, identify factors that appear frequently and cross-check one database against another, looking for matches.

While a reporter at *The Providence Journal-Bulletin*, Elliot Jaspin used computer tapes from several state agencies to analyze the records of 5,000 school bus drivers. The idea developed after three Rhode Island children were killed in separate incidents involving school buses.

Working from a computer list of bus drivers, Jaspin ran the names through separate databases for traffic violations and criminal convictions. He learned that several drivers had been convicted of felonies ranging from racketeering to dealing drugs, and identified drivers with more than 10 traffic violations.

Getting the Local Slant

Computers also create the opportunity for what one editor calls "niche journalism"—analyzing large national databases to focus on conditions in a particular city, county or state. The 1990 national census, available from a U.S. Census Bureau database, created such an opportunity.

Using a software program to sort and organize local census statistics, journalists can identify such social indicators as crime figures, hospital services and even mortgage lending practices by neighborhoods. While the Census Bureau provides its own analysis of national patterns, journalists with access to the same statistics can highlight local trends. Sometimes their analyses are ahead of the Census Bureau's.

The Atlanta *Journal and Constitution* produced an ongoing series of stories based on its computer analysis of the 1990 census. The coverage looked at national and local trends. One story showed that during the 1980s, divorce rates in the South surpassed the national average for the first time.

> Divorce, which transformed life in metropolitan areas in the 1970s, arrived at full power in Towns County and other bedrock Bible Belt communities in the 1980s, tumbling these last bastions of the traditional American family.
>
> Nationwide, one in every 10 adults is either separated or currently divorced, the U.S. Census Bureau reports. An analysis of the 1990 census shows that even more marriages are on the rocks in the South and Georgia, with 11 percent either divorced or separated in the region and 12 percent in the state.

Using the computer's sorting capability, the newspaper was able to identify individual counties in Georgia with the highest divorce rates.

> Dawson County led the state in divorce increases in the past decade. Divorced or separated people made up 5.7 percent of the population in 1980 and 9.8 percent in 1990. In South Georgia's Calhoun and Quitman counties, the percentage of divorced and separated people was among the highest in the state—13 percent and 14 percent, respectively.

Favorite investigative targets of computer-assisted reporting projects are state and county courts. Many newspapers will examine the sentencing patterns of judges, identifying discrimination in sentencing by crime, race or sex of the defendant.

The *San Jose Mercury News*, for example, used computer-assisted reporting to analyze 700,000 criminal cases in California during a 10-year period. The newspaper found that members of racial minority groups often were discriminated against in cases where judges had sentencing discretion.

The analysis of government records differs from the accessing of government databases described earlier. A reporter who looks up a person's driving record or criminal convictions from a newsroom terminal usually receives the information on a "read only" basis—that is, the data can't be changed or copied electronically.

A few state and county governments allow reporters to download to their computers from a remote terminal, but the more common method of obtaining the data is to purchase it on nine-track magnetic tape. When available, reporters purchase complete copies of the tapes—usually for a few hundred dollars—then analyze them on their own mainframe computer or with personal computers equipped with special conversion software.

Creating a Database

Sometimes reporters need public information not available from government computers, or at least not available in a usable form. When the information doesn't exist in electronic format, reporters will create their own "in-house" database by manually inputting the information from paper records. This tedious and time-consuming process was the only way to analyze records before the explosion in government computer data, and must still be done for some records.

When Dwight Morris of the *Los Angeles Times* decided to examine the availability of assault weapons in 1989, he discovered that the U.S. Bureau of Alcohol, Tobacco and Firearms collected data but had not entered it into its computers. Morris had to enter more than 45,000 agency documents into his database, which he accomplished with the help of commercial data entry services.

Personal Computers

Technological innovations have made it possible for journalists at medium and small newspapers to undertake ambitious computer-assisted reporting projects.

For many years, the enormous volume of information contained on government tapes could be analyzed only on large-capacity mainframe computers. Some reporters were allowed to use their newspaper's

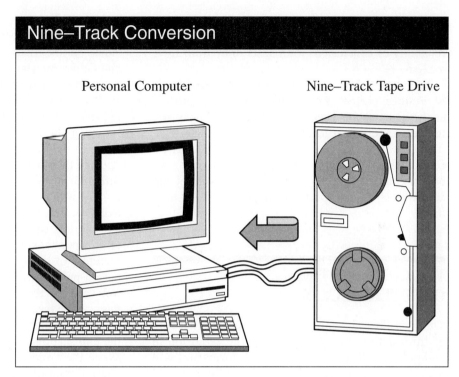

Nine–Track Conversion

Personal Computer   Nine–Track Tape Drive

business computers for projects, or they leased time from computer companies. While the number of newspapers doing projects grew, major investigations were usually limited to larger newspapers.

Many of the barriers facing journalists fell with development of equipment that can transfer nine-track computer tapes used by government computers onto personal computers equipped with software packages that can analyze the data (see Figure 3–1). As more and smaller newspapers have embarked on computer-assisted projects, larger ones have undertaken increasingly complex and ambitious investigations.

The Atlanta *Journal and Constitution* won a Pulitzer Prize for a 1988 series documenting racial discrimination in home mortgage lending patterns in the Atlanta area. The project was based on the records of 109,000 real estate loans reported to the federal government. The series, "The Color of Money," revealed that white applicants were five times as likely to get home loans as black applicants who earned similar incomes.

Four years later, the newspaper analyzed 4 million home mortgage applications across the country—

nearly 37 times the number of files examined for the 1988 series—and cross-checked the data with the 1990 census. The series showed that many of the discrimination patterns first identified in Atlanta also existed in cities across the United States.

Inaccuracy at the Source

Reporters must be alert to the possibility that the raw data they are using is inaccurate or was incorrectly keyboarded by the agency. Reporters at *The Hartford Courant* researching injury rates among prison guards were surprised when their analysis showed that guards were injured more frequently in fights with other guards than by prison inmates. It turned out that clerks had incorrectly coded injuries during data entry.

Such inconsistencies should be re-examined, with common sense being the rule. A statistical anomaly—something unusual or so unexpected that it immediately grabs the reporter's attention—always should be double-checked. The anomaly may indicate a big story or simply reveal tainted information.

Most ethical concerns emerging from this evolving field center on privacy issues, accuracy of data and the reliability of conclusions journalists draw from their analysis.

To guard against misusing this powerful tool, John R. Bender, editor of *FOI Notebook*, says reporters analyzing databases need a basic understanding of statistical measurement to draw correct inferences from their data. If necessary, they should consult experts to review their findings. Government records can become outdated, he says, and journalists who obtain computer tapes are expected to update and verify their data.

THE COMPLEXITIES OF PUBLIC ACCESS

The legislators who created federal and state Freedom of Information laws did so before the explosion in computer storage of government information and could not have anticipated the ways reporters would use that information. In recent years, states have had to grapple with the complex access issues raised by the computer revolution.

In the early days of computerized records, many states were cautious, even reluctant, to release information. (One state judge ruled that a computerized voting list was more like a piece of office equipment than a public record.) However, as journalists and policy-makers have come to understand the power of this technology, some progress has been made to bring FOI laws into the computer age.

Most state courts have ruled that computer tapes and disks are public records and must be made available, but some individual agencies still have great latitude in deciding how to make the information public, whether in paper form or on computer disk or tape.

A nationwide survey conducted in 1988 by the Public Records Division of the Massachusetts Secretary of State found no states that attempted to exempt computer records from public disclosure laws. However, some states allowed the agencies that collected them to decide in what form the records would be released.

Some agencies are generous in their policies, agreeing to sell computer tapes at a reasonable cost or providing on-line access to files from a newsroom terminal. Others are less obliging and may throw hurdles in a reporter's path, citing privacy concerns or limited staff resources as reasons for not complying with the request. Regulations guiding the use and availability of state, county and municipal information in computer form are still evolving and many agencies have not updated their open records policies to make computer information available. Reporters should become familiar with policies in their states and be prepared to negotiate for the release of information.

Reporters typically negotiate access conditions with an agency's ranking officials. Many agencies, such as a secretary of state's office or health department, may have a public records division. Both sides are usually well-versed in the law, and often an agreeable compromise can be reached.

These agencies often raise concerns that releasing the information may violate the privacy of individuals. When the *Syracuse Herald-Journal* attempted to purchase computer tapes from the New York Health Department containing millions of records on hospital admissions and discharges, many hospitals filed objections with the department's Data Protection Review Board. The board eventually released the records after the newspaper agreed to conditions that would protect the confidentiality of patients.

The ability of journalists to analyze government data presupposes that reporters can obtain those records in a usable form. Agencies accustomed to releasing copies of paper records may be reluctant to supply the information on computer tape or disks.

While some state laws specify that data should be made available in a form that is most practical or convenient to the user, other states allow the records custodian to determine the form, which may be reams of computer printouts.

Problems at the Local Level

Obtaining computer information in day-to-day reporting may pose different hurdles. At the city or county level, custodians of records such as municipal clerks or police desk sergeants might not be well-versed in computer access laws and may refuse to release information in a timely fashion.

Administrative reluctance can be most pronounced in smaller municipalities, where officials may have little experience with the issue. Those officials may cite time and staff constraints in refusing to grant the request.

A survey of municipal clerks in Connecticut, taken after passage of a new computer-access law in 1992, showed considerable resistance to computerization and a reluctance to release computerized information to reporters. Two thirds of the 169 municipalities surveyed had some or all of their records on computer, while the rest had none. Many clerks admitted they did not understand the law, and some said they feared accidentally releasing private records. Others said they did not know enough about computers to transfer information onto computer disks for reporters.

The reporter's best approach in such situations may be a reasoned and assertive manner, supported by a clear understanding of state laws. Reluctant custodians are a fact of life for all reporters. After an initial refusal, the reporter usually will be referred to a superior. Journalists would be wise to establish ground rules with an agency before records are needed on deadline.

Requests should be specific—a broad request for "all computer files about . . ." can be reason enough for denial. Reporters should be prepared to make the request in writing. They also should indicate they believe they have a legal right to the information, and that they will file a complaint with the appropriate review panel if the request is not granted. It also may be useful to cite specific cases at the same agency or in other communities where similar information was released.

Reporters who encounter continued resistance may find their only recourse is to file a complaint under their state FOI laws.

Recurring Concerns

Other key issues have emerged in the ongoing debate over access to computer records:

- **Confidential information.**   Some records contain both private and public information. For example,

state health departments collect information about hospitals that includes details on individual patients. While the number of people who underwent open-heart surgery may be a public record, the names of those patients are not. In some states, criminal court cases that have been dismissed become sealed and are no longer public.

When records contain both private and public information, agencies may refuse to release any information in those files, arguing that to do so would require creating a new record to delete private material. Most state laws only require the release of existing records, not the creation of new ones. However, some states allow for deleting confidential information if the newspaper pays processing costs.

- **Computer programs.**   Some states, while agreeing to release computer tapes, have refused to require the release of commercially produced software that agencies and municipalities use to process the information. Their argument is based on objections from commercial vendors.

- **Commercial information.**   Some states have attempted to control or deny access to any information that may have commercial value. The reason often given is that private individuals or businesses should not be able to reap large profits from information gathered with taxpayers' dollars. Some states charge higher fees for such information. Journalists have successfully argued that news gathering is not a commercial purpose.

Each of these issues has implications for reporting, and many states have reviewed their FOI laws to address at least some of them. Both the Massachusetts survey and a report by the Reporters' Committee for Freedom of the Press found wide variance among state policies. Those differences are expected to persist, in much the same way state FOI laws have varied.

Inconsistencies also exist at the federal level, where the Freedom of Information Act does little to instruct agencies about computer records. In 1991 the Justice Department surveyed federal agencies about their policies for releasing computer data under the federal FOIA. The survey found many disparities in compliance procedures, and recommended that the federal government develop uniform policies and practices for releasing information stored in the computers of federal agencies.

Some revisions to the federal FOIA are likely as demands for information increase.

A Resource List

Investigative Reporters and Editors Inc. has been a major force in promoting computer-assisted reporting and developing a network for journalists to share information. IRE conducts national and regional conferences annually, with several workshops dedicated to computer-assisted reporting. Its newsletter, the *IRE Journal*, regularly features innovative projects and how-to stories for launching investigations.

Formal training for journalists, students and educators is offered by several programs affiliated with large journalism schools: The National Institute for Advanced Reporting at the Indiana School of Journalism; the Missouri Institute for Computer-Assisted Reporting at the University of Missouri School of Journalism; and the University of North Carolina School of Journalism. The Freedom Forum Media Studies Center at Columbia University conducts studies and symposiums on computer-assisted reporting.

As database research continues to establish itself as a vital part of journalism, an increasing number of university journalism programs are teaching courses in database technology.

Traditional Reporting Still Needed

Despite its proven value and exotic allure, young reporters attracted to computer-assisted reporting should remember that it is just one reporting tool and that there are many potential pitfalls.

While computer analysis can point the way to important stories and provide solid documentation, reporters still must conduct interviews, develop sources and write concisely to bring the full effect of their computer work to readers and viewers in compelling, human terms.

Teresa Leonard, an experienced database user at *The News & Observer* in Raleigh, N.C., has cautioned

journalists about the realities of computer-assisted reporting.

It's tempting to take a gee-whiz approach at the almost magical way the information appears. However, it is important to remember that data analysis is still hard work and doesn't produce answers at the touch of a button or the blink of an eye. It takes an analytical mind to know what to ask of the data and how to interpret the results, and a careful, tenacious attitude to sort, check, cross-check, and recheck the numbers before building a story around them. Old-fashioned reporter doggedness is still an asset for dealing with obstacles along the way.

MONITORING PUBLIC OPINION

It had been a long and tiring day, but a fruitful one. The reporter's notebook was crammed with quotes from dozens of men and women, and the tally of yeses and noes marched across the white pages like stiff little soldiers.

The reporter had been measuring public opinion at a busy suburban mall, an assignment that had grown out of a newsroom decision to poll citizens on an important upcoming election.

In studying his notes later, however, the reporter was disturbed. Did the tally and the accompanying quotes designed to humanize and focus the cold statistics truly reflect the issues of the political race? He wasn't at all certain so he asked himself a few questions.

- Had he asked the right questions, and in the right way?
- Did the people he had interviewed truly represent the voting population?
- How would the resulting news story or stories affect the outcome of the race?

Suddenly the long hours in the parking lot closed in on the reporter, and some even more specific questions arose:

- How about the tired young mother who refused to answer any questions? Would she and others like her have affected the results of his survey if they had stopped to talk to him? Will their refusals to participate slant the survey?

The reporter was asking legitimate questions about an assignment that has become increasingly commonplace.

Measuring public opinion constitutes a vital and prevalent segment of modern mass communications, but polls and surveys must be conducted carefully and scientifically to truly represent the population.

Before the advent of professional polling organizations and increased knowledge among journalists about scientific polling methods, reporters often engaged in their own unofficial and amiable brand of polling. They talked to precinct captains in the big cities, counted crowds at staged political events, sampled the private views of hangers-on traveling with candidates and surveyed the opinions of other reporters on the campaign trail. Their results often were far from accurate.

The rise of precision journalism techniques has improved on that old, informal pattern. Reporters and editors now must have a minimum knowledge of modern survey methods to conduct and report polls accurately and to verify the validity of polls conducted by others.

Who's Doing It and Why?

Opinion surveys flood every public affairs beat. Political organizations, special-interest groups, business marketers and academic researchers all conduct public opinion surveys they hope will be covered by the press.

Care must be exercised in reporting on these polls because the sponsor may have a vested interest in the results, hoping to influence policy-makers or future public opinion. An environmental organization that can use a survey to show widespread public dissatisfaction with existing policies, for example, will improve its chances of swaying political leaders toward its priorities.

In-house polling by the news media extends well beyond tracking political contests. Reporters may seek to measure public opinion on social conditions, the performance of government, or other public concerns.

Sometimes particular populations are targeted for their views. For example, a newspaper may survey business leaders for their predictions on a struggling economy, or parents about the quality of the local schools.

Journalists may use surveys as part of larger projects, to add statistical strength to articles. As part of a major project on the causes of widespread racial segregation on Long Island, N.Y., *Newsday* conducted extensive surveys of black and white residents. The results, woven into news and feature stories, helped explain attitudes about segregation and why it has persisted (see Figure 3–2).

Checking the Pollsters

Care in conducting the reporter's own survey is only part of the obstacle to accurate polling reports. In *Newsroom Guide to Polls & Surveys*, G. Cleveland Wilhoit and David H. Weaver suggest important questions to be asked about other surveys:

- Who sponsored (or paid for) the poll and who conducted it?
- What population was sampled?
- What was the completion rate?
- How and when were the interviews done?
- What is the purpose of the survey or poll, and who is going to use the results for what purpose?
- Was anything found that is not being disclosed to the reporter?
- Is data being released selectively, raising the question that less-flattering results are being withheld?

The political campaign aide or public information officer who hands the reporter a press release containing a few selected findings from a poll should be asked for a copy of the poll itself and *all* the results.

This story, whose lead is based on a national poll, illustrates the care reporters must use when accepting material from paid professionals connected to a cause or interest group.

CHICAGO—The whole family suffers when employers don't pay a woman a full day's pay for a full day's work.

Newsday POLL

Thinking About The Schools

Question: In general, how would you rate the quality of the public schools in your community?

	Black %	Non-black %
Excellent	11	31
Good	44	48
Only fair	25	12
Poor	12	3

Question: If you had the opportunity, would you send your child to a public school in a different school district? (asked only of parents with children in public schools)

	Black %	Non-black %
Yes	44	17
No	53	79

Question: Do you feel that black children do better or worse if they go to schools that are racially mixed, or doesn't it make any difference? (asked of all respondents)

	Black %	Non-black %
Better	43	31
Worse	3	3
No difference	46	53

ABOUT THE POLL. For this Newsday Poll, the Gallup Organization conducted a telephone survey of 647 black Long Islanders and 650 non-black Long Islanders, all age 18 or older, from June 19 to July 8, 1989. The margin of sampling error is plus or minus 4 percentage points. Percentages may not add up to 100 because responses of "don't know" have been omitted.

Newsday POLL

Problems With Police

Question: How much confidence do you have in the ability of the police in your community to protect you?

	Black %	Non-black %
A great deal	21	35
Quite a bit	35	45
Not very much	29	15
None at all	8	2

Question: Do you think police protection in black neighborhoods is better, worse or about the same as in white neighborhoods? (asked only of blacks)

Better	5%
Worse	60%
About the same	25%

Question: Which of the following statements do you most agree with. . . (asked only of blacks)

Most cops are fair when dealing with black suspects	9%
Most cops view all blacks as suspects and are likely to arrest the wrong person	56%
Don't agree with either	27%

Question: Have you ever been harassed by police while driving through a largely white neighborhood on Long Island? (asked only of blacks)

Yes	16%
No	84%

ABOUT THE POLL. For this Newsday Poll, the Gallup Organization conducted a telephone survey of 647 black Long Islanders and 650 non-black Long Islanders, all age 18 or older, from June 19 to July 8, 1989. The margin of sampling error is plus or minus 4 percentage points. Percentages may not add up to 100 because responses of "don't know" have been omitted.

FIGURE 3–2
The Gallup Organization surveyed the views of Long Island residents on a range of topics, including schools, housing, police protection and race relations for a *Newsday* series on segregation. The results added effective statistical support for viewpoints expressed during interviews. (Note that each *Newsday* Poll includes "About the Poll," a brief explanation of how the poll was conducted. More detailed explanations often accompany survey results.)
Source: Gallup/Newsday Poll. Reprinted with permission.

And that makes unequal salaries based on sex a political issue that should be addressed in political campaigns.

That conclusion is the opinion of 77 percent of 1,000 registered voters interviewed by a professional research firm for the National Committee on Pay Equity.

The committee is a Washington-based, nonprofit advocacy coalition of unions, and women's and civil rights organizations.

The reporter made use of valuable Census Bureau statistics to support the committee's findings (men working full-time in 1990 averaged salaries of $27,800 while women averaged only $19,800). However, the "professional research firm" was never identified, nor was the reader given details about how the poll was conducted that might indicate a bias in the conclusions.

While it may be difficult to quarrel with the goals of the committee, this story illustrates how a special interest group can make sweeping recommendations based on research it has commissioned.

On the other hand, The Associated Press used material from a survey by another polling organization, and provided sufficient information about the process to explain its limitations.

WASHINGTON—In a reversal of past trends, people over 50 favor political change more than their younger contemporaries, according to a survey released Tuesday.

The survey by the Center for The People & The Press showed that more than four of 10 people over 50 agreed with the statement that it was time for political leaders to step aside and make room for new ones. Nearly half of those over 65 agreed.

Only 29 percent of those 18-to-24 years old expressed total agreement with the statement.

An explanation of polling details at the end of the story, while not complete, provided the reader with valuable information.

The survey, conducted from May 28 to June 10, was based on telephone interviews with 3,517 adults. The potential sampling error was plus or minus 2 percentage points.

Polling Methods

The way in which key elements of a poll are assembled—researchers call it methodology—determines whether or not the results are valid. In other words, if

the methods aren't sound by accepted polling standards, a conclusion that Candidate A is favored by most voters may be flatly wrong.

The shortcomings of the old and imperfect technique at the suburban mall can be analyzed by the reporter, and adjustments made that will assure a far more accurate reading of the issues. If the reporter is writing about polls and surveys conducted by others, this same analysis can reveal a weakness in the poll and perhaps a deliberate attempt to produce a desired result. These are some of the areas that require such analysis:

• **The questions.**   Before asking the first question— or in examining the poll results of others—the reporter carefully analyzes the type and wording of the questions to be asked for clarity, bias and imprecision. Are they loaded in favor of one answer? Do they assume too much knowledge on the part of the interviewee? Do they make poor comparisons? Are they too simplistic or too complex?

Questions should be checked to assure that they do not ask more than one question, yet allow for only one answer. People tend to favor the positive and prestigious over the negative, dangerous or unknown, and this should be taken into account in formulating questions. Questions should be carefully scrutinized to eliminate those that might be loaded, or weighted in favor of a particular answer.

Reporters can test the questions several ways, pre-testing them systematically or trying them out on colleagues. If the reporter stumbles over the questions while reading them aloud, chances are the people being polled will stumble, too. Asking filter questions, designed to determine whether some or all of the questions are really pertinent to the interviewee, also can be helpful before formal survey questioning begins.

Timing of the poll is important, too. Dramatic breaking news on the day of the poll, for example, can affect the way interviewees perceive the questions. A poll conducted the day before damaging disclosures about a candidate probably should not be reported because public opinion may have shifted substantially after the poll was taken.

• **Sampling.**   The key to successful sampling is the basic requirement that every person in a community or group, whatever its size, has an equal opportunity to be interviewed. The reporter must be able to assure readers or viewers that the sample surveyed is representative of the larger population or group from which it is drawn.

Stopping people on a street corner does not assure that the sample will be representative. Neither does drawing names out of a hat, although if all members of a group or community were represented in the hat, this could be a legitimate selection mechanism.

The manner in which the sampling is planned and conducted is vital. A telephone survey can be effective if a truly random sample can be systematically produced. Every 50th name in the directory might be contacted, but the 15 percent to 20 percent of the community with unlisted phone numbers would have no opportunity to be interviewed. Their exclusion might well affect the results. In the same way, using only half the directory names might improperly weight the sample in a community by dropping out a specific segment of the population.

Even time of day can be a factor. Calling in the early afternoon can exclude the opinions of the majority of people who work during business hours.

The reporter should be able to determine the range within which the survey has a good probability of representing the larger population or group of people. This sampling error depends on the size of the sample, the probability level and determination of the diversity or dissimilarity of the group being studied. These factors can be broken down into arithmetic terms and evaluated.

Size of the sample can play a part in its accuracy. Up to a point, the larger size, the more accurately the reporter can generalize to the larger populations.

But size alone does not ensure accuracy. Even the largest sample of the population may not be accurate if it is not representative—that is, if everyone in the sample did not have the same chance of being chosen.

The probability or "confidence" level—the odds that results of a survey lie within an acceptable error range—is important to the credibility of the survey. Because of these variables, the reporter must care-

fully study the type of sampling and survey methods used in his or her poll, or in the polls of others.

Sampling error, also called the margin of error, is an important variable in poll results and is therefore often included in the reporter's story. To say that Candidate A leads in the polls, 52 percent to 48 percent, would be inaccurate if the poll had a sampling error of plus or minus 5 percent. In that case Candidate A's actual support could range from 47 percent to 57 percent, while Candidate B's support might lie anywhere from 43 percent to 53 percent. Such a race would be too close to call.

- **Interviewing.** The basic interview techniques studied in advanced reporting courses can be quite valid for conducting surveys, although studies indicate that journalistic interviews are often flimsy instruments for accuracy. Respondents' answers tend to change depending on who's asking the questions. The presence or personality of the interviewer can affect results dramatically.

  Some studies suggest that "verbal conditioning" can affect the responses of an interviewee. Through subtle leadership, people can be encouraged to use or avoid certain words and phrases. An open-minded, nonjudgmental, low-profile approach to surveying is essential, all of these suggested by common sense and sensitivity to the task.

  Similar care should be exercised in making use of information supplied by polling organizations. Hiring and training practices can affect the data, and the reporter should attempt to determine the extent to which the polling organization has trained its interviewers. A familiarity with the respective advantages of face-to-face, mail and telephone interviewing is also desirable.

News accounts should include basic information about how the survey was conducted to help readers or viewers evaluate its accuracy. Newspapers often include sidebar stories or explanatory boxes outlining such details (see Box 3–2).

Polling boxes can go on to list a breakdown by educational level, age, or other characteristics. Mail surveys, whose response rate is generally lower than telephone surveys, may include the rate of response in the information box.

BOX 3–2

About the Survey

✳✳✳

The *Gazette* Poll on the Wilton mayor's race surveyed 478 people by telephone. The poll was conducted between Oct. 12 and Oct. 17 by Metro Media, a marketing and polling firm affiliated with Colsen College. Interviews were conducted by Metro Media employees and news staffers at the *Gazette*.

Only persons who said they were registered voters were interviewed. All respondents were residents of Wilton and at least 18 years of age.

Respondents were selected through a process called random digit dialing, a random list of telephone numbers generated by computer. While persons without telephones could not be contacted, the survey did include persons with unlisted telephone numbers.

The survey's sampling error was 4 percent, indicating that any result in the survey could vary plus or minus 4 percent. The poll has a confidence level of 95 percent, meaning there is only 1 chance in 20 that the results would vary more than plus or minus 4 percent.

Of the 478 persons interviewed, 41 percent were males and 59 percent were females. Eighty-eight percent were white, while 11 percent identified themselves as non-white.

To keep news articles from getting bogged down with long lists of numbers, newspapers frequently use tables, charts and graphs to illustrate major findings and highlight specific poll results.

- **Evaluating and reporting the results.**   In evaluating the material collected during a survey, the reporter asks the most important question of all: What do the figures say?

Other important questions will tell the reporter if the figures are accurate:

- What actual percentage of the planned sample was interviewed?
- How valid is the sample?
- Are missing answers a factor in the final results?
- Did filter questions, designed to determine whether some or all of the questionnaire is really pertinent to the interviewee, actually do their job in the sample of persons surveyed?

For the reporter, analyzing and communicating the results accurately is the bottom line.

Care should be taken in generalizing beyond the specific sample surveyed. The reporter also should be careful in drawing conclusions from only a few response categories or questions because this might create an unfair news report. Often the results of a single survey can be compared with another survey to improve the accuracy of any conclusions.

Such guidelines would have alerted the reporter surveying at the suburban mall that the effort he was undertaking had many deficiencies. The quality of the questions was suspect. Interviewing techniques were questionable. The survey failed the sampling test because merely stopping individuals at a shopping center does not provide a representative sample.

To call the reporter's effort a survey and generalize to a larger group would be misleading. The reporter's solution in this case is to make it clear in the story that only a group of people were questioned at a shopping center, and that their comments do not necessarily represent the opinions of the larger community.

The job of the reporter is to measure and report public opinion without misinforming thousands of readers or viewers. Without care and questioning, most newspaper and broadcast surveys will fail in their purpose of accurately measuring public opinion.

***

COMPUTER GLOSSARY

ACCESS CODE: A number, word or group of characters that must be entered before a computer will allow the user to access information. Also called a **Password** or **Personal identification number** (PIN).

BACKING UP: Making duplicate copies of programs or data files to prevent loss if originals are lost or damaged.

BOOLEAN LOGIC: A form of symbolic logic, similar to algebra, that uses words or syntax instead of numbers to define relationships. Database searching employs Boolean logic.

BULLETIN BOARD: A computer where users can leave messages, announcements, data and programs for other users.

CD-ROM: Short for Compact Disc-Read Only Memory. Discs containing text, illustrations and numeric entries on a variety of general and specialized subjects. Data are stored in binary codes and are accessed with a microcomputer equipped with special software. A low-cost alternative to on-line searching.

COMPUTER-ASSISTED REPORTING: A general term describing a range of computer uses in modern news gathering. Common techniques include retrieving information from computerized databases and using computers to organize and analyze large amounts of public information in government computers.

CONNECT TIME: The period of time a user is linked to an on-line database, from sign-on to sign-off. Fees are based in part on connect time.

CONNECTORS: Words used to define the relationship between topics or keywords being searched. Common connectors are AND, OR, and NOT.

CRUNCHING, NUMBER CRUNCHING: Informal terms used to describe the mathematical process a computer uses to analyze, sort and organize numerical data, such as census figures.

DATABASE: (1) A collection of data files maintained by and available from a commercial vendor, such as DataTimes, NEXIS, and Vu/Text. (2) A collection of unprocessed data that can be sorted, ordered and arranged by a computer program to satisfy a user's requirements.

"DIRTY DATA":   Erroneous or outdated information contained in a database, or information that was incorrectly entered at the source. Also called **Garbage** or **Tainted data**.

DISKETTE, FLOPPY DISK: A portable device for storing data. Most common disk formats are 5.25-inch and 3.5-inch. User inserts disk into a personal computer's disk drive to retrieve, read and print data. Data on hard drive may be copied onto floppy disk for safe-keeping. See **Backing up**.

DOWNLOAD: To transfer data from a central computer to a user's computer. Data can be transferred directly via modem or copied onto a floppy disk and then entered (uploaded) into the user's computer.

ELECTRONIC MAIL, E-MAIL: Messages sent between users of computer systems. Messages can be sent to a single user, a select group, or everyone in the system. Users need not be on-line to receive a message. PC users linked to a commercial E-mail service can correspond with others in the system.

FLOPPY DISK: See **Diskette**.

FULL-TEXT: Complete versions of articles, reports and other data available from a database. Material can be viewed on screen, copied or printed.

GATEWAY: A connection among two or more data networks. Commercial gateways, such as Dialcom and CompuServe, give users access to multiple database services for a single fee.

HARD COPY: Printed version of computer data.

HARDWARE: The equipment that makes up a computer system, including keyboard, monitor, printer and hard drives.

IN-HOUSE DATABASE: An original database created with information from other sources. Data may come from existing computer files or from printed material not available on computer. Printed material must be manually entered (keyboarded) into the database before it can be analyzed by computer.

KEYWORD: A word or words used in a database search to focus on a specific topic or to limit the scope of research. The computer attempts to match keywords selected by the user with the same or similar words in articles or documents.

MAINFRAME: A large, powerful computer system that can store and process a considerable volume of data. An organization's central computer is usually a mainframe.

MODEM: Short for MOdulator/DEModulator. A device that enables one computer to "talk" to another, allowing for two-way transfer of information along telephone lines. Digital computer signals are converted into a tone-wave signal for transmission, then converted back to digital signals for the receiving computer.

NINE-TRACK TAPE: A type of plastic magnetic tape commonly used by government and other institutional mainframe computers for storing data. Government tapes can be purchased by reporters and analyzed on a mainframe, or processed on a personal computer equipped with special hardware and conversion software.

NUMBER CRUNCHING: See **Crunching**.

ON-LINE: Being connected to a computer system, usually by a remote terminal or a personal computer connected to a modem.

ON-LINE DATABASE: A data library that can be accessed by a computer through telephone lines or other communication hook-up.

PASSWORD: See **Access code**.

PERSONAL COMPUTER (PC):   A general-purpose computer designed to be used by one person at a time. Programs and operating commands are intended to be understood by non-computer scientists.

PRECISION JOURNALISM: The application of social science and behavioral science techniques to news gathering to identify trends or increase reliability of conclusions. Common techniques include surveys, data analysis and field experiments. Computers are used to analyze large amounts of data.

PROTOCOL: Specific commands and procedures that govern the transmission of data between a user and a computer. Database vendors establish their own protocols that users must follow to access and transfer data.

READ ONLY: Computer data that can only be viewed on a screen or printed. "Read only" data cannot be altered, manipulated or analyzed by the user's computer.

SEARCH: To look for specific words, terms or topics in a database using keywords or combinations of keywords that the computer locates and isolates.

SEARCH SERVICE: A company that performs database searches for a fee.

SOFTWARE: Programs that enable a computer and related hardware to perform specific tasks.

SORTING: The process of arranging data in a usable form, usually numerically or alphabetically.

TRUNCATE: During a database search, a designated symbol is placed before or after the search term, serving as a "wild card" that represents every letter in the alphabet. Wild cards include ? and *. Thus, "histor*" would retrieve any reference to history, historian, historical and historicity.

UPLOAD: To transfer data from a local computer to a remote computer, or from a floppy disk to a PC.

***

POLLING GLOSSARY

BIAS: Factors that may affect the accuracy of polling results.

CONFIDENCE LEVEL, PROBABILITY LEVEL: The odds that the results of a survey are within the estimated sampling error range. Polls are usually reported at the 95 percent confidence level.

FILTER QUESTION: A survey item intended to test a respondent's knowledge or other characteristics to determine whether the questionnaire or parts of it are appropriate to the respondent.

GENERALIZE: To draw conclusions about the larger population based on results from the sample.

METHODOLOGY: The practices and procedures used by pollsters, including sampling system, selection and training of interviewers, and survey type.

NON-RESPONSE BIAS: Polling error that may result when people in a sample refuse to be interviewed, cannot be located, or fail to return questionnaires.

POPULATION, UNIVERSE: A group of items or people from which a survey sample is drawn.

RANDOM SAMPLING: Selection of a small number of people or units from a larger group in such a way that all units in the larger set have an equal chance of being chosen. Random sampling increases the likelihood that the sample chosen is representative of the larger group.

RESPONSE RATE: The percentage of people in the original sample who are actually interviewed. In a mail survey, the percentage of completed questionnaires returned. A low response rate, less than 70 percent, may affect the accuracy of survey results.

SAMPLING ERROR, MARGIN OF ERROR: The estimated range of possible error in survey results that can be attributed to random sampling, reflected as a percentage, plus or minus. The more diverse the sampled population, the greater the estimated sampling error.

SAMPLE SIZE: The number of individuals or units to be surveyed.

SOCIAL DESIRABILITY BIAS: A respondent's tendency to answer in ways that conform to socially acceptable views or to those of powerful groups. Bias can be created by the content of questions or by the personality and appearance of the interviewer.

WEIGHTING: To adjust, upward or downward, the results obtained from a sampling subgroup to more accurately reflect that group's representation in a larger population.

***

SUGGESTED READINGS

Jaspin, Elliot. *Out with the Paper Chase, In with the Data Base*. New York: Gannett Center for Media Studies, 1989.

Contains description of how journalists use database analysis in reporting. Simple explanation of analysis techniques.

Meyer, Philip. *The New Precision Journalism*. Bloomington: Indiana University Press, 1991.

Updated version of Meyer's original book, which introduced journalists to polling and other social science research methods. This version integrates tremendous changes in information gathering and computer use in reporting.

Weaver, David H., and G. Cleveland Wilhoit. *Newsroom Guide to Polls and Surveys*. Bloomington: Indiana University Press, 1990.

Practical introduction to using polls in news gathering and writing about polls conducted by others.

Part Two

Government

Legislative and Administrative

Chapter 4

Covering Municipal Government

The new homeowner stands on his front stoop, a smile on his face, gazing down the tree-lined street. Tomorrow is garbage pickup day, and neighbors are already placing cans along the curb.

A police car slowly cruises by, and the driver waves to the new resident. Cheers can be heard from a nearby playground as soccer players drive for a winning goal. Over the buzz of the cicadas and chirping birds, a distant fire truck warns drivers as it responds to an emergency.

The new owner smiles with satisfaction. The sights and sounds represent the reasons he has chosen to live in this municipality.

Municipal government exists to provide these and other services to an urban population and to establish regulations to assure order in the community.

A city maintains a police force, a fire department, crews to handle refuse removal, work crews to maintain the streets and highways, parks and other recreational facilities, and other amenities of urban life as determined by the mandate of the people.

There is an important implication for the new homeowner and city government reporter in this definition. Since services are being provided, someone has to pay for them. Most municipal governments use several sources to obtain funds that pay for services, and the mechanics of budgeting and collecting millions of dollars a year constitute one of the reporter's most important areas of involvement.

Little is more important to a taxpayer than a demand upon his or her wallet. The perceptive city hall reporter recognizes this, and always starts with these basic questions:

What is the service? Who wants it? What will it cost? Why is it necessary?

THE RANGE OF SERVICES AND INHERENT CONFLICT

Modern municipal government offers a broad range of services. Aside from those already mentioned, it provides parking in commercial areas, inspects buildings for safety, maintains public libraries, provides health services (often sharing these responsibilities with county government), and constructs arenas and civic centers.

But municipal government also exists to assure an orderly community in an urban setting. Police officers and judges do their share; so does a planning commission that promulgates and enforces zoning ordinances to protect property. The many prohibitions at the municipal level influence the flow of the news.

It is illegal to burn trash or garbage within city limits; residents may not maintain chicken or pigeon coops in their back yards; it is illegal to erect a structure without a building permit; and so on. Such restrictions, or the lack of them, are often what make news in a community.

"We don't want those people here."

Mental health officials have found a house in Southbridge, where three clients can live and readjust to society—but the patients' future neighbors don't want them.

"I'm not going to be a friendly neighbor," said John Pitger, who lives down the street from the three-bedroom home under contract to the Area Mental Health Services Agency.

Neighbors fear the stigma of having mental patients in the area will depress property values. They argue that the city zoning code prohibits such use. In short, they are unhappy.

So are the elected city officials who must sort out the problem and help reach a solution. The problem is quite sticky by most community standards. Even the federal government is a part of the dispute because Department of Housing and Urban Development (HUD) funds are being used to purchase the $130,000 home.

The city hall reporter will accumulate many of these "conflict" stories, and he or she will have to make sure other significant issues are not overlooked in deciding which ones to write about.

Criteria for such evaluation by the reporter include the number of people affected by the issue, the effect of the issue on a group and the depth of feeling over the issue. In this case, only neighbors in the area may be involved, but perceived problems can become very emotional. The setting in which the issue becomes public is also important. In this case, neighbors are arguing that officials had been secretive about the house purchase.

Julian Howell, who lives next door to the home at 4210 Forest Ave., tells the reporter that mental health officials should have talked to residents before deciding to locate there. He says he found out accidentally and alerted other neighbors.

The reporter also finds that establishment of other such facilities are in the planning stages. Suddenly, community interest in the issue becomes much broader and deeper.

Airing All Sides of an Issue

This issue offers another important lesson. In all stories dealing with such basic conflict, whether at the neighborhood or citywide level, the reporter must listen to all sides, not merely those most accessible.

In this case, the reporter quickly finds that two sets of neighbors are involved: those opposing use of the home by mental patients, and others who vigorously support the effort at rehabilitation. Any number of city employees will become involved—from mental health and zoning officials to the city manager and members of the city council.

What are the zoning restrictions for the area? What planning has gone into the process? What are the specific complaints by the neighbors who oppose the project? What are the arguments from officials in favor of establishing the home? What are the alternatives? How do other affected city officials view the issue?

The city hall reporter will anticipate these various "publics" and their points of view in answering questions and developing stories that illuminate the issue.

A Basic Rationale for Coverage

The mental health example helps answer the question, "Why is covering city government so important?" There are several answers:

- In contrast to state and federal government, city government is closer to those affected by its activities. For many, in fact, City Hall is right around the corner, or at least only a few minutes away. A council member or other official may be a neighbor.

- City government affects people more directly. Services provided are vital. Should a garbage truck neglect to service a neighborhood, citizen response will be prompt and noisy. Should city officials vote to change the traffic flow on a downtown street from two-way to one-way for the sake of efficiency, merchants may roar with indignation. Because of this multitude of limited-interest issues, city hall reporters often have a higher story count than those on other government beats, and the demands are greater.

- In smaller communities, a neighborhood atmosphere creates a more basic interest in the activities of city government. A zoning issue might involve families who have ties to other neighborhoods or who feel threatened by the fact that the issue is

affecting someone across town. Police negotiations with city officials on salary increases may hold more interest for a certain area because a police officer is a neighbor.

- Money is constantly flowing in and out at all government levels, and it's no different with municipal government. The public must ultimately pay for everything, so the acquisition and disbursement of money is of universal interest.

CREATING MUNICIPAL GOVERNMENT

Cities and towns are creatures of the states, and municipal government power flows from the states under their reserved rights of sovereignty, based on the 10th Amendment to the U.S. Constitution:

> The powers not delegated to the United States by the Constitution, nor prohibited by it to the States, are reserved to the States respectively, or to the people.

While city government is designed to satisfy the needs and desires of a specific group of citizens who are willing to pay for the costs, the typical municipality derives its powers (and some of its funding) from the state and is generally subordinate to state authority in many of its activities. For example, final budget approval for a municipality may lie with one of the state's fiscal agencies, and state legislation frequently influences the operation of local government.

The new city hall reporter should begin with a review of the municipality's enabling legislation, whether it be an original charter or "home rule" legislation that gives the city virtual autonomy in key areas. The specific legislation is important to the reporter's understanding of the basic structure of city government.

Many municipalities still work under a charter, the basic document originally granted by the state for governing the community. Whether it was granted in the 1800s or more recently, the charter spells out the powers and limitations on those who govern, identifying what can and cannot be done at the local level.

For example, the reporter may find that a city council has the power to change the districts from which members are elected, or that power may be vested in the state legislature or in the hands of the local electorate itself. The reporter should know the limitations imposed by the charter or home rule legislation as well as the powers specified by them.

DEALING WITH INTEREST GROUPS

The perceptive reporter knows that government is not neutral. It is the product of pressures from many groups, each of them working to assure some kind of access to government or some advantage. Many are working at cross-purposes.

One of the keys to effective coverage of municipal government is familiarity with all of these groups. The reporter must be able to communicate their ideas, goals and plans. As an issue develops, the reporter must ask the question "Who is going to be most intimately involved in it and its resolution?"

Many groups wield power as a traditional part of the local scene. The business community usually possesses influence that far exceeds the size of its membership. Labor groups, because of their size and composition, often form an important interest group. Other organizations such as church and ministerial organizations, civic clubs, women's clubs, minority organizations and neighborhood associations all influence municipal government.

Identifying Power Blocs

At the outset, the reporter will identify the groups that have a particular interest in the outcome of an issue, discussing with their leadership its perception of events and pressures that are being exerted, either in favor of or in opposition to it.

The political complexion of the municipality varies from city to city, and the power structures show immense variety. Paralleling the need for a background in government itself is another important requirement for the reporter: he or she must possess a practical knowledge of the socio-political system in the community.

Many municipal governments include the traditional political parties in their formation, while others label

---

BOX 4–1

Annexations Are Always Stories

✳✳✳

As an annexation effort develops, the reporter must ask these questions:

- Who is going to be most affected by it?
- What are the routes to resolution?

  For example, an effort is under way to annex six neighborhoods adjacent to the city limits. It is the largest such expansion since 1970, and people are already taking sides. The battle to remain outside the city and to become a part of it will rage unabated for months, even years.

- Who are the key players, and what are their positions?
- Aside from the neighborhoods affected by the proposal, who else has facts as well as opinions on the issues?
- What are the opinions of people inside the city, who will have to help pay for services to the annexed areas?

---

themselves nonpartisan. In some cities, a candidate for city council cannot even be a member of a political executive committee.

Whatever the designation and practice, alliances do form, and many of them are politically inspired and long-standing. Candidates find others with similar philosophical views toward government and run as a "slate," opposing other organized groups with divergent viewpoints. The City Hall reporter must be familiar with those alliances and their effect on local government.

While municipal government can be said to operate for the greater good of all, political decisions in practice stem from a working union of interests, institutions and individuals. The journalist understands and accepts this framework. As much as any social scientist, the reporter recognizes that local governments are not monolithic entities.

Government at this level is actually a complex of decision-making "islands" in the community, from which flow decisions and actions that shape the community. Participants are especially concerned with the decisions that affect their "island."

> "Your right to defend the value of your property is in jeopardy" is the headline on an unsigned flier being circulated in several west-side neighborhoods.
>
> The single sheet discusses a proposed amendment to an ordinance, which would allow developers to construct "multi-family dwellings" in R-4 zones without a public hearing.
>
> Under the current ordinance, a hearing is required. Planning Director Sara Bunn favors the amendment as one method for equalizing requirements for developers.

Implicit in this story is the pressure being exerted on resolution of the issue by some individuals or groups, usually the latter. The reporter realizes that each group does not wield the same amount of influence and that participants' strength varies from issue to issue. For example, the business community may act as a unit in discouraging a decision to permit a huge shopping mall on the edge of the city, yet take little interest in major extension of sewer lines to an undeveloped section of the city. However, the issue is substantially more important to an organized group of contractors who require the lines to construct new housing or to nearby homeowners who also want the sewer lines.

Interest groups can include environmental organizations, historic preservation groups, civic clubs or other organized groups. They may very well be neighborhoods, which frequently band together when their interests are threatened.

> Some people in the Highlawn area believe the city is trying to pull a fast one. Their leaders say the Board of Zoning Appeals didn't notify residents about a public hearing on a proposal to establish a private club in the area, and now they are petitioning to protest the move.
>
> Planning Director Amy Melvin argues that the city has done everything it is required to do—and more. A public hearing on the proposal to establish the club and a restaurant at 1400 Eastmoor St. is scheduled for 4 p.m. today in City Hall.

> "We think they tried to sneak it in on us," said John Sallivant, 270 Highlawn Ave., who initiated a petition he says contains 360 names.

Because such neighborhood groups and participants may be less accessible to the reporter than city officials, the reporter should be persistent in communicating their views. Getting other points of view into such a story is time-consuming but necessary.

FORMS OF CITY GOVERNMENT AND REPORTER ACCESS

Municipal government in this country generally takes these forms: the mayor-council, the city commission, the council-manager, and the fairly recent metropolitan form of government. The reporter should be familiar with all the forms. City charters are not written in concrete, and often are changed, as developments in metropolitan areas attest.

Traditional Mayor-Council Plan

The mayor-council form of city government is the oldest, growing out of the 19th century. It is a product of Jacksonian democracy, and it continues to reflect the spirit of the frontier with a skepticism of politicians and government itself. This form developed when the functions of city government were fewer, when local officials were "coordinated" through powerful political parties, and when people were reluctant to assign too much power to an individual or a group. In this way, a weak mayor-council form developed, with both the mayor and council elected to office and all sharing legislative and administrative power. In addition to setting policy through legislative action, the council appoints administrators such as a city attorney, city clerk, city engineer, police and fire chiefs, and municipal court judge. A committee of council is often responsible for preparing an annual budget. Some power accrues to the mayor because he or she presides at council meetings and sometimes a mayor's court, but the mayor is merely first among equals. As such, the power of the office is limited.

The potential problems in this form of government are apparent: no individual is responsible for seeing to it that ordinances and other rules are carried out. A weak administration usually develops.

The reporter operating in this environment may find many officials willing to discuss the issues, but few with actual power to dispose of them. The result may be many long-winded discussions of issues that remain in the news for a long time.

Strong Mayor-Council Form

Because of these deficiencies, the strong mayor-council form of municipal government began to develop at the end of the 19th century, differing from the weak form only in degree.

Administrative responsibility is concentrated in the hands of an elected and generally well-paid mayor, and the policy-making responsibility becomes a joint effort of the mayor and the council. The mayor exerts strong administrative leadership, appointing and dismissing department heads, making decisions that affect the running of a city. He or she usually prepares the annual budget, and the burden is on the council to alter it.

In sharing power with the mayor, the council is limited to legislative policy-making, and even this function must often be shared with the mayor. An additional factor must be considered: The mayor's position allows exertion of strong political leadership, further enhancing the mayor's role as the city's administrator. This is important to the mayor, who as an elected official must periodically renew his or her mandate from the voters, but it also offers the opportunity to exert leverage over a sometimes politically divided council.

Because of its provisions for vigorous political leadership, the strong mayor form has proved effective in large cities, where complexities of government and a diverse population call for firm leadership and direction. Its major advantage lies in the ability of the system to pinpoint responsibility and to plan city policy. And because it somewhat separates the legislative and executive functions, the strong mayor form offers a system of checks and balances not quite so clear with other forms of municipal government.

However, the form does have disadvantages. It appears to expect too much of a mayor, because few persons combine the talent of an adroit and electable politician and an expert administrator. The mayor must draw sufficient votes to remain in office, yet still make the difficult and often unpopular decisions expected of the administrator of a large city. The late Mayor Richard Daley of Chicago combined these qualities to create a powerful office, as did the late Mayor Fiorello LaGuardia of New York.

In recent decades, the office of mayor in major cities has been a stepping stone to higher office, increasing the political implications of a city's issues.

The reporter's coverage in this kind of government will focus on the administrative end, with a natural tendency to more fully illuminate the mayor's position. With all its power, a diffuse council—sometimes with more than two dozen members—does not easily offer the reporter the opportunity to focus on points of view.

Deadlocks are likely to develop between the mayor and council, and the reporter will find himself or herself a key element in communicating the arguments to the electorate. Care must be taken to keep the focus on the issues and arguments, and not solely on specific political personalities.

The Commission Plan

The commission form of government grew out of an emergency that gripped Galveston, Texas, in 1900. After a hurricane and tidal wave devastated the community, the state of Texas suspended local government in Galveston and substituted a temporary government of five local businessmen—the Galveston Commission.

So successful was the commission that this form was retained in the city and attracted wide attention as a "businessman's government." Within 10 years, the new form was in use in more than 100 cities, and by 1920 more than 500 cities had shifted to the commission plan. Growth continued at a slower pace up to World War II.

The outstanding characteristic of the form is the dual role of the commissioners, each acting individually as administrative head of a city department, while collectively acting as policy-makers for the city. There is no real separation of powers because commissioners perform both legislative and executive functions. It should be noted that the commission plan has evolved in different ways, and in some cities commissioners do not run departments.

This form has fallen into decline because of some basic disadvantages. For one thing, it is difficult to find citizens of professional caliber to operate city departments while overseeing their own affairs. Also, a small (generally five-person) commission allows little room for the important function of criticism, and a fraternity of tolerance is likely to result. Just as important, each commissioner tends to guard his or her territory jealously, and the top of the administrative pyramid is effectively sawed off. Overall city planning is apt to suffer.

Council-City Manager Form

The young reporter is more likely to encounter the city manager form of government because it prevails in many smaller and middle-sized cities where journalists often get their start. This form began to evolve early in this century when growth and complexity of cities dictated evolution of experts specifically trained to direct their affairs.

About 2,500 U.S. cities operate with this form of government today, with most of the growth occurring after World War II. An elected council or commission, composed of laypersons, is responsible for setting policy through ordinances and resolutions. This body hires a professional administrator to carry out its policies and oversee direction of the city. The administrator answers to the council. The manager form also is widely used at the county level.

The powers and duties of the city manager are outlined in the city charter, pointing to a plainly administrative role. He or she appoints and, when necessary, dismisses employees; prepares an annual budget and submits it to the council with a report on finances and administrative activities; submits regular statements to the council of all receipts, disbursements and unpaid accounts; and keeps the council advised of the needs of the city, making recommendations on them.

In this way a council entrusts to a professional the responsibility for day-to-day operation of municipal government. This form generally includes a merit plan to attract employees who are technically competent, but the manager is usually exempt, sometimes serving without a contract. A few employees are often excluded from the city manager's jurisdiction, among them a city clerk who answers to the council and a city attorney who advises the council as well as the city manager. As a result, the reporter will sometimes find the lines of responsibility unclear.

Emphasis on Technical Competence

Rapidly growing cities are likely to experiment with the council-manager form of government, and it also has proved popular in cities with heavy concentrations of young families or with mobile, middle-class populations. Bigger cities with major elements of working-class populations or heavy concentrations of ethnic groupings traditionally have endorsed the mayor-council form of government.

While city planners praise the city manager form for its businesslike approach, some complicating factors are important to the journalist who reports on its activities.

While the system places emphasis on technical competence, elected council or commission members continue to feel pressure from their constituencies to act in their behalf. So while a professional manager is deciding priorities impartially, citizen groups are pressuring policy-makers to influence the final decision.

The reporter often faces a dilemma: The manager may not always be the primary source of the decision, because the elected official or officials may actually be playing the major role. Such a diffusion of the decision-making process calls for knowledge of personalities and the real sources of power.

The council-manager system is often misunderstood. Some critics label it "dictatorial" because the city manager answers only to the council that appointed him or her. Supporters of the system respond that the electorate has adequate access to government through the elected council.

City managers, like the elected officials who hire them, come and go, with policy and politics playing a role in their arrivals and departures. In this respect, the council-manager system is not unlike other forms of local government. A change in administration at election time often foreshadows major changes, and the city hall reporter will be alert to such shake-ups.

> Stephen Weeks, the city's director of public works and perhaps the last vestige of the James Stillman administration, announced his resignation Tuesday, effective immediately.
>
> Weeks weathered the turmoil at City Hall for more than a year after the resignation of Stillman, the city manager who hired him in 1988.
>
> Weeks declined to discuss the turmoil of the past year. "I don't think any more discussion about the problems of City Hall is necessary," he said. "Enough has been said."

The reporter had monitored the departure of 20 other department heads and professional city employees who had left—some by resignation, others by elimination of jobs from the budget, and still others by outright dismissal by the new city manager.

Metropolitan Government

More than likely, the young journalist reporting for work at a metropolitan newspaper will be shunted to the far suburbs to cover one of the smaller governments. He or she may report solely for one of the neighborhood editions targeted to specific suburbs. There, the reporter is likely to find one of the traditional forms of municipal government.

Increasingly, however, new general-purpose governments are being created in metropolitan areas to cope with their problems. Most U.S. municipalities have encountered financial difficulties, caused partly by the increasing cost of providing services to burgeoning suburban areas. As the demand for such services has grown, so has the financial burden on city taxpayers. The problem has been exacerbated by the fragmentation of government—the rush to the suburbs and the decline of the central city.

> Marsha Wilcox, 35, moved to suburban Montgomery County to secure a better education for her 10-year-old daughter. The far suburb offered a first-rate school system and an array of after-school activities that saved her day-care costs, she said.

> The recession and its aftermath changed much of that. Montgomery County has slashed its school budget, eliminating the after-school programs and forcing Wilcox to begin paying for day care. The county is also raising taxes and considering more cutbacks and layoffs. Wilcox, a county employee, could be among them.
>
> "Everything was perfect," Wilcox said, "but the dream fizzled right out."

This working mother is among the growing number of people who realize that life in the suburbs can feel a lot like life in the cities they left behind. The reporter covering such an area has a permanent list of topics to cover: congested highways, a dramatic rise in the crime rate, unemployment, pollution and environmental neglect, inadequate public transportation, and other deteriorating services. Reporting on such a list strains the capabilities of even the best-organized newspapers and broadcast outlets.

Suburban taxpayers who fled the central city found many of the old problems had simply followed them to their new homes, and the older central city found itself surrounded by many square miles of crowded suburbs, often with their own local governments.

Directions of Reorganization

While the press tries to cope with reporting on this complex municipal maze, some government reformers have successfully restructured urban government to make it more capable of coping with the problems of the metropolis.

Three types of general-purpose city governments have been most popular:

1. A central city government that has been consolidated with the existing county government.

2. Internal reorganization of the county to create a more effective form of government.

3. Creation of a two-tier instrument of government, with one tier responsible for areawide services, and the other covering purely local functions.

There were early examples of consolidation—New Orleans in 1805, Boston in 1822, Philadelphia in 1854 and New York in 1898—but the movement languished until after World War II. Since that time, consolidation has been successful in cities like Baton Rouge,

La.; Nashville, Tenn.; Jacksonville, Fla.; Indianapolis; Lexington, Ky.; and Columbus, Ga.

Under the two-tier concept of metropolitan government adopted by Miami and Dade County, the restructured county government assumed responsibility for areawide services—mass transit, public health, some central police and fire services, and planning. Other more purely local functions were left to the 26 municipalities, school districts and other special districts in the county—police patrol, public education and control of local land use through zoning.

HOW MUNICIPAL GOVERNMENT OPERATES

When the sharp rap of a gavel signifies passage or rejection of an important proposal at a city council meeting, it is often merely the final curtain on a long-running drama. During the process, the city hall reporter has probed dozens of raw nerves in interviewing the actors. While it is important that the final act be reported, the extensive sparring that accompanies acceptance or rejection of an issue is the stuff of which useful news reports are made.

While the heart of municipal news coverage lies in the council chambers, the preliminary deliberations often cover weeks, even months, and take place in offices far removed from City Hall. While open-meetings laws have inhibited informal meetings leading to key decisions, the reporter may still expect them to take place. It is difficult to legislate visits to someone's home, an attorney's office, or even an upstairs hallway. While it is impractical to assume that the reporter will participate in all these informal meetings, he or she should try to follow the issues wherever they lead. The reporter has a responsibility to mirror the development of these issues rather than to cover only the final act of the drama.

How the Council Operates

A city council or commission is composed of a group of elected citizens, with regular meetings scheduled to conduct the policy-making aspects of municipal

business. Only at these official meetings are ordinances enacted and resolutions passed expressing the intent of the members. A preliminary meeting or "work session" is often conducted to prepare for the official meeting, although "sunshine" legislation in many states has inhibited this practice. Often the reporter will find this preliminary session is the more productive of the two sessions, because there is more informal give and take among members. The argument over a controversy may be resolved at the work session after some negotiation, and an ordinance may breeze through the official meeting with little or no discussion. Without benefit of the work session argument and compromise, the story is only half complete.

> An ordinance requiring registration of all charitable fund-raising drives in the city flew through Council last night after two members withdrew their opposition in an acrimonious work session earlier in the day. The ordinance, passed by a 5-0 vote on final reading, will go into effect immediately.
> "We're satisfied the ordinance will be enforced fairly," Councilman John Prudy said. Prudy and Councilman Charles Coors had objected to a clause requiring annual resubmittal of a request for registration by such agencies as the Salvation Army and Volunteers of America.

Most municipal councils operate through the traditional committee system. Standing committees study proposals on public safety, finance, public works, transportation, and recreation and health, then send them to the full council. Like the preliminary work session, many key decisions are reached in committee meetings, often not attended by members of the press.

> The proposal to adjust the cost of some city business licenses upward is apparently dead after Council's Finance Committee tabled the issue Wednesday.
> The action means that Council will have to vote unanimously to restore the proposal, an unlikely prospect in view of the fact that Council members John Keith and Wilma Stevens adamantly oppose seeking up to $250,000 in new funds from licenses.

Councils take official action through passage of *ordinances*, which are municipal regulations with the force of law, and *resolutions*, which merely express the intent, permission or opinion of the council. However, a resolution may often be far more important than a vote on a routine ordinance because it may indicate a new policy direction taken by the governing body.

A council resolution directing the city manager to execute a contract to construct a multimillion dollar sewer project that assures development of a major industrial park carries economic implications for the community, while an ordinance changing the method of applying reserve funds may be less vital to the average reader or viewer. The reporter will learn quickly to distinguish between important items and housekeeping measures.

An ordinance is introduced in an official session, read by the city clerk and assigned to an appropriate committee for study and further action. After a committee recommendation, the proposal is brought up for discussion and a second reading at a subsequent council meeting. Some municipalities provide for a third and final reading, and many councils can suspend the rules on an emergency basis and vote on two readings at the same session, resulting in quick enactment of the ordinance. The city hall reporter should have a good understanding of the patterns through which various proposals pass.

After passage, the ordinance becomes law, sometimes immediately, but often 30 or 60 days after passage.

Resolutions and other actions by the council, such as appointments to boards and agencies, usually require only one reading before the council.

A Typical Council Session

The importance of identifying and tracking government issues at any level cannot be overemphasized. Some newspapers are opting for a more issue-oriented approach, and minimizing long-winded official meetings. But final decisions are always built around official sessions of a city council or commission, and they are often vital to the process.

In advance of the official meeting, the city clerk has produced and distributed an agenda, a document that begins with roll call and a synopsis of the previous session. Some agendas provide little more than a mere listing of topics; others give pages of detail. The agenda offers the reporter assurance that an item will be up for discussion, and provides a good opportunity to check issues overlooked in the press of other City Hall coverage.

Here is a typical rundown of a council meeting:

- The city manager reports on contract bids for items such as new police cars, office supplies, and equipment for the streets department. A preliminary check often uncovers newsworthy items in seemingly routine contract discussions. Re-award of liability insurance for city employees offers an opportunity to explore the cost, effectiveness and usefulness of the insurance. Bids on a supply of street salt for winter enables the reporter to look ahead at plans to cope with the snow and ice that winter. The reporter also should be alert to no-bid contracts, and policies governing them.

- The council hears a second and final reading of an ordinance to modify parking along several neighborhood streets. Members approve the ordinance, which had received a unanimous aye vote at the previous meeting. This vote is routine, but should be noted.

- The council approves another ordinance on second reading, this one to amend a zoning ordinance to allow two-family dwellings in a changing neighborhood formerly restricted to one-family dwellings. As in the last council session, there are no objections.

- A council member introduces an ordinance to regulate taverns more closely, following complaints by residents of objectionable noise and activity outside some of them. With little discussion, the proposal is referred to the council's legal committee for study. (The reporter had written about the residents' complaints earlier.) Lack of discussion at a council meeting does not impute a lack of importance to an issue. At this stage, the reporter's obligation is to obtain a copy of the proposed ordinance and report its contents, while seeking follow-up comment from the council member who sponsored the ordinance and the people who will be affected by its passage—tavern operators and residents.

- A resolution is proposed, calling for a moratorium on major development in a sparsely populated section of the city until agreement is reached on extending water and sewer service to the area. Two developers have asked to address the council on the issue, and a city planner has been asked to comment. Several other people also want to address the council on the resolution. It is apparent that conflict has developed over the issue.

The council sidesteps the issue by tabling the resolution until the city planner studies it further. While no vote has been taken on final resolution, the arguments offer the reporter the opportunity to produce a detailed story on the issue. Comments of those addressing the council will be noted, and names and identifications double-checked. An important question is why they are involved.

The reporter will pursue the issue between sessions, because publication of the divergent points of view is important to its resolution.

- After routine requests for a parade permit and a donation to a local charity, the session is adjourned.

Official council meetings such as these require specific effort by the city hall reporter, who will arrive at council chambers early to determine the composition of that night's audience. Who are they? What issue or issues are they following? What interests are they representing? Such preliminary effort minimizes the risk of misspelled names and improper identification, and provides a better understanding of the issues.

The reporter should always research the agenda before the official session. A copy of an old ordinance should be obtained as soon as the reporter realizes that an attempt will be made to add important amendments. The process of selecting a new municipal judge should be reviewed carefully by the reporter *before* officials begin the discussions that will lead to appointment. Such preliminary work will pay off on deadline, when the reporter has to produce a clear, detailed story quickly.

Do's and Don'ts for the Reporter

The reporter usually will enjoy good rapport with a council and a cooperative city clerk, but sorting out the citizens who attend council meetings requires effort. A sparsely attended session or a full house can pose problems for a reporter on deadline. Information imparted at a council meeting can be abnormally heavy in a short amount of time, and confusion often

---

BOX 4–2

Avoiding the Label of 'Routine'

✳✳✳

Difficult as it may be, the label "routine" should be avoided in coverage of municipal government. To help drop the word from the reporter's vocabulary, he or she should begin asking questions that will pull any issue out of the "routine" category.

What seem to be "routine" appointments to boards and agencies often carry implications of major policy changes or initiatives. A new member on an 11-person Human Relations Commission may not materially affect the makeup of that commission (unless two factions are evenly split on important issues). But consider the effect of appointing a new member to the three-member Parking Authority, whose basic philosophy is to take all parking off downtown streets by constructing multimillion-dollar high-rise parking garages. A new board or commission lineup could substantially affect the policy of a governing body, and a good reporter will pursue this possibility.

Politics is often involved in such appointments, and council members are aware of their implications. The reporter should also be aware, and be able to articulate the various viewpoints to readers or viewers.

exists. To cut through it, here is some advice for the city hall reporter:

- Citizens addressing the council are usually, but not always, asked to sign in or otherwise identify themselves. Familiarity with the agenda and those who want to address the council permits the reporter to leave the press table briefly to obtain further details from those people.

- Many people attending a council meeting are interested only in a single issue and leave after their issue is disposed of. The reporter must be careful that someone vital to the story is not allowed to get away, because they might be unavailable later. It is best to follow the person outside for a brief interview.

- When the identity of someone making a significant point at a session is unavoidably missed, there will be a temptation to gloss over the point or even delete it from the story. Every effort should be made to identify the source, because the point may be too important to eliminate.

- A reporter will encounter frequent problems with the accuracy of citizen information at a council meeting. A complainer may state that 10 business establishments support her contentions, but the reporter's check may indicate that only four are involved. Tracking down and verifying such facts can be a headache, but it is important to the accuracy of the story. Making a practice of seeking verification on the spot is helpful.

- Reporters should always ask for copies of printed agreements, which the council usually makes for its own use but does not always circulate. Also ask for copies of all pertinent documents before council begins its session.

- The city clerk is a valuable source for verifying information, generally tape recording or otherwise collecting a verbatim account of the proceedings. While transcripts are not usually available immediately, confusing points can be cleared up with the clerk.

- Reporters should always be on the alert for "telegraphed information," the informal kind that indicates something is in the wind. If the reporter hears an aside by one official to another that a "short meeting" is scheduled in the mayor's office after the council meeting, he or she should try to determine the reason for it. A fine line exists between an informal meeting and an official executive session. While neither may produce newsworthy material, they can indicate important future developments. A reporter with good contacts usually can find out the purpose of such sessions.

- Why is a council member missing? He or she may be ill, merely indisposed or conducting specific business for the body. The reporter should be careful in dealing with specific votes when a council member is absent. A "unanimous 6–0 vote" on an ordinance is not really unanimous when the seventh member is absent. The missing member should be identified.

The Importance of Diligent Pursuit

The importance of pursuing budding issues before the council begins deliberating them cannot be overemphasized. Not every official will be happy with this approach, but it is best for the reader or viewer. How often the young reporter will hear from an official, "Why don't we wait until the council looks at it?"

An Ohio city manager was uncharacteristically frank with a reporter several years ago in arguing for tight parameters on news dissemination. "Until information is released through *official channels*, it is not in the public domain," the manager said.

"I believe," he continued, "that some reporters spend too much time digging for information that is not news yet, information that would soon be public anyway. The reporters who irritate me are the ones who dig for information about the inner workings of government, or who try to break a story ahead of time."

Part of the conflict noted in the city manager's comments appears to be disagreement over what constitutes "public information."

The official says, "It's public when I announce it."

The reporter should respectfully disagree, "It's already in the public domain, because people are talking about it."

In a common example, a city hall reporter hears through the grapevine that a tax increase is being considered to raise funds for the financially pressed municipal government. The new "development fee" would be tacked onto construction permits when they are issued.

These are some of the questions the reporter might ask to produce a complete story before council takes up the issue:

1. Whose idea is it? Such proposals rarely spring forth spontaneously, yet many people are unwilling to publicly commit themselves as sponsors of a project. Thus, the proposal takes on the appearance of an anonymous trial balloon. Every effort should be made to discuss the proposal with the sponsor.

FIGURE 4–1
Many of these working documents should be available to the reporter. These groups also interact informally with one another.

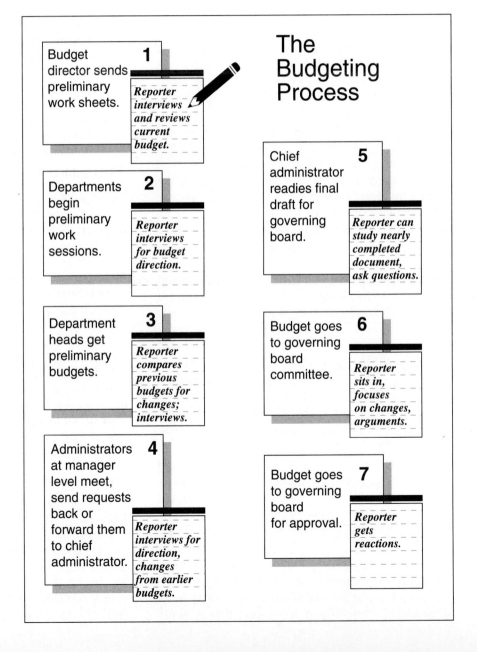

The Budgeting Process

1. Budget director sends preliminary work sheets.
Reporter interviews and reviews current budget.

2. Departments begin preliminary work sessions.
Reporter interviews for budget direction.

3. Department heads get preliminary budgets.
Reporter compares previous budgets for changes; interviews.

4. Administrators at manager level meet, send requests back or forward them to chief administrator.
Reporter interviews for direction, changes from earlier budgets.

5. Chief administrator readies final draft for governing board.
Reporter can study nearly completed document, ask questions.

6. Budget goes to governing board committee.
Reporter sits in, focuses on changes, arguments.

7. Budget goes to governing board for approval.
Reporter gets reactions.

2. When was it proposed to other officials in city government? How did they react to it? How were they persuaded to consider it? What alternatives were or are being considered?

3. What are the chances for the proposal's adoption? What will passage mean in terms of estimated revenue? What kind of stifling effect might it have on continued development in the city? What will passage mean in terms of the average taxpayer? Who will actually pay the tax—new homeowners and business enterprises or developers and contractors?

4. What is the reaction of those most closely involved—the developers and builders?

5. What created the need for the increased revenue in the first place? How will such a proposal affect other possible tax measures?

The sources are plentiful: the city manager and other officials, such as the planning director, council members and the treasurer or finance officer; organizations interested in the proposal, such as the Chamber of Commerce or the Development Office; builders and developers; and interested citizens.

Success in the early stages will turn on the reporter's persistence in following the story, which may get to the reader or viewer long before it is presented as an "official package" at a council meeting.

The Budget: Income and Outgo

Cyril Thornburg thumped the thick document on the desk in front of him. "Solid as the Rock of Gibraltar," the Rockmont Council president proclaimed of the proposed $49,570,500 municipal budget for next year. "No sir, there's no fat here," he announced proudly to three reporters in his office. "It's lean but it does the job."

Kevin Lockerby was not impressed. Later, down the hall in his office, the lone Democrat on the City Council bitterly denounced what he called "the Thornburg crowd's insensitivity to the need for greater human services at the local level."

"Every year," Lockerby complained, "they trim the help for the needier segments of the community, and add the money to those who support them at election time." He flipped open his copy of the new budget to offer an example.

In this developing economic scenario that will affect thousands in a community lies a host of charges and countercharges. The job of the public affairs reporter is not to start a controversy, but to follow it to a conclusion by communicating the issues involved.

In writing about the financial affairs of municipal government and the budgeting process, these questions are basic to the reporter's effectiveness:

- How much does it cost?
- Who is paying for it?
- How does it affect other programs?
- What are the citizens getting for their money?
- Do they really want it?

There are many other questions, and how the city hall reporter handles them dictates the quality of coverage. The budget is the single most important document issued by local government, and it constitutes a major policy statement by those in power. It indicates the bottom line on what services will be expanded or cut back during the coming year, how individuals and groups will be affected, and how much everyone will pay.

Although politics plays a major role in preparation of the budget, the reporter should not treat it primarily as a political document. He or she will have to balance the political aspects against the financial details of how millions of dollars will be spent during the coming year.

Just what does the city do with its $42.1 million annual budget? For one thing, a chunk of the money goes to agencies and services that aren't even controlled by City Hall.

About $5.6 million of it is distributed to two dozen agencies that range from the Regional Transit Authority, which receives $4.2 million, to the Kiwanis Day Nursery, which gets $17,000 to spend as it chooses.

Most of the agencies have been receiving money for years. Some are funded solely through contributions from the city. But all of them are finding themselves in the same budget crunch that is causing city officials to comb the budget these days looking for money to cover city pay raises.

Winners and Losers

One of the keys to effective coverage of a municipality's financial affairs lies in the changes a budget produces. Who will win and who will lose in the process? The pressures for new fire stations (and the subsequent savings in insurance rates to homeowners) may be outweighed by the increased incidence of crime that has forced police department priorities to the top. And departments such as streets and highways and public health may find themselves caught in the middle.

The reporter does not have to be a certified public accountant to follow the budget process, but should be able to digest technical financial information and to ask pertinent questions.

Budgeting, the reporter will find, is a series of political-economic decisions that come out of managers' coordination of city resources and expenditures. The paperwork on budgets is extensive and permanent, and follows regular patterns. This documentary evidence is a major tool for the reporter following the process.

Press tradition usually reports on the budget in its final form, rather than as an extensive and continuing series of decisions. But the reporter should follow the budget as a year-round process, because that is how city officials are looking at it. For example, the final budget approved by the council on Oct. 1 is a document that probably has been studied as an extensive series of decisions over many months.

> Service on 53 of the city's 76 bus routes would be cut back—in many cases drastically—if Metro Transit is forced to make budget cuts demanded by the City Council, according to a confidential budget document.
>
> Scores of routes would not operate after 8 p.m., and weekend service would be curtailed. The document being studied by various levels of transit officials also suggests as many as 100 transit workers would lose their jobs if the proposed cuts are made.
>
> "Listen, we are caught between a rock and a hard place," City Council President Lenore Ashby said. "We don't want to cripple the system," she said, adding that she would prefer a 5 percent to 10 percent fare increase to any cuts in service.

As this example shows, many documents and explanations by officials exist to illuminate a major issue—the future of public transportation. The budgeters have many studies at their fingertips that are also available to the reporter.

The reporter needs to look at the budget process as a series of arguments and negotiations followed by decisions (see Figure 4–1).

For example, the manager of an uncomplicated department such as street cleaning might be the first person involved in the process. Another manager, heading the streets maintenance division, will provide further input. The trail leads to the director of public works, possibly the budget director, the chief city administrator, the council's budget committee and finally council itself.

Participants in the process may alter figures (and make them stick) at any point. It is important for the reporter to know the budget participants, their political and organizational strengths, and the process that will lead to final figures.

Many of the lower-level participants in the process have familiarity and specialized competence in a particular area, giving them technical superiority on questions relating to program needs and the merits of the program itself.

It is to these people that the reporter should direct questions regarding program merits and needs, not an easy task if chief administrators see the reporter as "meddling" in the city's internal affairs. The reporter's job may be complicated by informal shirt-sleeve sessions that result in horse-trading. Reporters make officials nervous at such sessions.

The reporter also needs patience to deal with what may seem to be interminable preliminary sessions that indicate the direction officials are taking. The discussions of items, line by line, guide readers or viewers through preliminary coverage that points to final decisions.

After the initial presentation, the reporter has time to document a case history on funding for specific projects. Some examples:

- Crime statistics have forced city officials to study new ways to solve emerging law enforcement problems. Major expansion of the police academy, a costly project, is one issue under discussion. Many officials may be involved in finding the funds for such a project.

- Recycling, which has emerged as a major issue in many areas, is on the agenda of many communities.

Can the city afford to take over the planning and execution of a new program? City hall will be involved, but so will outside organizations and individuals.

- The reporter creates interest in the budget by writing about it in terms of people—those who prepare it, those who are served by it and those who are paying for it.

The Audit: A Special Tool for the Reporter

At the other end of the spectrum is another important document—the audit. The budget directs spending for a specified period; the audit evaluates the expenditures. Both documents are essential in covering municipal government. Most government units require audits—either in-house or by outside experts—and they are available to reporters as public documents.

The reporter should be familiar with the process, with the agents responsible for conducting and compiling them, and with the dates of their issuance. County and state governments often conduct such audits.

Some audits cover broad areas of government, while others are more limited in scope. All of them indicate the detailed record of expenditures: what, how and why.

Depending on whose figures one uses, the city's new Civic Center either earned a lot of money or lost a lot of money during its first year of operation. Last month, Civic Center Director William B. Leal displayed records that concluded the center had earned $160,000 during the period. However, a new audit released Monday concludes the facility lost $219,000 during the same time.

The $379,000 difference apparently is the result of a difference in how the depreciation "life" of the Civic Center is measured. Leal's "profit" was based on depreciation over a 100-year period, while the new audit used a 40-year depreciation figure.

Special audits are more visible than those routinely required by state law, and they usually are triggered by internal financial or personnel problems.

A special state audit of the city's financial records reveals "numerous violations" of the city charter requirement for competitive bidding on purchases over $2,500, City Manager Richard Bloom said Wednesday.

Although State Tax Department auditors completed their work Wednesday, the report must be forwarded to the city through the state tax commissioner's office.

The audit was prompted by the dismissal last month of city purchasing agent Lawrence Snow. A dispute had developed over purchase of a $303,000 insurance policy without the approval of council.

However, the city hall reporter does not have to wait for an official audit to check municipal spending. Financial documents are on file in most city offices. The reporter may not win any popularity contests in asking to review them, but the rewards are often worth the cost of popularity.

City officials have spent more than $85,000 since July 1 to "boost" the city through civic promotions, and have also spent $38,000 to join a variety of organizations, according to Finance Department documents. A review of canceled checks on file at City Hall indicates that thousands of dollars were spent in the last four months for Hershey "kisses," banners promoting athletic events, Christmas lights and keys to the city costing about $30 each.

In checking the records, the reporter found that "organizational dues" spent by city officials ranged from $48 on behalf of the city manager for membership in the American Academy of Political and Social Science to $16,460 for annual dues to the State Municipal League, which is listed as the official lobbying agency for the city. From this point, it is simple to check the budget for possible overspending.

With eight months remaining in the budget year, the current city budget lists total appropriations of $83,000 for "civic promotion" and $35,000 for organizational dues. Both budget items have already been exceeded, the records indicate.

Some familiarity with records location and accessibility is essential for the city hall reporter, who often relies on tips from insiders for questionable practices in handling city money.

A woman who has been named in employee complaints about salary inequities in the Police Department has accompanied Chief John Snider on three out-of-town trips at city expense, records show.

According to expense records filed in the Finance Office, Snider and department crime prevention officer

MaryAnn Mote had adjoining hotel rooms during trips to Raleigh, N.C., and Washington, D.C., and also traveled together to Stanton, Va.

Asked about his relationship with Mote Wednesday, Snider said, "It's basically nobody's business." He said any relationship between the pair has not affected his operation of the department, and that the trips were for legitimate city business. Mote, who could not be reached for comment, has been promoted to lieutenant and her annual salary has increased from $18,408 to $27,036 since she was hired Feb. 2, according to city payroll records.

Documentation is essential to these kinds of controversial stories. Breaking stories such as these give a reporter more credibility when larger financial issues are addressed.

Sources of Operating Funds

A typical municipality obtains operating and capital improvements funds in many ways (see Figure 4–2). These include property taxes, a sales tax, a business and occupational tax, a franchise tax on some businesses, a tax on utility bills, an amusement tax on theaters and other places of entertainment, a hotel-motel tax, parking meters, police court fines, building permits and refuse removal fees.

> Your neighbor sneaks out in the middle of the night and stuffs his garbage into your can. Or he allows his garbage to pile up on his front lawn or simply dumps it on the steps of City Hall.
>
> If the City Council goes ahead with a plan to impose garbage fees of $96 a year for residents, and require stickers on or near cans to indicate payment, how is the city going to deal with those who won't pay?

Officials and experts often raise such questions, and citizen groups are not shy about putting in their two cents worth. But the fact remains that the alert city hall reporter is one of the most effective questioners of municipal practices.

Income is only half the equation, of course. Expenditures qualify as the other essential element in the city hall reporter's mandate to cover financial affairs.

Typical expenditures include operation of City Hall offices, police and fire departments, the finance department, the court system, public health and welfare, parks and other recreation facilities, garbage removal and a host of minor services.

A city often subsidizes associated agencies that depend on it for funds without taking a direct part in their operation, or it may join with one or more county governments in assisting a metropolitan transit system or an areawide health services program. It also may contribute to the operation of a library system and civil defense offices. The relationships between the municipality and these other agencies are important to the city hall reporter.

> A $60 million bond issue to generate a "pool" for low-interest housing loans channeled through local banks has been agreed to in principle by officials of the city and county.
>
> "We're hammering out the details," Mayor Kevin Stanley said Thursday. "The money should be available in 90 days."
>
> The 40-year bond issue is designed to produce 30-year home loans with interest rates of 5 percent to 7 percent, somewhat below current bank rates. A family with a gross income of up to $35,000 will be able to apply for the loans, Stanley said. The city and county agreed on that level because it includes a majority of middle-income families, he said.

The City Hall 'Team'

The organization of municipal government is important to the reporter who must deal with personnel in many departments far removed from the policy-making council or commission (see Figure 4–3).

The best summaries of organization are found in the annual budget—where the reporter can determine allotment of funds and personnel and obtain insight into the breadth of services of the various departments.

The agency with the most personnel is public works, which also carries the most implications for the average resident. Included are subdepartments for traffic control, engineering, street maintenance, inspection bureaus, sanitation control and refuse removal, and maintenance and construction of public facilities.

Because of their intrinsic importance, size and visibility, the police and fire departments always constitute major divisions. The legal department, on the

FIGURE 4–2
Here are the major sources of revenue and major areas of expenditures in a typical municipality.

Based on sales of gasoline, cigarettes, alcohol, and automobile licenses within the city, the municipality also may receive substantial tax money from the state. Fees for bicycles and dog licenses are not overlooked, and many cities collect a local income tax as a major revenue source.

Funds are also received from state and federal governments through revenue sharing, some of it earmarked for specific purposes such as minority housing, education projects and a variety of health services. However, the federal grants that had become a major source of revenue gradually dissipated in the 1980s and created a need to generate more revenues locally.

Municipalities are constantly experiencing funding problems and searching for new sources. A proposal for a new tax or fee calls for legwork to determine the potential success or failure of the measure. The reporter may be the one who raises questions about the effectiveness of the proposal.

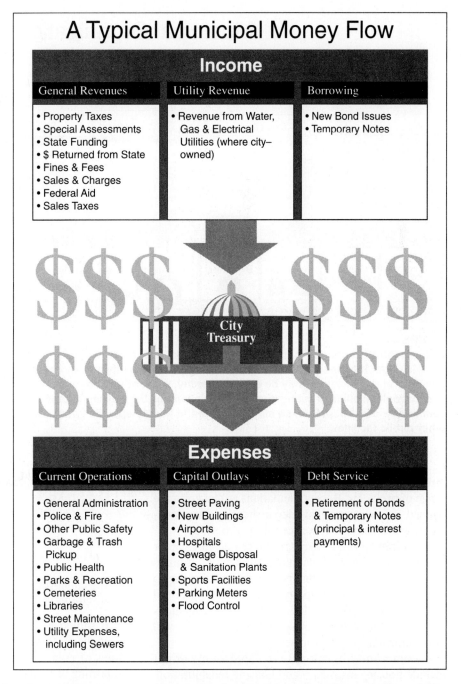

A Typical Municipal Money Flow

Income

General Revenues	Utility Revenue	Borrowing
• Property Taxes • Special Assessments • State Funding • $ Returned from State • Fines & Fees • Sales & Charges • Federal Aid • Sales Taxes	• Revenue from Water, Gas & Electrical Utilities (where city–owned)	• New Bond Issues • Temporary Notes

City Treasury

Expenses

Current Operations	Capital Outlays	Debt Service
• General Administration • Police & Fire • Other Public Safety • Garbage & Trash Pickup • Public Health • Parks & Recreation • Cemeteries • Libraries • Street Maintenance • Utility Expenses, including Sewers	• Street Paving • New Buildings • Airports • Hospitals • Sewage Disposal & Sanitation Plants • Sports Facilities • Parking Meters • Flood Control	• Retirement of Bonds & Temporary Notes (principal & interest payments)

other hand, may include only the city attorney, several aides and a few office workers. The finance department is somewhat broader, encompassing a purchasing department, controller and auditors, a data processing department to handle payrolls and city records, and employees to handle other fiscal affairs.

Most cities employ an expert to oversee the planning process. This official supervises study of future

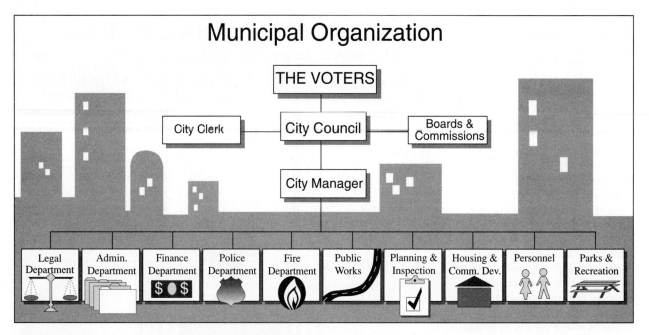

Municipal Organization

THE VOTERS

City Clerk — City Council — Boards & Commissions

City Manager

| Legal Department | Admin. Department | Finance Department | Police Department | Fire Department | Public Works | Planning & Inspection | Housing & Comm. Dev. | Personnel | Parks & Recreation |

FIGURE 4–3
This organization chart is fairly typical of municipal government, although details will vary. Sometimes the city clerk is under the jurisdiction of the city manager, and the city attorney answers directly to the council. Some boards and commissions may be elected directly, while others are appointed by the council and answer to it. In metropolitan cities, a safety director often oversees the police, fire and traffic departments. Depending on the community, other departments may be created to handle specific functions such as operating athletic arenas or other public facilities.

directions for the community and solutions to a broad range of problems. Recommendations are taken to the council for decisions. This department and its documents are a major news source for the reporter.

The zoning process, discussed more fully in Chapter 5, is an integral part of planning. An area of a municipality is restricted by ordinance to a particular use to protect the value of property there. A zoning board or commission oversees the process, which includes acceptance or rejection of appeals for variances and nonconforming use of property.

A community development department might include housing inspection and housing rehabilitation. A human resources department might oversee minority recruitment, selection of city employees on a merit basis, and employee relations and safety.

A child of city government, the Human Relations Commission, is investigating the employment practices of its own parent. The commission will meet with the City Council today at 4 p.m. to discuss the city's affirmative action practices.

At issue, Commission Chairman Joan Hesson said, is what she calls the "questionable hirings" of several city employees in recent months before the official advertising deadline had expired.

It should be pointed out that the official organization chart often differs somewhat from the unofficial lines of communication and authority, complicating reporting of municipal government.

An official organization chart may show the city clerk as answering to the city council and subject to dismissal by that body, but many of the clerk's duties might center on the city manager's office. That official may have no control over the city clerk. The director of an industrial development office may officially answer to the city manager, yet often deal directly with the policy-making council. These unofficial "lines of authority" should be a part of the reporter's arsenal of information.

The mayor, fearing that a financial crisis is brewing, calls a press conference after conferring with the finance director.

> City layoffs of 150–200 people and hiring freezes were recommended Tuesday by Mayor Ted Solomon, who said he fears a "budget crisis" because of revenue losses during the current economic downturn.
>
> Solomon called a news conference and issued a statement after conferring with Finance Director Gary White. Solomon said his statement was sparked by a 4 percent drop in revenues from the city's 2 percent sales tax. Declines also were recorded in business and occupational licenses.

Finance Director White nominally reports to the city manager, and is in fact subject to dismissal by that official, yet the normal chain of command is frequently disrupted by such developments. The city manager later told reporters that he was not briefed by the mayor before the news conference, but noted he is in basic agreement with the proposals.

However, the mayor's associates on the council may not agree with him on his emergency proposals and insist on detailing their side of the story.

> Mayor Ted Solomon's recommendations for layoffs of city employees and freezes on hiring during what he calls the city's "budget crisis" received a cool reception from other members of the city council Wednesday. Solomon suggested the measures in light of substantial drops in city revenues.
>
> Council members Dean Storm and Roberta Bailes objected to the proposal.
>
> "No matter if he says a 10 percent drop," Storm said. "There are six others of us on council, and what we collectively decide goes. I don't see any reason for panic."
>
> Bailes agreed. She said she considers layoffs "a last resort. We have a long way to go before we reach that point," she said.

BOX 4-3

These Bedevil the Reporter

✷✷✷

- Policy-making vs. administration in government.
- Relationships among governments.
- What to report in the public interest.
- How much reporting is too much?

Similar disruptions in the chain of command can arise with citizen access to the council in matters involving strong personal interest, although the director of an involved department answers to the city administrator. Members of boards and commissions may officially answer to the city council but in practice deal directly with the administrator or even department heads.

A safety director may exercise authority over the police and fire departments, yet actually retain little or no control over those departments. The legal department may answer to the city manager, yet find itself frequently questioned by the council. These unofficial lines of authority may be more effective in the practical governance of the municipality, and the reporter will benefit through an awareness of these sometimes unorthodox lines.

COMPLICATING FACTORS FOR THE JOURNALIST

Long after the reporter has passed the first hurdle at City Hall, learning to be comfortable in the role of information gatherer in often hostile territory, other factors intrude to complicate coverage. Some are merely mechanical problems, such as how to organize a story with complicating facets. Others carry deeper significance.

Policy-Making vs. Administration

Where does policy-making end and administration of policy begin? This question poses special problems for the journalist who covers the council-manager form of government, but it also can affect reporting on other forms of government. While most city charters identify the policy-makers, it is more difficult to draw the line in practice. And some administrators tend to draw the line much tighter than others to serve their own particular interests.

"I can't answer that question," the administrator tells the reporter. "That involves policy and you'll have to go to council for the answer to that." The administrator has probably drawn a sharper line than council would have, creating "dead space" in which neither an administrator nor the council will venture. Yet this "dead space" area may be important to the story—and to the public.

A major industry is considering moving to a municipality but wants the city to agree to provide sewer service. A municipal administrator may agree to provide that service, but as a practical matter, the final decision lies in the hands of the council as policy-maker.

If the council members decline to discuss the issue, sending it back to the administrator as "an administrative matter," the reporter is in limbo, with no one willing to discuss the issue.

While the apolitical position generally assigned to the city administrator often obscures the manager's contribution to the policy-making process, the professional administrator plays an important role in setting municipal policy.

The reporter often finds it difficult to draw a clear line of demarcation. The lead to this story illustrates the point:

City Manager Barry Evans is apparently bowing to the City Council's order not to release information to the news media before presenting that information to the Council.

"Council's the boss," Evans said Wednesday when he was asked about the reprimand.

Mayor William Schiller had sent Evans a letter reproaching him for telling a reporter he will recommend to the Council that downtown traffic patterns be drastically altered.

The city manager had discussed with the reporter what he saw as ineffective and antiquated traffic patterns. What a city manager does is often seen as politics by the policy-makers, and managers privately say the policy-makers too often poke their noses into the purely administrative aspects of city government.

But professional administrators cannot remain aloof from politics, and many of them recognize and deal with this fact of life.

Relationships with Other Governments

Involvement of municipal government with other agencies and governments also complicates the reporting process. There are long-standing associations, not only with other local governments but with the parent state and federal systems.

Grants of funds from the federal and state governments are channeled directly to officials charged with administering the programs produced by the money. After the original agreement is made, city council involvement is effectively bypassed and it takes additional legwork on the part of the reporter to follow the money.

State involvement adds a different perspective. Approval of local projects often must be obtained from state agencies. While approval is often merely a formality, the relationship adds another layer of officialdom with which the reporter must deal.

State powers over segments of local government operations can complicate relationships even further.

A legislative proposal to raise minimum pension benefits for police officers and firefighters would be a financial "catastrophe" for cities in the state if it is enacted, City Manager Gary Douglas said Tuesday.

Current minimum pension payments for retired and disabled police officers and firefighters are $350 a month. The General Assembly proposal would raise that minimum to $700 a month, or 60 percent of the person's income at the time of retirement, whichever is greater.

"I have no objection to increased pensions for retired persons," Douglas said in a letter to the bill's sponsors. "I must, however, express concern when added costs are placed upon cities without an offsetting income."

In this case, the city's budget for police and fire pensions totaled $830,000. The legislation, according to this city official, would raise the city's costs to nearly $2 million. Clearly, the state has the power to act in this manner, but communication among the various government sectors might have eased the tension for all involved. The city hall reporter must be constantly on the alert for such interaction.

Other local governments, often overlapping in jurisdiction, further complicate the reporter's work. They are all secure in the belief that theirs is the more important part of the equation.

A city and a county government are negotiating to construct and jointly operate a new animal shelter for the area, but discussions are sporadic. Both sides are working toward specific advantages, only one of which may be details of funding. How will the costs be met? Whose job will it be to construct the facility? Who will control it, and where will it be located? The best place for the city may not be the best place for the county.

Reporting is always more complex with the addition of another governmental unit to the equation.

The County Commission has postponed for 30 days any decision to allow Columbus to annex seven parcels of land northwest of the city. The postponement was agreed upon after Westerville City Manager Maynard Peek appealed to the commission to delay the annexation until Westerville is given an opportunity to annex the property.

The smaller city is complicating the annexation proposal by the larger city, the parcels being adjacent to both municipalities. The decision is further complicated by the county, which has the power to decide who will annex the land.

The reporter must answer these important questions:

- What is the county's role in the process?
- What are the political implications in the decision?
- What do the property owners prefer, and do they have a choice?
- Why does either municipality want to annex the land?
- What is its potential value on the tax rolls?
- What services would each city have to provide and how much would they cost?
- Who has analyzed the dispute for potential benefits to the total community?

Many sources exist to answer all these questions, including the county's Planning Commission itself, which probably has studied the issue. Covering such disputes among governments is part of the city hall reporter's job.

Reporting in the Public Interest

To what extent should the journalist report municipal government personnel matters? When is a personnel matter of legitimate public interest, and when should it be ignored as merely an "internal" matter?

None of these questions can be answered simply, and they further complicate the city hall reporter's job. A public body often closes a portion of its meeting, declaring an executive session to discuss a "personnel" matter. Is such closure really necessary or allowed by law?

Most public bodies close meetings in four specific areas:

- Personnel matters involving an individual's hiring, firing, pay, promotion or disciplining.
- Contract negotiations such as those involving sale or purchase of land or property, receipt of legal advice, and settlement of legal claims.
- Investigations involving allegations of criminal misconduct.
- Security subjects such as law enforcement planning or special investigations.

But the line drawn between public and private is a fine one. Is confidentiality necessary in interviewing candidates for an important city position? The search committee says it is unwilling to expose the job search to the prospect's current employers, but the community has a right to know a candidate's qualifications.

- An official being considered as city manager of a major city is plagued by a 30-year-old bankruptcy. Should the information be made public by the city hall reporter?

- A search committee operating in secret settles on a new city manager who is under fire in his present job in another state. He has been criticized for not bringing spending under better control. Do the people he will serve in his new job have a right to know his current problems?

The answer lies partly in the importance of the position to the well-being of the community. The candidate's positive qualifications will be aired after the decision is made. Should negative information be aired beforehand?

> Three finalists have been selected for the city manager's job in Brentwood, and all will be interviewed by the City Council during the next 14 days. All three are highly qualified for the position, vacated when City Manager John Playford departed for Houston, said Wilson McLean, head of the council committee charged with the search.
>
> Only one of the finalists has been identified—Ellison Snow, director of public works and acting city manager since Playford left. The job pays $94,000 a year.

The holes in this story are clear, but the council is trying to help the candidates from other areas maintain anonymity. No one wants their current employer to know they are considering another position. On the other hand, the public has a right to know the identity of anyone who will be intimately involved in operating a major public corporation.

The most important argument for leaning toward publication of most sensitive personnel matters is that those involved are on the public payroll and influence public policy in some manner. Rarely can this legitimate argument be refuted.

How Much Is Too Much?

The broad range of issues in the municipality creates another problem for the reporter. How much of the material should be covered?

The answer depends on the policy of the publication or station, and the editors' perception of community information needs. A council session may produce half a dozen major news stories and a dozen other reportable items, all with a need to be covered. "Better too much than too little," is a good rule.

The stories developed in the days before the official council session also help spread the material over a longer period. Constructing preliminary stories lessens the need to fully develop them after the council meeting, although official action should be noted. The reporter also should keep in mind an old rule, "Many major stories may require or deserve a follow-up."

After the council meeting, print reporters should break down the important material into separate news stories that will be easier to display and read. One of the stories can be used as a roundup of less important items:

> In other action, the Council:
>
> - Enacted an ordinance extending to 10 p.m. the operating hours of parking meters on downtown streets.
> - Approved requests for bicycle parades on Broad Street July 11 and 18.
> - Awarded a $31,456 contract to East End Cycle Sales for three Kawasaki motorcycles for the police department. East End was the only bidder.

The size of the city places a final burden on the reporter to determine what must be reported and in what depth. An ordinance closing a street will carry weight in a smaller city, yet be ignored in a metropolitan area as being of limited interest. The one-to-one relationships in smaller cities give way to different relationships in larger cities. It is often difficult for reporters in smaller cities to be as objective as a big-city counterpart, while the metropolitan reporter is often perceived as being more insensitive to issues close to people.

All these complications place on the journalist the burden of fitting together the pieces in the jigsaw puzzle of municipal government.

***

SUGGESTED READINGS

Banovetz, James M., ed. *Managing the Modern City*. Washington, D.C.: International City Management Association, 1971.

The student will find these chapters useful: Chapter 4, "The Environment and the Role of the Administrator"; Chapter 5, "Leadership Styles and Strategies"; Chapter 12, "City Planning"; and Chapter 15, "Public Relations."

Royko, Mike. *Boss: Richard Daley of Chicago*. New York: NAL/Dutton, 1971.

Chapter 1, Daley's Day: a Day in the Life of an Urban Mayor"; and Chapter 4, "The Machine and How It Works in the Big City."

Stillman, Richard. *Rise of the City Manager*. Albuquerque, N.M.: University of New Mexico Press, 1979.

"Introduction" and Chapter 6, "Some Perspectives on the Present Dilemmas and Future Directions of the Profession."

Chapter 5

Covering the County

"Overall, county governments are a mixed bag. They show signs of adaptability and inflexibility, of innovativeness and sluggishness, of being the most important local government of the future and of becoming practically lifeless."

Political scientist John C. Bollens' assessment of this venerable form of local government that exists in so many rich variations was made 40 years ago. Today, county government is more apt to be characterized by the positive terms—adaptability and innovativeness.

Although restricted to half a dozen basic forms, county government reveals all the shades of difference that an independent pioneer population could conjure up as it fanned out across the country. In fact, its diversity makes it difficult to provide a single meaningful model of county government for the public affairs reporter.

FIRST AT THE SCENE

Counties were there from the first—authorized by newly formed state governments to serve as their instruments—and, give or take a few, the number has changed little since the last wave of settlers spread west. Other forms of local government have proliferated, but for the most part they have merely been superimposed on the existing counties.

But times are changing in the county courthouse— the old brass spittoons have all but disappeared and the portly county commissioner, cigar in his teeth, has become a rarity. A mix of young and old, men and women, farmers and professionals now vie for seats on a county council or commission. Traditional county services, notably the court system and tax collection, are familiar parts of the scene, but expanding responsibilities have broadened the scope of county activity.

FOUNDATIONS OF THE MODERN COUNTY

Counties in this country developed from the English county form to administer rural areas under pioneer conditions. Some of their functions appear outmoded today, but most continue to thrive, even taking on many of the responsibilities of municipalities that overlay them.

Many of the old titles and offices still exist, albeit with somewhat different functions. The office of sheriff can be traced unbroken back to England; the justice of the peace, the coroner and the grand jury date to the 12th century in England.

While the system was borrowed from England, it was generously adapted to pioneer and near-pioneer conditions in the new land, and modified as Americans migrated west. By the time the western states were established, county government was a practical mixture of what had become four basic regional plans.

The New England Town

The New England town form evolved to accommodate the compact settlements in that section of the new country and performed the same functions as English counties. The popular assembly was most democratic; residents chose selectmen to administer the affairs of

the county, constables to enforce the law, officials to assess and collect taxes, and others to handle necessary civic duties. (Counties do exist in New England, but they are merely judicial districts.)

The form, characterized by strong self-government, proved effective because of the closely bound nature of people in the region. Town meetings continue to flourish and occasionally even influence broader political events. Those that took place during the Watergate scandal in the 1970s may have contributed to President Nixon's resignation from office. With the president under fire for his involvement in the Watergate cover-up, the subject of impeachment arose in at least 13 annual town meetings in Vermont in 1974. Resolutions calling for Nixon's impeachment were approved at eight of the meetings and were covered extensively by the national news media.

In a similar fashion, the national debate over U.S. involvement in Vietnam was escalated by the vigorous debate in the New England town meetings.

The Southern County Form

While New England was producing its special form of local government, the South was more faithfully reproducing the English version of the county. A more scattered settlement and the different character of the Southern settlers resulted in a county government with authority in the hands of a court composed of justices of the peace. They transacted the administrative, fiscal and judicial business of the community. Smaller political subdivisions, such as the town or township, were nonexistent in the Southern counties.

Townships and Supervisors

The township-supervisor form of county government, which originated in New York, was a compromise between the New England town and the Southern county, built on the principle of representation rather than on the direct town meeting format. Supervisors elected in their own towns served collectively as a county governing board while continuing to hold administrative power in their respective towns. Justices of the peace faded from the scene, and the county board of supervisors exercised administrative and fiscal responsibility in managing affairs of the county. Borrowing from the Southern plan, New York limited the range of countywide functions, leaving control over roads, public welfare and other functions to the town boards. The relatively stronger position of the county ultimately led to the demise of the town meeting, with the county board settling questions of policy and electing its officers by ballot.

The Commissioner Form

Both counties and townships existed in Pennsylvania, but the influence of the towns was much less pronounced. As a result, town government never became established, but the Southern system, with its centralized administration, was not favored either.

In Pennsylvania, county commissioners were elected at large and produced a strong but responsive county government. Counties were divided into townships for administrative purposes, but the townships never acquired the status of those in New York. The township was subordinate to the county board and was not represented on it.

Further Compromises

As the nation grew westward, the states created in the Great Plains, the Rocky Mountains and the Far West evolved further compromises in the original four plans. As in the Southern plan, there were no towns or townships, but most areas adopted the commission form of Pennsylvania. Many counties today have a five-member board, with a chairman elected by his or her peers, and a board-county manager rule.

Most of the 3,137 counties today use one of these basic forms of government, but a few areas have wholly or partly consolidated with municipal governments. Most are metropolitan areas, such as New York City, New Orleans, Boston, Philadelphia, San Francisco and Denver.

In recent years, further efforts have been made to modernize the structure. Many counties have established a form of government similar to the city manager plan. A specialist is hired to administer county government and is answerable to a board, which continues to establish policy.

SOME SUBTLE DIFFERENCES

There are subtle differences between the older counties and the more modern municipal corporations that have been superimposed on them. Although both were created by state government, the courts consider municipalities legal corporations, while counties are recognized as quasi-corporations, instruments of state government.

In most areas, a charter originally authorized by the state makes a municipality a corporation. The county has no such charter; it is subject to the action of that state—executive, legislative and judicial. It should be noted, however, that in recent years many states have given local governments substantial authority to handle their own affairs as "home rule."

As noted earlier, municipal services include refuse removal, water service, fire and police protection, parks and recreation, and other amenities of an urban community.

The modern county also provides some or all of these services, but it also is a convenient subdivision of the state—operating the judicial system and maintaining records. As the basic tax collection agency for the community, the county conducts elections, dispenses auto licenses and collects state fees. In areas where the municipality does not do so, it may also provide law enforcement, construction and maintenance of highways, and educational services.

Some New Functions—and Problems

Increasingly, however, counties are being called upon to expand their role of administrative functionaries by providing services and enforcing regulations once solely the function of towns and cities. Counties have responded by providing such services themselves or by creating subgovernments that do so. These are discussed more fully in Chapter 7.

This modern tendency to create new arms of government to dispense specific services has further fragmented local government, and created new demands on the government reporter. A county now finds itself carved up by an older metropolitan city, newer municipal suburbs and sometimes numerous special districts. Furthermore, the municipalities and newly created special districts spill over into adjacent counties, fragmenting metropolitan areas even more.

The antiquity of the county structure, its ties to state government as an administrative arm, and its increasingly complex relationship with its fellow local governments all challenge the reporter assigned to the county

FIGURE 5–1
Nowhere is the U.S. system of political governance more complicated than in a county with many divergent problems—urban, suburban and rural. The reporting challenge becomes similarly complex.

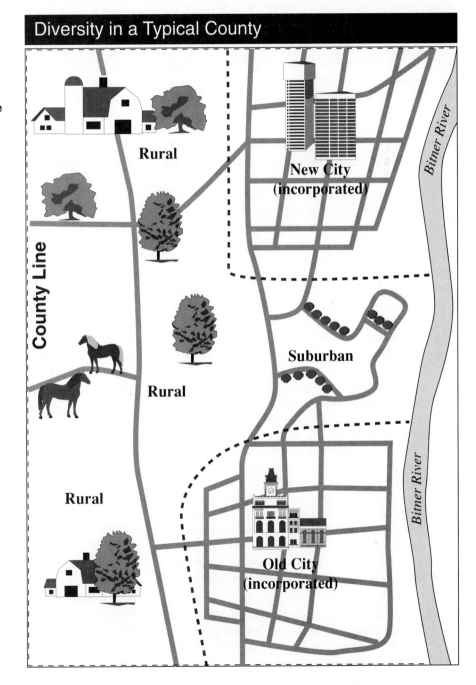

Diversity in a Typical County

Rural

New City
(incorporated)

County Line

Rural

Suburban

Rural

Old City
(incorporated)

Bitner River

beat. As with other forms of local government, the first rule for the journalist is to determine the character and composition of the government.

WHO GOVERNS THE COUNTY?

The county commissioner adjusted her horn-rimmed glasses on her nose, settled herself more comfortably in her chair, reflected for a moment, then responded to a questioning constituent:

"I know it's what you folks want, and I'd really like to help," she assured her visitor. "But our hands are tied. The state calls the shots on this and we have to go along."

This is best-known as "passing the buck," and the constituent is left little choice—drop the matter or take it to another level of government.

This is not an uncommon response at the county level. Historically, the county has been an arm of state government, administering state activities at the local level. Furthermore, counties increasingly have taken on a similar role for the federal government, which calls on county government to administer federal funds, sometimes overseeing multimillion-dollar public development, but more often running much smaller projects.

Within these basic limitations, which also serve as a political check-and-balance system, counties enjoy a considerable measure of self-government. County officials are popularly elected. The commissioner who brushed off the constituent also knew she could not afford too many negative responses if she hoped to run successful re-election campaigns.

While counties have some measure of independence, state constitutions and legislatures have attached strings to counties that limit their ability to act unilaterally in fiscal matters. The county reporter will anticipate these attachments to the parent government, partly because of the potential for conflict inherent in the relationship (see Figure 5–2).

> State Tax Commissioner David Hardesty has warned the Marshall County Commission he will not approve the county's new budget if it includes $138,500 in raises for the county's elected officials.

> The commissioners included the increases because state law provides for them when a county's tax base reaches $900 million.

> Although Marshall's tax base has topped that figure this year, the state constitution prohibits alteration of county officials' salaries during their terms of office.

The reporter will note a further subtle difference between county and municipal government. With its responsibility for administering state affairs at the local level, the county tends to be somewhat more administrative and judicial. Municipalities, with their ordinance-writing powers, tend to be more legislative. States have given counties more latitude in recent years, however, affording them greater powers to enact ordinances. The practical effect has been to allow officials to respond more positively to the demands of their constituents.

This has been effective in counties with substantial growth, but that growth has led to new challenges for the older county government. Demands are often made upon it by three diverse groups of citizens—the traditional rural population, urban residents and the mushrooming suburban citizenry.

Citizens of rural areas may seek services different from those sought by residents of more developed urban areas. And suburban residents may have yet another set of concerns. The county reporter will have to work hard to get feedback from such diverse sets of interests.

> The Earl County Commission voted yesterday to limit commercial growth on Western Highway by zoning the area for two-family residences.

> The effect, according to Commission Chairman John C. Wilson, will be to prohibit developers from constructing a 70-store shopping center along the highway.

> "It's far more important that we keep traffic moving along this stretch than allow new stores that will only jam up our roads," Wilson said.

For the suburbanite who must travel additional miles to the nearest shopping center, the decision may have a negative effect. For the urban resident who is trying to get to a job in the area each day, the effect may be positive. The same interest groups that operate within a municipality also influence decisions in the county environment.

A Typical County Organization

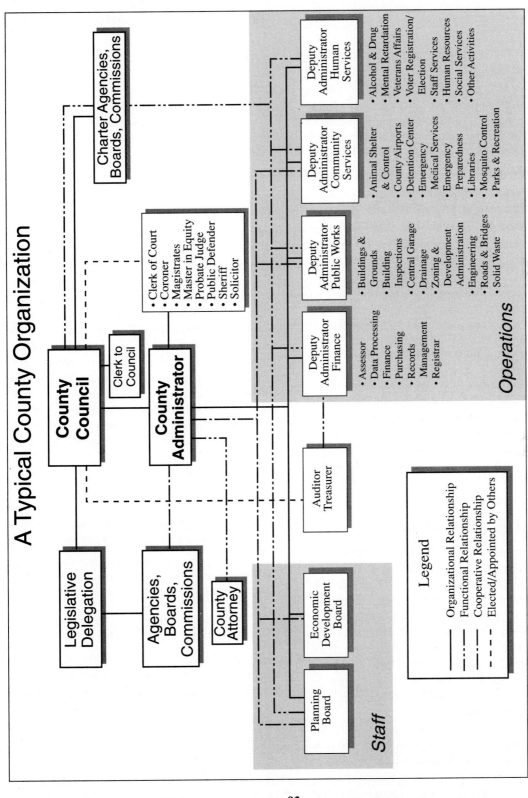

FIGURE 5–2
A traditional county government might be organized like this. In many areas, some of the elective offices are now appointed, or even have been eliminated.

Residents in an old rural area accustomed to their way of life may be thoroughly content with a two-lane road linking the city with nearby beaches. The county's efforts to expand the road to four lanes may bring heated objections, letters to the editor and threats to go to court. The county reporter will anticipate this, and collect the pertinent documents that will help illuminate the issue.

- What will the expanded highway mean to the rural character of the area?
- How many vehicles travel on the road now? How many and what kinds of accidents have occurred in the past few years?
- Who is leading or will lead the opposition to the highway improvements, and what kind of clout do they exert at the county and state levels?

Many documents exist to make a case for a decision either way. It is the county reporter's job to find and use them.

Whether these highway disputes take place in urban Columbus, Ohio (a limited access highway from downtown to the airport), or in coastal North Carolina (an expanded highway system from the city to ocean beaches through rural territory), pertinent studies and other public documents are always available to the reporter.

The Practical Exercises of Power

Contrary to popular belief, newly elected officeholders do not always dismiss their predecessors' entire staffs after a hotly contested election. It is undeniable that some displacement takes place, but there is considerable continuity in county government from election to election—usually a four-year span. Partisan politics is an integral component of the scene, becoming much more pronounced in election years. But the county employees who routinely handle the public's business usually belong to impartial civil service systems, providing employment stability.

The county's quasi-corporate character creates more stability. It can acquire property, enter into contracts, borrow money within limitations imposed by the state, and enjoy other privileges of a corporation.

Whatever the designation for the county governing board—and there are more than two dozen in use today*—it generally organizes or reorganizes after each election, selecting a chairperson or president from its ranks to preside at regular meetings.

Governing boards vary in size from three to as many as 100 members, but three to seven members on a board are most common. A tendency of the board to close ranks in the face of the press makes it somewhat more difficult for a reporter to cover a three-person county commission.

Even when the board is split by party affiliation, the county reporter often finds a certain unanimity among members, who usually find common ground for practical agreement. The unanimity makes the job of reporting the "why" of a decision more complicated.

Boards with larger memberships offer the reporter a better opportunity to identify dissenting and sometimes vocal minorities. The bigger boards permit broader representation but create administrative problems, resulting in more reliance on committees. The reporter's efforts, therefore, must also be directed toward interaction in these subunits; final action by the full board is often a mere formality.

The board meets regularly at a specified location to conduct its business. As with other governmental beats, however, the county reporter soon will learn that he or she cannot rely on official meetings for total coverage. Major and minor decisions are often thrashed out between sessions, and the reporter who is content to wait for the regular meeting will usually listen to the chair's gavel banging a *fait accompli.*

> Without discussion last night, the Blount County Commission approved guidelines tightening restrictions on admittance to the Aid for Senior Citizens program.
> "We've decided there must be real need before a person is enrolled," Commissioner Patricia Stone said.

Long before this official decision was reached, the matter was discussed at informal meetings, in telephone conversations and in hallway conferences. A study and an acrimonious public hearing preceded the

---

*Aside from the more prosaic designations of county commission and board of supervisors, names of county governing units include fiscal court, levy court, county court, board of chosen freeholders, board of revenue, quarterly court, police jury and county council.

decision. The reporter should have been at the center of these preliminary negotiations and arguments that led to the decision.

COLLECTING REVENUE: A COMPLICATED PROCESS

One of the county's indispensable functions is to collect and disburse the funds that provide services. Salaries, maintenance of public buildings and highways, special programs and costs of education are funded from a variety of county sources.

Property taxes are a primary source of funding, but many other sources exist. A county may assess an additional amount (called user fees) for garbage or refuse pickup, or for a county recycling program. It may levy a tax on businesses or a special accommodations tax on hotels and motels. A special county sales or income tax may be levied, and grants are received from state and federal government, many earmarked for specific programs. Some counties even impose an annual registration fee on pet owners.

The reporter new to the county beat should first study the current budget to determine the sources of all funding. (The budget also provides a helpful road map for country organization.)

Whatever the source and the use, the money flows into and out of the county treasury. The county sometimes serves as collecting agency for other governmental units within its borders, such as towns, cities and school districts.

Under authority conferred by the state, the county assesses property, levies and collects taxes based on those assessments, decides upon appropriations, incurs debt and makes arrangements to repay it, awards contracts and manages county property—all within a balanced county budget.

Collecting Taxes

The money-collecting process originates with a listing of all property in the county by the tax assessor, who places a value on it and assesses it for tax purposes. Many counties make a distinction between real and personal property, taxing separately. Real property includes land and the buildings or other improvements on it. Personal property judged taxable usually includes automobiles, boats, trailers, furniture and jewelry.

The tax assessor and staff are a gold mine of information for the county reporter. While a county council may have established special exemptions for primary residences, or senior citizen rates for residents over 65, the job of administering these rules falls to the assessor. What these items cost the budget, the effect they have on people, the number of people served by them, and other issues are all readily available to the reporter at the assessor's office.

Based on state restrictions or the policy of the county governing board, the assessment ranges from 10 percent to 100 percent of true value. Assessment ratio varies with the area. Some counties assess historic properties at the lowest rate, private residences at a higher rate, and commercial establishments at a still higher figure.

The key to what the taxpayer must pay is the country's current tax rate, which determines the tax. The rate is often expressed in terms of $X.xx per $100 of assessed valuation (see Figure 5–3). If the tax rate is $3 per $100 assessed valuation, for example, the owner of a home with a true value of $90,000 but assessed at 50 percent (or $45,000) will owe a tax of $1,350 on the property.

In covering tax matters, the reporter should always try to relate the decisions reached by officials directly to the reader or viewer, explaining how a specific increase or other change will affect an individual.

> Faced with rising salary costs, the board of supervisors increased the county's general tax rate 10 percent Wednesday.
>
> "We've opted for a continuation of services, rather than cutting what we believe is an irreducible minimum of services," Supervisor Roy Williamson said.
>
> The board added 32 cents to the current tax rate, bringing the rate to $3.52 per $100 of assessed valuation, with rates for special fire districts to be decided later.
>
> Under the new rate, the owner of an $80,000 home assessed at 35 percent of that figure will pay $985.60 next year.

A good way for the reporter to become even more familiar with the collection system is to study the tax bill mailed to property owners (see Figure 5–4). In

FIGURE 5–3

Here's how to figure your property taxes:

1.   Multiply the assessed value of your home by .04 (the assessment ratio of 4 percent).
     Example: $75,000 times .04 equals $3,000

2.   Take the result and multiply by .001 (a mill is 1/1,000 of a dollar).
     Example: $3,000 times .001 equals 3

3.   Take the result and multiply it by the total millage for your tax district.
     Example: 3 times 266.6 (for Sandy Run Tax District 4) equals $799.80

Your property tax bill will be $799.80

Lee County 1993 Tax District Millage Rates
     District 1 — Gaston   = 270.50
     District 2 — Springdale = 313.00
     District 3 — Richland   = 296.90
     District 4 — Sandy Run   = 266.60
     District 5 — Lexington   = 340.00

most places, it will reflect the basic county property tax, any applicable school taxes, assessments for specific fire or police districts, and any other special taxes.

All county property is reassessed at intervals, usually three to eight years. Outside specialists are often hired for that purpose, and improvements, additions to property and rising values are reflected in the new tax assessments. Reassessments offer the opportunity to use graphics to explain the steps that taxpayers can take to determine their bills. Many states limit tax increases caused by reassessment to specific percentages, and some counties have adopted the practice of reassessing a piece of property each time it changes hands, maintaining a truer picture of property values in a growing area.

To maintain a more up-to-date figure on county property values, Assessor Beatrice Stark said Monday her office will begin checking property transfers. Here is how Stark said the procedure will work:

Each week her office will study transfers, the price paid and the new owner or owners. The price will be checked against the current value of the property on the county tax rolls.

"If the price paid is more than 15 percent above current valuation, we will adjust the assessment and it will be reflected on the next tax bill," Stark said.

After the assessor has officially set the figures, a board of equalization meets to hear complaints from taxpayers who believe their assessment is too high. The board usually has the power to adjust the assessment. Often a county commission sits as a board of equalization or board of adjustment to review assessments itself.

A downward reassessment in the value of a residence owned by J.C. Tonley at 1600 Broad St. was granted yesterday by the Equalization Commission. It was the commission's only adjustment this year.

The Tonley assessment now more closely parallels adjacent property for tax purposes, Commissioner William Hands said. Six other requests for downward reassessment were denied by the commission.

Commercial property values, and their substantial effect on tax assessments, should be closely monitored by either the business reporter or the county beat reporter.

After assessments and allocations from other sources are completed, the county governing board draws up a budget and sets the tax rate designed to produce the revenue that will balance it. The rate determines whether the taxpayer will owe $300 or $2,000. The final step is to determine the amount of each bill and

GREENVILLE COUNTY TREASURER
GREENVILLE, SC 27902
1993 TAX BILL

FOR QUESTIONS CONCERNING
PERSONAL PROPERTY:

REAL ESTATE DATA CONTACT:

TAXES CONTACT:

COUNTY AUDITOR
(803) 522-6767

COUNTY ASSESSOR
(803) 522-4500

COUNTY TREASURER
(803) 522-7200

ACCOUNT KEY
10315605

ACCOUNT NO.
R300 020 00B 0123 1028

TOTAL TAXES PAYABLE NOW $1016.28

District: Henry Subdivision
TYPE PROPERTY CODE: 4113-11
ASSESSMENT RATIO: 4 percent

ACCOUNT DATA

ITEM	AMOUNT
Land Value	$ 69,313
Bldg Value	81,465
Taxable	150,778
Homestead	20,000
Assessed	5,231
No. of Lots	1.0
No. of Bldgs	1.0

JENNINGS, JOHN L. & ESTHER C.
JTROS
52 ST. HELENA DRIVE
GREENVILLE, SC 27920

BREAKDOWN OF 1993 TAXES

ACCOUNT	MILLS	TAXES
County	61.60	$322.23
School	102.10	534.09
Fire Dist	21.50	112.47
Indig. Care	2.30	12.03
Cont. Education	2.00	10.46
Recycling Charge		25.00
Totals	189.50	1,016.28

OUTSTANDING TAX RECAP

YEAR	TAX DUE	PENALTY	TOTAL
1993	1,016.28		1,016.28
Total	1,016.28		1,016.28

Lot 52   HENRY SUBDIVISION
         LOTS PB 31 P 161

FIGURE 5–4
The reporter can compare last year's tax bill with the current bill to focus on the changes. Using such figures, the reporter can provide exact comparisons. Be sure to drop the identification of the property owner to protect his or her privacy.

to send the bills to the taxpayers. In some counties, the sheriff is tax collector; in others, a county tax collector or treasurer fulfills this function.

A Sharing of Revenues

County governments accumulate operating funds from a variety of sources other than direct taxes. Fees are collected from users of county-operated facilities, such as civic centers, field houses and recreation complexes. Fees are often collected for documents filed with the county clerk and for handling the state's business in the courthouse. Most of the funds are returned to the county treasury to carry out the specific programs from which they were obtained.

A more recent source of funds has been revenue sharing by state and federal governments, particularly the latter. A typical state grant might include matching money to assist in purchasing or developing new facilities that would be operated by the county.

Money Flow in a Typical County

Revenues

Taxes: Property, Vehicular, Delinquent, Penalties

Licenses, Fees & Permits: Building, Electrical, Animal, Engineering, Vital Statistics

Intergovernmental: State Revenues from Gas, Income Tax, Liquor, Banking, Public Safety Funding, Public Health Funding & Federal Sources

Charges for Services: County Registrar, Court Fees, Emergency Medical Services, Waste Disposal Fees, Engineering & Other Inspections

Fines & Forfeitures

Interest

County Treasury

$ $ $ $ $ $

Expenses

Administrative: County Council, Financial Services, Personnel, Clerical, Accounting, etc.

Public Works: Roads, Bridges & Highways, Building Maintenance, County Docks

Courts: Magistrates, Civil & Criminal Systems, Family & Probate Courts, Jails

Human Services: Public Health & Hospitals, Welfare, Libraries, Parks & Recreation

FIGURE 5–5

CHARLESTON—Gov. John Roche yesterday approved a $650,000 allocation of state funds to help purchase a small airport in Cabell County.

The money, with $200,000 provided by the County Commission, will be used to purchase Kyle Field. Chairman William L. Dundee said the county will develop the property as a public general aviation facility.

Like municipal governments, counties have experienced substantial losses in federal contributions, but many specific programs remain. A typical list of federal grants to counties includes funds for judicial purposes, health and safety, law enforcement and jail facilities, and training. Some counties employ experts (also available to a reporter as sources) to study federal regulations and determine new sources of possible funding. These grants range from multimillion-dollar projects to more modest $15,000 matching grants for purchase of vans to transport the elderly.

Reporters should be aware that most of these federal grant programs require a careful accounting of funds spent at the local level. A county "monitor" is often appointed to investigate the efficacy of the programs.

> Following allegations of misconduct by county ambulance personnel, the County Commission Thursday transferred the Emergency Medical Service from the sheriff's office to a newly formed Department of Emergency Services.
>
> The report of misconduct was prepared by James C. Wesson, a county monitor for programs funded by the federal Jobs Programs Training Act. Part of the program funds the ambulance service.

Some county governments prepare two separate budgets, one based on local tax revenue and another detailing disbursement of up to 20 percent of the total that flows from federal sources (see Figure 5–5).

Disbursing: Who Gets the Money?

All money being collected by the county will be used for specific purposes. It may go to:

• The sheriff who wants funding for eight more deputies, citing the increased pressures of process serving and an increase in rural crime calls.

• The three circuit court judges who want their courtrooms renovated and a modern jury room installed in the courthouse.

- County clerical workers, joined in an informal "association" in lieu of an official union, who are asking for a 6 percent pay increase.

- Meeting the cost of skyrocketing auto supplies, and the needs of the county garage supervisor.

Each of these hypothetical requests, and many others, will be pondered by the county governing board before the budget is passed. And while the board ponders, the reporter writes—about the requests, their effect on county services, which ones seem to be frivolous and which ones appear legitimate. Some officials prefer to air their needs publicly through the press; others work quietly behind the scenes for funds they believe will enable their offices to function more smoothly.

So with the public watching through the eyes of the reporter, the budgeting and spending process in county government hinges on practical politics. Before a final budget is adopted, trade-offs will take place, new political alliances may be effected (and others rudely shattered), disappointments will occur among some, and taxes may even be raised to accommodate the major requests for funds.

> Franklin County commissioners adopted a hard line yesterday on a supplemental appropriation request made by Prosecutor George C. Allen.
>
> In deferring action on Allen's plea for an additional $285,000 to pay staff salaries and to cover costs of three major criminal trials this year, the commissioners indicated they will not honor the request.
>
> "The only way to hold back government spending is to say no," Commissioner Betty Dorrian said. "I'm not in favor of giving any more money unless we open the supplemental door to every officeholder."

With a convoluted budgeting and spending process that affects so many elected officials and their offices, the county reporter cannot afford to merely await the outcome of the negotiations. In analyzing the proposals, he or she also should be prepared to assess the current levels of services and spending.

- Are needy agencies receiving their fair share of county funds?

- Are favored agencies top-heavy with personnel?

- Are the proposals overlapping with each other or with other units of government?

- Is the county overextending itself with new programs that could mean substantial tax increases when they are put in place?

The reporter may be the only participant who takes the time to figure specific percentages on the changes in department funding, perhaps an important part of the process. He or she also can pursue many avenues in analyzing current and past budgets. County and state auditors, whose documents are all public record, are useful sources. Subordinates in the affected offices are often willing to discuss the effectiveness of the agency, and experts outside county government often can be counted on to provide a balanced opinion. Heads of other agencies should not be overlooked, although their opinions must be weighed for possible bias.

Just as revenue-sharing funds flow into the counties from state and federal governments, the county often earmarks grants to other local agencies for services deemed essential to the economic health of the area. A grant may be provided for regional bus service operated by a special district that draws funds from the federal government, several affected municipalities and the state as well as the county. The county governing board may participate in other programs such as regional airport facilities, public library systems and sewage disposal.

The relationships among these sponsoring government units become more important to the county reporter, who will monitor the movement of funds from one "jurisdiction" to another. Politics often plays a part in decisions to provide grants or withhold them from other agencies.

> The Seymour County Commission has decided to cut its $600,000 donation to the Regional Airport Commission in half next year, citing as its reason "major budgeting problems."
>
> The commission, which drastically changed its political complexion in the recent general elections, has been engaged in a running and often visible debate with the airport commission over selection of a director.

No one is more knowledgeable or better prepared to smoke out unnecessary "sweetheart arrangements" among officeholders than a perceptive reporter. One of the best rules is "follow the money."

THE PLANNING AND ZONING PROCESS

Where people live and under what conditions, how much it costs them, who makes use of the land around them and how, and their relationships with those persons and corporations provide an ever-changing tapestry of cooperation and conflict.

Planning boards that study land use are often the key to successful growth—at the city as well as at the county levels, and zoning is often the method used by counties to assure that growth moves in an orderly way.

Planning

The planning process is important to the county. Land use changes are constant, some brought about quickly by highway or industrial development, others brought about more slowly through changes in farming and forestry practices.

Old property records, some dating back hundreds of years, are constantly in a state of flux in all local jurisdictions as new owners are identified, taxes adjusted, buildings constructed, mortgages added and land uses changed. The records are an ever-renewable resource for the reporter.

Equally important are the studies produced by planning experts for the governing boards that oversee the process. Planners have varying degrees of responsibility and power. Some merely advise governing boards as to proper planning, others have the power to make planning decisions and enforce them. Some advise appropriate boards in planning for conservation of water and other natural resources.

The reporter is working at two levels in pursuing the consequences of planning—the deliberations of the planning commissions or boards, and separate interviews with the planning experts. The documents produced by the experts are also generally available to the reporter.

While these staff experts study land use and make recommendations to the board, their recommendations are not always followed. The governing board can approve, disapprove or change the recommendations. Most staffers are more than willing to discuss with a reporter their reasoning in reaching a conclusion.

Market value of land usually depends upon the designation placed on it by the planners, real estate brokers or developers, and the process becomes complicated as the board sorts out various options for land use.

Moreover, this process also creates a climate for manipulation and questionable actions that sometimes handsomely reward a few people. Unscrupulous public officials—and not a few intelligent hangers-on who intimately know the system—sometimes benefit from inside knowledge of potential planning decisions.

When specific changes are in the works, such as property being used for both commercial and residential purposes, the reporter is wise to spend some time identifying the property configurations, owners of major tracts of land and major players in the issue.

A high-rise residential development may come before a planning board, but the final occupant of the property may turn out to be high-rise offices, which yield a far more substantial return on an investment, or a sprawling shopping center, which yields an even more substantial return.

Increasingly, planning boards are also advising municipalities and special districts that lie within county boundaries. Often the planning process has become regional, approved by appropriate state and local legislation. Thus, other players are brought into the planning process.

Inclusion of such major issues as business and economic climate and environmental concerns, as well as the traditional city-county governmental issues, alter the playing field for the press. It is easy to see how reporters who also cover business, environment and health will become involved in such broad issue-oriented coverage. Many issues will surface on their own, but inquiring reporters can tap many that lie dormant.

Zoning: Outgrowth of Planning

Zoning a county or community for different land uses is a logical consequence of planning. A section of a political subdivision is restricted to a particular use to protect the value of the property, be it homes, rental units, businesses or industry. Sometimes the restrictions are minimal, as in rural areas of the county; at other times, uses are rigidly enforced, such as preventing a tavern from opening near a church or school.

Counties and municipalities control land use through zoning boards or commissions. Usually, but not always, a county or city council has the last word on its decisions. The reporter should be aware of the path that zoning issues travel to resolution.

Some counties possess only rudimentary zoning powers, responding to the will of people in unincorporated areas that zoning in those areas be minimal.

The tool shed you're building in your back yard may be a little illegal, says Robert Drinnon, county director of water, sewer and building permits.

Although anyone erecting a structure containing more than 100 square feet in the unincorporated sections of Harrison County must purchase a building permit, many residents ignore the regulation, according to Drinnon.

County commissioners want to rely on "education and persuasion," he said, and do not want to enforce the penalties, ranging from $25 to $100 a day for non-compliance.

"We want to assure people that these permits are not a step into zoning," Drinnon said. "We want to stay away from enforcement. We don't like that concept."

The obviously reluctant action was a response to the need for county compliance with the federal government's Flood Insurance Program requirements. The program provides low-cost flood insurance and other grants to the county.

Frequently the same zoning issues that make news in municipalities appear on the county scene and work their way into court. Residents may not object to a henhouse full of chickens in someone's back yard, but vehemently protest a proposed trailer court half a mile away.

The reporter's job is to assess the effect of zoning on an area. For example, a developer wants to construct a 10-story apartment building near a burgeoning suburban college.

- What would be the effect on road congestion and traffic patterns?
- Will parking be adequate and safe?
- What other zoning is needed to handle new businesses locating in the area?
- Is public transportation to the area adequate?

The reporter will answer these kinds of questions to clarify the issues and explain the final zoning decision.

Through changes in zoning, land values may be made to rise or fall. Speculators have amassed fortunes through manipulation of zoning ordinances and acquisition of preliminary information about changes in land use.

One area of a county might be zoned only for agriculture, but a change to industrial use could boost the value of thousands of acres, and foster an accompanying decline in nearby residential property values. Farmland that had gone begging at $500 an acre suddenly soars to $8,000 an acre, while contractors find they cannot sell subdivision homes at any price a mile away.

But the major zoning changes in a county or city should not be allowed to overshadow the seemingly minor ones that often affect neighborhoods.

Jerry Dykes awoke Monday morning to find his truck vandalized and a threatening message painted in vivid crimson on his house.

He told police that they are two more cases of harassment since a neighborhood dispute began four weeks ago over rezoning the 1800 block of Madison Avenue where he lives.

"This is my home, and I don't want a business going in behind me," he said, explaining that he opposes the efforts of several neighbors to have the area changed from a residential to a business zone.

While a police reporter might have covered this aspect of the issue, the county reporter will handle the larger zoning story.

When Planning and Zoning Conflict

Professional planners recommend basic zoning regulations, which have the force of law, but individuals and organizations often seek a different use for the property. A zoning variance allows them to use the property in nonconformance with the properties adjacent to it.

Counties and cities have special boards that deal with such requests. In some places they are called Board of Adjustments and Appeals; in others, Board of Zoning Appeals. Depending on the law, the boards may have the last word on variances. In other areas, the parent county board may have the right to overrule them (see Figure 5–6).

Zoning variances may be simple: A property owner wants to construct a garage on his property, but zoning regulations limit the structure to at least 12 feet from the property line. The owner wants to build 10 feet from the line.

Requests may also be complex: Regulations may call for single-family dwellings in an area, but a homeowner wants to convert a group of large old homes into Victorian-style apartments without destroying the appearance of single-family dwellings. The result

could actually be to upgrade the appearance of the neighborhood, but regulations limit the change. An industrial zone may permit only limited types of activity, and a developer wants to establish a meat-packing plant.

Variances forecast basic changes in zoning to the reporter, as well as raising legitimate questions about why the original zoning was adopted in the first place. Many questions must be answered:

- Who owns the property and who benefits from a variance?

- What board allowed the variance and what is its complexion?

- What are the board members' relationships with those who will benefit from the changes?

- And most important, who will be adversely affected by the variance?

> Johnson County Commissioner Roy Fleck has a sand mine on his property near Leesburg. He says establishing local regulations on mining would be a bad idea.
>
> Commissioner Lowell Spires works for a firm that operates two major mines in the county. Spires also opposes local mining regulations in Johnson County.
>
> Neither believes that his outside relationships constitute a conflict of interest on the commission, but some people who favor such regulations question whether Fleck and Spires should vote on or even discuss the issue.

In another area, this argument probably represents a clear conflict of interest on the part of the officials. But the local character of a community often dictates the direction of an argument, especially if the issue involves the economic lifeblood of the county. Covering an issue like this calls for reportorial sensitivity and persistence. Spotlighting the story will certainly help resolve the issue.

State regulations are often involved. The officials argued that they opposed local mining regulations because adequate state rules already protected the public health. However, such state regulations do not address whether mining would disrupt a neighborhood and lower property values. The reporter's trail would lead to state officials who have fewer axes to grind and to regulations that are public documents.

Route of a Zoning Appeal

1. Zoning board makes its decision. ✓

2. Owner appeals to zoning board of appeals.

3. Appeals board rules, sends to full county governing board.

4. County board upholds or overturns, sometimes after public hearing.

5. Property owner can appeal to courts for relief.

FIGURE 5–6

Using Land Records

It is not difficult to enlighten the public on issues surrounding variances as well as other property issues. Local and state regulations are public record, and property tax records offer valuable information. In addition to zoning board files, the recorder's office or register of deeds should be familiar territory to the county reporter. Real estate deeds, indexed by grantor and grantee, provide identities of buyer and seller, a description of the property including size and legal designation, and any mortgage agreements. Tax stamps affixed to the deed enable the reporter to determine the purchase price and date of purchase. Many counties now list the sale price in computer records.

Maps and plats in the recorder's office locate parcels of land, and it is relatively simple to convert the complex legal descriptions into plain English. The reporter is cautioned to doublecheck numbers because an error could result in description of totally different properties and people involved.

Most clerks are more than willing to lead a young reporter through the process, explaining limits and pointing to specific land maps that contain pertinent information.

The county or business reporter will follow who is buying and selling what, as well as the uses to which the property will be put.

THE CAST OF CHARACTERS

No structure houses so many public officials with such dissimilar functions as the county building. The county surveyor may be only a few feet down the hall from the county prosecutor. A magistrate may be across the hall from the county agricultural agent. The difference in jobs is worlds apart.

Not only do the functions of the offices differ, but the manner in which each official reaches the job varies from state to state and even from county to county. The health officer may be appointed by the county commission as a practicing professional, while the assessor or treasurer must be elected.

While the election process enables the public to toss out officials in whom it has lost confidence, election to office is somewhat more secure than it sounds, particularly if the candidate possesses some expertise, few skeletons in the closet, many friends and an effective campaign organization.

With all these dissimilarities, one constant remains—the jockeying for position and power that accompanies most units of government. Personalities of these officeholders and the jobs they hold play a major part in how the reporter covers the beat.

Nonjudicial County Officers

Depending upon the region, tradition or legislation, county officers function either directly under supervision of the governing board or under separate agencies or boards with varying degrees of autonomy. These officials may be dependent on the board for salaries and other financing, and subject to regular audit or other controls imposed by legislative action.

The county reporter should have a clear picture of the fiscal and legal lines of authority. One way to get this is to construct an organization chart, if one is not already available, looking at both the official lines as well as the unofficial ones.

For instance, a county board may employ a school superintendent and staff, or may delegate that responsibility to a separate collateral agency such as a board of education. A popularly elected county assessor may have no ties to the county commission aside from dependence on it for funding. A county commission may elect to abrogate its responsibilities and appoint an entirely separate advisory council to oversee a sensitive area of service.

> The first step in creating a countywide public service district to handle all water and sewer service was taken by the County Commission Monday.
>
> Commissioners voted 3–0 to abolish the Office of Water Supply, which now operates under direct supervision of the commission and services 60 percent of the county, and establish the new agency.
>
> Service would be expanded to the 40 percent of the county not being served.

This issue had already surfaced, and the reporter had obtained favorable reaction from members of the Planning Commission. The reporter had also put the water commissioner on record as objecting to plans for a separate agency. Also interviewed were some of the 17 other employees of the water office. Commissioners refused to comment on their future.

County Manager

In recent years, county boards have employed a professional manager, much like the city manager handling municipal affairs.

The manager answers to the county governing board, and is responsible for administrative functions, including preparing and administering the budget, hiring and dismissing nonelected employees and keeping the governing board informed of county affairs.

Like his or her city counterpart, the county manager treads a fine line between administration and policy-making, and the reporter should be aware of this.

County Clerk

The office of county clerk is nearly universal in some form, popularly elected in some states and appointed in others. The reporter will find this official and staff one of the most important on the county beat.

The clerk supervises the record-keeping of legal instruments such as deeds, mortgages, leases, property transfers, wills and trusts, often births and deaths, and election results.

The office may handle licensing for state agencies, such as drivers' licenses or vehicular tags. The clerk or a deputy often is the recorder for the county governing board, preparing the board's agenda and maintaining records of meetings. A cooperative clerk or assistant can provide unending assistance to a busy reporter as a source for all kinds of potential stories.

County Attorney

Most often appointed, the county attorney or county counsel serves as legal adviser to the county governing board and represents the county in legal actions. The attorney also draws up contracts and interprets board actions.

Sometimes the county attorney also acts as prosecutor, filing charges and assisting law enforcement officials in investigations.

Like the more visible county prosecutor, the attorney's position is often a stepping stone to higher office.

It is often filled by political appointment, with the party in power exercising control over the process.

> The Potomac County Commission appointed a new county attorney Thursday, but not without a dispute that ended when Commissioner William Schultz walked out of the meeting.
>
> Republican Commissioners Ted C. Johnson and Raymond L. Adams voted to employ George A. Mills, a 33-year-old Republican and partner in the law firm of Greene, Ketchum and Mills. Schultz, a Democrat, had objected to Mills' appointment.
>
> After the vote, Schultz stalked from the room.
>
> "What Potomac County needs is someone with experience in government, not someone with political connections," Schultz said later.

County Treasurer

The county treasurer is tax collector in many states, sending the tax bills after rates have been set and acting as custodian of all public funds. Often the treasurer is popularly elected. Records of county expenditures, maintained in that office, are available to the reporter.

The treasurer is often available as the reporter's source for impending changes in funding and should be cultivated for other developments. As a reasonably independent officeholder, the treasurer may not be as reluctant as other county officials to discuss controversial and negative developments.

> A "major crisis" in public service employment—the loss of up to 220 jobs—may befall the county by January, County Treasurer Barnett Ross warned yesterday.
>
> The loss of federal money will mean budget problems for the county, Ross said. "It's going to affect us quite drastically, particularly in the job area."
>
> Ross said his office had received notification from federal officials yesterday, citing formula changes in the Jobs Program Training Act.

County Assessor

Assessment of property for tax purposes, as previously noted, is a nearly universal function at the county level, and a popularly elected assessor fills that job in more than half the states. Where townships exist as a subdivision of the county, assessors at that level handle the function. Some states place assessment of property in the hands of a board of tax assessors.

The reporter should not wait for annual assessment time to look for news stories in this office. Changes in property values, methods of assessing valuation and general economic outlook often generate news through the assessor. The reporter should look to this official, usually an expert in the real estate field, as a valuable source of information. The assessor knows the community as well or better than anyone and is adept at spotting trends.

> The eastern—and much older—half of the county is more than pulling its weight in tax income.
>
> That's the assessment of one county official who has studied the trend and has the figures to back them up.
>
> "If you draw a line down Bull Street, the older half of the county is supplying 62 percent of the money," says Assessor Warren Shelton. That's $38.4 million of the $62 million collected by the county in property taxes.
>
> Shelton was responding to criticism by the Taxpayers Association that the recent revaluation tended to favor the older half of the city.

In many areas, a tax equalization board has been established to review any actions of the tax assessor, and confirm or modify any decision made. The reporter should make regular checks of the board.

County Auditor

Many states authorize a county auditor or comptroller who functions as chief budget officer or accountant. The designation is misleading because outside audits, often by the state itself, are conducted on county government every year.

In some states, the auditor serves as a county clerk, handling collection of personal property taxes, maintaining financial records for county agencies and paying county bills. Sometimes the auditor serves on a county budget commission, which mediates disputes among the various agencies.

Other County Officials

Many counties elect surveyors, whose offices maintain detailed county maps and determine boundaries in dispute. County engineers, usually required to be registered professionals, are authorized to perform the duties of a civil engineer, responsible for construction, maintenance and repair of roads and bridges. The engineer, sometimes elected but often appointed, prepares plans and specifications before public bidding on projects under that office's jurisdiction and prepares tax maps for other officials.

A health officer, usually a physician, is generally employed by the county, and the work is diagnostic or preventive. Selection of a chief health officer is often placed in the hands of a separate Board of Health, which develops services and conducts educational campaigns. The reporter whose beat includes health and medical care will find these offices valuable in collecting facts about the community.

> The Graham County Commission appointed a new health officer Friday, concluding a six-month search for a successor to retiring Dr. James L. Partin.
>
> Dr. Judith G. Giles, a general practitioner, will give up her private practice to take the position, which pays $72,000 a year.
>
> "The county deserves a full-time diagnostician," she said, "and that's what I intend to be."

Some county governments place sanitation and enforcement of pollution regulations in the health office, while others employ a sanitary engineer to oversee refuse regulations. As previously noted, counties are increasingly forming agencies with power to enforce environmental as well as medical regulations.

Larger counties appoint a finance director to provide fiscal control and coordinate operating and capital fund activity. This official may also assist in drawing up the annual budget. Increasingly, a central purchasing department coordinates all county purchases.

Another office often funded by county, state and federal money is that of the agricultural agent, which is a source of information on agricultural activities. As with other little-cultivated county offices, the reporter can find a broad range of news material, some of it important as well as interesting.

> Walter and Lona Hayes have lost more than $8,000 worth of cattle this year on their small East Lynn farm because packs of dogs—not necessarily wild—have literally run their livestock to death.

"This has been going on for several years," County Agricultural Agent Mary Crawford said. "The Hayeses are losing feeder calves, and so are others in that section of the county."

Crawford said the dogs run the calves until they are exhausted. "Older and larger cattle can usually take care of themselves," she said. "It's the young calves that are killed."

Many counties make provisions for an animal control department, which enforces laws requiring control and licensing of dogs and other animals. The board collects license fees and revenue-sharing funds to operate.

Officials of the Judiciary

The courts play a prominent role in the business of the county, and a substantial share of the budget is earmarked for housing and housing operations. Some states pay judges' salaries, as well as other costs, but counties usually share the cost of court operations.

The operation of the courts and the work of those who staff them are discussed in detail in later chapters.

Clerk of Court

A trial court of general jurisdiction is nearly always attached to the county courthouse. The clerk of court is its official record-keeper, with a staff to assist in expediting the judicial process. The office is often elective, and the clerk sometimes has duties other than those involving court recording, such as issuance of notary public commissions, real estate brokers' licenses and vehicular titles.

Sheriff

The office of sheriff is the most universal of all county offices, although the duties vary widely. The office is quite visible and carries substantial influence. The sheriff is generally elected, usually for a four-year term, and like the prosecuting attorney, the position is often a stepping stone to higher office.

As court officials, the sheriff and deputized employees assist in court operations, serving papers, swearing in witnesses, acting as bailiffs during trials and following instructions from the bench. In some states, the sheriff also collects county taxes.

The sheriff is traditionally the county's chief law enforcement officer, although growth of state police agencies has limited this function. Most sheriffs, however, maintain responsibility for enforcing the law in unincorporated areas of the county.

Criticism of the office usually centers on the wide range of responsibilities that may impinge on the quality of work produced. Often this criticism is answered with the argument that a lack of funding is responsible.

To have someone arrested, a warrant is needed and a law enforcement officer to serve it. Having that warrant served in Clay County, however, is easier said than done.

The backlog of unserved warrants on file totals 2,800, according to records in the Sheriff's Department, and appears to be increasing every month.

The reason, officials say, is an insufficient number of deputies.

"We don't have the manpower, and the men on the job don't have time to do it," Chief Deputy Lawrence Stephens said.

Stephens said a deputy requires at least 90 minutes to serve a warrant, take the suspect before a magistrate and complete the paperwork.

"That's if the deputy has no problems locating the suspect," Stephens said.

While the sheriff's law enforcement function may be minimized, the official continues to serve as custodian of prisoners, maintaining jail facilities. In many areas, the facilities to incarcerate municipal, state and federal prisoners have been combined and the keys given to the sheriff.

Prosecuting Attorney

Depending on the state, the attorney who conducts investigations and criminal prosecutions in the trial courts is identified as prosecuting attorney, solicitor, state's attorney or district attorney. It is an elective office in most states, and the occupant exercises considerable political power because of the visibility of the office. Successful prosecution in criminal cases often enhances the official's career and usually assures re-election.

Conversely, failure in visible criminal prosecutions often creates problems of tenancy in this office. Political organizations, seeing a negative effect developing before election time, have been known to withdraw their support for a candidate whose success has been questionable.

Justice of the Peace

Often elected, justices of the peace are still found in many states, serving mainly as judges of small claims courts and issuers of warrants. Because it is a court of original jurisdiction, the court reporter may monitor activities, noting that some potentially important or interesting cases are bound over to other courts. Newspapers tend to overlook JP activities unless there is some dramatic development, but many cases are begun at this level. Many state legislatures are modernizing their functions, even to the extent of abolishing them and transferring their functions to other offices.

Coroner

The primary duty of the coroner is to determine the exact cause, method and manner of death. As the county's medical examiner, the coroner conducts autopsies and hearings to determine whether a crime has been committed. This office, too, is being modernized, often changing from elective to appointive office. In the past, the coroner did not need a medical degree, but more counties are requiring it.

For the sake of efficiency, some states have created state examiners in central locations, and these officials must have a medical degree.

Collateral Boards and Agencies

Nearly every county governing board authorizes some form of independent board or agency that functions separately from the board itself. Sometimes they are composed of citizens who give their time as a public service, and exist to take essential county services "out of politics." In other cases, the boards are quite political.

The reporter must determine the relationship between the governing board and its independent agencies, learning what strings are attached and how much power the agencies actually possess.

Membership on the boards is often determined by the governing board through appointment, although some boards are elective. In either case, political friction is often created because of jurisdictional problems, sometimes culminating in court action.

> Legal suits pending between the Haskell County Commission and the County Parks Board were dismissed Friday by Circuit Court Judge Robert Dutton.
>
> Under terms of the dismissal, operation of the county fieldhouse will revert to the County Commission, and the Parks Board will continue to administer the adjacent playing fields.
>
> "I believe this is an equitable solution to the problem," County Commission Chairman Ted Durant said after the decision was announced.

Other agencies most often separated from direct control of the county governing board include a county health board, a board of education, a public welfare board, an elections commission and often a parks and recreation board.

Many counties have joined with municipalities to operate a joint library commission, aviation board to oversee airports, and alcohol and drug abuse boards.

While many are far less visible than the main governing board, issues they address are often more important to the county reporter than the main board's actions.

COPING WITH COMPLICATIONS

Three requirements are indispensable in competently covering county government:

- Familiarity with the system itself, the functions and powers of the various officials and their offices, and the relationships among them. The layered nature of government at the local level, both physical and fiscal, complicates straightforward reporting.

  To further complicate matters, the state Legislature is constantly imposing itself on county agencies through its actions, and the reporter must be alert to actions that affect county government.

Reporting requirements for counties handling juvenile offenders would be drastically altered under a bill introduced Tuesday in the state Senate.

The bill, introduced by Sen. Peter Crossland (D-Mansfield), would require each county to set up a local review board to outline a plan for handling youthful offenders.

Each county plan would have to include specific procedures for contracting foster home care, sheltered care services, group homes and home advocacy services.

Penalties for noncompliance are important. In this case, they range from letters of reprimand to cutoffs of state funding. The reporter's reading of the proposal also uncovered another mandate: Juveniles would not be jailed with adults.

- Understanding practical politics at the county level. Politics exists at every level and in every office. Every action by ambitious political figures will be weighed for its implications. Like the politicians, the reporter will learn to weigh them carefully, too.

   Who is backing the single-member redistricting plan, suggested as an alternative to the current at-large system? What are the political implications of the proposed consolidation between the county and its two cities? Who will benefit from the effort to "privatize" the county's wide-ranging sewer system? Will turning over the system to a private operator really take it "out of politics"?

   No one knows the skeletons in the courthouse closets better than the old-timers, but the reporter should be forewarned: Their views are often colored by old friendships or family alliances and shifting opportunities. The reporter should keep his or her own counsel and carefully weigh all "inside information." It is often unbalanced and sometimes unbelievable.

- An understanding of the character of the community in which the reporter is operating. Such an understanding will help place information in better perspective.

   The county may be predominantly rural or may contain strong agricultural elements that will color the governing power structure and affect the importance of some of the agencies.

Knowing these elements and understanding their interests, the reporter will find it easier to deal comfortably with all of them. A commissioner may have a responsibility toward a special constituency and has a dual role: representing that constituency as well as the county at large. A county board may include a representative from a citrus-producing section and another with divergent interests in a phosphate-producing area.

Some problems are more likely to occur within counties that contain different types of constituencies—rural, urban and suburban. Understanding these complications will help the reporter get a better handle on county coverage.

*** * * ***

SUGGESTED READING

Benjaminson, Peter, and David Anderson. *Investigative Reporting.* 2d ed. Ames, Iowa: Iowa State University Press, 1990.

Chapter 6

Reporting on State Government

With its usual terseness, the editor's memo is to the point.

> John: the gov. has news confab at noon today. Some kind of announcement in the wind. Drive up and see what's on his mind.

The order sets in motion a chain of events that often results in typical news coverage of the state's chief executive. In this case, the newspaper has been depending on wire service coverage of the governor's office for several months. The opportunity to staff an event in the capital—and to provide the reporter with time to re-establish personal contacts—has found favor with the editor.

The news conference is carefully staged in a small auditorium next to the governor's office. Present are two wire service reporters, a reporter for a three-newspaper group, three television camera crews who recognize that the event has visual importance, half a dozen reporters who traveled to the city to cover the conference, the governor's press secretary, and two other aides.

Of these, only the wire service reporters, the group reporter and two reporters for local newspapers regularly cover the governor's office.

The governor, with the director of the State Commission on Aging at his side, makes an announcement—a new $17 million program to provide grants for low-income and elderly residents, with funding by the federal Department of Housing and Urban Development. Eligible applicants will be served through county offices. The governor answers several questions on the subject, then responds to questions from reporters on unrelated issues. The conference concludes and the participants disperse.

With a few changes in personnel, timing and the issues involved, this scenario is repeated regularly in many states. Depending upon the resources of a newspaper or broadcast outlet and the impulses of editors or news directors, state government is covered in far more depth than this, in similar fashion or not at all.

The average newspaper and television station, not to mention the radio outlet, depends primarily on wire services or part-time stringers to monitor the state's activities, whether that state is the nation's biggest or smallest. Only during sessions of the Legislature is coverage expanded, and even then a newspaper may dispatch a staff reporter to ferret out material with a local angle, seeking out representatives from its home area and depending on wire services for general legislative coverage.

Thus, a vast array of state agencies, institutions and constitutional offices, staffed by thousands and operated with billion-dollar budgets, is often covered catch as catch can. Usually, only the most visible offices and agencies are selected for coverage.

But slim though the capital press corps may be, state governments are covered in countless ways by reporters at the local level. The long arm of state government reaches into every county and municipality. The local reporter who understands these ties and the issues involved can effectively blend state government news into local reports. If it were not for this, news of

state government would be sparse indeed. Here are some issues and events that link state and local government:

- The auditor for a state board of education checks a county school system's funding for construction, asking many questions.
- Even with home rule in place, a city government may have to seek approval from the Legislature to enact a local income tax.
- A county and its sheriff work on a plan to improve its outdated jail facilities, with the help of additional state funding.
- An investigative reporter digs into local pharmaceutical firms' questionable relationships with the State Board of Pharmacy.

All these local stories have another focus at the state level. The reporter covering and interpreting state government must sort out a complex mix of professional politicians, expert and inexpert administrators, and part-time citizen-legislators.

THE POWERS OF STATE GOVERNMENT

State government is organized much like its federal counterpart, assuming basic powers from a constitution and promulgating laws to carry out the various functions demanded or implied by the document.

Like their federal counterpart, the states have developed three distinct branches of government, with a legislative branch prescribing the law, an executive branch administering it, and a judiciary interpreting the statutes (see Figure 6–1). The judiciary is discussed in later chapters.

State government has evolved into a complex institution, with overlapping functions often leading to fuzzy jurisdictions and inevitable political arguments. Nowhere is this truer than in the relationships between state government and its various offspring—counties, cities, towns, special districts and single-purpose authorities.

These relationships are in a constant state of flux because of the flow of power among these government units, and the reporter covering the Statehouse will find politics the energizer that fires the system.

FIGURE 6–1

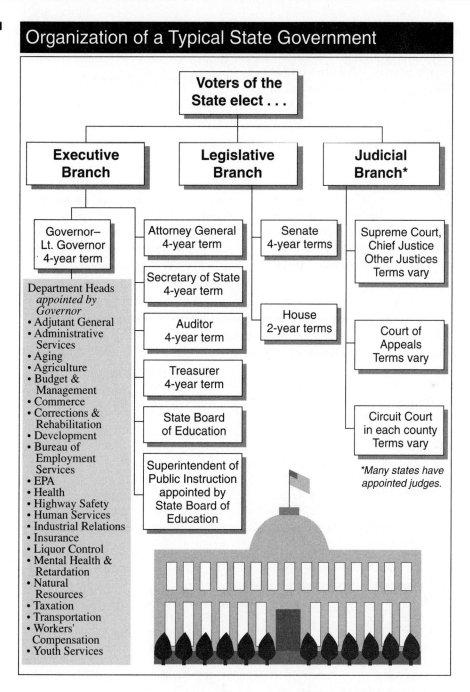

Organization of a Typical State Government

Voters of the State elect . . .

Executive Branch

Legislative Branch

Judicial Branch*

Governor–
Lt. Governor
4-year term

Attorney General
4-year term

Senate
4-year terms

Supreme Court,
Chief Justice
Other Justices
Terms vary

Department Heads
appointed by Governor
• Adjutant General
• Administrative
  Services
• Aging
• Agriculture
• Budget &
  Management
• Commerce
• Corrections &
  Rehabilitation
• Development
• Bureau of
  Employment
  Services
• EPA
• Health
• Highway Safety
• Human Services
• Industrial Relations
• Insurance
• Liquor Control
• Mental Health &
  Retardation
• Natural
  Resources
• Taxation
• Transportation
• Workers'
  Compensation
• Youth Services

Secretary of State
4-year term

Auditor
4-year term

House
2-year terms

Court of
Appeals
Terms vary

Treasurer
4-year term

State Board
of Education

Circuit Court
in each county
Terms vary

Superintendent of
Public Instruction
appointed by
State Board of
Education

*Many states have
appointed judges.*

The Federal-State Partnership

The framers of the federal Constitution delegated to the fledgling states many powers. While the original 1791 mandate provided a broad operating range, the federal government has steadily encroached upon the states' domain, providing increased financial and other assistance, while imposing guidelines and restraints that have created an interlocking federal-state partnership.

This has been accomplished through federal revenue sharing and an extensive grants system. The interstate highway system, with funding by the Federal Highway Administration, offers one example. The federal government underwrote 90 percent of the cost of the system; the states provided the remainder. But the states must follow federal guidelines in maintaining, policing and even beautifying the highways.

The States' Own Powers

Despite the ever-evolving federal-state partnership, states retain the power to raise taxes for many purposes and may borrow money to promote long-range projects. States also administer a vast body of their own civil and criminal laws.

Each year the nation's 50 state legislatures argue about, process and pass on to their governors new statutes, all dealing with specific measures regulating safety, health, education, law enforcement, welfare and transportation—and all affecting the lives of citizens in every city and hamlet.

TABLE 6–1

FUNDING THE STATE (or where the money goes)

Percentages and totals of a typical state government

Education	47.4% = $	3.534	billion
Health	15.3 =	1.141	billion
Corrections	6.9 =	515.4	million
Aid to Cities & Counties	6.8 =	512	million
Debt Service	3.7 =	277.4	million
Family Services	3.2 =	238.8	million
Public Safety	2.6 =	190.6	million
Environmental Protection	1 =	45.4	million
Other Services,* Costs	13 =	1.0	billion
TOTAL	99.9% = $	7.454	billion

*Includes such services as Transportation, Commerce & Industrial Development and Aid to the Arts

SOURCES OF FUNDING

Taxes and other revenue expected in 1994–95

Sales Tax	$ 2.6984	billion
Individual Income Tax	3.0837	billion
Corporate Tax	379.1	million
Other Taxes (alcohol, gift, estate, soft drink, etc.)	1.098	billion
Miscellaneous Fees (court fines, indirect,cost recoveries, etc.)	107	million
Waste Disposal Fees (interstate land fills)	93	million
TOTAL REVENUE	$ 7.459	billion

Huge budgets funded through taxes and other revenue sources provide for operation of colleges and universities, highway maintenance and construction, facilities for the ill and disabled, the election process, and control of commerce within the state. Funds are used to expand public facilities, establish new recreation areas, set up agencies to promote industrial development, create new programs to improve mental health . . . the list is endless. (See Table 6–1.)

Powers of the state do not end there. The average citizen is followed from the cradle to the grave. Birth statistics are recorded (often in county offices by direction of state officials), education records are maintained, marriages are approved, drivers licenses are issued to qualified motorists, state certificates are issued to college-trained pharmacologists or to new medical practitioners, and death certificates are recorded in the state archives. The final burial permit and adjudication of the deceased person's estate through a probate court concludes the cycle.

Practically all these documents are public record, a fact that is vital to any reporter who covers a beat for a newspaper or broadcast outlet.

With local government often acting as agent, the state's activities are all-pervasive. Whether a citizen wishes to hunt, fish, practice law, lease or purchase property, or operate a commercial enterprise, the state is the unseen arbiter through the code that permits the activity. While these regulatory activities are administered by the executive branch, they are scrutinized by the legislative branch, with the judiciary interpreting points of law.

Since all these activities affect every citizen, it is essential to report upon this accumulation of state-inspired do's and don'ts.

THE LEGISLATIVE BRANCH

Of the three branches of state government, the legislative is closest to the people. The lower house with a larger membership is generally called the House of Representatives, although some states distinguish it as the House of Delegates, the Assembly or the General Assembly. The upper house, the Senate, often has powers similar to its federal counterpart—confirmation of executive appointments and the power to impeach. Senators usually have longer terms of office.

Sizes of the houses vary across the country, with the Senate ranging from 18 members in Delaware to 67 in Minnesota. The lower house varies in size from 40 in Alaska to 400 in New Hampshire.

Like their federal counterparts, members of state legislatures are elected; participation in political party affairs is usually a prerequisite for nomination. Most states have fixed the term of office for members of the upper house at four years, but a two-year term is popular in some states. All but four states have fixed the term of office for lower houses at two years.

Seniority usually decides key leadership positions in the Legislature, and members with lengthy tenure assume the chairmanships of the committees.

Compensation fluctuates widely. More populous states pay legislators up to $60,000 annually; others pay as little as $200. The traditional practice of compensating legislators on a per diem basis has given way to annual salaries and in some cases full-time legislative responsibility.

Most state legislatures meet annually, but a few states continue to meet biennially. Nearly all legislatures begin their sessions in January with some meeting as few as 40 days per session, and other bodies meeting throughout the year.

Covering the Legislature

Organization of the state Legislature depends on its political complexion. The majority party controls the leadership positions, committee assignments and other organizational affairs. Party decisions are made at caucuses, meetings attended only by members of that party. They are not always open to the press, and reporters often must rely on second-hand information.

Leadership in the Legislature is determined by tenure, the power of a legislator's constituency, the ability to negotiate from positions of strength, friends in powerful places, and personality. Knowledge of these factors will help the reporter keep tabs on those at the top.

Party caucuses that meet regularly throughout the session guide the political direction of the lawmakers.

The degree of control the party exercises over its members depends on the state. A party agreement in caucus can result in major decisions to thwart or moderate legislation.

The executive branch, with its mandate to prepare and "sell" the state budget to the legislative branch, often attempts to influence the makeup of the legislative leadership. The governor is often able to effect selection of cooperative allies, even in the opposition party. Extensive behind-the-scenes maneuvering often takes place, continually affecting political relationships. The refusal of a key legislator to cooperate with the governor, for example, might signal a shift in alliance and power.

When party discipline is strong, political leaders can bring weight to bear on the legislators. Their word on a controversial measure often carries weight.

> The director of the State Development Commission wants the Senate to approve a plan to provide special tax incentives to auto manufacturers considering the location of new plants in the state.
>
> And it appears Richard Jensen has leaders on both sides of the aisle on his side.
>
> Republican Senate Leader James Axelrod and Democratic Minority Leader Lloyd Shell met jointly Tuesday to express support for the controversial measure.

Presiding officers are usually at the top of the power ladder. The lower house selects a speaker, the upper house is presided over by the state's lieutenant governor or by a president selected by the Senate membership. Other key positions include the majority and minority leaders who direct party activities on the floors of both houses. In some states, party "whips" enforce discipline and encourage attendance.

Committee assignments also determine the power structure in the Legislature. A position on a powerful rules committee, a steering committee, or a committee on committees is usually more important than chairmanship of a minor committee.

Leadership choices usually are made between sessions, and the reporter should remain close to sources during this time to pick up the first signs of those decisions. Legislatures often appoint interim committees to take up special problems between sessions or appoint legislative councils that function as permanent

joint committees. Regular meetings offer members high visibility when the Legislature is in recess.

Many states require legislative audits, and important stories are often developed through this source. Auditors regularly visit institutions and agencies, filing information with the Legislature. This office should be a regular stop on the statehouse reporter's beat.

> A legislative auditor's report has cited the State Tax Department for irregular mileage reimbursements.
>
> Assistant Tax Commissioner Anne Schwartz said the money has since been repaid.
>
> One member of the department, the audit showed, had been charging mileage of 125 miles between the capital and Williamson. The actual distance is 75 miles.

Such minor ensnarements are routine, but more important details often are disclosed through the auditing process. An audit might find improper bidding procedures by the State Highway Department or questionable expenditures by a state institution. The reporter's persistence will assure that these stories are not left uncovered.

Increasingly in recent years, legislative auditors have become a watchdog agency for state government, cataloguing problems and suggesting proposals to improve efficiency.

> The state could save $873 million in revenue during the next five years by adopting sweeping proposals to improve government efficiency, the Legislative Audit Council said Tuesday.
>
> In its most comprehensive review of state government efficiency, the Legislature's watchdog agency cited a litany of problems that keep the state from providing more cost-effective services.

Reaction to such a review would be swift—by the governor and agency heads, as well as legislative leaders, whose request for the review triggered the information. In this case, the reporter's study of the document would yield scores of ideas for follow-up stories:

> Among its findings, the audit council said the state:
> - Lacks travel policies that could save most state agencies thousands of dollars.
> - Grants costly tax breaks to a few.
> - Doesn't collect some of the money it's owed.
> - Subsidizes half the college tuition for out-of-state students.

- Owns surplus property, such as beach houses and homes for state officials that could be sold.

But the biggest single savings, the council reported, would come by tightening education expenses and instituting personnel policies that would lead to a smaller, more efficient work force.

The detail produced in such documents saves the reporter hundreds of hours of research time, and offers many inside views of how state government operates. Each of the audit findings represents major follow-up potential.

How a Bill Becomes Law

While the procedure varies from state to state, the lawmaking process embodies several principal stages on the road to passage. Most bills move ponderously from wind-testing discussion to formal introduction, on through a committee (a burial ground for much legislation), through debate and approval in each house, to a conference committee to iron out details, back to each house for final passage and finally to the governor's desk for signature or veto (see Figure 6–2).

Hundreds and even thousands of proposals are submitted each session, but relatively few survive the rigors of scrutiny and debate to become law.

The origin of proposals is important to the reporter. Some bills originate with individual legislators, others are launched in committees or legislative councils after much study. Still others are proposed by the governor or an agency official. Some come from special-interest groups such as teacher organizations, labor unions, environmental groups or business councils.

Legislators do not have to agree with a measure to introduce it. Many offer bills proposed by persistent constituents, even though they know the bill will go nowhere.

Organized labor constitutes one of the most important pressure groups, and the reporter should be alert to its interests as the session approaches. Sympathetic legislators can be counted on to introduce proposals backed by such groups and also to provide the reporter advance information.

The incoming Legislature quickly will see introduction of labor-backed legislation to increase unemployment compensation benefits and raise the ceiling on workmen's compensation benefits.

Passage of the proposals is being sought by the leadership of the 430,000-member State Federation of Labor, headed by Walter C. Mears.

Legislators whose constituencies contain such organized pressure groups are most likely to introduce and support such legislation. Often the size of the pressure group is less important than its visibility or activism. Law enforcement agencies, for example, would be likely to lobby for changes in laws that would make it easier for them to control criminal elements.

Two bills stiffening penalties for violent crimes were introduced in the House Wednesday by Rep. Charles E. Wilson (D-Logan).

One bill would restore the death penalty, abolished by the state in 1967. The other would require a mandatory 10-year prison term for anyone convicted of a crime in which a firearm was used.

Both measures are supported by the state Fraternal Order of Police, whose leadership has been vocal in its calls for tougher measures.

The major bill producer is often the governor, who delivers a message to the Legislature summing up proposals for the upcoming session. Supporters of the chief executive in both houses introduce the proposals and lobby for their approval, often with the expectation that the governor can improve their political prospects and give them a greater voice in filling appointive offices.

An administration-backed proposal to create a new agency to deal with state energy matters was introduced by five co-sponsoring senators Thursday.

One sponsor, Wilson Armstrong (D-Canton) said the "groundswell for the legislation" is strong enough to assure early passage in the Senate.

The five sponsors may not be enamored of the proposal, but their action may improve their relationship with the chief executive.

Dealing with Lobbyists

Advice to legislators—and often proposed bills—also comes from dozens of lobbyists who represent special-interest groups. Retail merchants, physicians, lawyers, teachers, beauticians, osteopaths, publishers, farmers,

FIGURE 6–2
At almost every point in the legislative process, the reporter can develop stories reflecting the bill's movement.

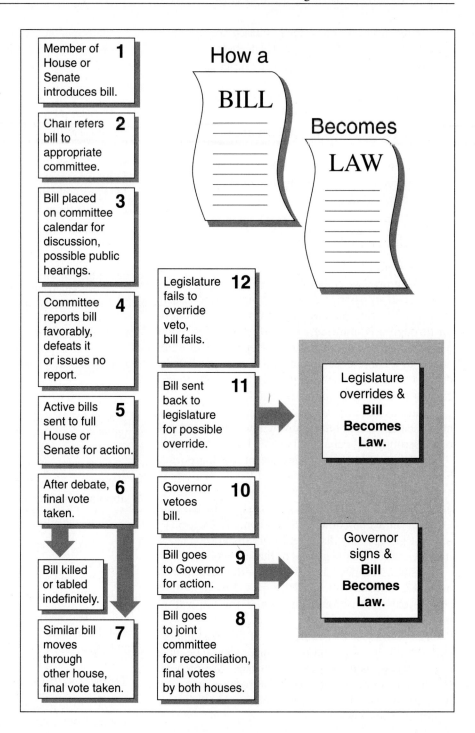

1 Member of House or Senate introduces bill.

2 Chair refers bill to appropriate committee.

3 Bill placed on committee calendar for discussion, possible public hearings.

4 Committee reports bill favorably, defeats it or issues no report.

5 Active bills sent to full House or Senate for action.

6 After debate, final vote taken.

Bill killed or tabled indefinitely.

7 Similar bill moves through other house, final vote taken.

How a BILL Becomes LAW

12 Legislature fails to override veto, bill fails.

11 Bill sent back to legislature for possible override.

10 Governor vetoes bill.

9 Bill goes to Governor for action.

8 Bill goes to joint committee for reconciliation, final votes by both houses.

Legislature overrides & **Bill Becomes Law.**

Governor signs & **Bill Becomes Law.**

public utilities and others may send experts to plead their causes in the capital during a session.

The identity of lobbyists is often crucial to the outcome of proposed legislation. Former state and local officials frequently represent special interests because of their expertise or connections. Most legislatures require official registration of lobbyists, a list helpful to reporters because it allows them to track the people who are putting pressure on legislators and other public officials.

Former House Speaker Julius R. Swain and former Welfare Commissioner Lee Winfrey were among 47 lobbyists who signed identification papers Thursday with the Senate clerk's office.

Swain, a Democrat from Morgan, said he represents the Mining Operators Association. Winfrey, a Republican from Scottsburg, said he is representing the state County Commissioners Association.

The other 45 lobbyists represented such disparate interests as utility firms, savings and loan associations, insurance boards, parent-teacher associations, state medical associations and a pharmaceutical group. Reporters should be familiar with the lobbyists and should be able to reach them on short notice, because their views on pending legislation are often important to a story. While lobbyists may try to use reporters as sounding boards, their priority is influencing legislators, and they are generally open in their relationships with the press.

In recent years, new types of lobbyists have descended on the halls adjacent to the floors of the legislatures. They include college students, senior citizens and others who lobby for broader constituencies. Citizen action groups and "people's lobby" organizations have proliferated, and other citizen organizations have formed new special-interest lobbies. Such groups represent old and new statewide organizations—the League of Women Voters, the State Abortion League, Common Cause, the Izaak Walton League and others.

College students fed up with spiraling tuition costs, larger classes and fewer course choices descend on the General Assembly today to appeal for more funding for higher education.

Student leaders from the state's publicly supported colleges are joining forces to try to send that message from constituents on their home campuses.

It can be difficult to identify illegal or unethical practices in the horse-trading and maneuvering that takes place during a session, but the reporter should be on the lookout for them, noting the pressures that may have been placed on specific legislators in an effort to influence a vote.

Sometimes legislators themselves "blow the whistle" on free-wheeling lobbyists.

A member of the House said Tuesday that a lobbyist for a Columbia small-loan firm handed him a $100 bill as he left the chamber during a recess.

In a speech on the House floor, Jerard Tighe (D-Winter) said he later returned the money.

A bill raising limits on loans such firms can make was at amendment stage in the House. The bill was tabled later in the day.

Tighe identified James T. Bailey, a registered lobbyist for Capitol Financial Services, as the person who handed him an envelope containing the money. Bailey could not be reached for comment. An official at the Capitol Hotel said Bailey had checked out Monday.

Conflicts of interest also appear in other forms. The roster of a legislative insurance and banking committee might include members with close associations with banks or insurance companies, information that is important to the public.

One example of conflict of interest might lie in a legislative subcommittee studying the issue of splitting retail gasoline outlets from their parent oil companies. If any of the members have interests or stock in oil companies, they could be said to have at least the appearance of conflict of interest.

The Committee System

Legislative committees often are the "proving ground" for proposed laws, and the effective reporter follows their work closely. Proposals die quietly in committee meetings, survive opposition attempts to table them indefinitely, or head for the floor on the heels of noisy public hearings.

After it is introduced in the Legislature, a bill is given first reading and is referred to an appropriate committee by the presiding officer of the House or Senate. Another key decision lies in the hands of the leadership—the ability to direct a proposal to a sympathetic committee or to one that will effectively kill the bill by ignoring it.

Although details differ from state to state, a bill must be placed on the committee calendar, sometimes survive public hearings, and be favorably reported out to the main legislative body. Most legislatures have the authority to bring up a bill that is bottled up in committee, but the process is difficult. The matter must be of sufficient importance to risk offending the committee membership and the legislative leadership.

The reporter should carefully follow the movement of legislation in committees, including any key meetings scheduled. Opposition and support surface at the public hearings, and the reporter who arrives early has a better chance of identifying the people who are working to influence the legislation through their testimony.

The reporter also must be on guard for intermediate votes that are often as important as the straight up-or-down votes on a bill. A committee vote to delay debate on a proposal, for example, might effectively kill it for the session or forever.

> The House Judiciary Committee has closed the book this year on rewriting the state's abortion laws.
>
> It held up a bill Tuesday requiring that women be given certain information before they have abortions.

There was no up-or-down vote on the measure. The committee, divided between abortion proponents and opponents, merely voted to delay consideration of the legislation until too late in the session for it to have a chance of passing.

The reporter also should be tuned into the tactics used by legislators to influence legislation.

> A bill weakening the state's 2-year-old open-meetings law narrowly survived a motion to table it permanently in the Senate Judiciary Committee on Monday, and was sent to a subcommittee for further consideration.
>
> "It's hurt but it's not dead," said the leader of the effort to weaken the law, Sen. Sylvester Powers (R-Mingo).
>
> Powers and others are seeking to remove the current requirement that governing bodies must notify the public of meetings by paid advertisements in the media.

A legislator may realize that he or she does not have the votes to move a bill out of committee and fail to appear when the vote on the proposal is scheduled. A courtesy move would temporarily sidetrack the bill, allowing the legislator time to corral the support necessary for passage. The alert reporter will understand that the legislator's absence is more than mere indifference, and report the story accordingly.

Committee hearings are also the center of citizen involvement in the legislative process. Such public hearings might include an impassioned plea for more school transportation funding by a parent-teacher group. An association of apartment owners might vigorously oppose legislation strengthening tenants' rights in disputes with landlords. The reporter armed with on-the-scene testimony can write a more accurate and compelling story.

Reporters also have the chance to ask pertinent questions at the scene, rather than being forced to track down pivotal figures later.

The Calendar

When a committee favorably reports a bill to the floor of the House or Senate, it is placed on a calendar already heavily laden with other legislation awaiting action. It is not uncommon for a bill to languish on the calendar until adjournment, effectively relegating it to limbo.

The leadership must be persuaded by the bill's proponents that the measure deserves consideration, which is where much horse-trading takes place. Power to obtain positive action on legislation is essential for the effective officeholder.

As the session nears its end, a special calendar becomes the springboard to success of a proposal reaching the floor. The leadership often constitutes itself as a special committee to determine what bills will be acted upon during the final hectic weeks, meeting each day to decide what will receive priority. Without this, bills usually have little chance of passage. Rules may differ, but the power to consider the order of bills nearly always lies in the hands of a few legislative leaders.

Floor Debate

For all its reputation as an exciting part of the process, floor debate is generally routine. However, it is a vital part and reporters must know formal parliamentary procedure to fully understand the process.

The Senate or House might meet formally only an hour or so each day, but the possibility of argument erupting over an issue is always present during the brief official sessions.

After successfully negotiating the committee, a bill heads to the floor for debate. Efforts may be made to amend the bill, sometimes amounting to a redrafting of the legislation. If the bill survives, it is placed on the calendar for a final reading. Special limitations often apply to final readings, such as consideration of it without the privilege of amending.

Approval through the final reading moves the bill into the other house where it must run a similar gauntlet. Frequently, however, a companion bill has been introduced in the other chamber, and agreement between the two houses is only a formality.

When amendments are added and the bills differ, the bill is referred to a conference committee composed of members of both houses that tries to reconcile the differences. Nowhere is political jockeying more evident than in the process of hammering out the conflicts between differing budget bills.

As members maneuver to keep their chamber's favorite projects, funding for a major health program might die or be weakened, pet school projects might be put aside for a year, or money for new state parks may disappear. In the struggles that ensue, the most powerful emerge winners, leaving behind political scars. Budget compromises are always reached. Other legislation may not be so fortunate. When agreement is impossible in conference committee, the proposal dies.

To the Governor's Desk

Of hundreds of original proposals during the session, a much smaller sheaf of successful legislation makes its way to the governor's desk where a final hurdle in most states—the veto—is encountered. This power, while essentially negative, assumes significant proportions at the end of the legislative session.

In most states, the governor is allowed from three to 30 days to sign a measure into law. If he or she vetoes it, the bill returns to the Legislature for further

consideration if it is still in session. For the bill to survive, the houses must vote to override the veto, generally by a two-thirds majority. Some states allow the governor to disallow specific items in an appropriation bill (called a line-item veto), and in other states the chief executive is allowed to reduce some budget items.

Coverage Is No 'Seasonal' Effort

The size and scope of activity by a state legislature requires the state government reporter to undertake major preparations. Simply tracking daily developments requires careful organization. Furthermore, far from being a "seasonal" effort, coverage of far-reaching legislative actions that reach into every community is a year-round responsibility.

The process is not only legislative but also political, as this example shows: The leaders of the city's police and firefighter's fraternal organizations have successfully appealed to local legislators to introduce a bill raising pensions for retired members of the two departments. But because the municipal government would have to absorb the $900,000 increase in its annual budget, those officials vigorously protest.

Compromise efforts fail and the proposal dies in the final stages of the session, but it remains a major community issue. When the Legislature reconvenes, municipal officials persuade another local legislator to introduce a bill that would transfer the power to regulate pensions from the Legislature to municipal officials, who argue that their lack of control over the fund runs counter to community interest.

Coverage of such a story ranges from the legislative maneuvering in the state capital, to the police and fire officials back home who have demanded changes, to the municipal officials who have their own ideas about how to balance a budget, and on to the pensioners themselves and the community in which the issue has been raised.

Documents will help the reporter illuminate the issue, and while they may not be easy to find, people with unbiased opinions will balance the strong statements sure to be made.

In this case, and in similar ones, the issue spills outside the legislative chambers and into different arenas, creating the need for broader coverage.

The Journalist's Checklist

The reporter about to be drawn into the maelstrom of a session for the first time has some vital preliminary work to do. The best way to begin is to compile a checklist:

• Area legislators should be contacted and asked about their plans to introduce potential legislation. The reporter should record where they will stay and get their phone numbers.

Some members of a local delegation rarely submit legislative proposals, involving themselves instead in their favorite statewide issues; others are active in submitting local bills. Preliminary stories provide readers and viewers with advance information on pending activity.

A new legislative session usually brings with it a shower of new proposals, and tomorrow's opening is no exception.

Harrison County's all-Republican delegation promises a range of activity from "a great number of bills" to virtually none.

Sen. Charles Palumbo says he plans to introduce "a great number of bills, because they are nothing more than concepts or ideas whose time may or may not have come."

At the other extreme, Rep. Patricia Hart says she plans to introduce no bills.

"Virtually everything worthy of merit will be introduced by someone else," Hart says.

Potential legislation with important local implications should be identified early, through local legislators and other community officials. The process through which purely local legislation is enacted also should be reviewed.

• The reporter should become familiar with legislators in leadership roles, especially those who have been selected to those roles for the first time, and with the key members of the House and Senate committees.

Major legislation should be researched, with special attention to the lines that will be drawn on the issues.

• Newcomers should review the rules of the two houses, and visit the legislative chambers before the start of the session. Offices often are shifted between sessions, information services relocated and new procedures established. For the new reporter, a review of the sections of the state constitution dealing with the Legislature can be helpful

• A good backgrounding in the current relationship between the Legislature and the executive branch is essential to competent legislative reporting. Which legislators are crucial to passage of the governor's program? Who are expected to be most hostile to the executive branch's requests for funds? Which state agencies will be making special requests?

Officials from state agencies often are called to testify on legislative proposals that affect their operations. The state commissioner of finance might be quizzed on mushrooming operating losses in the state parks system. The state banking commissioner might be asked to tell the House Banking Committee why some banks are obtaining short-term loans to circumvent investment laws, then selling the loans after they are checked by the State Banking Commission. Conflict between counties and the state over the auto license fee may require testimony before a finance committee by the state motor vehicles commissioner.

Many state officials ask to appear before committees considering legislation because they have an interest in the outcome.

The seal of a notary public on a legal document is intended as proof that the signatures on it have been witnessed and verified. But state law does not make that as clear as Secretary of State James A. Mandell would like.

In a letter to leaders of both houses, Mandell sought to explain Monday why stronger legislation covering notaries public is needed.

Conflicting testimony from state officials often leads to appearances by members of the executive branch, particularly when more than one agency is involved in the legislation.

Alcoholic Beverage Commissioner Jack T. Baldini said Thursday he initiated the proposal to dismantle the State Beer Commission and merge it with the Alcoholic Beverage Control Board.

Baldini said he believes the present system of beer and liquor commissions constitutes a duplication of effort. Legislation dismantling the beer commission has been promised.

• The reporter should enter the new session with a working knowledge of the previous session's business. What important bills were passed? What are the prospects for the bills that died in the previous session? How did the governor and others fare in passage of programs, and who was responsible? What new political alliances were made at the last session, and where do they stand this year? Out of the past often come the answers to future action.

• Knowledge of the routine in the Statehouse is important. Reporters should get to know personnel who handle legislative services, processing new bills and amendments. A knowledge of committee meeting locations can make or break a reporter's day, particularly if the site has not been announced. Most capitals are overcrowded mazes, and a 30-minute search for an important committee hearing can be fatal to on-the-scene reporting.

Most legislatures employ specialists to help members deal with complex fiscal matters. Reporters should get to know them. Clerks are employed around the clock to follow legislation, furnishing copies of the bills introduced, the journal covering the previous day's activity and agendas for the houses. Like the legislator, the reporter has access to these services, which eases the task of assembling detail.

Much of the reporter's time will be spent checking new proposals; chasing down legislators, state officials and lobbyists for comment; monitoring floor debate; sitting in on important committee hearings; and keeping up with behind-the-scenes maneuvering. Often this last activity is the most important part of the reporter's efforts. An issue may die in this manner, never reaching a committee room hearing or a floor argument. It is the reporter's responsibility to try to accurately portray the death of such issues.

The lobbyist for the State Pharmaceutical Association wore a broad smile in the hallway. A Senate bill calling for posting of all medicinal prices, opposed by Tom T. Broadmoor and his organization, was dead.

No one wanted to be quoted on the issue, but the consensus was that the proposal was killed by agreement among the legislative leadership to support a House measure requiring posting only prices of life-supporting drugs.

• Reporters in the capital should maintain close contact with their home offices to keep track of local officials. Absence of the city manager from his or her office may occasion little notice at home, but that official may in fact be attending a committee hearing at the capital in which the city has a strong interest.

The city manager may be pressing for legislation taking control of the city's water system rates away from State Public Service Commission jurisdiction. County officials may be visiting their legislators to promote a bill allowing them to establish a regional planning and zoning board. A public service district official may be seeking legislation raising the district's bonding capacity.

Close cooperation among news staffers at the capital and at home is necessary to track the movements of such officials.

• The reporter should be prepared for cramped quarters. Facilities for the press in statehouses may include spacious quarters with electronic hookups to the home office, but are more likely to be in a cramped basement containing a desktop computer and a telephone. Most legislatures reserve press tables in the main chambers and provide access to reference material.

• The reporter also should be prepared for stress. As the session progresses, its tempo increases. What seemed to be a leisurely pace during the first weeks, with brief afternoon floor sessions, suddenly becomes a rat race. Floor sessions begin at 9 a.m., and the days get longer. Evening sessions are scheduled, and adjournments for four-day weekends to allow members time for trips home become rarer. The final days of the session are often frantic.

BOX 6–1

Local Legislation

✳✳✳

The reporter will be concerned with two distinct levels of legislative activity: the "local" bills that affect only the home community and the state-wide proposals. Both of these must be addressed in some manner, despite the tendency of many newspapers to leave the general legislation to the wire services.

Legislation that applies to a particular area sometimes proceeds quite differently. As noted, the growth of "home rule" at the local level has given towns and cities much more power to handle their own affairs. In some states, local bills are still passed as a courtesy to local legislators unless those officials are divided on the issue. When there is a conflict among the delegation, the proposal usually dies unless a compromise is found. The reporter must take care that such local proposals are not lost in the shuffle of more general issues affecting the entire state.

These levels of legislation also create a subtle problem for the reporter—the frequently conflicting responsibilities of the legislators who must represent the interests of the constituents who elected them to office, and also vote in the best interests of the state.

These interests may not always coincide, and the attentive reporter reflects this in news accounts whenever possible. One such method is to publish the "shopping list" of a local legislator, asking him or her to reconcile the needs of the constituency with those of the state at large.

Easing environmental standards on burning of coal, for example, might be beneficial to the legislator's industrial area but not in the best interest of the state.

When Legislation Becomes Law

Problems also exist in two other important areas of coverage closely related to the legislative process:

1. Far from the debate in the legislative chambers, someone must gauge the reaction of public officials and others who have a direct interest in the outcome of an issue. The busy legislative reporter may be half a state away from such reaction, so the responsibility falls on reporters at home.

2. Someone must be responsible for assessing the workability of new legislation. Passage of a law is only the beginning. Now the reporter must explain how it affects people. Is the new law working? Is it reasonable? Is it doing the job it was designed to do? Is it more costly than its proponents argued it would be? Has it had the effect of merely giving people jobs, without any other justification for existence? Who is going to answer these questions?

For example, two years after establishment of a state Commission on the Spanish Speaking, it would be time to assess its effect. The task could fall to the state government reporter rather than to those who are on the payroll of the commission. Some of the reporter's logical sources include those who originally supported the legislation, those who opposed it, the officials who set up the commission, the people who are most closely affected by it and experts who have no axes to grind, whatever the findings.

Public documents also probably will include regular audits of the agency.

Depending on the legislation, this kind of assessment might also fall to city hall, county, education, police or business reporters. Reporters on each beat should possess a sound knowledge of legislative action and its possible effects on those they cover.

Has the 3-year-old State Commission on the Aging been a worthwhile community investment?

The verdict is still in doubt, but its original opponents contend the $1.2 million a year it costs could have been much better spent.

"The commission has only served to fragment services to the elderly," said Will F. Spearman, president of the State Taxpayers Association.

But its supporters, including the state chapter of the American Association of Retired Persons, argue that the commission's accomplishments have outweighed its frequent problems.

Evaluating the programs created by legislation requires rigorous fairness and balance from the reporter.

No one in the state is in charge of helping migrant farm workers, and the governor won't take on the task either.

Gov. Dan Field has rejected a recommendation by the state Migrant Farm Workers Commission to set up a migrant affairs division in his office.

That sends the problem back to the commission, which has neither money nor authority to help the 26,000 workers and their families who visit the state each year to harvest peaches, apples, tomatoes and tobacco.

In this case, coverage fell to a reporter whose beat is the agricultural community. The reporter found that the recommendation was the first the commission had made in its 10 years of existence. The Legislature had created the body but given it no enforcement power and only $18,000 a year to employ a part-time secretary.

However, public pressure following the disclosure forced the governor to reconsider, and within days he asked another agency to come up with a solution to the problem.

Gov. Dan Field has asked the State Budget and Control Board to come up with a comprehensive plan by March 15 to assist migrant farm workers.

The goal of the plan will be to put someone in government in charge, for the first time, of protecting and helping the 26,000 workers and dependents who pass through the state each year.

"At least four agencies have a piece of the pie," said Lucy Caldwell, Field's spokesperson.

She cited the Departments of Agriculture, Labor, Social Services and Health & Environmental Control. "No one department pulls this together."

Closer assessment of new legislation might have picked up the deficiencies long before 10 years had gone by. The state government reporter followed this story after it surfaced, but such issues should be monitored regularly.

The state's migrant farm workers and their dependents will have an advocate in state government by this year's growing season.

A monthlong study recommends that the Migrant Labor Division of the state Department of Labor be restructured by creating an executive director's slot.

Other recommendations by the Budget and Control Board include immediate appointment of a migrant advocate to serve as executive director of the Migrant

BOX 6-2

Interpreting and Analyzing Events

✳✳✳

Special care must be taken by the reporter in interpreting and analyzing the course of legislation, particularly in predicting what may or may not occur. Careful analysis of an issue, clearly labeled, does have a place in legislative reporting. It cannot replace, however, the straight reporting necessary to public knowledge.

Interpretation of a complex proposal, such as major changes in a state's Cabinet system, with a discussion of its chances of passage, may often be necessary to public understanding. Like an analysis, it should be undertaken carefully.

The safest course is to clearly label analysis and interpretation and to avoid them entirely if publication threatens even a hint of misunderstanding of the reporter's motives.

Workers Commission and installing toll-free telephone lines with bilingual assistance.

Gov. Dan Field promised to act quickly to implement all of the recommendations.

A final caution: The reporter should be familiar with the "sunset laws" governing state agencies, boards and commissions. Most states are enacting legislation designed to terminate an agency when its usefulness has ended, and the process should be a part of the state government report.

THE EXECUTIVE BRANCH

The size and scope of state government today create a formidable obstacle to thorough coverage. The reporter must rely on a combination of effective sources, knowledge of agencies and issues, aggressive instincts and a dash of luck to do the job well.

The problem: What stories have priority? Even a team of capital reporters has to wrestle with the problem, much less a single reporter covering the state for a distant newspaper.

The Agriculture Department announces important changes in its million-dollar meat inspection program; the governor makes a hurried visit to a flood-ravaged community; the Alcoholic Beverage Commission schedules an important meeting; the State Education Commission plans a special hearing on funding changes. On any given day in the capital, these and dozens of other legitimate news stories compete for coverage.

The executive branch includes many different agencies, boards, commissions or departments. Some are gold mines of information, others yield little of interest to the reader or viewer. Some agencies are nearly invisible because their activities are routine; others work deliberately to maintain a low profile.

A reporter might be tempted to report on the most visible personalities and agencies in state government, but those are not always the most important agencies. Some are important because they reach into local communities, such as a board of higher education that oversees colleges and universities as well as local school boards. Some agencies are nearly independent

of the executive branch; others are highly political in character.

The reporter's challenge is to uncover the most important as well as the most interesting stories. The task can never be complete, no matter how extensive the staffing, but it can be acceptable.

Roadblocks to Effective Coverage

Besides the size of state government and the limits to reportorial personnel, other factors create roadblocks to effective coverage of the executive branch.

Agencies that serve no real purpose abound in some states, and archaic procedures are preserved in some constitutions, creating administrative labyrinths with political overtones.

There are many pressures for agency autonomy, and long-term officials jealously guard their sinecure. In addition, powerful political allies support their position. Disputes between agencies are common, and often the governor or the Legislature must mediate.

> State Finance Director Miles Sinnet says he can't figure out what the Commission on Mental Retardation does and is trying to abolish it.
>
> But the commission has survived at least two other attempts on its life, both foiled by action in the Legislature.
>
> "Its function as a grantsman agency as well as a lobbying unit should hardly be financed by the state," Sinnet said Thursday.
>
> With a budget of $637,000 and a director who is paid $76,500 a year, the commission coordinates federal grants to communities.

Relationships between the executive and legislative branches also complicate news coverage. Many basic decisions of the executive are subject to review by the Legislature, and the reporter should be able to identify the political ramifications.

Despite the move toward professionalism in public service, the "spoils system" remains and even thrives in many states.

> A key state senator said Monday he would oppose confirmation of a mental health expert as director of the State Health Department.

Committee hearings on confirmation of Dr. John C. Oskenhirt, who was appointed acting director of the department by the governor Nov. 1, are nearing an end.

"I still have too many questions about his background in diagnostic health services," said Sen. Sam Killian (R-Lowery), who said he would vote against confirmation.

Pressures of many special-interest groups also intrude on operation of state agencies, and the reporter should be able to convey the origin of such pressures. For example, trucking firms may exert pressure on the Highway Department to allow heavier loads through special permits. The permits may not be in the best interest of the public, partly because highway maintenance costs could go up.

Antiquated facilities in the state mental health system may be kept open despite recommendations of a study commission that they be closed. Pressures to keep them open come from a community that argues it cannot afford the loss of jobs.

The "clients" of many state agencies also influence policies of the offices. Welfare recipients, while individually seeming to have little voice in policy-making, in fact may constitute a formidable interest group. The journalist should be aware of the pressures that leaders of such "client" organizations exert on agencies. News accounts ultimately may reflect the fact that the "clients" forced an important policy change rather than a political figure.

A farm leader threatened to organize a march on the state capital next week to press for changes in the system of figuring tax credits for using land for agricultural purposes.

"It's outdated and costly, and needs to be revised," said Thurman Whitley, president of the State Grange.

The Agriculture Department maintains it cannot change the rules without legislative approval.

The reporter operates in a climate where there is often widespread feeling that some agencies should be "above politics," closing doors to the reporter that should be open. Especially susceptible to this belief are areas such as education, prisons, correction and parole procedure, promotion of fair employment practices, law enforcement, management of state resources and many personnel matters.

These areas are no more nonpolitical than others, but the effect of this attitude makes the task of covering the agencies more difficult.

The Parole Commission on Thursday rejected a newspaper's request for records of parole violators, despite assurances that the publication is interested in total figures rather than individual involvement.

Education officials are especially touchy on this subject. They believe they qualify as experts who know what is best for the public school system and often resent press scrutiny. It is not an attitude easily overcome.

Another obstacle to good reporting is the relationship between state government and the federal government's aid programs. Reporters need to monitor and report upon these two levels of government.

A new congressional proposal to limit funds supplied to state governments for secondary highway construction has drawn criticism from the director of the State Highway Commission.

"A cut in matching funds will endanger our whole program," John T. Blasik said Tuesday. "It's already five years behind our neighboring states."

The reporter must reconcile the response of an angry state official with the actual federal proposal under scrutiny, which first means double-checking the proposal at the federal level.

How much is the reduction? When will it be scheduled? What are its chances of congressional passage? What areas are threatened? What is the response of the state's congressional delegation? Many questions at other levels must be asked, to balance the word of one state official.

The Governor and the Office

The pivotal and commanding figure in the executive branch is the governor—ceremonial, legal and political chief of the state.

A peculiar overlay of personalities and functions is embodied in the one official. As the state's chief administrative officer, mandated to supply efficient government to a broad constituency, the governor must exude confidence.

But a seemingly contradictory personality emerges from the same official—the cautious politician staging a "media event" at just the right time, often unwilling to commit to a direct answer and always hedging a little to avoid alienating any segment of the electorate.

To the reporter, who realizes that public office is part of a recurring pattern—politics, election and re-election—it is one of the realities of covering state government.

The governorship is the state's chief political prize, because of the power of the office to influence public policy and the role of the governor as spokesperson for the state. The governor also is head of his or her political party, which adds strength to the office. The governor also has the capacity to dilute somewhat the power of the legislative branch and give the executive's initiatives a better chance of succeeding.

Several factors intrude to limit these powers, however. One factor is the need to make contradictory campaign promises. A gubernatorial candidate may promise tax relief, while assuring that a proposed new and expensive highway program will solve all transportation difficulties. The two promises may be wholly incompatible, and the candidate's position might be weakened by the reporter's insistence upon pointing out such contradictions.

The governor also must share power with other elected officials—a lieutenant governor, an attorney general, a secretary of state, a treasurer and/or a comptroller. Independent agencies also help to decentralize authority. It is within this framework of state bureaucracy that the reporter must operate.

So while the governor may propose, the Legislature may finally dispose—and possibly in a manner quite contrary to the way the chief executive wishes it resolved. The legislative leadership often has its own priorities.

The Senate's president and Finance Committee chairman took off in a different direction Monday from Gov. Will Hochman on proposed tax relief.

President Bruce Angelo (R-Fanning) and Chairman Patrick Donovan (R-Cayman) introduced a bill to raise the personal exemption on the state income tax from $1,500 to $2,350, the same level as the federal exemption.

In his state of the state address Monday, the governor had asked for removal of food from the 5 percent sales tax, at a cost to the state of $615 million a year.

But the governor also gets help from friends and political appointees, who can be counted on to pressure the Legislature to enact the chief executive's programs.

Gov. Will Hochman's tax relief plan is superior because only it can provide a tax cut to all 5.7 million residents of the state, Tax Commissioner Mary C. Hardy Jr. said Wednesday.

Hardy commented during a briefing with reporters on Hochman's proposal, an indication of the administration's resolve to remove food from the 5 percent state sales tax during the current legislative session.

The governor also wields extensive administrative authority, appointing and removing many state officials, and conducting the day-to-day business of the state.

The reporter's regular access to the governor will be determined mainly by those around the chief executive. The ability to penetrate the sometimes formidable barriers of press secretary, personal secretary or any number of other aides depends upon several factors—persistence and personality of the reporter, openness of the chief executive, and willingness on the part of the governor's aides to encourage such openness.

Information filtering from the top "through channels" is rarely as effective as firsthand material, and every effort should be made to speak regularly with the person in charge.

Lacking direct access to the governor, the reporter must turn to aides for needed information and acceptable detail for stories. The most helpful will be those closest to the governor. Reporters will need to be able to distinguish the mere errand-runners from the real decision-makers around the chief executive.

Other State Officials

Also influencing the governor's full use of the powers spelled out by the state constitution are the other elected officials over whom the chief executive has little or no control.

Secretary of State.   The secretary of state, popularly elected to constitutional office in 37 states, often rivals the governor in prestige if not in power, directing a state department that reaches into every community.

As the state's chief election officer, the secretary registers political parties and determines ballot eligibility, files nominating papers, assumes responsibility for referendums and initiative petitions, decides on the form of the ballot, files candidates' expense papers and publishes election results. Outside election years, the secretary of state's office yields regular news material for the state government reporter. The secretary rules on irregularities in the election process or takes them to court, and oversees local election laws as well as those involving statewide contests.

The three unlocked ballot boxes in Wayne County's First Precinct did not constitute a deliberate fraud, and won't affect the county's school bond levy election, Secretary of State James A. Manchin ruled yesterday.

"I am convinced it was wholly accidental," Manchin said after his office completed an investigation of the incident. The $14.5 million levy passed by a wide margin last week.

Licensing and registration constitute another area of responsibility. Depending upon the state, the secretary's office may register vehicles, license business and professional enterprises, supervise banking and securities legislation, commission notaries public, register trademarks and prepare extradition papers.

Custodial duties include maintaining records of state lands, filing articles of corporation and issuing charters. Because of these functions, the office is a constant source of news.

Depending on the requirements of the constitution or the legislative process, the secretary of state depends on the work by local government officials, such as city and county clerks, creating a need for reporters to check these levels for news developments, too.

Secretary of State Wilson M. Morris ruled Monday that the city's effort to obtain property next to City Hall for parking lots had to go through the condemnation process, even if the property owners are willing to sell to the city.

In a letter to City Clerk Mary L. Neeley, Morris stated that City Council's agreement to buy the land must be taken to Circuit Court.

The secretary of state also maintains the state archives and collects data from other agencies, making that office a prime collection point of vital statistics.

The watchdog function of the office occasionally intrudes on the prerogatives of other state agencies.

With his usual flair, Secretary of State Sam "Slim" Black announced Tuesday that his office will investigate a country music promoter accused of deceiving country music star Tammy Wynette, which resulted in cancellation of a concert in Arlington last week.

The investigation stems from Wynette's complaint that she was lied to about weather conditions in the state, causing her to abandon the trip to Arlington.

Attorney General.   The attorney general, popularly elected in most states, is another important constitutional figure. As the state's chief law officer, the attorney general issues official advice to the governor and other agencies, interprets statutes or regulations, prepares or reviews legal documents and represents the public before state agencies. In some states, the official exercises authority over local prosecuting attorneys.

Providing opinions on issues gives the attorney general's office considerable prestige as well as power. While the opinions can be overturned by judicial action, the rulings often take on the force of law.

In recent years, legislation has allowed the attorney general wide latitude in the field of consumer protection. In many states, that office can commence civil or criminal proceedings in consumer protection cases, and in other ways handle consumer complaints. Many states give the attorney general power to prosecute complaints against merchants in the courts.

The reporter should be familiar with routine responsibilities handled by all the major state officials. For example, the attorney general also may be responsible for awarding state legal work to outside law firms. Politics also can intrude on this process.

Attorney General Thomas Medlin has approved millions of dollars in state legal work for law firms that are also major donors to his campaign.

About three-quarters of the 72 firms approved to defend state government against lawsuits contributed at least $1,000 each to Medlin since 1986, according to records in the secretary of state's office.

The top 22 contributors to Medlin received from $141,000 to $1.7 million in state business since 1986, the records show.

To get the story, the reporter looked up public records of attorneys doing work for the state as well as records of campaign contributions.

In this case, the attorney general is considered a potential contender for the Republican gubernatorial nomination. Early in the story, the reporter has a responsibility to allow the official to respond.

> Medlin, who must approve virtually all contracts going to private attorneys for state work, denied that the donations have any influence.
>
> "Campaign contributions absolutely have no effect on this program," he said. "It's totally random."

Detail is important to this story, and the reporter should provide specific examples, as well as comments from other people involved.

> Lawyers who have donated money to Medlin also denied the contributions have anything to do with the work they sought.
>
> "Thomas Medlin is a friend of mine," attorney Benjamin Morris said. "If I never got a dime's worth of business from him, I would still contribute to his campaign because I think he is a good public servant."
>
> Morris has donated $6,625 to Medlin while collecting $989,000 in legal fees from the state.

Stories like these refuse to disappear, particularly if the reporter is persistent. In this case, the attorney general capitulated weeks later.

> Attorney General Thomas Medlin, seeking an end to an ethics controversy, announced he will no longer take campaign contributions from private attorneys approved by his office to do legal work for the state.
>
> Medlin has been on the defensive for several weeks after a newspaper reported that his office consistently approved state legal work for top campaign contributors.

State Treasurer.   An aura of financial wizardry and a measure of public trust characterize the office of state

treasurer. The office, filled by popular election in most states, is the custodian of state funds and disburses them as authorized by law.

Wise investment of idle funds, which might sit in banks for months, constitutes a significant source of state revenue. The treasurer is often guided by state depository legislation requiring a board to designate banks for depositing such funds.

With millions of dollars at stake in deposits, politics often plays a role in determining where the funds will be deposited. The reporter who carefully checks depository agencies and records may find that certain banking institutions have received the lion's share of state deposits, sometimes under questionable circumstances. As noted, the records can be checked against political contributions, also public record.

State Auditor.   Only about half the states continue to elect a state auditor, whose duties are to periodically audit the accounts of the treasurer and other state officials. The auditor also acts as a check on the treasurer, authorizing disbursements from the treasury through a pre-audit.

At the state level, the auditor acts as a check on boards, agencies and officials at the local level. Regular checks of the office are essential to thorough coverage.

> Perry County Water District officials spent more than $30,000 to pay the bills of a private company owned by three members of the district's board of trustees, State Auditor Joan Frank said Monday.
>
> Frank's auditors said they also found that nine former and current trustees had improperly doubled their own pay.
>
> In both cases, Frank has ordered repayment.

Results of the audit of the water district books were forwarded to the county prosecutor and the State Ethics Commission, so other reporters may be pursuing the story at another level.

The state auditor may be investigating procedures used in awarding printing contracts, and may ask for help from criminal investigative agencies. But increasingly, other state agencies are wielding the power to audit their subsidiary agencies.

A state Department of Mental Health may regularly audit county governments in search of funds owed drug treatment programs at the state level. A state

Division of Insurance Services, which handles health insurance for thousands of state employees, may audit the company hired to administer the state's dental plan and find discrepancies.

> An audit of the state School for the Blind's Medicare program has found no evidence of fraud, although the school must repay the federal government $14,250 for improper billings.
>
> The audit, conducted by the state Health and Human Services Commission, found 172 cases of improper documentation and 83 instances of overbilling affecting about 7 percent of all claims submitted by the school, documents released Friday show.

State Agencies: A Logistical Nightmare

Without a working knowledge of the specific functions of the various government agencies and the staff that directs them, the reporter will always be playing catch-up.

Reporters new to the beat should first identify the agencies headed by officials generally appointed by the governor. Also on the list are multimember boards or commissions whose operations become more complex with addition of local or regional offices, often with substantial autonomy.

The first step is to identify each agency's functions and personnel. What are the basic services provided? How is it organized? Who are the key personnel? What is its budget? What is the best way to cover its activities efficiently? Who are the people who can most effectively provide information?

Similar questions apply to regulatory agencies. Who are the regulators? What are the rules under which they operate? At what levels does the reporter best obtain information? In answering such specific questions, the reporter will more quickly solve the problems of time, red tape and resistance to pursuit of information.

Although degree and direction vary considerably, these are the major services provided at the state level: education, health and welfare programs, public protection, transportation, protection of natural resources, housing and development, labor relations and a revenue and taxation unit to collect funds to provide for those services.

Education

The education reporter often detects an undercurrent of anxiety in local school board offices, not necessarily connected with day-to-day administration of local school affairs.

The reason is not complex: While local governmental units have responsibility for education, a "higher" authority—the state Legislature—enacts most of the laws governing the public school system.

The Legislature determines how local units will be organized, who will govern them, and how they will be selected and funded. Statutes are enforced by a state board of education.

Whatever authority school boards possess, the state government reporter recognizes that a state-level school board or commission also has important responsibilities. Officials at this level may set teacher certification, prescribe subjects to be taught in the classroom and the textbooks to be used, promulgate compulsory attendance laws, and establish salary standards. No matter what the state, some educational policies are determined at the state level.

A familiarity with the authority of the state governing board and the "strings" it attaches to local school systems are essential if the reporter is to coordinate coverage at both levels of government.

> State Board of Education Chairman Robert C. Myer charged Thursday that the Warren County Board of Education failed to comply with state guidelines in spending school construction funds.
>
> Myer appointed a three-member committee to review procedures used by the Department of Education to assure that local school boards are spending funds in compliance with the law.
>
> In a report issued to other board members, Myer stated that the Warren board had failed to show in its budget proposed sources of income to complete construction projects at seven schools in the system.

On the surface the dispute appears to center on reporting policies of local school units, but the persistent reporter may find that other factors are involved, such as improper transfers or melding of funds.

> Controversies in Warren and Lincoln counties appear to have been factors in the sudden resignation Friday

of State School Superintendent James C. Wilson from his $85,000-a-year position.

Wilson, who has had the job for nine years, announced his resignation effective June 1.

Handling of a Warren school construction controversy and a Lincoln tax dispute which poses a threat to the state's educational funding formula led to Wilson's differences with some Board of Education members, including Chairman Robert C. Myer.

Strings of a different nature bind institutions of higher education to special state boards that govern them. While operating control resides at the level of the institution, a board of regents or education commissioners develop general guidelines and enforce statutory demands, which often include a role in the budgeting process for the institutions.

Duties and selection of these boards vary, with some established by constitution, others by legislation. But whatever the composition of the boards, the pragmatic reporter recognizes once again that politics often plays a part in the process.

"Politics," observed Board of Regents Chairman Rogers Thornby on Monday, "is the art of people working together or not working together."

With that observation, Thornby dodged a direct question on whether the board's Higher Education Resources Fund has become a political football.

At its monthly meeting in the capital Tuesday, the board will discuss the fate of the $234 million fund, collected as student fees and used for athletic equipment, travel and other current expenses.

State Tax Commissioner Warren C. Still has criticized the regents' handling of the fund.

While the regents' chairman dodged the question, others directly involved might be willing to discuss the issue: the state tax commissioner, other regents, legislative officials interested in the outcome of the argument, university officials charged with disbursing the funds and even the students from whom the funds are collected.

Health and Welfare

The elderly pensioner clutched his robe more tightly about his thin shoulders and responded slowly to the reporter's question:

Yes, he said, the new facility for the elderly and disabled seems "just fine." The nurses are efficient, the food is adequate, proper medication is always available, television and radio sets are nearby. But, the pensioner sighed, something is lacking. Despite all its controlled activity, the place seems lonely, he said.

The reporter was questioning an aid recipient in depth, a familiar device to illustrate how a state welfare agency is performing its function. In covering human services, the effective reporter works both at the administrative level and at the individual level. An interview with the state welfare commissioner is only half the story. The response from the recipients is equally important.

Health and welfare programs affect nearly everyone, and they are an integral part of state coverage. Cost of human services may not match that of public education, but substantial funds are required to provide health care, aid to indigent persons not fully covered by federal programs, and special services for the disabled and aging. As with other service agencies, department types vary from state to state.

Total funds budgeted are not always a factor in intrinsic news value. A modest department designed to ease the burdens on the elderly may possess only vague powers, but still yield important story material.

Half the pharmacies in the state are ignoring a new law requiring substitution of cheaper generic drugs for brand-name prescriptions, the director of the State Commission on Aging said Friday.

Annabelle C. Gerrard said the commission completed a spot check this week indicating problems implementing the law, which went into effect July 1.

Public health has increasingly become the responsibility of all levels of government, contributing to the difficulty of news coverage. Health care was traditionally the responsibility of the states, with diagnostics rather than specific care the original goal. The federal government, with a Cabinet-level Department of Health and Human Services, has involved itself in many programs, among them extensive grants-in-aid to states for investigating maternity and child health, industrial health, communicable diseases, heart disease and cancer.

Early emphasis centered on medical care for the indigent and control of epidemics. Today's services are a far cry from those limited programs and now include mental as well as physical well-being. A study by the Public Health Service lists up to 36 health services performed by the states, including disease control, sanitation, collection of vital statistics, operation of state hospitals, regulation of health insurance, and specific hygiene programs.

The state maintains some authority over local health units, including private hospitals and other facilities. Local health departments turn to state units in policy matters, while maintaining the freedom to handle their own administrative affairs.

> The Wheeling Hospital will be permitted to proceed with construction of a four-floor addition without delay, the State Board of Health announced Wednesday.
>
> The board had withheld certification while considering whether a new maternity ward was warranted in the community of 90,000.

Welfare services also have expanded beyond their original scope. Services for certain disadvantaged groups now embrace dependent as well as underprivileged children, disabled people and delinquents through a broad range of public services.

A state welfare department also coordinates federal funding and guides local agencies. The substantial nature of the funding calls for coverage from a technical as well as a human standpoint.

> The State Welfare Department Tuesday revised its standards for supplying minimum payments to the indigent, to conform to new federal guidelines.
>
> The effect of the action, Director Yvonne Salinger said, would be to increase the monthly payment by $31 to $447, effective in July. Half the annual $67 million cost will be borne by federal revenue-sharing, she said.

A host of new programs, many of them controversial and more newsworthy than traditional services, has cropped up in recent years. The reporter may find it difficult to identify the programs because they are federally funded and no accounting needs to be made to state legislatures.

> Family planning has become big business for the state, which dispenses more than $27 million a year in federal funds to hold down its population.

The State Department of Health's project pays for a male's vasectomy and a female's tubal ligation, and dispenses free birth control pills and other contraceptives, according to department literature.

A Health Department spokesman said the line is drawn at providing free abortions, but callers to the project's toll-free number are told where they can obtain abortions at little or no cost.

Public Protection

The trooper carefully backed his vehicle, its radar pointed at the long curve on the interstate highway, onto the median and turned off the ignition. Passing motorists checked their speedometers. While the trooper represents state law enforcement in its more visible form, this is only the tip of the public protection iceberg.

The range of agencies assuming responsibility for protecting the public is far more extensive, from the state highway patrol and National Guard contingents to public utilities regulators, medical and dental licensors, and consumer protection agencies.

> SACRAMENTO—The Public Utilities Commission issued orders Friday to keep the San Francisco Bay mass transit tunnel closed until city crews correct the problems that led to a fatal, terrifying fire during rush hour Wednesday.
>
> Bay Area Rapid Transit General Manager Keith Bernard told the commission that the fire, which claimed one life and injured 45, "could happen again." He said the precise cause of the accident was not known.

Under a mandate to protect the public, states prescribe general qualifications that must be met by applicants who wish to practice most of the professions, as well as other occupational callings. In most states these include lawyers, accountants, architects, chiropractors, engineers, nurses, pharmacists, physicians, teachers and veterinarians.

Some states also regulate barbers, beauticians, insurance and real estate brokers, and surveyors. Licensing boards or commissioners, composed wholly or partly of members of the profession, examine and approve applicants. The boards also consider revocation or suspension of licenses for reasons such as incompetency, malpractice or unprofessional conduct.

The State Medical Licensing Board has agreed to hear a petition by Dr. David Johnson of Forest Hills, which asks the agency to reverse its decision to revoke Johnson's medical license.

The board revoked his license Jan. 13 as a result of his conviction last year on charges of possessing marijuana with intent to deliver it. The physician served six months at the prison camp at Rosewood.

Because public utilities generally enjoy monopolies, they are regulated by states in the public interest. The complex decisions involving these enterprises are among the most difficult to report in state government. Some technical and financial expertise will help in reporting on such essential services as electricity, gas, water and sewage facilities, telephone services, and transportation services.

State utility commissions, with staffs of experts, regulate rates to ensure a fair return to private investors, issue certificates of convenience and necessity for expansion of services, and approve corporate actions construed as affecting the public interest.

The reporter will see a constant stream of legislation directed at these various agencies, including those involved in public protection. Often the legislation is unclear, and officials must sort out the options while the law is clarified.

The Highway Patrol has suspended enforcement of the state's new window-tinting law until the Legislature clarifies the law.

Highway Department spokesperson Jennifer Brokaw said Tuesday that the patrol will ticket a driver only "when the glass is so dark that you can't tell there's a driver inside."

The controversy centers on the issue of whether windows are to be tested with hand-held laser-operated "tint meters," or with a special card issued by the Highway Patrol. The card gives a different reading than the meter.

In this and similar cases, the issue may be only temporarily sidetracked until the Legislature clarifies the law.

Transportation

Nowhere is the multilevel structure of government more evident than in the field of transportation,

particularly in construction and maintenance of highways and roads.

The reporter backs out of the driveway onto a city street, purely the responsibility of the municipality in which the reporter resides. The route to work leads through an unincorporated area where the county maintains the roads, and along a highway constructed and maintained by the state. Before parking the car in still another municipality with its own street program, the reporter travels a brief stretch of interstate highway, constructed mainly with federal funds but maintained by the state.

The journalist is reporting on transportation for a nation on wheels. Unrepaired potholes and mileslong traffic snarls rank among the most-reported stories. There are many others, however, and reporters should be aware of the technicalities of highway construction and traffic control:

Why is the state's interstate system composed mainly of concrete, while a neighboring state sports macadam surfacing? Is it politics or good highway construction? What percentage of the cost does the state Highway Department pay for farm-to-market county roads? How are road funds apportioned among counties, and what's the formula? Who controls the funds? Is politics involved in the sudden transfer of district road supervisors in the area? What will the governor's highway reorganization mean to the public?

The transportation beat wends a winding course from the Legislature, which appropriates funds for highways and increases gasoline taxes for that purpose from time to time, to the executive branch, which administers the system.

The pothole repairs, in fact, may be the simplest story of all. A knowledge of classes of roads is important—generally designated as primary and secondary highways, farm-to-market roads and city streets. But, more important, the reporter should know who is responsible for maintenance and traffic control.

Every mile of new pavement, every square yard of road resurfacing and other improvement probably involves some degree of politics—be it the decision of the state highway board, a district commissioner or the many local advisory boards that are asked for recommendations. The reporter covering this area needs to understand the hierarchy that puts plans into effect.

A state highway improvement fund would be broken up and used to draw in matching federal highway funds under a legislative proposal made Thursday.

Sen. Doris Gray (D-Marion) said turning direct control of the $160 million fund over to the highway department would give the agency the money it needs to match federal funds.

To communicate this story to readers or viewers, the reporter must be familiar with federal matching-funds policy and know how the state road-funding programs work.

States have increasingly become involved in mass transportation projects, and many support bus and rail systems. Such systems cross county and even state lines, necessitating special governing units to administer such programs. Federal funds often provide the bulk of the financial assistance, with help from state and local units.

Natural Resources

The tree-lined bluff overlooking the blue waters of the sound was crowded with people of all ages. The group carried a sign that proclaimed "SAVE OUR STATE'S WATERFRONT!" Representing various conservation organizations, they were protesting the decision of state officials to allow an industrial plant to locate nearby on the sound.

Urban or rural? Mountainous terrain or flatland? Agricultural economy or industrial heartland? Mile after mile of timber or rich mineral deposits? Open prairie or ocean vistas? The mix of natural resources a state possesses dictates the direction a state government reporter follows in covering their development. Every state has a mix of such resources, and the importance of each varies.

An Agriculture Department is less important in the industrial East than environmental regulation and pollution control, for example. Whatever the locale, natural resources are regulated through similar boards, agencies and commissions.

Some states provide an umbrella agency, a Department of Natural Resources, to cope with the complex problems of forest management, soil and wildlife conservation, flood control, state parks and other recreation facilities, and agriculture.

Others have developed several separate administrative agencies, often with overlapping jurisdiction, and sometimes with conflicting roles in protection of resources.

Two state agencies are arguing over disposition of federal funds for conservation, and the governor says he'll mediate the dispute.

The Agriculture Department has earmarked the $21 million windfall for soil conservation purposes, but the Forestry Service claims that a share of the funds belongs in its forest management account.

In some states, the new importance of energy conservation has led to creation of departments addressing themselves specifically to energy, often with overlapping responsibilities with Departments of Conservation and Public Utility Commissions.

A new emphasis on recreation has fostered important State Parks Departments, which operate extensive lodging and recreational facilities. Because income from use of the facilities rarely covers the cost, such agencies are dependent on the state Legislature for additional funding.

Business and Labor

Responsibility for regulatory action in the fields of private enterprise and labor, often with those groups in conflict, lies with state government.

A Department or Bureau of Labor, headed by a director appointed by the governor, deals with health and safety standards, liability of employers, unemployment and disability compensation, and compilation of labor statistics. These functions are discussed in detail in Chapters 15 and 16.

An increasing emphasis on business and industrial development as aids in protecting and expanding the state's economy also has led to creation of special agencies to deal with the issue.

Seeking new employment opportunities for citizens and new sources of tax revenue, departments of industrial development send representatives to other regions, enticing industrial firms to locate facilities in the state. Some states offer lucrative tax write-offs; others offer to underwrite bond issues to remain competitive. Reporters will find these agencies secretive about their affairs because the field is so competitive. With tax shelters a part of the negotiations, however, the public interest is involved, and the state government or business reporter should monitor the issue.

State planning commissions sometimes assume these recruiting functions and go further, assisting private industry and business in securing outside contracts for state-produced goods.

The Institutions

The state's institutions, many in inaccessible rural areas, pose a special problem for the state government reporter.

Dozens of such facilities are scattered around most states—educational, correctional and vocational institutions, and facilities for the indigent and disabled. Educational centers are among those best covered, while mental institutions, health-care facilities and prisons are among those with the poorest coverage.

The problem: Day-to-day activities of the facilities are carried on far from the scene of the policy-making activities—the agency offices in the state capital. Meanwhile, many of the financial functions may be carried out in still another office, and the auditing process may be located elsewhere.

Some newspapers tend to leave the reporting of state institutions to the state government reporter, who may be far from the physical facilities. As a result, coverage of institutional affairs often is fragmented and minimal, with those possessing great public visibility enjoying the most coverage.

Editors and reporters should maintain an effective checking system to assure that such institutions do not become invisible to the public except during emergencies. Access to these institutions often poses the biggest problems of coverage for reporters.

Chapter 7

Authorities and Other Special Districts

Laughter echoed behind the closed door, then dropped to a hum of conversation as the small group got down to business. The monthly meeting of the Johnstown Development Authority was under way.

The chairman brought the meeting to order, asked the executive director for a financial report, heard briefings on activity that included efforts to lure a West Coast industry to the area, then called for discussion of the major topic of the meeting: changing the fee schedule in three industrial parks to meet increased bond payments.

A consensus was apparent, and after hearing the executive director's recommendation, the group voted for it. The meeting concluded, and the group adjourned to a nearby restaurant for lunch and a return to each member's private affairs.

No illegalities had occurred, and the public had not been bilked. It merely had not been consulted on a matter that could deeply affect it later. This was one public body's method of doing business. Although a public body, the group had not announced date, time and place of the meeting. As a matter of fact, the press probably was not aware of it.

Thousands of meetings are being conducted all over the United States each month by these little-known public bodies—special district government.

In 1917, H.S. Gilbertson labeled county government, which up to that time had been subjected to little study or analysis by political scientists, as "the dark continent of American politics."

Forty years and two world wars later, political scientist John C. Bollens respectfully disagreed. The term, he contended, should be applied to the special district (or special purpose) governments that have proliferated during this century.

These new units, sometimes called "phantom governments" because of their low visibility, are far more numerous than all municipal and county governments combined. In studying them, Bollens reported:

> "People who receive services from them often do not know they exist or exactly where they function. Although most districts have definite areas and boundaries which limit their jurisdiction, there is seldom visible evidence of these facts."

Few public affairs reporters will work in a community that does not have at least one of these special districts or "authorities." And while it may take a bit of research, the reporter will find special purpose government units provide a vast range of services. The spectrum reaches from public transportation, sewage disposal and recreation facilities to cultural arts complexes and industrial development zones. Figure 7–1 outlines the funding for a typical special district.

The original special districts, the ones still most familiar to the public, were the traditional school districts, which were conceived to provide funds for public education. School districts used to outnumber other types of special districts, but they have been consolidated drastically during the past several decades. School districts in the United States totaled 108,579 in

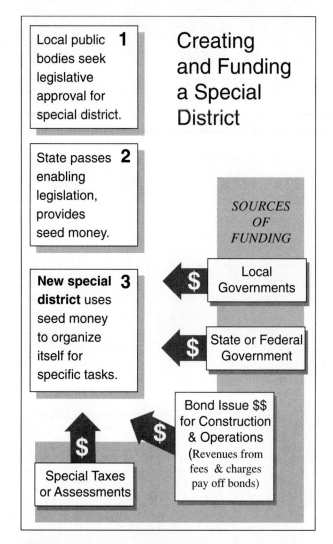

FIGURE 7–1
The documents covering all these operations and funding sources are public record, making it easier for a reporter to follow the operations of the special district.

1942. By 1990, consolidation had cut that number to only 14,721.

Meanwhile, new limited-purpose special districts have grown dramatically. Those districts, which totaled only 8,299 nationwide in 1942, proliferated to 29,532 by 1990, nearly a four-fold increase.

U.S. Bureau of the Census reports put Illinois special districts at 2,599, and California districts at 2,497. Pennsylvania has 2,039. Other states with heavy concentrations include Texas with 1,697, Kansas with 1,377, Missouri with 1,187, Nebraska with 1,152, Washington with 1,129 and Colorado with 1,031. Many less populous states also have experienced dramatic growth. South Carolina, for example, has more than 500 special purpose districts superimposed over its 46 counties and 271 cities and towns.

These nearly 30,000 units of special government make up more than 43 percent of total local governments. (There are 3,137 counties, 19,200 municipalities, and 16,691 towns and townships in the United States.)

The passage of time has helped outline the distinction between the terms *special district* and the more recently popular *authority,* basically a special district, too. Thirty years ago, *special districts* were generally defined as independent government units; *authorities* were characterized as being dependent on another governmental unit, either fiscally or administratively. As these authorities have grown and their functions have broadened, this distinction has changed.

Today, special districts are considered units that rely primarily on special taxes to fulfill their function. Public authorities are considered units that rely primarily on borrowed funds, raised through revenue bonds, to handle a specific function, such as a toll road or a convention center. The money is paid off through collection of fees or charges to the users. The distinction is not all-encompassing, however, because many of these special units of government rely on both sources of revenue. In some areas they are called public service districts (or PSDs), in others they are known as special purpose districts (or SPDs).

Whatever their revenue sources, special districts and authorities operate outside the traditional structure of government. They are easily confused because many combine functions and names, which vary from state to state. Furthermore, many are tied in some manner to other local governments, either as dependent children tied to apron strings or as grown-up children subject to little or no scrutiny.

So many special districts and authorities have been created in the last 50 years that it is impossible to classify them, except generally. As their numbers—and functions—continue to expand, so do the arguments for and against their existence.

An examination of these units will help the government reporter prepare to cover their activities.

ORIGINS OF SPECIAL DISTRICT GOVERNMENT

While the origins of these special units of government reach back to the 18th century, the term *authority* is fairly recent. When a Port of London special district was created in England in 1908, the problem of labeling it arose. David Lloyd George, then chancellor of the exchequer, was unable to decide on a name for this nontraditional mold of government. The story may be apocryphal, but a reporter for the *Observer* in London suggested the solution: With so much repetition of the term *authority* in the enabling legislation, the new unit should simply be called an authority. The name stuck.

Special district governments, however, date back to 1790 in the United States, when the city of Philadelphia established a governmental unit to combine administration of city and suburban prisons. Then, as now, the intractable nature of political boundaries created jurisdictional problems, solved in the case of Philadelphia with a new, overlapping government fulfilling one specific function.

Others followed in Philadelphia—a board of port wardens with jurisdiction over the waterfront district, an areawide board of health, a consolidated school district and a special metropolitan police district.

By 1900 half a dozen other metropolitan special districts had been established, with various functions and powers. They included a sewage and water district in Boston; sewage districts in Chicago, New York and northern New Jersey; a levee district in New Orleans to protect the city from the excesses of the Mississippi River; and a port district in Portland, Ore.

These original metropolitan units were given powers similar to those bestowed by states on authorities and special districts today: the right to borrow money by issuing long-term revenue bonds, to spend the money in operations, and a certain degree of autonomy.

A new interstate dimension to the growth of these new forms of government was added in 1921 with formation of the New York Port Authority, created through agreement between the states of New York and New Jersey to develop the commerce of the port of New York.

Seven years earlier, the *American Political Science Review* had begun reporting on "special municipal corporations." In one of the early reports, Charles Kettleborough wrote:

> "In the past few years there has been a significant increase in the number and diversity of municipal corporations, and the creation and development of interesting political units seems to be only in its infancy."

In retrospect, Kettleborough's modest prediction was an understatement.

DEFINING THEIR FUNCTIONS

The reporter asks a legitimate question: Why would a community need yet another government to clutter the landscape? Doesn't it have enough now to do the job?

The answer lies at least partly in the growing pressures by the public for more services. Another answer may lie in a story passed along by an official for the New York Port Authority:

> An executive for the authority once conducted a seminar in the Midwest for municipal officials. After the executive concluded his talk, a fiscal officer from a nearby community approached him and said, "Mr. Speaker, what you just said about the port authority hits the nail on the head in my town. We have been wanting to build a playground in my city, but the taxpayers don't want to spend any money and raise taxes. But I told the mayor, "Why don't we have a Playground Authority? The taxpayers have heard all about the wonders of the Tennessee Valley Authority and the New York Port Authority. If we just call this project the Playground Authority, the taxpayers will fall for it like a ton of bricks."

An unpublic approach perhaps, but the story exemplifies to some degree the basic function of an authority: It is generally created to accomplish some public or quasi-public purpose that cannot be accomplished through traditional methods.

Residents of an area, for example, want a new airport that will serve a growing region. The state Legislature is petitioned to enact a law permitting formation of an agency to oversee the airport. It will function outside the regular structure of government because it overlaps so many of the traditional units. The sole purpose of the special district (in this case labeled an authority) will be to finance, construct and operate the regional airport.

Often the issue will have been argued at the local level, or a reporter might pick up the story through a new legislative proposal. Enabling legislation already may be present statewide, and affirmation by the voters is all that is needed to bring the government unit into being.

The legislation gives the authority corporate form in an effort to make it more businesslike, assure greater efficiency and create a climate in which lending institutions will be more likely to provide the capital for construction of the facilities. Those same lending institutions see the new government unit as serving a strictly public function; thus, it obtains funds at a more reasonable rate, backed by its public status.

To protect the other governmental units unable or unwilling to finance the proposed facility because of limited resources, the state Legislature usually limits their liability. Thus, the new government cannot impinge on the credit of the older governments.

All of these powers, with their accompanying limitations, suggest a working definition for these authorities:

> A limited legislative agency of corporate form intended to accomplish specific purposes calling for long-range financing of specific public facilities without legally impinging on the credit of the state or local governing unit in which it operates.

Different authorities have so many functions that they have been grouped into basic categories: Health and sanitation; protection to persons and property; road transportation facilities and aids; other transportation facilities and aids; utilities; housing; natural

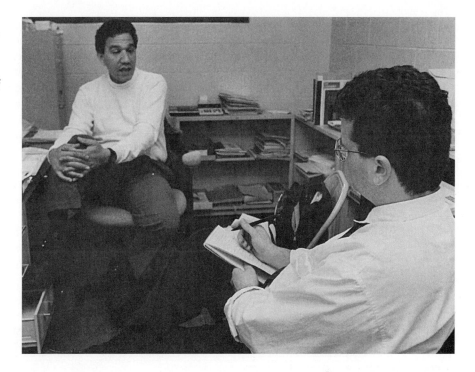

A reporter interviews a source about violence at a city housing project. Federally funded housing projects often are administered by quasi-public authorities whose members are appointed by local officials.
Photo by Andrea Hoy.

resource and agricultural assistance; education; parks and recreation; and cemeteries.

Many authorities have been designed to foster industrial growth or enhance the tourist industry. Most recreation facilities, such as civic centers and riverfront complexes, and major sports facilities in the country are operated by such special purpose governments.

The lack of ability by traditional government units to legally finance the major capital improvements often demanded by the public or its elected officials is only one of the reasons for the growth of special districts. Another is the overlapping jurisdictions of local governments, including growth of populations across state as well as county borders. The reporter frequently will find such amenities as intercity bus and rail transportation heavily funded by the federal government with substantial financial assistance from various local governments. Such facilities are feasible because the cities and counties involved can turn to an umbrella unit of government to handle the operation.

Municipalities in two states, separated only by a major river, discuss establishment of a port facility that will enhance the industrial growth of the entire region.

New industry and increased river traffic is the goal. However, there is a problem: Two states and two state legislatures are involved. Legislative action will have to be taken on both sides of the river to establish the authority that can find the financing, construct and ultimately operate the facility.

A reporter covering this complex story must obtain answers to these questions: What legislation does each state possess that will allow such cooperation? What are the limitations imposed by each? Will one or both of the communities have to go to state government for special legislation? How will the proposed unit of government be set up? Who will establish policies and supervise the operation? How will these leaders be selected? How will the facility be financed initially? What will its permanent financing be, and who will ultimately pay off the bonds that will be floated to finance construction? What ties will the new unit have with present governments, and to whom will it be responsible—if to anyone?

The new unit often takes on a life of its own. Its governing board probably will be appointed by the traditional governments that were responsible for creating the new unit, or by state officials. In rare cases, the board may be elected. The relationships between the new unit and its "parent" governing bodies can become complex.

The new port authority can be funded through any of several methods. Grants might be obtained from the federal or state governments, contributions solicited from the local "parent" units, and funds obtained by floating long-term revenue bonds, which must be repaid out of fees collected by the authority. Even private contributions sometimes are solicited.

The new umbrella government can tie together these various revenue sources, cut across traditional political boundaries and provide a specific facility or service to communities that might not otherwise be feasible (see Figure 7–2).

A legislature often takes an old measure and beefs up the power of special districts. This was the case when the Ohio Legislature enacted a law giving state port authorities new powers that would allow local governments to subsidize them. Under the new law, a port authority need not have a body of water within its territory, an obvious effort to allow authorities to develop industrial parks at military bases that were undergoing closure.

Claims for Their Effectiveness

The rapid growth of these special units of government is only one manifestation of their effectiveness. The sheer volume of physical facilities they have produced is another. But every government has its advocates

FIGURE 7–2

Why a Need for a Special District?

Overlapping Government Lines

- Afford flexibility to cooperating governments to work together more effectively

- Provide more logical lines of jurisdiction

- Offer possibility of joint ventures not possible in the past

Financing Options

- Provide special taxation benefits

- Offer creative bond funding

- Spread costs more fairly and more effectively

- Avoid restrictive debt ceilings of local or state governments

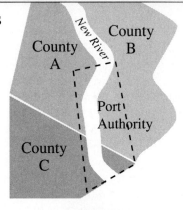

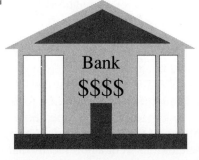

and its detractors. The reporter should be aware of some of the claims of proponents of special districts:

- These new governmental units can arrange financing of capital construction that otherwise would be impossible under restrictive debt ceilings in some states. This is done by floating bonds in the name of the authority, usually without obligation to existing governments. Facilities constructed by the authorities revert to traditional governments when the bonds have been paid off. For example, a toll highway would revert to the state after money from highway users retired the long-term bonds.

  Increasing numbers of special districts also may be attributable to annexation laws that prevent some cities from expanding into new, urbanized areas.

  For example, after a series of burglaries, residents of an unincorporated area vote to create a minigovernment that supplies only street lighting, then tax themselves to pay for it.

- Because these authorities engage in only one important function, more professional people are attracted to it, enhancing governance.

- Authorities must be businesslike because they do not normally rely on direct taxation, but instead finance themselves through sale of revenue bonds. A businesslike approach assures a good bond rating, which means that interest on the loans is reduced. Proponents argue that, while the authorities' objectives are in the public interest, the agency takes on the cast of the private sector, enhancing the businesslike approach.

- By establishing a new unit of government, free of traditional restraints, its operators take the functions of the new unit out of politics. By bringing in citizens with successful records of community service and allowing them to operate in a businesslike manner, a nonpolitical cast is placed on the authority, suggesting greater effectiveness.

- Through their flexibility, authorities make possible the formation of more logical lines of jurisdiction, no longer tied to intractable political boundaries established in another century. Cities, counties and states can cooperate to establish ventures not possible in the past.

Opponents Argue the Deficiencies

Not everyone agrees on the effectiveness of these governmental units. Critics say the special districts and authorities can create more problems than they solve including:

- Lack of accountability to the public.
- Inflated sense of importance.
- Undue bondholder influence.
- Fractionalization of effort among governments.
- Not necessarily nonpolitical.
- Unrepresentative boards.
- Tendency to self-perpetuate.

Following are some of the critics' arguments against special units of government.

Accountability

These authorities are not sufficiently accountable to the public for their actions. Those actions, critics say, often involve the social and economic development of the community and directly affect the people residing under the umbrella of the unit.

The reporter may find authority officials reluctant to provide any but the most superficial information. Administrative operations, particularly the financial aspects, are often difficult to obtain. Persistence, moreover, does not always pay off, and even a trip to the courts trying to force compliance may not bring results.

After the *New York Post* filed a lawsuit to inspect contract records of New York City's Triborough Bridge Authority, the court ruled that the authority did not have to provide the records or other information to the newspaper. It ruled that body "is a legal entity, separate and apart from the state which created it, and the city and counties which it serves."

But while the press was denied access, the court did suggest other avenues of accountability: New York's State Investigation Commission could investigate and audit the authority. So could the comptrollers of New York State and New York City. The authority was required to submit an annual detailed report of its operations to the governor of New York. The bank serving as trustee of the bonds for the bridge authority had the right to investigate the authority's financial operations. The bondholders themselves could investigate the authority if they desired.

There is a potential problem with "investigations" by these officeholders, because most are political animals themselves. This could not be imputed to an impartial reporter asking pertinent questions.

The result of the court ruling: The public's involvement in this authority's accountability process is peripheral only.

Critics contend that because members of authority governing boards usually are appointed, they are not as accountable to the public as officeholders who must regularly return to the electorate for a mandate. Governing board members tend to be more insulated from the public and its representatives—the press— and from parent governing bodies. In fact, some authorities are given the power to perpetuate themselves by selecting members to vacancies on the board themselves.

The function of an authority is sometimes given as the reason for refusing to make its records available for public inspection. A mental health program, set up to provide privacy to its clients, may have the concurrent effect of closing its financial operations to the press and the public. It defends its accountability to the public by pointing to independent audits that may be scrutinized by other public agencies but not by the press.

Critics argue that district officials are sometimes sloppy about their bidding process, and in fact often ignore the process.

The Ohio Building Authority chose architects for the new State Office Tower without accepting bids or formally interviewing candidates for the job, a Senate committee investigating the OBA learned Thursday.

Sen. Leon Fleischman (D-Cleveland), a member of the Transportation and Public Improvements Committee, said he saw a "grave cause for concern whether the OBA had any basis whatsoever to choose these architects."

"You've conducted no formal interviews and scheduled no meetings or discussions," Fleischman said. The Senate committee is trying to determine whether the OBA is building the facility as efficiently as a private builder would.

Lack of accountability raises potential for abuse of power by these special districts. During the past five years, reporters have investigated many of them, with the conclusions not always attractive. Jack Newfield, who researched New York public authorities in the 1980s, was harsh in his indictments:

"Public authorities are a powerful, self-perpetuating, unaccountable fourth branch of state government. Relatively obscure 'public benefit corporations' such as the Urban Development Corporation, the Dormitory Authority, the Battery Park City Authority and the State of New York Mortgage Agency have become private empires of profligate patronage. Public authorities are not responsible to the electorate in the same way that other government agencies are. They are exempt from most of the restraints on the other agencies of state government."

Answers are not always easy for the reporter to obtain, and it often involves subterfuge, such as obtaining fragmentary information from dissident employees or secondhand information from another public agency.

Inflated Sense of Importance

Many observers, including journalists, concede that these special governments possess the potential for a more efficient and businesslike approach to their functions. However, political scientist Kirk Porter complains:

"The prime evil of the special district is that it grossly decentralizes administration. It tends to exalt each little service, and tends to make those in charge lose their sense of proportion."

A Southern community, which had created an authority to capture new industry, bringing more jobs to the area and enhancing economic growth, offers an example. After months of maneuvering in secrecy, the authority announced with much fanfare that a "major outside industry" would acquire and construct facilities on prime riverfront property. The public euphoria was short-lived, however, because the "major" firm finally was identified as a cement storage plant that would employ only 17 people when the facilities were completed. And a half-dozen of those would be engineers brought in from the parent company in another state.

This poses a further problem for the reporter, who probably is privy to the information. Does he or she hold it until the deal is consummated or pass it along to the public and allow inevitable public discussion? In the case of the cement storage plant, public discussion might have been beneficial. But in other cases, the publication could be blamed if a story is published and negotiations fall through.

Critics also argue that the single-function approach of the special district can be inimical to a community's interests. Says Luther Gulick:

> "When you set up a function in a single authority, that single authority knows it was designated by God to do a certain job and its work is the most important in the world. Nothing can stand in the way of what the authority is planning to accomplish. They don't care if they bankrupt the town—they're going to get their job done because it's the only job they have to do."

A state water resources authority in Massachusetts was criticized by local contractors who charged that the authority was steering major contracts to out-of-state firms, unfairly excluding in-state companies from bidding, and depriving area workers of jobs.

For the reporter, this paper trail should be easy to follow. Bid specifications, the method of bidding and the bids themselves should be available to the press, and angry local contractors might provide excellent leads.

Journalists also cite as one of the complicating factors the ability of authorities to shift into and out of the public and private sectors whenever they wish. When a reporter asks to check their records, they are a "private" agency. When they submit an annual budget request to a parent government unit, they become a "public" agency serving the community. To deal with this ambivalent attitude, the reporter needs persistence and a knowledge of how the authority operates.

Undue Bondholder Influence

Critics say the influence of bondholders on the operation of an authority may be disproportionate to that held by other individuals and groups.

Holders of the bonds have a right to assurance they will get their money. But critics argue that their influence is not always in the public interest.

The late Robert Moses, who was chairman of the Triborough Bridge Authority, used investors as an excuse for withholding information on the authority from the press and public. Moses vigorously opposed legislation to have all records of public authorities declared public records, open to inspection by reporters at all times subject to reasonable regulations. He argued:

> "The general dissemination of information, alleged to be culled from authority files, which distorts and twists the facts in the interest of sensationalism, would erode investor confidence in authority operations."

Because they are the financiers, investors gain a pre-eminent role in the operation of an authority. Critics contend that they are a distant but useful tool that officials can use as an excuse for maintaining secrecy.

In a 1992 report to bondholders, researchers for one fund wrote that the bond market's most overburdened participants were "the smallest governmental units—the special districts." Many special districts issued bonds to build local infrastructure, counting on substantial housing growth in their areas to provide the tax base to service their bond issues. When real estate markets weakened in regions such as Texas and Colorado, development halted, and the districts were faced with an inadequate tax base to cover their obligations. Default followed in numerous cases.

Economic conditions and the condition of special districts' financial bases go hand in hand, and the reporter should monitor both regularly. A willing financial expert can help the reporter analyze the material.

Fractionalization of Effort

While more logical lines of jurisdiction are possible through special districts, critics say most of the new districts have the same boundary lines as existing governments. They point out that the lines are merely superimposed over those of traditional governments, resulting in a "disguised" government.

These superimpositions may be one reason for public ignorance of these special governments and for lack of coverage by reporters. An example of such a disguise would be a county government that decides to establish a water and sewer district to serve the unincorporated area of the county. The district would not overlap into adjacent counties or the municipalities currently in the county. It would merely be an administrative device for the county commissioners.

Creation of such special districts has resulted in awkward relationships with existing governments, and the cumulative effect may further fractionalize planning and cooperative efforts at the very time that coordination may be a major concern. Carl H. Chatters, a planning expert, argued:

> "Freezing a single function or activity into an authority may prevent the unification of all government. A careful look ahead is needed in any metropolitan area before the 'fractionating' is frozen even more thoroughly into the governmental structure."

After they studied Pennsylvania authorities, researchers Tina V. Weintraub and James D. Patterson concluded:

> "There is virtually nothing an authority can do which could not be done by a regular unit of government, except where the need exists to unify functions and services across municipal or state boundaries."

The reporter may even find that this fractionalization engenders competition among the government units involved, a far cry from cooperation. It may be merely a case of personality conflict, or it might be much more serious—a feeling by two governments that their mandate is the more important. A housing authority may be seeking federal funds for a major project, for example, and realize that another local government unit is vying for the same money.

A growth community dependent on inadequate water sources decides to pursue new avenues of supply. A municipal government sees its role as coordinating the effort, but older special districts currently supplying the water object vigorously. It is their function, they argue, to supply the water. Before the smoke has cleared, a regional water-sewer authority has entered the picture as a possible supplier, and the

town government is bickering with the older special districts over jurisdiction.

The state legislator representing the community seems unclear on the question of legal authority.

"What I'm trying to find out," she tells a reporter, "is who has any authority over the public service districts."

The directors of the special districts quickly give her an answer: Neither the municipality nor the regional water authority have any authority over the districts, which were created by state legislation.

It will take an arbitrator with uncommon ability to find a solution to this problem, much less sell it to the disputants.

Not Necessarily Nonpolitical

The boards of many special districts stress their nonpolitical composition, selling themselves to the public as incorruptible units acting only in the public interest. These units of government do offer a certain insulation between the boards and political pressures.

The quality of the insulation, however, depends on the locale. One New Jersey county established an authority to handle a single countywide function and then appointed itself as the new unit's governing body. The all-Republican board in effect established itself as another political entity.

As the reporter knows, practical politics continues to play a part in the relationships between the old and the new government units. Citizens who serve on such boards are often political amateurs. This danger was cited by Dennis O'Harrow of the American Society of Planning Officials.

O'Harrow warned that, by use of special districts or authorities, a city "exchanged one set of intelligent politicians, sensitive to the citizens' wishes, for a group of inept politicians who, because of their amateur standing, didn't give a damn about the citizens."

The policy-making board of a special district may in fact be ignorant of day-to-day affairs, meeting only occasionally to put a routine stamp of approval on actions of its administrators. *The Star-Ledger* in Newark, N.J., exposed major corruption in a sewage authority and found the governing board unaware of the problems: falsified records, double-billing, retroactive bids, misuse of county and state funds, faulty materials used in construction, phony tests and illegal payoffs.

Politics is often played at a much higher level. Elected officials have a vested interest in high-profile authorities that deal in multimillion dollar figures.

Alarmed by the Massachusetts Turnpike Authority's plans to float a new series of bonds, the governor has launched a fast-track study into ways to "privatize" the turnpike.

Top aides to the governor said Wednesday they will hire an investment banking firm to examine the feasibility of placing the semiautonomous turnpike authority's highway assets in private hands.

John Marchetti, the governor's press secretary, indicated the cash-strapped state administration has its eye on the revenues generated by the turnpike—which amounted to $161.5 million in 1991.

"Maybe those dollars could be used better in other ways," Marchetti said.

As a practical matter, the idea that creation of a semiautonomous unit of government automatically "takes it out of politics" is too disarming. Politics and special-interest pressures are much too pervasive.

Unrepresentative Boards

While many well-informed citizens sit on authority boards, research into the makeup of boards in Pennsylvania found that members did not mirror the characteristics of the people they were supposed to represent. In his research, Paul A. Pfretzchner of Lafayette College "firmly establishes that Pennsylvania authority members are thoroughly unrepresentative of their communities in terms of their age, education, income, occupation, politics and race."

A further restrictive element in adequate representation lies in the built-in requirements that some members of governing boards be selected from certain groups. Often the enabling legislation for an authority calls for appointments from structured lists: a member of a board of trade or chamber of commerce, a merchant, a banker, an industrialist with specific expertise, or even a tugboat captain in the case of a Southern port authority.

The authority in one community charged with acquiring new industry for the community listed on its governing board the managers of two of the city's biggest industries, the presidents of the gas and electric companies and two bankers representing the major financial institutions of the city. The mayor of the city served on the board—but merely ex officio. After the local press pointed out that the board appeared unrepresentative of the community, far-reaching changes were made in the composition of the authority.

Tendency to Self-Perpetuate

A final criticism of authorities is that they have a tendency to perpetuate themselves. Because of the decades necessary to retire long-term money obligations, it is difficult to fully assess this criticism.

It is a fact, however, that few authorities have gone out of business. One exception was a New Jersey city's parking authority. Board members decided they could eliminate awkward relationships with the city and save nearly $700,000 in future interest payments by dissolving themselves and turning the authority's functions over to the city. Assets were deeded to the parent government and the authority went out of business.

The tendency toward self-perpetuation is epitomized in actions of the New Jersey Highway Authority, which operates the Garden State Parkway. Its original function was to construct and maintain a toll highway. Substantial funds were generated by the users, which were plowed back into expansion of the highway. However, the authority decided to expand further by constructing a major arts center, accessible only from the toll road. Despite public controversy generated by this expansion the arts center finally became a reality.

Layers of Administration

Special districts have evolved differently in various sections of the country. Many are bound loosely to a county council or commission, area or regional government board, or even to state government itself. Consider the government units or subunits involved in the story produced by this reporter:

In many states, bridge projects are financed through bond issues and run by quasi-public bridge authorities. Other services administered by autonomous agencies are public transportation projects, water systems, utilities and airports.
Photo by Robert Patterson, courtesy of The Day, New London, Conn.

Hoping for higher Medicare funds from the state, Talcott Nursing Home administrators are seeking to lease that facility to the Talcott County Hospital Authority, officials said Friday.

The 478-bed public nursing home, which has projected a $700,000 deficit next year, could receive a financial lifeline if the authority agrees to a lease and the home is designated a "hospital-based" facility.

In researching the story, the reporter found that such a lease must first be approved by the State Health Planning and Development Agency, a state regulatory agency that reviews such proposals under federal law. The hospital authority, which oversees the County Medical Center, must also approve the agreement.

The home, now classified as free-standing, could receive an additional $1.2 million a year with the change. All of the parties to this proposal are prime sources for the reporter.

Each special district labors under different layers of decision-making bodies. For example, the Massachusetts Bay Transportation Authority, which supplies mass transit in the Boston area, is subject to an advisory board, whose approval is needed for most fare increases. The board is composed of representatives from the 78 cities and towns that make up the authority's district.

While the authority can propose a fare increase, the advisory board has the power to review and veto it. The board may ask for more details on the proposal, information that a reporter will find useful in writing about a complex fare-increase issue.

REPORTING QUESTIONABLE PRACTICES

Special districts, especially the authorities that have proliferated, are often the subject of investigations. Prestigious journalism prizes have been awarded to reporters and their newspapers for uncovering questionable practices.

The *Chicago Tribune* won a Pulitzer Prize for accounts of scandal in the Metropolitan Sanitary District of Greater Chicago, resulting in the discharge of more than 100 employees. A Pulitzer Prize for public service was awarded to the *St. Petersburg Times* in Florida for its investigation of spending by the Florida State Turnpike Authority.

The Star-Ledger detailed many abuses in a patchwork of local authorities in northern New Jersey, calling the freewheeling system of independent authorities "a jungle of confusion and red tape that has bred and fostered the mismanagement of millions of dollars of taxpayers' money."

The authorities were created profusely in the late 1970s and '80s, mainly to finance sewage treatment projects that became too expensive for municipal and county governments. One law enforcement official described the system as a "grab bag" for unscrupulous but politically well-connected administrators, lawyers, engineers and contractors, whose fees and salaries often bear little relation to their abilities and performance.

One lawyer, who admitted developing an expertise in sewer authority-related matters because it was a lucrative field, collected $500,000 in fees from sewer authorities he represents. He also collected an additional $370,000 during the same period from the municipality which he served as town attorney, doing much the same legal work that he did for the authorities.

The Star-Ledger's investigation raised further questions about the validity of superimposed government, even in such a key area as waste disposal in urban settings.

> TRENTON—The New Jersey Commission of Investigation urged the Legislature on Monday to delay passage of bills appropriating more than $200 million for local sewer projects.
>
> The commission said the funds should be withheld until legislation could be enacted to ensure that the money "won't be squandered or stolen."
>
> The recommendation came at the end of public hearings into the operation of local sewerage and utility authorities, after some witnesses detailed mismanagement and corruption in several northern New Jersey authorities.

Individual instances of wrongdoing often surface, despite the pervasive secrecy provided in authority operation, and court action is sometimes involved. Newspaper accounts of questionable activity by officials of the Port Authority of New York offer a good example:

> John Tillman, former director of public affairs for the Port Authority of New York and New Jersey, who admitted last year that he had systematically padded his expense account, was indicted Monday on criminal charges of defrauding the authority of more than $2,700.
>
> In an 80-count indictment brought by the Manhattan district attorney, Tillman, 61, was accused of grand larceny and falsifying business records. If found guilty, he could face seven years in jail.
>
> Tillman pleaded not guilty to all charges at his arraignment.

In this case, authority officials would not comment and the reporter obtained all of his information through the court. Without access to agency records, reporters must rely on law enforcement officials for information.

Tillman was suspended briefly from his job, but was reinstated as an assistant director after he repaid the Port Authority $2,619.91. He maintained that in falsifying his expenses, he was merely following the accepted practice of colleagues and predecessors. Despite this stated defense, the information is a sobering statement on the operation of such special districts.

THE ROLE OF THE REPORTER

A study of the arguments for and against these units of government indicates the complexities that the public affairs reporter faces in dealing with special districts. Because of their role as quasi-public institutions, it is more difficult to cover their activities, despite the growth of sunshine laws in many states designed to open certain meetings to the public.

Many boards are secretive about their financial condition and personnel matters. Asked for details of an authority's operation by a reporter, one administrator declined to reply except for a cryptic comment: "We simply engage in sound business practices. The public will have to trust us to do a professional job." A response such as this should only inspire a good reporter to dig further into operations that are legitimate public business.

A Midwest newspaper routinely reported the resignation of the general manager of an area transit authority. Only after police reported that the official was later hospitalized for an overdose of sleeping pills did reporters discover that the resignation was more than routine. The press finally uncovered the details of an audit of the authority's operations. After the audit, the official had been asked to repay more than $3,000 in unauthorized personal expenses, then allowed to resign his job. Many authorities tend to operate in similar secrecy.

The reporter whose beat includes these authorities should have a working knowledge of their reasons for existence, which includes how they were created—that in itself will tell a reporter much about the unit. Here are other "must" questions:

What are their powers and limitations? What checks and balances keep them accountable to the public? What are their relationships with their parent government? Whom do they employ, and how many? What are the roles and duties of the employees?

The reporter also should be aware of the means employed by the authority to keep its parent government informed of its activities, for this may be a key to important information. If it takes the form of annual reports, the reporter should maintain permanent files to compare them from year to year, researching possible changing functions in the unit or its operations that might never be publicly announced.

Because of funding requirements, audits may be regularly sought by state and federal governments. The reporter should consider these a means of monitoring the local authority. This may be particularly true of housing authorities that handle substantial federal funds.

> Open conflict has erupted between the Metropolitan Housing Authority and the U.S. Department of Housing and Urban Development over a HUD report criticizing MHA management.
>
> The report states that the MHA has too many vacant housing units and is not using its financial resources to best advantage.

The reporter obtains a copy of the audit which raises questions about the competence of MHA's property management staff, policies regarding staff travel, the use of MHA cars and executives' salaries. MHA Executive Director Stephen J. Bollinger is bitter about the report.

> "It fails to acknowledge the tremendous progress we've made here in the last two years," he said.

> When he became director two years ago, Bollinger said, MHA was more than $1.2 million in debt. When the books were closed last month, MHA was in the black by $1.1 million, Bollinger argued.

Reporters always should be trying to obtain hard-to-get information on authority operations. In this case, a reporter who had cultivated friendships with personnel inside the agency might have known earlier about the problems being encountered.

Another area that should be cultivated by the reporter is the client-agency relationship. Driving into the housing areas and talking to tenants can reveal problems that will surface later in official audits. Many of these housing developments also have active tenant organizations whose members will provide the reporter with detailed information about operations.

During the 1990s, the reporter covering local government should pay special attention to developing problems that affect special purpose districts. Although they are nearly impossible to dissolve, the districts are finding it increasingly more difficult to operate because of more stringent health standards on drinking water and sewage disposal.

Experts suggest that larger general-purpose governments can handle such standard changes more efficiently.

> The city of North Charleston, in the midst of an annexation campaign, boasts that it can provide more services at half the cost of adjacent special purpose districts.
>
> The city's annexation coordinator, Robert Holladay, predicts that the city will soon take in 20,000–30,000 residents.
>
> That would make North Charleston the largest incorporated city in South Carolina—about 107,000 residents, he said.

In cases such as these, the reporter should study the sources of financing for both the district and the adjacent city, comparing costs for the taxpayers. While scenarios such as these are being played out in a community, the reporter also should watch for parallel developments in the state Legislature. Despite legislators' protests that these special districts "run their own show," many legislators may have a closer relationship to the districts than they profess.

Authority sources often dry up in proportion to lack of contact with officials. Many officials would prefer that reporters busy themselves on other beats, far removed from their activities.

Reporters should keep their superiors informed about the problems of covering such secretive units of government. Authority officials usually respect power, and if they know the editor or news director is especially interested in the district's operations, they can be more likely to open doors to reporters.

Whatever their amateur or professional status, officials often play pressure politics in attempting to operate by their own rules. It is the job of the public affairs reporter to assure that those officials play by the public's rules.

Becoming Familiar with Special Districts

Some research is necessary to learn more about these units of government. Here are some suggestions:

1. Identify the authorities or special districts in the community and study them to determine their functions and methods of operation. Study their enabling legislation.

2. Compile all documents available on the units, including any organization charts, mailing brochures and other published information.

3. Determine how (if at all) the units are accountable to the public, fiscally or otherwise. What accountability to or relationships do they have with other governmental bodies? Interview officials of the "parent" government for their perceptions of the relationship.

4. Conduct a survey of citizens in the community, asking questions that will help determine their awareness or knowledge of these special units of government.

5. Identify the sources of funding. Ask for budgets or other documents, and identify outside agencies or auditing bodies that scrutinize their affairs.

6. Determine whether other governmental agencies offer similar services, and ask officials of other political units what they think of the special governments in question.

***

SUGGESTED READINGS

Caro, Robert A. *The Power Broker*. New York: Knopf, 1974.

Chapter 28, "The Warp on the Loom," and Chapter 43, "Late Arrival," offer insight into the operations of special district government in a metropolitan area.

Walsh, Annmarie Hauck. *The Public's Business*. Cambridge, Mass.: MIT Press, 1980.

Chapter 12, "Reappraisal," should have special interest for the beginning reporter.

Chapter 8

Reporting at the Federal Level

The word is out, and the newsroom of the Midwest newspaper is rampant with speculation. There's an opening on the staff of the Washington bureau.

Who's going to get the job?

Thousands of young journalists cherish a secret ambition to cover the nation's capital, asking probing questions at presidential news conferences, interviewing powerful and charismatic figures in congressional cloakrooms, and poring over federal documents to break the "big story" that shocks the nation.

It is only a dream for most. Only a small percentage of those thousands of print and broadcast reporters will ever be stationed in Washington to report on the vast bureaucracy on the Potomac River.

However, most of those reporters will find solace in another important fact: Most of them working at the local level will regularly cross countless thresholds of federal offices to dig out stories with a "federal" angle as genuine as the Washington article. More than that, they can rest assured that their news coverage equals the importance of their more visible counterparts in the nation's capital. For instance:

- The Commerce Department's decision to sharply restrict imports of foreign-produced automobiles will affect a Midwest city's job market, which has been weakening for many months. The decision will affect other economic segments of the community. The roundup story belongs to the reporter at the local level.

- A major local industry, whose efforts to cut pollution along the region's major river have not proved entirely successful, is directed by the U.S. Environmental Protection Agency to place a timetable on its efforts. A local reporter with the right contacts will be the likely recipient of this news break.

- The White House has proposed a new cutback in funding for a federally assisted summer work program in urban communities. The home folks must find alternate solutions for funding, and the local reporter will tie the story together.

However, stories like these will fall not to the reporter who merely observes the routine, but to the one who knows the various federal agencies, their responsibilities and their potential effect on the local community.

AT THE LOCAL LEVEL

Before attempting to cover the federal beat at the local level, reporters should answer three basic questions:

- **What agency am I looking for?**   The reporter is always probing for the federal angle. If it is a transportation development, how will the federal government be involved? Perhaps there is a discussion of funding for a regional mass transit system. A basic reassessment of the city's postal facilities? Will federal officials inform local government leaders? Will

rehabilitation of the local jail facilities involve federal assistance?

- **Where do I go for the answers?**   Questions like these demand good answers. Many of them will be developed in the local offices of federal agencies. How will new Social Security Administration regulations affect retired people in the city? The agency maintains offices in most communities, and its employees are alert to new federal initiatives involving the elderly and disabled. Who has the answers to how the new jobs program will work? Many important federal agencies staff only regional offices, and the reporter also should be familiar with them.

- **Who do I see for the answers?**   The clerk in a local federal office may be able to answer one question for the reporter but refer others to a superior. One of the first stops on the road to a federally related story may be the local office, but the reporter should be prepared to be sent elsewhere. The Agriculture Department maintains a local office, but its staff may refer policy questions to other officials. The reporter should remember that there is always a "higher-up" to whom he or she can turn for more decisive responses. The nation's capital is as close as the reporter's telephone.

The reporter's route to the answers, however, is not always direct. Responsibility for many new federal programs is constantly changing—because of action by Congress and the executive branch. Administration of the water pollution program over the years is one example.

In 1965, the Federal Water Pollution Control Administration answered to the secretary of health, education and welfare. A year later the agency was transferred to the Department of the Interior. In 1970, the pollution designation was dropped from the name, and the agency became the Water Quality Administration. Soon after that, the entire agency was abolished by a federal reorganization, and its functions were transferred to the EPA. It is now under the direction of the assistant administrator for water and waste management. Not every federal enforcement program undergoes this kind of metamorphosis, but enough of them do to make coverage more complex for the reporter.

Where to Go

The indispensable element in collecting accurate and useful information from the federal bureaucracy is knowing where to begin. No freedom of information act can help a reporter who is knocking at the wrong door. The simple quiz in Box 8–1 will prove instructive. Choose the answer you believe to be correct, then read on to determine whether you have the answer.

The reporter whose beat includes any of hundreds of such diverse federal angles will discover that talking to the right official in the right department can save much time and effort, particularly on deadline. Whether plotting a course to get federal reaction to a local airplane crash or checking a report that tobacco subsidies are being adjusted sharply downward, the reporter's goal is the same—getting to the source quickly and efficiently.

The reporter should acquire a sense of the kinds of questions that probably can be answered at the local level, as well as those that probably will be "bucked up" to the district or regional office.

The list of federal offices in a community depends on its size, location and the characteristics of the people who live there. A river port in the Midwest will house an extensive Coast Guard operation, directed by a captain of the port. A knowledge of the agency's functions is important, both for routine coverage and in case of emergencies on the river or in the port.

The duties of the Coast Guard touch several beats: It engages in search-and-rescue operations on navigable waters of the United States (police reporter); maintains aids to navigation (outdoors editor); enforces rules involving use of ports within its jurisdiction (financial reporter); supervises loading and unloading of dangerous cargo (labor or environmental reporter); operates a program of prevention, detection and control of pollution in all navigable waters (environmental reporter); and operates boating safety programs (education writer).

In nonriver communities, other agencies might be more visible. A city in the Sun Belt with many elderly retirees provides more extensive services from the Department of Health and Human Services or the Social Security Administration. A Farm Belt city's Agriculture Department offices are more extensive than most other federal agency offices in that region, and a metropolitan area is the focus of offices for the Department of Housing and Urban Development.

THE LONG FEDERAL ARM

Signs of the federal hierarchy are everywhere. Cities of any size include a basic complex of federal offices, many of them a regular source of information for the press. A nearby airport facility is almost certain to include offices of the National Weather Service, for example.

The independent U.S. Postal Service handles more than 100 billion pieces of mail a year nationwide, a portion of that eagerly awaited by thousands in the reporter's hometown each day. The postmaster and subordinates are a source of local news—new postal regulations, changes in routes and in type of service, issuance of new stamps and even registration of aliens in the United States.

The Internal Revenue Service, the tax-collecting arm of the Treasury Department, is visible at all levels. The decentralized nature of the agency allows reporters access to much information of public interest. Collection of income taxes, only a part of the IRS responsibilities, and general information on audits create interesting news stories. Statistical information is also available on filing of returns and refunds. Federal wagering stamps are sold by the IRS, and professional gamblers can be identified through agency records.

Nearly every action taken in Washington invites reaction at the local level, but only alert reporters who follow the daily flow of national news and who can translate it quickly into questions will generate a worthwhile local news story. The opportunities are endless:

- Congress takes action on a program to improve counseling services for veterans of the Vietnam War. At the local level, the reporter can discuss the changes with officials at the Veterans Health Administration, who explain how counseling is

BOX 8–1

Quiz

✳ ✳ ✳

1. The U.S. Botanic Gardens' purpose is to collect and cultivate various vegetable productions for exhibit and study. Who supervises the Botanic Gardens?

   a. Commerce Department
   b. Agriculture Department
   c. The Congress
   d. Interior Department
   e. It is independent

2. Who oversees the Government Printing Office, which prints all government documents?

   a. Treasury Department
   b. The Congress
   c. Commerce Department
   d. Interior Department
   e. The executive branch

3. The Forest Service manages federal forest reserves throughout the United States. To whom does it answer?

   a. Bureau of Land Management
   b. Commerce Department
   c. Agriculture Department
   d. Interior Department
   e. None of these

4. To whom does the U.S. Court of Military Appeals answer?

   a. Supreme Court
   b. Administrative Office of the U.S. Courts
   c. Defense Department
   d. Department of the Army
   e. It is independent

5. The Federal Aviation Administration is charged with regulating air commerce to foster aviation safety. Under whose jurisdiction does it lie?

   a. National Transportation Safety Board
   b. Commerce Department
   c. Department of Transportation
   d. Interstate Commerce Commission
   e. It is independent

ANSWERS:

1. The Botanic Gardens, founded in 1820, is under the control of the Joint Committee of Congress on the Library, which funds it directly from congressional appropriations. Garden officials usually can answer any question about a rare, unidentified plant specimen, whatever the region.

2. The Government Printing Office is controlled by the Congress and executes orders for printing and binding for all establishments of the federal government.

3. The Forest Service is under the jurisdiction of the Agriculture Department, since being transferred there from the Interior Department in 1905. Sources for a news story on the spread of a tree parasite through a region would include the field office for the Forest Service.

4. The U.S. Court of Military Appeals is judicially independent, although it operates administratively out of the Defense Department. Problems at a nearby military installation which lead to disciplinary action might conclude with a need for a reporter to contact the appeals court clerk in Washington.

5. The Federal Aviation Administration, formerly an independent agency, became a part of the Department of Transportation in 1967. In researching a story on the air controllers who operate the city's flight control towers, the reporter's path might lead to the regional office of the FAA.

handled locally and how the changes might affect older veterans.

- The Department of Energy wants to create information centers in cities around the country. Who will staff them? What information will they provide? How soon will they open?

Many federal offices at the local level do not publicize their activities, so reporters should check in regularly to collect information that might become a significant news story. Decisions of the Labor Department's Wage and Hour Division may affect dozens of local businesses and industries, and the reporter might have to make personal contact to obtain the information.

> Six area industries have been ordered to revise their application to minimum wage regulations, and 11 others are under investigation for similar problems, the local office of the Labor Department's Wage and Hour Division reported yesterday.

Not every local federal office has the same news value. Some agencies empower their offices to release substantial quantities of useful information to the public, others authorize little.

The Legislative Branch at Work

The long arm of the federal government reaches into each community in many ways. The legislative branch initiates hundreds of measures during each session that affect various segments of the community. A typical session of Congress might result in stories like these:

- Authorization for a pilot project for a new mineral extraction process near a community can create an instant business boom.
- More funds can be provided for the needy through a new program aimed at community block development.
- A new foreign trade program, which includes duty-free ports of entry, can affect the economy of an entire region.

Such information is often visible because of the national news media's interest in it, requiring only an enterprising reporter to come up with local angles. However, other developments of purely local interest

may be buried in catch-all legislation, stagnating for months in agency offices until an official acts to implement a particular project.

A $5 million grant allowing a city to extend sewer service to an adjacent area will create new jobs, additional housing and the potential for new industrial development, yet the enabling legislation may have been approved by Congress several years before. Responsibility for applying for the funds lies in the hands of local officials; informing the public that the funds are available is up to the reporter.

The Congressional Representative as a Source

The congressman answered the phone himself. After the usual pleasantries, he got down to business. Yes, he told the reporter calling from one of the cities in his district, he had heard that federal funding for the health services facility was in danger. Clearing his throat, the representative expounded:

"The battle has just begun to save that facility. I don't care what the other problems are. The people of this district are my first priority."

It's a quotable quote and certainly part of the story the reporter was pursuing. But it was not the entire story, and that is the key to the reporter's relationship with his or her congressional delegation.

As a practical matter, the pivotal offices in the nation's capital for many such stories are occupied by the state's senators and congressional members. Officials of federal agencies have learned to allow representatives and senators the privilege of formally announcing programs and decisions that enhance a political image. Particularly during election years, the announcements will come with a flourish.

- New medical facilities, including a psychiatric wing, have been approved for the veterans hospital in the district, and the representative for the district duly announces details, sketchy though they may be.
- An $8.9 million contract to renovate 333 family housing units at the local Air Force installation has been awarded, and the senator representing the state makes the announcement. Left unsaid for the moment is the implication that the base would not be closing for the time being. Other officials confirmed that important information.

• The Office of Personnel Management, formerly the Civil Service Commission, is planning a new job-information service, with a full-time office staff in the city, and the representative's office leads with the announcement.

• A federal committee is planning a fact-finding agricultural tour to assess the district's potential, and the representative hurries to make the announcement.

Meanwhile, the same federal officials learn to make the "problem" announcement themselves when it is necessary, such as plans to close a postal facility, trim the personnel of a nearby Army installation, or cut funds for agricultural research in the area.

Elected officials are jealous of their prerogatives and often put pressure on agencies to give endangered projects another look. Part of the strategy may include a visible news story.

While the congressional news conference announcing such matters is inescapable, agencies themselves often provide more detail than is found in the news release handed out by the representative's office. The political figure often seeks only visibility; the reporter seeks details of an important decision affecting the community.

This is not to suggest that a close relationship between the members of Congress and the reporter on the federal beat is not desirable. The representative's office is usually the first to know about developments affecting the reporter's community, and close ties with that office are useful. The reporter can put the informational expertise of the elected official and his or her staff to good use, and usually the office is eager to help.

WASHINGTON—Family farmers say the Agriculture Department is inflating its estimates of net farm worth to hide economic troubles in rural America.

USDA's estimates of net farm income—historically a barometer of financial health in the countryside—are in the billions of dollars each year.

But Internal Revenue Service figures show total taxable farm income amounts to be merely a fraction of USDA's count.

This story was triggered by Sen. Bob Kerrey (D-Neb.) who provided the preliminary figures needed by the reporter to pursue the story. In 1988, the Agriculture Department estimated net farm income at nearly $42 billion. IRS figures showed total taxable farm income from individuals, partnerships and corporations totaled $527 million that year.

As a result of the discrepancy, the General Accounting Office, the congressional watchdog agency, launched an investigation. Such stories often develop in congressional offices.

A spending program moving ponderously through Congress may contain items targeted for the reporter's territory, and the representative's office will be more aware of it than anyone else.

Sometimes it may be in the best interests of the representative to avoid spotlighting a proposal, and in this case the reporter needs the eyes and ears of competent Washington associates or wire services.

WASHINGTON—The Senate wants to use $229 million in defense spending for programs designed to help people and communities hurt by the shrinking Pentagon budget.

The bill is loaded with spending for lawmakers' home districts, including $672,000 for management of small estuaries in South Carolina—home state of Democratic Sen. Ernest Hollings, who chairs the Appropriations subcommittee that wrote the bill.

This information was generated from several sources, and constitutes only the first of many stories at the local level. The reporter's strategy should be to develop important news stories through good contacts and then by digging beyond the brief references to important issues.

THE FEDERAL STRUCTURE

To even categorize, much less fully cover, the vast bureaucracy that is the federal establishment is a Herculean task. To make sense out of the maze of offices, duties, relationships and often conflicting functions, the reporter must begin with guidelines that will help him or her sort out the information to be sought.

These guidelines can help the reporter fight the natural tendency to allow the bureaucracy to set the agenda instead of the reverse. The reporter is seeking *useful* information; officials are not always interested

BOX 8–2

Letting the 'Strings' Work for You

✳ ✳ ✳

Washington has many "strings" to the reporter's hometown. By monitoring the strings that tie local government to the federal establishment, the reporter often can obtain both ends of a story rather than merely one end.

The federal government has $3.1 million to loan, and Mayor William L. Anderson said he wants the city to apply.

"The money is there for the asking," Anderson said.

However, R.J. Gibson, regional service officer for the Department of Housing and Urban Development, said the city will be competing with agencies from nine other counties for the funds, which must be used to construct 200 units of multi-family housing.

Federal grants are also available to many non-profit organizations in a community, some of them specifically to implement federally funded projects. Identification of these organizations is essential to effectively cover the federal-local spectrum.

The Southern Community Action Council has been awarded a grant for $317,000 for a major new program to help preschool children acquire basic skills.

Funds will be provided to the private agency by the Department of Health and Human Services, Council Director Jane Bevin said yesterday.

The project, which will be conducted with help from the Board of Education, "will provide continuity in programming basic skills as children move from development centers to the elementary school classrooms," Bevin said.

Whether the reporter who handled the original story follows up the program or leaves it to the education reporter, a later assessment of the value of the project is also important. Follow-up stories are all too often ignored in favor of new projects.

While federal grants generally focus on education, health, housing and employment, other fields receive funding, too. Arts centers receive funds for cultural purposes, and historic preservation has become an important federal item.

in that criterion, preferring instead to promote successful projects and ignore problem areas. In setting his or her own agenda for coverage, the reporter should ask these basic questions:

• What agencies, programs and developments among the thousands affect the most people in the community, and why?

• Which are considered important in terms of public policy?

• Is the information of interest to the public, and in what way?

• Are major changes being effected, new programs being developed or new facilities being added?

• Are the federal programs that are constantly being developed in the community working?

Armed with answers to these questions, the reporter is in a better position to set an agenda for coverage more closely attuned to the needs of readers. The place to begin is with the composition and functions of the departments and agencies.

With a few major exceptions, the basic departments of the executive branch have remained unchanged. The traditional departments at the Cabinet level are Agriculture, Commerce, Defense, Housing and Urban Development, Interior, Justice, Labor, State, Transportation and Treasury. Two Cabinet departments were created out of the Department of Health,

Education & Welfare—Health & Human Services and Education. Newer departments include Energy and Veterans Affairs.

Every reporter should have the most recent edition of the *U.S. Government Manual*, which offers specific information and easy access to location and personnel of all government departments and agencies. The 920-page manual, available in paperback from the Superintendent of Documents, provides superior references by subject, agency and personnel identification. The reporter quickly can determine the functions of an agency, location of regional offices, sources of information and even telephone numbers to obtain specific public information. Included are detailed listings of the executive, legislative and judicial branches.

These are some of the departments with which the local reporter should be familiar in covering the federal beat.

Department of Agriculture

No industry in the United States has a greater effect on people than agriculture. Its economic status and collective problems are a constant source of news.

Whether the reporter's beat encompasses a Farm Belt community or an Eastern metropolitan city dependent upon a constant supply of produce, there is news in "agriculture." Preceding the first planting, through the growing process and the harvesting, and on through marketing, the Department of Agriculture coordinates programs to assure stability and a constant food supply.

With the objective of aiding the producer and coordinating the complex process of putting food on the table for 250 million people, the department operates worldwide.

Research, education and conservation are carried on through the Agricultural Research Service, which provides information to help farmers produce efficiently while conserving the environment.

An office found in nearly every county is the Extension Service, the education agency of the Agriculture Department. Area and county agents work with individuals and groups in supplying the technology for effective agricultural production. The service has been broadened in recent years to include home economics and nutrition for its primary audience—nonmetropolitan families.

A national soil and water conservation program is carried out through the Soil Conservation Service, another agency that operates in nearly every county. Cooperating with landowner, land user and developer, the service offers technical assistance to more than 3,000 conservation districts, developing watershed projects and flood control plans.

At planting time, the Farmers Home Administration provides financial credit to rural Americans, and is a good source of statistical information. However, as already noted, reporters must be on the lookout for changes in the mission of any agency.

> Setting up a new government agency is a big enough headache without having to worry about the aftereffects of Hurricane Andrew.
>
> That's the position William Ball finds himself in as newly appointed regional director of the Rural Development Administration.
>
> The RDA, a division of the U.S. Agriculture Department, was created to handle many of the federal grant programs formerly handled by the Farmers Home Administration.

A good share of the federal loans arising out of such natural disasters as hurricanes will be handled by the new agency. The reporter will want to find out the ability of the agency to make loans for community projects, such as courthouses, schools, water and sewer systems, and even for private industry projects.

Other agencies within the department offer different assistance. The Rural Electrification Administration helps finance electric and telephone service; the Rural Development Service coordinates a program with emphasis on community development.

In efforts to stabilize food production and coordinate it with demand, the Agricultural Stabilization and Conservation Service administers programs for wheat, corn, cotton, peanuts, rice, tobacco, sugar, milk and other products grown in every area of the country. Often little noticed, this "coordination" affects the prices that consumers pay.

A drop in price supports for a major commodity can create powerful and emotional copy for the reporter. Nothing is closer to the farmer's pocketbook than federal assistance that stabilizes the agricultural economy. The Commodity Credit Corporation administers the federal government's price support policies, purchasing excess production and disposing of it through domestic and international sales. The Federal Crop Insurance Corporation provides crop insurance against loss from unavoidable causes, such as weather, insects and disease.

Assistance in marketing of farm products comes from the Agricultural Marketing Service, which offers current, unbiased market information to producers, processors, distributors and consumers to assure orderly marketing of products. The service establishes grade standards for produce and administers regulatory programs. Changes in these standards often are newsworthy, both to farmers and consumers.

The Food and Nutrition Service administers federal food assistance programs, including the Food Stamp Program and the National School Lunch Program. Both these areas are high on the list of newsworthy topics, because millions of recipients are involved. The strengths and weaknesses of both programs have been widely publicized, and they continue to provoke broad public response. The reporter, whether in an urban or rural setting, should monitor them closely.

An education reporter seeking statistics on nutritive value of cafeteria food might find answers in the Human Nutritional Information Service, which conducts research in human nutrition and the nutritional adequacy of diets.

Another important agency is the Forest Service, an unlikely Agriculture Department offspring, which manages federal forest reserves. The service administers 155 national forests and 19 additional grasslands in 41 states and cooperates with state and local governments in protection, reforestation and utilization of forests. Sale of timber to private interests has been an important nationwide issue in recent years.

Another little noticed board is the World Agricultural Outlook Board that coordinates development of all commodity and agricultural forecasts issued by the Agriculture Department. The board, in concert with the National Oceanic and Atmospheric Administration,

continually monitors world weather and assesses its effects on agriculture.

Department of Commerce

"Everybody talks about the weather but nobody does anything about it."

This remains fairly accurate, but the editorialist who penned these words in the *The Hartford Courant* in 1897 could not imagine the growth of weather reporting during the next 100 years, or the sophisticated methods it has developed. Satellite systems now monitor weather conditions around the world, and the reporter has technology at his or her fingertips to provide slices of the weather—past, present and future.

The National Weather Service is only one of the missions of the National Oceanic and Atmospheric Administration, probably the most visible. But there are others.

The NOAA explores, maps and charts the oceans of the globe, and manages and conserves them. It is also charged with assessing the consequences of inadvertent environmental changes, and disseminates long-term environmental information. The NOAA also operates a national environmental satellite system.

The Commerce Department's mission, however, is more far-reaching. It promotes the nation's economic development and technological advancement through its nearly 40,000 employees. The department approaches its role in several ways—through business development and links with other nations; the Maritime Administration, which oversees the merchant fleet; an Office of Minority Business Enterprise, which aids ethnic minorities throughout the nation; U.S. Travel Service, which stimulates travel to other countries; the National Bureau of Standards, which sets weights and measurements; and an Office of Telecommunications, which develops new systems and services for communication.

The department is continually expanding. Recent additions to its responsibilities include a Fire Prevention and Control Administration, whose function is to reduce loss of life and property through improved fire prevention procedures.

At the local level, the Economic Development Administration aids areas with severe unemployment and low-income problems. The EDA cooperates with local governments to provide employment opportunities by financing needed public projects.

> A $3.7 million grant from the Economic Development Administration will enable the city to proceed with plans for an expanded sewage treatment plant in the south end.
>
> The city's share of the project will bring the total cost to about $5.5 million, Mayor Miriam Potter said yesterday.

The "whys" of such actions are also important to the reporter, and a call to an official of the federal agency will often disclose the reasoning behind the awarding of substantial grants to cities.

> An unemployment rate of nearly 10 percent, caused by plant closings, was a significant factor in the Economic Development Administration's decision to grant funds to expand the city's sewage treatment facilities.
>
> The effect, according to R.C. Hobbs, regional director, will be to add construction jobs over a one-year period. He cited other factors that led to the EDA decision:
>
> • Surveys by the EDA indicated continuing economic problems in the region.
> • Average income per household in the city had dropped substantially during the past 24 months.
>
> "The need for infusion of new jobs, even on a temporary basis, was implicit in these statistics," Hobbs said.

Another visible reminder of the Commerce Department is its practice of collecting a vast amount of social and economic data every 10 years. The Bureau of Census is the center for collection, compilation and analysis of a broad range of information, most of it available to the news media. A section devoted to using census statistics is included later in this chapter.

Department of Defense

Few federal departments are as all-encompassing at the local level as the Department of Defense. Military installations and their importance to the economic well-being of the communities in which they are located create a regular and potent news source.

While the reporter should be alert to major developments in the secretary of defense's office in the Pentagon, subsidiary departments of this giant umbrella agency are more often the sources of information—the Air Force, Army, Navy and Marine Corps. Whatever the installation, the reporter should be familiar with the chain of command, the exact nature of the units at the base, and the public information officers and their availability.

Movement of personnel, shifts in housing practices, changes in purchasing procedures and other military activities can affect an entire region. The reporter who is sensitive to such changes and to the effect of the military units will find this beat a gold mine of information.

Reduction of the military after the end of the Cold War has added a new dimension to defense coverage. Base closings and transfers have created a near logjam of continuing stories.

> MYRTLE BEACH, S.C.—A battle is brewing between Myrtle Beach and Horry County over how to develop the Myrtle Beach Air Force Base after it closes next year.
>
> "There is bound to be some blood-letting before it is all over," City Councilman Harry Charles said.

Such disputes are far more frequent with the base closures of the 1990s. The Myrtle Beach base is inside the city limits, but the county operates a commercial jetport on 170 acres of land leased from the federal government. When the base closed, the county had to pick up the costs of operating the runway, the air traffic tower and a fire station. The city wanted the golf course, fire station and radar building.

A redevelopment group studying the base closing complicated the issue—and added other sources for the reporter.

Shifts of personnel from reduced bases are also a continuing story. Moving a 400-person maintenance unit from a Southern air force base to the Midwest would cost the community 200 civilian jobs with an annual payroll of more than $3 million a year. The Chamber of Commerce supplied the figures but Defense Department officials in Washington confirmed them.

Political officeholders are finely tuned to developments affecting their constituents, and news regarding

Employees of a U.S. Navy submarine base in Connecticut protest the Defense Department's plan to "downsize" the installation and eliminate jobs. Across the country, the effect of base closings and other military spending cuts are important local topics.

Photo by Gordon Alexander, courtesy of The Day, New London, Conn.

military installations in their districts frequently receive an initial airing through a congressional office. Reporters usually can count on a good quote or two from these sources.

Sometimes other agencies will be involved in military affairs and trigger news developments. The General Accounting Office, the investigative arm of Congress, might question the need to continue commissary activities at an Air Force base that is closing. Military officials, backed by pressure from retired service personnel in the area, may seek to continue the commissary, which is subsidized by federal taxes.

The reporter covering the proposed closing of Chanute Air Force Base in Rantoul, Ill. used Washington as well as local sources to confirm that Maharishi International University, an arm of the Transcendental Meditation Movement, had applied to the Pentagon to turn the 2,500-acre base into a university and conference center.

The director of the Air Force Base Disposal Agency said he must consider "all reasonable alternatives for reuse of the base." City officials were concerned that

the new owner, as an educational institution, would not have to pay property taxes.

Pentagon military cuts also are heavily affecting civilians. The Scripps Howard News Service found that those left behind after a base closing or reduction are forced to scrounge for jobs in an often-devastated economy.

> At Portsmouth Naval Shipyard in New Hampshire, the employment level is being slashed from 9,000 workers in 1985 to 5,500 by 1994. And there is no guarantee that reductions will stop there.
>
> Five miles away, the area's only other major employer, Pease Air Force Base, has been closed completely, putting hundreds more civilians out of work.

Reporters must ask military and community officials specific questions to round out stories like these. What are employment figures, state by state and community by community? What benefits are being offered to civilian workers, and to military personnel? What systems have been set up to help civilians and military find new jobs? What steps are being taken to retrain laid-off personnel? How have the cuts affected the recruiting process? (Although recruiting has been cut to its lowest level in many years, 200,700 new enlistees and 19,000 new officers enter the services each year.)

A close relationship with public information officers on military installations in the area is helpful to the reporter covering this beat, but the reporter is again forewarned: Many gaps in stories may have to be filled by calling on officials at higher levels.

An Air Force information officer may be able to quickly connect a reporter to fighter pilots who are awaiting assignments, but the statistics may have to come from other levels.

SUMTER—The smell of jet fuel and the sight of cottony clouds on the horizon should be bringing out the gung-ho fighter jock in 1st. Lt. John Adams.

Instead, his surroundings at Shaw Air Force Base brings on a touch of melancholy.

That's because the Air Force has a lot more pilots than planes, forcing qualified officers to sit on the sidelines. For Adams, a 1991 Air Force Academy graduate, it could be two years before he gets a chance to fly his own jet.

To get the statistics on the pilot backlog, the reporter moves up the ladder to the Pentagon. The Air Force, officials explain, is shrinking from 36 "wings" of 72 planes each to only $26\frac{1}{2}$ wings, creating a logjam for officers in one of the military's most glamorous occupations.

The Air Force also said it is cutting by two-thirds the number of graduates it sends to pilot training— from 600 to 800 a year to 225. So while the reporter focuses on Lt. Adams, the larger picture is sketched through the statistics provided by Defense Department planners. An important military story with national implications is localized through this process.

An often overlooked military area are the reserve units scattered around the country. Their size and visibility dictate considerable general interest, and often stories emerge from their activities, including activation and deactivation of units, training programs and maneuvers, and personnel changes.

Reduction of the military also has affected these reserves, as well as National Guard units. The story may begin at the local level, but quickly can reach into state and federal offices.

Soldiers from a National Guard artillery unit headquartered in Moline have been using weekend drill time to lobby against proposed Pentagon cuts in Guard strength.

The soldiers, attached to the 3rd Battalion of the 78th Field Artillery unit, gathered signatures on petitions opposing cutbacks during weekend drills in May.

The petition drive was part of a nationwide effort by Guard commanders to ensure that National Guard strength is not cut below 420,000 troops. The Pentagon had proposed cutting forces to well below 400,000.

One of the battalion's officers told the reporter the local unit's activity was acceptable conduct.

"All the states are doing this, some on drill time," Sgt. John Lawford of the 78th said. "All of us are concerned over the cuts."

But the Center for Defense Information, a military watchdog agency in Washington, D.C., told the reporter that on-duty politicking violates unwritten rules of military conduct. Before the story was completed, Pentagon sources and major Guard figures had been pulled into the issue.

The reporter should not overlook the recruiting offices operated by the military in cities across the country. They can provide periodic statistics on enlistment and sometimes offer social implications of military changes.

The Corps of Engineers

Another major source of news is the Army Corps of Engineers, a traditional part of the military structure. Functioning under the Department of the Army, the corps maintains offices in many cities along rivers, the ocean coasts and lakes.

As a military agency, the corps plans and carries out construction and maintenance of military facilities, such as harbor and waterway work. But the civilian activities of the corps are an important part of community growth and activity.

An indication of the magnitude of the agency's functions, and its importance to the federal beat reporter, can be seen in the U.S. Government Manual's delineation of its duties:

"These (engineering) works provide flood protection for cities and major river valleys, reduce the cost of transportation, supply water for municipal and industrial use, generate hydroelectric power, provide recreational activities for vast numbers of people, regulate the rivers for many purposes, improve water quality, protect the shores of oceans and lakes, and provide other types of benefits."

The corps also provides planning assistance to states and other nonfederal entities for comprehensive management of water resources, including pollution abatement.

Activities of the corps affect water transportation, the economic character of the communities along the waterways, and even the lives of residents. For example, the complex of locks and dams that enable giant barges to move smoothly along the nation's rivers directly influences nearby communities.

> New high-lift dams along the Ohio River are creating major soil erosion problems for hundreds of farmers and homeowners whose land abuts the river bank, a private agency charges.
>
>   In a 26-page memorandum to the Corps of Engineers, the Taxpayers Council details specific instances of acreage being lost to the river because of channel changes along a 120-mile stretch of the waterway.

A reporter must contact many sources in pursuit of this story: the affected farmers and homeowners, the corps itself, county agricultural agents, local tax officials whose books are being affected by the loss of property, and legislators whose constituency includes both the landowners and the barge operators who are benefiting from the high-level dams. Geological experts will also be useful.

Dams also provide recreation and enhance the potential for tourism in an area. Relationships between the Corps of Engineers and local government units become important when each shares in funding a complex that will encompass elements of protection and recreation.

> The State Parks Commission and the Army Corps of Engineers have reached agreement on financing the new Mill Run Dam recreation project, which will cost about $38 million when it is completed next year.
>
>   Access roads and boat ramps to the 17-square-mile lake will be provided by the federal government. A 300-

site camping area and public facilities to accommodate the thousands of visitors will be financed by the state.

District offices of the corps are excellent sources of information on continuing flood prevention activities. One of the major issues of the 1990s is protection of U.S. wetlands, a current function of the Corps of Engineers. The reporter will find many different voices speaking on the same issue.

In 1992, a wire service reporter obtained documents summarizing proposed changes in definition of the term *wetlands*, and various federal agencies have analyzed them.

> WASHINGTON—Government wetlands experts have concluded that the administration's redefinition of the term is unworkable, unscientific and would leave "many obvious wetlands" unprotected.

The analyses reflected the views of experts at the Corps, the Environmental Protection Agency and the Fish and Wildlife Service. The reporter should be aware of the many agencies that play a part in resolving such issues.

In widening a U.S. highway, for example, a state agency might oversee part of the adjacent tidal waters. However, the Corps of Engineers might have jurisdiction over the major part of the land.

> Officials inspected the wetland area near the Johns Island Airport yesterday, to determine which agencies have jurisdiction over the proposed site for a new runway.
>
>   After conducting a field analysis, permit biologist James Dowling said 10 percent of the land is tidal wetland and subject to state Coastal Council jurisdiction.
>
>   The remaining 90 percent of the 20 acres falls under the U.S. Army Corps of Engineers, he said. That means decision-making for the bulk of the project would be handled by the corps.

The reporter should monitor all new responsibilities that fall to various federal agencies because of their inevitable local connections.

Department of Energy

A major reorganization of agencies in 1977 placed many energy-related offices under the Cabinet-level Department of Energy.

The department consolidated the major federal energy offices, including the Energy Research and Development Administration, the Federal Energy Administration and the Federal Power Commission. Also transferred were some functions previously handled by other departments. The department today encompasses issues that involve environmental, business, safety and other concerns.

One of the most important—and visible—is the Office of Environmental Restoration and Waste Management. The office manages the assessment and cleanup of inactive waste sites and facilities, helps ensure safe and effective waste management operations, and funds programs to find permanent disposal solutions.

A spill of highly radioactive tritium into the Savannah River late in 1991 triggered many stories about its effects on two states. The spill, affecting communities more than 100 miles downstream, came as the Energy Department sought to reopen the Savannah River Site, a major producer of nuclear materials.

> The Savannah River Site's answer for immobilizing 34 million gallons of intensely radioactive waste is beset by technical problems, poor management and overruns that nearly doubled its $1.2 billion cost, a congressional study has found.
>
> A 62-page report released Friday by the General Accounting Office stated that the cleanup is five years behind schedule.
>
> Energy Department officials originally estimated the complex operation would begin treating waste by 1989. The department now expects to begin in 1994.

The GAO faulted the Energy Department. "Much of the cost growth and schedule slippages resulted from ineffective management."

Reporters covering the issue used local sources as well as those at the Washington level. The department owns the nuclear facility and Westinghouse Co. operates it. The GAO spread the blame for the spill equally between the government agency and the private contractor, and its political and environmental repercussions will last for years.

Grants are also awarded to states and local government for energy conservation projects and safety programs. As with other agencies, the department provides an inspector general to monitor such projects.

> NASHVILLE, Tenn.—A federal audit has questioned the propriety of nearly $3 million in grants approved by the governor's office and intended to promote energy conservation and fuel efficiency.
>
> The audit, conducted by the Energy Department's inspector general, said three grants totaling $1.6 million do not meet legal requirements and should be withdrawn.
>
> Grants for another $1.3 million are questionable and require additional review, the report stated.

An independent, five-member commission within the department—the Federal Energy Regulatory Commission—sets rates and charges for transportation and sale of natural gas, and for transmission and sale of electricity.

Department of Health and Human Services

Even without its former education component, the Department of Health and Human Services surpasses most of the other Cabinet departments in size and scope. The importance of its services dictates a need for regular, comprehensive and often sensitive coverage of its activities, although federal legislation assuring privacy for individuals limits some reporting. The department reaches out with monetary assistance and a multitude of programs such as old-age and survivors' insurance, child welfare and aid to disabled and dependent persons.

No federal agency touches the lives of so many so often:

- A new senior citizens center is dedicated, after being constructed with joint funding from local and federal sources. Staffing and other services are also provided through federal grants. The reporter should ask: Who is using the facility, and how is it affecting the lives of those who do?

- An added provision in federal law brings new recipients under supplemental funding providing assistance to families with emotional problems. How will it be administered, what kinds of problems will it be expected to solve, and how will local and federal government be involved?

- A new federal grant changes and expands the foster home program in the city. What are its implications, and how will it affect current local efforts to find homes for abandoned children?

WASHINGTON—A record 13.4 million people are receiving money from the government's welfare program to help families pay for food, clothing and shelter. That is almost 2 million more than when the recession began in 1990.

The rising tide of poverty and the accompanying public costs is focusing attention on Aid to Families with Dependent Children.

Sources for this story included political figures, who agreed that the program does not help people become self-sufficient, and state welfare agency officials. Others were officials of the Administration for Children and Families, the agency that oversees the AFDC program, and an American Public Welfare Association study. Most such stories include sources from different levels.

The Public Health Service, another agency of Health and Human Services, operates public hospitals, collects vital statistics, helps local health planning and offers grants for a variety of health protection.

Because of their emphasis on research, several elements of the agency are often useful to the press. The National Institutes of Health, for example, are an important source of information. They are scattered about the country and include research agencies in cancer, AIDS, heart and lung disease, allergies and infectious diseases, child health and environmental health.

ATLANTA—The federal Centers for Disease Control is reaching out of its laboratories into violent urban neighborhoods to try to curb the injuries that are the top killers of young people.

"We do not call them accidents because that carries the idea that they are acts of God that cannot be prevented," CDC Director William Roper said.

"We believe that by subjecting them to study and using the techniques of public health, programs can be constructed to avoid injuries and violence."

The CDC's injury control division was being upgraded to a full-fledged national center, the National Center for Injury Prevention and Control. Reporters covering inner city neighborhoods will find a wealth of material in the research and actions of this agency.

Health and Human Services provides other facilities in communities, including the resources of the Office of Equal Employment Opportunity, an agency active in assuring equal opportunity for all those in the workplace.

Department of Housing and Urban Development

This department also reaches into local communities with a variety of programs—mortgage insurance for families, rental assistance for low-income families, programs that encourage fair housing, aid to communities for neighborhood development and preservation, and protection for the home buyer in the marketplace.

The reporter will find HUD making direct loans for construction or rehabilitation of housing projects for the elderly and disabled.

It's unusual for an agency to return federal grant money, but that's what the York Housing Authority is doing with a $2.1 million housing grant.

The authority received the grant from the U.S. Department of Housing and Urban Development to buy 30 houses to rent to low-income families.

But authority officials said the program would deplete the city's tax base by $58,400 during the next decade. The authority pays about half what a normal homeowner pays in taxes.

This story is complicated by the fact that two local real estate agencies negotiated the contracts with HUD—and are threatening to sue the authority if it does not complete the deal. The reporter's other sources include the federal agency's officials in the area, regional HUD officials and city officials.

Grants from HUD flow into city, county and state governmental units, housing and other authorities that are set up to make use of such aid, and private agencies that use matching money to improve the quality of life in such communities.

The reporter should be familiar with the relationships these units have with the federal agency. New programs also should be scrutinized when they affect the local area in which the reporter operates.

Federal grants designed specifically to eliminate drug problems at public housing developments have been given to Tennessee housing developments that documented little or no drug-related crime, government auditors say.

An audit of two such grants made to Tennessee housing agencies has prompted a wider examination to determine whether there are problems with similar grants throughout the U.S. Department of Housing and Urban Development's southern region.

In checking the audit, the reporter found that the housing units were not eligible for grants because the application did not prove the neighborhoods had significant drug-related crime.

The grants were made under the Public Housing Drug Elimination Program, a nationwide program with a $151 million budget. In this case, the reporter and the auditors worked together to cast light on deficiencies in a major program. Such government audits are usually open to press scrutiny.

However, as many positive as negative stories can come out of this agency.

The federal government awarded money yesterday to study a proposal to let residents in publicly owned apartment complexes in Kansas City buy their units.

The grants are $120,000 for North Park Village, the state's largest single public housing complex, and $84,000 for Harms Terrace.

This is the first step in arranging for residents to buy their units, according to the Department of Housing and Urban Development.

Other HUD organizations include the Interagency Council on the Homeless, which reviews federal programs designed to help the homeless; the Office of Administrative Law Judges, which hears and decides federal housing equal opportunity cases; and the Board of Contract Appeals, which issues decisions on appeals of HUD actions in contracting and awarding grants.

The Inspector General's Office conducts independent audits and investigations of departmental activities, and the reporter should know who can provide the results of the investigations. The reporter is limited only by the time needed to monitor HUD actions that affect his or her community.

Department of the Interior

The Department of Interior is custodian of the nation's natural resources. The department administers half a billion acres of federal land and 50 million more acres of native Indian reservations, oversees conservation and development of mineral and water resources, and is responsible for conservation of fish and wildlife resources.

Interior helps formulate policy on the nation's outdoors. Other functions include Job Corps Conservation Centers and Youth Corps programs, and preservation of scenic and historic sites.

Common news sources in the western United States include the Bureau of Indian Affairs and the Bureau of Reclamation. The National Park Service and the Bureau of Land Management are more widely known in other sections of the country. The reporter also should be familiar with the functions of the other agencies under direction of Interior, including the Geological Survey, the Bureau of Outdoor Recreation, the Bureau of Mines, the Mining and Enforcement Administration, and the various hydroelectric projects.

Department of Transportation

Whether you board a flight to Los Angeles, wheel your auto onto Interstate 10, step aboard a Canada-bound ferry on Lake Erie, or board an intercity passenger train for Chicago, the Department of Transportation is looking over your shoulder.

The department coordinates the nation's transportation programs and, depending on the subsidiary agency, is either directly or peripherally involved at the local level.

- A community's bus service is near collapse, mainly because of the defection of riders to the ubiquitous automobile. The role of the Urban Mass Transportation Administration is to assist in developing an efficient and successful system. It supplies techniques, equipment and financial assistance, with federal experts becoming deeply involved.

- The final phase of the interstate highway network nears completion at one end of the city, with only a few miles remaining to be opened to traffic. Financing has been arranged through a grant from the Federal Highway Administration, which pays 90 percent of the cost; the other 10 percent comes through the state. In the middle are local officials who want desperately to complete the link. The holdup lies in the priorities established by the state—and this particular interstate linkup is obviously not one of them.

Spot news is often affected by one of the investigative agencies of the department.

> VERNON, N.J.—A bus that crashed on a steep and winding road, killing six people and injuring 40, did not belong on the rural road and was not properly registered, authorities said Monday.
>
> The bus was taking a group from New York City to a Vernon amusement park when it went off the road, rolled over and caught fire.
>
> A preliminary check showed the bus was not registered with either of the two agencies that certify buses for safety: the Department of Transportation or the Interstate Commerce Commission.

Evidence of the Federal Highway Administration's presence is everywhere. Its funding is used to eliminate road hazards and initiate safety improvements, and preserve the natural beauty of the countryside.

The reporter will deal with officials and experts at the local, state and federal levels to pull together major highway stories.

> Interstate 77, the major highway between Columbia and Charlotte, is wearing out faster than experts planned, and repair costs are soaring.
>
> Taxpayers have spent at least $10 million on four projects to repair cracks and potholes that riddle the interstate, according to state highway department records.
>
> This year, the department is beginning two more projects totaling $9.2 million to repair sections completed 11 years ago. Federal Highway Administration engineers expected the pavement to last 20 years without major work.

State and federal engineers told the reporter that the problems were not caused by shoddy construction but by the fact that the road design plans did not account for the slow-draining soil of the region. The reporter used these facts to get to the heart of the matter: state engineers blamed the failures on reinforced concrete construction, a once-popular highway design espoused by the federal agency. Most states have abandoned the design, which seems better suited to arid climates.

Other current issues affecting relationships between state highway departments and the FHA include new rules removing billboards on federal highways, and long-range planning for highway congestion.

Another subsidiary agency, the Federal Aviation Administration, regulates air transportation, a vital component of a community's well-being. Related assignments can originate on the financial desk or the federal beat.

> ORLANDO—It began as a project to be financed strictly by the private sector, but the city's proposed magnetically levitated tourist train keeps calling for taxpayer dollars.
>
> The latest request by the city, Orange County and local transportation officials calls for Federal Aviation Administration money to be used for two terminals estimated to cost $443 million.

Others involved in the issue include the Florida Department of Transportation's public transportation office and regional planning agencies.

The day of the steam locomotive puffing 'round the bend with scores of passengers may be gone forever, replaced by a few sleek diesel engines pulling a handful of aluminum cars to and from a selected few cities. The Federal Railroad Administration consolidates federal support of rail transportation, enforces safety regulations and provides financial assistance to some railroads in need of help.

But the national passenger system today is administered by a quasi-official agency, the National Railroad Passenger Corporation (Amtrak), which operates independently of the Transportation Department. Amtrak was conceived on a for-profit basis, with operating losses currently made up with federal financing. The agency provides 90 percent of intercity rail passenger service, operating its own trains between points designated by the secretary of transportation.

With Amtrak's ever-shrinking rail service in doubt, reporters in cities along its routes will find frequent newsworthy developments in the system's future.

Department of the Treasury

- An incoming traveler arrives at O'Hare Airport. Customs Service agents find 16 balloons containing heroin hidden in his intestines. Police reporters have a field day.

- A prominent businessman is convicted of income tax evasion and is sentenced to prison. While the case has concluded in the courts, Internal Revenue Service officials provide specific financial details on the case, explaining the statutes that apply.

- A ring of counterfeiters has been traced to the city, and local police cooperate with federal agencies to arrest and charge the suspects. Police reporters may deal with several agencies in producing stories, but the Secret Service is basically responsible for enforcement.

Journalism students should not be misled into believing that law enforcement activities underlie the Treasury Department's total mission. Money and other currency is a part of every family, governmental and corporate action. The treasury secretary, a Cabinet officer appointed by the president, presides over a vast bureaucracy driven by money.

In addition to overseeing the department's major law enforcement responsibilities, the secretary recommends domestic and international financial, economic and tax policy, manages the public debt and participates in formulation of the broad fiscal policies that affect the public.

- A business reporter may be seeking information on two local banks that have just been taken over by the Office of Thrift Supervision. As regulator of savings and loans institutions, the office will provide statistics on the banks' well-being, as well as details that interest depositors in the community.

- An education reporter may be seeking information on new tax rulings regarding the several private schools operating in the area, using as a source the Internal Revenue Service.

- A medical and science reporter may be seeking specific information on the French-produced abortion pill RU486, which a U.S. citizen attempted to bring into this country in 1992. Since the pills were not approved by the Food and Drug Administration, the Customs Service confiscated them as the woman entered the United States.

This action became a law enforcement, medical and legal issue, and could have been covered by several reporters.

Probably the most often used sources for the local reporter are the Customs Service and the IRS. At more than 300 ports of entry, Customs inspects, controls and intercepts contraband items.

> MIAMI—Boys and girls at the Sheridan Facility are going to be wearing a whole lot of brand-new blue jeans, thanks to the U.S. Customs Service.
>
> Federal inspectors seized 2,103 pairs of the counterfeit jeans when they were flown in from Hong Kong. The forfeited jeans were donated to the facility that offers programs for troubled school-age youngsters.

The Coast Guard may board a boat and find 10,000 pounds of cocaine aboard, but forfeiture action against the vessel and its owners will be initiated by the Customs Service. Good sources are indispensable to reporters covering these agencies.

Veterans Affairs

The Department of Veterans Affairs administers a wide range of benefits for former members of the armed forces and their beneficiaries. Its health care system includes 172 medical centers, 27 domiciliaries, 260 outpatient clinics, 122 nursing homes and 198 Vietnam Veteran Outreach Centers throughout the United States.

Communities also are affected by the broad programs in medical research and the education and training of health workers. And nearly every city has an office to handle veterans' claims for disability compensation and pensions, auto allowances, and special adaptive equipment.

Changes in programs, development of new facilities and new procedures for filing claims create news stories of interest to a substantial segment of the community.

> WASHINGTON—Congress has authorized $48 million in each of the next three years to finance services for homeless veterans.
>
> The bill directs the Department of Veterans Affairs to set up four comprehensive centers to counsel home-

less veterans. Counselors also would be located in 83 other VA facilities.

VA officials and sponsors of the legislation provided further details for the story, which will have several follow-ups.

"Thirty percent of the homeless people in this country are veterans," said Rep. G.V. Montgomery (D-Miss.), chairman of the House Veterans Affairs Committee. "Our veterans deserve better."

The Federal Regulators

- They decide that factory stairways must be at least 22 inches wide, and they protect bank depositors from losing billions of dollars in savings.
- They bungle, and drive a toymaker to the edge of bankruptcy. They succeed, and save motorists' lives.
- They have a voice in what Americans eat, breathe, wear and drive.

"They" are the unelected federal regulators, a growing band that now makes more rules directly affecting the people than do the elected members of Congress.

That's how The Associated Press characterized the reach and power of the federal regulatory process.

More than two dozen major agencies currently set the rules for millions of Americans. Critics, numerous and vociferous, point to resulting high costs, delays, overzealous regulation and conflicting rules. Proponents counter that regulation, while occasionally cumbersome, has improved the quality of life. Even the auto manufacturers concede that federal auto safety regulations have saved thousands of lives. And America's air is measurably cleaner since regulators began regulating.

As the arguments swirl about proposed reform of regulatory agencies, the reporter's role remains to report on new rules and their effects and to assess old ones.

The regulators have become a sea of alphabet soup, with the reporter and readers awash in it. Abbreviations such as FDA (Food and Drug Administration), FTC (Federal Trade Commission), FCC (Federal Communications Commission), ICC (Interstate Commerce Commission) and SEC (Securities and Exchange Commission) have become household

fixtures, along with those not so well-known: National Transportation Safety Board, Nuclear Regulatory Commission, Equal Employment Opportunity Commission, Occupational Safety and Health Review Commission, and the Consumer Product Safety Commission. Most actions of these agencies create a ripple effect, and the reporter must explain action and effect to the reader.

Wire services report that the Food and Drug Administration is "working very hard" to eliminate methapyrilene, a cancer-causing antihistamine, from over-the-counter sleep aids and other drugs. What are the implications of this unpronounceable substance for the public? And what is the reaction of the pharmaceutical community? No story like this would be complete without checking pharmacies, physicians and other health agencies.

Inspections by the federal government to assure completion of local projects also lead to investigation of questionable practices, followed by court action. The reporter should always be alert to such possibilities. A knowledge of the standard under which projects are evaluated is often helpful in explaining action.

A federal investigator researching the scaffold collapse that left 11 men dead at Oak Hill April 12 says the concrete supplier should have known there were problems the day before the disaster.

In a report submitted to the Occupational Safety and Health Administration, investigator Tillman C. Moody said tests indicated numerous air pockets in the concrete used on the Midwest Power Co.'s Mississippi River project.

Federal agencies often take their cases to court to protect what they perceive to be the public's interest and sometimes to protect themselves as well.

A federal judge yesterday issued a restraining order, halting FMC Corp.'s production of carbon tetrachloride and emission of the chemical into the Soloway River.

Judge Charles V. Kelley acted after the Environmental Protection Agency filed a lawsuit earlier in the week to prevent what it termed "the repeated history" of FMC spills into the river.

An EPA spokesman said the action was taken under the emergency provisions of the Safe Drinking Water Act and the Federal Water Pollution Control Act.

Local law enforcement agencies often are involved in investigating practices carried on through federally funded programs. The FBI, which is nominally responsible for enforcement in such areas, may be only casually involved.

> Armed with 23 payroll fraud arrest warrants, police took into custody 19 workers and administrators of the federally funded Reading Application and Practice Center yesterday.
>
> Conviction on charges of public payroll fraud carries a maximum sentence of 10 years in prison.

In this case, the reading program was under the direction of the State Department of Education, but most of its local employees were being compensated through the federal Department of Education. Sometimes an alert reporter, assessing the quality of such programs in search of a story, will ask the right questions and obtain the information before the auditors get to it.

In constructing regulation stories, the reporter should not overlook one of the most active auditing bodies, the General Accounting Office. GAO auditors reach into every federal agency.

It might investigate charges that an oil company is making unfounded environmental claims about its plastic trash bags, trumpeting to buyers that its bags offer a significant environmental benefit compared with competitors' bags. The investigation might lead to a settlement with the Federal Trade Commission.

Or the GAO may use regulators' findings about industries they police.

> WASHINGTON—The country's migrant farm workers have no guaranteed minimum wage, work in fields sprayed with pesticide, and lack access to drinking water and toilet facilities on the job, congressional investigators say.
>
> As a result, the country's hired farm workers face serious health hazards, the General Accounting Office concluded in its first look at the plight of migrant workers since 1973.

GAO investigators used statistics from several regulatory agencies, including EPA figures that show pesticide exposure causes up to 300,000 acute illnesses and injuries among farm workers each year.

Whether the agency is regulating overtime pay (Labor Department), poisoning of coyotes in the Rocky Mountains (EPA), or use of antibiotics to treat cattle (FDA), the reporter far from the Washington scene handles the best part of the story—how those rules affect people in his or her world.

USING FEDERAL STATISTICS AND STUDIES

Whatever the newspaper beat, statistics compiled at the federal level are indispensable to good reporting. Combined with companion state and local statistics, the information can be used to generate or round out innumerable stories.

The most visible source of this massive collection of statistics is the U.S. Census Bureau, but other sources abound. Many of them, of course, are other federal agencies, but nongovernmental associations and groups also collect data covering important social and economic issues, frequently issuing studies that suggest stories at the local level.

To keep from being buried by figures, the reporter should study what's available and how best to use the material. The best place to begin is the Census Bureau.

The Census Bureau

The reporter analyzing long-range trends in the community will find a wealth of data from the Census Bureau on housing, income levels, age factors in the population, job opportunities and many other specific demographic facts.

The bureau, which operates under the Commerce Department, is a general purpose, statistical agency that collects, tabulates and publishes a variety of data about the people and the economy of the nation.

The statistics are as available to the public as they are to business, industry and government officials, but it is often the reporter who can best put the material in perspective.

> Statistics show an emerging dramatic change in the community's way of life, a Census Bureau official said yesterday.

"Preliminary compilation indicates that more than four of 10 dwelling units in the city contain no married people," said Rodney White, field supervisor for the regional office.

He suggested that research into issuance of marriage licenses, coupled with new figures on residences, will yield important implications in the city's changing lifestyles.

Census data offer only one facet of the issue. A community's planning department, financial and service agencies, and university researchers all may have pertinent observations and specific information to round out the story.

While the best-known of the Census Bureau's activities is the decennial census of population and housing, this giant statistical machine also produces many monthly, annual and biannual reports.

For example, censuses of agriculture, state and local government, manufacturers, construction industries and transportation are produced every five years—outside the major 10-year effort. Reporters also can obtain current reports on manufacturing, retail and wholesale trade, service industries, construction, and imports and exports.

Government Finance Reports are compiled annually, and include revenues, expenditures, indebtedness and assets of local governments. The information makes it easier for a reporter to compare costs of doing city business in communities of similar size.

The bureau makes available its statistical results through printed reports, computer tape and microfiche. It also produces catalogs, guides and directories that are useful in locating information on specific subjects.

What's Available

Two basic types of material are produced from census figures—demographic and economic.

Demographics is the statistical study of human populations, especially with regard to size and density, distribution, and vital statistics. The capacity exists to study their expansion or decline, important to the reporter's efforts. Population statistics are only part of the package. The reporter can find the median age in a community, percentage of elderly and school-age children, median family income, how much black renters

pay for apartments compared with white renters, and the home values in different neighborhoods.

The bureau's economic statistics relate to production, distribution and consumption of goods and services, and their practical or industrial significance.

For a reporter, one of the keys to using census data is tying the demographic and economic data together, then "humanizing" the material with comments from people who have something to say about it.

Here's what a reporter can do for starters:

Indicate Change.   Look at "sales zones" in a community, study the income of families in the area, then talk to local planning and zoning officials about the findings.

Compare Places.   Compare suburbs around the community, studying income, housing, education levels, size of families, and retail sales. School districts as well as city tracts can be checked. Identify differences as well as similarities, and talk to experts about reasons for those differences and the prospects for change.

Profile a Community.   Draw a demographic profile of a specific area of the city, using figures to show income, home ownership, family size, number of minority families, education levels. Compare with state and national averages.

Study Social Patterns.   Demographic information can be correlated to reveal social patterns. Suppose many four-bedroom homes are for sale. Statistics will show their location, average time it takes to sell them, how close to the asking price the houses are selling for, and changes in family size over the years. The reporter can track the effect of changes on the community's school system and tax structure.

An Associated Press reporter tracked living arrangements and marital status through the 1990 census, and focused on figures that suggested a serious trend.

WASHINGTON—More than half of the nation's black children lived with only one parent in 1990, according to new Census Bureau data.

The report on the living arrangements and marital status of Americans shows that the percentage of black children living with only one parent increased from 31.8 percent in 1970 to 45.8 percent in 1980 and 57.5 percent by 1990.

The bureau also reported that the majority of the 5.8 million black children living with one parent (5.5 million) reside with the mother. Impartial experts help provide analysis of the census figures.

> "The numbers reflect the deterioration of the American family structure and the growing social acceptability of a woman having a child without getting married," said Sar Levitan, director of social policy studies at George Washington University.
>
> The trend is serious, he said, because one-parent families more often live in poverty.

These are complex issues, and in pursuing them, the reporter also should seek out experts who can shed light on solutions.

Track Political Patterns. Demographics can be related to politics by studying officeholders' wards or districts, checking government spending on specific projects such as environmental improvement or crime control.

The 1990 census, for example, triggered a massive redistricting at the local and state levels. As a result, politicians—and the public—are studying possible changes in political composition of their communities.

> A local voting rights expert yesterday urged the Boston City Council to redraw council and School Committee districts to take the city's rising minority populations into account—or face a potentially disruptive lawsuit.
>
> Alan Rom, an attorney with the Lawyers Committee for Civil Rights Under Law, said a coalition of minority groups believes the city must redraw nine municipal districts based on 1990 federal census data.

Since 1983, minority members of the City Council and School Committee have come from two of the city's nine districts. But the new census data show that minorities make up 41 percent of the city's population. The redistricting plan would put more than 60 percent of minorities in four of the districts.

Predict the Future. Study a specific area and draw up a "scenario" based on your research. Get reactions from various officials to develop the scenario.

What Data Reveal

Part of the key to developing useful stories lies in comparisons. Figures from 1960, 1970 and 1980 all play a part in analyzing the 1990 statistics for important trends.

A reporter for *The Miami Herald* researched worker occupations through the 1980–90 decade in the South Florida market, looking for those growing the fastest and slowest. Then she tracked down officials willing to discuss and analyze the results.

> A decade of rising crime made security work South Florida's fastest-growing occupation, new U.S. Census figures reveal.
>
> The number of police, firefighters, jail guards and private security officers leaped by 74 percent in 10 years to 45,500, while the overall work force grew by 33 percent.

The reporter easily found public and private officials willing to offer reasons for the dramatic growth.

> "Crime has changed the way we look at our neighbors, the way we look at our communities," said Robert Kneip, vice president at Wackenhut, the major private security firm in the area.
>
> Drug-related crime and rapid growth in demand for home and condominium security have helped fuel the increase, he added.

The great value of the 10-year census lies in the figures for the 250 largest cities, all 3,137 counties, 318 metropolitan areas and more than 2,600 smaller communities with populations as small as 10,000. Inside these tables lie stories about income gaps, immigration patterns, effect of immigration on incomes, where people live and why, and countless other social patterns.

In searching for clues to use of public transportation, for example, a reporter collected figures and comments from local officials, then turned to census figures for additional information: What are commuters in a community doing besides using public transportation, where are they going, how many miles are they driving, who's riding in the car with them, and how much time does it take to get where they are going?

Reporters in rapidly growing regions are producing stories about the state and local community's immigration patterns, using census figures and humanizing them with stories of the people moving in.

> Maybe you assumed your grocery store is offering Sunbeam white bread, bagels and pita bread because your neighbors are becoming more cosmopolitan, expanding their tastes beyond state borders.

Instead, your store might be responding to the fact that three out of 10 of your neighbors—and maybe you, too—grew up in a state where bratwurst and tamales are home-grown chow.

The 1990 census shows 30.6 percent of us were born in another state.

Past census figures help put the current data into perspective: "The shift from homefolk to transplants has been steady during the past 30 years," according to census officials.

A reporter with these statewide figures can easily localize the material, discovering, for example, that the shift has been dramatic in the coastal counties. Natives are outnumbered nearly 2 to 1 by incoming residents.

A reporter also can take state and local census figures on poverty to peripheral agencies whose officials can provide perspective.

The percentage of state residents living below the poverty level dropped to an all-time low in 1990, according to census figures released Tuesday.

Advocates for the poor, however, found little to cheer about, noting that the census data was compiled before the recent recession knocked many people back below the poverty line.

"What's a real shame is that the census was taken right before the recession," said Sue Berkowitz, director of the state Legal Services Division, which provides legal help to poor people.

Sources Are the Key

Few newspapers have the resources to handle the multitude and depth of stories that emerge from the decennial census, much less the constant flow of statistics that come out during the other nine years of a decade. Issues are bound to be lost in the shuffle.

But good sources can help focus on the important ones. The Census Bureau and state agencies that collect statistical information can provide "problems" and facts about specific demographics such as general housing characteristics, population characteristics and block statistics.

The bureau also offers guides to the concepts it uses to collect its statistics. Its public affairs office provides lists of state data centers, a network of offices that provide facts and advice.

To supplement these sources, reporters and editors are advised to follow an old rule: Watch other publications and media for ways to localize important findings. Wire services, and general and special interest magazines often produce stories that merit local application. Data on the so-called middle class offers an example.

WASHINGTON—Fresh evidence was provided Thursday that the nation's middle class is shrinking.

A Census Bureau report shows that the percentage of people with middle incomes dropped from 71.2 percent in 1970 to 63.3 percent in 1990.

"The conclusion is obviously that income inequality has grown rather substantially over the last 20 years," bureau economist Jack McNeil said. "We're getting clusters toward both ends of the income scale."

The report may first have surfaced in a wire service story, but it can be localized to any city, state or region. By the time the reporter has finished a local story on the issue, readers may have learned that the elderly are doing better than any other group, signs of improvement are emerging among blacks, and that families headed by single mothers who are less likely to work are increasing.

A cautionary note: Early in any story like this, the reporter must define "middle class." In this case, low incomes are defined as those below $18,576 for a family of four, while high incomes are defined as $74,304 for a family of four.

Many sources can help the reporter localize a story. An analysis of the 1990 census by the Children's Defense Fund showed that with nearly 1 in 3 preschoolers living in poverty, Minneapolis and St. Paul have higher percentages of poor young children than Los Angeles; Washington, D.C.; or Montgomery, Ala.

Defense fund officials said the increase was disturbing because Minnesota's wealth, and therefore, presumably, its capacity to end child poverty, improved substantially during the decade. Reporters in other states are looking at different kinds of demographics.

The average Hoosier is getting older as the state's ability to replenish its population is reduced, according to Census Bureau figures made public Tuesday.

In this case, the figures were analyzed by the Indiana Business Research Center, which assists local officials with challenges of census data. It is important to identify sources of such analyses.

Many such organizations join the bureau in analyzing the data. Newspapers also have the capability of producing computer analyses.

Some Census Cautions

While figures rarely lie, the ways in which they are used can be misleading. Here are some cautions:

- Before using a number, the reporter should know what it means and be sure the number is the correct one for the story.

- Is only one figure being used to indicate change? This could lead to a simplistic analysis. Perhaps more than one indicator is needed.

- Is a projection that the reporter may be taking to planning officials to comment on based only on limited population analyses, and not really meaningful? Be sure the information is grounded in longer-term trends.

- Figures should not reflect atypical situations (such as using figures about new water connections just as major new housing developments are being built) that could skew the results or conclusions.

- When looking at an area of growth, are rates for adjacent areas projected to grow similarly, as one might expect? If not, why not?

Reporters also should be sure to understand and define or translate terms that census officials tend to toss around. "Independent variables," "SMSAs," "enumeration districts," and "block groups (BGs)" are but a few.

Definitions are important to understanding much census data, and the reporter should point out what a designation actually means.

The state's population has shifted from rural to urban areas during the past 40 years, although that hardly means residents have found a love for the big city.

The 1990 U.S. Census found 54.7 percent of the state's residents live in urban areas, compared with 45.3 percent in rural areas. Of those rural residents, however, only 1.3 percent live in what the census calls "farm population."

Some of the "urbanites" live in places that hardly match New York, Atlanta or Kansas City. *Urban* is defined as a place with 2,500 persons or more, including such towns as Smithville with 2,105 residents.

Dealing with Noncensus Statistics

While nearly every federal agency produces studies useful to reporters, an entire publishing industry has grown up around nonfederal groups that have an interest in researching specific issues and publicizing them.

PHILADELPHIA—Banks, auto dealers and credit card companies—any outfit that lends money to consumers—often try to sell credit life insurance.

But credit life insurance, which pays off loans when a person dies, "is still the nation's worst insurance rip-off," according to a report by two consumer groups.

"Consumers are overcharged more than $500 million annually for this insurance, and most consumers don't need the coverage," states the report by the Consumer Federation of America and the National Consumer Insurance Organization.

The reporter used officials of the two consumer groups as sources, but balanced the story with comments from an insurance industry trade group and insurance experts at a university.

Economic surveys abound, both in and out of the federal agency hierarchy.

If you think you earn less today than you did in 1990, you are right.

A report by the Economic Policy Institute in Washington shows that 80 percent of the U.S. work force has experienced substantial pay losses during the past five years, regardless of education.

The drop began before the recession and is likely to continue, says economist Lawrence Mishel, co-author of the study.

The study also showed that the wage gap between men and women is starting to close, but only because the earnings of males is falling. The U.S. Labor Department also can provide input for a story such as this.

Researchers at institutions of higher learning throughout the United States constantly are being funded by both federal and nonfederal groups to do research on a specific area.

> Boosting daily calcium intake well above the recommended levels significantly increased the bone mass of children—a step that might reduce the risk of future skeletal injuries, according to a study by Indiana University researchers.
>
> The findings are expected to lead to a re-examination of guidelines for calcium intake by youngsters.

The study was funded by the National Institute for the Aging, but overseen by the National Academy of Sciences' Food and Nutrition Board, the body that sets recommended dietary allowances. The institute is part of the National Institutes of Health, and so are more than 20 other research-oriented institutes.

Federal task forces also generate useful statistics on different issues. A recent study by the federal Task Force on Homelessness showed that a third of them are veterans. Other sources for such information include the Department of Veterans Affairs; members of Congress; and the National Coalition for Homeless Veteran Service Providers, a group of community organizations across the country.

SPECIAL INTEREST GROUPS

The reporter cannot lose sight of the special-interest groups, both in Washington and at the local level, that influence actions of the federal bureaucracy. Such individuals and groups affect not only the decisions, but also the process through which the reporter covers the federal beat. At nearly every turn, the reporter will find that a thrust brings a counterthrust, a charge calls for a countercharge, and a preliminary decision often brings a later decision overturning that decision. It is part of the process of government.

The reality of such special-interest groups was made clearer by Donald Kennedy, former commissioner of the Food and Drug Administration. Asked about the power of special interests in Washington, he admitted they are competitive and effective:

"I think that they can delay legislation, but I don't think they can delay a good piece of legislation indefi-

nitely," Kennedy said. "I would say they are strong, they try to get their way, but that they don't win all the time."

A federal highway agency makes a preliminary decision to toughen standards governing weights of trucks on interstate highways. The reporter should ask: What pressures are going to be generated and from whom?

The reporter contacts the trucking associations, who are certain to growl that they are being discriminated against, and to others known to favor the trucking industry. The truckers on the highway deserve equal time, and consumer activists concerned with safety and highway maintenance spring up to do battle. State officials, who are often subject to similar pressures, may exert pressure themselves.

So, while the decision is purely "preliminary," it passes through a period of uncertainty. How public and how visible this argument becomes depends on the ability of the reporter to cover the substantial areas of disagreement.

> Industry pressure and election-year politics are driving the Food and Drug Administration to back away from some consumer protection policies it favored as recently as last fall, consumer advocates charge.
>
> FDA's retreat is especially marked in the key areas of enforcement and food labeling, the critics say.

The reporter pointed out that earlier FDA policy had been to seek stronger enforcement powers, but now the agency says it doesn't need them. The agency also wants to relax the deadline for industry compliance with the tough food-labeling regulations it proposed months earlier.

> "FDA is showing an over-willingness to respond to industry pressure," said Ellen Haas, director of Public Voice for Food Health Policy, a consumer advocacy group based in Washington.
>
> "The food industry has been lobbying very hard," she said. "So has the White House and the Office of Management and Budget. I think FDA just hasn't stood up to the pressure."

Food industry associations, among them the Grocery Manufacturers Association, were putting pressure on federal officials at both the legislative as well as administrative levels to soften the proposed requirements.

It is often difficult to identify the players in such disputes. The federal beat, as much as any, is susceptible to endless efforts by special interests to influence public policy.

***

SUGGESTED READINGS

Congressional Quarterly staff. *Federal Regulatory Directory*. Washington: Congressional Quarterly, 1990.

Provides profiles of the major regulatory agencies, including key personnel, organization and information resources.

Herbers, John. *No Thank You, Mr. President*. New York: Norton, 1976.

A White House reporter discusses the beat. Chapter 3, "A Beat Without Sources," and Chapter 4, "Down on the Plantation."

Investigative Reporters and Editors. *The Reporter's Handbook*. 2d ed. New York: St. Martin's Press, 1991.

An investigator's guide to documents and techniques at local and federal levels.

Peters, Charles. *How Washington Really Works*. Reading, Mass.: Addison-Wesley, 1992.

Anecdotal accounts of how the nation's capital works, as viewed by a veteran reporter.

Part Three

Law Enforcement and the Courts

Chapter 9

The Judicial Process

- A small loan company files a lawsuit in court to recover more than $23,000 in funds it says were misappropriated by one of its employees.

- A mother files a lawsuit to regain custody of her two children, asking the court for an order to force her former husband to return them.

- A person caught stealing from a home may be a burglar supporting a drug habit or a juvenile seeking excitement. While procedures may differ, the process is the same. Law enforcement officials file charges and the courts begin the process of determining guilt or innocence.

- An industrial firm discharges a dangerous chemical into a nearby lake—a criminal charge punishable by fines and possible prison terms for employees found responsible.

All these examples represent the law in action—rules of conduct or procedure formally recognized as binding and enforced by a controlling authority. Our system of courts exists to adjudicate the arguments that arise when people believe wrongs have been committed.

This chapter offers the student-reporter a view of the federal and state judicial systems; Chapter 10 covers civil actions, and Chapter 12 discusses criminal proceedings.

It is important that the reporter distinguish between a civil action and a criminal proceeding. While some of the procedures are similar, the philosophies underlying the process and the final actions reached are vastly different.

Civil actions are filed by individuals or corporations against other individuals or corporations seeking enforcement or protection of a right or redress or prevention of a wrong. The court arbitrates between the parties, with a judge or a jury deciding in favor of one litigant or the other. Judgment in a civil action can result in award of financial compensation, in some other form of compensation, or in an order directing a defendant to comply with an order of the court.

> A woman who claimed that she developed a disabling condition from birth control pills prescribed by a local physician was awarded $280,000 by a Circuit Court jury Tuesday.
>
> Mrs. Joyce T. Nether, a Lancaster computer programmer, had sought $1.1 million from gynecologist Edward L. Humphrey, charging that he was negligent in failing to inform her of "untoward side effects" from use of the contraceptive Ovral.

However, judgment in a civil action such as this does not impute criminality. If a law had been deemed to have been broken, a criminal action would have been filed against the physician.

Criminal actions are instituted to punish a person or group of people who commit acts that injure society. A public official files the charge.

In such cases the defendant is considered innocent until judged guilty by a carefully selected jury. Furthermore, that process is preceded by another that first determines whether such a trial is warranted.

Because the defendant's reputation and possibly freedom are at stake, the criminal process offers the accused person many safeguards, not the least of which is the potentially lengthy process leading to a finding of guilty or not guilty. Conviction in a criminal trial can result in imprisonment, a fine or both.

> Logan County Sheriff-elect Johnson C. Waggoner was indicted Thursday by a special grand jury investigating charges of vote fraud in the county's primary election in May.
>
> Waggoner was charged with "conspiring to defraud the county of Logan of true, honest and uncorrupted services of its election officials." The indictment also charged Waggoner with deceiving and intimidating voters.

In this case, conviction might mean a prison term for the official of up to five years, a fine of up to $20,000, or both.

THE COMPLEXITIES OF COURT REPORTING

No area of public affairs reporting is more complex or more far-reaching in scope, attracts greater interest or demands more diligent accuracy and impartiality than reporting the judicial process. Further, the journalist whose major effort is directed toward the court system will find that the process spills over into every other public affairs beat.

- A labor union seeks an injunction in court to prohibit the manager of an industrial plant from locking out workers during a dispute. Coverage may fall to the court reporter, the labor reporter or the business reporter.

- The state government, acting through its attorney general's office, asks a circuit court judge to forbid a county commission from paying additional funds to public defenders. Coverage could fall to the state government reporter, the county reporter or the court reporter. All governments, in fact, are often in the process of suing or being sued, of forcing judicial action or being forced to act through judicial action.

> Attorney General S. Baird Singleton is girding for court battle in the state's effort to recapture more than $20 million of overpayments to highway contractors during the past 15 months.
>
> Singleton contends that highway contracts did not reflect the federal government's insistence on additional

negotiation of penalty clauses for failure to meet agreed-upon deadlines.

- A school district defends itself in court against charges that it illegally disbursed funds from the federal government for a project not yet officially sanctioned. One of several reporters might be assigned, including the education writer who has followed the dispute.

As these examples show, the court beat requires much more than knowledge of legal principles and procedures. The court reporter must be an adaptable "generalist," with a grounding in all areas of public affairs. The ability to translate legal terms and actions into terminology understandable to the average reader or viewer is also essential.

Methods of Coverage

No consensus exists on how to cover the courts, and every newspaper and broadcast outlet covers them somewhat differently. The police reporter may take responsibility for covering the municipal court or police court, mainly because he or she is familiar with the cases there. The county beat reporter may cover the circuit or county court, and general assignment reporters often check with the clerk of court for possible stories. State appellate courts are often covered by the state government reporter, mainly because many of those courts are located in the state capital.

The full-time court reporter has become scarcer, but that specific assignment continues to be the best way to cover the judiciary completely.

There is an ever-present need for regular cross-checking among beats to guarantee quality coverage. A tip to the state government reporter, for example, can pay off with a timely story that might otherwise be overlooked.

Six nursing homes have filed a lawsuit against the State Department of Public Welfare, charging that they were incorrectly reimbursed for services to Medicaid patients for the years 1988 through 1992.

The lawsuit, filed Wednesday in Common Pleas Court in Columbia, charged that the state failed to use the correct inflation factor in reimbursing the nursing homes as required by law.

BOX 9–1

Cases Clog the Court System

✳ ✳ ✳

The number of actions filed in state courts topped 100 million in 1990, according to the National Center for State Courts.

U.S. population rose 5 percent between 1984 and 1990. During the same period:

- Criminal actions filed increased 33 percent, to 13 million.
- Civil actions filed increased 30 percent, to 18.4 million.
- Juvenile cases increased 28 percent, to 1.5 million.
- Traffic and other minor cases increased 12 percent, to 67 million.

Other information: There are about 800,000 lawyers practicing in the United States today. A report from the National Center for State Courts also says:

- The most dramatic growth in civil actions involves contracts and property disputes.
- Much of the growth in the criminal actions comes from stepped-up prosecution of drug cases.

Outside the court action lie other questions germane to the state government beat: What agency ultimately will have to provide the reimbursement? What effect will the action have on the other 600 nursing homes in the state? What will be the final cost? In this and many other instances, more than one reporter may be grappling with details of court actions that have other implications—and other sources of information.

Going About It

Covering the courts is often laborious, particularly if the case is complicated. The reporter obtains information by examining court records; covering judicial proceedings, including trials; and interviewing court officials, attorneys for the litigants and the litigants themselves.

Access to material depends on the willingness of the court officials to make it available to the reporter on a timely basis. Few special journalistic rights to court records exist, and the reporter relies instead on the public's basic right of access. This includes attendance at most judicial proceedings and the right to inspect official court records.

Attendance at judicial proceedings, such as preliminary hearings or trials, is a right granted to the public rather than specifically to the press. A judge may order such proceedings closed to the public to protect the rights of a defendant, to shield a minor or to maintain courtroom order. In practice, reporters are seldom excluded from such proceedings.

Some court records, such as actions of a grand jury, are not public record until they reach the judge of a court or are read in open court.

Much of the information obtained through the courts is conditionally privileged, which means that a reporter can use such material without fear of libel, provided that it is reported fairly and accurately, and without malice.

Errors can destroy conditional privilege (sometimes called "qualified privilege"). Careless note-taking by a reporter at a trial or in copying details of a civil complaint is a danger. Most states insist that the report must be of a "public and official proceeding," not related material that emerges outside the proceeding. This privilege extends through courts of record.

DIFFERENT KINDS OF LAW

The term *law* actually applies to a multitude of different rules and regulations, ranging from the Constitution—the most important set of laws—to the administrative law decided by officials in government agencies and equitable relief provided by judges.

Custom and conduct dictate adherence to prescribed laws. An old and obscure state statute may forbid all smoking on school property, yet custom allows school administrators to smoke in their private offices. An old municipal statute still on the books may prohibit

gambling within corporate limits, yet bingo games and raffles may flourish in many churches. Old laws may prohibit the sale of merchandise on Sunday, but officials in a community may look the other way and allow it.

All law has its origins in morality, custom, religious treaties, institutions, legislation and judicial decisions.

The Constitution

The most important law in this country is embodied in the Constitution, which is the basis for the U.S. legal system. It sets up the structure of the federal government and defines federal-state relationships.

It divides authority among the three branches of government, and reserves a number of powers for states and their subdivisions—counties, cities and towns. The reporter should remember that no law can be enacted by statute that conflicts with the Constitution.

The Common Law

Common law grows out of usage and custom, and is an outgrowth of English judicial tradition. It accumulated over generations, and was produced by cases decided through the litigation process. It is often referred to as the law of decided cases. Unless specifically changed by statute, common law is generally observed in the United States. One of its significant characteristics is precedent, under which the judiciary makes use of a previous decision to adjudicate a case.

Although common law is not codified like statutory law, much of it appears in written form through the judgments in cases that are decided and reported. Since most courts maintain records, the ability of the judiciary—and reporters—to research precedent-setting decisions has contributed to the continuing strength of the system.

Actions in Equity

Although not actually a law, equity is an important alternative to common law. Equity also originated in England, where "law courts" were established to administer the common law. However, common law held that damages (usually in the form of money) would right a wrong. Equity was developed to correct instances when faithfully applying the common law did not help an injured party.

Equity began where the law ended, taking the form of judicial decrees rather than merely a judgment of "yes" or "no." Under equity, judgments take the form of preventive or remedial measures, such as an order calling for specific performance or a restraining order. Equity is designed to provide remedies not otherwise obtainable.

- A wife, fearful that her estranged husband will harm her, asks a court to issue an order restraining him from threatening her.

- A glass-making firm may seek an injunction from a judge to restrain employees who are about to strike from leaving their jobs until they bank the furnaces in the plant.

- A property owner may ask a court to restrain a county highway department from cutting down a 150-year-old tree at the edge of his property until a hearing is scheduled on the dispute.

- The county might respond by asking for a court order restraining the property owner from threatening road crews working in the area.

The court reporter will find a wealth of interesting stories in such orders, and, more important, many are vital to the cases in progress in the courts.

The Statutory Law

While this country operates under systems based on English common law, the framework for both the federal and state judiciary is a mixture of common and statutory law.

Statutory law is created by legislation, and thousands of government bodies, from tiny towns to the U.S. Congress, are constantly in the process of enacting them. Statutory law may replace common law and other judicial precedent. Sections of a code, or body of laws, may be revised, updated or replaced outright.

The influence of statutory law upon the public depends on many factors—enforcement, exemptions to its provisions, type of statute and jurisdiction. A

state legislature would enact a statute requiring registration of firearms, for example, and authorities would enforce the statute. The courts then would adjudicate the disputes that arise over that enforcement.

Much of this country's statutory law provides for reasonable discretion on the part of the judge, with a judge or jury reaching a decision and a judge pronouncing sentence. A guilty verdict by a jury in a criminal case may give the judge discretion to set the sentence as long as it does not breach the maximum and minimum penalties provided by the statute.

> Frank J. Hern, a prominent Swiss County coal broker, was sentenced to four years in prison Tuesday after his conviction for interstate transportation of stolen coal.
>
> Hern had been convicted Sept. 1 of fraudulently disposing of more than 2,300 tons of coal taken from Consolidated Coal Co.'s local mine in 1991.
>
> U.S. District Judge Charles M. Francis recommended that Hern serve at least two years of the sentence and also imposed a $20,000 fine.

Under the statute, the broker could have been sentenced to as much as 10 years in prison and been fined up to $50,000.

Administrative Law

Early in his or her career, the reporter will produce stories based on still another kind of law—administrative law. Agencies at the federal, state and local levels often wield the power to adopt and enforce administrative regulations which have the force of law.

Thousands of federal agencies have such rule-making power, and regularly promulgate regulations that affect private citizens and corporations.

> WASHINGTON—The U.S. Environmental Protection Agency proposed regulations Monday to require the nation's smoggiest cities to toughen automobile emissions inspections by using high-tech tests that will flunk more vehicles.
>
> The EPA directive expanding requirements for basic emissions testing would affect 55 more urban areas, for a total of 177 nationwide.

The EPA received such enforcement power from the 1990 Clean Air Act that required the agency to write performance standards for tighter inspections.

Other areas of widely watched administrative law include such agencies as the Food and Drug Administration, the Interstate Commerce Commission and the Consumer Product Safety Commission.

Substantive vs. Procedural Law

The home purchaser who files a lawsuit charging a breach of contract by the firm constructing her house is basing her case on a statute regulating such contracts. **Substantive law** creates, defines and regulates such rights.

After the lawsuit is filed, both the plaintiff, the party who alleges injury, and the defendant, the party against whom the lawsuit is filed, follow **procedural law**, the body of rules through which the substantive law is administered.

Procedural law, with which the reporter must be thoroughly familiar, dictates the progress of the civil or criminal action and the stories that will be written during the course of litigation.

- A defendant charged with passing several fraudulent checks after forging another's name to them is brought to court under substantive law forbidding such action and making it a criminal offense. In appearing at an arraignment before a magistrate who orders a preliminary hearing to determine whether the defendant should be bound over to a grand jury, procedural law is being followed.

- The chairman of the Airport Commission who files a civil lawsuit to force the county government to fulfill its financial commitment is relying on substantive law binding the agreement between the two bodies. But the complaint, the answer and subsequent pleadings flow out of the procedural law that governs the process.

While substantive law and its ramifications constitute the basis for news reporting, the court reporter should not overlook the news inherent in the judicial process itself.

Prosecutors will be allowed to use a list of rape victims as evidence in the case against Edward C. Mears when his trial begins March 21.

Circuit Court Judge Frank W. Pardue, in a written decision Tuesday, overruled a motion by Mears'

attorneys to suppress evidence seized in a Nov. 3 search of the optometrist's apartment.

Mears is charged in a 78-count indictment with committing 17 rapes and 27 aggravated burglaries over a four-year period.

This procedural decision, and many others similar to it, is important to coverage of a major court action.

Changes in a court system's process of jury selection, for example, are newsworthy because they affect the residents of entire communities. New legislation, such as the federal statute calling for speedier trials for defendants, often changes the procedures under which courts operate. The reporter should stay abreast of such procedural developments through judicial journals and local court sources.

Jurisdiction

The attorney leaned back in his chair and studied the ceiling, pondering the question by his client. Finally he responded:

"Our best bet in winning this case is over in Judge Lander's court. That's where you drew up the contract and filed it, even though you live over here now."

The attorney subsequently files a complaint in Lander's court and the lawsuit begins its course through the litigation process. The power or right to interpret or apply the law is called **jurisdiction**. Jurisdiction also sets the limits of that power. The U.S. Constitution or statutes of each state and the federal government determine the jurisdiction of the courts.

In the lawsuit noted, Judge Lander may dismiss it, claiming lack of jurisdiction and recommending that it be refiled with another court.

Original jurisdiction is the power to hear a civil or criminal action and pursue it through the trial process. The district court is the court of original jurisdiction in the federal system; each state has its own court of original jurisdiction.

Appellate jurisdiction is the power to consider a judgment in a civil or criminal action and to uphold or reverse it. Both the state and federal systems embody a system of appellate courts.

Courts of limited jurisdiction are bound by statute to a specified area, such as magistrate, police or municipal courts. Many states limit these inferior courts to cases involving a maximum of $500, $1,500 or $5,000 in damages, or to minor infractions of the law, such as traffic violations. Judgments of these courts are usually subject to review in higher courts.

OUR DUAL SYSTEM OF COURTS

"Don't make a federal case out of it."

How often have we heard someone use that expression in an effort to minimize the importance of an action? While the importance of a state "case" often far outweighs that of a federal "case," the expression helps to explain our dual system of national and state courts.

The process of justice proceeds at two levels—a federal system that exists throughout the 50 states and the state systems. Although the state judicial systems are similar, differences exist in selection of court officers, organization, jurisdiction and even terminology.

Most of the legal business of the nation is transacted at these state levels, with the federal judiciary empowered to handle only those actions specified by the U.S. Constitution. All powers not specifically delegated to the federal government by the Constitution fall automatically to the states, and so each state's judicial process is unique.

The Federal Courts

A simple fork in the judicial highway leads to either a federal case or a state case. The reporter should be able to identify the fork and understand the scope and role of the two systems. The federal system is detailed in Figure 9–1.

FIGURE 9–1

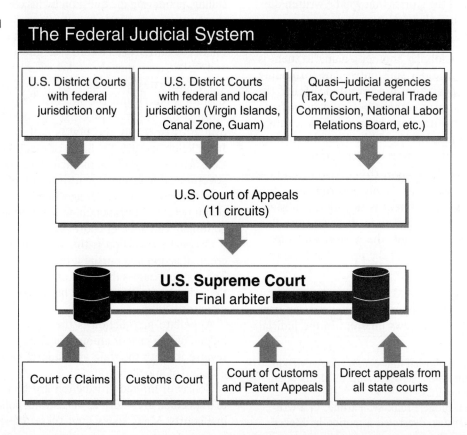

What makes an issue a federal question? Article 3 of the U.S. Constitution explains:

> The judicial Power shall extend to all cases in Law and Equity arising under this Constitution, the laws of the United States, the Treaties made, or which shall be made, under their Authority:
>
> - to all cases affecting ambassadors, other public ministers and consuls;
> - to all cases of admiralty and maritime jurisdiction;
> - to controversies to which the United States shall be a party;
> - to controversies between two or more states, between a state and citizens of another state, between citizens of different states, between citizens of the same state claiming lands under grants of different states, and between a state, or the citizens thereof, and foreign states, citizens or subjects.

The Constitution also vests the U.S. Supreme Court with original jurisdiction in all cases affecting ambassadors and other public ministers and cases in which a state is a litigant. With these constitutional limits in mind, paths in the fork of the judicial terrain become comparatively easy to identify.

For example, the federal government's power to regulate interstate commerce and copyright laws relies on a broad body of legislation covering those areas.

After the framers of the Constitution set such limits for the federal judiciary, they left all other judicial proceedings to the states.

The U.S. District Court is the federal court of original jurisdiction and serves as the trial court. Most cases deserving public notice originate in the district court, and many conclude at that level, although an extensive appellate process exists.

> A former teller for the Guaranty National Bank pleaded guilty Monday in U.S. District Court to embezzling $17,700 from the bank last year.
>
> Caesar Willmarco, 30, 1206 Martinez St., was employed in Guaranty's main office for five years. He will be sentenced Aug. 23, after probation reports are completed and submitted to the court.

Because federal banking laws cover such criminal activity, these cases are heard in the federal courts. Congress has enacted thousands of such pieces of legislation, which provide for settlement of disputes in the federal system.

The Federal District Courts

Every state has at least one federal district court; more populous states have as many as four. There are 90 in all, and each court maintains from one to 27 judges, depending upon the case load within each jurisdiction. Federal appeals courts are empowered to review all final decisions of district courts, except where the law provides for a direct review by the Supreme Court.

These are some of the types of cases that would be adjudicated in the federal rather than the state courts:

- A seaman is injured while working on a dredge in the Mississippi River. He files a lawsuit, claiming negligence on the part of the firm operating the equipment. The river is considered a maritime jurisdiction and the firm being sued has its headquarters in another state.

- Natural gas customers claim they were cheated out of millions of dollars because the firm from whom they bought fuel misused funds in their exploration operations. The firm was charged with violating provisions of the federal Racketeer Influenced, Corrupt Organizations Act.

- A California resident vacationing in Nevada is struck by a car driven by a Nevada resident. Claiming negligence on the part of the Nevada driver and major injuries (and if the damages asked were high enough), the California resident would sue in federal court. If both were residents of the same state, the lawsuit would be filed in state court.

- A dispute over the right of way for a proposed bridge spanning the Ohio River between West Virginia and Ohio would be litigated in the federal courts, because two states are involved.

Since the Constitution delegated power over a broad range of activity to the federal government, the federal courts also hold jurisdiction in such areas as bankruptcy, postal and currency activity, and taxation. Meanwhile, legislation working its way through Congress is annually expanding the jurisdiction of the federal judiciary.

> Joe E. Bales admitted Tuesday in federal court that he conspired to take kickbacks while he was responsible for the state Department of Education's school bus fleet.

Bales pleaded guilty to conspiracy to violate the Hobbs Act, an anti-corruption law that prohibits public officials from taking money or gifts for performing their jobs.

The official had received cash, golf games, meals and use of a vacation condominium for steering bus repairs to a particular truck repair firm. He also can be prosecuted in the state courts.

A charge of forgery, for example, would be prosecuted in the state courts, but if use of the mail system was involved, the case would be sent to federal district court for action.

Four men who Federal Bureau of Investigation agents say were part of an interstate theft operation were charged Monday by a federal grand jury with stealing bulldozers and other construction equipment in Illinois and disposing of them in Ohio.

At least $600,000 in equipment has been identified as part of the ring's thefts, the Justice Department said.

A huge body of federal laws has grown through legislative action, and a multitude of agencies possesses the power to prosecute those who break the laws.

FORT VALLEY, Ga.—A local peach harvester was fined $1.1 million Friday by the Immigration and Naturalization Service, the largest such fine in the agency's history.

INS officials said four employees of the harvester, Lane Packing Co., had smuggled thousands of aliens into the country over the past two years and had employed many of them, keeping them in conditions akin to bondage while they worked to pay off the fees charged by the smugglers.

Prosecution stemmed from the Immigration Reform Act of 1986, which gave the agency the power to levy such penalties.

Theft of dynamite would be prosecuted by the Bureau of Alcohol, Tobacco and Firearms. Interception of illegal drugs being transported from the East to the West Coast might be prosecuted by several agencies at the federal level, including the FBI and the Drug Enforcement Administration.

Discrimination cases have become common in the federal system because of legislation giving the Equal Employment Opportunity Commission power to bring a lawsuit.

A longtime clerk for a Richland County master in equity has filed a federal lawsuit against him after he fired her in 1991 when she lodged a discrimination claim with the U.S. Equal Employment Opportunity Commission.

Cecilia W. Moffett was dismissed the day that Joseph M. Keplinger learned she'd been to the EEOC, according to the lawsuit filed Monday in U.S. District Court. It also states that Keplinger threw papers at Moffett and accused her of being "a spy for the Democrats."

The judge was so angry that Moffett feared he would physically attack her, she said in the lawsuit, which asks for lost pay with interest.

It should be noted, however, that most states have enacted substantial discrimination laws, so the reporter will find similar types of actions in both the state and federal court systems.

How the Federal Courts Operate

The district court is the workhorse for the federal judiciary. Dockets are separated into criminal cases, civil disputes and admiralty actions. Lawsuits are filed with the clerk of district court, whether they are "local" actions or emanate from an executive agency in Washington. Federal civil proceedings become public record when the pleadings are filed.

WASHINGTON—The Bush Administration, arguing that legal challenges to the forced return of Haitians to their country amounted to an "unprecedented assault" on the prerogatives of the executive branch, asked the Supreme Court on Friday to reject a plea by lawyers for Haitian refugees that repatriation be halted.

More than 15,000 Haitians have been picked up at sea trying to flee Haiti since a military coup overthrew the elected government of President Jean-Bertrand Aristide in late 1991.

The range of cases working their way through the federal system is vast. Dissatisfied workers at the Charleston, S.C., Naval Shipyard ask a federal judge to prevent officials from destroying personnel files in a layoff dispute. A Milwaukee firm is awarded $25 million in punitive damages from an insurance company in another state after the insurance firm is convicted of fraud.

The chambers of federal judges often serve as courts of last resort for groups seeking extraordinary legal remedies.

> Plans by the Navy to slaughter more than 3,000 goats living wild on a Navy-owned island off southern California were disrupted Tuesday when a consortium of humane groups obtained a temporary restraining order barring a helicopter hunt scheduled to begin tomorrow.
>
> The order, which expires in 10 days, was issued by Federal Judge Irma Yamaguchi in Los Angeles a few hours after it was sought by groups asserting that the planned killing on San Clemente Island was unnecessary and inhumane.

Such orders often postpone action for days or months while the issue is sorted out in court hearings.

District court judges are provided with an assortment of assistants to help carry out the work of the court, including magistrates, law clerks, bailiffs, court reporters, probation officers and professional administrators. The U.S. magistrate is indispensable to the system, with authority to take action on many preliminary legal moves in federal cases. As a federal justice of the peace, the magistrate issues arrest warrants, holds preliminary examinations to determine whether to detain an accused person for federal grand jury action, and sets bail for the accused.

Much of the reporter's contact at the courthouse will be with the magistrate and his or her assistants, who may assume responsibility in some minor federal cases when the defendant waives his or her right to have the case heard by judge and jury.

Working closely with the magistrate is the marshal, who is empowered to make arrests, guards and transports prisoners, and maintains order in the federal courtrooms. The marshal is also an administrative official, with responsibility for disbursing federal judicial funds, serving court orders and transporting federal documents.

The federal judge, marshal and the U.S. attorney, another important officer of the district court, are appointed by the president, with the advice and consent of the U.S. Senate. Patronage and the wishes of influential members of the president's political party often play a major part in the selection of these federal officials.

The Federal Appellate Courts

Decisions rendered in the federal district courts can be taken to the U.S. Court of Appeals and in some cases directly to the Supreme Court. The 13 appeals courts also possess statutory power to review and enforce the actions of many federal agencies, among them some rulings of the National Labor Relations Board, the Department of Labor, the Federal Communications Commission, the Federal Aviation Administration and the Interstate Commerce Commission.

But most of the work of these courts is of an appellate nature, because it is the first stop from the district courts.

Other Federal Courts

Other federal courts with special functions include the U.S. Claims Court, the U.S. Tax Court, the U.S. Court of International Trade, the U.S. Court of Military Appeals and the U.S. Court of Veterans Appeals.

The Court of Claims adjudicates lawsuits brought by citizens against the federal government, most of them involving government contracts. Some involve attempts to collect damages for injuries by negligent behavior of federal employees; others are brought in an effort to collect compensation for the taking of private property for public purposes. This court represents an institutional arrangement whereby the federal government can be sued within a fairly narrow range.

The Tax Court redetermines excise taxes and penalties imposed on private foundations, pension plans and real estate investment trusts. It also renders judgments relating to qualification of retirement plans, and reviews the tax-exempt status of charitable organizations.

The Court of International Trade has jurisdiction over any civil action arising from federal laws governing import transactions. This court is used by the federal government to recover customs duties or for civil penalties involving fraud or negligence. Its decisions can be appealed to the federal circuit court.

The Court of Military Appeals, staffed by civilians, reviews decisions concerning military personnel.

The newest court in the federal system is the Court of Veterans Appeals, established in 1988 to review decisions made by the Board of Veterans Appeals.

The U.S. Supreme Court

At the pinnacle of the federal judiciary, the Supreme Court sits as the ultimate arbiter in the judicial process. Its decisions are final. In practice, however, the court has the discretion to reject an appeal on the ground that the federal issue is inappropriate or insubstantial, leaving the outcome of the case in the hands of a lower court. This discretionary power has cut down on the appeals from state courts, but the Supreme Court's caseload remains heavy—more than 5,000 cases docketed annually. While full written opinions may number fewer than 200 annually, most of the cases brought before the court are disposed of in some manner— affirmed, reversed, dismissed or returned to a lower court.

Disputes between or among states are taken directly to the Supreme Court, and the pleadings can take several terms of court.

> Fish and game officials in Kentucky and Ohio are watching carefully as fishermen slip in and out of what they call the "gray areas" of the Ohio River.
>
> The uncertainty is caused by the boundary dispute currently before the U.S. Supreme Court.

This lawsuit was filed by the Ohio attorney general and sought to establish how much of the Ohio River is owned by Kentucky. The court studied the case for more than 14 years before ruling on it.

> WASHINGTON—Like the sands of time, the banks of rivers may shift. But the boundary between the states of Ohio and Kentucky remains fixed where it was two centuries ago, the Supreme Court ruled Monday.
>
> In a 6–3 decision, the court said the boundary line between the two states is the low-water mark on the northern shore of the Ohio River as it existed in 1792 when Kentucky was admitted to the union.

There is regular interaction between the federal judiciary and the legislative and executive branches, and many court decisions provide potential local angles for reporters.

Disputes over new or existing legislation are common at the federal level, and they often conclude in the high court.

> WASHINGTON—The Supreme Court Thursday limited the ability of threatened children to sue state agencies that fail to protect them properly from their abusive parents or that needlessly split their families.
>
> In a 7–2 vote, the justices said the Adoption and Child Welfare Assistance Act of 1980, enacted to help children from troubled homes, does not give people the right to sue its violators.
>
> The law provides federal funds to states to use in foster care and other child welfare programs. In return, states must make "reasonable efforts" to keep families together and assure proper care for children who are removed from their homes.

In this case, the law had been in place for more than a decade before some of its provisions were questioned by a group of Illinois guardians. Lower courts had ruled that the guardians could sue the state agency, but the Supreme Court reversed that decision.

Controversial legislation often makes its way to the high court more quickly. Federal legislation that allowed limited timber harvests in Oregon and Washington forests populated by the endangered species of northern spotted owl moved quickly to the court where it was unanimously upheld in 1992.

The State Courts

The gavel bangs and the municipal court judge pronounces the verdict: guilty, he says of the defendant charged with allowing his dog to run loose on the streets. The dog's owner is fined $35 and charged an additional $25 in court costs.

The defendant does not deny the offense, which had led to the dog's biting the daughter of another resident, but pleads that it was unintentional. A youngster had left a screen door ajar, and the dog had escaped. After rejecting the defendant's argument and assessing the fine, the judge makes a final comment: "This is the limit of jurisdiction of this court," he tells the parties. "For further relief you will have to file action in another court."

The defendant judged guilty decides not to appeal his sentence to a higher court. But the other party files a civil action in circuit court to recover substantial hospital costs and other damages alleged to have been inflicted on the family.

Each state constitution, codification of statutes, or combination of both specifies the jurisdiction and function of a system of courts. Although different terminology is used among the states, the lowest courts—magistrate, municipal and police—generally are known as **courts of limited jurisdiction**. Minor cases begin in these courts and can be appealed to higher courts. Many limited courts also provide for trial by jury if demanded. More serious cases begin in **courts of general jurisdiction**. Cases in these courts can be appealed to the appellate courts (see Figure 9–2).

Disposal of a traffic charge may conclude the case in municipal or city court. Suppose, however, that a motorist strikes and injures a pedestrian in a crosswalk while running a red light. The injured pedestrian may seek relief in a trial court, initiating action to recover thousands of dollars in hospital and other medical costs.

The identity of the court of general jurisdiction in which the pedestrian seeks relief depends on the state. In Alabama it is known as Circuit Court; in Colorado it is District Court; in Ohio it is the Court of Common Pleas.

Some court systems provide for judges to handle both civil and criminal cases; other systems separate them; and still others operate separate chancery

FIGURE 9–2

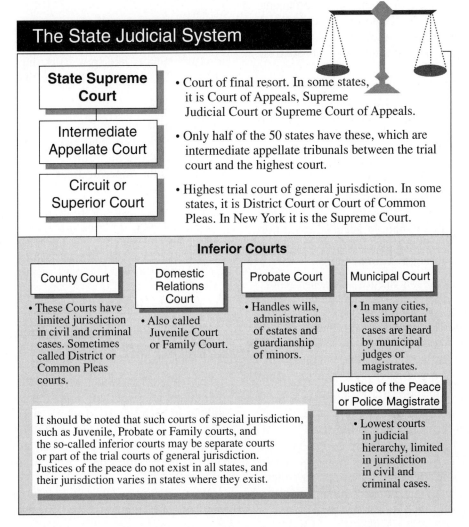

The State Judicial System

State Supreme Court
• Court of final resort. In some states, it is Court of Appeals, Supreme Judicial Court or Supreme Court of Appeals.

Intermediate Appellate Court
• Only half of the 50 states have these, which are intermediate appellate tribunals between the trial court and the highest court.

Circuit or Superior Court
• Highest trial court of general jurisdiction. In some states, it is District Court or Court of Common Pleas. In New York it is the Supreme Court.

Inferior Courts

County Court
• These Courts have limited jurisdiction in civil and criminal cases. Sometimes called District or Common Pleas courts.

Domestic Relations Court
• Also called Juvenile Court or Family Court.

Probate Court
• Handles wills, administration of estates and guardianship of minors.

Municipal Court
• In many cities, less important cases are heard by municipal judges or magistrates.

Justice of the Peace or Police Magistrate
• Lowest courts in judicial hierarchy, limited in jurisdiction in civil and criminal cases.

It should be noted that such courts of special jurisdiction, such as Juvenile, Probate or Family courts, and the so-called inferior courts may be separate courts or part of the trial courts of general jurisdiction. Justices of the peace do not exist in all states, and their jurisdiction varies in states where they exist.

(equity) courts. In sparsely populated areas, a single judge will serve a judicial district. Many urban counties provide for trial courts to handle cases that originate in them and intermediate appellate courts to handle the first appeal in the long process toward the state supreme court.

A Hierarchy of Functions

The lowest court in many states is justice of the peace. It is called Magistrate's Court, Municipal Court or Mayor's Court, administering justice in minor matters. Sometimes appointed, often elected, the justice of the peace need not possess a law degree in some areas of the country and is elected for a term of office ranging from two to 10 years. Many JPs perform quasi-judicial duties such as conducting civil marriages for a fee, signing county documents and issuing warrants of arrest to law enforcement agents.

Such courts have specific limits, usually set by the state Legislature, often hearing civil cases involving no more than $2,000 and criminal cases involving only misdemeanors. Judgments can be appealed to the next level of court jurisdiction.

The JP's office is an excellent source of news because of the justice's close relationship with police. Aside from issuing warrants, JP courts are often empowered to schedule preliminary hearings for people charged with crimes, set bail for people accused of minor crimes, and bind over people accused of more serious crimes to a higher court or to a grand jury.

> A Wellington salesman was charged with armed robbery Tuesday after the victim of a knife-point confrontation pointed him out to police.
>
> Arrest records identified the suspect as Paul D. Haynes, 28, 1500 Sussman Ave., who was jailed in lieu of $30,000 bail set by Magistrate William R. Baker.

Whatever the identity of these inferior courts, their jurisdiction remains limited to misdemeanors and small claims court action. For a filing fee of as little as $15, a person can seek recompense for any wrong or injury. Usually there is no need to hire a lawyer. Buyers of merchandise can sue for damages to the merchandise, people in business may sue to collect unpaid bills, baby sitters or day-care workers may sue for unpaid wages.

The reporter can find a wealth of feature material in the inferior courts. A resident filed a 75-cent lawsuit against a soft-drink firm, charging that she had purchased a defective can of soda. The firm settled out of court, settling for five cases of soda and the 75 cents. Another woman collected $150 in damages after filing a lawsuit against a laundry firm and charging that it had shrunk her lingerie to a point where it would not fit.

As the courts of general jurisdiction, the county or area trial courts originate the bulk of important cases for the state judiciary. It is these courts that the reporter will monitor most carefully, because more serious civil and criminal litigation will work its way through these systems.

More than half the states have an intermediate Court of Appeals, which is almost wholly appellate in nature. Some, like New York, have an elaborate intermediate structure, with more than 150 appellate courts.

Major litigation can work its way to a final court of appeals, whose main purpose is to determine the law rather than the facts. The highest state court may be designated as the Supreme Court, but some states refer to it as the Supreme Judicial Court or the Court of Appeals.

> The state is not liable for the death or injury of people in state-owned parks if the victims didn't pay to enter the grounds, the state Supreme Court ruled Wednesday.
>
> The case involved a damage claim by the mother of a girl who drowned in a park accident involving a rented canoe.

STAFFING THE COURTS

Judicial officials and the paperwork that flows through their offices are important to the reporter. The responsibilities of each official are fairly clear-cut—from the judge to the probation officer. Other offices in the system include the clerk of court, jury commission, bailiff, court reporter, prosecuting attorney and public defender.

Other officials might include a friend of the court, commissioner, referee, master, receiver and monitor.

As already noted, two of the most significant officers at the federal level are the marshal and the U.S. attorney.

The Judge

The chief officer in the judicial process is the judge. Records may be maintained in the clerk's office, but the decisions at nearly every point in the process are the judge's responsibility.

The clerk prepares trial lists called dockets or calendars, with the concurrence of the presiding judge, and final approval rests with the judge.

Most of the more than 12,000 judges in state and local courts are elected, but the appointive method is used exclusively at the federal level. Judges are drawn almost entirely from the legal profession. The federal judges are appointed by the president, subject to confirmation by a Senate majority, but other factors complicate the selection process. The administration usually needs to consult with the political powers in the home state of the judicial candidate.

Another group that plays an important role in the appointment of federal judges is the American Bar Association's Committee on the Federal Judiciary, which is asked to evaluate potential candidates. The 12-member committee, established in 1946, is a powerful factor in the nominating process.

Politics also plays a part in selection of judges at the state level. Proponents of the election method, which is used most often, argue that it is better to select a judge through a partisan ballot method than to engage in what they refer to as horse-trading and the "wheeling-dealing" of political figures. Proponents of the appointive method argue that the judicial candidate who must run on a partisan ballot cannot possibly serve as an impartial judge. Such a political process, they argue, impinges on the basic need for total impartiality on the bench. Furthermore, they say, the uninformed electorate may not be in a position to evaluate the legal abilities of the candidates.

Increasingly, civil rights groups in various states are questioning the way judges are selected.

Armed with a state report saying that the system of selecting New York Supreme Court judges could not withstand a legal challenge under the federal Voting Rights Act, a civil rights organization went into federal court Tuesday in an effort to give minority voters a bigger voice.

The action came a week after a judicial task force concluded that the way justices are nominated and elected in the state "cannot pass muster" under the federal law according stronger protection for racial minorities.

While some states call for candidacy on bipartisan or nonpartisan tickets, long and loyal service in partisan politics is generally a prerequisite for nomination. Elective terms of office are considerably longer than they are in other public jobs, ranging from four to 12 years, and some terms extend to life.

The judge rules supreme within the jurisdiction of his or her court, be it inside the courtroom during a trial or regarding the administrative details surrounding that proceeding. The clerk of court may summon a prospective juror, but the judge usually decides whether to excuse the juror for whatever reason.

As the presiding official, the judge exercises what is known as "inherent power" to assure impartial and efficient administration of justice. He or she demands decorum in the courtroom, assures attendance by all involved in the disposition of a case, and in other ways safeguards the administration of justice. The judge may punish a recalcitrant witness with contempt of court, an attorney who is seeking to unduly delay disposition of the case, or a reporter who the judge believes has interfered with administration of justice.

Nathan J. Rexrod told Judge Robert Maxwell on Friday that he had more important things to do, such as handle his business affairs, than be sworn in as a juror in Maxwell's court.

Maxwell wasn't sympathetic. He fined Rexrod $350 for failing to show up for jury duty and ordered him to spend 24 hours in the Randolph County jail.

While actions are pending, the judge issues orders (often called rulings or rules) which are directives rather than judgments. Orders are issued orally or in writing, often on a motion by one of the attorneys involved in the action. The order might require a witness to appear in court with specific records or it might delay proceedings while a defendant obtains information from another jurisdiction.

In jurisdictions in which two or more judges handle actions, a chief judge is appointed—through seniority, rotation or election—and serves as administrative officer, assigning cases and ruling on technical matters within that jurisdiction. Occasionally a judge with too many criminal cases routinely overturned in the appeals process will be reassigned to minor civil litigation. The careful reporter will keep track of such reversals, and, while a story of record may be an embarrassment to the judge in question, it is of interest to the public.

In cases where conflict of interest is possible, the presiding judge may also assign a different judge to hear the case.

Many actions of judges are routine, but others are worthy of coverage, depending upon the importance of the case. The reporter's working relationship with the judge is important, and often a court clerk will send the reporter to the judge's office for information about a pending case. Most judges will take the time to explain the significance of a ruling to a reporter.

The Clerk of Court

The clerk and assistants are the officials with whom the reporter will have the most contact. The clerk is the custodian of all court records, including the papers and exhibits scheduled to be taken into trial court. Money paid to the court is in the safekeeping of the clerk, who makes regular accountings and keeps records of funds received.

During the course of a day, the reporter will consult with the clerk or assistants to determine lawsuits filed, preliminary motions in pending trials, or papers filed during the course of a trial. Cooperative clerks can assist the reporter in assessing the importance of a development in a pending case, although the experienced journalist will make his or her own decision on whether to cover it.

The clerk or a deputy serves as secretary to the court during trial proceedings, helping draw jury panels, administering oaths to witnesses and jurors, reading verdicts of the jury, polling jurors when necessary, and entering judgments made by the presiding judge.

The clerk is also a source of information for periodic reports on fines collected and forfeitures, comparing them with those of previous years, problems with

bonds, and other court-related issues. The attorney for an aggrieved party makes the clerk's office the official point of first contact, filing a civil action there. The clerk assigns a number to it, and it is this number that the reporter uses to call up information on a pending case as it progresses through the judicial process. Through these filings with the clerk, the reporter determines the identity of attorneys retained by the parties in the dispute and often contacts them for additional details.

Commissioners, Masters and Referees

Most states appoint special officials to assist the judge in carrying out the work of the court. Some of the duties are partly judicial and partly clerical, such as the taking of affidavits and depositions, approval of bond and examination of sureties in civil cases, and administration of oaths. Court commissioners also handle details of probate and other proceedings.

Masters or referees are appointed at the judicial level to handle special cases, such as those involving technical evaluations. The judge may appoint a master to merely ascertain the facts or to actually try the case, subject to the judge's review.

Receivers are also appointed by the court to serve as temporary custodians of a business while issues in a lawsuit are determined by the court.

Growth of the courts has led to a variety of ways to try to keep up with the caseloads, and not all of them are universally accepted.

> When 14-year-old Louis Pilchner was convicted of aggravated murder April 4 in Statler County Juvenile Court, it was not by a jury or a judge.
>
> Administrative Judge John Mills was on vacation, and the three-day trial was heard by Referee Winifred Potter, who rendered the guilty verdict.
>
> Referees, who are employees of the court, hear all preliminary hearings and most juvenile court trials. A judge must approve of their decisions, but criticism of the referee system has surfaced.
>
> Prosecuting Attorney Henry Givens, who handled the juvenile case, said he found it "ridiculous" that a referee handled an aggravated murder trial.

This story was given impetus by a group called the Court Watching Project Inc., which uses observers to evaluate judicial effectiveness. In this case, the court watchers wanted juvenile court matters given a higher priority. The reporter can call on other sources on an issue such as this, including the public defender's office and officials of family agencies.

The reporter also has other sources in evaluating how the court systems are working. The American Bar Association and state legal groups have policies covering such court procedures, all available to the press.

Perceptive court officials often will seek out a reporter when an innovative project is about to be started, but the reporter cannot always depend on public information specialists. It is best to be aware of new projects as well as developing problems.

> A custody mediation service, designed to help divorced parents resolve by themselves any problems concerning custody of their children, will be started Jan. 1 in Starke County Domestic Relations Court.
>
> Domestic Relations Judge Rosanne Wilder said she believes the arrangement will be better than having a judge dictate custody, visitation and support decisions.
>
> The program will be funded by the Starke County Commission, but Wilder said many of the program's expenses can be collected as court costs.

The Jury Commission

The task of selecting prospective trial jurors falls to a jury commission, and the clerk of court sometimes acts as a jury commissioner. Clerks comb the voter lists (sometimes using the telephone directory, the city directory or tax rolls) for a representative list, called a **venire**, to appear as prospective jurors. Prospective grand jurors are selected in a similar manner.

Although little attention is given to the process of choosing people to serve in the jury system, thousands of citizens are selected each year to participate, drawing many who normally have little or no business with the courts.

Increasingly, states are changing the way jurors are selected, and the issue is rarely a cut-and-dried matter.

> Greenville County Solicitor Joseph Watson wants to stop choosing jurors from lists of people with driver's licenses and return to the old way of selecting them from the lists of registered voters.
>
> Watson said the change made in the jury selection pool in 1991 hasn't accomplished the goal of ensuring more jurors.

On this issue, as most others, the reporter has a wide range of sources. The state public defenders association might take a strong stand on the issue. Legislators who backed the new method are yet to be heard from. Sufficient time has elapsed to provide specific figures from representative courts and add detail to a nebulous issue. As with any new project that affects the public, the reporter always should take the time to ascertain whether it is working.

Human interest stories abound in the laborious selection and rejection process, and the reporter learns to watch for information that leads to such material. Stories detailing the cost of maintaining jury systems are interesting, and the people who operate them often provide human interest material.

Attorneys

Other court officials include private and public attorneys, who represent litigants before the bench. All are technically officers of the court.

A prosecuting attorney, sometimes called a district attorney or solicitor, is paid with public funds and represents the state in criminal cases. Under a constitutional guarantee of counsel, a public defender is often employed to represent people who cannot afford private counsel.

Private attorneys who represent clients in court are paid by them, making special arrangements for remuneration. Often a lawsuit is brought by a private party based on a contingency fee—a portion of the court award to be paid to the attorney who takes the case. The reporter should be familiar with lawyers in the community, and remember that many are helpful in explaining technical points in cases such as bankruptcy proceedings, tax litigation and real estate cases. Other lawyers specialize in condemnation proceedings and antitrust litigation.

Other Court Officials

The court reporter is important to the journalist covering the courts, taking verbatim accounts of all that transpires during a trial and at depositions. Attention to detail is important to this official, who prepares a complete record of the proceedings, known as the transcript, and makes those records available to reporters upon request. The transcripts constitute a public record that is used through the appeals process. This record is invaluable to the reporter in assembling an accurate account of an important proceeding, although deadlines often interfere with quick acquisition of a total transcript. But nothing breathes confidence into a reporter covering a complicated trial more than being able to quickly obtain an exact quotation by a witness or attorney. Oral instructions rendered by the judge and summations by attorneys are all detailed in the transcript.

Law enforcement agencies generally supply a **bailiff**, who acts as a sergeant at arms for the court, maintaining order, administering oaths to prospective jurors, serving subpoenas for the court, and otherwise assisting the judge in the courtroom.

> More than 400 people with knives have visited the Clay County Courthouse since Jan. 1, but the new security system in place kept them from carrying the knives into the building.
>
> Since the system went into effect, 422 knives with blades 3 inches or longer were left with security guards, Court Bailiff James Mejia said.
>
> The knives are returned when the people, who have been given receipts, leave the building.

The bailiff is an excellent source of news tips, identifying people scheduled to appear and providing information on coming events. Bailiffs ensure privacy for the jury during deliberations and remain with jurors if they are sequestered in important cases.

A party who desires to participate in a proceeding but without standing as plaintiff or defendant is given permission by the judge to act as a **friend of the court** (*amicus curiae*), offering advice or presenting other evidence. Such outsiders in the court process may present briefs or offer testimony because their interests may be directly or indirectly affected by the outcome of the case.

CONTEMPT OF COURT

Like the public, the reporter operates under a special condition: the judge's power to cite for contempt of court. Any act the judge construes as hindering or obstructing the court in its effort to fairly administer justice subjects a person to contempt. Even an action that embarrasses the court might bring on a contempt citation.

The judge possesses the arbitrary power to fine or imprison anyone determined to be in contempt of court. A presiding judge has the power to send a reporter to the lockup overnight for what the judge perceives to be an infraction of his or her rules.

Such penalties are enforceable unless they are reversed on appeal to a higher court. Reporters should remember that they are as susceptible to contempt as anyone else.

In a pending trial of a public official on sexual misconduct charges, the presiding judge took steps to limit the coverage of the case.

> Although the trial was expected to receive extensive publicity, Judge George J. McGillivery has placed limits on some aspects of that coverage.
>
> He has prohibited news interviews with witnesses, or photographing and interviewing of jurors.
>
> McGillivery has also forbidden the photographing of any women called to testify. Some female witnesses previously were reluctant to testify because television cameras are being allowed in the courtroom.

The reporter or photographer who breaks such rules does so at his or her own peril.

Publication of stories that include criticism of a pending case, which the judge believes has obstructed justice, has landed reporters in jail, sometimes for a specified length of time, sometimes for an indefinite period.

Reasons for contempt citations include publication of grand jury testimony which has not been made public by the court; serious inaccuracies in reporting a trial, including what the judge perceives as an incomplete or unbalanced report; publication of stories deemed prejudicial to the case; or refusal of a reporter to break a confidence while testifying on the witness stand. Often a reporter will be in possession of information that the court considers important to a case.

> A federal judge jailed four reporters Wednesday when they refused to testify in the corruption trial of State Sen. J.R. Stinson (R-Macon).
>
> One by one the reporters were held in contempt of court for declining to answer questions about their

interviews with Stinson in 1991 when his campaign records were seized in an investigation by the Federal Bureau of Investigation.

In this case, the reporters' attorney said they were "united in resistance" to a court order compelling them to testify in the legislator's trial. After the reporters spent five hours in jail, the judge freed them, saying it did not appear that his action would change their minds.

The courts are not clear whether reporters have special rights that protect them from testifying in a trial. Press advocates say that forcing reporters to testify violates the First Amendment to the Constitution protecting freedom of the press.

The issue of confidentiality between the reporter and his or her sources continues to be debated, and some journalists have spent weeks in jail after refusing an order by a judge to disclose a source. More than half the states have enacted shield laws designed to protect the reporter, but the debate continues over whether the press should bow to legislative decree for the protection it needs.

The contempt process extends to the public and is often newsworthy, as this story shows.

> Each month a diverse collection of divorced fathers who have consistently failed to make regular child support payments is called to Warren Circuit Court to explain why they should not be sent to jail.
>
> The pageant of wheedling, mumbling, last-minute bargaining and tall-tale telling that ensues during these court sessions is known as Contempt Day.
>
> Tuesday's session offered an education in extenuating circumstances as parents in arrears tried to explain themselves to Judge Wanda Peers.
>
> "I've been trying to get a business started for five years," explained a father who had fallen more than $3,000 behind in child support payments.
>
> But why hadn't he showed up in court last month?
>
> "I didn't see my name on the docket," he said. The judge was not convinced. She sentenced the man to 90 days in the Warren County Detention Center for contempt of court.
>
> The bailiff closed in on the father, snapped the handcuffs on and took him away. It had a chastening effect on the 35 persons waiting to plead their cases.

Attorneys involved in a court case are also susceptible to citations for contempt. Sometimes the jury's verdict in a case is accompanied by a judge's order directing an attorney to pay a fine for contempt, on grounds he or she exceeded the bounds of propriety in handling a case.

MONITORING THE COURTS

Because the court system is all-pervasive, used by both individuals and public bodies to litigate arguments, the records path becomes a pipeline of valuable information for reporters on many beats. The information moves both ways—into the courts from ongoing issues in government, and out into the hands of governmental bodies themselves.

The pipeline can be a valuable and sometimes unexpected source of information. Facts that can't be had in either the private or public sector often turn up in seemingly unrelated court actions. The business reporter might be at a dead end in pursuing details of a developer's questionable activities, for example, then find relevant information in a court action brought by disgruntled contractors.

Often a bankruptcy action will trigger information that a reporter can use to put a business story into better perspective.

> Creditors of Mark R. Savage, accusing the prominent Boston developer of "pervasive looting," have asked U.S. Bankruptcy Court for approval to directly supervise his companies' holdings.
>
> Savage, a well-known philanthropist and political contributor, filed for Chapter 11 bankruptcy protection May 13.
>
> The creditors claim Savage improperly took money and spent it on his 70-foot yacht, landscaping for his oceanfront home in South Dartmouth, and an inflated salary for himself.

In this instance, as in most bankruptcy cases, abundant detail helps the reporter put a complicated financial story into perspective. The number of bankruptcy filings has grown immensely in the past 10 years, and all are public record. The reporter only needs the name of the principal or the filing number to obtain access to the case.

The bribery trial of an Indiana mayor several years ago provided reporters with details of improper city purchasing practices not always easy for reporters to obtain.

> Prosecution witness John Trippe told an Indianapolis jury Tuesday how he determined whether city officials were susceptible to bribery.
>
> Trippe made his first appearance on the witness stand in the bribery trial of Seymour Mayor Christopher D. Moritz, and explained how he upped his earnings from $300 a week to $1,500 a week:
>
> Before approaching city officials, Trippe said, he visited the city's garage to check product labels.
>
> "If I found legitimate firms' products, I wouldn't even bother to sell to that city," Trippe testified. "But if I found labels of Century, Correlated Products or American Associates, I would figure somebody was either on the take or ignorant that those firms paid kickbacks." Trippe testified that he then would approach the person in charge of the city's purchasing department.

In another court case, a New Jersey salesman of chemicals used by sewage treatment plants testified that he had to pay a 20 percent kickback to plant operators if he wanted to stay in business.

"Everybody's doing it," the salesman said of his competition. He testified under immunity from prosecution in bribery-kickback schemes.

The court reporter should regularly take time to analyze the quality of service the public receives from judges and court staffs. This entails assessment of details of court operation, such as how the budget is being spent and the currency of court dockets. As the plea bargaining patterns of district attorneys are scrutinized, so should sentencing patterns among judges be monitored.

Reporters also should be familiar with public and private groups that monitor the courts. They are a mix of private, nonprofit organizations trying to improve the courts and educate the public, as well as bar associations that maintain monitoring committees.

> County judges suspended prison time or fines in 58 percent of convictions in 1991, according to the Court Watching Project.
>
> The project, a nonprofit organization that monitors the local courts, said its members followed 1,309 felony charges that ended in 670 convictions. Prison time was suspended in 41 percent of the convictions and fines in 16 percent.

Crime victims' groups also have become active in monitoring the courts, some of them state commissions created by legislation. Civil rights groups, too, watch the courts, and their material is often newsworthy. However, reporters must take care in attributing the figures disseminated by all of these organizations because they cannot be assumed to be impartial or accurate.

***

LEGAL GLOSSARY

Knowledge of these basic legal terms will help the student-reporter explain court actions in more understandable terms.

ACTION IN PERSONAM: An action against the person, based on a personal liability.

ACTION IN REM: An action to recover a specific object, usually an item of personal property, such as jewelry or a car.

ADVERSARY SYSTEM: The system in use in this country in which each of the opposing, or adversary, parties is given the opportunity to present and establish opposing contentions in court.

AFFIDAVIT: A written statement given before a notary public or other official who has the authority to administer an oath.

ALLEGATION: The statement to a party in an action, submitted in a pleading, setting out what the party expects to prove.

AMICUS CURIAE: A friend of the court; one who joins an action, with permission of the court, and volunteers information.

ANSWER: A pleading by which a defendant seeks to resist a plaintiff's allegations.

APPELLATE COURT: A court that has jurisdiction of appeal and review, as opposed to a trial court.

ARRAIGNMENT: The process of bringing a prisoner to court to officially hear and respond to the criminal charge(s) against him or her.

ASSIGNMENT: An act by which a person assigns his or her rights to property to another.

ATTACHMENT: A remedy that enables a plaintiff to acquire a lien upon property for satisfaction of judgment.

ATTORNEY OF RECORD: The attorney whose name appears in the permanent files or record of a case.

BAIL: Security obtained by the court which allows a person to go free pending appearance in court.

BENCH WARRANT: A demand issued by the court for the arrest of a person or attachment of property.

BINDING INSTRUCTION: Process by which the jury is told that if it finds certain facts to be true, it must find for the plaintiff or the defendant.

BIND OVER: To hold on bail or for trial.

BRIEF: A document filed by counsel in court, usually setting forth facts and law in support of his or her case.

BURDEN OF PROOF: In the law of evidence, the necessity of indisputably proving a fact or facts.

CERTIORARI: A writ directing judges or officers of inferior courts to certify or to return the records of proceedings to the higher court for judicial review.

CHATTEL: Tangible property, such as personal possessions, machinery, stocks and bonds, as distinguished from real property.

CIRCUMSTANTIAL EVIDENCE: Evidence of an indirect nature.

COLLUSION: A secret, deceitful arrangement between two or more people.

COMPLAINT (CIVIL):   The initial pleading on the part of plaintiff in a civil action.

COMPLAINT (CRIMINAL):   A sworn application for a warrant of arrest, alleging that a law has been broken.

CONTEMPT OF COURT: Any act that a judge considers has embarrassed or hindered the court in its effort to administer justice.

CONTRACT: A written or oral agreement between two parties which is considered enforceable by law.

DECLARATORY JUDGMENT: Court decree that declares the rights of a party to an action or expresses the opinion of the court on a question of law.

DECREE: An order or a decision by the court. Decrees can be final or interlocutory, provisional or preliminary.

DEMUR: A pleading admitting the truth of the facts in a civil complaint, or answer, but contending the legal insufficiency of the complaint. Also, **Demurrer**.

DEPOSITION: Testimony of a witness taken outside of court.

DISCOVERY: A proceeding that enables one party to become informed of the facts known by other parties to the action.

DOUBLE JEOPARDY: The constitutional prohibition against more than one prosecution for the same crime.

EASEMENT: A privilege or right acquired to use the land of another. A public easement is acquired by condemnation, such as a public utility's right to place power or telephone lines across property.

EMBEZZLEMENT: Fraudulent appropriation of money or property entrusted to one person by another.

EMINENT DOMAIN: The right of a government to take private property for public use.

ENJOIN: To require a person through court action to perform or abstain from an act.

ESCROW: A fund into which a party to a pending agreement deposits something of value, often a deed or money, to be surrendered to a second party when final action is taken in a proceeding.

EXTRADITION: The surrender by one state or jurisdiction to another of an individual accused or convicted of an offense outside its own territory and within the territorial jurisdiction of another.

FELONY: A serious crime, generally punishable by imprisonment in a penitentiary.

FORGERY: Altering or falsely copying, with intent to defraud, any material which, if genuine, might be the foundation of a legal liability, such as a check or deed.

FRAUD: Intentional perversion of the truth; a deceitful practice undertaken with intent to deprive another of his or her rights.

GARNISHMENT: A court decree that applies (garnishees) money or property of a person toward the debts owed to a creditor.

GRAND JURY: A body whose duty is to study complaints and accusations in criminal cases and to indict or dismiss persons accused. (As distinguished from a **Petit jury**, the ordinary jury of 12 or fewer people who sit at the trial in civil or criminal actions).

HABEAS CORPUS: A writ directing a person to appear before a court or judge. Most commonly, it is directed to an official detaining another, commanding him or her to produce that person, so the court can determine whether due process of law has been observed.

INDICTMENT: A written accusation by a grand jury, charging that a person has committed a crime.

INJUNCTION: A mandatory or prohibitive order issued by a court.

INSTRUCTION: Directions given by a judge to a jury concerning the law.

INTERROGATORIES: Written questions by a party to an action served on the other party who must provide written responses under oath.

LIBEL: Defamation of a person or group by print, pictures or signs.

LIEN: A charge imposed on specific property, which is security for a debt.

MANDAMUS: A court order that compels action.

MANSLAUGHTER: The unlawful killing of another without malice. It may be voluntary, upon sudden impulse, or involuntary in the commission of an unlawful act.

MASTER: A court officer, usually an attorney, who takes testimony in proceedings such as divorce hearings, and reports to the court.

MISDEMEANOR: Minor offense, often punishable by less than a year in jail or a fine, or both.

MISTRIAL: An invalid trial, usually aborted because of irregular procedure or disregard of a fundamental requisite.

NO BILL: Returns of a "no bill" by a grand jury that decides evidence is insufficient to warrant charging the accused.

NOLLE PROSEQUI: The prosecuting officer in a criminal case declares that he or she will no longer prosecute a case, effectively dropping the charge or charges. Also, **Nol pros**.

NOLO CONTENDERE: A pleading by defendants in criminal cases, which literally means "I will not contest it." The defendant is, in effect, throwing him- or herself on the mercy of the court. Corporations often plead to this, agreeing to pay damages but without admitting guilt.

PLAINTIFF: A person who brings an action in court.

PLEADING: The process in which parties to an action alternately present written contentions, narrowing the field of controversy.

PRELIMINARY HEARING: A hearing to determine whether a person charged with a crime should be held for trial.

PRESENTMENT: A statement in writing by a grand jury to the court that a public offense has been committed without a bill of indictment being first submitted to the jury.

PRIVILEGE: A protection that allows the journalist to report judicial and other public proceedings without the risk of libel.

PROBATE: The process of proving that a will is valid.

PROBATION: The process of allowing a person convicted of a crime to remain free, usually under supervision of a probation officer.

PROSECUTOR: An official who initiates prosecution of someone accused of a crime and who performs the function of a trial lawyer on behalf of the public.

QUASH: To overturn, annul or void a summons or indictment.

REMAND: To send a prisoner back to custody after a hearing that has not resulted in final judgment; also, the action of an appellate court in returning a case to the court of original jurisdiction for final disposal.

SEARCH WARRANT: An order directing an officer to search a specified property to determine whether a crime has been committed.

SLANDER: Defamatory words spoken that tend to prejudice another in reputation or livelihood.

SPECIFIC PERFORMANCE: A mandatory order in equity to perform a specific action.

SUBPOENA: An order for a witness to appear and give testimony before a court.

SUBSTANTIVE LAW: Law dealing with rights, duties and liabilities, as distinguished from adjective law, the law regulating procedure.

SUMMONS: An order directing the sheriff or another officer to notify a person that an action has commenced against him or her in court, and requiring appearance to answer the complaint.

TORT: An injury or wrong committed against the person or property of another.

TRANSCRIPT: The official record of a proceeding.

TRESPASS: Any action in which entry is made or unlawful injury is done to another's property.

TRUE BILL: A grand jury's endorsement of a bill of indictment when the jury believes there is sufficient evidence to support a criminal charge.

VENIRE: A writ summoning people to court to act as jurors but used popularly to identify the group of names summoned.

VENUE: The location in which the events take place from which a legal action arises. A change of venue removes an action from one geographical or judicial area to another.

VOIR DIRE: Literally, to speak the truth. The preliminary examination of prospective jurors or witnesses to determine their qualifications.

WARRANT OF ARREST: An order issued by a magistrate or other authority to a sheriff or other officer directing the arrest of a person to be brought to court.

WARRANTY DEED: A document giving title to land or other property, including the covenant guaranteeing the validity of the title.

WRIT: A court order requiring the performance of a specified act or providing the authority to have it done.

*** * ***

SUGGESTED READINGS

Denniston, Lyle W. *The Reporter and the Law*. New York: Columbia University Press, 1992.

A respected reporter discusses techniques for covering the courts.

Franklin, Marc A., and David A. Anderson. *Mass Media Law: Cases and Materials*. 4th ed. Westbury, N.Y.: Foundation Press, 1990.

Chapter 10

Covering
Civil Actions

The reporter pores over her notes in the court clerk's office, reviewing a 2-year-old lawsuit about to go to trial. Several stories have been written during that time, the first reporting a prominent citizen's grievance with the operators of a local cemetery and asking for a substantial money award. Another story reported the cemetery operators' response to the civil action.

The most recent story several months ago detailed an unsuccessful effort to make the city, nominal owner of the cemetery property, a party to the lawsuit.

A clerk interrupts the reporter. The case will not go to trial after all, he says. It has been settled out of court for an undisclosed sum.

The reporter's final story is brief. Despite her earnest efforts to obtain information from attorneys and from the principals themselves, the amount of the settlement remains a secret—at least for the moment. Sometimes the amount of the settlement will appear on the record later—through filing of a related court action by one of the parties to the original lawsuit. The reporter will note this possibility for future reference.

As in this example, most of the civil actions begun in the courts never reach the trial stage, but many are worth covering. Controversy arising from the legal process is part of what makes civil litigation news. The identity of the individuals or corporations involved is another element, and the decisions reached by judge or jury are others.

Diligence and persistence, coupled with the ability to organize information as actions inch their way through the legal process, are indispensable elements in covering the courts. A knowledge of the process itself, of course, is basic.

THE ACTION COMMENCES

Civil action begins with a dispute between two parties. One contends that a wrong has been committed and seeks redress. Advice is usually sought from an attorney, who identifies relevant law, helping to decide whether the issue should be pursued through the courts and estimating the chances for recovery.

The proper court system is identified, and legal action begins when the aggrieved party, called the **plaintiff**, retains an attorney to present the grievance as a formal complaint. The complaint details the grievance and asks for relief in the form of a monetary award or equitable action.

A Middletown physician has filed a $3 million lawsuit in U.S. District Court against Central Hospital Inc., charging discrimination in the hospital's decision to limit her staff privileges there.

Dr. May Kho Lim, whose office is at 300 West St., is also seeking an injunction to force the hospital's executive committee to grant her full surgery privileges.

In her lawsuit, Lim alleged that she had been granted surgical privileges from 1989 until this year

when the executive committee voted to deny them without giving a reason.

After the complaint is formally brought to the attention of the other party (the **defendant**), the attorney for that party drafts and files an answer. These basic actions constitute the beginning of the process called pleadings, which may or may not culminate in trial.

Some newspapers use the term **respondent** instead of defendant to help the reader distinguish between a civil and a criminal defendant.

Between filing the complaint and the trial lie months, even years, of pretrial activities that narrow the issues in the dispute and force both sides to share information about the case.

Failure to settle the dispute leads to the judge's decision that the case is **at issue** and ready for trial. A civil lawsuit is decided by judge or jury, with a judgment order issued if the judge concludes that the jury's verdict was correct, calling for payment of damages. After the trial, an appeal may be made to a higher court.

The scope of the judicial process, and the large number of actions filed, prevent comprehensive coverage of the courts. Because only a small percentage of actions will be reported, news judgment plays an important role.

The individuals or corporations involved in the action, amount of damages and circumstances surrounding the dispute are all critical in the decision to report and follow a civil action.

The reporter should be careful with "I am going to file a suit" stories. The best rule is to wait for official filing of an action before reporting it, but major legal controversies are often an exception. If the mayor of a municipality threatens to sue the county government to force release of matching federal funds, the threat is clearly newsworthy. But the attorney for a wronged party who advises the press that he is "about" to file a lawsuit for his client may be fishing for a way to frighten the potential defendant into settling the grievance. The reporter is wise to wait until the lawsuit is filed to do a story on it.

Following through is important after the initial story is written because the complaint merely outlines the grievance of one party and does not necessarily constitute fact. Many newspapers now point this out in stories about originating lawsuits, adding this parenthetical note:

(A lawsuit outlines the grievance of one party against another and does not present both sides of the issue in question.)

Fairness dictates that the reporter try to obtain the defendant's side of the story when a complaint is filed. Because the defendant probably has not seen the complaint, the reporter may get a "no comment," but the effort should be made. Lacking that, a follow-up story should detail the defendant's response.

The city Tuesday defended its action in dismissing three police officers on official charges they were derelict in their duties.

Answering a complaint by Officers Harry S. Reed, Willis J. Sims and Joseph P. Ridell that the city unjustly discriminated against them by its action, City Attorney G.S. Merritt alleged that the men "illegally conspired to call in for each other during night patrol, allowing each other to remain away from their posts for long periods of time."

"This serious action," the lawsuit's answer stated, "resulted in a dangerous and unwarranted reduction in police patrol."

If news judgment dictates that a story be written on the filing of a civil lawsuit, its progress should be followed through the final disposition of the case—even if it is years later. Many newspapers hire clerks to compile and publish lists of lawsuits filed, with final judgments listed as a public service when they occur. Separate news stories highlight court actions deemed of general interest.

Details of a Complaint

A civil complaint (not to be confused with a complaint filed in the criminal process) officially advises the defendant of the existence and nature of the grievance and puts the defendant on notice that the action is being brought.

Complaints include the following basic information: Identity of the plaintiff and the defendant, location and identity of the court, serial number of the case, a factual statement of the plaintiff's claim or claims, and a demand for relief.

The plaintiff may be parent or guardian for a minor child or for a person who is otherwise incompetent to pursue the case. Often a substitution is made in identity of a plaintiff or a defendant upon the death of one of the original parties to the lawsuit. Other parties may join the lawsuit as intervenors, and the court retains the discretion to consolidate actions where several relate to the same dispute.

A judge has ordered six nursing homes to consolidate civil suits filed against the state, seeking reimbursement for service to Medicaid patients during the last four years.

In most complaints, the plaintiff details the specific circumstances which led to the action, such as time and place, exactly what is alleged to have occurred, and the parties involved. After the allegations, the plaintiff lists the damages demanded or equitable relief asked, such as money, issuance of an injunction or granting of a divorce.

The amount of money damages is often deliberately exaggerated, and the reporter should take this into account in assessing the value of the news story. The law provides for general damages, presumed to have resulted from an injury, and special damages, which must be proven. A businessman may allege that his income has been affected by breach of a contract, and the actual amount of damages must be determined by jury or judge. Punitive damages sometimes are assessed with the object of punishing the defendant. Nominal damages sometimes are awarded merely as vindication of the plaintiff's character. Awards of $1 are not uncommon.

How to Deal with a Complaint

This complaint against the Sisters of the Pallotine Missionary Society, filed in state court, provides an example of the type of information available to the reporter. A news story is culled from the basic information.

Plaintiff ID is frequently inadequate, and the reporter must carefully flesh out a full identification. In this case, a few phone calls were sufficient to establish Ms. Hodges' home address, age and occupation.

IN THE CIRCUIT COURT OF CALE COUNTY, WEST VIRGINIA
MACEL HODGES
   Plaintiff

vs.

SISTERS OF THE PALLOTINE MISSIONARY SOCIETY,
a corporation d/b/a ST. MARY'S HOSPITAL
   Defendant

doing business as

                                    CIVIL ACTION NO. 92-2747

The reporter will find it easy to return to records years later through this permanent court number.

COMPLAINT

I.

On November 26, 1992, plaintiff Macel Hodges was a patient in St. Mary's Hospital in the City of Greenville, WV and was being treated in said hospital for a nervous condition and was kept on 4 East, a locked ward of said hospital. Said hospital is owned and operated by Sisters of the Pallotine Missionary Society, a corporation doing business as St. Mary's Hospital.

Suits are frequently filed years later. The reporter should always doublecheck the year in which the grievance was alleged to have occurred.

II.

It was necessary in order for the patients on 4 East to use the toilet, that they walk through a shower room. Said shower room had developed a leak so that floor from time to time became wet and slippery. The employees of said hospital were aware of this condition and failed to use due care to make the premises reasonably safe and to protect the patients on 4 East from injury.

Charges like these are privileged in court actions, but the reporter must always qualify the material that is picked up. It must always be remembered that this represents only one side's version.

III.

Plaintiff had an occasion to use the toilet on November 26, and as she stepped from the hall into said shower room she suddenly slipped on the wet floor and was thrown violently to the floor. On the way down she attempted to catch herself on the lavatories and as a result she suffered a severe wretching of her shoulders, back and neck and also took a severe blow on her left hip. When plaintiff recovered her senses, she was able to get to her feet and inform the nurses she had fallen. Plaintiff had planned to go home for a Thanksgiving visit the next morning, but was unable to go by reason of the fall. Plaintiff suffered what is commonly known as a severe

Like other areas in which direct quotation is used, the reporter must never take liberties. If a suit uses the term "wretching," and the reporter wishes to use it, he or she should pick it up exactly.

Often the reporter must draw a line between "trying the case" in the newspaper and ignoring it completely. So many months or years will elapse before possible trial, there is little likelihood of the former. A suit may appear frivolous, but it is not so to the parties involved.

whiplash, and for a period of several months suffered great pain in both shoulders and neck. At the present time, the pain in plaintiff's left shoulder has been alleviated, but the pain in the right shoulder is so severe that she is unable to perform any task without suffering great pain. Since the fall, plaintiff has on at least a dozen occasions, when the pain radiates from her neck down into her back, fainted and completely lost her senses. Since said fall, she has feared to travel any place without being accompanied by some other member of her family, and when she is forced to travel alone she is continually apprehensive that she might faint and fall upon the street.

IV.

Plaintiff alleges that it was the duty of said hospital to use all due care to keep the premises in a reasonably safe condition in order that patients confined therein would suffer no injury, but that St. Mary's Hospital breached the aforesaid duty and failed to use due care, and that the failure constituted actionable negligence against the defendant; that the negligence of defendant was the sole and proximate cause of plaintiff's injury, and that by reason of the aforesaid negligence plaintiff has been injured and suffered great pain of body and mind and will continue to suffer great pain of both body and mind for the rest of her life. As a direct consequence of the wrong and injury, plaintiff has been damaged to the amount of $420,000.00.

WHEREFORE, plaintiff demands judgment in the amount of $420,000.00 and costs.

The key to most suits lies in amount of damages sought, but that should be only one yardstick used by the reporter in deciding how much of a story to produce.

MACEL HODGES,
by counsel

Most newspapers consider publication of attorneys' names and their firms a necessary part of the court story. Others look upon it as a form of free advertising for lawyers. The reporter is advised to add the attorney's name unless there is a rule against it.

BARR, NAPIER & COLEMAN

Attorneys for plaintiff
630 Fifth Street
Greenville, West Virginia

By _William K. Napier_
May 30, 1993

IN THE CIRCUIT COURT OF CALE COUNTY, WEST VIRGINIA
MACEL HODGES
    Plaintiff

vs.

SISTERS OF THE PALLOTINE MISSIONARY SOCIETY,
a corporation d/b/a ST. MARY'S HOSPITAL
    Defendant

ANSWER OF DEFENDANT

Like many answers, this is a fairly general defense and there is little the reporter can do about it, unless the party is willing to discuss it further. Most defendants cloak themselves in as much anonymity as possible and hunker down for the long litigation.

FIRST DEFENSE: As its first defense to the Complaint of the plaintiff against it, said defendant states as follows:

    1. As its answer to Paragraph I of the Complaint of the plaintiff against it, said defendant admits that St. Mary's Hospital is owned and operated by the Sisters of the Pallotine Missionary Society, a corporation d/b/a St. Mary's Hospital, but specifically denies each and every other allegation contained therein and demands strict proof thereof.

    2. As its answer to Paragraph II of the Complaint of the plaintiff against it, said defendant denies each and every allegation contained therein and demands strict proof thereof.

SECOND DEFENSE: As its second defense to the Complaint of the plaintiff against it, said defendant states that the plaintiff herself was guilty of acts of negligence which contributed directly and proximately to the incident involved in this legal action, and the alleged injuries and damages suffered by her, therefore was guilty of contributory negligence, and as a result thereof may not recover of this defendant in this action.

The key to this news story probably lies in this second defense—in alleging that Ms. Hodges was herself guilty of negligence which contributed to her fall.

WHEREFORE, defendant, Sisters of the Pallotine Missionary Society, a corporation d/b/a St. Mary's Hospital, demands that the Complaint of the plaintiff against it be dismissed, and that it be awarded its costs of action.

Peter C. Jenkins
_____
Counsel for Defendant

Be consistent. If you used lawyer for the plaintiff weeks before, you should pick up the counsel for the defendant as well.

PETER C. JENKINS
1190 Wood St.
Greenville, WV

Counsel for Defendant

In this case, the complaint was accompanied by an affidavit signed by Macel Hodges certifying the truth of the allegations. It is often necessary for the reporter to contact the parties involved or their attorneys for ages, addresses, occupations and other explanatory information. With this material in hand and added to the complaint, the reporter is ready to write the first story on the action:

> A 77-year-old retired bookkeeper sued the operators of St. Mary's Hospital for $420,000 Tuesday, claiming that she was severely injured in a shower room fall while she was a patient.
>
> In the lawsuit filed in Cale County Circuit Court, Macel Hodges, 1920 Earl St., alleged that while being treated for a nervous condition Nov. 26, 1992, she slipped in a shower room, suffering "a severe wretching of her shoulders, back and neck," and whiplash. Since the accident, Hodges contends, she has fainted on at least a dozen occasions and fears to travel alone.
>
> Hospital personnel, although aware of the leak in the shower room, were negligent in allowing the condition to exist, Hodges contends. She charged that the Sisters of the Pallotine Missionary Society, who operate the hospital, failed to keep the facility in a "reasonably safe condition."
>
> William K. Napier is attorney for Hodges.

Important to this story is the claim of injuries suffered by Hodges, the total damages sought, and identity of the defendant and the religious society that operates the hospital. Hodges is suing the operators of the hospital rather than the hospital itself.

The Defendant Answers

In the parlance of the prize fight ring, the first blow has been struck. As defendant, the hospital operators must respond to the complaint with a formal answer within a specified time, usually within 30 days, or risk a default judgment (see legal answer on p. 205).

The defendant may deny some or all of the allegations in the complaint, setting the stage for the pleadings which lead to eventual trial or settlement. The purpose of the pleadings is to identify the issues to be tried.

An answer to Hodges' complaint was filed several weeks later by the attorney for the operators of the hospital. The answer was accompanied by a Certificate of Service, certifying that the defendant's attorney had provided a copy of the answer to the attorney for the plaintiff.

The operators of the hospital, who have declined until now to respond to any questions concerning the lawsuit, have officially responded to the court. Armed with the court record, the reporter can write a story detailing that response to Hodges' action.

> The operators of St. Mary's Hospital Thursday denied charges that its employees were negligent in caring for one of its elderly patients, who said she sustained injuries in a severe fall during her stay in the hospital.
>
> In answering a $420,000 civil suit brought by Macel Hodges, Sisters of the Pallotine Missionary Society, who operate the hospital, alleged that Hodges herself was guilty of negligence that contributed to her fall in a shower room Nov. 26, 1992.
>
> The hospital operators also argued that Hodges knew the risks involved when she became a patient and voluntarily assumed those risks. They asked for dismissal.
>
> The answer to Hodges' charges was filed in Cale County Circuit Court. Peter C. Jenkins is attorney for the hospital operators.

It should be noted that the complaint generally has greater news value than the defendant's answer weeks later. Whatever that newsworthiness, fairness dictates equitable play for both sides of the argument.

While civil actions may be far more complex than this, most of them begin with this basic procedure—a document laying out the complaint of one party and an answer by the other.

Other Responses

A defendant has recourse to responses other than denial of allegations through a formal answer. His or her attorney may file a **demurrer**, stating that the plaintiff's action has no basis in law, or a **plea in abatement**, objecting to the manner in which the plaintiff filed the action. The defendant may cite a **lack of jurisdiction** over the person or subject matter; object that the **venue**, the court in which the action is filed, is improper; or cite lack of a capacity to sue in the first place. The defendant may plead that another action is pending and, thus, the complaint is invalid or the action has been brought prematurely. All of these tactics require rulings by the presiding judge.

The reporter must be able to explain the legal terminology, while moving the story along. Here is how a demurrer action might be handled in a news story:

> The attorney for Langmuir County Monday asked for dismissal of a Circuit Court suit brought against it by the District Authority, *arguing there is no legal basis for the claim.*
>
> *In a demurrer* filed with Judge John T. Scopes, County Attorney Paul L. Craig submitted detailed federal regulations specifying the $6.9 million to which the county claims the authority is limited.
>
> "None of us has anything to say about how the pie is sliced," Craig argued. "It's all spelled out in these federal regulations."
>
> The authority is suing to increase the amount due it from the county to $10.6 million.

A defendant might think he or she not only owes nothing to the plaintiff but also that the plaintiff in fact owes something to the defendant. Then the answer may include a **counterclaim**, which calls for a further reply from the plaintiff. Often an automobile collision is the catalyst in such actions, with each party asserting that the other is responsible and should pay damages.

JUDGMENTS WITHOUT TRIAL

In any court on any day, routine motions are heard that affect the course of litigation in civil actions. Not all of them are newsworthy. They include efforts to extend the time allowed for filing a pleading, changes in attorneys and other such requests.

In some circumstances, judgment can be made without going through the trial process, and the reporter should be alert to these proceedings that affect the final outcome of an action. Often an abrupt decision to drop an action is as newsworthy as the original filing of the action.

The attorney for one party may move for a **summary judgment** if he or she believes the defendant's answer is clearly inadequate. Arguments on a motion for summary judgment can be as extensive as a full trial. This motion is used to compel the other party to disclose the kind of proof he or she intends to present later and attacks the facts in the case. Denial of a motion for summary judgment implies that the judge believes that there are genuine issues of fact, and the case proceeds.

Rather than contest the action, a defendant may acknowledge the legitimacy of the plaintiff's claim and consent to a verdict for a stipulated amount. This motion is known as **judgment by consent** or **judgment by confession**. The advantage to the reporter is obvious: The specifics of the settlement are easily obtainable, in contrast to the problems of secrecy in the usual out-of-court settlements.

In some proceedings, the parties in dispute may jointly produce a **consent decree** under sanction of the court. While not a judgment, such an action allows both parties to withdraw with an adequate determination of their rights. Antitrust suits are often settled through consent decrees between private corporations and the government agencies that oversee their operations.

> WASHINGTON—The federal government and 22 manufacturers of folding cartons have agreed to settle a 4-year-old civil antitrust suit, the Justice Department announced Thursday.
>
> The consent agreement is subject to approval by a federal district court judge in Chicago.
>
> The government had charged that the firms conspired to fix prices on folding cartons from 1984 to 1991.
>
> A companion criminal case was resolved earlier this year with the 71 corporate and individual defendants pleading no contest to the charges. Fines against the 71 totaled $7.2 million.
>
> Under Thursday's proposed settlement, the firms will be barred by court order from conspiring to fix prices, allocating customers or exchanging pricing information.

DISCOVERY

While procedures vary depending on the jurisdiction, the law assures that information in the hands of one party in a legal action be made available to the other to properly answer the lawsuit.

This disclosure by parties possessing relevant documents or knowledge is called **discovery**. Either the plaintiff or the defendant might be ordered to produce contracts, letters, certificates, photographs, books, bills of lading, promissory notes or other acknowledgements of debt. Discovery helps to narrow the issues in a case by eliminating the need to prove the authenticity of documents later in court.

Another method of discovery involves the taking of **depositions**, testimony in writing of a party or witness to the lawsuit taken outside of open court. Depositions are ordered by the judge, often specifying the subject matter and whether they are to be oral depositions or written interrogatories. Out-of-state witnesses unable to testify in person often respond in this manner. The deposition is similar to the affidavit, except that notice of deposition must be given to the other party. Interrogatories taken in important actions often yield newsworthy information.

Discovery petitions are routine, but they are sometimes crucial to a civil action in controversial cases. The right of reporters to attend discovery examinations has been affirmed in some jurisdictions and denied in others. They are privileged material when made a part of the court record, and the reporter then has a right to it.

While discovery is basically a provision to help the litigants in an action, the reporter should be alert for newsworthy information that surfaces.

REMEDIES

The judicial process itself is the basic remedy for settling grievances, but special remedies are available to compel enforcement of rights and equitable determination of the issues.

Such remedies might surface in an action such as one involving environmental issues. They can be newsworthy, and reporters should be alert to the significance of **provisional remedies** as a lawsuit commences and **extraordinary remedies**, legal procedures that are often used when ordinary measures might prove inadequate.

Provisional Remedies

Included among provisional remedies in civil actions are the injunction, attachment, arrest and bail, receivership, garnishment, and claim and delivery.

To restrain performance or require a specific act, the court issues an **injunction** when no other equitable remedy exists. After a hearing, a judge may issue a temporary injunction barring striking workers from picketing a plant until their leaders can appear in court to show cause why the order should not be made permanent.

A temporary injunction might delay an official meeting scheduled by the owners of a business firm or protect the holder of a patent by forbidding start of work on a new product. Such an injunction remains in force until it is vacated by an appeal or trial or is otherwise discontinued by the presiding judge. Terms of an injunction also may be modified to allow some action or extended when the order is about to expire without the rights of those involved being determined. Many injunctions have specific time deadlines.

WASHINGTON—U.S. District Judge William R. Greene on Friday temporarily blocked the Labor Department's efforts to cancel the Armstrong Corp.'s $86 million in government contracts.

Greene said the firm had raised "substantial legal questions" in challenging the department's move, which was based on allegations of sex discrimination.

Greene will hear arguments July 12 on whether he should issue a longer-term injunction blocking the government's action.

An injunction may be secured for an individual while that person's rights are being determined or for a city government that contends its rights are being violated.

Human Rights Commissioner Alice Deegan asked for a restraining order against the city Monday so she can continue in office until a court hearing is held.

Deegan was dismissed suddenly Friday by City Manager Alfred Williston on unspecific charges after a series of meetings in Williston's office.

The attorney for the official had filed suit in the circuit court, asking for a temporary order blocking the city manager's action. At a hearing, the judge will attempt to determine the validity of the request and either issue or deny the order.

Issues like these constantly cross beat boundaries, and the city government reporter might join the court reporter in collaborating on the ensuing stories.

Most injunctions prevent action rather than compel it, and judicial officials usually act quickly so that neither party will be unduly injured by a lengthy impasse.

A taxpayer might file a lawsuit to restrain a public agency from collecting taxes while the citizen questions the agency's disbursement of funds. An individual or public official might question the manner in which another public official is performing his or her duties, seeking an injunction to restrain that official from exceeding the authority of the office. A person being sued by others claiming title to the same property may seek an injunction to protect himself or herself. Federal agencies and private organizations frequently make use of the injunction process to restrain or force action in many kinds of matters.

> PIERRE, S.D.—A federal judge ruled Thursday that ranchers must temporarily stop using the chemical toxaphene to combat an infestation of grasshoppers.
>
> District Judge Donald Porter granted a temporary injunction sought by the National Audubon Society which contended that toxaphene is dangerous to wildlife.
>
> The U.S. Environmental Protection Agency had approved emergency use of the chemical June 22 on 600,000 acres of rangeland after grasshoppers swarmed over the area—as many as several hundred per square yard.

The judge added that he had weighed the Audubon Society's chances of winning a permanent injunction and decided that it had "a strong chance of success." With further court maneuvers by ranchers a strong possibility, this injunction is part of a continuing story dominated by judicial action.

Other provisional remedies are available to the plaintiff in a court action. A request may be made for a **writ of attachment** before judgment to assure that the defendant will not dispose of the property in dispute. Such a writ can be requested if there is danger that the defendant might leave the court's jurisdiction with the property. A court official, usually the sheriff, is directed to take possession of the property.

If a party in a civil suit has reason to believe that another party might depart a jurisdiction or dispose of property in dispute, he or she can request **arrest and bail**. The party may be required to post suitable bond with the court before being released from custody.

The court often appoints a knowledgeable person to manage property while the dispute works its way toward trial. The property is said to be in **receivership**, and the appointee is called the **receiver**.

Wages of an employee can be taken by the court through a **garnishment** order and the money redirected to a plaintiff who has successfully argued that the defendant owes him or her money. This is common practice in the business community and in child support cases.

A remedy similar to attachment is available when a plaintiff seeks property, claiming that it is wrongfully possessed by the defendant. In an action of **claim and delivery**, a court official is directed to take possession of property and deliver it to the plaintiff, with the plaintiff assuring fairness by posting bond.

Extraordinary Remedies

The reporter should be familiar with several extraordinary legal remedies available to litigants in the courts—habeas corpus, mandamus, prohibition, and certiorari.

The oldest is **habeas corpus** (you have the body), a constitutional remedy that assures a person's right to appear before a court. The remedy stems from efforts to protect people from arbitrary arrest and indefinite confinement and is often used by prisoners to obtain further court hearings on their imprisonment.

This remedy is often used to force the arraignment of prisoners who have not yet been officially charged.

After other remedies have been exhausted, the attorney for a convicted person often uses the procedure to challenge the jurisdiction of the court or to question the validity of parts of the legal process used in the conviction.

> The court-appointed attorney for 3-year-old Sheila Bond sought a hearing Tuesday on a Welfare Department decision to place the child in a foster home.
>
> Diane L. Selden, representing the daughter of Mrs. Wilson S. Bond, filed a petition of habeas corpus in Domestic Relations Court in an effort to force another hearing in the case, this time in court.
>
> The Welfare Department decision had followed agency hearings in the dispute, in which Mrs. Bond is seeking to retain custody of Sheila.

When a public official refuses to perform his or her official, nondiscretionary duty, a citizen may institute a **writ of mandamus** (we command) to force the official to comply with the law. The writ usually orders the official to appear in court to show cause why the writ should not be made permanent.

Controversies involving quasi-public agencies, such as special district governments and publicly supported hospitals, often surface, with active citizen groups trying to force action on an issue.

> A citizens organization has sued to force the Central Valley Water District to share its new $43.5 million federal grant with the city of Bennettsville.
>
> Alleging that federal regulations call for sharing water conservation funds with overlapping governmental units, the Action Council asked Superior Court Judge Tanhill Barnes on Thursday to issue a writ of mandamus, directing the district to appropriate $8 million to the city as its share of the grant.

The writ of mandamus does not apply to public officials when another remedy is available, nor is it applicable when discretionary action on the part of the official is at issue. A citizen's group may seek a writ of mandamus directing the police department to enforce anti-fireworks legislation which the department has ignored in the past. Or it may command a sheriff to take action on tax collections, but it has no power over setting a specific tax rate.

Individuals often make use of the remedy. A stockholder might file a lawsuit to compel a corporation to open its books for inspection. A lawyer might file a lawsuit against a court, asking that his name be restored to its rolls.

> A Huntsville barber has asked Circuit Court to force the State Barber Board to restore his license.
>
> In a petition for a writ of mandamus filed Friday, William J. Dennison, 77, stated that the board's refusal to reactivate his expired license was "arbitrary and capricious, for nowhere in the law is there a mandatory retirement policy for barbers."

Application for a **writ of prohibition** is made to a superior court in an effort to restrain an inferior court from exceeding its jurisdiction. The effect of the order is to halt the proceedings of the inferior court before final judgment in an action. Both public bodies and individuals make use of this remedy.

Lawyers confer with a Superior Court judge in a lawsuit brought by private citizens seeking state enforcement of desegregation laws in public schools. Civil cases whose outcome will influence public policy often receive intense news coverage.
Photo by Stephen Dunn, courtesy of The Hartford Courant.

Arguing that the Argus Construction Co.'s lawsuit to evade payment of $180,000 for damage to county roads has no standing in Circuit Court, the Doane County Commission asked an appeals court Friday to halt action and forestall judgment.

In the writ of prohibition filed with the Court of Appeals, the commission argued that its contract with Argus clearly specified that the firm would be responsible for damage to county roads during construction of the new $75 million County Administration Center.

The writ of prohibition only seeks to prevent an inferior court from exercising jurisdiction; it does not change a final judgment in a case. The **writ of certiorari** is a form of appeal, petitioning another court to direct an inferior court to send the records to determine whether it has exceeded its authority in a particular case.

Lt. John Steen, charging that the city's Civil Service Commission had exceeded its authority in upholding his dismissal from the police force, asked Superior Court on Wednesday to take jurisdiction in the dispute.

Steen's attorney, Olive Sammons, filed a petition for a writ of certiorari, stating that the commission's action was without legal foundation and was politically inspired.

Steen, a 24-year veteran of the force, was dismissed June 14 after testimony in commission hearings that he took 42 days of unauthorized leave of absence last year.

FINAL PRETRIAL PROCEDURE

Not all pretrial conference actions are newsworthy, but regular attention to the schedules of judges and clerks will help assure that the newsworthy ones will be reported.

After all the pleadings have been filed and all motions disposed of, the civil action is said to be at issue—that is, ready for trial. Attorneys for the litigants meet with the judge in a pretrial conference to eliminate uncontested questions from the trial proceedings.

After the conference, the judge may issue a pretrial order, listing the agreements of the parties and the issues in the case. Here is an example of a pretrial order produced after a conference between counsel for a pedestrian injured during a car collision and the defendant who was operating the vehicle:

Parties agreed:

- That plaintiff was struck by defendant's automobile.
- That hospital records may be introduced into evidence without objections.

Issues in the case:

- What degree of care did defendant owe plaintiff at the intersection?
- Did defendant commit any act of negligence?
- Did insurance release defendant from any further claims?
- What amount of damages, if any, is plaintiff entitled to recover?

With the issues narrowed to these questions, the case is placed on the trial calendar or docket. Often a pretrial order after the conference is newsworthy because of the time that will elapse between its filing and the trial itself, which could be months.

Only three questions will be at issue during the trial to determine ownership of the popular White Horse Cafe in suburban Lucasville:

- What steps did former owner Jake Carlisle take to validate the contract selling the cafe to Wendy Lawson for $880,000 in 1990?
- What is the current marital relationship between Carlisle and Lawson?
- Who actually owns the White Horse Cafe now?

These questions were included in a pretrial order by Circuit Court Judge Jane Spottswood Wednesday directing the long dispute to a jury trial during the next term of court, which begins in October.

THE TRIAL CALENDAR

Several times a year the clerk's office, which has been mired in routine filings and correspondence, is galvanized into action. The catalyst is the beginning of a new term of court, important because it produces so many decisions.

The clerk's office publishes a trial calendar, listing the parties to each action, dates of trial and case numbers. The calendar, the reporter will learn, is only a general guide to the activities of the court, because cases often are delayed and switched for many reasons. Out-of-court settlements right before the trial date often change the schedules for the term.

> Amos Johnson's $1 million lawsuit against the Peerless Water Co. was suddenly settled Tuesday when attorneys for both parties requested dismissal during opening arguments in the long dispute.
>
> Johnson had charged the firm with illegally tapping an underground water supply, which he claimed had affected the water supply to his 3,000-acre farm near Theopolis.
>
> No settlement figures were supplied by the parties in the dispute, but Johnson's attorney, Steven Womack, said his client "is entirely satisfied with the settlement."
>
> Peerless attorney William Snider declined to comment, but a source in the clerk's office indicated that the Peerless water tap would remain in place.

A typical notation in the civil jury trial calendar provides this basic information:

90-9534 RLG-B&C James Horne vs. Allegheny Railroad Corp. May 3

The first number is the case to which the notation refers. Identifying this number in the clerk's office brings up the file for scrutiny. The permanent file number makes access to the material easy for the reporter.

The initials indicate the attorneys of record for the parties in the dispute—in this case Ralph L. Goodwin for the plaintiff and Bostick & Carruthers for the defendant. The plaintiff is James V. Horne, who has filed the action against the Allegheny Railroad Corp. Tentative date for trial is May 3. The reporter often will find it helpful to contact the attorneys in a pending trial. Often they can help set the stage and provide specifics about the parties' reasoning. They also confirm court dates and times.

THE TRIAL

Litigation that reaches the trial stage usually has endured protracted pretrial argument, and such jockeying for the best position continues into the trial. Lawsuits often are settled while a jury is being chosen.

Many cases that reach the trial stage are not newsworthy and merit only a few paragraphs in a daily listing of routine cases. Little or no space is devoted to jury selection, arguments or other phases of these trials.

In newsworthy civil litigation, however, such proceedings are often important to the story, and the reporter must possess a sound knowledge of the trial process and the issues in the case.

In covering major cases, the reporter may write a daily trial story; in others, he or she may cover a two-day trial, then write it in a single story. This Washington reporter covered a three-day trial, then produced this wrap-up:

> A District of Columbia landlord has been ordered by a Superior Court jury to pay $104,000 to a tenant who was seriously injured when he fell through a stairway that the landlord had been charged with failing to repair.
>
> Robert Walker, a bookkeeper, testified in court that his landlord, William J. Davis Inc., had not properly maintained the fire escape that Walker used to leave his fourth-floor apartment May 20, 1992.
>
> Walker testified he climbed down the metal stairs to the first floor in search of his dog. The bottom step had apparently rusted away, he said, and he fell when he stepped on it.

Impaneling of the Jury

The clerk calls the case, and the trial begins with selection of a jury. Both plaintiff and defendant have a right to demand that a jury determine issues of fact in common law disputes.

Juries of six to 12 members are chosen from a venire (a group of prospective jurors summoned to court) and are closely questioned by the attorneys and the judge regarding their qualifications and impartiality through a process called **voir dire** (to speak the truth). Depending on the court and the jurisdiction, attorneys may challenge (or reject) prospective jurors for cause when they have reason to believe that they may adversely affect their client's case. The attorneys also are entitled to a specified number of peremptory challenges, allowing them to reject jurors without giving a reason.

After the jurors are chosen, they are sworn in and the trial proceeds.

Presenting the Evidence

Opening statements are made by the attorneys for the plaintiff and defendant. The plaintiff's counsel attempts to explain the lawsuit to the jury and identify the evidence that he or she plans to introduce to prove the plaintiff's case. The defendant's attorney follows with a statement explaining his or her client's side to the jury. The defendant's attorney might delay the opening statement until the plaintiff's evidence has been presented.

In presenting evidence, the plaintiff's attorney must establish a case, attempting through witnesses and introduction of exhibits to show that there is a cause for the action. Questions are asked in an effort to show that the plaintiff has been wronged, with corroborating testimony from others.

Following direct testimony by witnesses for the plaintiff, the defendant's attorney is entitled to cross-examine them, seeking to discredit their testimony by pointing up contradictory statements or raising questions about the witness's interest in the case.

Defense Motions

When the plaintiff's attorney has concluded his or her case, the defendant's counsel can preface presentation of the defense with a series of motions in an effort to end the trial. The attorney may ask for a directed verdict or a demurrer to the evidence (in some jurisdictions), or move for a nonsuit.

In asking for a **directed verdict**, the defense asks the judge to determine whether sufficient evidence has been presented to justify submitting the matter to the jury. Either party may move for a directed verdict, which, if granted, effectively concludes the case.

In moving for a **nonsuit**, the defense argues that there is no legal basis for the action, while conceding the truth of the plaintiff's evidence. Such a motion attacks the sufficiency of the evidence rather than the pleading itself. The motion for nonsuit has generally replaced the **demurrer to the evidence**, the defendant's argument that there is insufficient evidence to support the case.

Defendant's Arguments

The attorney for the defendant now presents his or her case; the defendant may take the witness stand to testify. Efforts are made to disprove the statements made by witnesses for the plaintiff. Requests are often made for the jury to visit the scene of a dispute, such as land in a condemnation suit for highway construction.

After both sides have presented their arguments, attorneys summarize their cases with closing statements, attempting to emphasize the points they believe necessary to win their case.

Conclusion of the Trial

Before the jury begins its deliberations, the judge charges the panel, instructing jurors on points of law. The judge identifies the evidence that the jurors are to consider and what verdicts they may return. The jurors then retire to deliberate.

Many states require a unanimous verdict from the jury; others permit split verdicts in civil suits. Juries often rule that more than one party contributed to damages in auto accidents and product lawsuits. For example, a jury might decide that a plaintiff suffered damages of $100,000 in an accident, but was 25 percent at fault. In that case, the plaintiff would be entitled to only $75,000 from the defendant.

After the verdict, the attorney for the losing party has several options for motions, including a motion to set aside the verdict and grant a new trial. The defendant's attorney also may seek a reduction of damages.

Either party not satisfied with the judgment can appeal the verdict—usually to a higher court, and at further expense. Judgment in the action is satisfied when the clerk issues a writ of execution and the defeated party pays the amount to the clerk. The clerk then dispenses the judgment to the plaintiff, concluding the case.

Chapter 11

Law Enforcement

"**T**en-Four."

The rasping signal ending the exchange crackled over the receiver in the dispatcher's office. The dispatcher, a young uniformed police officer with a ready smile, flipped a switch, leaned back in his chair and picked up a steaming mug of coffee.

Almost apologetically, he turned to pass the word to the waiting police reporter. "Units all say it's quiet out there." He shrugged. "Two drunks in the can and a minor fender bender out on Eighth Avenue. Pretty dead night, I'd say," he concluded.

With a sigh, the reporter checked the clock on the wall, then picked up a telephone to call the newspaper office. It was nearing deadline for the final, 1:04 a.m., and there was nothing to report. She checked out for the night.

Total output for the evening's tour of duty: Two minor break-ins at local businesses, reported earlier in the evening; an auto-truck collision on the nearby interstate, a spectacular affair resulting in major damage but minor injuries; unreported was a family quarrel patched up without incident by a sympathetic police officer.

It was in sharp contrast to the previous day's report. A gun-wielding robber had invaded a local tavern, forced patrons to the floor and left with $2,200 in bar receipts and a sackful of valuables collected from the patrons. The reporter was fortunate. She managed to reach the scene shortly after conclusion of a high-speed police chase resulting in capture of the gunman. She got a front-page story.

That breaking story, coupled with an announcement earlier in the day of a detective bureau reorganization and an assortment of minor stories, created a logjam for the reporter.

Coverage of the police beat is often characterized by these alternating bursts of activity and lull periods.

COMPLICATING FACTORS

Unlike other areas of coverage, the work of the police reporter has special complications. The unpredictability of news developments creates a great deal of pressure, particularly on deadline. Consider these factors:

Irregular Hours.   Police departments operate around the clock, generally on a three-shift basis. Reporters must adjust to and work around these shifts. The "lobster shift" may begin at 11 p.m. and conclude at 7 a.m. or begin at midnight and end at 8 a.m. A normally cooperative police officer can become very uncooperative when roused by an inquiring reporter at 10 a.m., just after drifting off to sleep after a night's work.

Newspapers handle the shift problem in different ways. Metropolitan dailies may staff police headquarters around the clock, while a morning newspaper in a smaller city may staff the station only during the evening hours, being content with occasional telephone checks during the day and relying on an office radio monitor to check police frequencies.

The busiest time for the police reporter often occurs at what are usually considered "off hours" for other beats. Inaccessibility of public officials during evening hours sometimes complicates reporters' efforts to get comments on police-related developments.

> A police officer was charged with using excessive force last night in arresting a runaway juvenile. Officer Alvin Donovan was suspended from duty by Lt. Allen Bragg, who filed the charge.
>
> Bragg said the youth, a 14-year-old Detroit resident, had been beaten with a nightstick. Police Department officials could not be reached for comment last night.

Disillusioning Associations.   Law enforcement deals at somewhat greater depth with a "criminal element." The average citizen rarely runs afoul of the law, so the lawbreaker is much more apt to occupy the police officer's time. Their stories are also more significant and interesting. Reporter and police officer alike should avoid the tendency to become cynical after spending time in that world.

Violence is much more common on the police beat than on other beats, and it appears in the form of homicide, rape, robbery and other major crimes. The perpetrator may be a common purse snatcher, a serial rapist or the leader of an organized theft ring.

Because police beat reporters are likely to become disillusioned, newspapers often transfer them off the beat after a time, rotating the coverage among several staffers. This too has its disadvantages, because contacts carefully nurtured must be regularly updated by new beat reporters.

Many police reporters also have been transferred because their loyalty to police sources transcended the need for healthy skepticism. There is romance in being an insider in police work, but readers and viewers are ill-served by a reporter whose major obligation is to glorify the force and ignore its mistakes.

Unpleasant Duties.   The police reporter should be prepared for obscenities, blood and occasional violence—they are intrinsic to the beat. A newspaper account of a violent death in a Florida field some years ago was all the more vivid because the reporter had inspected the site and gathered details that might otherwise have gone unnoticed. A prisoner trying to escape from a county road gang had been struck down by a bolt of lightning in an open field. Still lying in the field after the body had been taken away were the man's blackened shoes, torn from his body by the lightning.

After reading a reporter's account of a fatal auto collision, an editor may ask: "Did you check out the intersection yourself?" A visit to the emergency room of a local hospital or morgue may be useful in covering an accident, albeit unsettling. In reconstructing a gruesome unsolved murder, the reporter might find it helpful to visit the scene of the crime.

> The trail of blood began behind the old farmhouse, big dark splotches leading grimly across the open ground to the brick well 40 feet distant.
>
> Lt. Walsh pointed to the porch, where there were many more splotches. "It looks like she put up a real fight, then she fell and was dragged to the well," he said.

Reporters with "inside connections" might manage to accompany deputies on a drug raid, collecting vivid details for their news accounts. They should be prepared to take cover on short notice, however. Law enforcement officers are paid to accept the danger; police reporters are paid to survive and write the story.

> Police raided an illegal after-hours club early Tuesday, arresting seven unruly patrons who scuffled with officers and the club's operator.
>
> Joseph Turnbull, operator of the club located at 600 Elm Ave., threatened police with a meat cleaver and had to be subdued by force after emergency backup units arrived.

Reporters will obtain a much better story at the scene, but they sometimes stand in the same danger zone as do the police. It is best to be careful and not take chances.

> Sgt. R.A. Gabbert cut a slightly comical figure as he tiptoed out of the Benson High School science lab, gingerly holding a small brown bottle at arm's length.
>
> But the bottle's contents were no laughing matter. "I have respect for explosives," said Gabbert, a demolition expert with the state police's hazardous device team.
>
> "If somebody tells me something might blow up, I always take their word for it," he said. Gabbert was at the school to detonate a bottle of picric acid, a volatile

substance that has created a minor crisis in several area schools during the past week.

The Constant Danger of Libel.   Danger of defamation is always present in law enforcement, and the reporter must constantly be on guard. Criminal accusations are particularly sensitive. In addition to knowing the law, the reporter must take painstaking care with names, addresses, exact charges and other vital facts. Minor errors, such as a wrong address, can stir libel suits.

> George M. Jones, an unemployed carpenter *who listed his address* as 124 Elm St., was charged with robbery of Daniels Candy Store last night.
>
> A substance *believed to be* cocaine was found in his possession, *Detective Sgt. Ollie Vance said*.

Careful attribution is necessary. Precision is also required in identifying the charge against a person. The difference between the charge of sexual abuse and the charge of incest, for example, is sufficient to cause a publication grave problems if the facts are not accurate. A simple charge of robbery carries a far lesser sentence than armed robbery. The reporter loses some of his or her protection against legal action when the published charge is found to be imprecise.

Inaccurate and Uncooperative Sources.   The pressures of the police beat create a greater likelihood that inaccuracies will creep into news accounts. The lodging of official criminal charges often makes normally open news sources more uncooperative. Police become unavailable to the press when they believe it is in their best interest to close informational doors.

Lack of cooperation can bedevil a seemingly routine effort on the part of the reporter. Pursuit of a story on an often-robbed convenience store might be frustrated by the reluctant merchant or by police officials who fear that visibility of the issue might hamper investigations.

With so many "official" and "unofficial" sources, the reporter must make special efforts to establish reliable contacts that can be critical to a story. Developing human interest stories about members of the police force can earn a reporter the appreciation of the officers, who then might be more cooperative when a sensitive story is sizzling in the frying pan. Feature story possibilities are endless—unusual outside interests, husband-wife patrol teams, officers who volunteer their time to worthwhile causes, interesting part-time jobs.

One teaches chops.

Another cuts them.

And still another checks them.

All of that chopping is done by city police officers supplementing their income by moonlighting on part-time jobs.

The teacher is Detective Dan Lane. He delivers karate chops at a local self-defense school, and lays claim to ownership of the coveted black belt.

Detective Sam Blackman cuts chops as a meat cutter for a local wholesale food distributor.

Guarding chops, as in pork and lamb, is Police Officer Arnold Ross, who spots shoplifters at a supermarket.

They are three of more than 90 city police officers who make ends meet by holding second jobs. Under department regulations, they can work up to 20 hours a week elsewhere.

Such stories are relevant, interesting and often sociologically important. As a further benefit, they offer the reporter an opportunity to make friends.

From One End of the City to The Other.   Finally, the police reporter must deal with the enormous variety and scope of material on the beat. A major accident on the western edge of the city may be balanced by a simultaneous emergency at the other end. The reporter and editor might have to decide quickly whether to cover a major church fire or an imminent bridge collapse.

Some police beat stories have little or no connection to crime. Police are generally the first to know about fires, weather-related problems or other natural conditions, power outages and special events in the community, such as parades. From originating police sources, the reporter can move to others for more information:

On-the-scene reporting of accidents and disasters provides important details on the police beat.
Photo by John Ligos, courtesy of The Day, New London, Conn.

- A citizen reports a leaking gas main to police, or worse, an explosion caused by gas. The utility handles the details.

- A fall down the stairs necessitates an ambulance trip to the hospital. Police forward the call to the emergency squad.

- Fire calls are forwarded to the fire department, but police usually remain involved to some degree.

THE LAW ENFORCERS

The big-city police detective and the rural constable work under dissimilar conditions, but they have a lot in common. The detective might be questioning witnesses after a drug raid that resulted in a violent death. At the same time, the constable might be checking into the theft of cows from Arlie Jacobs' farm over on East Ridge.

Law enforcers come from many backgrounds and bring different skills to their jobs, which are varied and diverse:

- The small-town constable might be the only law enforcement agent in a Farm Belt community. He might have an unrelated full-time job and act as cop part-time, earning as little as $6,000 a year to protect the town's 450 people.

- The thousands of police officers across the United States include substantial numbers of women and ethnic and racial minorities.

- An agent for the FBI might have a college degree in accounting or in law. Hundreds of such agents operate at the federal level, investigating an interstate theft ring, auditing records of a corporation accused of defrauding the government, or cooperating with local authorities in a kidnapping case.

- A sheriff in the South may be charged with keeping the peace over a wide area and also be responsible for collecting taxes and serving legal papers for the court system.

Reporting in all these jurisdictions falls to the police reporter, who may be a full-time journalist or merely a part-time "stringer" for a publication. Whatever the background, the first step is to sublimate any preconceived notions about the people who enforce the laws. An open mind, along with a dose of healthy skepticism, is essential on the police beat.

To most people, uniformed police officers assume an aura of power unlike other public employees. Some of this stems from early encounters with the law, often unpleasant but occasionally more than that. A dressing-down by a police officer for trying to beat a red light can be most uncomfortable, particularly when it is coupled with a summons to appear in court.

The police reporter must clear away any such biases and adopt the principle that law enforcement officers are like other people—some kind and understanding, a few ill-tempered and intransigent. Considering the pressures of the job, most officers are well-adjusted, even-tempered personalities. Few people could withstand the pressure of easing 20,000 vehicles through a busy intersection every day without occasionally letting off a little steam. But few citizens are more sensitive than a beat police officer who offers first aid to a stricken pedestrian while awaiting an ambulance.

The typical police officer is a high school graduate although many also have college degrees. He or she also has completed a basic instruction course in police work.

While law enforcement traditionally has been dominated by men, women are becoming an integral part of the criminal justice system. Twenty years ago, their function was limited to passing out parking tickets and acting as decoys in high-crime areas. Today they perform the same tasks as their male counterparts.

POLICE DEPARTMENT ORGANIZATION

The office was bustling with controlled activity. At the rear of the room, a secretary guarded the entrance to the police chief's office. Personnel worked quietly at computers or answered telephones. At the front counter a uniformed sergeant explained to an anxious woman: "We don't take parking tickets here, ma'am. Go down the hall and look for a door that says 'Finance Department.'"

In a smaller community, the reporter's regular contact with a police department may be with a desk sergeant who presides over and compiles a 24-hour record of activity within the department. A fire call, a traffic accident, a police car out of service, a robbery report with bare details—all are described briefly on the *blotter* or police log.

In larger cities, which might have as many as 30 stations or precinct headquarters, that function is being replaced by a service bureau with an office director, a secretary and an official callboard for the press. In a medium-size city, one police station is usually sufficient.

The informal structure of the department is as important as the formal structure. Who is actually in charge in the central office? How much day-to-day responsibility does the police chief retain? Who are the department's chief policy-makers? Who is authorized to act as spokesperson? Such organizational questions are important if the reporter is to cut through the red tape and quickly get to the source of news stories.

Setting Basic Policy

While the police chief sets much of the policy for the department, the pragmatic reporter will look beyond that office to the elected officials in the community. It is they who are finally responsible for propounding the laws, and they often are more involved in law enforcement than they seem to be.

Whether a city council, a city commission, a municipal board or police commission, the governing body retains ultimate responsibility for and control over the police department. Another level of control lies with a city manager or other city administrator, such as a safety director. The degree and nature of their involvement in police department affairs depend on the personalities of the individuals and the tradition of the community.

An ordinance to limit sale of alcoholic beverages after midnight is approved by the City Council, with a provision in the ordinance for enforcement by the police department. A council member may informally pass on to the department a complaint from a constituent that teen-age gangs are engaging in frequent free-for-alls on neighborhood streets.

An ordinance designed to regulate the growing number of massage parlors in the city was introduced by Mayor George Ballinger last night.

The key limitation in the proposal, which would be enforced by the police department, would prohibit operation of the parlors between midnight and 6 a.m. daily.

Police would also have the power to make on-the-scene spot checks of the businesses, some of which have been called thinly disguised houses of prostitution.

On a smaller newspaper, the same reporter might cover the council session and the police beat, and the sources for this issue would be the same: the police, who would enforce the ordinance; the Finance Department, which would collect the business licenses; the Fire and Building departments, which would enforce related regulations; and the massage parlor operators.

The police chief often is selected by the city manager, with concurrence of the City Council. Despite the increasingly professional character of law enforcement, the appointment often has political overtones. An unpopular police department can create major problems for political figures seeking re-election, and police chiefs are occasionally caught in the crossfire between political opponents at election time.

> George P. Slater, heading the slate of independent candidates seeking City Council seats next month, has promised to dismiss Police Chief O.T. Wilkins and reorganize the department if he and his group are elected.
>
> The current campaign has been characterized by frequent criticism of Wilkins and the department.

While the political reporter may be covering the campaign, the police reporter's knowledge of police department organization and operation can add an important dimension to the coverage.

For these reasons, the philosophy of the governing body concerning law enforcement is important to the police reporter, who should follow developments at City Hall as closely as the government affairs reporter.

Removal of top police officials is sometimes in the hands of a police governing board or council, but more often it is the responsibility of the city manager.

> Clarksburg Police Chief James Shield was relieved of his duties yesterday and returned to the rank of lieutenant, effective immediately.

City Manager Pat Tremont, who ordered the change, said his action had nothing to do with an internal investigation of the department, conducted after two confiscated slot machines disappeared from the collections room.

"It was just time for a change," Tremont said.

The governing body of the municipality usually decides on a basic pay scale, often negotiating with police fraternal organizations or organized labor unions in setting annual increases. It also allots funds for equipment and determines whether increases in staffing are necessary. In this not-too-subtle manner, a council or commission effectively controls the police department.

Units of the Department

Day-to-day responsibilities are in the hands of the police chief, who appoints division officers, promotes and demotes, transfers and suspends, approves procedures and requests equipment purchases, and often personally checks on important investigations. In most personnel matters, the reporter will deal directly with the chief, who is often reluctant to delegate authority to release information concerning departmental policy and personnel.

Regular, personal contact with the chief often helps the reporter keep abreast of future plans.

Foot patrols will return to the city tomorrow when two police officers begin walking the controversial 20th Street bar area from 4 p.m. to midnight in an effort to reduce complaints.

Records show that most of the complaints have been logged after midnight, but Police Chief Louis Sarran explained that the evening hours have been ordered "for show."

"This way, the business people will see them for a few hours and the bar customers will know they're there," he said.

Departments are organized in paramilitary fashion, with captains, lieutenants, sergeants and patrol officers. Functions of the various subdepartments have become increasingly specialized, and many departments have an administrative unit, a patrol or traffic unit, an investigations division containing a detective

bureau, and a crime prevention unit that deals with the public in education matters (see Figure 11–1).

The administrative unit operates the headquarters, maintains records and the communications system, and is responsible for property disposition. A service bureau often maintains records and operates a fingerprint and scientific laboratory.

The patrol division operates the squad cars and often includes a traffic unit. It is within this unit that the reporter obtains information about collisions and other traffic problems. The reporter is often much closer to this unit because it responds first to emergencies. Some departments refuse to allow patrol officers to discuss police work with reporters, but most investigating officers cooperate in providing firsthand information.

"Too much snow and too little salt," Patrol Officer Leo Otis said last night after traffic was disrupted on slippery Fifth Avenue by a spectacular pileup that caused extensive property damage.

Twelve vehicles were involved in the snowy jam, Otis reported. There were no injuries. Asked about damage, he responded: "I can only guess. It was a mess." Otis' educated guess: about $60,000.

The reporter can look to the investigations unit for a broad range of information on criminal activity, much of it a result of today's vastly superior scientific methods. Larger municipalities break down the unit, often separating crimes against property and crimes against persons. Also a separate juvenile section and drug abuse unit might be established.

Recovery of stolen property, car theft, fraud and robbery fall under the jurisdiction of the investigations unit. Detectives are usually veterans of the department and operate as a nonuniformed unit.

When a shopper at the Central Mall saw three people tossing empty coat hangers under a parked car, she became suspicious.

Her suspicions led to the recovery of more than $30,000 in merchandise shoplifted from area stores during the Christmas season.

"It was a minishoplifting ring, three outsiders trying to cash in," Don L. Morris, chief of the city's Detective Bureau, said yesterday.

Detectives traced the trio to 115 Burke St., where the goods were recovered, Morris said.

FIGURE 11–1
An organizational chart for a typical municipal police department.

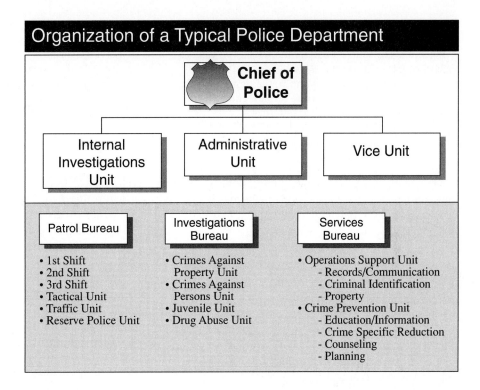

Organization of a Typical Police Department

Chief of Police

- Internal Investigations Unit
- Administrative Unit
- Vice Unit

Patrol Bureau
- 1st Shift
- 2nd Shift
- 3rd Shift
- Tactical Unit
- Traffic Unit
- Reserve Police Unit

Investigations Bureau
- Crimes Against Property Unit
- Crimes Against Persons Unit
- Juvenile Unit
- Drug Abuse Unit

Services Bureau
- Operations Support Unit
  - Records/Communication
  - Criminal Identification
  - Property
- Crime Prevention Unit
  - Education/Information
  - Crime Specific Reduction
  - Counseling
  - Planning

A reporter will find an interesting follow-up story by talking to the alert shopper and merchants involved.

Using Statistical Information

The process of educating the public to ways in which it can best protect itself often falls to the crime prevention division.

Statistical information gathered by the division is shared with the press as well as with other police units. Modern police departments also provide other informational services through such a division.

> The doors of more than half of the cars stolen in the city last year were unlocked, a statistical breakdown by the Crime Prevention Bureau shows.
>
> Of 486 motorists whose vehicles were stolen in 1993, 255 failed to lock their doors, according to a study of stolen vehicle reports.
>
> "Locking your car may not deter a professional car thief, but it most certainly will cut losses to amateurs," said William Dawson, chief of the unit.

This division also produces useful annual crime summaries, comparing the past year with other years and the rate of increases. But the reporter should remember that law enforcement officials, like other public officials, often have a vested interest in placing the best light possible on such summaries. Every effort should be made to portray the material accurately and completely.

An increase of 7 percent in major crimes, for example, might be accompanied by an increase of 17 percent in arrests for those crimes. The key might lie in the conviction rate of those arrested and accused of the crimes.

The computer age has brought this statistical process to a high level, and the reporter will find a wealth of such detail in the records.

The department's statistics bureau uses data in department planning and staffing, but much material is also pertinent to the public. High-crime areas, for example, can be located through use of the computer, and detailed incidents in the area compiled for a story.

The intersection of Central Avenue and Fifth Street, under state study for possible relocation, has averaged five traffic accidents a week for more than two years, a Statistical Bureau analysis shows.

"Collisions at that point and traffic tie-ups are the reason work needs to be done straightening it out," Supervisor Robert Reane said yesterday.

A computer analysis shows that 517 traffic collisions occurred within one block of the intersection during the two-year period ending yesterday.

Many wire service stories contain national statistics that can be localized by a reporter who has access to similar statistics in department files. Such national stories are good local story generators.

Dealing with Disputes

Departmental disputes often find their way into print, either from police sources or from officials themselves. A new manual of objectives, for example, may reflect a desire by the chief to make each officer a generalist rather than a specialist. The detective division may object privately but strenuously to the reporter.

The police chief is usually a key figure in these disputes, occasionally with less control over their outcome than he or she desires.

Following a three-hour meeting with the Civil Service Commission, Police Chief William Squire has postponed an order that eight members of the Police Department undergo training.

Squire confirmed that he had postponed the action, but declined to discuss the matter with a reporter.

He had issued a memorandum last week identifying the police officers as "needing immediate basic retraining" after receiving written reports from their commanders indicating poor performance.

Police department morale is a recurring issue, sometimes involving the reporter on the beat. The reporter must resist aligning with one faction or another, and work to produce impersonal stories about the dispute.

The final word in many department personnel disputes lies with civil service commissions, established to decide merit disputes and other personnel matters, rather than with a city council, police board or mayor.

A 90-day suspension and reduction in rank for Police Capt. Henry Playford was sustained today by the Civil Service Board.

Playford was reduced in rank to lieutenant and suspended May 10 for failure to take a polygraph test upon order of Police Chief Willis Henson. Playford had appealed the order to the board.

Outside Relationships

The police department's relationships with outside organizations and agencies can get rocky. It may be a dispute with the American Civil Liberties Union, the judiciary, the county sheriff or a state investigations unit. It may be professionally motivated or purely political.

An active chapter of the American Civil Liberties Union in a city will sometimes become embroiled in police actions that it believes to be excessive. Acting as an ombudsman for the public, the ACLU may attempt to force a limit on the use of deadly force by police officers. It may propose that police training include instruction on alternatives to the use of deadly force.

Depending on the area, there are often as many disputes with outside agencies as there are areas of cooperation. A police officer may sometimes have a much different perspective than a judge or prosecuting attorney.

Thirty-four armed robberies have occurred in the city so far this year, and the police chief believes "the entire judicial system is making it tougher for officers to cope with the problem."

The department reported 21 armed robberies in January, 10 last month and three so far this month. That's half the number reported during all of last year.

"I don't want to blame any one person—magistrates, prosecutors or judges," Chief Earl Durden said, "but I am saying the judicial system is just not working right."

Durden said 12 of the 17 people charged in connection with 25 of the 34 armed robberies this year "are back on the streets after posting bond."

Depending upon the size of the community, police may have an arms-length or "cozy" relationship with the district attorney, who is charged with prosecuting the cases brought by officers. Prosecutors often want more evidence than police are able to procure for a case, which can lead to strained feelings on both sides.

The field of law enforcement, like other areas in which the public has an abiding interest, is complicated by the role of peripheral agencies in the enforcement process.

> In the midst of a rise in juvenile crime in the city, Solicitor Charles Condon said Monday he will take steps to get tough with juvenile offenders.
>
> Condon said the increase is caused by some young people who have no sense of right or wrong.
>
> "The juvenile justice system was designed 75 years ago when there was a quite different society," he said. "Children are growing up much faster these days."
>
> The solicitor said his office would be more aggressive in recommending that family court judges send juveniles accused of violent crimes or repeat offenders to general sessions courts.

Proposals such as these affect law enforcement officers, and the reporter should seek out all the agencies involved for feedback.

Issues also emerge at the state level. A local story involving juvenile mob attacks may benefit from statistics produced in a state agency.

> Three days after her son was charged in a mob attack on two police officers, Renee Dalton shook her head and sadly said:
>
> "I'm afraid I'm never going to see Desmond again." Desmond Dalton, 16, was one of 11 young people charged with throwing chunks of concrete at the officers Feb. 4.
>
> But while there was conviction in Mrs. Dalton's voice, police and counselors think she is probably wrong. Young offenders who commit violent crimes in the state are receiving lighter penalties than adults receive for the same crimes.

A state's Department of Youth Services tracks youthful offenders, making their statistics available to the press, and police departments and juvenile courts provide similar information at the local level.

Important to this story were statistics showing the increase in juvenile violent crime at the state level (5 percent compared with the previous year), and at the local level (nearly 50 percent).

COVERING THE POLICE BEAT

Crime reporting has changed over the years, paralleling similar changes on other public affairs beats. There is a new emphasis on the *why* of crime rather than merely the *what*.

But an important basic principle remains. Press surveillance of the law enforcement process always will be necessary to assure the rights of citizens. The reporting of crime, and its subsequent resolution through the judicial process, is an outgrowth of this need.

In smaller communities, the police beat is not a full-time assignment. A city hall reporter might include it as part of the daily rounds. Some newspapers provide their staffers with radio receivers or "scanners" at home, and it is common for a reporter to head to the scene of a fatal accident outside his or her regular hours.

Metropolitan newspapers usually assign reporters to the police beat on a full-time basis, some rarely seeing the newsroom. Reporters operate out of a press room at police headquarters, keeping in touch with their office through telephone and computer. The reporter's car is usually equipped with a police radio to monitor calls, and a radio telephone may connect the car with the newsroom.

The police reporter in the smaller city begins the day by studying the running, 24-hour account of all activity. Incoming complaints, vehicles dispatched, traffic accidents, burglary reports and routine messages are all listed, although often with scant information. The police message board, sometimes called a blotter or log, alerts the reporter to nearly all the activity occurring during the past 24 hours. Not everything is always transmitted, however. The reporter in smaller communities should be alert to references to sensitive incidents that may be absent from the report. For that reason, arrest and complaint reports should be carefully checked (see Figure 11–2).

The report's brevity can be expanded with details from the desk sergeant, investigating officer and the police chief.

Many departments have abolished the old blotter, using instead a complaint board containing official reports. A service bureau is responsible for collecting and dispensing such information, which remains accessible to the press for as long as 48 hours.

The reporter checks a general complaint board for information on all crimes committed within the department's jurisdiction and an accident board, which contains official reports of all traffic accidents. These are privileged documents, along with an arrest record, often called a rap sheet, that become part of department records. The rap sheet is a compilation of information regarding any arrest or temporary detention and includes the identity of the person arrested or detained, the nature of the police contact, the charge (if any), and the disposition or current status of the case.

If the case results in a conviction, police also maintain a conviction record and often compile investigative reports or "statements of fact," which are not generally available to the reporter.

An overnight burglary will be noted on the complaint board identifying the homeowner, valuables taken, method of entry and so forth. The reporter should check with the supervisor on duty in the investigations

A reporter checks the daily police log with an officer. Logs are an introduction to police activity, and reporters must be able to identify newsworthy items from the numerous routine entries.
Photo by Andrea Hoy.

unit and with the detective who responded to the complaint. Is the burglary part of a pattern? Has there been a rash of them in the area? Was someone at home during the burglary? What was taken?

The detective's comments on the complaint board are privileged as part of the public record, which means the reporter is free to use the material. However, any oral statements are not privileged.

Generally, the reporter also will be able to speak with prisoners in the lockup, although the trend today is to provide jail facilities in a county-operated central location, so the prisoner might not be available. In such cases, identical arrest records are also maintained at the jail by the agency in charge of the facility.

Finding out the identity of victims of criminal acts and witnesses is one of the prime goals of the police

FIGURE 11–2
Incident reports contain details of incidents investigated by police and are usually a public record. The narrative section contains the investigating officer's description of the incident, while other coded sections supply additional details. Arrest information may be contained in an incident report or may be recorded in a separate booking report, also available to reporters.

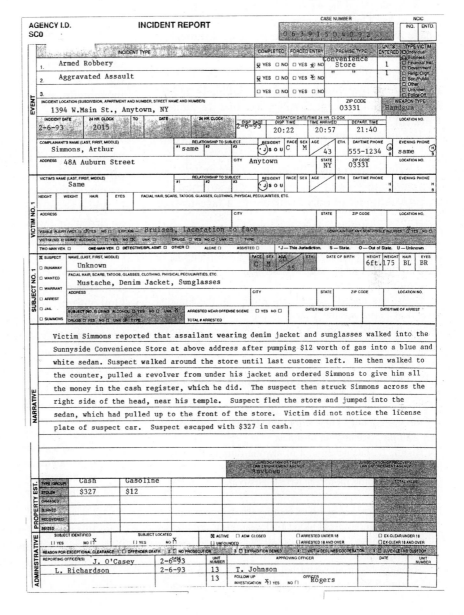

reporter, who seeks out eyewitness accounts for more accurate and vivid news stories.

> Two bandits slipped into Willis Drugs this morning, held two employees and three customers at gunpoint and escaped with nearly $4,000 in cash.
>
> "They held us in the corner, grabbed the money and went," said Ted Willis, operator of the store at 2020 3rd Ave. "It all happened in less than five minutes."
>
> Willis described the men as tall, dark-haired with red face masks. "One put the gun (a pistol) to my head and made me face the wall while the other went through the cash register," he said. "I was scared to death."

Under deadline conditions, a preliminary story on the capture of three men suspected of killing two Ohio men provided only scant details of the arrests: identity of the three men and the two who were killed, and location of the interstate exit where state troopers captured them.

But armed with extra time, the reporter tracked down and interviewed the trooper who stopped the car, providing detail only available in a face-to-face interview.

> His hands were clammy with sweat, his heart was racing, and swirling through his mind was the warning he had just heard on his radio: "These men are armed and dangerous."
>
> But in the end, 18 months of training at the State Highway Patrol Academy paid off for Trooper Nicolas Ream when he stopped a silver-colored car carrying three suspects in the slaying of two Greenville men an hour earlier.

The reporter asked Ream what it was like, and how he felt about the assignment:

> "I was scared, but I knew what to do by reflex and from my training," Ream said Monday.
>
> Ream, 27, has never shot at anyone during his four years as a trooper. He spends most days stopping speeders, helping motorists whose cars conk out, or filing reports.
>
> That changed about 4 p.m. Sunday when he was sent to wait for a getaway car along I-70 west. Four minutes after he'd parked his cruiser south of the Rt. 97 exit, the car zipped by.
>
> "I almost lost it all when they drove by," the 6-foot, 185-pound Ream said, "but I couldn't let those suckers go."

Ream told the reporter he had radioed for backup cruisers by then. He followed the car off the exit ramp and pulled the vehicle over.

> "I got out of the car with my shotgun and yelled at them to freeze," Ream said. "All I could think was 'Why is it taking the backup so long?' It seemed like forever."
>
> Within minutes, two more troopers arrived to help arrest the suspects. Four loaded pistols were found in the car.

Because of good legwork, the reporter also provided personal information on the trooper, whose wife was expecting their first child any day. Effort such as this often turns a routine story into a more readable and meaningful account.

Use of Force

The use of force and sometimes deadly force by police officers has stirred emotions across the country. The reporter's questions are legitimate:

When should an officer use deadly force in making an arrest or defending himself or herself? When the officer does so, what agency should decide whether he or she has acted properly? How do the officers themselves feel? Figure 11–3 shows a form that many departments require officers to fill out after using any kind of force.

Police theoreticians are arguing over the issue, cases are constantly in the courts, and legislators have politicized the debate.

> Police Officer Jeffrey Wingate has faced the wrong end of a revolver before, and it nearly cost him his life.
>
> That's why he is alarmed about his own reaction this week when he and his partner encountered another man wielding a cocked pistol.
>
> "I'd say six months ago I probably would have shot him," Wingate said.
>
> But he says public criticism since then about the use of deadly force has made him—and many fellow police officers—somewhat more hesitant to fire their weapons.

So this time, Wingate told the reporter, he lunged for the man and subdued him with the help of his partner, Sam Longdon. The gun, it turned out, was not loaded.

But there's always the next time, Wingate said. The officer, who was wounded in the line of duty in 1979,

FIGURE 11–3
Some departments have developed their own forms, like this one.

STATEMENT OF FORCE

Date/Time _10/23/93   1400hrs_ UCR # _0428_

Name _Johnson   Will   Earnest_
       (Last)   (First)   (Middle)

Address _Apt 4, 928 First St._

_____

Sex: _M_   Race: _W_   Date of Birth _06/19/7c_

Social Security # _426-78-4429_

ARRESTED AT (Time, Date, Location): _0230 on 10/23/93_
at rear of McCrea Hardware, Jasper St.

ARRESTING OFFICER: _Cpl Henry Hansen_

ARRESTING OFFICER WHO USED CAP-STUN: _same_

OTHER OFFICERS ON THE SCENE: _Patrolman William_
Eason and Patrolman Sam Elridge

FORCE USED (check one)

Physical _X_   Cap-Stun _X_   PR-24 _____

Other (Explain) _____

CIRCUMSTANCES: _Subject caught coming out of_
back door, refused to be placed in
cruiser, had to be restrained with
force. Threatened officers.

Date/Time placed in detention: _0330 on 10/23/93_

INJURIES OBSERVED/CLAIMED: _Subject claimed back_
and arm injuries

MEDICAL TREATMENT PROVIDED (First Aid Administered,
                             Transport to Hospital)

John Sears and Earl Johnson, EMS
(List Name(s)/Title/Organization)

_____

TYPE OF TREATMENT: _Subject obviously intoxicated_
was checked by EMS and taken
to county lockup

pointed out that just a moment of hesitation could prove fatal.

"I think there is a lot of hesitation. I look for an officer to get killed out of it," Wingate said.

The Rodney King beating by Los Angeles police, videotaped by an onlooker, provided new impetus to the issue in 1991-92, and it has not lessened.

Even after acquittal of the officers involved in the beating, there is little consensus about the events of March 3, 1991.

King was stopped by police after a chase on the Foothill Freeway. Police said he was traveling at 100 mph; King maintained he was traveling 45 mph in a 35 mph speed zone. Officers said King came at them in a threatening manner after he was stopped, and had to subdue him by force.

George Holliday, 31, awakened by the clamor outside, aimed his videocamera at the scene and filmed the beating. King's swollen face was proof that the taped events were real. His leg was broken, bones in his face were fractured, some of his teeth were knocked out, and gravel was embedded in his face from being dragged along the ground.

Within weeks, four officers were indicted on charges of felony assault. A year later, a jury decided the men had not used excessive force, triggering the worst riots in Los Angeles history.

In the wake of the King incident, police departments again studied the guidelines they are using to determine excessive force. State and federal agencies are also involved.

WASHINGTON—New Orleans police lead the nation in brutality complaints to the federal government—35 a year on average, according to a study undertaken after the Rodney King beating.

The Los Angeles Police Department, focus of a Justice Department civil rights investigation, ranked 11th with an average of 14 complaints annually.

The reporter covering this sensitive issue will find a wide range of sources: state and federal officials, university criminologists and sociologists who research law enforcement issues, and local district attorneys.

A former London police officer was indicted Friday on charges he used excessive force in the arrest of a suspect.

Kevin Shorter, who has been suspended from his duties in the wake of the incident, was charged with assault and battery of a high and aggravated nature by a Slocum County Grand Jury.

In this case, the reporter used as sources the grand jury's indictment, the testimony of a state law enforcement official, the city's police chief and the prosecuting attorney. The officer did not want to comment. Specifics of the indictment are important.

The indictment charges that Shorter used his "hands, fist and feet" on a male suspect before and after the suspect was handcuffed. Police Chief Charles Durden said the incident was said to have occurred during a drug raid.

The city's Civil Service Commission often will become involved in such disputes, disagreeing with a prosecuting attorney's findings.

Four police officers will be punished for their roles in an incident last month when a 14-year-old boy said he was held over a bridge railing and threatened.

While the prosecutor in this case ruled that the officers had used excessive force against the juvenile, the commission disagreed. The issue is headed for the courts, where it will be followed by either the police reporter who originated the story or a courts reporter.

New Approaches in Law Enforcement

It is common practice for trained dogs to sniff out marijuana and other drugs in school locker searches, but the use of hypnosis in the crimefighting arsenal is not nearly so common. Medical examiners have new techniques to determine exactly when a person died.

Imagine seeing a police officer stab the ground with a metal tube able to sense a decomposing body buried 12 feet deep.

That item is not on the market now, but check again in a few years, says John Jupin, county medical examiner.

Such futuristic equipment is an example of the investigative techniques being researched across the country.

The advances will enable police and medical examiners to diagnose more accurately when and how a crime occurred.

Answering all questions that arise when new police defense weapons are introduced is a basic job for the reporter.

Imagine someone holding a blowtorch to your face, having your head shoved onto a barbecue grill or being stung in the face by a jellyfish.

These were the descriptions used by Grandview police officers to describe the intense temporary pain caused by the newest defense against violent suspects.

It's called Cap-Stun, and Major Paul Quinn said he hopes it will put an end to physical conflicts between officers and suspects.

The reporter graphically explained officers' reactions to the new weapon when they were exposed to it, and also answered other logical questions about it.

Cap-Stun solution is derived from the oil of cayenne pepper and swells the mucous membranes, causing the immediate closing of the eyelids and uncontrollable coughing and gasping for air, Quinn said.

It is not like Mace, which has been shown to be more of an irritant than a preventive measure against attacks, he said.

There has been controversy over another new device to test drunken driving suspects, and at least one judge has refused to allow police officers to use it. The reporter's role is to explain the older and new devices.

The controversy involves the new DataMaster 2000 machine, which is being supplied to State Highway Patrol officers as funds become available.

Law enforcement officials believe the self-contained, computerized machine is a more efficient way to test blood alcohol content than the Model 900 Breathalyzer.

The new equipment uses infrared technology and can produce an accurate chemical analysis of a person's breath, officials said.

"The DataMaster is a newer, faster model," spokesman Hugh Morse said. "It's not any more reliable. It just does it more efficiently, and it's self-contained, needing no operator."

Police are usually first to see new problems in violence brought about by technology. Told about possible child abuse in several local neighborhoods, a reporter researched the issue and produced a story.

Police officers and doctors are being warned about a new form of child abuse: burns from stun guns.

Designed as a nonlethal method of self-protection, and for use by police in subduing violent subjects, stun guns use high-voltage electrical charges, which are most effective if they touch skin or clothing.

Police said the guns inflict small, whitish circular burns, and do not inflict long-term physical damage, although they cause severe pain and numbness that lasts about 15 minutes. Local hospital physicians corroborated and added to the police accounts.

New programs are an important source of news, and the reporter has a responsibility to assess their effectiveness. Inner-city housing programs that involve police officers are an example.

A new approach to fighting crime in Greenwood that stresses problem-solving as much as law enforcement has begun to win converts across the United States.

The catch phrase is "community-oriented policing," and based on statistics and response, the 2-year-old program is working, Police Chief Charles P. Silvers said.

Greenwood's crime rate is down 17 percent from a year earlier, and the murder rate has fallen even more dramatically—44 percent, with five deaths so far this year compared with nine last year at this time.

The reporter used many sources to assess the program, which puts satellite police stations in the community and allows officers to become friendly with people living nearby.

Time must also be budgeted to develop stories that cover other areas of law enforcement. Growth of special police units, and how and why they operate, would be an important story. Many cities have trained officers in handling nuclear material and in responding to nuclear accidents. Others have become skilled in terrorist activity, including handling the sensitive issue of hostages. Both topics are unusual and interesting.

Monitoring Detainees

The function of habeas corpus, a remedy to compel police to either charge a person who has been detained or release the person from custody, also has important implications for the press. The police reporter should be familiar with the jail population, determining why prisoners are being detained and the length of their stays in jail. Informative and useful stories often result.

It's only a few feet from the Dean County jail to the magistrate's court in the courthouse basement, but it sometimes takes a long time to cover that distance.

Donald C. Wilson, 27, was charged with robbery 13 days ago. He was finally granted a preliminary hearing yesterday afternoon.

The problem, according to Prosecutor Keith Lyons, was that no one was available to bring Wilson from the jail to the court for a hearing.

As it turned out, Wilson was bound over to the grand jury. "But if the magistrate had decided we didn't have enough to hold him on, that would have been 13 days out of his life," Lyons said.

The reporter tracked down Public Defender John Simpson, who acted as counsel for Wilson. Simpson disagreed with the prosecutor. "That was 13 days out of his life anyway," he argued.

Officials are rarely willing to publicize conditions in jails or other detention areas, and the reporter must dig beneath officialdom for a more accurate picture of how detainees are being treated. It is often "out of sight, out of mind" for the public. Within some limitations, reporters usually have access to prisoners, and their views are often newsworthy.

"There's no stability of mind here," said Charley Gibson, who has been a Rikers Island inmate for three months. "You're better off taking a plea and letting them send you on to prison."

In a series of interviews, Gibson and others at the city's House of Detention for Men sketched a picture of life so bleak that some inmates plead guilty, they said, so they will be moved to the better conditions of the state prison.

The police reporter should guard against becoming bogged down in day-to-day stories, which creates interesting but specific news accounts that ignore the bigger picture of law enforcement activity. Figure 11–4 shows the path a suspect follows from arrest to trial.

WRITING THE STORY

The basic rules for writing the police-beat story include a need to be straightforward, precise, fair and accurate, requiring both curiosity and care on the part of the reporter. Choice of words is important.

Cliches should be avoided on every beat, but the field of law enforcement has its own peculiar brand. The reporter should resist the temptation to "launch an investigation," describe an officer as "grim-faced," or write that a bank robber has fled with "an undisclosed amount of cash."

By the end of their first month on the police beat, most reporters probably have covered their first big fire, with a few succumbing to the temptation to turn in the most overwritten of all leads:

Fire of undetermined origin swept through an East Side home about 9 p.m. Wednesday, killing a 72-year-old invalid.

Editors have been rejecting this overworked beginning to fire stories for years, sending the reporter back to the video display terminal for something fresher.

A 72-year-old invalid collapsed and died at her front door as fire swept through her East Side home about 9 p.m. Wednesday.

Police identified her as Florence L. Wolfe, 806 Kenton Ave. She lived alone, they said.

Assistant Fire Chief Neal Mills said the fire might have been caused by a lighted cigarette that burned a living room chair after Mrs. Wolfe fell asleep.

While most fires do bear the label "undetermined origin" during preliminary investigation, officials often provide information that takes the reader or viewer beyond that bare fact.

Exaggerated reports of crime should be avoided at all costs, but literary techniques that will be effective in telling a story should be sought out. Good writing that focuses on the heart of an issue is important, but content is also necessary.

John Turner slammed his fist on the table, snatched his woolen cap from his head, jumped from his seat and shouted at the gray-haired man who was examining the parking ticket.

"Give that ticket back to me," he yelled at the examiner, Herman Dorfman. "You're going to find me guilty anyway. I'm just wasting my time."

Turner is one of 15,000 motorists who sought hearings last year at the Parking Violations Bureau because they felt themselves unjustly served with parking tickets.

And while in the past, few could expect to win the battles, today the Davids of the driving world are often winning disputes with the Goliathlike bureaucracy responsible for adjudicating parking tickets.

More than 80 percent of the people who show up for hearings have their cases dismissed or fines reduced, according to the bureau.

Careless identification is one of the chief causes of libel suits against publications. That's why the police

reporter must exercise great care in obtaining middle initials and correct addresses. When there is doubt, writing "police listed Jones's address as 124 Cardinal St." will help when an address can't be verified on deadline.

Clothing a story with "alleged" and "the suspect" offer only partial defense in libel lawsuits and should

FIGURE 11–4
The sequence of events that leads a criminal suspect from arrest to trial.

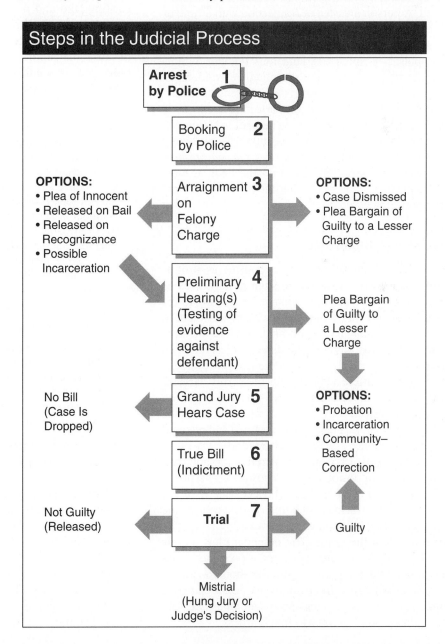

Steps in the Judicial Process

Arrest by Police 1

Booking by Police 2

OPTIONS:
• Plea of Innocent
• Released on Bail
• Released on Recognizance
• Possible Incarceration

Arraignment on Felony Charge 3

OPTIONS:
• Case Dismissed
• Plea Bargain of Guilty to a Lesser Charge

Preliminary Hearing(s) (Testing of evidence against defendant) 4

Plea Bargain of Guilty to a Lesser Charge

No Bill (Case Is Dropped)

Grand Jury Hears Case 5

OPTIONS:
• Probation
• Incarceration
• Community–Based Correction

True Bill (Indictment) 6

Not Guilty (Released)

Trial 7

Guilty

Mistrial (Hung Jury or Judge's Decision)

be avoided. Referring to a person, particularly one who has not been charged, as "the alleged intruder" or "the alleged robber" is not only unfair but unsafe. The writer should refer to the person by name, as "the detainee" or as "the person in custody."

The reporter should avoid another danger zone—writing about a specific charge before it is formally placed. A person arrested in connection with a rape or robbery constitutes a legitimate story. But adding to the story, "Brown will likely be charged with rape, according to police," is unfair and dangerous. Quoting authorities as to their future intentions should be avoided.

Caution should also be exercised in incidents involving domestic arguments, a routine complaint in most cities. While poignant stories can be written about wife and child abuse, care should be taken in reporting what a distraught wife says about her recalcitrant husband. She may be willing to "throw the book at him" one night, then deny everything the next day, leaving the reporter high and dry.

Precision Is Important

The reporter must be precise in routine as well as major crime stories, avoiding such generalities as "Jones was jailed on an open charge," conveying to the reader or viewer that some kind of charge was filed. In fact, no charge may have been filed. Instead, the story should state: "Jones is being detained but has not been charged."

There is a difference between the terms "arrest" and "detain." Should a reporter observe a person being taken into custody, then later released, he or she should write that the person was "detained and released for lack of evidence" rather than "arrested."

Even correct words can be rendered unfair and dangerous by the imposition of a preposition. The police reporter should avoid writing "A Reedsville man has been indicted *for* armed robbery." This oversteps the bounds of fairness because the phrase implies that he has committed the crime. The defendant has merely been held for trial on the charge and is presumed innocent until found guilty. So the reporter should write:

"A Reedsville man has been *indicted on a charge of* armed robbery," or "*in connection with* an armed robbery." Precision is essential to total fairness.

Qualifying the Information

The importance of qualifying information cannot be overemphasized. While the word of law enforcement officials is not an absolute defense for a reporter on deadline, it is certainly a mitigating factor.

The temptation would be strong to provide an exciting lead and fast-paced account of the arrest of a husband who shot his wife, then engaged in a shoot-out with police before being shot himself. But because the reporter did not witness the affair, the story requires substantial qualification. Note the care with which the reporter presented the information.

> A former member of the city School Board *was found shot to death* in her home yesterday, and police are holding her husband *for investigation*.
>
> The dead woman is Mrs. Simon Gideon, 54, who served three terms on the board from 1976 to 1988 and did not seek re-election. Her body was found in the bedroom of her home at 3200 High St. by police who were called *when neighbors heard shooting*.
>
> Police *took into custody* Mrs. Gideon's husband, who is 57, after an exchange of shots.
>
> *Det. Sgt. Dan Williams said* police found Gideon, an insurance adjuster, in the kitchen armed with a .45-caliber pistol. He fired several shots before surrendering, *Williams said*, and was wounded in the left arm by shots fired by police. Gideon was taken to Riverside Hospital, then to the police lockup.
>
> Police had been called to the house once before, *Williams said*, and *added that* there was a record of trouble between Mr. and Mrs. Gideon.
>
> Mrs. Gideon was an accountant who worked for several firms in the city. The couple had no children.

Despite the temptation to handle this story somewhat differently, it is always best to qualify the information.

Fairness dictates similar caution in reporting traffic accidents. Claims by persons injured in collisions often conclude in court, with judge or jury deciding the outcome. Reporters are often dependent on accident reports turned in hours after the incident occurred and on the investigating officer who arrived at the scene after it happened. The reporter also should take care in reporting damage estimates as well as other questionable data.

Equal caution should be observed in writing a story concerning a suicide or a homicide. The careful reporter avoids use of the words "suicide" or "murder," just as competent police investigators do. There may be every indication that a person took his or her own life, but until an official ruling is made, the reporter should carefully imply it through the circumstances. The occasion is rare when a reporter can write in a straightforward manner that a person "committed suicide."

Instead, police and press will be circumspect until a coroner's jury conducts a hearing and makes a finding of suicide or murder.

> Harlan County Judge William E. Sparkman died Tuesday morning of a gunshot wound in the head. Sparkman's body was discovered in the bathroom of his chambers at the county courthouse.
>
> "It appears that the wound was self-inflicted," Coroner Michael L. Smithson said, but added that circumstances surrounding Sparkman's death were being investigated.

Days, even weeks, can pass before an official ruling is returned.

POLICE-PRESS RELATIONSHIPS

Although most law enforcement officials recognize the function of the press as communicator and interpreter for the public, relationships between police and press often become strained.

Police tend to see themselves as "the good guys in the white hats," fighting crime and keeping the community safe. This image is encouraged because, as former Los Angeles Police Chief Quinn Tamm said, "The police officer, upon whom we depend for the maintenance of peace and order in our society, can function most effectively in a community where he can depend on the support and assistance of the citizens."

The police reporter's goal—to communicate accurate and timely information whether or not it pleases officials—does not always coincide with those articulated by police officials. Stories that are perceived as inimical to a police department's interests cannot be ignored or hidden, making way for only the "positive" stories. The police reporter is not a press agent.

Police often resent what they regard as publicity that the press sometimes gives to notorious criminals. By creating a glamorous image, police believe, the press makes it more difficult for them to build a case against someone they believe has broken the law. What a reporter sees as a fair story, police may perceive as detrimental to law enforcement.

Despite the reporter's best intentions, information is occasionally published that complicates police efforts to solve a sensitive case. The news story might contain sufficient detail about a case to enable a missing suspect to continue to elude authorities, for example. Police see many stories as jeopardizing their investigations.

In their zeal to get close to the scene of emergencies, reporters, particularly those lugging heavy camera and broadcast equipment, sometimes get in the way. If other irritating factors are already present, such perceived clumsiness on the part of the press can deteriorate press-police relationships even further.

To counteract these impediments to good communication, trustworthy contacts should be developed at all levels of law enforcement without compromising the integrity of the reporter or that of his or her news organization.

A fine, often shifting, line separates cooperation from cooptation. The reporter must learn how not to cross it. The ranks of law enforcement officials, like other public employees, contain their share of self-serving men and women. The reporter should identify and work around them, recognizing that most law enforcement people are dedicated to their jobs and desire a good relationship with the press.

To Print or Not to Print

New approaches to protecting individual rights have complicated the traditional considerations of the press in deciding whether to print or suppress information. To help assure the right to a fair trial, police, generally with the cooperation of the press, limit some information they once would have provided without question. Because at least some of this information is considered public record, the constitutional issues of freedom of the press (First Amendment) and the right to a fair trial (Sixth Amendment) have come into conflict.

Guidelines protecting both these constitutional issues were given strong impetus in 1966 with recommended standards on release of material before criminal trials. The so-called Reardon Rules, formulated by a committee headed by Paul C. Reardon, justice of the Supreme Judicial Court of Massachusetts, were designed to restrict law enforcement officials and attorneys in dissemination of information that could hinder a defendant's right to a fair trial.

One of the effects of the Reardon Committee report has been the growth of voluntary agreements among the press, law enforcement officials and the judiciary. But despite the proliferation of such agreements, editors usually reserve the right to decide what they will publish or broadcast, while agreeing in principle to adhere to the accepted guidelines.

Law enforcement agencies today make public factual matters about a criminal case, but avoid subjective observations.

Identity of a defendant, vital statistics, specific charge or charges, identity of the arresting officer and circumstances surrounding the arrest are considered usable facts. But police often avoid releasing details that might compromise the defendant's right to a fair trial, such as a person's past criminal record, confessions or alibis, or material such as lie detector tests or laboratory tests.

In all of these cases, there is nothing to keep a reporter from using the material if he or she can obtain it from another source, such as court records or a district attorney. But the reporter must determine whether justice is fully served by using it.

Similar sensitivity applies to coverage of crimes involving juveniles. Newspapers generally avoid identifying juveniles unless they are charged with a capital crime, but this practice is changing. One of the reasons is a Supreme Court ruling in 1979 that a state cannot punish a newspaper for accurately publishing the name of a juvenile charged with a crime.

Fairness also dictates caution in cases in which publishing the name of one person involved might compromise the privacy of a sex victim or a juvenile. A juvenile who accuses her father of incest, for example, is identified for all practical purposes when the father is arrested. At the very least, identification should await formal charges and be handled with care. The problem is often intensified when juvenile cases involve the children or relatives of prominent individuals. Editors are divided on the issue of using the juvenile's name when that name is news.

A single standard for reporting all juvenile crime news is unlikely, but setting some general guidelines acceptable to press, law enforcement agencies and the courts appears to be a reasonable approach.

The police reporter is occasionally asked by sources to withhold a story from publication on grounds that publication would hinder an investigation in progress or endanger victims, such as hostages. Each instance should be studied and decided individually.

Police-Press Guidelines

Guidelines are useful in clarifying the relationship between police and the press and in minimizing friction—especially if both sides have a hand in developing them.

The objective of the reporter and editor in working out any set of guidelines should be to produce a flexible document, not one that is cast in stone. The final decision on what to print, however, always rests with the editor.

Police officials, aware of the influence of the press upon public opinion, are usually agreeable to considering formulas that will facilitate the flow of information when it does not interfere with law enforcement.

In a typical memorandum to members of the force, the chief of a Midwest police department directs them "to engage in a program of complete fairness and frankness with the news media and their representatives."

The memo directs members of the department to facilitate "the maximum flow of information to the public through the media." Such general directives can help the reporter, but specifics can be even more helpful.

Desirable goals include rules to obtain information at the lowest possible administrative level within the department, easing the pressures at deadline time. Sometimes designation of specific officers to release information can help.

A typical police memo authorizes bureau, shift and unit commanders or their designated representatives "to release news items regarding the general or overall activities of their respective elements, that is, matters of public record about which they have personal knowledge. This would include information as to violations, crimes reported, arrests made and, where possible, the disposition of the case."

A central file or "booking register" that is easily accessible to the reporter should be a major goal. One typical department memo spells out this responsibility:

> It shall be the responsibility of the commanding officer of the Services Bureau to ensure that a copy of preliminary field case reports is placed on the designated board at the Information Counter, for use by representatives of the news media. Such reports shall be retained on this board for a minimum of 48 hours. The central booking register and other "public records" shall also be made available to representatives of the news media upon request.

Police and press in Connecticut produced the following voluntary guidelines containing minimum specifics several years ago. They are useful to the reporter, whatever the locale.

Information to be released before arrest:

• Description of the offense, including brief summary of events, location, time, injuries, damage, victims and other information pertinent to the incident; information necessary to investigation of the crime, to solicit public assistance or alert the public to danger (examples include a fugitive warrant, warnings that a fugitive may be armed or dangerous, release of criminal background when a public alert to danger is necessitated); method of complaint, such as officer observation, warrant or indictment; length of investigation, name of officer involved, public agencies involved.

Information not to be released before arrest:

• Identity of suspect interviewed but not charged; identity of victims of sex crimes or juveniles; exact identifying information about weapon or other physical evidence where release of such information would prejudice the investigation; information that could be known only to the guilty party; identity of victims, when a clear danger to them exists or if it would impair an ongoing investigation.

Information to be released after arrest:

• Identity of person accused or charged; suspect's name, address, age, employment, marital status; circumstances of arrest including time, place, resistance or pursuit, possession/use of weapons; description of physical items seized, provided the information will not compromise individual rights or investigations; name, address, age of victim, except victims of sex crimes; exact charge and its classification; identity of agency, unit and arresting officer; duration of the investigation; pretrial release or detention arrangements, including amount of bond, detention location; scheduled arraignment date (generally open to the press).

Information not to be released after arrest:

• Existence or contents of any statement or admission made by the accused person, or his/her refusal to make such a statement; statements concerning the character, reputation or guilt of an accused person; information that could lead to identity or specific address of a juvenile offender; identity of witnesses or victims, when a clear danger to them exists, or when identification would impair an ongoing investigation.

Press access to scenes of disasters or other emergencies has been complicated in recent years by the equipment necessary for quality broadcast coverage. Press identification cards are as useful as authorities are disposed to make them. The reporter's objective should be to convince authorities that the press has a right to be present, provided there is no interference with personnel at the scene.

No set of police-press guidelines is perfect, however, and gray areas will continue to exist because of the discretionary nature of information in the hands of officials. Good working relationships between reporter and police continue to constitute the major building blocks of effective access.

Covering Hospitals

Guidelines are also effective in dealing with hospitals and other emergency facilities. Disputes over access to information traditionally surround requests for facts involving emergency treatment in hospitals or by emergency units.

While the media's responsibility to report the news promptly is recognized by most officials, they retain a moral and legal responsibility for the care and privacy of their patients. Good guidelines recognize both sets of responsibilities.

The reporter's major effort should be encouraging release of information on cases of public record that are reportable by law to public authorities. Examples of these are people under arrest or under police surveillance; people taken to the hospital by police, firefighters or other public officials; or cases involving violence, poisoning or traffic accidents.

Unless hospital officials determine that release of information jeopardizes the health or welfare of the patient, pertinent information often will be released with or without the patient's consent in cases of public record.

The reporter should encourage officials to release these basic facts concerning patients brought to the hospital: Identification of the person, including name, address, age, sex, marital status and occupation; nature of the accident if an accident is involved; condition of the patient, including whether he or she is conscious or unconscious and whether there are fractures, head injuries or internal injuries; whether poisoning is involved and the nature of the substance, if so; whether a shooting or stabbing has occurred and the number and location of wounds.

The reporter will find officials reluctant to answer questions about child abuse, drug abuse or sexual assault, but often they can be persuaded to offer a statement on the medical condition of the patient.

Hospital administrators should be encouraged to designate hospital personnel to release information 24 hours a day, when possible. Public information officers can facilitate the flow of such information, although they occasionally may balk at releasing sensitive information.

No matter what guidelines are developed to facilitate information flow from the hospital, the old rules still apply. Reporters should be sufficiently familiar with the incident to ask specific questions. Such reporters are more difficult to turn away, and there is no substitute for being on the scene at the hospital rather than relying on the telephone.

STATE AND FEDERAL AGENCIES

Growth of law enforcement agencies at the federal level has been dramatic—to more than 115. One-third of those agencies did not exist before 1970. Police reporters are finding an increasing cooperative effort among local, state and federal agencies.

Local police departments must file regular reports with federal and state agencies, and turn to them frequently for assistance.

While police reporters may never deal daily with this multitude of agencies, they should be familiar with their operations. Regular contacts should be developed with agencies that frequently deal with enforcement problems at the local level. A current U.S. Government Manual and state manuals provide up-to-date addresses, telephone numbers and personnel for agencies.

State Police Agencies

State crime fighting units generally are made up of a highway patrol, a state militia, a bureau of identification and a division of criminal investigation.

The police reporter most often will deal with the highway patrol, which enforces the laws on federal and state highways. The reporter should maintain regular contact with district offices and substations of the patrol, but local police departments usually keep tabs on emergencies involving the patrol through their radios.

Police reporters should cultivate contacts with highway patrol personnel because patrol headquarters are often far from central police facilities and media offices. The key to dealing with the patrol lies with the dispatchers, and reporters who have taken the time to get to know them will have an easier time getting information, particularly on late-breaking stories.

A 6-year-old girl was shot and killed, and her father arrested after a high-speed chase with a highway patrolman along Interstate 70.

Mary Julia Swift, whom neighbors described as a "quiet, loving and sweet little girl," was shot as her father, Joseph C. Swift, 27, and Trooper W.A. Birke wrestled for a gun after a car chase Thursday night, officials reported.

The news pipeline tends to become sluggish when detailed investigations are involved, but the reporter who cultivates sources at the outset should have little trouble gathering information.

Most states provide a criminal investigation agency and an identification service, used by local officials as well as state agencies. The trend is also toward establishment of state coroner's offices in central locations for autopsies and scientific labs.

Miscellaneous law enforcement agencies include those dealing with enforcement of fish and game laws or alcoholic beverage laws, the state fire marshal's office, revenue agents and mine inspectors.

Federal Police Agencies

Local police departments turn most often to the FBI, the federal government's principal law enforcement agency, which has field offices scattered about the country. Agents investigate a wide range of criminal, civil and national security violations, including espionage, sabotage, kidnapping, extortion, bank robbery, interstate transportation of stolen property, civil rights violations, fraud against the federal government, and interstate gambling violations. The FBI often sharply restricts its release of information.

FBI services used by other law enforcement agencies include fingerprint identification, laboratory services and police training. Sophisticated police techniques offer new approaches to apprehending criminals.

> An FBI profile of a man suspected of committing 19 rapes in the Tricounty area shows he most likely is a soft-spoken family man who drives an older model car and lives in the southern end of Wake County.

Some of the directions the agency is taking point to changing trends in law enforcement. For example, law enforcement officials and juvenile advocates say creation of a nationwide fingerprinting system to track violent juvenile offenders reflects a growing trend to treat them like adults.

The FBI also works with state and local law enforcement agencies to extradite suspects from other states and investigate civil rights violations. A magistrate may ask the agency to investigate accusations of police brutality, or to join in a search for a missing state legislator who has been charged with a crime.

> A cargo plane registered in Nicaragua and crammed with 10 tons of marijuana crashed and burst into flames on a Tristate Airport runway yesterday.
>
> None of the eight persons aboard the DC-6 was injured. All eight face federal charges, and three face additional state charges.
>
> Authorities said the aircraft may have been stolen. Street value of the marijuana was estimated at nearly $10 million by authorities.

Several federal agencies joined the FBI in the case—including the Federal Aviation Administration and the U.S. Attorney's office. Before the investigation is completed, the Drug Enforcement Administration, the Immigration and Naturalization Service and the Customs Service may have a hand in it.

Like the FBI, the DEA is an arm of the Justice Department, enforcing laws relating to narcotics and controlled substances. The agency investigates drug trafficking at the national and international levels, but it also works closely with local law enforcement agencies, providing specialized training in dangerous drug control.

The Bureau of Alcohol, Tobacco and Firearms, an arm of the Treasury Department, has substantial contact at the local level. Its agents are responsible for enforcing firearms, explosives, gambling taxes, alcoholic beverages and tobacco products laws. The bureau has two distinct functions: criminal and regulatory enforcement.

Criminal enforcement activities include eliminating illegal possession and use of firearms and explosives, suppressing traffic in illicit distilled spirits and enforcing gambling tax legislation.

Its regulatory functions include collection of revenue from legal alcohol and tobacco industries, and efforts to prevent bribery, consumer deception and other improper practices in the distilled spirits industry.

One of the most dramatic stories of 1993 involved agents of the bureau, four of whom died in an abortive raid on the compound of a religious cult near Waco, Texas, on Feb. 28, 1993.

The ATF, with assistance from local police, had organized the raid to arrest the cult leader, David Koresh, on charges of illegal possession of fully automatic weapons and explosive devices.

The compound of the Branch Davidians burned to the ground April 19 in what the FBI, also involved in the 51-day standoff, described as a mass suicide. The remains of at least 86 cult members were recovered, including the bodies of at least 17 children.

The stories focused attention on the relationships among local, state and federal law enforcement agencies.

The Immigration and Naturalization Service enforces legislation covering admission, exclusion, deportation and naturalization of aliens. Its Border Patrol tries to prevent illegal entry into the country. Many stories are prompted by INS deportation proceedings.

Like the DEA, the Customs Service works to suppress illegal drug traffic, but its functions are broader. Customs enforces regulations on importation of goods into the United States and fights fraud and smuggling through its interdiction program.

A special division of the Postal Service, the Inspection Service, protects the mails, postal funds and property, apprehends those who are suspected of violating postal laws and investigates internal conditions.

One of the best-known agencies because of its responsibilities in protecting the president, the Secret Service enforces legislation relating to coins, currency and securities. As the main enforcement arm for the Treasury Department, the service also investigates forgery, counterfeiting and alteration of U.S. and foreign currencies.

It was a perfect hiding place—almost.

But because of the persistence of a Secret Service agent, Colbert Hale, 27, 800 20th St., was in the county jail today, charged with counterfeiting.

Agent Sam Winslow, acting on a tip by an informant, found Hale hiding in the chimney over the fireplace in his apartment.

Winslow had earlier checked the premises without success and had called the informant who insisted Hale was in the apartment. Winslow returned, noticed a wood slat ajar in the fireplace, and found Hale's hiding place.

The Law Enforcement Assistance Administration was established by Congress to help reduce crime.

One of its programs, the National Institute of Law Enforcement and Criminal Justice, is a national clearinghouse for exchange of criminal justice information. Another program, the Criminal Justice Information and Statistics Service, collects, evaluates and disseminates statistics on crime and justice, all available to the press.

The U.S. Marshal is one of the nation's oldest law enforcement jobs, dating from 1789. Traditionally, the marshal's office serves process papers produced by the federal courts, but the office's responsibilities have expanded. Marshals make arrests on the basis of federal warrants and serve as officers of the federal court.

The Coast Guard, a division of the Department of Transportation in time of peace, is responsible for enforcing federal laws on navigable coastal and interior waters. The service also enforces conservation and marine environmental laws, cooperating with other law enforcement agencies in use of its transportation facilities.

Enforcement of wildlife laws is the responsibility of the Fish and Wildlife Service, which manages and protects wildlife resources. Representatives often engage in cooperative ventures with state wildlife officers.

Other agencies generate law enforcement stories on occasion, some of them significant, and the reporter should be familiar with these sources.

✳✳✳

SUGGESTED READINGS

Cohen, Howard S., and Michael Feldberg. *Power and Restraint: The Moral Dimension of Police Work.* Westport, Conn.: Praeger, 1991.

More, Harry W., ed. *Managerial Control of the Police: Internal Affairs and Audits.* Springfield, Ill.: C.D. Thomas, 1991.

McArdle, Phil, and Karen McArdle. *Fatal Fascination: Where Fact Meets Fiction in Police Work.* Boston: Houghton Mifflin, 1988.

Chapter 12

Covering the Criminal Courts

The police reporter is pleased with herself. So is her editor.

With little time remaining before deadline, the reporter has produced a highly readable account of arrests of two men suspected of committing a series of armed robberies to supply their drug habits. An exciting midnight auto chase has resulted in arrest of the pair.

The police reporter brought into play all the skills she possesses to tie up the story in time for the newspaper's final edition: good communications with the police, reliable sources, a knack for being in the right place at the right time, and the ability to organize and write a complicated story under deadline pressure. It has been a good news day.

However, in the days after the heavy door of the lockup slams shut on the jailed suspects, a different kind of drama will emerge.

239

Noisy street scenes and police station confrontations will give way to quiet courtrooms as the case begins its journey through the judicial process. And while its interest and importance to the public may not diminish, different kinds of stories emerge from the courts.

A FORUM FOR SOCIETY

Citizens can depend on the court system to help them settle their disputes before an impartial tribunal. But the courts serve another important function—providing a mechanism by which a person charged with a public offense is brought to trial, with subsequent punishment or acquittal. Through this process, the state punishes a person who commits an act deemed to be injurious to society.

A criminal action in the courts is prosecuted by a public official—called a district attorney, a prosecuting attorney or a state's attorney—and follows a nearly universal process of arrest, accusation, pleadings and trial. The process may be lengthened by an appeal.

The state must prove criminal guilt beyond reasonable doubt. Anything less demands acquittal of the accused. The proceedings in a criminal action are designed to safeguard the rights of the accused person, the most important truth in the criminal process for the reporter.

From the beginning, the reporter must be sure that news accounts reflect the presumed innocence of the accused. At most, the accused is only *charged* with a specific crime, even if details seemingly point to guilt.

In the case of a suspect who is charged with assault and robbery, for example, it is not only unfair but dangerous for the reporter to predict on the basis of conversations with law enforcement authorities that further charges will be made.

> A police department spokesman said two counts of rape, two counts of aggravated robbery and one count of kidnapping *probably will be filed* against Smith this week.

Reporting in this manner is totally inappropriate. Only *after* a suspect is officially charged with such crimes should they be reported.

Nowhere else in public affairs reporting do the rights of the people to know and the concomitant rights of the individual stand in such constant danger of collision.

How much detail should the reporter provide in pretrial stories? Who should be quoted and at what length? How should incriminating evidence be handled in news stories? How much and what kind of detail should be provided on the suspect's background?

The press has attempted to balance conscientious reporting of crime with sensitivity in dealing with its sensational aspects and protecting the rights of the accused. Policies differ from newspaper to newspaper and among broadcast newsrooms. Metropolitan newspapers have been accused of sensationalism in reporting crime news, while publications in smaller communities often are accused of suppressing similar information deemed to be important to the public interest.

The answer lies in a thoughtful commitment to coverage that balances the public's right to pertinent details in criminal actions with the accused person's right to fair treatment in the courts.

Levels of Jurisdiction

Two members of a political party argue in a hallway over a long-standing difference. Suddenly one of them strikes the other, sending him to the hospital with a fractured jaw and other injuries. The injured man swears out a complaint that a law prohibiting such assaults has been breached, and the attacker is charged with simple assault. After hearing the evidence, a city court judge pronounces the defendant guilty of violating the law, suspends a 30-day sentence and fines him $300.

Unless the injured politician seeks an appeal to a higher court, this concludes the "criminal" aspects of the case.

However, the injured party can file a civil action to recover medical costs and other damages he believes he has sustained. The reporter should remember that civil action often follows a criminal case in court.

Depending upon the nature of the crime, criminal actions can be pursued in federal as well as in state courts. The celebrated break-in at the headquarters of the Democratic National Committee in Washington's Watergate Complex in 1972 offers an example of overlapping local and federal criminal cases.

- The Watergate scandal began when five intruders were arrested at the Democratic headquarters June 17, 1972. At that point, only District of Columbia police were involved in the "local" burglary.

- The affair became a federal criminal case Sept. 15, 1972, when a grand jury indicted seven people (including two former White House aides) on charges of conspiring to break into the Democratic headquarters. The charges included illegal wiretapping, a federal offense.

- Watergate also became a federal civil action when the Democratic Party filed a $1 million lawsuit against the Committee to Re-Elect the President, a Republican organization.

- An out-of-court settlement later concluded the civil action, while most of those involved in the criminal proceedings were convicted and imprisoned for varying terms. The case illustrates how a single criminal action can expand to other courts.

The Nature of Crime

crime: the commission of an act that is forbidden.

Stripped to its simplest definition, a crime is an offensive act committed against all the people in a community rather than merely a wrong that one individual perceives another as committing against him or her.

But the nature of crime itself and the multitude of offenses create a more complex relationship between those who commit crime and those responsible for punishing the criminal. Some crimes are inherently wrong (*mala in se*, or wrongs in themselves), such as robbery or assault. Others are merely prohibited by law, such as failure to register as an alien in this country.

Newsworthiness often depends upon the seriousness of a criminal act. A misdemeanor implies a minor offense, such as a traffic violation or a gambling charge. More serious crimes, such as burglary, extortion, kidnapping and murder, are identified as felonies, with conviction calling for longer prison terms or fines.

```
                    BOX 12-1

                  Kinds of Crime
                      ✲✲✲

     Against the person
     Against property
     Against the habitation
     Against the public peace
     Against authority
```

The reporter should learn to distinguish the specific classes of criminal acts. Conviction on a simple robbery charge might be punishable by two years in prison, while a more serious charge of armed robbery could result in up to 20 years in prison. Still another charge, robbery with a deadly weapon, might be punishable with a sentence of up to life imprisonment.

Kinds of Crime

Common law differentiates among the kinds of crime: crimes against the person, crimes against the habitation, crimes against property, crimes against the public peace and crimes against authority.

Crimes Against the Person

Crimes against the person range from simple assault, merely threatening someone without actual physical violence, through homicide, the gravest of all crimes against the person. Simple assault may be punishable by up to 30 days in jail, while assault with intent to maim could draw up to 20 years in prison.

The reporter must always take care to identify the exact charge in a crime. When a person forcibly takes a person against his or her will, the charge may be kidnapping; when a person is taken by persuasion but without violence, the charge might be abduction. Unlawful carnal knowledge of a person without his or her consent is rape, but less serious charges can be lodged against a person in this category—molestation or sexual harassment. Most newspapers mask the identity of victims of crimes involving sex, and some explain they are doing so in a footnote to the story:

> (*The Morning News* does not normally use the names of people who report incidents of sexual abuse to law enforcement agencies.)

This is a difficult area, and policies differ as the press tries to balance the rights of victims, who have legitimate fears of retaliation and humiliation, with the right of defendants to face their accusers.

The most serious crime is homicide. The killing of another human being, either intentional or by accident, is always among the most newsworthy of criminal actions. And because the punishment is generally most severe, its news coverage is the one that calls for the most care.

The law recognizes two types of homicide: justifiable and felonious. A police officer who shoots and kills someone in the line of duty might be charged with justifiable homicide and in fact may not go to trial. A charge of homicide might be placed against a homeowner protecting her family against an intruder, but the charge may be a mitigating justifiable homicide.

Different degrees of felonious homicide range from first-degree murder—a premeditated act with intent to do harm, to second-degree murder—an intentional act committed as the result of extreme provocation, to murder in the third degree—known as manslaughter.

A manslaughter charge is often filed after a fatal automobile accident. The charge becomes more serious if the defendant has broken a traffic law or acted irresponsibly. The charge may be dropped in its entirety if the defendant has been found to be acting within the law.

Crimes Against the Habitation

The original concept of "habitation" as a dwelling place has been expanded to include almost any building in which people live, work or engage in recreation. Arson, the act of burning such a building, and burglary, the act of entering a building for a felonious purpose, are recognized as crimes against the habitation.

These felony charges often are coupled with others, such as burglary with intent to commit bodily harm or burglary with intent to sexually assault. Possession of a dangerous weapon while burglarizing a home carries a more serious sentence than simple burglary. Willfully setting fire to another's property, including setting fire to one's own property for fraudulent insurance purposes, is known as arson. This charge becomes murder if a person is killed as a result of a deliberately set fire.

> A murder charge will be placed against the arsonist who touched off a fire that gutted the vacant Marshall Building on State Street Monday, police said.
>
> Firefighter Wilson Jent, 28, was killed instantly when a falling timber struck him as he and 22 other firefighters fought to contain the blaze that State Fire Marshal Soward Fell said was deliberately set.

Crimes Against Property

The right of a person to be secure against theft is undisputed in common law, but statutory legislation also has been enacted to meet changing conditions and further protect the individual. Degrees of crimes against property range from theft of a purse to robbery with a dangerous weapon to extortion or embezzlement of funds from a company.

Larceny or Theft.   Taking property that belongs to someone else is known as larceny, although some places have abandoned that term and use theft, including embezzlement and obtaining money under false pretenses. Lack of violence generally characterizes this charge, and the sentence varies with its seriousness.

Robbery.   Larceny or theft through intimidation or force, implying violence or potential violence is robbery. The victim need only be placed in a state of fear for the robbery charge to hold. The instrument used is often the determining factor in degree of seriousness. Robbery with a weapon such as a knife or gun carries a more serious charge.

Cliches abound in describing details of robberies, and the reporter should steer clear of words like "stickup men," "bandits" and "thugs."

Embezzlement.   Appropriation of a person's property through fraudulent means is embezzlement. Often the charge is brought against people handling money or property of others, such as bank or other business establishment employees, servants and public officials.

False Pretenses.   Deliberately misrepresenting facts with intent to deceive or defraud is using false pretenses and has been established as a statutory crime. The swindler might represent himself as a successful businessman in an effort to persuade a friend to assign property to him before marriage.

Malicious Mischief.   Deliberately destroying property belonging to another is called malicious mischief and carries different penalties, depending upon the seriousness. Tampering with another's automobile, damaging trees and shrubs on another's property, or harming pets or animals belonging to another are all classified as malicious mischief.

Receiving property stolen by another is punishable by a prison term. Concealing or reselling the goods, often by professionals known as "fences," leads to this charge. Other common offenses against property include extortion or blackmail, an effort to obtain money or property through the use of threats or intimidation, and forgery, the signing or creating of a written instrument with intent to deceive or defraud. Altering a check is considered to be a forgery.

Crimes Against the Public Peace

The statutes of most states are weighty with laws governing public morality and decency. The apartment dweller who offends the neighborhood with frequent and raucous parties or the homeowner who has turned his front lawn into a graveyard for junked automobiles can be prosecuted for disturbing the peace. Accepted standards of social conduct govern these incidences.

Depending on the area and statutes, such crimes include adultery, bigamy, incest, prostitution, gambling, obscenity, indecency, and contributing to the delinquency of a minor. Civil liberties legislation, for example, has led to the demise of several statutes, such as vagrancy or loitering, which formerly was the vehicle for arresting people just to get them off the streets.

Obscenity laws also are in a state of uncertainty; definitions of the term depend on the jurisdiction and the accepted social values of the people who live there. The same applies to riot actions or disturbance of public assembly.

Crimes Against Authority and Justice

A body of legislation deals with willful interference in recognized functions of government. They include statutes forbidding obstruction of justice, such as interference with a police officer performing his or her duty; resisting arrest or hindering the arrest of another; breaking out of prison or helping another avoid custody; withholding evidence leading to disposition of a crime; giving false testimony under oath in a judicial proceeding (perjury); and offering a bribe or giving a reward to a public official, with intent to corrupt the official.

Tax evasion, postal violations such as theft of mail, and contempt, which is a willful violation or disregard for judicial proceedings, also are classified as crimes against justice or authority.

State and federal codes include a variety of other statutes prohibiting specific offenses. These include traffic laws, food and drug laws, and fish and game statutes. Many are punishable by fines; others carry jail or prison sentences.

Rights of the Accused

The rights of the accused person are safeguarded by the Fifth Amendment to the U.S. Constitution. In all the proceedings that will be covered and reported by the press, a person is presumed innocent until proved guilty. Thus, the reporter should avoid writing that a jury "has found the defendant innocent." The defendant cannot be *found* innocent, because he or she *is* innocent until found guilty or convicted. Technically, the defendant is acquitted of the charges. The terms of the Fifth Amendment protection are unequivocal:

> No person shall be deprived of life, liberty or property without due process of law.

Other basic rights also are important to the reporter in the criminal process. The accused person is guaranteed the right to:

- Notice of the nature and cause of the accusation.
- Have the assistance of counsel, even if the public must provide it.
- Reasonable bail, as determined by law.

- A speedy and public trial by an impartial jury.
- Refuse to testify against himself or herself.
- Confront and examine his or her accusers.
- Be tried only once for the same crime.

Recognizing each of these basic guarantees, the reporter will cover the court developments that reflect each step through the often lengthy process. Although the process may take different paths, the guarantees remain the same.

Every story should reflect a responsibility to protect the rights of an accused person. No one should be incriminated, and speculation regarding guilt or innocence or imputed motive should always be avoided.

The reporter should beware of such off-hand comments from arresting officers as "We caught them red-handed," or "I had a hunch he was the one who did it." Most law enforcement officers are more cautious today, but such incidents persist and the reporter should understand the dangers they pose to fairness.

ARREST, ACCUSATION AND PLEADING

The point at which the reporter most often enters the law enforcement picture is the arrest. Commission of a crime does not have to be observed for an arrest to take place, but there must be reasonable suspicion that a person has been involved.

The arrest can be observed by the reporter at the scene, or it can be verified through police or court records. Because of its serious nature, however, the reporter should always verify that the action occurred.

> A man *who police said* used a dozen aliases was charged Tuesday with passing $20 counterfeit bills in the Front Street district.
>
> He was arrested after a suspicious jewelry store clerk quietly called police while ostensibly making change for a purchase.

After the arrest, the police officer swears out a formal complaint with a court official, usually a magistrate, who issues a warrant of arrest. The process is sometimes reversed when the officer first files the complaint and the court official issues the warrant, after which the arrest is made.

The suspect is **booked**, with the arrest formally recorded at a jail, in a police station or in a magistrate's office. The defendant may be jailed until arraignment or released on bail or on personal recognizance (a promise to appear in court) if the charge is not serious or if the individual is well-known. In serious offenses where there is danger that the accused person may flee, a judge may refuse to set bail.

> An oil worker at the Marine Terminal was arrested this morning and charged with the murders of a Tilly woman and her three children whose battered bodies were discovered Monday in her stucco house on Broad Street.
>
> Wesley S. David, 28, who gave his address as 1905 Oak St., was charged with four counts of murder and placed in the Dale County jail shortly after 10 a.m. without bail.

The accused has a right to a speedy arraignment, whose purpose is to identify the defendant, to advise of the charges filed, and to inform the defendant of his or her constitutional rights. The reporter covers an arraignment to determine the specific charges that the defendant faces and the defendant's plea.

> Arrington physician Louis C. Milton pleaded not guilty this morning to three separate indictments charging trafficking in drugs.
>
> The 55-year-old Milton, who has been practicing medicine at 710 S. 11th St. for 27 years, sat pensively throughout the 10-minute arraignment in Lawrence County Common Pleas Court, only answering a few questions from Judge Forrest McClanahan. Bail was set at $50,000.
>
> The indictments, returned July 31 by the county grand jury, accused the physician of "aiding and abetting and trafficking in drugs" during a 13-month period concluding with the indictments.

The accused offers one of these pleas:

- Guilty.
- Not guilty.
- *Nolo contendere* (I will not contest it). With this plea, the defendant admits no guilt but throws himself on the mercy of the court. The plea amounts to a guilty plea but is often used to avoid use of an admission of guilt in a later civil action.

• Not guilty by reason of insanity. (The defendant may admit the crime, but argues that she was not in control of her faculties when the crime was committed.)

Plea Bargaining

The defendant also may use a bargaining process, pleading guilty to a lesser charge. In return for such a plea, a costly trial is often avoided. Plea bargaining is a popular—and controversial—part of the judicial process, and the reporter should be sufficiently familiar with pending cases to present the details accurately.

A defendant often will bargain with authorities for a reduced or suspended sentence in return for testimony that will implicate other people in the case. Prosecutors who fear a jury trial because their case is not strong enough often seek plea bargains with defendants.

> Lawyers for seven remaining defendants awaiting trial in the $7.1 million robbery of a Hartford Wells Fargo depot have reached a plea agreement with federal prosecutors.
> Under the agreement, a U.S. District Court memorandum states, the defendants will plead guilty to reduced charges and serve some time in prison.
> The action is intended to prevent a long and costly trial, according to the memorandum.

Plea bargaining takes place throughout the judicial process—even after a trial is over. It can complicate the reporting process, because much of it is closeted in private negotiations among attorneys in the case.

The reporter is generally forced to rely on vague reports of a "deal" being struck, speculation by other officials and other inappropriate sources. It is a dangerous reporting area, but important to thorough coverage of the courts.

> LOS ANGELES—A Ventura County flower grower charged with enslaving hundreds of Mexican laborers has agreed to plead guilty to corporate racketeering and to pay $1.5 million in back wages to former workers, the stiffest fine ever levied in a U.S. immigration case, prosecutors said Monday.
> In exchange for the plea from rancher Edwin M. Ives, 55, the U.S. Attorney's office agreed to dismiss extortion and slavery counts.

Even after a deal is struck, the parties to the agreement sometimes argue at length in court over coercion and violation of the plea bargain agreement itself.

> WASHINGTON—A federal appeals court has upheld the guilty plea and life sentence for intelligence analyst Jonathan Pollard, who sold secrets to Israel.
> By a 2–1 vote Friday, the Court of Appeals for the District of Columbia rejected Pollard's claim that the government violated the plea bargain on how harsh a sentence to seek.

In this celebrated case, the defendant argued that the government had coerced him to plead guilty. The judges granted that the federal government had "engaged in hard-nosed dealings" with Pollard, but found he had not mounted a sufficient challenge to the actions of the prosecutors.

Further complicating the reporter's job, plea bargaining often is criticized as promoting a double standard of justice. Powerful and wealthy individuals have been accused of using their money and stature to extract better deals from the justice system. In some states, efforts are under way to outlaw plea bargaining through legislative changes, but most prosecutors see plea bargaining as a necessary part of the judicial system. They argue that it eliminates costly trials and helps unclog the crowded court system.

Preliminary Hearings

Unless an indictment already has been returned by a grand jury, the defendant is entitled to a preliminary hearing (sometimes called a preliminary examination). Its purpose is to determine whether a crime has been committed and whether there are reasonable grounds to believe the defendant was involved.

At this hearing, the defendant is confronted with the evidence to support the charges against him or her. The reporter is reminded that the hearing is essentially one-sided because the defendant presents no witnesses, and the reporter must take special care to avoid a prejudiced news report. In some jurisdictions the defendant can request a closed preliminary hearing to prevent publication of only prosecution testimony, which might hinder selection of an impartial jury.

Closed pretrial hearings were given new impetus in 1979 when the U.S. Supreme Court gave trial judges wide latitude in barring reporters and the public from pretrial hearings if the judge believes publicity might be a threat to a fair trial.

In a 5–4 opinion, then-Justice Potter Stewart wrote, "To safeguard the due process rights of the accused, a trial judge has an affirmative constitutional duty to minimize the effects of prejudicial pretrial publicity." Following the ruling, some judges closed preliminary hearings as well as pretrial hearings to the press, but the effects on information-gathering appear to be minimal.

After the prosecuting attorney has presented the state's case in a preliminary hearing, the presiding judge may order the case to trial or dismiss the case and release the defendant if he or she feels that the evidence is insufficient.

Other Routes to Trial

Felony cases reach trial court by two routes other than the sworn complaint:

1. Through an **information**, which is an accusation by a prosecutor of a criminal offense. If the prosecuting attorney has knowledge that a crime has been committed, the official may swear out an information and submit it to the court for action. The defendant is entitled to a preliminary hearing to determine whether a trial is warranted. The filing of an information has the advantage of speed, with the district attorney sidestepping the often time-consuming grand jury process.

2. Through the **grand jury**. A specially impaneled group of men and women meets to consider whether people accused of crimes should go to trial. The prosecuting attorney presents the evidence and requests that an indictment be returned. After hearing testimony, the grand jury votes a "true bill" if it believes evidence supports a trial. It votes a "no bill" if it believes there is insufficient evidence.

The Grand Jury System

"The grand jury," legal scholar Henry J. Abraham observed, "may well be cumbersome, amateurish,

time-consuming, annoying, emotional and the fifth wheel in the legal process, but on balance—as was well-demonstrated by the persistent 1973–74 Watergate grand jury—it does appear to serve as a potentially powerful arm of direct democracy, *if* one is willing to accept the philosophy of the institution in the first place and if one has faith in the competence and intelligence of one's fellow citizens."

The grand jury system, which serves as a body of inquiry in most states, remains a major means of determining whether there is sufficient evidence to warrant a trial on criminal charges.

A grand jury can open an investigation on its own, or it can rely on the prosecuting attorney to prepare cases for consideration. It considers evidence in cases of persons arrested and being held in jail or who have been released on bond. During the course of an investigation, the jury members can subpoena witnesses, call the accused as a witness, and seek any information that will help them make a decision.

Grand jury sessions are usually secret, mainly to protect innocent people. Many indictments are considered but never returned. The jury generally considers only the prosecuting attorney's evidence in a case, and the accused may have little or no opportunity to present his or her own case or to cross-examine witnesses.

As a practical matter, the reporter should be aware that the prosecutor may not always be objective in treatment of a pending case. Human frailty or overriding ambition on the part of an official sometimes obstructs justice. Public pressure often has been responsible for prosecution of notoriously weak cases by police and prosecutors. Cases that appear politically motivated should be analyzed closely by interviewing both sides and independent legal experts.

A reporter with good investigative instincts and a healthy skepticism can avoid publicizing such actions by scrutinizing the details of the case and asking probing questions.

In some states, the grand jury also acts as an investigative body to public agencies. Operations of county facilities, such as nursing homes, hospitals and jail facilities, are often investigated. Questionable bail practices by bondsmen in a city may be investigated by a grand jury, leading to changes in the system and even to indictments on conspiracy and extortion charges.

When a grand jury conducts its own investigation and returns an accusation, it is called a **presentment**.

The prosecutor also plays an important role in grand jury investigations of public agencies, which may be complicated by the political character of that official. This example illustrates how an official might sidestep political fallout.

> The prosecutor for York County is letting grand juries decide whether to bring indictments in public corruption cases, instead of first telling jurors what he thinks they should do.
>
> Solicitor Frank Wilson said the new approach is fairer and less political.
>
> County solicitors traditionally have led jurors through the investigation process. Wilson said that now he will only answer jurors' questions and prepare indictments.

There are other questions important to this story: What triggered the change in policy? What is the reaction of defense lawyers? How do judges who will receive the indictments feel about the new policy? How do nearby counties handle similar grand jury investigations?

While press access to the grand jury is limited, the alert reporter can figure out who is being investigated and why, often by observing who enters and departs from the grand jury room.

Grand jurors are sworn to secrecy, but witnesses are free to discuss their own testimony unless they have been specifically admonished to secrecy by the presiding judge. General information is often available from a prosecuting attorney and the presiding judge, if they choose to divulge it.

> A special grand jury will examine the records of the Oxford Urban Renewal Authority to determine whether relocated families have been cheated out of thousands of dollars.
>
> A subpoena issued Monday by Circuit Court Judge Henry L. Mannington directed URA Director Thomas R. Wilson to bring records on relocation before the grand jury tomorrow.
>
> Requested records span the period from Jan. 1, 1991 to July 12 of this year.

In this case, the prosecutor, who accompanied deputies when the subpoena was served, was willing to go on the record. He told the reporter there was reason to believe that unidentified officials might have pocketed money earmarked for families forced to leave their homes and move elsewhere.

Access to grand jury transcripts is usually regulated by the judge, and transcripts are not available until after the indictments have been returned and the grand jury dismissed. A portion of a transcript may be sealed by the judge until the trial has begun.

> The Prince County grand jury has charged three area fire chiefs with falsifying records and providing misleading information to insurance companies.
>
> The grand jury initiated the indictments after reviewing state reports involving Fire Chiefs James Wilson of District 3, Weston Houck of District 7 and Carl Dickert of District 8.
>
> Conviction on the felony charges carries a prison sentence of two years or a $5,000 fine, or both.
>
> The chiefs, according to the indictment, passed among themselves thousands of dollars in equipment to upgrade insurance ratings during the past three years.

The federal government also impanels grand juries for purposes similar to the county bodies, with the federal bodies binding over defendants for trial and investigating possible abuses by officeholders and government employees.

Grand juries have from six to 30 members, chosen at random from among the public. Terms are limited, ranging from a month to a year before jurors are discharged, but a presiding judge may occasionally extend a jury's term if its business has not been completed. The presiding judge instructs the jury, which appoints its own foreman and secretary. Length of sessions varies, with some juries meeting every day for a week before recessing, and others meeting one day a week for longer periods.

The reporter should watch for new procedural developments in the juries as well as in the courts. Sometimes they are more newsworthy than the lists of indictments returned.

> A new procedure for grand jury deliberations promises "far more efficiency," County Prosecutor John J. Cummings announced yesterday.
>
> Cummings said he would break with tradition, calling the grand jury into session every two weeks throughout the course of the three-month term. In the past, juries have convened only once every three months.

"Things will come up as they occur, instead of waiting and waiting and waiting," Cummings said. "Cases essentially will be fresh when they go before the grand jury," he added, giving jurors a more accurate account of each case.

Pretrial Pleading

Before trial, many courses of action are open to the defendant through his or her attorney, mainly through motions attacking the accusation. The defendant may file a demurrer, challenging the accusation on the grounds that the facts stated in it do not constitute a crime or that a crime is charged for which the defendant does not have to respond. If the judge sustains a demurrer, the case is dropped unless the complaint, information or indictment can be amended and resubmitted.

The defendant can deny that the court has jurisdiction to try him or her for the offense charged (plea to the jurisdiction) or can request a change of venue when there is a question as to whether the defendant can obtain a fair trial in that area.

Ronald Wilmer's request to change the site of his trial on charges of murder was denied Tuesday, but Circuit Court Judge Wanda Haswell left the door open to reconsideration later.

Wilmer, 24, is scheduled to go to trial Monday on charges that he killed three people during a March 12 crime spree along the coast.

Haswell said she denied the request "based on the showing here today." Defense attorney Cleveland Eames based his motion on pretrial publicity and a fund-raising effort for one of the victims.

"Monday morning when we start to impanel a jury, if I get the idea this is not the place for the trial, I'll change the venue," Haswell said.

A motion may be made to set aside the charge for factual or procedural deficiencies. The defense attorney might argue that the prosecuting attorney's complaint, based on evidence presented at a preliminary hearing, is not sufficient to prove what it charges.

The defense attorney may move to suppress evidence that is not admissible in court, such as that obtained through an illegal police search and seizure.

The defense attorney also might ask the judge to dismiss the charge because the defendant has been denied due process, if notice of his or her constitutional rights is not given when an arrest is made.

Lengthy legal maneuvering often takes place during efforts to extradite a person accused or convicted of an offense to a court that demands his or her surrender. Proof is demanded that the person is indeed a fugitive. Uniform extradition legislation has standardized the procedure, but often such efforts are newsworthy.

Michele Sindona, an Italian financier who once controlled the Franklin National Bank, won a court decision Wednesday that bars his extradition to his native Italy.

The decision by Federal District Judge Herman L. Werkman represents a significant victory for Sindona, who has conducted a two-year struggle to avoid extradition on fraud charges involving the collapse of Italian banks he had controlled.

CRIMINAL TRIAL

As a bailiff intones, "All rise," the black-robed judge strides into the courtroom, and the crowded chamber quiets. The judge takes a seat on the raised bench, and the crowd settles back expectantly. A trial is about to begin.

Across the land, the cast of characters in this drama of an American institution is similar: In front of the judge and closest to the action sits a court reporter, expert fingers ready to negotiate the keyboard of the stenotype equipment. Every question asked, every answer given will be recorded with efficiency in a complete transcript of the proceedings.

At a table facing the bench sits a defendant formally accused of committing a crime, flanked by one or more attorneys.

At an adjacent table, public officials charged with prosecuting the indictment against the accused whisper last-minute comments. The prosecuting attorney, often with several assistants in major cases, orchestrates the effort.

The bailiff, present to maintain the decorum of the court, stands near the door to the judge's chambers.

Lined up at a nearby table are reporters awaiting opening arguments in what promises to be a news-worthy case. The jury of 12 people has been chosen and sworn.

Although the scenario is unchanging, the participants are as dissimilar as are the elements of the population. The defendant may be indigent, with public defenders, or a wealthy industrialist, with a half a dozen well-known attorneys. Two witnesses may be scheduled, or 25. Testimony may be dramatic, or it may be cut-and-dried as the trial proceeds.

Most trials lack the newsworthiness to compel a reporter to cover them daily, listening to all of the evidence and carefully sorting it out for the reader. Instead, the major interest is in the final result, and the reporter checks regularly for the judgment or judgments—guilty, not guilty or case dismissed.

Daily checks with court clerks should be adequate to keep up with the less important cases. But the story should not be left hanging. If preliminary stories have been written concerning a case, a final story should be written when the trial ends.

Officers of the Court

The chief officer of the court is the judge, who presides over the trial and issues rulings on all points of law dealing with procedure, submission of evidence and witnesses, and determination of the substantive law in each case. The judge leaves the determination of facts to the jury, except when the case is tried without one.

A court clerk is the judge's right arm during the trial and is an important source of information to the reporter. Records of the judicial proceedings are kept in the clerk's office and are indispensable to the accuracy of trial stories.

All proceedings of the trial are recorded by the court recorder, also indispensable to the reporter. Exact testimony of witnesses, details of evidence, objections made by attorneys, and court rulings are taken verbatim through shorthand, stenotype or tape recorder. In important trials, newspapers often arrange to obtain a daily transcript of the proceedings for accuracy and

thoroughness. Despite this vital backup, however, the news reporter should depend on his or her own note-taking, checking confusing testimony with the court's recorder.

Setting the Stage

While the reporter should avoid interpreting actions, events and testimony, important trials often merit a description of the setting, the principals and drama of the event. Overly descriptive "labels" for those involved should be avoided, with the reporter concentrating instead on helping the reader or viewer understand the issues involved.

The reporter often offers to the reader a picture of the trial scene that only can be obtained by sitting in on the trial.

CONOVER—As though he were only a passerby, former State Liquor Commissioner Brian L. Jeffries has listened quietly to the shrill arguments that have resounded for 10 days in the courtroom where he is on trial.

Jeffries is charged with defrauding the state of thousands of dollars while he was commissioner from 1985 to 1992.

Jeffries has remained a passive figure on the fringes of the proceedings.

Defense attorneys Rudolph Bulgari and John Barber offer a vivid contrast to one another. Bulgari's red suspenders and folksy manner disarm witnesses, who are startled when the fatherly, friendly voice switches suddenly to a booming, accusing baritone.

Barber, polished and sophisticated, hammers at witnesses from the outset of his questioning. Some of his remarks have provoked the ire of presiding Judge Ernestine Wills, who keeps a tight rein on courtroom procedure.

Basic Elements of the Trial

While specifics vary from state to state, these are the basic steps of a criminal trial on a felony charge (also, see Figure 12–1):

• The jury is selected and sworn.

• The accusation is read in open court, and the defendant's plea is recorded.

- The prosecution makes an opening statement, explaining to the jury how it intends to prove its case. Stories are often written based on the opening remarks of both prosecution and defense.

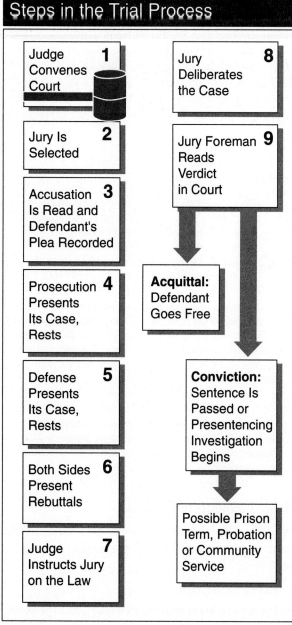

Steps in the Trial Process

1 Judge Convenes Court	**8** Jury Deliberates the Case
2 Jury Is Selected	**9** Jury Foreman Reads Verdict in Court
3 Accusation Is Read and Defendant's Plea Recorded	**Acquittal:** Defendant Goes Free
4 Prosecution Presents Its Case, Rests	**Conviction:** Sentence Is Passed or Presentencing Investigation Begins
5 Defense Presents Its Case, Rests	
6 Both Sides Present Rebuttals	Possible Prison Term, Probation or Community Service
7 Judge Instructs Jury on the Law	

FIGURE 12–1

- The prosecution presents its case, calling witnesses and presenting evidence that it believes will help convict the defendant.
- The defense makes its opening statement, explaining how it will show the defendant to be innocent of the charge. This opening statement is sometimes made immediately after the prosecution offers its opening statement.
- The defense presents its evidence, with the burden of proof on the prosecution. The defense merely has to prove reasonable doubt that the defendant committed the crime.
- Both sides present rebuttal evidence in an effort to weaken the other side's case.
- Both parties sum up their case to the jury, seeking to strengthen their cause.
- The judge instructs the jury on the law, explaining the jury's limitations and what possible verdicts can be returned.
- The jury retires to deliberate and return a verdict. If it cannot reach a verdict in a reasonable time, the judge can rule a mistrial, and the case may be retried or dropped.
- If the defendant is convicted, sentence is passed, sometimes after extensive presentencing investigation by court officials. Judgment is then executed, with the convicted defendant remanded to custody or to probation proceedings.

Course of the Trial

Selection of the jurors who will render final judgment is important to both sides as well as to the public. Traditionally 12 jurors are chosen, with alternates selected in potentially lengthy and complex cases so that illness of a juror does not abort the proceedings. Alternates do not vote unless they must substitute for one of the 12 jurors in the case. Many states have adopted legislation permitting fewer than that number, except in capital cases.

Some cases are heard, at the defendant's request, by a judge or a panel of judges.

The story covering the verdict in a criminal case should be written in a straightforward manner, with

Two judges examine a bloody rag, a key piece of evidence in a murder trial.

Photo by John Long, courtesy of The Hartford Courant.

prompt efforts made to determine from the principals whether appeals will be made.

> A federal court jury convicted John and Edward Schneider Thursday of plotting to blow up the Olde Mill Elementary School in October, a plot the brothers claimed was promoted by undercover police.
>
> The jury returned its verdict against the Schneiders—John W., 28, and Edward S., 26—less than two hours after it received the case from District Judge Joseph Kinnear.
>
> Each brother was convicted of conspiring to violate the rights of schoolchildren, of attempting to damage an institution receiving federal aid, and attempting to interfere with a federal court order to adjust the ratio of minority students in city schools.
>
> Attorneys for both defendants said they will appeal the verdict.

As the trial proceeds, there are points at which the reporter must take particular care, such as the introduction of a defendant's confession or an admission of a fact that indicates guilt. Admittance of a confession must be preceded by proof that it was given voluntarily, without intimidation.

The reporter should use the appropriate words in writing about testimony. There is a vast difference between *testified* and *admitted* and between *acknowledged* and *described.*

During cross-examination, the reporter should be aware of the significance of previous testimony. A witness who earlier may have stated flatly that a marriage was legal may admit under cross-examination that he

is not certain. Such nuances can change the course of a trial and add dramatic interest to a story.

To cover a trial effectively, the reporter should anticipate developments, checking with attorneys for both sides during court recesses. Some information is worth advance notice in a news story. Whether the defendant will testify in his or her own behalf, "surprise" witnesses who may be called to testify, shifts in the order of key witnesses—all provide clues to the course of the trial. Conversations with the attorneys and the court clerk help the reporter monitor the daily proceedings.

While the ubiquitous telephone is a necessity for the reporter, it cannot replace actual presence at the courthouse. Legwork often provides the kind of additional information that humanizes court coverage.

> A mistrial was declared in a Superior Court case Tuesday after two members of a deadlocked jury became locked in combat.
>
> Judge Nelson C. Rivers stopped the jury's deliberations, declared the mistrial and sent the bristling jurors home after squeals and sounds of a scuffle filtered into the courtroom from the adjacent jury room.
>
> The jury had been deliberating for two days in the trial of three men charged with armed robbery when an argument broke out between the two women over the evidence in the case, according to witnesses.

The official court record is, of course, available to the reporter, but timeliness dictates on-the-spot coverage in important trials. Only personal coverage could produce material such as this:

A key witness in the murder trial of James H. Allen testified Monday that the killer of 19-year-old Mark Patterson "appeared to be laughing" when he pulled the trigger of a gun as Patterson ran from him.

But the Common Pleas Court jury sitting in the case won't be allowed to consider that testimony.

The witness, Carol Jean Hale, testified she saw Patterson shot to death Jan. 9 after a scuffle with two men behind his father's business, Auto Parts Inc. on Cleveland Avenue.

Of four witnesses to the scuffle, only Hale has identified Allen, 20, as the killer. She said he pointed the gun at Patterson and fired three times, hitting Patterson from about 20 feet away.

Judge Corinne Meyer told the jury to disregard Hale's conclusion that Allen was laughing. But she did allow her to testify, "I could see his teeth. His lips were turned up. His eyes were bright."

Hale, a psychiatric nurse, said she watched the shooting from her second-floor office just north of the Auto Parts parking lot.

The reporter must have the patience to wait through lengthy deliberations by a jury in important cases, often piecing together details that will convey much more than a cut-and-dried acquittal in a murder case.

FREE PRESS VS. FAIR TRIAL

After Richard Speck was apprehended and charged with murdering eight women in Chicago in 1966, a local minister visited the suspect in jail. As the minister emerged, he told reporters that the suspect seemed remorseful. The comment was duly reported, but the propriety of publishing such a damaging comment before a trial has been debated since.

At the heart of the debate lie two basic rights as expressed in the U.S. Constitution:

1. Congress shall make no law . . . abridging the freedom of speech, or of the press (First Amendment).

2. In all criminal prosecutions, the accused shall enjoy the right to a speedy and public trial, by an impartial jury of the state and district wherein the crime shall have been committed (Sixth Amendment).

Any actions abridging these basic rights are forbidden, yet each traditionally encroaches upon the domain of the other. Today the journalist faces the same responsibility in determining whether publication of such a statement as the minister's is in the interest of a fair trial because the comment implies the accused is guilty. The merits of publishing certain information about criminal cases must be weighed as must the shifting, often contradictory, judicial opinions that have further confused the issue.

The U.S. Supreme Court ruled in 1976 that judges may not generally impose orders on the press forbidding publication of information about criminal cases. The same court did an about-face three years later and granted judges broad discretionary power to order courtrooms closed to the press and the public during pretrial hearings.

In the celebrated "Nebraska case" in 1976 (Nebraska Press Assn. vs. Stuart), the court ruled that judges could not gag the press in criminal cases, even if the judge believes that such an order will help to assure the defendant a fair trial by preventing prejudicial publicity.

But in 1979, in Gannett vs. DePasquale, the court ruled that a trial judge has an "affirmative constitutional duty to minimize the effects of prejudicial pretrial publicity" and has the right to bar the press from pretrial hearings.

The court's rulings created confusion among the nation's judiciary and the press.

Individual justices made unofficial efforts to explain the rulings. Justice John Paul Stevens said, for example, that the effects of the ruling had been exaggerated and warned that the country's trial judges should not use the latest ruling "to unnecessarily exclude the public from judicial proceedings."

Supreme Court justices were not unanimous in their opinions limiting press access to court proceedings. Justice Harry Blackmun, a dissenter, said the result of the Supreme Court action "is that the important interests of the public and the press in open judicial proceedings are rejected and cast aside as of little value or significance."

Press spokespersons opposed the ruling, arguing that 90 percent of criminal cases are disposed of before coming to trial and that pretrial limitations violate the right of a defendant to a public trial.

The court clarified its position somewhat in a significant 1980 decision, holding for the first time that the First Amendment to the Constitution gives the public and the press an all but absolute right to attend criminal trials.

Ruling in the case of a Virginia judge who had closed a murder trial to reporters and spectators (Richmond Newspapers Inc. vs. the Commonwealth of Virginia), the court held that "absent an overriding interest" to the contrary, the trial in a criminal case must be open to the public.

While the ruling did not clear up all of the problems associated with the Gannett vs. DePasquale opinion on pretrial procedures, it repudiated much of the reasoning in that case. The press applauded the 1980 ruling, pointing out that it was the first time the court had recognized there was a constitutional right of access to information.

Conflicts between constitutional rights to a fair trial and to a free press only emphasize the importance of both in a free society, says Connecticut Chief Justice Ellen A. Peters. The courts and the news media must find new ways to achieve a better balance between their often competing demands.

The conflicts are often difficult to resolve, she says, because "whatever the outcome, we put some burden on some constitutional right. We all need to search for accommodations that will strike a better balance between competing constitutional demands that are pressing and serious."

SECRECY AS A PROBLEM

Not all records of judicial proceedings are available to reporters. Actions in domestic relations courts, for example, are sometimes sealed, and judges often seal sections of sensitive hearings to protect the trial process.

Protective orders often are issued in court settlements to ensure secrecy. Files in product liability lawsuits and medical malpractice lawsuits are routinely sealed by the court.

Wilson Turnbull won his medical malpractice case last year against two physicians who, he said, had botched

his kidney surgery. In October, six years after he filed his lawsuit, the doctors agreed to settle the case.

But there was one condition:

Their names would have to be kept secret. The settlement was thus kept secret from the public and off a national list of doctors who had lost or settled malpractice lawsuits.

When Turnbull learned of the secrecy condition, he said, he was outraged. But he was deeply in debt from pursuing the case and felt he had no choice but to agree to the order.

"It was a slap in the face," he told a reporter. Turnbull said he wanted to see justice done, and the doctors' names made public.

Cases like these have become more common in recent years. Lawsuits involving toxic chemicals released into the environment also are often sealed when they are settled, sometimes with a significant bearing on the agencies that regulate the use of the chemicals. Sealing the records makes it more difficult for state and federal agencies to promulgate changes in usage and pass on to the public possible dangers.

According to the Food and Drug Administration, documents that reveal the dangers of a heart valve that is prone to sudden, deadly failure were kept from the public and the agency. Lawyers for clients in a lawsuit against the manufacturer found pertinent documents, but the company insisted they be kept secret as a condition of allowing the lawyers to pursue their cases. Court orders guaranteed secrecy.

In the case of silicone breast implants, trial lawyers first saw the documents that cast doubt on the implants' safety years before the FDA, which is charged with protecting the public from unsafe drugs and medical devices, saw them.

Arthur Bryant, director of Trial Lawyers for Public Justice, said companies use the protective orders to keep damaging documents from state and federal regulators. But supporters of the secrecy orders argue that they induce parties to settle and reduce litigation. Some states are passing laws to restrict use of the legal tool.

Bryant's Washington-based group is pushing a national project to petition courts to lift secrecy orders in cases where they believe the orders endanger the public.

Part Four

The Specialized Reporter

Chapter 13

The Education Beat

Silence engulfs the newsroom of *The Gazette*. It is the last gasp of summer—the long Labor Day weekend. A lone reporter pecks out an accident roundup on a terminal as the city editor wrestles with beat assignments for the coming week.

"Vacation's over," he grumbles to himself. "Johnson's got to get on schools Tuesday." As the summer nears an end, thousands of children are preparing to troop back to the classrooms, and the education pipeline is creakily returning to full steam.

But while children and teachers have been on vacation, the system has continued to study issues and make decisions that affect the school population. Administrators have put the summer to good use:

- They have evaluated and made major adjustments to the school system's programs for the gifted. (Is there a story here?)

- They have completed a preliminary report to a state-mandated commission seeking methods to deal with the problem of weapons in the schools. (Another story?)

- They have spent the summer evaluating a pupil survey that will have far-reaching effects on the redistricting of the system. (Still another story?)

- They have responded in detail to a state-mandated plan to use new tools in assessing students' work. (Another story?)

School machinery is operating year-round to produce programs and make decisions that affect thousands of students and their families.

THE REPORTING CHALLENGE

A study of education coverage at newspapers in the Midwest exposed several shortcomings, including an over-reliance on public school board meetings for news about education. The shortcomings are not unlike those found elsewhere.

Coverage at many newspapers tended to be passive, the study showed, with reporters waiting for controversy and issues to surface at meetings rather than identifying them through independent reporting. Stories often focused on citizen complaints, or a skimming of financial matters. Education issues not raised at meetings were rarely covered. Reporting that assessed the quality of local education, that would inform the community about how and whether their children were learning, also was minimal.

Such a routine, uninspired approach to reporting fails to recognize education's importance to the community. The Education Writers Association, a national group of reporters who cover education, presented a strong case for better education reporting:

"No other assignment sweeps across people's lives from infancy to old age. In most communities, education is a major industry. In most states, it consumes the largest share of tax dollars. A reporter or other journalist writing on education will cover everything from budgets to blustery encounters over values, from threatened local lawsuits to U.S. Supreme Court rulings, from clever products by students in woodworking to the role of education in competition for global markets, from back-to-school features to assessments of the worth of a college degree."

The challenge for education reporters is to move beyond public board meetings to the important matters inside the schools that citizens want and need to be informed about. Meeting that challenge begins with understanding how school systems operate and how decisions are made.

Why Cover Education?

Education systems cost far more money than any other form of local government. A typical county with a population of 130,000 may spend $30 million on general services, while the municipal budget for the 75,000 people in its principal city may total $35 million for services. In comparison, the budget to educate the county's children during the same year might reach more than $60 million. The huge share of tax dollars spent on education creates the need to determine how and why the money is being spent.

- Nearly everyone is involved in or affected by the education process—parents, teachers, students, taxpayers, employers.

- Most parents are concerned with how their children are being educated. It is important to translate developments into understandable language.

- Capital construction, maintenance of buildings, operation of fleets of vehicles, and employment of a substantial segment of the population in the education "industry" are important to the economic life of the community.

WHO RUNS THE SCHOOLS?

When the presiding officer of the Board of Education bangs the gavel and announces the board's vote, the action symbolizes conclusion of a decision-making process of school governance that is different from other forms of local government.

The system's various "publics" who range from parents and taxpayers to a large number of employees (some of whom work nine months while others work 12 months) to the composition of the school population create the need for an authoritative governing board. That board also must be responsive to the thousands affected by its decisions.

Each decision affects people in different ways. Can the school district afford to maintain programs for the gifted students? What should be done about violence in the schools and the increasing problem of truancy?

Is competency testing fair, and should it be mandatory in the school system?

The School District

The vehicle that has evolved to respond to these needs is the independent school district. Most states provide for these governmental units that handle education needs at the local level. Figure 13-1 illustrates the administrative organization of a typical school district.

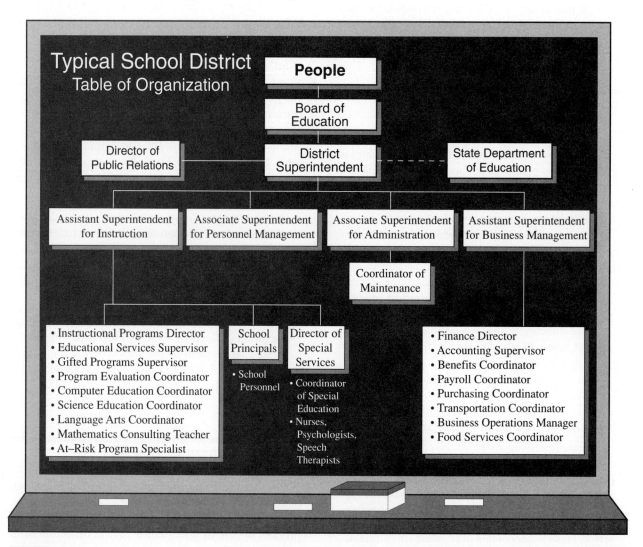

FIGURE 13-1

School districts have substantial legal and financial autonomy. They are direct suppliers of education, and their policy-making board usually answers to the public through elections.

Many of them, however, are tied financially to counties and cities in which they exist, often providing a budget to another governing body that sets tax rates and collects the operating funds. The many variations offer a guide to the checks and balances system of government developed at the state and local levels.

> The Greer County Council angered public school district officials Monday by ordering cuts in their proposed millage rate for 1993–94.
>
> Voting 9–2, the council told the school board to pare its proposed millage increase from 12 to 7 mills. The council has the final word on setting the school district's tax rates.

In this case, school officials had prepared the proposed budget, and passed it to their school board, which in turn gave it to the council for action.

The story will answer other important questions, such as money totals, what the ordered cuts will mean to residents, and how school officials will respond to the order. But the process and the players will be a major part of future stories. Politics, personalities and public pressures all play a part in the financing process.

School districts also answer to some degree to state school boards. State legislation may set maximum class loads for teachers, specific hours of instruction, class sizes for state-mandated special programs, or call for specific financial procedures, subject to state board approval.

The national trend toward consolidation of local school districts has been dramatic in the past several decades—from 127,000 districts in 1932, to 67,346 in 1952, 15,781 in 1972, and 14,721 by 1988. Efficiency of larger districts, population shifts and outmoded facilities of many smaller districts all played a part.

The Governing Boards

School districts operate under a governing board that sets basic policy and employs an administrator to carry it out. Called a board of education, a board of school trustees or something similar, the policy-makers are usually elected by popular vote. When nonelective procedures are used, the appointing individuals or groups include grand juries, the governing board of a county, the mayor or council of a municipality, or a board of higher education.

While usually less overt, the political character of the governing process remains to some degree on the school board. Who serves in these policy-making positions?

Retired schoolteachers often run for a spot on the board, urged on by friends. A parent who has been active in parent-teacher associations and who has high recognition in the district might be encouraged to seek a position. A successful business executive, encouraged by board members with a kindred philosophy, might run for election. A member of a local taxpayer group that is trying to hold down taxes might run on a platform of forcing greater fiscal accountability on school operations.

Politics is subtly different at the education level, but it can be highly emotional. The reporter should be forewarned: Campaigns are often fiercely waged, with sore losers and sometimes court battles in the aftermath.

The powers of board members are defined by the state constitution and legislative action, with members retaining responsibility for the quality, extent and cost of primary education in their district.

Some boards determine the school tax rate themselves after preparing and adopting a budget. A board also might have the power to raise revenue for capital construction by issuing bonds, often after approval of voters in a referendum.

> County Board of Education members said Tuesday they need to spend more time discussing the school district's proposed 10-year building plan before deciding how it can be implemented and funded.
>
> Some board members said public perception of the plan, called "Project 2001" is askew.

The board also selects building sites and authorizes new construction, sometimes after bitter arguments over details. It selects new textbooks for the district, often after special parent-teacher committees have studied the alternatives and offered a recommendation. The board employs, dismisses and transfers teachers, usually within the framework of a well-defined tenure program, and employs, discharges and transfers nonteaching personnel, who may include principals and custodians. The reporter will find potential conflict in any or all of these decisions.

It is not always easy to know how to cover the governing boards:

• The textbook committee for the Board of Education, which includes teachers and administrators, has completed its selection work for the coming year. While the action seems routine, the reporter learns privately that some of the selections have created friction among members of the committee. However, the vote has been cast, and the issue apparently is closed. Does the reporter move on to other assignments or determine what the problem was?

• The waiting list for teaching jobs in the district is long, and there is little turnover. A reporter learns that No. 13 on the list has been given an available opening because she has the "requisite background." Many of the teachers with lower numbers are unhappy but unwilling to jeopardize their places on the list by complaining publicly. The Board of Education says it is a "personnel matter" and declines to discuss it.

These are the kinds of administrative matters with which the governing board and the education reporter must grapple. School boards, which deal with multi-million-dollar budgets, also make all reasonable rules and regulations within the district, disciplining both students and teachers, and admitting and excluding children for sufficient cause.

Some of these actions end up in court, particularly in districts whose teachers are members of strong unions. Within this framework, school board decisions are usually final, subject to judicial action or the reaction of the electorate at the polls.

COVERING THE SCHOOL BOARD

While the education beat needs a more thorough approach to coverage than merely reporting action at official meetings, the importance of those meetings

should not be underestimated. And, as with other local governments, the reporter will discover that major issues probably have been thrashed out before the official session. Like other administrators, school officials prefer smoothly functioning machinery in government. Issues discussed at length in public have a way of "making waves."

Members of the Wilkes Board of Education met Monday in an unannounced session that ended abruptly when a reporter for the *News-Dispatch* appeared.

President Clarence Tooey said the meeting did not end because the reporter appeared. "It was simply time for the meeting to be over," he said.

School Superintendent William Cryce said later that the informal meeting was called to discuss the federally ordered realignment in the school district to bring about better racial balance.

While such meetings may be illegal under some states' open meeting laws, their nature is often disguised as informal or called to discuss "legal" or "personnel" matters. Yet the issues discussed, and often reconciled, affect thousands of people in the school district.

One of the functions of official meetings is to provide a forum for the public, and feedback on issues is important in a system the size of most school districts. Unless the reporter identifies issues beforehand, however, citizens must rely on informal community grapevines for information.

The board of education's agenda, and the reporter's ability to identify issues before official discussion and action, are an important part of the communications pipeline. Preliminary stories set the stage for discussion and often outweigh coverage of the event itself.

The Younts County Board of Education will decide tomorrow whether to continue to provide bus transportation to students who live between one and two miles from schools they attend.

State law mandates bus service only to students living two miles or more from school, but the Younts board has regularly reduced that figure to one mile.

"Transportation funding is short," Board President T.S. Hite said yesterday, "and we can't decide where to cut costs. We'll just have to vote tomorrow and hope we're doing the right thing."

Governing boards must grapple with difficult decisions, and a probing reporter may not always make dealing with them any easier. That said, however, it is the reporter's responsibility to follow the process that culminates in the decision. Closing schools in areas where school-age populations are diminishing, for example, poses special problems for educators concerned with holding the line on expenses—and taxes.

A student assignment plan proposed for the Columbus school district would spell the end of Beechcroft and Centennial High Schools, Superintendent Joan L. Hendrix said yesterday.

Both schools would become alternative schools, giving the district five such schools. If the school board approves the proposal, the district would drop to 15 high schools, housing an average of 920 students each.

Many factors affect such closings, and the reporter will have to collect all of them. Building capacities, enrollment figures, future projections and changes in the curriculum all play a part in resolving such issues.

The problem of major repairs to aging, outmoded and overcrowded school buildings also requires a broad range of sources, including construction, real estate and appraisal experts. A visit to the scene often helps the reporter better convey the problems.

Part of the front lawn at Berkeley Terrace School, built in 1931, is roped off to keep children out of the path of bricks falling from the crumbling cornice. The First Avenue School, built in 1929 for 350 children, accommodates 720, with 40 children to a class. The cafeteria is also the gym. There is no art or music room. The library was removed to make way for a second grade class, and classes meet in the basement.

Only personal inspection by a reporter (and comment from an official intimately involved) can bring detail to an issue-oriented story such as this:

There are three science labs at Morrell High School. One is only five years old, and a second was upgraded in 1953, with power cables cut into the floors.

But the third is still furnished with long black tables that are equipped with outmoded inkwells and scarred with the initials of pupils now in their 80s.

"We have new computers we could install, but we don't have the power for them," said James Ross, chief of maintenance for the school district.

Other questions must also be answered. How have these problems been addressed in other communities? How are school board members reaching decisions on these issues?

Board decisions often bring it into conflict with its constituencies. Teachers may object to new rules governing maternity leave or other fringe benefits, for example. The way a board handles procedures regarding staff misconduct may bring major reaction from teachers.

Very few things will make school officials wince faster than a case of serious misconduct by a teacher.

They must walk a legal and moral tightrope, trying to balance the students' best interests, their moral obligations to the community, and the legal rights of the accused.

Hoping to make a clear statement that quiet settlements have no place in the district, the Board of Education has adopted a policy that establishes a specific procedure for investigating and reporting misconduct cases.

"It's aimed at ensuring that we're not exposing children to abusive teachers," board member Kate Albright said.

The issue of student abuse, both by teachers and classmates, arises frequently. Incidents are not being hushed up as they once were, and the reporter is advised to handle the stories with sensitivity, accuracy and thoroughness. Charges of serious professional misconduct should not be ignored.

Many governing boards employ public information officers to disseminate information deemed useful to the public. While these officials may be helpful to the reporter in broadening the range of story possibilities, it is important to remember that the PIOs are employed by the school system and may be pushing an agenda that does not coincide with that of the press.

The School Board Agenda

There is no typical school board agenda. One district's policy may be to prepare a detailed 40-page agenda that lists every ream of paper to be purchased on bids and every can of paint to be bought. Another agenda might be as superficial as this:

Borden County Agenda, April 20

1. Reading and approval of minutes from previous meetings.
2. Reports from the superintendent.
3. Transfers of nontenured teaching personnel.
4. Report from budget committee on new federal grants.
5. School calendar adoption for coming year.

Such agendas tend to disguise the important elements. The transfer of nontenured personnel may involve key athletic coaches and prove to be a major issue, or the system of transfers itself may be undergoing a metamorphosis. The new federal grants may involve major construction possibilities or an indication that another portion of the financial pipeline from Washington is being closed. The school calendar may also be undergoing some major changes, with abrupt shifts in snow-day scheduling and spring vacation shuffling.

This is not to suggest that the longer, 40-page agenda will offer fewer disguises. Longer agendas may merely bury important elements in detail.

Longer agendas also suggest that a policy-making board may have become bogged down in nitpicking details. By the time the board gets through detailed pages of minor bids to be awarded and requests for use of school facilities, it has little time to discuss more important issues that confront it. The policy-making function may effectively be turned over to administrators.

A 30-page school board agenda listed these items the board had to consider during its twice-a-month official meeting:

Request for out-of-state travel by a guidance counselor; employment of two substitute teachers during a partial school year; hiring of substitute cooks for cafeterias in several schools; the resignation of a teacher who was leaving the district; a request for verbal support for a summer camp program designed for superior science students; a request for bus service to transport a class to the science and cultural center in a nearby city; a change order in a plumbing contract at a junior high school; and so on.

Lost in the shuffle and still on the desk of the superintendent were the major issues of truancy, the problem of what to do with the elementary school to be permanently closed in the spring, and whether to allow city police to search student lockers for drugs and alcohol.

The education reporter should cut through such routine items and focus on major issues as well as those whose importance is not immediately apparent. A routine listing of medical expenses, for instance, might not tell the whole story. Who were the physicians paid by the school system last year? Who is on the payroll this year? How were they chosen? How much are they being paid and why?

What are the major firms doing business with the school system, what do they supply and how much? The unanswered questions and story possibilities at the administrative level are endless.

As with other governing boards, an active committee system provides the reporter with further avenues for researching and reporting on issues. Special committees named to "look into" a specific problem inside the system are good sources. Additional issues are often raised, as this reporter discovered.

A county school board committee formed to examine the nutritional value of school menus discovered other problems at school cafeterias.

Members of the committee complained Wednesday that the food was poorly prepared and the workers sometimes humiliate children.

The harshest criticism came from Luray Evans, vice president of the Parents and Teachers Association, who said the committee found that the cafeteria food is inadequate, the milk is not refrigerated and is often sour.

Another committee member said the menus are fine—it's the cafeteria service and food quality that is uneven from school to school.

In this case, the committee report triggered a major new set of cafeteria policies throughout the school system.

OVERCOMING SECRECY

One of the problems in many school systems is a tendency by some officials toward secretiveness.

The Orange County Board of Education, embroiled in a controversy that resulted in resignation of

Superintendent James Lang last week, met privately last night to discuss the problem.

Four of the five members refused to discuss the unannounced meeting, but the fifth member confirmed it took place. R.C. McCoy said the board discussed the qualifications that would be sought in Lang's successor.

To combat this problem of secrecy, which may be rare or common depending on the community and its attitude toward employees of its school system, the reporter should rely on the most powerful weapon in the journalist's arsenal—the truth.

He or she must prove through ability that an accurate portrayal of the system's actions is possible. This is important to breaking down barriers to better and more open relationships with school board officials. The reporter also must aggressively pursue the story if it is considered information the public should know. Nothing helps to open closed doors shielding secret conferences more than accurate accounts of the meetings. Officials often decide to allow reporters access to information in self-defense, reasoning that it will be at least more accurate that way. Maintaining an even disposition is important, too. A good humor can often cool the worst-tempered public official.

Most states have enacted legislation prohibiting closed meetings by public officials and also have enacted open-records legislation. Legislation in many states mandates notice by public officials when any formal meeting takes place. While the laws are often cumbersome and ambiguous, they can help the reporter gain access to information through judicial action.

> Citing the right of the public to know how tax dollars are being spent, the publisher of *The News* on Monday filed a legal action to obtain details of an audit performed for the Sutton County Board of Education.
>
> Attorneys for Publisher Harold Burton filed a lawsuit in circuit court to compel the board to release the information. Reporters have been denied access to the audit since it was completed last week.

Many school officials view hiring of personnel and contract negotiations with teachers and staff as issues to be taken up in closed meetings—often called *executive sessions* by boards and commissions—where personnel matters may be discussed in private. Legal matters are another area of secrecy, and the reporter is often dependent upon after-the-fact comments by officials for information.

> The County Board of Education voted 7–2 Tuesday not to renew the contract of Linville High School Principal Richard K. Phebus when it expires in June.
>
> No reason was given, but one board member said the decision had nothing to do with a mixup last year in which Linville's teachers originally were denied incentive pay they had earned. The teachers were ultimately awarded the pay.
>
> The vote was taken after Phebus addressed the board in executive session for an hour after the regularly scheduled meeting.

Such closed meetings are common in school districts, and most are allowed by freedom of information legislation. This issue is discussed in detail in Chapter 19. The education beat is as susceptible to problems of secrecy as other areas of local government, and the reporter should be aware of his or her rights of access.

Reporting Personnel Matters

Because many school decisions involve personnel matters, the education reporter must learn to identify and report those matters that legitimately call for public exposure and to reject those that may not fall into the "public" domain.

A fine line exists between the public's right to know and the right of a public employee to privacy. It is too simplistic to use the argument that because the teacher is on the public payroll, his or her affairs are public. The question instead is whether it is in the interests of the public to pursue and publish. The education reporter, with advice from editors, should be part of the decision-making process in determining whether to publish a sensitive story.

> The Cale County Board of Education approved certification of 11 teachers yesterday, but held up action on one because the teacher's application for state approval is still pending.
>
> Certification of Sally Ann Hager, who is the daughter of Assistant School Superintendent Wilson Hager, will be delayed until the state acts, the board decided.
>
> "It is a minor point," Board President Watson Sims said, "but we should be correct about it."

In this instance, the reporter must decide whether a minor point on a personnel matter becomes a public issue because the teacher in question is the daughter of a school administrator.

School officials sometimes reprimand a teacher or other employee and refuse to make details public. Often the effect is to raise more questions than if the details had been made public. The reporter will have to be persistent if he or she is to play a role in deciding whether to make such an issue public.

This story was deliberately withheld from the press on the grounds that the employee in question had resigned, settling the matter. A persistent reporter ultimately uncovered the pertinent facts and wrote the story.

> Charles C. Sites, former director of the County Vocational Center, repaid more than $2,450 to the Board of Education after the board determined that certain purchases were "improper and illegal."
>
> The information was obtained from a board audit obtained by the *News-Dispatch*.
>
> Sites resigned last week, but the Board of Education members have refused to reveal reasons for his sudden resignation.

Education officials reasoned that no purpose would be served by publicizing the fact that the employee had resigned after returning the funds. The reporter, deciding the official's responsibilities in handling public money was sufficiently important, confirmed the facts and wrote about them.

MONEY OILS THE MACHINE

An education system is a sophisticated pipeline. Uneducated youngsters and money are plugged into the system, and, ideally, educated students march out the other end. In between lies complicated machinery, much of it human, that converts the money into salaries, educational facilities, and a multitude of equipment and services (see Figure 13–2).

Figures swarm over the pages of a 100-page budget, but this document is only the starting point for the reporter trying to make sense of a multimillion dollar operation.

Funding for the School System

Income

Taxes
est. $20 million
- Property Taxes
- Vehicular Taxes
- Delinquent Taxes
- Other Personal Property Taxes

Miscellaneous
est. $2 million
- Rental of School Properties
- Summer School Tuition
- Parking Fees
- Instructional Fees
- Athletic Revenue

State Revenue
est. $23 million
- Base Revenue
- Salary Increases
- Bus Driver Salaries
- Fringe Benefits
- Home Instruction
- Special Programs

Federal Revenue
est. $1.5 million
- Vocational Training
- Handicapped Services
- Lunch Programs
- Other Services

Disbursing Agent

Expenses

Teaching
- Salaries & Benefits
- Supplies & Equipment
- Libraries & Supplies
- Music & Art
- Driver Education
- Travel & Conferences
- Periodicals
- Special Education

Teaching Support
- Salaries & Benefits
- Food Service
- Services & Clerical
- Computer Services
- Guidance Counseling
- Psychological Services
- Speech & Hearing Therapy

Administration
- Salaries & Benefits
- Maintenance
- Communications
- Transportation
- Health Care
- Cleaning Services
- Computer Services
- Accounting & Payroll
- Payroll Services

Debt Service
- Bond Payments
- Interest

FIGURE 13–2

Funding comes from a broad range of sources. A county property tax may raise 60 percent, state government sources may provide another 30 percent and federal funding may total 3 percent. A special merchants' inventory tax, rental of school properties, summer school tuition and parking fees might make up the rest. These sources are broken down to give the reporter specific figures needed to write detailed stories.

On the other side of the balance sheet are costs, detailed down to fire extinguisher maintenance and piano tuning. The reporter can study different schools to compare administrative and teacher salaries, bus transportation, special programs and supplies.

The Budgeting Process

In a nutshell, the role of the education reporter is to audit the entire process—from *laying the levy*, a fiscal term for deciding the rate at which citizens will be taxed to pay for the schools, to the graduation exercises.

Good coverage demands generalists who can translate specialized legal and fiscal language for the average reader or viewer. The broadcast reporter faces special problems because of time constraints. Two minutes of air time leave little room for a detailed explanation of a multimillion-dollar school budget. But broadcast reporters, as well as print journalists, must be able to translate a tax decision into lay terms.

After the tax assessor has appraised a piece of property for tax purposes, the property is assessed at a percentage of its value—from 10 to 60 percent. When a board of education decides upon a tax levy of 91.8 cents the reporter must be able to explain:

> The school board's rate is 91.8 cents on each $100 of assessed property valuation, which is one half the appraised value of the property. For example, if a home is appraised at $80,000, its assessed value is one half or $40,000. The homeowner can figure the tax by dividing the assessment by 100 and then multiplying by .918. The tax bill will be $367.20.

There are other methods for determining the citizen's tax rate and tax bill, and the reporter need only explain any of them simply and clearly.

Most of the education budget is spent on salaries and employee benefits. Details of a proposed budget,

often published as legal advertisements, provide the reporter with the opportunity to check salary ranges and specific expenditures. Some line items, for example, will list "contracted services." What specifically are they, the reporter should ask, and how do they fit into the system's other services? A line item of $315,000 for "consultants" should raise other questions. Who are they, how are they selected, and what are they going to do to earn the money?

Reporting on huge outlays of funds for education can be made more meaningful if the writer breaks down the figures and tells the reader or viewer what they mean. For example, a school system's budget increase may total a modest 4 percent over the previous year. Where is the increase going to be spent? Here is how one reporter addressed the question.

> School officials call it "holding the line."
>
> Of the $2 million increase in the Roane County school budget, $1.7 million will be used for salaries and fringe benefits, an analysis of the $48.8 million proposed budget shows. The school board will vote on the budget tomorrow.
>
> Nearly 81 percent (more than $39.5 million) of next year's budget total will be spent on personnel. Surveys indicate the national average percentage ranges from 77 percent to 84 percent, Treasurer Will McCabe said.
>
> The Roane system employs 1,461 full-time personnel and 200 part-time workers.

A schedule of disbursements offers the best opportunity for the reporter to compare categories of school expenditures, and specifics always put figures into perspective. Funding for a system's speech and hearing therapists, for example, may be story material, particularly when interviews with the therapists reveal that their workloads are far above (or below) state guidelines. Also newsworthy are listings of new positions, such as "gender-equity specialists" to monitor complaints of sexual harassment.

Each of these categories will yield to the right questions from the reporter. What substantial changes are being made and why? How does a category differ from the previous year? What are "contracted services" and why are they listed? What efforts are being made to build efficiency into each category?

The reporter should not overlook the audits used to monitor the spending process. Armed with breakdowns in the budget and audits, the reporter can question expenditures at all levels. Financial records in school, city and county offices are also available. A tip regarding spending practices can yield newsworthy stories.

> The Glenn County school district has spent more than $1,400 on alcoholic beverages for school board members to drink at conventions and private parties at the home of Superintendent Ernest Caldwell.
>
> Documents show the district has also picked up the tab for two $100 tickets to fund-raisers for State School Superintendent Mary Sentac, who is running for re-election.

The situation was complicated by the fact that school administrators and board members were guests at the affairs. Records of purchases, which were public record, made it easy to locate the liquor store operators who billed the school system. After the story was published, the practice of using school money for liquor and beer was halted. At the state level, there were notices of reprimand and a job shuffle.

Relationships with Other Governments

The traditional physical overlap between school districts and the other, more political forms of local government complicates the relationships among them. All these local governments compete for funding, and education needs are generally paramount.

Two school districts may appeal to the same county government for funding, leading to conflicts and potential for unequal treatment. Disputes among local leaders often point to divergent sets of priorities, to be sorted out by the education reporter.

A broad range of federal money also can be found at the local school level. The funds come from the U.S. Department of Education under automatic formulas embodied in programs such as Title I of the Elementary and Secondary Education Act. Funds are allocated to systems based on a broad poverty index. Much of it is earmarked for special programs, such as lunches for needy students, aid to disabled students and special instructional materials. The details of such funding are important. Often a computer printout will provide the education reporter with a breakdown of federal fund-

ing areas in the total school budget. Responsible reporting should follow implementation of the programs and periodically assess their effectiveness.

> Cook County teachers have found the federally funded slow-learners program difficult to administer but effective for most of the students.
>
> "The paperwork is terrible. It takes all our time," moaned Neal Workman, coordinator for the select group of 35 teachers who have been organizing the program with a $780,000 grant from the Department of Health and Human Services.
>
> "But it's working for most of our slow learners," Workman said. Under the program, special classrooms are being set up in 35 schools.

Relationships between school districts and other governments often reach beyond fiscal matters. Joint library services might be established, and recreation facilities are often shared. Responsibility may be shared for costs of adult and vocational education. Law enforcement also can get involved with the school system.

> A Rockford Police Department detective has been assigned to each of Stiles County's public schools in an effort to deal more effectively with juvenile problems.
>
> The detectives will not patrol the 13 schools, Superintendent John Stinson said, but will be on call to the principal of their assigned school.
>
> "The whole idea is for schools and police to have better communications with each other," Stinson said.

After innovative programs such as these have been in place for a while, it is the reporter's responsibility to assess the reaction of students and teachers and, most important, help to evaluate them for the public.

A reminder file can help the reporter keep track of these developing stories. After a program has been publicly launched, for example, the reporter should later trigger a "success story" or at least a progress report.

> The 6-month-old plan to deal with juvenile crime in Stiles County schools has not been effective, Superintendent John Stinson admitted Friday.
>
> "It's been too complicated to work smoothly," he said. Each school had been assigned a Rockford Police Department detective, who has been on call when needed.

Stinson and police officials will meet next week to discuss ways to improve the program.

Lines to State Government

Depending upon the state, the ties between local school systems and the state education department might be loose or stringent. Some states have passed legislation mandating staffing guidelines and extensive lists of minimum standards for schools, while others have left such decisions to state education boards or local governing boards.

A battle is brewing over a proposal that could cost the state's financially troubled schools millions of dollars by requiring them to add more classroom teachers and some other staffers.

Opposition has already surfaced to staffing guidelines contained in a proposed revision of minimum school standards.

Public hearings are scheduled on the standards, which were developed by a 30-member advisory committee to the State Board of Education.

"There will be a furor over it. The word is just starting to get out," said John Slade, chief lobbyist for the State School Boards Association.

Several state teacher associations have already thrown their weight behind the new guidelines. The only certainty for the reporter covering this issue is the debate ahead.

Covering education at the state level is difficult for the reporter at the local level because there is little time to pursue issues in the state capital many miles

---

BOX 13–1

Generating Stories at the State Level

✳✳✳

Many issues surface at the state level, but quickly generate debate locally.

- A bill that would provide an alternative way for parents to qualify to teach their children at home would give the State Association of Independent Home Schools the authority to act as an accrediting board in overseeing home schooling. However, local school boards would still oversee parents. Arguments quickly arise at the local level.

- A state board of education passes a resolution endorsing silent meditation in public schools, an alternative to voluntary silent prayer. While the U.S. Supreme Court ruled in 1962 that organized school prayer violates student's religious freedom, the issue persists in many states. In 1992, the court banned prayer at graduations, leading to sometimes heated debate at the local level.

- Some states have passed legislation requiring competency testing for teachers, but the issue continues to be debated in others. Teacher associations resist the proposal, and many state officials support it. Interest at the local level is high.

- Some state education departments are trying to develop new tests that will better determine how students are progressing. But officials argue that too many tests are being given, and ask the wrong questions. A state school superintendent argues that the tests are constructed merely to measure memory regurgitation and she demands legislative changes in testing. If the Legislature must approve changes in a testing system, the issue becomes three-pronged—local and state school levels and a politicized Legislature.

distant. But it is important to watch developments at the state level because they are sure to affect local schools one way or another. Education officials may take on the role of "equalizer" in some states, for example, attempting to help school systems where academic performance lags behind state averages.

> Alarmed by the poor academic record of city school children, state education officials are considering a plan to intervene in one or more of the state's urban school districts.
>
> Education Commissioner Gerald Nigrelli outlined a proposal Monday in which state consultants would help review curriculum, run professional workshops, examine school organization and help solicit money for schools in the state's four largest cities.

The state already had made a number of efforts to help urban schools, including increased state financial support and better teacher salaries, but city children continue to score considerably lower on various academic measures. The reporter should cover this continuing story at both local and state levels.

Colleges and universities also require thorough coverage. Many newspapers assign a reporter to cover a college in their community, but the importance of the institutions transcends local boundaries. Giant public college systems in some states can make coverage difficult.

A TRIP INTO THE SCHOOL SYSTEM

Whatever the distance from the central school offices to the individual schools, each school is a self-contained world. A familiar figure, the principal, figuratively guards the front door. Whether stern-visaged or kindly in demeanor, the principal is ruler of his or her domain and is the point of initial contact for the reporter.

The reporter must first breach this battlement to entertain any hope of covering the system from the inside. Access to the offices always precedes the freedom to roam halls and classrooms where "people" stories abound, and officials recognize the visibility—both positive and negative—that news stories offer their schools.

The principal is apt to be far more supportive of a feature story about a spelling champion than publication of an ugly incident that has created policing problems at the school. Doing the first story and doing it well often can open the door to covering more sensitive issues that arise.

At the classroom level, the teacher is boss. He or she can help a reporter produce a good story or effectively kill one, so a good relationship with the teacher is as important as one with the supervisor.

> Students about to become "two-time losers" sit down with Eileen Jennings at 8 o'clock every morning in Santa Rosa High School.
>
> Jennings, a teacher at Santa Rosa for six years, tries to help students who are about to fail a course for the second time.
>
> "It's a tough challenge," she admits, but says some potential dropouts seem to be helped by the program.

The size of the school system dictates the need to spend time inside, listening to officials, teachers, guidance counselors, custodians and students. Reporters who simply rewrite press releases may not get the whole story.

One press release noted that a prominent judge and the county prosecutor would address a parent-student meeting at the junior high school, discussing the problems of alcohol and drug use. An advance story was duly published, and the reporter covered the meeting. It was well-attended, and provided substantial quotes, including the comment from the principal that the session was merely a preventive measure. "We have no problems here, of course," he said.

If the reporter had acted on the principle that "where there's smoke, there's fire," he or she would have learned that the school did have problems. A serious case of alcohol poisoning during a class excursion to a nearby city had sent one student to a hospital, and all out-of-city class trips had been canceled for the rest of the year. In addition, student suspensions for alcohol consumption had been numerous.

The reporter who had gotten inside the system would have written a much different story.

No administrator or public information officer can provide the personal view of the school system that teachers and students can. The reporter with the confidence of administrators and others will be better able to penetrate the red tape that often ambushes easy access to the schools.

The Wide Range of 'Publics'

To effectively cover the education beat, the reporter must address many publics, all of them with different interests in school affairs. Separately, they constitute special-interest groups, often with unique responses toward decisions reached in the school system. At the same time, the reporter must remember that, collectively, they represent the community.

The Teachers

As a part of the school system, teachers are an important element.

Well-organized through associations and labor unions, they constitute a powerful voice in the community, and the education reporter must take care to note their actions and reactions to current issues.

> A newly formed teachers' political action committee will consider endorsing candidates for two Board of Education seats in the May 9 election.

> Questionnaires will be mailed to the seven candidates, Fran Sellers, chairperson of the County Classroom Teachers Association, said yesterday.

> "People who run for the school board affect all of us—teachers, children, schools," Sellers said. "We have a responsibility to take a position in politics." About 350 teachers are members of the association.

Teachers are interested in new programs but perceive them somewhat differently than do administrators or parents. The parent asks: How will the program affect my child? The teacher asks: How will the program affect me as well as my students? The reporter must answer questions for both.

With their safety at stake, teachers also are concerned with the problem of violence in the schools. What legal rights do they have in protecting themselves from unruly students? How are teacher roles changing in the classroom? How do they perceive outside influences, such as television, as affecting their jobs? Many of the major education issues directly affect teachers, who are among the reporter's key sources in effectively covering the beat.

Teachers not only are good sources for news and feature stories but they also can be excellent sounding boards in the reporter's efforts to broaden a story's bases.

A third-grade teacher reads to his class. Education reporters often visit classrooms to find stories about innovative teachers and instruction methods.
Photo by Tom Stevens, courtesy of The Hartford Courant.

Teacher groups, many of them activist in nature, are also important in developing stories. Good sources in the teacher associations and their working committees identify the many issues inside the system.

> Hundreds of teachers are debating what some say is a frequently neglected subject—what and how students should be taught.
>
> While participants in the State Curriculum Congress teach different grades and subjects, common concerns and goals seem to be emerging from the group charged with writing what one member called a new constitution for the state's 2,200 schools.
>
> That constitution will outline the core knowledge and skills that students should learn in seven key areas—math, foreign language, health and physical education, art, history, language, and science.

Groups such as these provide good direction for future, more detailed stories on the issue. In this case, the reporter was told that academic subjects need to be more closely linked. Common themes can be explored schoolwide, whether in an art class or advanced algebra.

> "The math teacher needs to talk to the English teacher," said Nancy Townsend, who led the language arts group through discussion. "We aren't always doing what we need to support one another."

The debate over the need to emphasize "real world skills" that students will use as adults can make an interesting story. A teacher might insist that showing students how to find and analyze data is more important than simply teaching facts.

> "Is it more important for students to know what the capital of North Dakota is or to know how to find it when they need to know?" teacher Dennis Bartell asked.

If the reporter is to tell the reader or viewer about what the student is doing in the classroom, from kindergarten to college, the teacher is vital as a source.

Parents and Taxpayers

Because their interests often diverge, taxpayers and parents are sometimes seen as two separate publics. The parent might be willing to pay higher taxes to assure continued quality education and, in fact, might be adamant about it. But taxpayers without children might be reluctant to support a proposed increase in taxes to maintain current programs.

The education reporter must portray this dichotomy as accurately and objectively as possible.

> The mushrooming student population in suburban Wilkes County means higher taxes if the school system is to maintain its high standards, Cheryl Whitten, president of the Parent-Teacher Association, warned yesterday.
>
> "Parents are going to have to choose between higher costs and reduced services—and soon," she said.
>
> Whitten called on the Board of Education to provide the public with a "balance sheet" so that it can study alternatives and make an informed decision.
>
> "The PTA has in it both taxpayer and parent," she said, "and the roles don't always coincide."

For the reporter, sources at the parent level are nearly endless, and provide graphic detail to what could be dull financial issues. This story on personnel costs focuses on administrators:

> School districts trying to balance their budgets find that personnel costs take the biggest chunk of money, and the employee taking home the most is the superintendent.
>
> Some parents struggling to get programs approved while keeping taxes down are questioning top officials' pay.
>
> "My husband's out there working his little heinie off every day to pay for someone who's basically just in charge of delegating," Richmond parent Victoria Gill said.
>
> The object of her wrath is Superintendent Wendel Clamp, who earns $98,311 a year. Gill is a resident of District 2, which is considering a 20 percent tax increase next year.

For balance, the reporter will talk to several sources to round out the story, including board of education members, teachers and others involved in the issue. By the time the story is complete, it will include a chart showing the state's major school districts, enrollment, budget, and superintendents' salary and fringe benefits such as car and travel budget.

In addressing taxpayers and parents, the reporter should keep two objectives in mind:

1. New developments in education must be quickly and accurately reported and fairly interpreted.

2. The potential costs of any new program must be accurately assessed. It is important to obtain such assessment from objective school officials and experts who do not have a vested interest in seeing a program adopted. The manner in which the reporter portrays such programs and their costs often will have a bearing on whether they are finally adopted.

The Students

If for no other reason than it lacks an organized spokesperson, the student population should be considered one of the education reporter's important publics. In part, the school beat exists to inform the "educatees" about what educators are thinking and doing that affects the classroom itself. The school "grapevine" is a poor substitute for the work of an informed reporter.

No matter that students at the lower grade levels are not the most avid newspaper readers in the community. It is for this public that the reporter must pursue information into the schools themselves rather than rely on the occasional public relations release on scholarship winners.

At graduation time, the reporter should seek more than merely the valedictorian's comments and the graduation lists, and look for trends that bespeak future issues and problems in the system.

> The number of graduates at Washington County's four public high schools has dropped below 4,600 for the first time since 1968, statistics from the superintendent's office show.
>
> A decreasing birth rate, both locally and nationwide, was cited by administrators as the major reason for the drop, but residential movement to the far suburbs was also mentioned as a factor.

The reporter can round out this story with specific figures on growth of other school districts, the prospects for future consolidation and possible uses for empty school buildings.

Student successes also can be used to mirror innovative programs instituted by school districts.

> Pam Thornhill remembers what it meant to flunk the seventh grade.

> "All my friends left me and went on to the eighth grade, so we couldn't talk about the same things anymore," she said. "I stopped caring if I passed or failed. The teachers didn't seem to notice."
>
> Isolated and frustrated, she dropped out in high school. But thanks to a special dropout prevention program, Thornhill, now 20, will receive her diploma Saturday.

This student was a survivor of what many researchers say is one of the worst ideas in education. Educators call it retention, or keeping students from advancing to the next grade. To students, it's simply flunking.

The reporter used a good device to lead into a story of vital importance to students. Also used as sources were statistics from the State Department of Education, the National Dropout Prevention Center at Clemson University and the Center for Policy Research in Education at Rutgers University.

Other issues that interest as well as affect students include quality of school lunch programs and bus transportation, changes in length of the school day, new truancy regulations, police searches of school lockers, and policies for smoking on the school grounds.

News that touches on these as well as more far-reaching issues will interest and attract student readers. The education reporter also will not leave athletics solely to the newspaper's sports department. Funding, changes in coaching personnel and changes in the sports ethic itself are more important to many readers and viewers than who won or lost a game.

Other Publics

Other special-interest groups can be easy to overlook on the school beat. Business and industrial firms, for example, have a special stake in the quantity and quality of graduates from the system. As employers, such corporations naturally are interested in the quality of young adults who emerge from the educational system. How many and which ones will go on to college? Who will constitute the job pool right out of high school and what skills are they being taught? Such questions are important to the economic segments of the community.

> Nearly 80 percent of the 2,650 Duchess County high school graduates will go on to college in the fall, affecting the job market here next year.

"That seems to be an accurate reading," Schools Superintendent Joseph Slash said about a survey conducted by the *Morning News* this week.

"The rush to college is certainly going to affect employment practices in Duchess during the coming year or more," he added.

As with other taxpayers, members of the business community are sensitive to financial matters, and changes in the community's tax base affect them as deeply as individual homeowners. Tax abatements to bring new industry and business to a city are often hotly debated.

> The Board of Education decided Tuesday it will not support future tax abatements for businesses and industry unless the school system is reimbursed for the loss of tax revenue.
>
> The city has offered tax abatements to lure business and industry, but the policy has been criticized because it weakens the tax base that supports the school system.
>
> "Tax abatement is not an innocuous tool that stimulates the economy," said board member Gary T. Holland after the 5–1 vote against abatements. "It is detrimental to the schools and the community."

The alumni in the school system constitute another important public. While graduates ultimately become taxpayers and parents themselves, their alumni status requires that they be addressed in a special way. What's happening in their schools will be of long-term interest to them.

Most education stories will interest even wider segments of the community, but an awareness of these various publics as sources, readers and viewers will assure more thorough coverage of education.

ACCOUNTABILITY

> "Fathers themselves ought every few days to test their children, and not rest their hopes on the disposition of a hired teacher; for even those persons will devote more attention to the children if they know they must from time to time render an account."

The admonition by the Greek essayist Plutarch is a reminder that the education reporter plays a major role in the accountability process. Feedback to the various publics in the system is essential to a good education system. However, parents are less able to evaluate instruction for several reasons:

- Children are acquiring more and different formal knowledge than their parents did.
- Larger, more bureaucratic school systems discourage parents from individually evaluating their children's education.
- Growth of the school curriculum and longer school days also have been a deterrent.
- The official use of education jargon can make it harder for parents to understand completely what is happening in the school. Thus the reporter has another important role to play: that of translator.

The public depends on the reporting process to provide some form of accountability. The reporter becomes the observer, helping to answer parents' questions.

Assessing Educational Quality

Much education reporting falls into one of two categories—"good" stories, features that cast some aspect of school life in positive terms; or "bad" stories, news that reflects conflict or controversy in the school system.

There is a third type of story, however, that more reporters are producing: the enterprise story. This indepth approach informs the public about its schools in a less polarized fashion, attempting to show where schools are both failing and succeeding. It draws comparisons with the best schools to promote improvement, and focuses more on educational solutions than political disagreements.

Enterprise reporting involves evaluating local policies and programs, but in a larger context. The reporter might look at a school's methods for teaching reading and science or the way it selects textbooks or its philosophy about teaching vocational skills.

The reporter can assemble the informed views of people in the education system with those of other experts to give the public an unglossed view of how well a program or educational approach is working.

Drawing meaningful comparisons among school systems can be an effective evaluation tool. If students in one system consistently score below the state average on standardized reading tests, for example, a reporter might examine a similar school where students always score well, looking for the factors that may have contributed to the high scores.

In any comparison, several questions and issues must be raised. What conditions at the second school enable its students to score so much higher? Do teachers have more experience in teaching reading, or are they using newer approaches? Are their textbooks, computers or other learning aids more up to date? The reporter who probes for differences and similarities can provide valuable suggestions about how schools might be improved.

Help in evaluating school programs can come from education experts at colleges and universities, or from within the state education department. Most education departments have research offices that evaluate programs, especially those mandated by the federal government. They usually compile comparative information on test scores, funding and teacher salaries that can help the reporter in the evaluation process.

Two additional sources for statistical information are the Center for Education Statistics in the U.S. Department of Education, and the State Education Assessment Center, operated by the Council of Chief State School Officers in Washington, D.C. The latter can supply information on individual states, and its data are collected in ways that allow meaningful comparisons among states.

Incisive reporting on education requires more than numbers, however. Many aspects of learning—motivation, creativity and growth—are difficult to measure, yet are vital components of a good education. The reporter must take care to incorporate a range of views on those topics, too, when assessing programs and teaching methods.

The reporter evaluating any aspect of a system can expect to encounter some form of resistance. Teachers, school officials and others vested in the system may resist attempts to scrutinize their performance, especially by a "nonexpert" reporter. Their concerns should be considered but should not deter the fair-minded reporter from keeping schools accountable to their publics.

SOURCES AND ISSUES

The issues inside the education system are nearly endless, and each year brings new ones. Some issues drop into limbo only to recur after a period of time. Many endure, such as balancing costs against available tax money.

The reporter's task is twofold: to pursue current issues inside the system, and identify new ones as they emerge. Broad issues arise out of changes in the national social and economic climates, and the astute reporter should pursue as many as time permits.

> For retired Col. James Hunt, moving from the Army post to the classroom wasn't exactly what he expected, but it wasn't bad either.
>
> "Pedagogy is common sense," says Hunt, a 56-year-old career military officer who is chairman of the math department at Glades High School.
>
> Hunt's classroom rules are shaped by his military experience. He doesn't "give away" grades and he doesn't "pop popcorn or throw parties for his students."
>
> "I just put the information out there for them and if they absorb it, and work on it, they will be successful," said Hunt, a soft-spoken West Point graduate who has a master's degree in business.

The reporter has identified two related issues: cutbacks in the military since the end of the Cold War, and the chronic shortages of competent teachers in math and science. Good sources offer important statistics:

> In the next three years, there could be a lot more James Hunts in public schools. Pentagon statistics show that 100,000 military personnel capable of teaching math and science will leave the service between now and 1996.

The U.S. Department of Education offers further statistics to the reporter: More than 37 percent of all math teachers in secondary schools do not have math degrees. Only 47 percent of chemistry teachers majored in chemistry in college while fewer than 20 percent of physics teachers studied physics.

To tie this together, the reporter contacts the state's Critical Needs Program, which certifies teachers in hard-to-fill specialties. Other military retirees who are seeking certification provide additional examples and human interest to the story.

Other sources include the state Department of Education, the state's Center for Teacher Recruitment, and officials in the state university's College of Education. The story is a continuing one.

Good sources also assure similar types of stories at the county level.

> Virginia Miller, a retired secretary, works 13 hours a week with students in the computer lab at Early Elementary School.
>
> Like many retirees, Miller is on a limited income, and like many school districts, the Fulton schools need community involvement.
>
> Thanks to a new program, Miller can not only share her computer skills with students but also get a break on her school taxes.

The subject of this story is among a dozen senior citizens paid near-minimum wage for sharing their expertise with students. As a bonus, the program also reimburses the participants up to $500 in property taxes.

But stories like this tend to reappear, and the reporter recognizes it as a fact of life. After two successful years, the program is quietly being phased out because of budget difficulties, and a new education reporter on the beat quickly picks it up.

Other important issues in the 1990s include ability grouping, grouping students based on their academic and creative abilities; multi-age classes that combine two grades in one and allow students to move at their own pace through the lower grades, and the proper role for computers in education, including at what age to introduce computer skills.

Another issue emerging in the 1990s is tests to determine whether first-graders are ready for school. Many states have established "transition" classes for students whom officials have determined are not ready for the first grade. By taking a typical transition class and relating it to statewide testing figures, the reporter can put the issue into better perspective for the public.

A major issue that emerged during the 1992 presidential campaign was the concept of allowing parents to choose the school their child will attend. Many state legislatures have followed suit since Minnesota adopted a "choice" plan in 1987, and the education reporter should watch for studies and statistics that advance the issue.

BOX 13–2

Sources at Every Level

✳✳✳

WASHINGTON—In an effort to tackle growing violence in the nation's schools, the National Education Association called on the Clinton administration Thursday to fully enforce a federal law that makes it a crime to carry firearms onto school property.

> The nation's largest teachers' union cited Justice Department statistics that show about 100,000 of the country's 45 million students bring guns to school each day.

NEA President Keith Geiger contended that the Bush administration had done little to make school officials aware of the law, administered through the Bureau of Alcohol, Tobacco and Firearms. ATF officials countered that the agency meets regularly with local law enforcement agencies, which then work with the schools.

> According to the National Association of School Psychologists, 900 teachers were threatened each hour and 40 teachers were assaulted each hour on school property in 1991.

Sources, both at the local and national levels, are plentiful for the education reporter trying to get a handle on one of the major stories of the 1990s. They range from the school systems and students and law enforcement agencies to state sources and educational associations.

WASHINGTON—Most American parents would rather see improvements to their neighborhood public schools than choose another for their children to attend, a new study says.

The study, by the Carnegie Foundation for the Advancement of Teaching, does not take a position on the issue of school choice, but makes recommendations on how such programs could be made to work for jurisdictions that want to use them.

The reporter may find other studies that show the pressure for school choice is coming more from theoreticians and politicians than from parents.

The issue of sex discrimination continues to be a major issue in the school system—at both student and teacher levels. Title IX of the Education Act of 1972 offers a powerful weapon against sex discrimination, and people are taking advantage of it in the courts. The reporter should be familiar with the law.

Sexual harassment in schools at all levels is another issue that should be watched closely.

Sexual harassment, a hotly debated subject in the nation's workplaces and on college campuses, is also a serious problem among adolescents in schools, according to a nationwide study released Monday.

"America's schools are experiencing a sexual harassment epidemic," said Alice McKee, president of the American Association of University Women's Educational Foundation, which sponsored the study.

The survey found that four out of five eighth- through 11th-graders in public schools, including boys, reported some form of sexual harassment. More than one in 10 of those surveyed reported being forced by fellow students or adults to engage in sexual conduct beyond kissing.

Faced with such reports, local school administrations must decide if and how to respond, and their actions can provide a valuable local angle to a national story.

The problem of sexual harassment can be a difficult one for schools, said Frank R. Turcotte, executive director of the state's Association of Public School Superintendents.

"What happens when some clown pinches a young lady at a prom or a basketball game?" Turcotte asked. "The real solution is to change the attitudes of young men and women about what's appropriate and inappropriate."

At the local level, the sources are many: Students, parents and teachers are interviewed and school officials are asked how they will address the issue. Will legislators enact, as have several states, laws requiring schools to adopt sexual harassment policies covering students?

Emotional issues include sex education in the schools, school prayer and transportation of students for purposes of racial integration. The reporter's job is to address such issues dispassionately, trying not to fan the flames.

When Richard Branch began to discuss the sex education class he teaches, the 50 assembled parents grew still.

Suddenly the silence was shattered by a man in the rear of the room who tried to shout down Branch.

Margaret Wilson, chairperson of the committee on sex education for Middleton County, immediately told the man he was out of order, but his comments prompted lengthy committee debate.

Could the committee, members asked, ever debate the sex education issue if it allowed parents at its meetings? The committee finally agreed that parents should play a role.

An equally sensitive emerging issue is competency testing, which would require passing standardized tests to move from one grade to another or to graduate with a high school diploma. Many educators support such a plan. As with the issue of sex education, the reporter has an obligation to write about the issue while recognizing its emotional aspects.

Reporters also can find stories in how well school systems provide educational opportunities for different segments of the student population: Are the schools providing special help for so-called at-risk students, such as new immigrants, potential dropouts, pregnant teen-agers? How are the needs of gifted students being met? Are some students benefiting while others are being shortchanged? How does the system establish priorities to meet increasing demands for scarce resources?

Local and national studies also are a good source of story ideas and can help identify important issues in the schools. The Educational Testing Service studies many levels of education, and the National Report Card offers school assessments. The National Assessment of

BOX 13–3

Monitoring the System

✳ ✳ ✳

A checklist is indispensable in assuring that stories are not lost in the shuffle. This partial listing identifies areas of coverage. Statistics for some categories are available in census reports and local tax studies.

• Expenditures for services like teacher salaries, library and media services, guidance counseling and psychological services, vocational education, and special education.

• Disciplinary procedures; changes in student dropout, suspension, truancy and turnover rates; teacher assaults and crime rates; drug and alcohol abuse programs.

• Advanced placement, computer science, career education, and community and adult education programs; changes in graduation requirements.

• Student government; summer enrichment programs; music, art and speech programs; and remedial programs.

• Changes in transportation and building facilities policies.

• Changing neighborhoods and the effect on the school population; accreditation procedures and their effect on students.

• Athletic policies; costs of administering sports programs.

• Pupil assignment policies and long-range planning in the school system, relating to building repairs, school system size, and pupil performance.

Educational Progress and the National Education Goals Panel are federally funded study groups.

A forecast of the ethnic makeup of public schools predicts that by 1995 a third of U.S. students will be from minority groups, and that such students will make up a majority of high school graduates in four states.

The study was released Thursday by The College Board and the Western Interstate Commission for Higher Education.

The report provides voluminous statistics that will help the reporter sort out local story possibilities.

A REPORTER'S RESOURCES

Reporters can get assistance in covering the education beat and information for specific stories from several specialized sources.

The Education Writers Association, with more than 600 members, offers an informational network for education reporters. The association produces regular and special publications, including a comprehensive guide to education reporting, *Covering the Education Beat*, that lists contacts, story ideas and detailed backgrounders on a range of school issues. The guide and other information are available from the association at 1001 Connecticut Ave. NW, Suite 310, Washington, D.C., 20036.

The national trade publications *The Chronicle of Higher Education, Education Week* and *Phi Delta Kappan* can help the reporter get background and track education issues and trends.

Several indexes and reference books, available at most university and many public libraries, are another valuable resource:

The Condition of Education. This reference book, updated annually, examines current conditions, trends and issues at all levels of American education.

The Facts on File Dictionary of Education. A comprehensive treatment of education terminology at all levels, including information about important laws and court cases.

Education Index. Provides references to more than 350 education journals, and includes indexes of books and government publications.

The Encyclopedia of Educational Research. Contains articles that summarize and interpret studies in education.

Current Index to Journals in Education. Contains monthly indexes of articles appearing in hundreds of journals related to education.

The Encyclopedia of Education. Provides good historical perspective on history, theory and philosophy of education.

Standard Education Almanac. A compilation of education statistics pertaining to enrollment, financing, degrees and other topics.

***

EDUCATION GLOSSARY

AMERICAN COLLEGE TEST (ACT):   Administered to high school students seeking college admission and used to predict how well a student might perform in college subjects.

BASE SALARY: The basic schedule for a teacher with a bachelor's degree and no professional experience, usually the step from which all other positions on the salary schedule are calculated.

CATEGORICAL AID: Federal or state funding earmarked for a specific purpose, such as transportation, special or vocational education, or school lunches.

CERTIFICATE: A document certifying that a teacher has fulfilled the requirements for employment. A **Provisional certificate** is usually issued by the state board of education to beginning teachers; a **Temporary certificate** may be issued on a limited basis to those who have not met the requirement for a standard certificate (usually issued when there is a scarcity of qualified teachers); a **Professional certifi-** cate is issued after a specified length of teaching service and additional education.

DISTRIBUTIVE EDUCATION: An instruction program for students who are preparing to enter such occupations as marketing, merchandising or other careers. Part of the school day is spent on the job.

EDUCATION SERVICE PERSONNEL (ESP):   Supporting staff such as librarians, counselors, school nurses and visiting teachers; many districts must employ such personnel at specific rates per 1,000 pupils.

EDUCATIONAL TESTING SERVICE: An organization based in Princeton, N.J., that administers the Scholastic Assessment Test (SAT) for the College Board in New York.

FAIR DISMISSAL: Entitlement of a teacher to continued employment until such time as just cause for termination exists; assurance of due process before employment is terminated.

GRADE RETENTION RATE: A method of forecasting school enrollment by relating to grade-to-grade enrollment in a system over a long period.

HETEROGENEOUS GROUPING: Assignment of students to classes according to a general cross section of the school population. Homogeneous grouping assigns students to classes on the basis of test scores or achievement in one subject or activity.

INDIVIDUALIZED INSTRUCTION: Process under which each child is allowed to progress at his or her own learning pace using programs designed to meet the diagnosed needs of individual students.

IN-SERVICE TRAINING: On-the-job activities and assistance provided to teachers to promote professional growth.

LEARNING CENTER: Space containing equipment and supplies for use by students or small groups pursuing independent or special study.

LESSON PLAN: An outline prepared by the teacher that arranges important points in a lesson, usually including objectives, key questions, assignments and reference materials.

MAINSTREAMING: Moving disabled children from their special education classrooms and integrating them into regular classes.

MODULAR SCHEDULING: Class periods arranged in modules of time, such as 15, 30, 40 or 50 minutes. Also known as flexible scheduling or flexible modular scheduling.

NONGRADING: System in which students are allowed to proceed according to individual ability rather than being assigned to specific grade levels.

PARAPROFESSIONAL: A noncertified assistant to teachers in nonteaching roles; also called teacher aides or educational aides.

PERCENTILE RANK: A way of ranking test scores. For example, if a student scores in the 70th percentile, his or her score would be as good or better than 70 percent of all students taking the same test.

PHONICS: Learning the sounds of letters and building words from them.

SCHOLASTIC ASSESSMENT TEST (SAT): Test taken by students seeking college admission. It is used to predict how well the student might perform in college subjects. (Note: The name, Scholastic Aptitude Test, was changed in 1993 because of concern that it implied measuring innate intelligence.)

SHARED TIME: Private school students are allowed to attend public schools for special classes not available in the private school.

STANINE SCORE: A method of comparing a student's performance with others on the same test. Similar to percentile ranking.

STUDENT TEACHER: A college senior participating in classroom experience under the supervision of a regular teacher, usually a requirement for graduation.

SUPPLEMENTAL CONTRACT: Written agreement setting forth any duties to be performed and salary paid beyond the normal classroom day, usually for extracurricular activities such as athletics, band, drama and debate clubs.

TEACHING LOAD: A teacher's entire daily responsibilities, including classes taught, class preparation and grading time, number of students in classes, and supervisory assignments.

TITLE I: A segment of the Elementary and Secondary Education Act that provides funds for instructional programs to meet the needs of educationally disadvantaged children living in areas with high concentrations of low-income families. Programs for disabled children and children of migrant workers are included in this legislation.

TITLE IX: The portion of the Education Amendments of 1972 that prohibits sex discrimination in federally assisted education programs with regard to admissions, treatment of students and employment.

WORK-STUDY: A program in which a high school student is permitted to divide time between attending school and working in business or industry.

***

SUGGESTED READINGS

Lutz, Frank, and Carol Merz. *The Politics of School-Community Relations*. New York: Teachers College, 1992.

Wirt, Frederick, and Michael Kirst. *Schools in Conflict: The Politics of Education*. 2d ed. Berkeley, Calif.: McCutchan, 1989.

Wynne, Edward. *The Politics of School Accountability: Public Information About Public Schools*. Berkeley, Calif.: McCutchan, 1972.

Fact-finding in the school system, with a chapter aimed at education reporters.

Chapter 14

Politics and the Reporter

"All of the Great Patriots now engaged in edging and squirming their way toward the Presidency of the Republic run true to form. This is to say, they are all extremely wary, and all more or less palpable frauds. What they want primarily is the job; the necessary equipment of unescapable issues, immutable principles and soaring ideals can wait until it becomes more certain which way the mob will be whooping."

With these pithy generalities, the late H.L. Mencken marched into the battleground of the 1920 presidential political campaign. But he was capable of being far more specific about his favorite subjects—the political candidates of that day:

> Of the whole crowd at present in the ring, it is probable that only Hoover would make a respectable president. General Wood is a simple-minded old dodo with a delusion of persecution; Palmer is a political mountebank of the first water; Harding is a second-rate provincial; Borah is steadily diminishing in size as he gets closer to the fight; Gerard and the rest are simply bad jokes.

Political commentators continue to wield a sharp scalpel 72 years later. Joseph Sobran, senior editor of *National Review*, issued what he called a safe prediction in 1992:

Neither of this year's major presidential candidates will say anything worth remembering. Extended stretches of reasoning are out of the question. Autumn holds out the prospect of relentless cliche.

While political commentary today is somewhat more restrained, the reality of 1920 remains—almost any thing goes in politics. The political reporter of the 1990s must still negotiate through land mines that dot the landscape—politicians who attempt to use the press, sources that mysteriously dry up at inopportune times, and outright lies and deception, all perpetrated in the name of "good government."

politics: the art of science of government; the conducting of or participation in political affairs, often as a profession; political methods, tactics, etc.

Webster's definition does not nearly encompass the complexities of the process by which this country is governed. Companion definitions are necessary to clarify the journalist's role: **political** is defined as "being concerned with government, the state of politics; engaged in taking sides in politics."

Taking sides is one of the most important elements in the political process, and the reporter who does not recognize its implications will encounter far more formidable land mines in the political battle zone. Political office—the legal position from which individuals or groups design and implement public policy—and politics itself are inevitably intertwined.

The effective politician is usually an officeholder—but not always. Whatever the role of a politician, be it U.S. senator, unpaid adviser to a governor or the secretary of a political organization, the individual wields some measure of power. All or part of that power lies in effective organization.

Edmund Burke's 18th century description of a political party is not realistic today. He suggested it was "a body of men united, for promoting by their joint endeavors the national interest, upon some particular principle on which they are all agreed." Because organized political parties in this country tend to sidestep many major issues and to avoid views that might alienate important segments of the party, the practical political structure today does not embrace that ideal. Its strength lies in its ability to compromise differing viewpoints.

A more practical approach today would be to categorize political parties as organizations of diverse groups that seek to acquire office and direct policies, often for mutual gain. Be it a farm organization, a labor union or an association of business executives, the group often promotes its own interests ahead of others.

The State Council of Retail Merchants put public pressure on Democratic members of the state Legislature Friday to resist a sales tax increase and turn instead to some other method of balancing the budget.

In this instance, a pressure group is aiming at avoiding placing other burdens on business establishments. Many organizations, such as chambers of commerce, industrial development groups, labor unions, businesses and churches, see themselves as part of the political process. The reporter should be sufficiently familiar with the groups to identify their roles.

RHETORIC VS. REALITY

rhetoric: insincere or grandiloquent language.
reality: the quality or state of being real.

The political reporter needs more than a sharp pencil to deal with the realities of the job. He or she needs an instinct for what is real and unreal, so the public can be assured the reality it requires to make informed decisions.

Political officeholders and would-be officeholders lean toward ornate oration, declamation and occasionally verbal tub-thumping. One of the most important jobs of the political reporter is to cut through the shrubbery to reach the roots of the verbiage. Thus, the reporter will correctly translate to the reader or viewer this exchange with Vice President Nelson Rockefeller in 1976:

REPORTER: Mr. Vice President, do you see the possibility that you will be nominated at this year's Republican National Convention?

ROCKEFELLER: I cannot conceive of any scenario in which that could eventuate.

TRANSLATION: The vice president sees no possibility that he will be nominated.

Many such responses by politicians are far more detailed than this comparatively simple exchange, and they are not limited to a single section of the country. West Coast candidates are often as obscure, as reporters covering California Gov. Jerry Brown discovered during the same 1976 primaries:

REPORTER: Gov. Brown, isn't your 1976 candidacy really aimed at a 1980 candidacy?

BROWN: My equation is sufficiently complex to admit of various outcomes.

TRANSLATION: It certainly is possible.

The reporter's other responsibilities include total fairness and balance in coverage, the ability to work with disparate interest groups, and an intimate knowledge of those involved in politics and the organizations in which they function.

A good political reporter must be willing to go the extra mile to put a politician's remarks in perspective. During the 1992 presidential campaign, independent candidate Ross Perot displayed a politician's flair for avoiding a direct answer to a question.

Asked by a Californian whether he would defend Saudi Arabia from attack, Perot instead criticized the longtime U.S. support for Iraq's Saddam Hussein.

"We made this sucker," Perot said. "You don't have to prove your manhood by running a television war and shoot smart bombs down airshafts and let every-

body think that, you know, war has become a Super Bowl."

A reporter tracked down the Los Angeles caller, who told him, "Unfortunately, he didn't answer my question."

The Reporter's Role and Goals

Whether print- or broadcast-oriented, the political reporter must first understand the difference between his or her role and that of the political figure:

Politician: actively engaged in conducting the business of government or party politics, or trying to reach that level.

Political reporter: actively engaged in reporting the affairs of the politician and the party, whatever those affairs may be and wherever they may lead, as they affect the public interest.

The politician is attempting to secure power, generally through popular election. The journalist is seeking to make public the truth. Politicians, even those most nearly at the level of angels, do not always care to find the truth emblazoned across the front page of a newspaper or coldly broadcast to constituents across the region.

Political figures cultivate a certain amount of calculated mystery, particularly when the facts may not enhance their images or advance their political causes. On the other hand, the reporter should be concerned with sweeping away such cobwebs, watching what political figures do, rather than merely listening to what they say.

FIGURE 14–1

Doonesbury   BY GARRY TRUDEAU

Here are some questions a good reporter will ask: What's their record? What have they accomplished in office and in private life? What does the campaign platform say, and how does it square with the record? What kind of approach do they have? What are their philosophies? Who is backing them and why?

Also important is a candidate's consistency throughout the campaign, and from one campaign to another. What changes has the candidate made in style, philosophy and positions on issues? Such questions are at the heart of the political reporting process.

To begin, the reporter must know the people in a political organization, how and where they function as a hierarchy, and what they see as their goals. Also necessary is a knowledge of the legislation governing the political process and judicial action that affects it.

The successful reporter operates closely with politicians, often obtaining important stories through personal approaches.

> State Sen. James B. Taylor, whose stand on abortion upon demand has made him a controversial political figure, has decided to seek a second term in the Legislature, a source close to Taylor indicated Monday.

In this case, the "source" was the senator himself, acting to foreclose other candidacies within his own party without publicly committing himself. The reporter's interest lay in alerting readers or viewers to the candidacy. So while the goals of reporter and politician differed sharply, the instrument used to achieve the goals was the same.

But the reporter must be sure the working relationship with a political figure still will pass the reporter's ethical tests. Carefully constructed ground rules are necessary to protect the reporter and the public from being compromised by the relationship that brought the news break in the first place and to assure that the story was not merely a trial balloon floated by a cautious politician to test public reaction without committing to a position. The reporter's instinct plays a big part in determining whether the political figure is merely using the press as a sounding board.

Instinct aside, basic ground rules should be set in cases like these. For instance, before floating any trial balloon for a public official or candidate, the reporter should weigh its real importance to the public. Another rule might specify that any "floated" material include a public warning that could prove embarrassing to the politician who floated it.

Reporters also should recognize the danger of prejudging information from political sources. There is a natural tendency for every person to view kindred philosophies in a more favorable light. Reporters are no exception to this natural bias. To minimize the tendency to entertain preconceived notions, the reporter should maintain a healthy skepticism, whoever the party and whatever the issue. Figure 14–2 shows how the political learnings of journalists have changed over two decades.

The reporter must forever ask why, adopting a cooperative attitude but maintaining a certain aloofness. Author William L. Rivers, a former reporter, is led to the conclusion that the proper role of the political reporter is that of adversary:

> However friendly an official and a reporter may seem to be, however often they may drink together or have lunch together, however happily they may remember

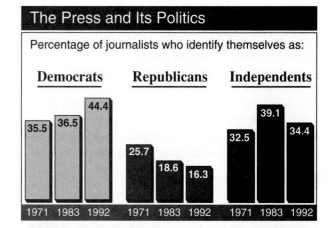

FIGURE 14–2
A 1992 survey of 1,400 journalists, sponsored by The Freedom Forum, indicated that an increasing number identified themselves as Democrats. Conservative critics said the results illustrated a strong liberal bias that affects the fairness of news coverage. However, those identifying themselves as either Republicans or independents totaled 50.7 percent, still higher than the 44.1 percent for Democrats.
Source: The Freedom Forum.

their college years together, there should be a degree of tension between them when they serve their professional roles.

Rivers concludes that a proper adversarial relationship is a balance of tact and antagonism, of cooperation and conflict. How effectively political reporters maintain that balance is one measure of how well they do their job.

POLITICAL PARTY STRUCTURE

Political parties constitute the principal medium through which the people can influence public policy. While there is a sizable contingent of independent voters and candidates, most of the electorate depends upon organized parties to choose officials and determine policy in government.

The reasoning is sound: There is strength in numbers. Most of those who say they belong to one of the two major parties—Democratic and Republican—do not normally participate in day-to-day functioning of the parties. That is left to a far smaller group of interested persons who wield the power and influence to affect decisions at the top echelons of local, state and national government. These are the party members that reporters depend on for politics to be fully and accurately portrayed to the public.

Officeholders are often important members of this party machinery, and thus public office and organized politics are part and parcel of each other.

> Republicans unanimously elected Sheriff Ted C. Farr chairman of the County Republican Executive Committee last night.
>
> After the meeting, Farr, 51, who is serving his second term as sheriff, said party harmony would be his major objective.
>
> "We are a minority party," he said, "and it is essential that this committee work together if all our goals are to be met."

From Precinct to National Committee

Political parties are structured like a pyramid, with a multitude of local organizations operating at the

bottom levels and the national committee functioning at the top, with headquarters in the nation's capital.

The party's strength lies in the effectiveness of the precinct, the smallest political unit. Voters are registered in specific precincts, which range in size from a few dozen persons in rural areas to more than a thousand in metropolitan communities.

Precinct workers, under the direction of the precinct committee head, ring doorbells during political campaigns, watch polls on Election Day, and handle many other volunteer jobs. The key to winning elections, particularly in the big cities, often lies with the party's precinct chief, who knows the people in the district and their motivations, and can effectively get out the vote on Election Day.

Depending upon the size of the community, the next level in the party's structure may be the ward, city or township committee, or legislative district. The ward committee usually consists of precinct committee members who elect a chairperson. These are the groups that select candidates for local tickets and often influence officeholders.

Although the bottom of the pyramid, with its proximity to the "grass roots," wields substantial influence on the success of the party, it is much less visible than the national offices. Party power gravitates to the candidates who win office; after an election their influence is far more pervasive, for they control the purse strings and patronage.

Between the top and bottom of the party pyramid lie the county and state committees, which tie the local and national organization together.

An active party leader might serve as a county official and also be elected to state party office. Thus, Sheriff Farr, while heading the county executive committee, also could be a member of the State Republican Executive Committee. Furthermore, he also might be a delegate to the Republican National Convention, completing the chain of office as a successful power broker in the typical political party.

The federal government regulates many of the parties' activities through the legislative process, setting dates for primary elections and determining deadlines for candidates. The parties themselves have adopted rules under which members conduct party business. They determine their candidates through primary elections or conventions, and successful primary candidates represent the party in general elections.

As members of organized parties, elected state officials look to their party's interest as the Legislature dictates dates for primary elections.

> Gov. Randall Dole today asked the state Legislature to enact a law setting the first Tuesday in June as primary election day. The first Tuesday in May is presently primary day.
>
> Shortening the time between primary and general elections will enable candidates with fewer resources to better compete with wealthy candidates, Dole said.

The reporter can be sure that the shift in primary dates is in the interest of the governor's party as well as the candidates he espouses.

Legislatures also enact laws governing campaign contributions and the method in which they are reported to the public.

A party is only as effective as its committees at the local level, and efforts are made to develop strong local organizations. However, factionalism is bound to disrupt the organization now and then. When it does, officials at the next level attempt to contain it while preserving an outward show of unanimity.

> Depending on which faction is correct, the chairman of the County Democratic Executive Committee is either State Sen. Robert Morris or Sheriff Herbert Gartin.
>
> The executive committee was evenly split last night, with 16 members voting to re-elect Morris and 14 members supporting Gartin. Two proxies from absent committeemen were cast for Gartin, but Morris ruled them invalid. The Gartin faction walked out, met in an adjacent courthouse room and elected Gartin chairman.

Power in political parties is not always where it appears to be, and the effective reporter knows where to find it.

Is the party chairman the real boss or merely a figurehead? Who is actually running the party at this level? What are the background and interests of the dissident factions and how much strength do they possess? Who owes what to whom, and why?

Armed with the answers to these and similar questions, the reporter can more accurately cover the party processes. Party organizations operate in comparative

secrecy, and the reporter should know how to dig through to the truth.

The chairperson calls meetings of the local committee, presides at them and leads the party at the local level. Because much of the effort at the precinct level is voluntary, the successful party leader—and the reporter—must be able to recognize the factors that motivate people, whether philosophical, social or acquisitive.

A change in status of a party worker at the local level can be the result of bad political choices, which the alert reporter can pass along.

> Clyde C. Stephens, a wealthy local businessman who backed an unsuccessful candidate for governor, was succeeded as chairman of the Caine County Democratic Committee by Homer L. Harris, a retired railroad employee.

Reporters were aware that Stephens lost the chairmanship and most of his political power because he could not overcome the handicap of backing a losing candidate. Harris, however, had remained neutral in the governor's race, which paid off in the race for chairman.

In time, the political reporter will develop a fine antenna that points out areas of greatest influence and those who are actually making party decisions. Many factors produce this influence—wealth, prestige, family ties, length of service to the party, organizational ability, and personal or professional friendships.

By following local party affairs closely, even the routine events, the reporter should be able to recognize and report on political developments long before they become campaign fodder at election time.

The Road to the Polls

The highlight of the political process is Election Day, when arguments over public policy and political figures are settled by the voters. The process begins with registration of eligible citizens, continues through an often frenetic campaign to the voting and tabulation, and finally to an official canvass by an elections committee that certifies the winners.

The process does not always end there, however, because legislation provides for legal challenges, which often are taken to state election officials or the judiciary.

> Jody Snedden, unsuccessful candidate for the House, complained that her Democratic opponent, Rep. Albert Ensign, the winning candidate, had violated election rules.
>
> Her complaints were detailed yesterday in a letter to Secretary of State Virginia A. Munck, whose office said it is investigating the matter.
>
> Munck's office has the authority to appeal to Circuit Court for relief for Snedden.

Voter registration differs from state to state. Some still have complex, exclusionary systems, while others have made it increasingly easy to register. Political parties act as a catalyst in registering potential voters, and tend to concentrate their efforts in areas they believe will produce more support for their side. The reporter should keep in mind, though, that sometimes the interests of a minority party are better served by a low voter turnout than a high one.

> Based on registration figures, heavy rain forecast for tomorrow may keep voter turnout low and enhance Democratic State Sen. William Woodbury's chances for re-election.
>
> Registered Republican voters outnumber their Democratic counterparts in Wayne County 36,416 to 29,677.

Some states still permit nomination of candidates by caucus or convention, but most have shifted to the direct primary election. The primary process also differs from state to state, and is often confusing. In states dominated by one party, the primary election IS the election. In others, hard-fought primaries create the most interesting and important political coverage.

Local conventions are generally cut-and-dried affairs, with delegates routinely elected to the state conventions, which nominate the candidates. State convention delegates adopt a platform and select members of the state executive committee. The reporter should try to gauge sentiment for the candidates at the caucus level because delegates often take party instructions to the state level.

Caucuses, once the mainstay of the systems for choosing party candidates, are not used as much anymore, but they continue to serve a function. Political leaders at all levels of government call caucuses to determine party matters. Some are tightly controlled, others are freewheeling affairs. Either way, the press is usually barred from the sessions, and informed of the results afterward. A persistent political reporter with good sources inside the party usually can find people who will provide interesting details and perspective.

The 1992 presidential campaign spotlighted a growing group of politicians and voters—the independent. Wealthy Texan Ross Perot opened up the political process with his unusual campaign, creating a need for new sources at all levels for the reporter.

Covering the Campaign

When the filing deadline has passed, and candidates know who their opponents are, the campaigns begin in earnest. But even before the deadline, they are putting together their team, developing marketing strategies and planning the campaign week by week. The astute reporter won't wait for the deadline to pass either.

This is the time for preliminary stories that set the stage and cast of characters, and for planning coverage for the weeks and months ahead. Spot developments undoubtedly will force a change in plans more than once, but the preparations will keep straight the basic plans for coverage.

This is also a good time to research the candidate's background and sources of funding. A reporter once found that a candidate managed a marketing firm whose clients included the State Association of County Commissioners.

The association hired the candidate's firm to lobby voters to approve a local sales tax option. Later, after the lobbyist had become a candidate, he admitted he favored the option. The admission shed more light on his political motives.

Some reporters see the campaign trail as boring, covering the same speeches by candidates day after day. But it can be quite interesting and productive; there are plenty of avenues the reporter can explore to get at the issues.

• What's the candidate's style? How does he or she react to breaking events that expand the scope of the campaign? What reception is the candidate getting at various functions organized by civic, fraternal and political organizations?

- Who's supporting the campaign? What are their backgrounds and political philosophies, and how are they directing the candidate?

' What kind of help is the candidate getting from friends or political allies? Will the governor speak on behalf of the candidate, or even appear at a rally? Have any state officials agreed to appear in public with an endorsement? Has the community received substantial funds recently? It is not unusual for an official at the state or federal level to announce a substantial state grant to a community just before an election.

DEARBORN, Mich.—In what has become a popular campaign strategy, President Bush opened his sack of presidential goodies Friday, handing out concessions to ailing U.S. automakers just four days before Michigan's primary.

Bush announced in a speech that he is killing a plan that would have forced automakers to equip new cars with canisters to capture polluting gasoline fumes that escape during refueling.

Instead, the canisters must be installed at gas pumps, a move certain to anger oil companies in Texas, whose primary took place last week. Bush won that one handily.

Such favors, often systematic efforts to coordinate the policies and actions of government with the operations of a re-election campaign, can be found at local, state and federal levels. At the federal level, it is known as "the funnel," and daily meetings are scheduled to coordinate efforts.

WASHINGTON—The nation's savings and loan industry more than doubled its profits in the first three months of 1992 to about $1.5 billion, the best performance in six years, the Office of Thrift Supervision announced Tuesday.

The reporter turned to private analysts, who said the agency—an arm of the Treasury Department—appeared to be releasing its report piecemeal in an attempt to put a favorable gloss on it.

A gubernatorial candidate on the stump greets local party supporters.
Photo by Daniel G. Dunn, courtesy of The Narragansett Times

"They're sitting on a key part of the story. The question is 'why,'" said Bert Ely, a financial institutions analyst. "From a taxpayer's perspective, the fact that 90 percent of the industry is doing well is secondary to how the worst 5 or 10 percent are doing, because that's where the threat lies."

During a campaign, the reporter helps put such information into perspective, and asks others for their views. If such moves are political, the reporter should pursue them as such.

Political charges and countercharges can run rampant during a campaign, and require special care by reporters. It should not be enough merely to report the charges, attributing them to the opponent or political ally who made them. When one candidate levels charges against another, the reporter is obligated to try to verify them.

James Miller accused Democratic U.S. Sen. Fritz Hollings Tuesday of running a dishonest television ad campaign in an effort to remake his image as a fiscal conservative.

Miller, Republican secretary of state, cited an ad that opens with a shot of the Watchdog of the Treasury Award and an announcer noting that Hollings has been "honored time and again" for his battles to save taxpayers money.

The ad is cleverly worded, giving the impression that Hollings has received the Watchdog award several times.

The reporter checked the organization, a nonprofit group committed to fiscal responsibility, and found that Hollings had won the award only once—in 1988. That was duly noted in the campaign story, along with the fact that Hollings' Republican opponent, a former congressman, had won the Watchdog award five times.

The "reality checks" undertaken by newspaper and broadcast reporters during the 1992 political campaign offer good examples of press efforts to make candidates toe the honesty line.

Charges that an opponent is "unfit and unqualified" are easier to handle than more serious charges against an opponent's ethics, but most can be addressed by the reporter who takes the time to research the charges and countercharges.

Many of a person's qualifications are verifiable and lie in his or her background and record as a public official and, to some degree, as a private citizen. Ethics charges are more difficult to assess, but are by no means impossible.

The candidate who in private life represents companies that stand to gain from his or her election should become an open book to the voters, who ultimately will decide whether to accept the conflict of interest.

Reporters should not allow candidates the luxury of making general charges without providing specifics. They should ask for detail when a candidate representing herself as an "outsider" charges that her opponent is "one of the good old boys." Demanding specific examples or other verification can do wonders in casting light on such general slogans.

Campaigns also are notorious for political "dirty tricks," deliberate sabotage by the workers of one candidate against the campaign of another. They have ranged from ethically questionable campaign advertising to infiltration of major campaigns by the other side.

Political operatives might acknowledge they are "building a file" on the opposition, but usually deny they are planting negative stories about a candidate. The weapon of opposition research, informally known as "oppo," moved to a new level of sophistication in the 1970s when Republican operative Donald Segretti and his associates engaged in high-tech political sabotage. Segretti eventually landed in jail for distributing false campaign literature.

The bungled Watergate break-in in 1972 has evolved into computer-dominated tracking systems that collect virtually all speeches, public statements, votes or major financial transactions by candidates. Like the investigative reporter, political aides study annual corporate reports, government files and court records to find out as much as they can about the other side.

Information developed by campaign workers is either leaked to political reporters or turned into paid advertising. The leaks usually come first, then the material is used over and over in TV spots or newspaper advertising. The reporter covering a specific campaign should be familiar with the operatives who do this work, and, as always, conduct independent research to verify or debunk their claims.

During the 1992 presidential campaign, Ross Perot charged that the White House had engaged in a dirty tricks campaign to discredit his character. He also denied that he had investigated President Bush and his sons. The press' extensive efforts to verify the charges and countercharges about alleged dirty tricks helped clarify the Bush-Clinton-Perot campaigns.

Two other important tools that have gained widespread use in campaigns are polls and studies by special interest groups. Candidates' strategists use polls when it benefits their candidate, research groups add their own conclusions, and media organizations have found the poll a convenient news peg. The political poll has become an inescapable part of the campaign process.

The reporter must be careful when writing about polls, including those commissioned by media organizations. Political scientists have criticized polls, charging they contribute to a "horse-race mentality," focusing mainly on "who's ahead" rather than the more important "why." Used carefully, however, polls can be an illuminating part of the political story. (Polls are discussed at greater length in Chapter 3.)

Similar caution should be used in writing about reports and studies commissioned by special interest groups. They should be carefully attributed, so the reader or viewer can determine their origin. Special effort should be made to get reaction from other candidates and groups.

Exploring the Issues

Some issues endure, others change with campaigns, the candidates and the nature of society. What may have been an overriding issue two or four years ago, such as protecting the environment or dealing with the federal budget deficit, may merit little attention this year.

Abortion, a highly emotional and visible issue, can be counted on to remain volatile in many elections. The tax issue also maintains a high level of interest from year to year. Other issues change with the locale and level of government. In 1992, candidates running for national office said little about the quality of public education, but it was a burning issue in many local and state election campaigns.

In a 1992 report on the public's discontent with the state of affairs in America, pollster Daniel Yankelovich found that people were deeply concerned about several problems:

Schools they do not perceive as preparing children for life; racial tensions exacerbated by the Los Angeles riots; vanishing jobs in many sections of the country, and the struggle to make ends meet; the skyrocketing cost of health care; crime, drugs and violence in both urban and rural areas; and the perception that their government doesn't work.

In the wake of such polls, many journalists began discussing reform in political reporting. The process began evolving which called for the media to police the political process, rather than merely describe it; to refuse to automatically broadcast or write about staged events or manipulative, repetitive messages; and to determine how candidates and their records relate to the public's concerns.

During the 1992 campaigns, broadcast and print reporters made sustained efforts to cut through candidates' rhetoric and put the issues in perspective by providing actual statistics and material from impartial sources. The objective, balanced reporting, including an airing of the public record, is the most effective way to give the voters the facts they need to make informed choices.

Changes in the Process

Dramatic changes have occurred on the political scene during the last 20 years, some of them in the form of legislation designed to make political campaigns more open and to limit campaign spending.

The Federal Election Commission, established in 1971, administers laws that provide for public disclosure of the financial activities of political committees involved in federal elections, and limits or prohibits contributions and expenditures made to influence federal elections.

Detailed forms must be completed for the FEC regularly, and the agency offers efficient, computerized record searches. The completed forms also are available in the state where the candidate seeks federal election. The secretary of state is usually the designated official. (Most states also have their own reporting regulations for candidates and officeholders.)

The federal process begins with a candidate designating a principal campaign committee. Contribution limits are complicated, and the reporter should study

FEC literature for guidelines to coverage. For example, the limit on contributions to a candidate by individuals is $1,000 per election, and the limit for political action committees is $5,000. However, in reality the amount is twice that, because the law regards primary and general elections as two separate elections. Also the individual or PAC may spend as much as it cares to on behalf of a candidate—buying campaign advertising, for example. Political action committees have proliferated in recent years, and their financial contributions dominate campaigns.

The candidate's designation of principal campaign committee and statement of organization provides names of the officers and the banks used to deposit campaign funds. Reports of receipts and expenditures by all of the candidate's committees provide names, addresses and occupations of contributors giving more than $200 (see Figures 14–3 and 14–4).

Through indexes, the FEC also provides names of all contributors to a candidate or political action committee. Officials can obtain PAC identification numbers for the reporter, making it easier to track down the special interests the candidates represent.

Special-interest groups often contribute to *both* parties and opposing candidates. A Democrat running for office often has the same financial donors as his or her Republican opponent. Through research of public records, the reporter can point out how such interests are "hedging their bets."

The states also have passed legislation opening candidates' and elected officials' financial records to public scrutiny. The relationships between contributors and candidates' votes on legislation are important.

> TALLAHASSEE, Fla.—Medical lobbies, beverage distributors, cigarette makers and pari-mutuels funneled thousands of dollars to the Florida Democratic Party this year while the Legislature considered laws affecting their interests.
>
> The Democrats raised $1,026,000 in the first three months of the year. The gambling industry, medical professions and bottlers were among the most generous.

Many of these "generous" donors also contributed to the Republican Party. In cases like these, only the press of time hinders reporters trying to follow the trail of funds flowing into the treasuries of political parties and officeholders.

At the local level, the reporter will find much financial detail that is worth pursuing:

> William Haley and Dolly Snowden spent a combined $173,051 in the race for the Senate District 44 seat that pays $12,500 annually.
>
> Campaign disclosure forms show Haley's campaign spent $122,500 in a losing effort in the Republican primary for the post—about three times the amount Snowden spent to win both the primary and the general election—$50,551.
>
> In the Aug. 25 face-off between the two, Snowden received 67 percent of the votes cast—10,150 votes to Haley's 4,964.

The reporter collected this material from the state's Senate Ethics Committee, but probably also could have found it at the state Board of Elections, which often requires such financial detail. Sometimes the details come from legislative offices or disclosure ordinances enacted by smaller communities.

> JONESBORO—Elected town officials will have to disclose their property holdings in Bishop County by July 1, to comply with a new town ethics ordinance.
>
> The Board of Aldermen voted 6–1 Tuesday to require property disclosures of aldermen and their spouses.

Election Day Coverage

The key to successful Election Day coverage lies in planning. Long before Election Day, editorial staffs lay out assignments for the team that will fan out over the community and state to collect election statistics.

Reporters will be assigned to monitor Elections Board offices, campaign headquarters and other key candidate locations, and key precincts. Questions will be developed for exit polling.

While statistical detail is vital to the Election Day report, the individuals and their stories should not be ignored: Democrats with an uncontested primary of their own "cross over" to vote in the Republican primary, hoping to force the election of someone they think their own candidate can beat in the state race. Two candidates help each other in school board races and are both elected. A young candidate with a pro-choice stance on abortion is elected by a surprising margin. The reporter responds to all of these in the

MICHIGAN DEPARTMENT OF STATE
Bureau of Elections

**ITEMIZED RECEIPTS
SCHEDULE 1A
CANDIDATE COMMITTEE**

1. Committee I.D. Number	2. Committee Name
0001147-1	SCHULTZ FOR SENATE

3. Name and Address from whom received.	4. Type of Contribution or Other Receipt	5. Date of Receipt	6a. Contribution of Money	6b. In-Kind Contribution Received	6c. Other Receipts	7. Cumulative for election cycle	8. If over $200.00 cumulative, enter Contributor's Occupation, Employer and Business Address
Lincoln Republican Club	**Contributions:** ☒ Direct ☐ Loan (describe) ☐ In-Kind (describe) **Other Receipts:** ☐ Interest ☐ Loan from lending institution ☐ Misc (specify)	9-5-92	600.00			600.00	850 N. Jones Lincoln, MI 48864
IRENE MARTIN 910 West Ave. LINCOLN, MI 48864	**Contributions:** ☒ Direct ☐ Loan (describe) ☐ In-Kind (describe) **Other Receipts:** ☐ Interest ☐ Loan from lending institution ☐ Misc (specify)	9-11-92	250.00			250.00	TEACHER LINCOLN HIGH LINCOLN, MI 8862
JOHN WILSON 427 KNIGHT ST. LINCOLN, MI 48862	**Contributions:** ☒ Direct ☐ Loan (describe) ☐ In-Kind (describe) **Other Receipts:** ☐ Interest ☐ Loan from lending institution ☐ Misc (specify)	9-13-92	150.00			150.00	
MARY SCHULTZ 2400 Newton LANSING, MI 49104	**Contributions:** ☒ Direct ☐ Loan (describe) ☐ In-Kind (describe) **Other Receipts:** ☐ Interest ☐ Loan from lending institution ☐ Misc (specify)	9-17-92	1000.00			1000.00	CANDIDATE/ATTORNEY 118 N. MICHIGAN SUITE A LANSING, MI 48933
CITIZEN'S PAC 1800 RIVER GRAND LEDGE, MI 48837	**Contributions:** ☒ Direct ☐ Loan (describe) ☐ In-Kind (describe) **Other Receipts:** ☐ Interest ☐ Loan from lending institution ☐ Misc (specify)	10-13-92	5000.00			5,000.00	
JOHN CHAPMAN 1200 FIELD ST. KALAZAMOO, MI 49103	**Contributions:** ☐ Direct ☐ Loan from a person ☒ In-Kind (describe) LUMBER **Other Receipts:** ☐ Interest ☐ Loan from lending institution ☐ Misc (specify)	10-15-92	150.00			150.00	

Page Subtotal: 7,150.00 | 0 | 0

Grand Total of All Schedule 1A's
(Complete on last page of Schedule)

Enter this total on line 3a of Summary Page | Enter this total on line 8a of Summary Page | Enter this total on line 4 of Summary Page

Authority granted under P.A. 388 of 1976.

FIGURE 14–3
Itemized receipts form that must be filed with the state election commission. All are available to reporters as public records.

MICHIGAN DEPARTMENT OF STATE
Bureau of Elections

ITEMIZED EXPENDITURES
SCHEDULE 1B
CANDIDATE COMMITTEE

1. Committee I.D. Number	2. Committee Name
000147-1	SCHULTZ FOR SENATE

3. Name and Address of person to whom paid.	4. Purpose (be specific)	5. Date	6. Amount Expended
ARCO MEDIA 110 HILL AVE, LANSING, MI 48915	MEDIA CONSULTING ☐ Payment of Debt or Obligation	10-3-92	10,000.00
FIRESIDE INN 3400 TWIN LAKE RD. LANSING, MI 48917	SCHULTZ SHARE OF FUNDRAISER HELD ON 10-10-92 ☐ Payment of Debt or Obligation	10-10-92	740.32
SPEEDY PRINT 1456 NORTH ST LANSING, MI 48927	BROCHURE PRINTING FUNDRAISER TICKETS (10-10-92) ☐ Payment of Debt or Obligation	10-2-92 10-3-92	354.17 75.00
WXIX RADIO 600 W. OAK LANSING, MI 48910	RADIO SPOTS 10-28-92 10-29-92 10-31-92 11-1-92 11-3-92 11-5-92 ☐ Payment of Debt or Obligation	10-25-92	3,600.00
ELSIE LONG 115 N. OTTAWA LANSING, MI 48915	SALARY ☐ Payment of Debt or Obligation	10-25-92	500.00
DREW'S GAS 'N GO 1400 PINE LANSING, MI 48910	GAS (LESS THAN $20 EACH DATE) ☐ Payment of Debt or Obligation	VARIOUS	85.00
		Page Subtotal	15354.49
		Grand Total of All Schedule 1B's (Complete on last page of Schedule)	

Enter this total on line 6a of Summary Page

Page 1 of 2

Authority granted under P.A. 388 of 1976.

FIGURE 14–4
Itemized expenditures form that must be filed with the state election commission.

A candidate and his supporters watch early returns on election night. For some, a long campaign culminates in elation; for others, disappointment. Reporters are there to capture both

Photo by Robert Patterson, courtesy of The Day, New London, Conn.

aftermath of the election hoping to answer the questions many voters will ask:

How and why did the candidate or party win? How will the outcome affect public policy? Did voter turnout make a difference? Some of the answers will be found in the post-campaign rhetoric, some in follow-up interviews with the winners. An effective and often untapped source are the losers, who are often more candid than during the heat of the campaign. Recapitulation is always important following an election.

COMMON PITFALLS
AND DILEMMAS

Sooner or later, the political reporter will be confronted with a version of each of the following situations. Depending on the specifics and personalities involved, each reporter will find ways to handle them without compromising basic journalistic virtue.

Keeping Confidences

The soundness of keeping the confidence of a source applies to any beat. But in the world of politics, where confidences are sacred, a slip of the tongue on the part of a reporter can result in the loss of trust of many sources. While others in the political battle zone take sides, the reporter should maintain an objective view and try to earn the respect, if not always the confidence, of both sides. Political figures usually deal with the independent reporter on the assumption that they will get at least an "even break." Most do not—and should not—ask more than that.

In *Politics and the Press*, Richard Lee suggests some qualities that politicians respect in a reporter, including enterprise and correct interpretation of events.

"They can spot a phony a mile away," one politician said. "There is enough sophistication in the press that you can't put something over on them."

A final note of caution: Reporters who value their reputations will avoid making promises. The philosophy of "You do this for me and I'll do that for you" prevails in the world of politics, and the wise reporter understands that no story is worth being in debt to a source. The political reporter will leave the business of making promises to the candidates or officeholders.

Selective Perception

Psychologists define perception as the process through which we become aware of our environment by organizing and interpreting the evidence of our senses. Yet from childhood on, people subconsciously tend to see what they want to see.

The problem of selective perception confronts reporters as well as other mortals, but journalists can be especially vulnerable. The nature of the business places reporters close to current events and issues and it is to be expected that they will develop opinions about these events just as other people do. Usually, though, journalists recognize this tendency and make a point of keeping their opinions out of their stories. But the problem becomes more complicated with the kaleidoscope of activity during a political campaign. The danger is always present that the busy reporter might remember only the facts that unconsciously enhance his or her own views.

The reporter must constantly be on guard against this danger of selective perception. For example, a candidate has finally endorsed a project with which the reporter privately agrees, but which the reporter did not expect the candidate to endorse.

County Commissioner Jules Simon on Tuesday reluctantly endorsed the proposal to create a $30 million watershed in the south of Lake County.

Simon's opponent, John Jennings, had enthusiastically endorsed the project last week.

Nowhere in the remainder of the account is Simon's "reluctance" reflected. The insertion of the word merely emerged from the reporter's subconscious feelings about the candidate's timing of the announcement. Selective perception might involve only the use of a word or phrase, but it can affect the meaning of an entire story.

Another example suggests that the problem of selective perception can worsen under deadline pressure. Coverage of two presidential inaugurations by the same

newspaper contained a certain amount of "color" in the accounts. Although the integrity of the reporters was unquestioned, a charge of selective perception could have been lodged after a careful study of these leads:

WASHINGTON—Richard Milhous Nixon was inaugurated for a second term as president today and appealed to the nation and its allies to show greater self-reliance "as we stand on the threshold of a new era of peace." In a ceremony that mingled the martial spirit of brass bands and cannon, the peace prayers of clergymen and the distant shouts of protesters, the 60-year-old president took the oath of office. . . . Inauguration day broke cold, and a sharp wind sliced across the dirty Potomac, snapping the half-staff flags as it swept up Pennsylvania Avenue past the $235,000 presidential reviewing stand and on up to the Capitol.

Jan. 20, 1973

In contrast to this lead was another four years later in the same newspaper but by a different reporter:

WASHINGTON—Jimmy Carter today became the 39th president of the United States and spoke softly but passionately of a new beginning for the country. In the gentle cadence of his native Georgia, the 52-year-old Democrat took the oath of office. . . . "I have no new dream to set forth today, but rather urge a fresh faith in the old dream," he said in a brief inaugural address that, in homiletic style and moralistic tone, reiterated many of the populist themes of his long campaign . . . a 12-minute address that reflected the strong religious tone of the ceremonies and focused on the nation's spiritual lineage, stressing human rights, human dignity and a new role for the country as an international symbol of decency, compassion and strength.

Jan. 20, 1977

The reporters' use of the phrases "sharp wind slicing across the dirty Potomac" and "homiletic style and moralistic tone" take simple description and observation a step toward editorialization. Characterizing the nation's "spiritual lineage" as he did, the writer became an editorial writer.

In these cases, both reporters probably inserted themselves into the descriptions more than they should have.

Political reporters can cope with selective perception by remembering that the potential is always present for misrepresentation.

Setting the Scene

Proper background in political stories helps readers and viewers understand them, and the amount of detail needed depends upon the story and the setting of an event. The background might consist of a long history or a brief paragraph to bring the reader or viewer up to date: The announcement by a candidate for governor of West Virginia that he favored liberalizing strip mining laws in the coal fields could not have been placed in proper perspective by the reader or viewer unless the candidate's opposition to that issue four years earlier was pointed out. A long memory is as important to the reporter as it is to the politician.

Equally important is setting the tone of a political event. The demeanor of a candidate is important; so is that of the dignitaries on the platform and the mood of the crowd. Public officials and candidates do not function in a vacuum. They are affected by people and events, and the political reporter should fairly reflect this in coverage.

This 1962 Associated Press story provides an example of the importance of setting the tone for a political event:

BEVERLY HILLS, Calif.—An embittered Richard M. Nixon, his hopes for a political comeback in ruins, congratulated Gov. Edmund G. Brown Wednesday, bade farewell to public life and, in an angry denunciation of the press, told newsmen:

"You won't have Nixon to kick around any longer. Because this, gentlemen, is my last press conference."

The 49-year-old Republican former vice president, eyes swollen from lack of sleep and flashing anger, accused the press of distorting his statements. In one breath he said he had no complaints. Then he aired a few.

"Thank God for radio and TV," Nixon said through tightly compressed lips, "for keeping the newspapers a little more honest."

Nixon, who lost the 1960 presidential election by the narrowest of margins, lost his usual polished composure before newsmen and television cameras in the ballroom of the Beverly Hilton.

In this story, the emotional element needed to be stressed to put the scene in perspective. However, reporters should beware of using unnecessary adjectives that might subtly alter the focus of the story.

The Importance of Following Through

What did he say? When did he say it?

There is a tendency to separate the political campaign and assumption of office into two distinct worlds—one of promises, the other of performance. In fact, the two are inseparable. What more capable person to assess the official's performance than the reporter who transcribed the promises as they were being made?

What were those promises? How will they be implemented? Who will be affected and how do they feel about that? Where is the money coming from? How will keeping or breaking the promises affect present policies?

In theory, the office-seeker becomes the policymaker, with a higher duty. In practice, the politician remains the politician, donning a candidate's hat for frequent forays back into the world of campaigning. The officeholder must be carefully monitored as he or she replaces promises with reality.

The politician-officeholder may in fact come under scrutiny of another reporter covering a different beat, but the need to compare past promises with present practices is inescapable.

"Following through" encompasses many levels of reporting, and the political arena is no exception. With persistence and knowledge of the subject, a reporter is less likely to let a politician "off the hook."

In 1992, Cable News Network interviewer Larry King asked Ross Perot whether he would run for president. Twice Perot responded that he did not want to run. King later reworded his question, asking what circumstances would prompt Perot to enter the presidential race. This time Perot declared that he would run if supporters put him on the ballot in all 50 states.

The 1992 presidential campaign was characterized by such appearances on television talk shows, and the need for reporters to do their homework on the issues was inescapable. Late in 1992, President Bush appeared on King's TV show and was asked about the administration's support of Iraqi leader Saddam Hussein before the Persian Gulf War:

KING: "Did you have any knowledge of this going on?"

BUSH: "Of what going on?"

KING: "Sales of stuff to Iraq."

BUSH: "Against our policy?"

KING: "Right."

BUSH: "No."

The discussion continued, but inconclusively, and the president was let off the hook. More knowledge on King's part and willingness to discuss specifics of the Iraq issue might have forced a better answer.

It is common for politicians—even sitting presidents— to avoid sensitive issues, and the role of the reporter is to gently but firmly force them to allow the public some insight into their thinking. Every effort should be made to obtain responses on the reporter's terms, rather than the politician's.

Establishing Ground Rules

The adversarial relationship between the press and politicians dictates that ground rules be established to ensure that each side understands the role and goals of the other.

Rules may be specific or implied, but they should be consistent and apply to all situations that might arise.

The following are some gray areas that ground rules should cover:

"Off the record" remarks.   With shirt unbuttoned, tie tossed carelessly on a nearby chair and cocktail in hand, the candidate stretches out on the divan and expansively says, "Now, gentlemen, this is off the record but. . . ."

Long before this scene unfolds, the rules should be spelled out between the reporter and the candidate. Nothing is ever "off the record." The reporter will get far more stories than he or she will lose with such a rule. At the very least, the question should be addressed before the comments are made, not after.

"Exclusive" stories.   Often a politician will offer a reporter an "exclusive" story on the condition that it is

tailored to suit the desires of the politician. It usually boils down to how much the reporter will give in return for the exclusive, and the ground rules should be clear: The final decision on how a story is to be handled always rests with the journalist.

Gratuities.   Most news organizations have strict policies about accepting gifts from sources, usually based on questions such as these: Is lunch or dinner going to be "on the candidate"? Will accepting a ride on the candidate's aircraft affect the reporter's coverage? Will simply accepting such gratuities destroy the reporter's credibility? Should a reporter attend a candidate's private party on his or her own time? Usually, the news organization will insist on paying the reporter's share of the bill.

Departures from prepared texts.   Texts of speeches are often prepared ahead of time for the press, but candidates often depart from them in the course of changing audiences and conditions. Material might be added or deleted. The reporter should immediately ask why the material was changed to determine whether the omission should be noted in the subsequent news story.

Other problems will arise, necessitating similar decisions. For example, a campaigning candidate might give an informal, negative response to a question on a campaign issue. In the activity of the campaign, the almost offhand comment is temporarily forgotten. Later, in a more formal setting, the candidate offers a different, positive response to the issue, duly included in the news reports. The reporter's dilemma: How to deal with the candidate's earlier, possibly more candid, comment? The importance of the issue should determine whether the reporter should add it to the news report.

Listening to Dissidents

That ancient slogan "Never put all your eggs in one basket" is never so pertinent as on the political beat. The friendly source of yesterday may be the hostile nonsource of tomorrow. By cultivating sources at all points of the political spectrum, the reporter can continue to provide a solid news report.

Another slogan is equally apt: "Always cultivate the dissidents." They are present in all political hierarchies and are often able to clarify murky actions of those in power. They will be present at the secret caucuses in which political decisions are thrashed out—often with bitter exchanges.

> The Clay County Republican Council has decided to drop its opposition to changes in state laws governing campaign contributions, it was learned last night.
> The council met informally last week at the home of Chairman Douglas Monroe to resolve the controversy, according to reliable sources who attended the meeting. None of the council's officers would discuss the action.

In such cases, it is always best to obtain confirmation from two sources, to corroborate the events as fully as possible. No source should be underestimated in keeping track of the inner workings of the political parties, but as with any source, the reporter should seek verification to assure that information supplied by dissidents is not colored by bias.

A Common Interest

The political reporter's relationship with his or her sources constitutes a curious mixture of friendship and animosity. It is natural for the politician to attempt to place the emphasis or "spin" on the points that will enhance his or her position. It is just as natural for the reporter to probe for the truths in the process.

But being close to the mainstream of current events, and following them in depth, reporter and politician also find much in common. There is always a current subject that interests everyone. Furthermore, the long campaigns, with many hours on the road, create a certain camaraderie among reporter, candidate and candidate's staff. But the reporter should maintain an arms-length position to assure reportorial fairness and balance. Potential problems often can be avoided by setting ground rules up front regarding the level of involvement the candidate can expect from the reporter.

✳✳✳

POLITICAL GLOSSARY

Some of these common terms are jargon or slang that generally should be explained or avoided.

BIPARTISAN: Cooperative efforts among parties on issues where there is usually disagreement; nonpartisan issues are assumed to be above politics.

CRAWFISH: Regional slang for backing out of a stated position.

CROSSOVER VOTER: One who votes for the person rather than the party; also **Swing voter** or **Floater**.

DEMOCRACY: A government in which the people exercise their political powers directly or through elected representatives; the people exercise those powers through elected representatives in a republic, but the terms are now interchangeable.

DIRTY TRICKS: Unethical and often illegal political practices, including ballot box stuffing, character assassination and wiretapping of opposition candidates and offices; also **Political tricks**.

EXIT POLLING: Questioning of voters as they leave the polling place, to forecast early results.

FISHING EXPEDITION: An investigation undertaken without a specific goal, usually with intent to embarrass the opposition.

FRONT-RUNNER: The leading candidate for nomination or election to office.

GOOD SOLDIER: An ardent party supporter who places the party first.

GRASS ROOTS: People at the local level rather than at the center of major political activity; implies spontaneous public support.

GROUNDSWELL: A gathering of force, as of public opinion.

HACK: Slang for one who is willing to undertake distasteful tasks for money or other reward, putting it ahead of principle; also, **Political hack**.

HATCHET MAN: Slang for one who is hired to take on an unpleasant task or unscrupulous order.

HECKLE: To try to annoy or embarrass a speaker by questions, gibes or comments.

HORSE-TRADING: A transaction characterized by shrewd and vigorous bargaining.

HUSTINGS: Humorous expression for the campaign trail.

IDEOLOGY: The body of ideas and policies reflecting the aspirations and beliefs of a political group.

INFLUENCE PEDDLER: Someone who, for a fee, attempts to change the policies or actions of a politician, usually involving favors.

JUNKET: An excursion at the taxpayer's expense, usually having little or no official usefulness.

KEYNOTER: Speaker at a convention whose address sets the tone and rouses listeners.

KINGMAKER: One with sufficient political power to influence the selection of a candidate.

KITCHEN CABINET: Unofficial advisers to a politician or officeholder.

LAME DUCK: A retiring or defeated officeholder whose power is diluted because of the retirement.

LEAK: Disclosure of information through unauthorized channels; also **Courtesy leak**, **Authorized leak**.

LOGROLLING: The exchange of political favors or votes among legislators to achieve passage of projects of common interest.

LOVE FEAST: A gathering intended to promote good will among political groups, usually humorously applied.

LOYAL OPPOSITION: The political opposition in government uses this phrase to imply it opposes those in power for patriotic reasons.

MACHINE POLITICS: The power of a political organization to advance its cause and candidates, usually used in a derogatory way.

MANAGED NEWS: Information distributed by government officials to place it in a light consistent with their own interests.

MANDATE: A successful candidate's authority to carry out programs espoused during a campaign, usually associated with a landslide election.

MAVERICK: A person who bolts his or her political party; also **Mugwump**.

McCARTHYISM: An investigation that sublimates the rights of individuals in pursuit of its goals, from the late Sen. Joseph McCarthy's efforts to identify Communists in and out of government.

MUCKRAKERS: Journalists who search for and expose political or commercial corruption.

MUDSLINGING: Use of unsubstantiated charges in a campaign.

MUZZLE: An attempt to stifle criticism within one's party or government.

NEPOTISM: Preferential treatment for family members in government jobs.

NOT FOR ATTRIBUTION: Agreement by a journalist to use information without revealing the source. Off-the-record information is only for the reporter's knowledge, and is not to be taken to another source in hopes of getting confirmation. The reporter may use background information only on condition that a general source is used, such as "a source close to the candidate."

NUMBERS GAME: Misleading use of statistics to advance a cause.

OPEN CONVENTION: Convention in which no candidate has the votes to assure nomination.

OPPOSITION RESEARCH: Search by supporters of a candidate for information that will make the opposition look bad; also **Oppo**.

OPPORTUNIST: One who selects expediency over principle, frequently used against fast-rising political figures.

PARTY FAITHFUL: Slang for the rank-and-file regular voters.

PARTY LINE: Official position of the organization.

PATRONAGE: Government appointments given as a reward for loyalty and effort.

PEAKING: A campaign technique of building momentum to peak at Election Day.

PERORATION: Stirring speech, usually more inspirational than informative.

PLAYING POLITICS: Taking a stand on an issue mainly to create political mileage; sublimation of the public interest to partisan gain.

POLITICAL SUICIDE: An unpopular action or stand, which could lead to defeat in an election.

POLLSTER: One who measures opinion, with an eye to predicting election results; polling is popular in the political arena.

POPULIST: A politician seen as closely attuned to the average voter.

POSITION PAPER: A statement of policy on a specific issue.

POWER BASE: Foundation for a politician's support, usually a section of his or her constituency.

POWER BROKERS: Those who use political power, generally behind the scenes, on behalf of others.

POWER GRAB: An attempt to take over leadership; power politics implies running roughshod over the opposition.

PRECINCT CAPTAIN: One who directs political troops at the local level.

PREFERENCE POLL: Poll used to determine the mood of voters in specific venues; also **Trial heat**.

PRESSING THE FLESH: Shaking hands on the campaign trail; now seen as any form of physical contact between the voters and the candidate.

PRIMARY: A preliminary election to select candidates for the general election; closed primaries are restricted to registered voters of a specific party; voters can cross party lines in an open primary.

PROGRESSIVE: Originally, a movement for economic reforms, but now an alternative label for those not wishing to be called *liberal*.

PROTEST VOTE: Registering dissatisfaction with a candidate by casting a ballot for someone who stands little or no chance of winning.

PSEUDO EVENT: An event scheduled primarily for the coverage it will receive.

PUNDIT: Slang for a political analyst.

PURGE: Eliminating opposition within an organization.

RED HERRING: A side issue raised to draw attention away from the main issue.

RUMP SESSION: A legislative body that refuses to adjourn; a meeting of dissidents.

SHOO-IN: A candidate who is perceived as unbeatable.

SLOGAN: Rallying phrase for a candidate or a party.

SLUSH FUND: Money collected for personal use without proper accounting, or for payoffs.

SPELLBINDER: A speaker who can persuade an audience through his or her oratory.

SPIN DOCTOR: Campaign worker employed by candidates to put their own particular cast or "spin" on a breaking news event.

SPLINTER GROUP: A group of dissidents that breaks away from a larger group; organized, it becomes a splinter party.

SPLIT TICKET: A ballot cast by a voter without regard for party designation; the party prefers voting a straight ticket.

SPOILER: A candidate who can split an opponent's vote, spoiling his or her chances for victory.

STALKING HORSE: A candidate whose aim is to split a vote, creating problems for another candidate.

STEMWINDER: A loud, partisan speech.

STEPPINGSTONE: An advantageous position, usually employed to demean a candidate who has his or her sights set on higher office.

STRAW VOTE: An informal survey of a small group to determine opinion; increasingly becoming a large-scale, scientifically conducted poll; also **straw poll**.

TAKING A WALK: A person who bolts the party after a dispute.

TRIAL BALLOON: A preliminary statement or idea issued by a candidate to test public reaction before committing to it.

TRUTH SQUAD: A team of party members organized to harass an opposition candidate by quickly refuting his or her statements.

WAFFLE: A politician or officeholder who refuses to commit, straddling the fence.

WAR HORSE: A campaigner who has been in politics for a long time.

WHEEL HORSE: A dependable party regular.

WHIP: A party official chosen to assure that members are on hand for important votes, usually a steppingstone to higher party office.

WHISTLE-STOP: A tour by train or bus, during which the candidate gives short speeches as the tour passes through small communities.

WRITE-IN: A candidate not on the printed ballot, who the voter writes in.

YOUNG TURKS: Insurgents within a party; any faction impatient with things as they are.

✳✳✳

SUGGESTED READINGS

Crouse, Timothy. *The Boys on the Bus*. New York: Random House, 1973.

Chapter 4, "The Heavies" and Chapter 5, "More Heavies."

Lee, Richard, ed. *Politics and the Press*. Herndon, Va.: Acropolis, 1970.

"Appraising Press Coverage of Politics," William Rivers, and "Politicians and Biased Political Information," David Broder.

Chapter 15

Business and Consumerism

The date: anytime during the 1940s, 1950s or 1960s.

The place: the business desk of almost any newsroom in the United States. Editors are busy putting the final touches on these stories:

An open house is planned for Saturday at the new distribution facility of the Buckeye Biscuit Co.

***

David J. Cooper has been named national sales manager for Nulook Fashions Inc., importer and wholesaler of wigs and hairpieces.

***

Central Bag & Burlap, in its 50th year of distributing textile bags and specialties, is becoming a full-service supplier with emphasis on supplying the bag needs of industry and agriculture in the area.

The date: anytime after 1970.

The place: the same desk, where editors are adding a new dimension to the business beat, along with a different kind of copy.

> Here's good news for all of you 45 and older. You're not aging. You're "de-youthing."
>
>   Listen up, business folks. That crowd is a big potential market, but researchers advise you to be careful in your sales pitches. The word "aging" is a turnoff. So is that gentler description, "senior citizen."
>
> ***
>
> In Wrigley Field it's two guys, Fred and Darryl, changing cards; in Los Angeles it's an 11-person production crew; and in Toronto it's a $30 million whopper, nine stories wide, that lights up the sky. Baseball scoreboards run the gamut, but they are also rich sources of advertising revenue.
>
> ***
>
> Contrary to widely discussed orthodoxies of modern economics, raising the minimum wage might not prompt employers to trim jobs, new studies suggest, and might not be such a bad way to help America's working poor.

These examples of traditional content and the more contemporary approach illustrate the dramatic changes that have taken place during the last 30 years in reporting economics.

THE 'OLD' AND THE 'NEW'

The traditional business beat included announcements of personnel changes, new store openings and reports of record earnings by local industry. The page was fleshed out with a look at the real estate market, a national business column and a feature story about a downtown merchant.

These staples are still the backbone of many a newspaper's business page, but the emphasis has shifted to a new generation of subjects and issues:

- The city offers tax abatements to new industry as an inducement to locate in the area. But not everyone is happy. Officials of financially strapped school districts criticize the eroding tax base.
- The tobacco industry aims an anti-smoking campaign at children, but critics charge that the method is inappropriate.

- Executive changes in a troubled industrial firm signal major shifts in the company's objectives and possible economic consequences for the community.

The approach to business news is broader and deeper today, with an emphasis on "what it means" and "what's ahead" for readers and viewers.

A Broader Beat

The business beat today encompasses a whole stable of beats—from extraction of raw materials from the Earth through production into marketable items, on to marketers and distributors, and finally to sellers and buyers.

The term *business* has a broader meaning. Industrial production, transportation and distribution, and the role of the financial community are equally important.

There are many reasons for this dramatic growth:

1. New relationships between private enterprise and government at all levels, characterized by more involved regulatory practices.

2. The public's heightened awareness of global economic affairs has created a new and dynamic market for news. The old question, "How does it affect me and my pocketbook?" is addressed from a worldwide perspective.

3. The age of technology has highlighted the influence of the "business world" on where people work, where they live, what they earn and what they consume.

4. Joining this new technology is a new consumerism with its probing questions, and new marketing strategies on the part of private enterprise to cope with them. Consumerism is discussed later in this chapter.

The old "business beat" has expanded to become the "economics of the private sector" and one of the most important assignments in any newsroom.

The Range of Story Ideas

The story possibilities include Main Street, U.S.A., New York's financial centers, the global trading markets and the U.S. breadbasket.

Today's readers and viewers are likely to understand how the drop in the U.S. dollar's value overseas affects the dollar in his or her wallet and the interest earned on the dollar in the bank.

Other types of economic developments can be turned into interesting, important stories:

- The elderly owner of a neighborhood drugstore capitulates to a huge new "superpharmacy" nearby that offers thousands more items at far cheaper prices. The proprietor retires, discharges his four employees, and negotiates sale of his property as a beauty shop. It is a poignant story that affects more than a neighborhood; it is a sign of the times.

- Poor folks aren't necessarily poor credit risks. In fact, bank loans to the inner city can bring in solid profits, a message getting out to the banking industry, which for years was criticized for rejecting qualified low-income and minority borrowers.

- An industrial firm announces that it will close its local plant, a rumor for months, putting 1,000 people out of work. The reporter begins to assess the damage to the area's economy.

- The electric utility, a privately owned enterprise, petitions to raise rates, citing increased costs and a drop in return to its financial investors. To cover the story, the reporter must understand complex rate structures and be able to present the important points clearly to a concerned public.

All of these matters will require considerable legwork on the part of a reporter to develop fully. Reporting the economics of the private sector is a mixture of minor items and major developments, all in some way affecting the readership or viewership.

THE PRIVATE SECTOR: PROFIT AND RISK

While both are basic to the U.S. economic system, there is a formidable difference between the "private" and "public" sectors. The goal of any business system, which includes its industrial capacity and its financial manipulations, is to produce goods and services that satisfy the wishes and needs of the consumer public with maximum efficiency.

All businesses also operate on a profit or loss system—and this involves risk-taking. Profit is essential, providing a return on the owner's investment in the business, whether it is a one-person operation or a multinational corporation employing thousands.

If a business executive forecasts correctly about customers' needs, and meets these needs efficiently, the firm is rewarded with good earnings. If the forecast is inaccurate, the firm suffers a loss. The profit motive is uppermost through the various stages—from planning to production to distribution and sales.

On the other hand, the journalist's interest often lies in how that business, its operations and products affect the public. Some conflict is inevitable.

Complaints about the Media

"Can't the press ever get anything right?"

That complaint, often unjustified but sometimes containing elements of truth, points up the antagonism that often exists between the press and the businesses it covers.

Writer Carl Tucker pointed out that "both a free press and profits are essential to the workings of our system of governance." He urged that "newsmen and business people recognize each other as legitimate partners in our national enterprise."

Specific complaints against the media include publication of careless news stories, misquoting business executives, comparing "apples with oranges" in controversial business stories, and committing errors of fact.

Other charges include ignorant reporting, drawing erroneous conclusions from complex financial facts; oversimplification; ignoring "constructive" progress and focusing on the "bizarre, odd, inconsequential or exceptional."

Business people often complain that good news is seldom printed or broadcast, while the accident in the plant, the environmental control problem or a slur from a competitor is surefire copy for news stories.

Complaints about Business

Journalists argue that business and financial leaders are secretive and inaccessible, and respond inefficiently to media inquiries. They also charge frequent and deliberate distortion. As a consequence, the reporter's relationships with a company suffer, and his or her sources become unwilling to communicate at all or are defensive, belligerent and uncooperative.

The business world's desire for a favorable public image also creates barriers to better press-business relations. A public information office will distribute vast amounts of routine information in news releases, much of it designed to enhance the corporate image. Important information often is absent or camouflaged in jargon: Layoffs of hundreds of workers at a major plant become "production adjustments;" the loss of an important production contract becomes a "contractual renegotiation."

Journalists argue that this tendency to minimize adverse developments fosters mistrust of the business community. Many are convinced that facts routinely are withheld or twisted. One reporter says,

> You call a company president, get referred to a public relations man who gives you a prepared handout telling you about the excellent state of that business, and adds a few well-chosen "no comments" and you are supposed to write a story.

A corporation may be receiving exhaustive media coverage, yet none that it approves. Executives often fail to understand that the press cannot operate merely as a public relations tool, a business blotter or a booster of the corporation.

Many corporation executives believe their companies should receive unquestioned exposure, yet become hostile when reporters ask for specific details about the firms. Some worry that the wrong information will wind up in the hands of competitors.

Mindful of this problem, the business reporter will be open-minded in dealing with business and industrial sources, and persistent in his or her attempts to produce complete and accurate news accounts.

MONITORING THE COMMUNITY

At its most basic level, each segment of the private sector affects the public in many different ways: A

merchant opens for business. What he produces and sells may be news, as well as his relationship with the community. People are employed by him, deal with him as brokers, sell to him and earn money by investing in his firm as stockholders.

Depending on the firm, many readers and viewers have a vested interest in a firm's activity—whether it is a retail business, an industry or a privately owned utility.

One of the major functions of the press is to monitor the economic well-being of the community. The traditional approach at the local level has been to present an annual "business review" packaged in a special section containing advertising from those being reviewed, and offering a generally upbeat report to the public.

However, a more honest and thoughtful monitoring does not await the packaged review but instead deals daily with the ongoing economic successes and reverses encountered by any community.

It is easier to monitor the business community when all indicators are positive rather than negative: What retail merchant wants to discuss with a reporter his grim six-month sales figures? "It's all downturn, as much as 20 percent." What real estate broker is eager to tell a reporter that her staff is selling "far fewer properties" and admit that the immediate future is not bright? And what president of an industrial firm wants to admit that a major work force layoff is imminent?

But fairness demands reporting the entire spectrum of business news. The key to successfully handling the negative reports is to monitor the community regularly, reporting the good news as well.

The reporter cannot assess a community's well-being through press releases extolling the virtues of sale-priced merchandise during "Spring Sale Days." He or she should be seeking out more important indicators:

• Changes in the city's bond ratings. Such changes often indicate localized economic problems.

• A survey of new orders being placed with local industrial firms. Such information will often reveal slowdowns or speedups in the local economy. Also important are delays or speedups in planned expansion by business and industrial firms. Coupled with unemployment figures at the local level, these statistics often will offer a more accurate picture of economic activity than the traditional roundup of comments by well-known civic figures.

- Changes in activity in banks and savings and loan institutions. Declines and increases in loans to corporations and individuals are indicators of economic activity.
- Changes in government's funding. Problems with the tax base and the city's spending plans are good local economic indicators.

Other indicators include housing sales, production of public utilities, postal receipts, vehicular sales in the area, the average workweek and plans for purchasing new equipment.

Agencies such as the local Chamber of Commerce, development boards and university schools of business often can shed light on a community's economic well-being. Even the courts are a source: Increased bankruptcy filings might signal a slip in the community's vitality.

The Reporter as Monitor

Competent monitoring of the community's economic life requires knowledge of business and industry, and an ability to explain them in understandable terms.

The prepared reporter won't have to resort to a glossary to reconcile a proposed new excise tax with a firm's future growth. Nor will it be necessary to consult a dictionary for definitions when a company decides to reorganize under pressure from its stockholders.

The news organization's business office can teach the reporter how to read a financial report, pointing out the intricacies of the double-entry process—the basic accounting system of most corporations, public and private. Merrill Lynch produces a booklet, "How to Read a Financial Report," that will help a reporter grasp the facts in corporate annual reports.

As already noted, the tendency on the business beat is to depend on spokespersons trained to provide data in the interest of their company. Information from spokespersons often begins the news story process, but additional interviews with the decision-makers concludes it. Between these are other sources that will provide a complete and balanced story: experts such as market analysts and researchers who know the company and how it operates, the company's critics and competitors, and published figures that offer an even more accurate portrait of the company.

Delay or postponement of an important project may be newsworthy, but officials often would rather not emphasize such negative aspects of the program. Reporters should ask specific questions until they have the whole story.

Another important part of the reporter's job is to monitor continuing stories so they won't get lost in the welter of new stories that are constantly breaking. A "tickler file," designed to jog a reporter's memory, is helpful in assuring that such stories are not forgotten.

Legal advertisements should be watched closely, because overlooked business developments often show up there.

A new downtown bank designed to provide services especially to the elderly has been proposed by a group of nine local businessmen, physicians and lawyers.

The application to organize the new firm has been filed with the Comptroller of the Currency in Washington, according to published legal notices.

Attorney Leon S. Oxnard, a spokesman for the proposed bank, said efforts are being made to lease the vacant facility formerly occupied by the Downtown Athletic Club at 410 Front St.

Reporters also should regularly check new corporations chartered by the state. Many newspapers routinely publish the names of new firms, but such a list offers few clues to their makeup. Identity of the incorporators often provides information of greater interest. Business people can get a state charter for as little as $100, but capitalization is usually far in excess of that figure, and the effect on the community may be much greater. Figure 15–1 lists more statistics available to the reporter.

The Players in the Private Sector

Most major segments of the private sector are interrelated. The reporter cannot assess the housing market, for example, without considering the real estate brokers and sales agents who power sales and rentals. Neither can the mortgage loan banks or construction

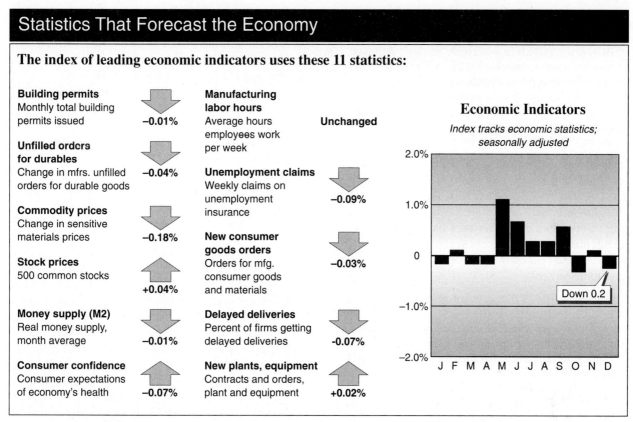

Statistics That Forecast the Economy

The index of leading economic indicators uses these 11 statistics:

Building permits
Monthly total building
permits issued   –0.01%

**Unfilled orders
for durables**
Change in mfrs. unfilled   –0.04%
orders for durable goods

Commodity prices
Change in sensitive
materials prices   –0.18%

Stock prices
500 common stocks
                                 +0.04%

Money supply (M2)
Real money supply,
month average   –0.01%

Consumer confidence
Consumer expectations
of economy's health   –0.07%

**Manufacturing
labor hours**
Average hours   **Unchanged**
employees work
per week

Unemployment claims
Weekly claims on
unemployment   –0.09%
insurance

**New consumer
goods orders**
Orders for mfg.   –0.03%
consumer goods
and materials

Delayed deliveries
Percent of firms getting
delayed deliveries   -0.07%

New plants, equipment
Contracts and orders,
plant and equipment   +0.02%

Economic Indicators

*Index tracks economic statistics;
seasonally adjusted*

Down 0.2

J F M A M J J A S O N D

FIGURE 15–1
Following these statistics at the local level helps the reporter monitor a specific community.
Source: Bureau of Economic Analysis.

industry be ignored. Following is a look at the various components.

Retail and Wholesale Sales

The purchase of a tie for a relative at Christmas represents only a miniscule portion of the chain that binds the consumer who made the purchase to the U.S., Korean or Brazilian textile worker who produced it.

Months or years before the last-minute purchase, the economic system is at work filling stores across America with finished goods for sale. At any point along the chain—the merchant who sells, the wholesaler who supplies, the driver who transports, the warehouse operator who stocks, the broker who facili-

tates the transaction, the manufacturer and the industry that supplies the fiber—there is a story with continuing interest and importance.

Whether on a downtown street in Moline or in a suburban mall near San Diego, the reporter who studies the commercial establishments will find a vast range of activity.

Who are the people doing business on the street (or in the mall)? What is the consumer buying, and at what prices? Where was the item manufactured and why? What are the implications of the purchase? Simplistic perhaps, but from such analyses are trends and issues stories born.

The reporter monitoring this business community is looking for more than economic health. What is working and not working? What are the trends? How is the buyer coping with them?

> BOCA RATON, Fla.—Walking through 7-Eleven, someone takes a candy bar off the shelf and puts it in a bag. Shoplifting or merely forgetful?
>
> Suddenly a voice booms out from the ceiling:
>
> "Attention. This is Southland Security. This store and all its activities are being monitored." The candy bar is replaced. Video surveillance has entered a new age.

The firm that controls 6,500 7-Eleven stores nationwide was testing an interactive audio-video surveillance system throughout its chain. But the new protective device is only one of the business stories generated. Surveillance at businesses has raised new concerns about privacy. Researching this story, the reporter finds others worried about the ever-present eye of the camera.

> Is there an end to the proliferation of video cameras, monitors and security devices?
>
> Go to a gas station, and you're being watched. Walk up to an office building at night and you're on TV. Enter a dressing room, and signs tell you that you have no guarantee of privacy.

Business stories are everywhere in the retail marketplace. The reporter at the end of a long line in a supermarket when the bar scanner refuses to work may be onto a story.

> There's nothing like a long delay in an "express" checkout lane to turn a relaxed buyer into a crank.
>
> The culprit is often a bar code—the ubiquitous 1-inch square of black lines printed on nearly every commercial product.
>
> A bar code stubbornly resists as the clerk drags it across the scanner—once, twice, three, four times.
>
> By the time the clerk gives up and begins entering the price manually, customers at the end of the line are desperately searching for a shorter one.

But relief may be on the way. The retailers tell the reporter that a growing alliance of angry shopkeepers, fed up with strained customer relations and lost productivity, is clamping down on manufacturers who don't print dependable bar codes on products.

The reporter checks available statistics: Bar codes now work 80 percent the first time they are passed over a scanner. Retailers want that figure improved to at least 95 percent. Such issues interest more than the retailers—they affect the buying public.

Stories detailing such controversies—along with explicit graphics showing how bar scanners work—are an important part of the business beat.

> Two empty storefronts stare blankly out on the street. Another has a mass of signs proclaiming: "GOING OUT OF BUSINESS. PRICES CUT 80%! LAST WEEK!"

Why are the merchants going out of business? What is the problem, if there is one? What are the reactions of the remaining merchants to these developments? What do elected officials say? What's the effect on the city's tax base? What is the reaction of city planners? Nearly every such development incurs a reaction, and a news story should not be far behind.

The reporter monitoring the community has a lot of help. Many local, state and federal agencies are gathering statistics and surveying all levels of business. The Small Business Administration collects income and other figures, compiling them and issuing periodic reports. Income of an area's small merchants may be rising while the national statistics show much slower growth. The reporter's task is to determine the reasons. Other SBA statistics are also worth localizing: The number of jobs created by small businesses, the sectors that are creating the most new jobs, and the number of people who are self-employed all generate story ideas.

Private research firms also compile consumer buying statistics. DYG Inc., a research firm, finds that more and more younger car buyers are switching to U.S.-made autos. A reporter can determine whether the trend exists in his or her community.

Business and trade associations also are valuable sources of information, but the reporter is again warned that they serve as support groups for their clients. Names, addresses and phone numbers for most associations can be located in the Encyclopedia of Associations, available in most libraries.

The Service Industry

The service industry also is composed of a broad spectrum of individuals and corporations. Professionals such as physicians, dentists, chiropractors and psychologists dot the landscape. Rug cleaners, hair stylists, marinas, weight control services, auto towing, electronics repair, restaurants and plumbers vie for the privilege of serving the public.

Service industry jobs proliferated during the last decade, and are likely to be the future for many more Americans. One of the business reporter's tasks will be to follow this trend, using statistics from many sources, community-based groups such as Alliance for Fair Employment, service industries themselves, and the people who work in them.

> The Hudsons were smiling.
>
> Gypsy, the Wonder Dog, had scored, sniffing out termites at the corner of the house they were about to purchase and assuring Robert and Betty Hudson that the seller would remedy the problem at no cost to them.
>
> Gypsy's owner, James Hill of Hill Exterminating Services, would like to put a cape around her neck so she would look more like the "Wonder Dog" she is.
>
> But that might get in her way as she goes about her business of sniffing out termites.

Such stories as this offer interesting insights into a community's service industry. The beagle who has graduated from bug college—and is incredibly accurate—is only one of the possibilities for the business page.

News developments emerge from many sources, and new consumer protection codes provide a wealth of information. A city's plan to begin a food service inspection program generates comment from local health department officials who will administer the program. The reporter also should talk to a cross-section of the establishments that will be affected, and to officials about how the program will work and what it means to the consumer. Many newspapers routinely publish violations of health codes, listing the establishments and the violation.

An afternoon tour with an inspector can give the reporter an opportunity for a close-up view of the program and its effectiveness. No business is immune from local, state or federal scrutiny.

Sometimes, as in a Federal Trade Commission order, the story out of Washington suggests an in-depth look at the financial relationships between rental car agencies and airport taxes and other charges.

> WASHINGTON—Two major rental car companies have agreed to stop advertising misleading rates that

do not include mandatory extra costs such as airport and fuel surcharges, the Federal Trade Commission announced Thursday.

> Dollar Rent-A-Car Systems and Value Rent-A-Car Inc. have settled FTC complaints against them by promising to state clearly the additional charges in the future, the agency said.

While seeking a follow-up story on the misleading advertising story, the reporter discovered that auto manufacturers had stopped giving discounts to rental agencies, forcing up rental rates.

National and international events also shape business at the local level. When the U.S. dollar weakens against European currencies, for example, travel agencies are affected, since tourists going overseas find the trip much more costly. At the same time, visitors from abroad find vacations in this country are cheaper, boosting segments of the retail and service industries.

Housing and Other Real Estate

Nearly everyone has a stake in the housing market—either as a homeowner, a renter or a landlord.

Rock-bottom interest rates can be expected to bring a rush of homeowners seeking to refinance homes purchased when rates were much higher a dozen years before. Bank officials can help the reporter determine the spread between the old and new rates at which it makes sense to refinance.

Statistics help put the refinancing stories in perspective (see Figure 15–2), but specific examples of families who are opting to do so add human interest to the coverage.

Conversely, high interest rates may soften a city's real estate market, visible through sharp drops in classified advertising in local newspapers and in real estate closings, all available statistics. Because potential homebuyers often cannot raise necessary down payments, the rental market booms. Several approaches to coverage suggest themselves, from the statistics-based hard news story to the human interest angle of the couple who is forced to keep renting.

Don't forget the plight of real estate people whose livelihoods depend on sales in the housing market.

> Lois Jackson didn't show up for the weekly meeting at Specialty Realty Co. yesterday.

FIGURE 15–2
Statistics like these offer
the reporter a benchmark for
studying a specific state or
community.
Source: National Association of
Realtors and AP/Carl Fox. Reprinted
with permission of AP/Wide World
Photos.

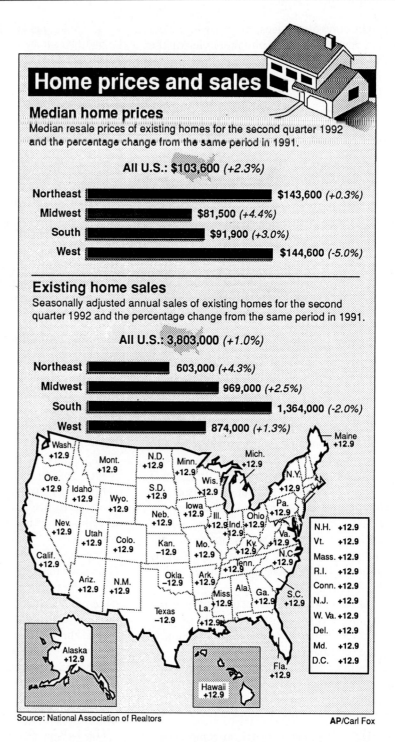

Home prices and sales

Median home prices

Median resale prices of existing homes for the second quarter 1992
and the percentage change from the same period in 1991.

All U.S.: $103,600 *(+2.3%)*

Northeast **$143,600** *(+0.3%)*
Midwest **$81,500** *(+4.4%)*
South **$91,900** *(+3.0%)*
West **$144,600** *(-5.0%)*

Existing home sales

Seasonally adjusted annual sales of existing homes for the second
quarter 1992 and the percentage change from the same period in 1991.

All U.S.: 3,803,000 *(+1.0%)*

Northeast **603,000** *(+4.3%)*
Midwest **969,000** *(+2.5%)*
South **1,364,000** *(-2.0%)*
West **874,000** *(+1.3%)*

Wash. +12.9
Ore. +12.9
Idaho +12.9
Mont. +12.9
N.D. +12.9
Minn. +12.9
Mich. +12.9
Maine +12.9
Wis. +12.9
S.D. +12.9
Wyo. +12.9
Nev. +12.9
Utah +12.9
Neb. +12.9
Iowa +12.9
Ill. +12.9
Ind. +12.9
Ohio +12.9
Pa. +12.9
N.Y. +12.9
Calif. +12.9
Colo. +12.9
Kan. -12.9
Mo. +12.9
Ky. +12.9
Va. +12.9
N.C. +12.9
Tenn. +12.9
Ariz. +12.9
N.M. +12.9
Okla. -12.9
Ark. +12.9
Ala. +12.9
Ga. +12.9
S.C. +12.9
Miss. +12.9
La. +12.9
Texas -12.9
Fla. +12.9
Alaska +12.9
Hawaii +12.9

N.H. +12.9
Vt. +12.9
Mass. +12.9
R.I. +12.9
Conn. +12.9
N.J. +12.9
W. Va. +12.9
Del. +12.9
Md. +12.9
D.C. +12.9

Source: National Association of Realtors   **AP/Carl Fox**

Instead, she watched the morning talk shows, then planted tulip bulbs in the afternoon. Mrs. Jackson is one of the victims of the dramatic drop in the real estate market that has sent her and hundreds of other part-time real estate salespeople to the sidelines.

"It's just a temporary thing," she theorized over coffee in the Oak Ridge home she occupies with engineer husband Herbert and two teen-age children. "When the market improves, I'll plunge back in. Meanwhile, there's lots of reading to catch up on."

The reporter has uncovered at least one reason why salespeople do not suffer quite as much during such periods of real estate inactivity. Many have other sources of income, including those of spouses.

Public records are helpful in monitoring the housing industry, but are more important in studying commercial real estate activity. Property transfers and tax records show ownership, last price paid for the property and taxes levied on it. Identifying transfer of important property in anticipation of major activity is easy through county maps.

Local as well as federal agencies conduct regular surveys of various segments of the real estate market, including vacancy rates for apartments—which often are tracked by regional or county planning councils—and the asking prices on available commercial space.

Federal agencies also produce a wealth of real estate statistics that can add perspective to local stories on similar subjects. If national housing starts do not parallel the local statistics, the reasons should be explored. Local and regional breakdowns between multiple and single family units might offer more insight.

Sales of new homes are an important tracking indicator, but so are statistics of older home sales.

Developers and speculators abound in the real estate market, and the reporter should be familiar with the firms and individuals who do business in his or her area. A federal agency may create affordable housing for low-income families in a city, but developers are usually the ones who set up and administer the operation.

Commercial developers often strike deals with governmental units that control the federal funding for such projects. The county reporter or a business reporter may be following the negotiations that lead to construction.

A zoning change that paves the way for a $23 million housing development on the West Side was approved yesterday by the Municipal Planning Commission.

The development, which will include 206 rental townhouses and 100 apartment units, has been proposed by Brush Industries, a firm that has built extensively in the midstate.

Harold M. Denning, president of the firm, said the project is being financed with loans from the state's Housing Development Fund.

Reporters also should monitor the foreclosure rate of both private and commercial property and attend the sales on the courthouse steps, looking for changes in ownership and land use.

Other questions a reporter should ask: How do current property listings compare with the totals of six months, 12 months or two years before? What are the availability and price range of specific kinds of real estate? The Multiple Listing Service can provide the figures. The Multiple Listing Service is a private service for clients that tracks most of the real estate on the market. Local real estate agents are members and list their current property for sale or rent in binders that are constantly updated. A helpful agent will let a reporter study the trends.

The reporter also can compare new building permits with previous figures, and check permits for improvement and alteration of businesses and warehouses.

Alternative housing trends provide impetus for coverage. The growth of the apartment and attached townhouse market should be monitored for changes in direction.

BOSTON—During the real estate boom of the 1980s, the condominium seemed the answer to yuppies longing for property and city chic. But after the bust, some residents say they are living in Condo Hell.

Condo associations are having trouble raising the monthly fees to pay for trash, sewer and maintenance. And with declining real estate values, condo owners cannot afford to move.

Statistics and figures are important to this story; so are the individual owners who are used as sources. What are the fees? Monthly fees for a two-bedroom Boston condo have crept up 30 percent, for example—

to $192 a month. Annual "special assessments" cost the same owner about $2,000. Where does that money go?

Although the condo associations are private, the reporter usually can negotiate information from disgruntled owners.

Owner Bruce Hopper said that even with the higher payments, his group's bills are paid so late that notices are sometimes posted in his building threatening service shutoffs.

Reporters can explore many such issues in the real estate market.

The historically low interest rates in the early 1990s led to major changes in apartment availability.

The city's apartment communities are feeling the competitive crunch these days, and that's good news for would-be tenants.

Area vacancy rates are higher this summer than in the past because low mortgage rates are luring many renters to buy homes. Compounding the glut of rental units is an improving economy that has led to a surge in new apartment construction.

The reporter who researched this story used vacancy rate surveys compiled by the city's apartment association, and figures supplied by banks' mortgage departments and construction industry officials. Even her newspaper's advertising department offered figures to show the surge in classified ads for vacant apartments. She also tracked down new homeowners to provide a personal view of the changes.

Still another aspect to the story are the concessions being given to prospective apartment tenants—in the form of lower rates, washer/dryer giveaways, slashed security deposits and free rent in exchange for longer leases.

Keeping tuned to the changing economy and people's lifestyles is a good way to focus on such stories.

Industry

The health of an industrial firm that produces goods and employs hundreds or thousands directly affects the health of a community. Industry is tied to the community—through its purchasing practices and labor

requirements, environmental concerns and not least, the tax base it provides.

The firm may be a specialized ornamental glass company that employs only 10 people, but ships all over the country. It may be a giant auto assembly plant employing thousands of skilled workers.

The corn crop in Kansas, or the shrimp businesses off the Atlantic and Gulf coasts are important "industrial" segments of their communities. Lobster catches in Boston might go for $2 a pound or $10, depending on the season and the conditions—the reporter should monitor both.

The business reporter should follow these industries regularly, and not wait until an event occurs to develop a story. Monthly and yearly statistics on crops, catches and auto loadings are always available for study and can signal up or down trends in the business. Loss of farm land to development, precipitous drops in corn production, or loss of fishing boats to a hurricane are important parts of the business beat.

Other important areas of coverage: marketing conditions that cause changes in crop production, drops in cigarette consumption that affect Southern tobacco growers, and a decision to direct more of the nation's corn crop toward production of ethanol, alcohol used as a fuel additive. Statistics can add substance to comments by officials and growers.

Translating federal statistics to the local level helps the reader or viewer see how the community is affected. The Federal Reserve Board, for example, regularly produces an industrial production index, which measures output at the nation's factories, mines and utilities.

WASHINGTON—The nation's factory output fell in June, and analysts saw that as more evidence the recovery has stalled.

Officials at the Federal Reserve blamed the 0.3 percent drop on a slowdown in auto manufacturing and a two-day national rail shutdown.

At the least, these statistics should trigger questions about industrial production at the local level. The Commerce Department also provides regular statistics on the industrial sector, including an index of factory orders for durable goods (items expected to last three or more years, like furniture and appliances).

Lower factory orders could bring responses from local securities dealers, economists and industrial officials. And retailers of durable goods are logical sources of information.

Industry incentives, such as money, tax abatement and even land, should be monitored constantly. The announcement in 1992 that German automaker BMW would construct a new plant in South Carolina raised questions about such incentives.

Is a BMW plant worth $145 million to the taxpayers of South Carolina?

That's the amount that Gov. Carroll Campbell and his economic advisers have ordered up to lure the German automaker to build a plant near Spartanburg.

Months before, the state had promised $3 million in roads, sewer systems and other infrastructure support to clinch a $500 million pharmaceutical plant for another area of the state. In the case of BMW, the final announcement that the plant would locate in the state offered two faces to the public.

SPARTANBURG—State officials beamed Tuesday as BMW officials finally said the Munich-based automaker will build its first U.S. plant in Spartanburg County.

But the celebration was semisweet. BMW said the plant will employ 2,000 workers by the year 2000, not the 4,000 originally estimated.

BMW also dashed hopes that its high German wages would mean high-paying jobs in the state. "We aren't here to pay what we pay in Germany," the BMW official said.

Questions about the secrecy involved in such negotiations also bedevil reporters. Many states' freedom of information acts exempt public disclosure requirements for most government industry-hunting efforts. Not every state provides such incentives, but reporters should be aware of the trend for local and state governments to provide them.

One of the important industrial stories during the 1990s is the "downsizing" or "restructuring" of the nation's work force. The business reporter watches announcements from distant headquarters for clues to a local firm's future. For employees, news that an employer is getting "leaner and meaner" sometimes means losing their jobs.

Money and Banking

Money drives the private sector. Its availability, the cost of acquiring it and what people are doing with it are daily newsmakers. The homeowners who earn incomes, the businesses and industries that require loans and mortgages, all depend upon banks, which makes them among the most important commercial institutions at the local level.

What does the reporter—and ultimately the reader or viewer—need to know about local banks and the system itself? Undoubtedly the most important item is the safety and stability of individual banks as well as the system. The national savings and loan crisis, brought about by the failure of hundreds of lenders in the late 1980s and early 1990s, resulted in a new focus on the condition of S&Ls and banks all over the United States.

Reporters have had to learn about a new range of statistics—much of it generated by federal agencies dealing with the crisis. More than ever, readers and viewers want to know the bottom line of the components of their banking system, along with detailed analysis from solid sources.

A still-developing wave of bank mergers also has created a dynamic news source, and with a language all its own.

Now what does this sound like?

The offensive manager for tactical decisions will start right away, but the defensive manager for tactical decisions won't start until the second quarter.

Football? No.

These are new corporate banking executives who will run the $116 billion NationsBank when it begins operations this year. New departments include "Corporate Banking, Investment Banking, Global Trading & Distribution, Secured Lending Group and Corporate Investments Group."

It is easy to see that the first task for the banking reporter is to identify the functions of these new departments. The job might not be easy.

Some of the bank's new jobs are downright obscure:

Joseph Whitman will be the "offensive manager" in the area of "Market Strategy and Tactical Decisions." His defensive counterpart, Marta Hollins, won't be on board until the second quarter of the year.

Vice President Lee Dodd will be in charge of "Portfolio Analytics and Specialized Collateral Lending."

Banking officials often speak a language of their own, and reporters must translate. They must also be familiar with banks and their various systems. New offerings, such as private banking services to attract affluent customers, new branches in the suburbs, and special attention to retirees are all a part of the banking beat.

Despite the wave of mergers, intense competition for the public's business continues among lending institutions. Services peripheral to banks' main business, such as stock brokering and the credit card industry, are worth dissecting for readers or viewers.

The banks of the United States are regulated by the Federal Reserve System, the central point for administering and making policy for the nation's credit and monetary affairs. Banks must file annual reports with the Federal Reserve, showing financial condition and shareholder information. Because most banks are public corporations, valuable information also exists with the Securities and Exchange Commission and with state agencies.

The Federal Reserve influences the lending and investing activities in most communities through its regulation of commercial banks, including tightening and loosening the cost and availability of money and credit. Its influence over credit conditions affects public borrowing and lending, and the reporter should be familiar with the Federal Reserve's reporting procedures.

Cuts to the Federal Reserve's interest rates might be good news for borrowers, but could be costly for savers who rely on interest income.

The cuts have led banks to drop their prime lending rate to 6 percent, a rate that forms the base for some credit lines and for savings accounts and certificates of deposit.

"It is unfortunate, but retirees and others on fixed incomes are going to be hurt," People's Bank Vice President Donna Wilcox said Tuesday.

As public corporations, most of their activities can be monitored—at the state as well as federal levels.

The Resolution Trust Corp. was created to manage and dispose of insured depository institutions that go into receivership. The assets often include failed business properties and foreclosed residential property. A catfish farm and processing plant may be auctioned on the courthouse steps; a condominium development may suffer the same fate.

Much of the financial detail is public record, and the reporter usually can obtain other information from court records.

CHARLESTON, S.C.—A federal court ruled Wednesday that the Resolution Trust Corp. can take control of and sell Kiawah Island, an upscale resort on the coast.

Control of the resort has been at the center of a 14-month tug of war between the agency and Landmark Land Co., which owned the extensive amenities on the island.

The banking industry, with its ties to the public, is often the beginning point for stories that touch the lifestyles of a community. Research uncovers economic stories—two-job families that become one-job families during a recession, for example.

Families that relied on two or more paychecks to qualify for a San Jose home are finding the going increasingly tough as unemployment takes a bigger bite.

"We are getting some families with problems," Ralph G. Staper, vice president of Downtown Savings and Loan Association, said this week. "We're trying to work with them until they get on their feet again."

Staper estimated that up to 20 percent of the association's customers are in danger of losing one of the family paychecks.

Stories like these abound in the banking industry, but the reporter should be forewarned: Officials can be choosy about the subjects they wish to explore with the press. Many bank records, such as reports by examiners, are private. So are company trade secrets and some types of financial information.

For example, a Southern bank involved in an accounting dispute with the Securities and Exchange Commission did not want the public to see some of the records of the dispute. The reason: Some banks sell off bonds with profits, while holding on to those with losses. It is known as **gains trading** or **"cherry picking"** of profits.

Since the dispute involved $25 billion in bonds, the SEC sought to force banks to adopt accounting rules that reflect the losses in their bank holdings. Such stories are complicated by efforts to keep the records private.

Other Community Segments

The reporter should not overlook other major segments of the business community—the construction industry, transportation, agriculture and mining, and utilities.

Contractors, building materials retailers and wholesalers, architects and planners are good sources for construction updates. So are building trade associations.

For example, growth of prefabricated building materials are providing home buyers with new opportunities for savings. It also raises new questions about reliability, and sends reporters to county building offices for answers.

A wire service story containing specific figures on spending for private and public construction around the nation offers the opportunity for similar local surveys of the construction industry.

> A surge in apartment construction fueled by major developers is helping the city avoid the downward national trend in new construction, the city's Development Board said yesterday.
>
> "We're optimistic this difference will continue into next year," said Daniel C. Fogerty, executive director of the board. But, he added, "a long-term national slowdown will inevitably affect us."
>
> A U.S. Commerce Department report this week placed the nation's spending for new construction at 11.8 percent below the same period last year.

The business of transportation is also economically important to a community, whether it is a taxi company regulated by a municipality or a fleet of 18-wheelers overseen by the Interstate Commerce Commission. The ICC was created by Congress to regulate carriers engaged in interstate transportation, including trucking companies, railroads, bus lines, freight forwarders, water carriers, transportation brokers and express agencies.

The commission settles conflicts over rates and charges among competing modes of carrier; rules on applications for mergers, acquisitions and consolidations; prescribes rules for operation; and investigates complaints against firms. Records of protests, complaints and investigations are available to the press.

Privately owned utilities—supplying power and gas, water, telephone and sewer service—pose a special challenge. Because utilities usually operate under franchise in a community and have no competition, they are closely regulated and their rates are set by special commissions and agencies. These elaborate and complicated rate structures are sometimes Greek to the reporter trying to translate the material.

Most of the material is public record, the hearings are public, and regulatory commission staffers usually are willing to help the reporter follow complicated rate increase requests.

Using Other Economic Data

New information-gathering techniques, coupled with the ability to quickly and efficiently process material through computers, has resulted in a massive outpouring of economic data from government agencies.

The reporter can effectively localize much material, making it more meaningful to the community. A city's unemployment rate, for example, with attendant breakdowns of various industries, is just as important as the periodic announcement of national unemployment figures.

Economic indicators have been developed to cover just about every aspect of national life. All are interrelated, and most can be localized. One of the most widely watched indicators, the Consumer Price Index (Commerce Department), tracks retail prices. The Producer Price Index for finished goods (Labor Department) tracks wholesale prices and is an indicator for the near future.

Many of these indicators break down into specific categories, important to a reporter trying to localize national statistics.

> Food prices, which have fallen or stayed unchanged in 11 of the past 13 months, remained frozen in July although there were big swings in different categories.
>
> Fruit prices were down 14.7 percent, the biggest one-month drop in 20 years, while vegetable prices shot up 19.7 percent.

Analysts can provide the reporter with the reasons for the swings: An unusually wet and mild summer has resulted in bumper fruit crops in many regions but has sharply reduced vegetable yields, especially in the West and Midwest. The statistics show even more detail.

Among the vegetable prices that skyrocketed were potatoes, up 79.7 percent; carrots, up 74.9 percent; and eggplant, up 32.6 percent.
Declining fruit prices included peaches, down 44.5 percent; strawberries, down 41.2 percent; and melon prices, down 32.6 percent.

The reporter also can monitor changes in food and beverage prices, energy prices such as gasoline pump prices, airline fares, new and used car prices and apparel prices.
Regular monitoring of this index at the national level also yields regional and local figures. The Bureau

of Labor Statistics breaks down figures for various areas and offers detailed reasons for upward or downward changes in the indexes.

Consumer prices continued to rise in the Tristate area last month, reflecting higher costs for housing, transportation and medical care, the Bureau of Labor Statistics reported Thursday.
However, the national Consumer Price Index continued to outpace the regional figure, rising at an annual rate of 6.6 percent.
The comparable area figure was at an annual rate of 5.7 percent, Warren Norwood, regional commissioner for the agency, said.

Often, the effect of national trends on local communities can be translated into very specific and personal stories.

FIGURE 15–3
This widely watched federal indicator provides material for locally generated sidebar stories about the economy of a specific community.
Source: The Conference Board. Reprinted with permission.

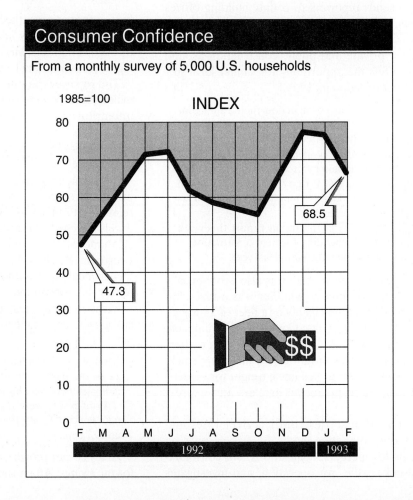

The Consumer Confidence Index, which tracks the willingness of Americans to buy and invest, is also a widely watched indicator (see Figure 15–3). It is produced by the Conference Board, which analyzes its components for significant changes. In complicated indicators such as these, it is always helpful to explain them to the reader or viewer.

> The Consumer Confidence Index, calculated on a 1985 base rate of 100, is compiled from responses to questionnaires sent to 5,000 households nationally to assess financial and job security.
>
> Economists pay close attention to the index, which offers insight into attitudes toward spending and borrowing.

Another important indicator of economic growth or lack of it lies in the Index of Economic Activity, produced by the National Association of Purchasing Management. The monthly index is compiled from a survey of more than 300 purchasing managers at a wide range of industrial companies. It is considered important because it is the first significant indicator of economic activity during the previous month.

As with other indicators, an effort is always made to explain why the index has risen or fallen.

> The decline from 56.3 percent in July to 52.8 percent in August was largely a result of slower growth in production, mainly in the auto industry, the association noted.

Included in the main indicator are other categories, like production, employment, new orders and new orders for products for export. There also are breakdowns for various industries, such as glass, stone and aggregates.

> The employment component of the index, however, continued to decline. Nineteen percent of the more than 300 companies polled reported smaller payrolls in July; 14 percent reported they had more employees than in the previous month. The remainder were unchanged.

Employment statistics come from several sources. The most widely watched and commented upon is the Labor Department's unemployment rate.

> WASHINGTON—The nation's unemployment rate fell slightly to 7.1 percent in August as a federal summer jobs program helped send payroll employment up by the largest amount in two years, the government said Thursday.

The department also provided a separate payroll survey that showed the economy created 198,000 jobs in August, the biggest gain in two years. Statistics also showed widespread weakness in defense-related industries. New technology also enables agencies to break down figures by group: white, black, Hispanic, men and women.

Such announcements often trigger other actions among government agencies. The Federal Reserve might be prompted to cut key interest rates, for example.

New claims for unemployment benefits is another important Labor Department indicator. The department also analyzes the reasons for changes in the statistics.

> WASHINGTON—The number of Americans filing new claims for jobless benefits took its largest jump in more than 10 years early this month as a result of a two-week shutdown of General Motors operations, the Labor Department reported Thursday.

The Commerce Department also tracks growth or decline in the personal income of Americans, analyzing the effect. Private organizations also offer analyses of figures.

> "We can't blame consumers," said economist David Wyss of DRI-McGraw Hill, a forecasting firm. "Consumers are doing their part. They just don't have much income. To cure that, we need more employment."

Another forecasting firm pointed out that "income weakness goes hand in hand with the employment weakness."

Trade associations regularly monitor their specific businesses, providing forecasts and other information that can be checked locally.

> Delays in pickups and deliveries, caused by shortages of diesel fuel, will frustrate the estimated 4.3 million people moving to distant cities this summer.
>
> "Loaded vans are already running into the problem," said Cliff C. Knowles, director of the Household Goods Carriers Bureau, a trade organization representing 80 percent of the nation's moving firms. "We expect it to be much worse when business peaks this summer."

For further information, the reporter has access to the American Movers Conference, another major trade association representing the industry; the

Interstate Commerce Commission; and local sources. An ICC official provided even more information:

> While families planning interstate moves can expect problems, the 17.4 million people planning local or intrastate moves will have far fewer problems.

Many indicators, such as the U.S. trade deficit or occasional surplus, involve figures of billions of dollars. The gross domestic product, the broadest measure of U.S. economic health, is another, and the reporter is often hard-pressed to relate them to the average reader or viewer. Experts and analysts often can comment on the reasons for any changes.

> WASHINGTON—The U.S. trade deficit widened to $7.38 million, the worst showing in two years, as sales of American aircraft and farm products dropped sharply, the Commerce Department said Friday.
>
> One economist called the report the "worst of all worlds," and others said the figures indicate the year "is beginning to look ominously like 1992 when a budding recovery faltered in late summer."

Experts also can reflect upon the significance of changes in specific exports.

GOVERNMENT INVOLVEMENT

Through regulation, direct and indirect assistance, and credit agencies, government is involved in the business and industrial sector. Some involvement concerns significant regulation, important to the reporter, while the rest concerns bookkeeping measures designed to secure data for census or survey purposes.

Nearly 100 federal agencies regulate private enterprise in the United States, creating massive paperwork networks. Business complains that many of the rules are unnecessary and that the cost of complying with regulations forces firms to pass on the costs to the consumer.

Whatever the veracity of the complaints, the economics reporter will have to face a fact of life: the work of many government agencies affects this beat, and a knowledge of their work is essential. Few reporters have the time to monitor the 80,000 pages produced annually in the *Federal Register*, the daily

publication that announces most of the proposed federal regulations. Most reporters rely on well-placed sources to keep them informed of developments that affect the economics of the local community.

Wire service stories and reports in business journals also can alert the reporter to stories that could be localized.

> WASHINGTON—Under heavy pressure from bankers, the Federal Deposit Insurance Corp. board Tuesday postponed an increase in its insurance premiums until next year, when it hopes to have a system for charging risky banks more than safe banks.
>
> Members of the Senate Banking Committee and other lawmakers have been pressing for an increase this year to ensure repayment of money borrowed by the agency from U.S. taxpayers.

Other federal agencies also are players in this game, including officials of the Federal Reserve System and the Treasury Department, who warned that raising the fees paid by banks could hurt their ability to make loans needed to stimulate the economic recovery.

While this story was generated in the nation's capital, it can be localized. What is the reaction of area lending institutions? Will they cushion a predicted decline in mortgage lending and homebuilding activity? What is the reaction of congressional representatives?

The Executive Agencies

The executive agencies, which possess regulatory powers and the means to assist business, also impart important economic information.

One of the most important agencies is the Department of Commerce, which encourages and promotes the nation's economic development and technological advancement. Its many divisions offer sound and factual data that affect local communities, such as information on finances, growth and production in industries.

The department provides background on companies that may be considering locating in a community, including size and organization, sales area, products, financial references and general reputation. (Banks often offer credit information on foreign firms that are proposing a U.S. location.)

The Departments of the Treasury and Energy also are good sources of economic information. The Comptroller of the Currency regulates currency and banks; the Customs Service administers the tariff laws; and the Internal Revenue Service administers most of the tax laws in this country. The Energy Department regulates firms dealing with power production and supply, and documents ownership, organization and financial structure of privately owned firms.

The Regulators

Many independent federal boards and agencies can provide documentation on the industries and individual companies they regulate, including annual reports, financial statements, economic impact statements, and records of complaints and investigations. A reporter can research firms affecting the public interest through documents and other information.

For this reason, reporters should take the time to become familiar with the various boards and agencies, their functions and operational formats.

One of the most important independent agencies is the Securities and Exchange Commission, and a knowledge of its role is indispensable to the economics reporter. Legislation creating the SEC in 1934 provided for rules to protect the public against malpractice in the securities and financial markets. A wealth of information is available to the reporter concerning many major corporations with local ties, with the information often more accessible from the agency than from the firm itself.

WASHINGTON—Federal regulators have proposed requiring corporations to spell out how much top executives are paid and to compare stock performance to similar firms for stockholders.

The Securities and Exchange Commission also proposed changes that would loosen restrictions on communications among shareholders on corporate matters.

If approved, the changes would give stockholders more details about how the people who run their companies are compensated and more freedom to speak out about how the companies are run.

Before the changes are adopted, they would be published in the *Federal Register* to give the public and business groups who may be critical of the changes an opportunity to reply.

More than 11,000 companies selling shares of stock to the public come under the scrutiny of the SEC, and many basic documents that must be filed by the firms to do business are part of the SEC's public files. Through easy-to-obtain reports such as Form 10K, the reporter can obtain a description of the company and its subsidiaries, location and description of all properties owned, major lawsuits in progress, and identification and relationships of all the officers of the firm.

Also available are possible bankruptcy proceedings; major disposition of assets; and changes in methods of doing business, indebtedness and competitive conditions.

Local firms that have a substantial effect on the community can often be monitored through these public records. Through records alone, the reporter can determine sales, revenues, sources and application of funds, gross profits and net revenue, any defaults or nonpayment of dividends, and identities of principal security holders.

The journalist can stay abreast of current developments, such as changes in control of the firm, the nature of the transaction, loans and contracts that could result in future changes, and major acquisitions and their effect on the local plant. Even the sources used to purchase such acquisitions are available. Armed with such information, the reporter is better equipped to produce accurate stories on local developments that affect the community.

Other agencies scrutinize firms doing business in specialized areas. The Federal Communications Commission, for example, requires annual reports and other documents from areas such as radio and television broadcasting; telephone and telegraph operation; two-way radio and radio operators; and satellite communication. Such firms do business via the public airwaves, and therefore are more closely monitored than many other private corporations.

The Occupational Safety and Health Review Commission makes available transcripts and decisions concerning any firm involved in interstate commerce. The National Transportation Safety Board provides safety reports on aircraft, railroads and pipelines, and reporters can obtain accident reports and hearing transcripts on agency investigations.

The reporter's access to agency information often is restricted only by time and effort. Activities in commodities trading that affect consumers as well as the firms doing business on the various trading exchanges, are regulated by the Commodity Futures Trading Commission. Registration is required for brokerage firms, including financial statements, and names and addresses of principals in the firms.

Legislative Involvement

A steady stream of legislation governing the business sector moves through Congress, and much of it has local application.

> WASHINGTON—Homeowners refinancing their mortgages are about to get the same consumer protection federal law guarantees as applicants for new home loans.
>
> The Senate has passed a bill plugging two statutory loopholes—the failure of both the Truth-in-Lending Act and mortgage settlement anti-kickback laws to cover home refinancings.

The bill requires lenders to make identical disclosures on refinancings as they do with new mortgages. With this information in hand, the reporter seeks out officials for comment. The law, one said, should eliminate "settlement day ambushes," last-minute discoveries by consumers of extra fees and costs that were not disclosed at the time of application.

Congress frequently calls on various departments and agencies to undertake specific investigations involving economic issues. The results are often newsworthy and easy to localize:

> Less than half of 1 percent of American farmland was owned by foreigners or American corporations with 5 percent foreign ownership Oct. 31, the Agriculture Department reported yesterday.
>
> In an analysis of congressionally mandated reports on foreign ownership of farmland, the department said such ownership is so small that it probably would cause few problems overall but might affect local areas where such ownership is high.

The report details areas in which such foreign ownership is heavier, such as Oregon, South Carolina, Nevada and New Mexico. Economic activity in the federal bureaucracy is so widespread that it is impossible for a single reporter to keep track of it. The key is to adapt the needs of a story to what is available among the agencies. To do this successfully, the reporter must have a handle on the agencies that affect his or her area of specific economic activity.

State and Local Government

At the state level, insurance companies, utilities, retail outlets and many other private businesses are regulated to some degree. Some state offices regulate pharmaceuticals and cosmetics; most control water and air pollution. Economic development agencies work actively to acquire industry for depressed areas of the state.

Like the national Congress, the state Legislature plays a continuing role in the business community. For example, the Florida Legislature in 1992 took a look at changes it had made in the state's Condominium Act. New legislation modified objectionable provisions in the law, introduced new regulations and imposed limitations on areas previously unregulated by the state.

Local government also has a hand in local economic developments. Many cities have established development offices to assure even economic growth, gathering local statistics and serving as a clearinghouse for information that focuses on economic issues.

> The City Council, looking for new business downtown, has doubled its allocation to the local Chamber of Commerce this year.
>
> But one council member, Hamilton Jent, complained that the $140,000 supplement approved Wednesday simply represents a taxpayer bailout of an organization that has made some poor business decisions.

While this also may be a political issue, the decaying downtown business section is on the minds of all the council members.

Many communities are establishing industrial parks, often with a combination of government and private funding, to lure industries to their area. New jobs and an improved sales climate are usually the reasons for such efforts.

The reporter must study the financing structure of the proposed park—how much public money is involved in its creation?—and determine what the park will mean to the community. Park tenants are not always successful, and the public should be kept aware of the failures as well as the successes.

> When Prime Aquaculture Inc. was sold at a forced bankruptcy auction last week, local and federal government agencies were left holding worthless documents.
>
> The Council of Governments and its Development Corporation, the major backers of the catfish farm enterprise, will lose more than $1 million, according to documents.

Also losing money were the federal Farmers Home Administration and several hundred shareholders in the business. In this case, the reporter wanted to know how and why the failure occurred—and what will be done to keep it from happening again.

The Courts

The courts are a rich source of business news. Regular checks of the local, state and federal systems are probably the province of the courts reporter, but the business desk should become involved with cases that involve commercial activity. The federal bankruptcy court is an important part of the business reporter's beat.

Dramatic increases in court filings have paralleled the increases in business failures in the early 1990s, brought on by the sluggish national economy. In 1991, 87,266 businesses failed, a significant increase over prior years, and the 1992 failure rate was 17 percent higher than that year.

In nearly every sector of the community, the reporter will find troubled corporations seeking relief, and many cases are newsworthy.

> A slumping economy and "misjudgment" has forced Winsco Builders Inc. to file for bankruptcy protection.
>
> The 20-year-old Naples building firm filed for Chapter 11 protection Tuesday, which allows a "breathing space" from 341 creditors, according to owner John Bari.
>
> Winsco has 120 days to file a reorganization plan to restructure the company and pay off the debts.

Because the firm was involved in developing a 220,000-square-foot shopping center in the county, this

will be a priority story. The 110-person staff has been cut to 25, and full recovery of the company is in doubt.

The reporter should be familiar with the various kinds of protection afforded petitioners. Chapter 11 filing provides for reorganization and payment of debts to creditors. The court separates the creditors into priority claims and nonsecured claims, all of these actions public record and available to the reporter.

Chapter 7 bankruptcy calls for liquidation of the company. Its assets are sold, and creditors are paid according to how much money is received from the sale.

Such actions in bankruptcy court often generate lawsuits in other courts, and the reporter should look for newsworthy disputes.

> The developers of Pinetree Golf Club have filed for protection from creditors under Chapter 7 of the U.S. Bankruptcy Code.
>
> Raintree Investors Inc., owners of the upscale development near Lake Nelson, also face actions in another court for breach of contract and breach of fiduciary duty.

The other action, in the Court of Common Pleas, charges that the developers diverted funds from other projects to the golf club. Before this story runs its course, other actions may be filed.

The consequences of a bankruptcy filing also are newsworthy: Details of the proposed reorganization plan are public record, and the reporter has access to volumes of specifics when they are filed.

> Caught in a cash crunch when he sought protection in 1991, Jennings listed $135 million in assets, much of it in undeveloped land, and $110 million in debts.
>
> Attorneys said Jennings' creditors are being paid 100 cents on the dollar, plus interest, Jennings' employees didn't miss a day of work, and the firm is prepared to resume full operations.

The documents will reveal, however, that Jennings lost major holdings in apartment developments valued at $25 million.

Larger stories also emerge from the bankruptcy courts. Statistics on total bankruptcies, and the corporations affected are always news.

> WASHINGTON—Establishment of a group to monitor bankruptcy fees to ensure they are not excessive and

do not threaten a company's pension benefits was announced Friday by Labor Secretary Lynn Martin.

"There is ample evidence of exorbitant fees being paid in bankruptcy cases where PBGC (Pension Benefit Guaranty Corp.) has substantial liability for pension benefits," she said.

The PBGC is the Labor Department agency responsible for guaranteeing payment of benefits for private pension plans that cover 40 million workers and are often major creditors in bankruptcy cases.

Attorney fees in bankruptcy actions also are a major concern, and the reporter should try to localize the issue. Such fees are part of the public record, and became an issue in 1993 when a proposal was made to give the U.S. Trustee's office the authority to set fee guidelines.

The reporter can compare specific court fee schedules with state rules governing attorney fees. In some states, attorneys can charge no more than $150 an hour; in others, such as New York, charges can reach $550 an hour. Fees approved by judges in an action can be checked against these standards.

Another alternative in bankruptcy actions is Chapter 13, which is used mostly by individual proprietors whose business and personal affairs are intertwined—such as painting contractors, plumbers and carpenters.

CONSUMERISM

The wire service story caught the attention of a telegraph editor, who routed it to a reporter for localizing.

WASHINGTON—Children who eat a school lunch are getting too much butter and oil with every meal, because the federal government is dumping fatty farm products on school cafeterias, a consumer group charged Thursday.

Public Voice for Food and Health Policy said the Agriculture Department has spent twice as much money on butter and cheese for the national school lunch program as on fruits and vegetables.

"School lunch program" rang a bell with the editor, and she routed the story to the education reporter. But the story easily could have been sent to the farm reporter, the food editor, the federal reporter or the business desk because it also qualified as a "consumer" issue.

Since 1979, the consumer group said, the Agriculture Department has spent $3.3 billion of its $10.2 billion budget to buy high-fat items like butter and cheese. During that time, the agency spent $1.6 billion on fruits and vegetables, nearly all of it canned.

Whoever pursues this story, it qualifies as a "consumer" issue, and the billions of tax dollars need to be translated into terms understandable to the reader or viewer.

Cafeteria officials, for example, can supply figures that will be more digestible to the reader than the "billions of dollars" detailed by federal agencies.

Stories such as these qualify as "consumer affairs," which cross several beats. The relationship between distribution of goods and services and individuals who purchase and use them constitutes the modern consumer movement. Midway between producer and consumer, the journalist functions as an honest information broker, providing perspective on a complex marketplace.

The reporter's objective is to make certain everyone receives a fair hearing—producer, distributor, marketer, sales representative, deliverer and consumer.

THE REPORTER AND THE CONSUMER MOVEMENT

Yesteryear's questions were simple: Where can I buy the product and how much does it cost?

Today's questions, from more sophisticated consumers, are more complex: How dependable is the product? How does it compare with others of its kind? How safe is it? What are the production conditions, and how do they affect me? What are the social and environmental costs involved in making the product? These questions also are pertinent as efforts are made to cut spending in government agencies that monitor the marketplace.

The issue is made more complicated because of the media's involvement in a part of the process—as an advertising and marketing vehicle for many of the products. Nonetheless, the press today is responding to this surge in information demand. One reporter's in-depth account of an aborted fraud scheme, months in the making, may be epic; another's account of a manufacturer's warning about a deficient electrical device may be a routine paragraph.

No matter what the length of the story or difficulty of assignment, consumer affairs reporting reaches every desk in today's news or broadcast office:

- A financial reporter reports the closing of three outlets for a major national hardware store chain and then discusses the problem of their customers' service warranties on recent purchases.

- The editor of the Family Living section ponders publication of a story warning of cancer-causing agents in various hormonal treatments, looking ahead to local angles and sources—physicians, pharmacists, healthcare agencies and the university's research center.

- A sports writer, noting a deficiency in quality and quantity of parking around a popular city stadium, identifies what he considers the safest, most efficient and most affordable sites. Meanwhile he prepares for his next step—discussing the issue with city officials and stadium operators.

- The travel editor investigates complaints against a travel agency operating in the community, exposing discrepancies in fees and in guarantees of resort bookings. A reporter already has checked the state attorney general's office for possible violations of law and other agencies for their fee schedules.

- The court reporter covers a series of consumer complaints originating in small claims court, resulting in editorials on the newspaper's opinion page that the municipal court system be updated. Many consumer stories conclude in the judicial process and wind up in the hands of the court reporter.

- In the case of the butter and oil story, the education reporter, with help from nutritionists, produces a comprehensive story on food values in local school lunch programs.

Historical Dimensions

It was only when the whole ham was spoiled that it came into the department of Elzbieta. Cut up by the two-thousand-revolutions-a-minute flyers, and mixed with half a ton of other meat, no odor that ever was in a ham could make any difference. There was never the least attention paid to what was cut up for sausage; there would come all the way back from Europe old sausage that had been rejected, and that was moldy and white. It would be dosed with borax and glycerine, and dumped into the hoppers, and made over again for home consumption.

Most consumer historians date the consumer protection movement from these and like passages written by Upton Sinclair in *The Jungle*, published in 1906 and possessing a fiery strength that lit up the country. Sinclair's novel about the Chicago stockyards was a smashing success. For all its melodrama, the book carried with it the conviction that all the injustices actually occurred, if not to the immigrant hero, then to other mistreated workers of that period.

The Jungle was not designed for reading at the breakfast table. Sinclair, who as a young writer spent weeks roaming the stockyards, wearing old clothes and carrying a workman's dinner pail, designed his novel as a potent propaganda tool. Few politicians could withstand the angry, naked words as their constituents read the stomach-turning accounts of how their main courses were being prepared.

The graphic passages galvanized Congress in 1906 and led to enactment of the first Pure Food and Drug Act, which provided the public with limited protection from impure foods and drugs. Sinclair's expose of the meat packing industry and the subsequent uproar was the opening chapter in the battle for consumer protection.

The 1906 legislation stimulated growth of consumer groups—called leagues, committees and clubs—and encouraged further reform, but weaknesses in legislation gradually brought on a lethargy that lasted into the 1920s.

It fell to two other writer-researchers, Stuart Chase and F.J. Schlink, to again galvanize the public and politicians into action in 1927.

In their book *Your Money's Worth*, they pictured the consumer scene as a "wonderland of conflicting claims, bright promises, fancy packages, soaring words and almost impenetrable ignorance." Chase and Schlink attacked high-pressure salesmanship and called for scientific testing and establishment of product standards to protect consumers.

In contrast to Sinclair's novel, *Your Money's Worth* was readable nonfiction produced by a certified public accountant and an engineer-physicist. Their approach was factual and their material sounded much like a reporter's investigative story might today:

> The firm (Mack, Miller Candle Co.) sold as "beeswax altar candles" a candle containing less than 50 percent of beeswax, although the practice of the Catholic Church required more than a 50 percent beeswax content. Analysis by the Bureau of Standards showed that the company's candles contained only 11.5 percent of beeswax.

In their chapter on adulteration and misrepresentation, the authors covered dozens of examples, from cotton blankets labeled as "woolnap" but containing no wool, to firms selling pure food gelatin in which glue had been substituted for gelatin. Much of their information came from findings by federal agencies and from congressional hearings.

Chase and Schlink checked the findings of the National Fire Protection Association and reported:

> Four worthless and unsafe electric irons selling for $1.00 each were found to burn out in from 3 to 35 minutes. 15,000 dozen of these were imported by one New York dealer.

Your Money's Worth focused a discontent among consumers into new product-testing laboratories and by the early 1930s led to updating of the Food and Drug Act.

After World War II, there was a new upsurge in consumer protection interest, and consumer groups mobilized against product problems. President Kennedy laid out a "Consumer's Bill of Rights" in 1962:

• The right to safety, to be protected against goods hazardous to health or life.

• The right to be informed, to be protected against fraudulent, deceitful or grossly misleading information, advertising, labeling or other practices and to be given the facts needed to make an informed choice.

• The right to be assured access to a variety of products and services at competitive prices; in those industries in which government regulations are substituted, an assurance of satisfactory quality and service at fair prices.

• The right to be heard, to be assured that consumer interests will receive full and sympathetic consideration in the formulation of government policy.

Development of consumer programs was spurred by pressure from organized consumer groups, and legislation was enacted requiring that drugs be proven effective and approved by the federal government before they could be marketed. Subsequent administrations

---

BOX 15–1

A Consumer Checklist

✳✳✳

The reporter should monitor such special publications as *Home Furnishings Daily*, *The Wall Street Journal*, *Changing Times*, *Consumer Reports* and *Money*. The *Federal Register* lists regulations about to go into effect, and many federal agencies publish newsletters on consumer affairs, such as the Federal Trade Commission, which publishes *FTC News*.

The American Council on Consumer Interests produces a newsletter, and the Agriculture Department publishes *Farm Economics Review*. Many attorneys general and consumer affairs offices at the state level produce bulletins warning of shady practices, and other agencies offer guides to use of public services.

Trade associations' publications also can be useful in researching business and consumer stories. The *Encyclopedia of Associations*, available in most libraries, is a guide to national and international organizations—including trade, business and commercial. Updated annually, it contains addresses, telephone numbers, membership identification, publications produced and newsletters.

continued to reflect the new consumer awareness: "truth-in-packaging" legislation in 1966, a National Commission on Product Safety in 1967, and a Consumer Product Safety Act in 1971 that established an independent commission with power to set and enforce safety standards for thousands of household, school and recreation products.

Consumer advocate groups sprang up in the wake of publication of Ralph Nader's book *Unsafe at Any Speed*, published in 1965. Nader charged that the high incidence of death and injury on U.S. highways was largely the fault of automakers who sacrificed safety for styling in the interest of higher profits.

By 1970, Congress had enacted a national traffic and motor vehicle safety act, a wholesome-meat act, a natural gas pipeline safety act, an occupational safety and health act, and truth-in-lending legislation.

Today the Office of Consumer Affairs, operating within the Department of Health and Human Services, analyzes and coordinates federal activities in the field of consumer protection.

Six Viewpoints

Nowhere will the reporter deal with sources offering greater divergence in their perception of the marketplace than on the consumer affairs beat. The point of view shifts with the individual:

- The **householder** wants assurance that a just-purchased item has been carefully tested.

- The **store owner** recognizes this, but has a different priority: selling enough of these items to cover the cost of doing business and make a reasonable profit.

- The **advertising sales representative** may be sympathetic to the householder's demands but is focused on how to help the store owner create a strong demand for the product.

- The **manufacturer** wants to produce the product cheaply enough and in sufficient quantity to assure a profit.

- The **consumer advocate**, persistent and sometimes strident, wants assurance of the product's quality and safety and a fair sales approach.

- The **government official**, armed with a directive to assure quality, safety and performance, cannot promise it absolutely without an army of agency inspectors.

The reporter must see the marketplace through the eyes of all these, and add an additional ingredient—the impartial communications link.

A news story may alert the public to a problem, but it also runs the risk of injuring someone's business, sometimes unfairly, or of wrongly impugning the motives of a professional group.

The reporter who digs up unsavory but accurate accounts of a fraudulent roofing contractor must be sure not to tarnish the entire roofing industry in the story.

Another reporter uncovers details of questionable real estate transactions by a broker and follows it through its resolution before the state Real Estate Board. The story about the revocation of the broker's license should reflect the fact that it is a specific incident, not necessarily an industrywide approach.

Demands on the Reporter

With so many voices clamoring to be heard, the consumer affairs reporter might find it difficult to decide what to cover, and when. Following are some challenges the reporter faces:

Reluctant Sources.   The target of an investigation is uncooperative and threatening, drying up information pipelines and tying up the reporter's time in trying to pursue a legitimate story.

Every effort should be made to convince the subject that it is in everyone's best interest to clear the air with a news account. Failing that, the reporter can turn to agencies and other sources that may have information relating to the story.

While government agencies are helpful, offices are often located in other cities, and telephone contact is not always effective in obtaining detailed information. Some officials may be difficult to reach and indifferent to requests for information. But a good reporter refuses to give up.

Private sources often offer information to the consumer affairs reporter not easily obtained elsewhere.

For example, the Association of Home Appliance Manufacturers compiles product performance reports that show how products of various manufacturers measure up to uniform standards.

Testing New Ground.   Traditional beats at least offer the reporter some patterns, but consumer affairs reporting often tests new ground. The question, "Is there a story here?" must be answered carefully.

The business sector encourages upbeat news stories, but the consumer affairs reporter is often cast in the role of the "heavy" because the stories are often confrontational. A series detailing the incidence of warranty complaints to the Better Business Bureau is not likely to make the business community happy. Neither is a story that examines the shortage of downtown parking, for it could send potential customers to the suburban shopping malls. What the consumer sees as a positive and productive story may threaten the business community.

Advertising departments of newspapers and broadcast outlets sometimes come under pressure from retail outlets, lending institutions and public utilities. While pressure from special interests should never dictate news coverage, the reporter is well-advised to solicit the advice of his or her editor on potentially controversial consumer stories. It is most important that the reporter have the backing of the news organization. Many consumer stories will be difficult if not impossible to cover without such support.

The Reporter as Translator.   The consumer affairs reporter must wrestle with the problem of translating highly technical material into the language of laypersons. Coping with information on musical "woofers and tweeters" can be as complicated as a pharmaceutical development requiring the posting of names of generic drugs. Similar problems exist in the "legalese" in the small print of a product warranty.

The reporter should not be shy about asking questions of experts. It's far better to display one's ignorance before one expert than in a story sent to thousands of readers or viewers.

Fairness.   Reporters and editors are constantly asking themselves if they are being fair in pursuing a controversial story?

A reporter interviewed a former used-car salesman who shared some of his tricks of the trade: stuffing banana peels into axles to disguise rear-end noises; hiring a man to set back mileage figures on speedometers for $10 a car; and warming up engines each morning to assure they would start right up.

The reporter believed that the story, called "Confessions of a Used-Car Salesman," represented a sincere effort to alert the public to unscrupulous vendors, but the army of used car dealers who descended on the newspaper did not feel the same way.

Reviewing the problem, the editor listed the basic errors in reporting the story:

- We placed too much faith in the word of one person, however expert he may have sounded.
- We were lulled by a naive belief that if it's good for the consumer, how much can it hurt?
- We didn't give other used-car dealers a chance to respond to charges from one of their former salesmen.

Such broad-brush consumer reporting is unfair and should be avoided.

Potential for Defamation.   Consumer reporting faces a somewhat greater risk of defamation than many other public affairs beats. An expert's opinion that training procedures at a local school of cosmetology appear to be "incompetent" should be edited as closely as another's comment that a recent business transaction seemed "unprofessional."

Here are some other "red flag" words and phrases that could endanger an otherwise impartial consumer affairs story—and the interests of the public—unless thoroughly documented:

altered records	sharp dealing or
adulteration of products	wheeler-dealer
cheats or cheating	short in accounts
collusion	shyster
corruption	smooth and tricky
credit risk	sold out to a rival
defaults	swindle
false weights	unethical
fraud or fraudulent	unworthy of credit
illegitimate	

Sources, Contacts and 'Expert' Advice

Consumer reporting helps people cope with changes in buying practices, business practices and legislation affecting those practices. Out of this variety flows contact with many levels of citizens, corporate enterprises, government officials and private organizations. The reporter must be able to relate to sources at every level:

The Consumer.   Readers and viewers will identify with the issues in a story and often contact reporters to discuss their concerns. It might be merely to air a personal complaint, but often the telephone call, letter or personal visit will open the door to a problem that leads to a major story. A complaint about the practices of one small loan firm, for example, may lead to exposure of a communitywide problem and subsequent legislative action.

Media Ombudsmen.   The average reader or viewer may subscribe to a broader definition of "consumer affairs reporting" than the journalist. A review of a visit to a restaurant, concert or movie provides consumers with information enabling them to make intelligent choices in spending money.

The same can be said of the numerous ombudsman services adopted by newspapers and broadcast outlets, often cast as "action lines" or "consumer hotline" columns. To consumers, these question-and-answer columns often hit much closer to home than major news developments.

Federal, State and Local Agencies.   Whether information is obtained from the federal government's Consumer Product Safety Commission or from the local Better Business Bureau, the "official" imprimateur of the agency offers a safe umbrella for the reporter.

Any number of state agencies have a hand in consumer protection: State property commissions, which investigate land-grabbing schemes; legal firms; police agencies; and agriculture departments, to name a few.

> Meat quality in the state has improved in recent years, and artificial preservatives have largely been eliminated from meat, an Agriculture Department official says.
>
> Of 885 meat samples taken by employees of the department's consumer protection division last year, only 37 violations were found, G. Harold Arms, director of the division, said Monday.
>
> "None of the violations involved preservatives," he said. "We used to find preservatives all the time, but we broke that up."

Many communities today have some form of local consumer protection agency, and their officials are key contacts. Such agencies can point a reporter to consumer-oriented stories that otherwise might never see the light of day.

> If someone offers you a "free vacation" in Las Vegas, the best thing to do is call his bluff.
>
> Bogus certificates for three-day/two-night vacations in the gambling city are apparently being sold throughout the area, says Jon Reed, director of the Consumer Protection Office.

While law enforcement aspects of such consumer protection agencies provide the most dramatic stories, their education function can trigger many routine but important stories. A consumer credit counseling service may offer assistance to anyone who asks for it, for example. Cities have established agencies with different functions: reporting services, complaint resolution offices, and even courtlike agencies that deal more efficiently with the problems of the marketplace.

> The Community Service Council has proposed a new system to provide the public with a faster and easier way to settle grievances against merchants and manufacturers.
>
> The system would provide for establishment of consumer-claim centers around the city, with officers empowered to award quick judgments and pay settlements to people with legitimate complaints.
>
> Because the money would come from a government-organized fund, the problem of collecting Small Claims Court judgments from recalcitrants would be overcome, says a CSC official.

Consumer Advocates.   Consumer advocate offices have been built into state government systems, and are helpful to reporters in identifying consumer issues. The state attorney general often acts as consumer advocate, but many states have a special office to handle the responsibility.

Consumer officials and hired experts take the public's part in hearings before the Legislature, and rate cases heard before state public utility commissions.

State Consumer Advocate Steve Hamm criticized the state's Mobile Home Licensing Board on Thursday after it briefly relicensed a salesman who admitted he had faked bank documents for buyers.

The board renewed Glen Conway's sales license Wednesday—even though board members knew he had pleaded guilty two months ago to wire fraud in mobile home sales.

However, the board rescinded the license Thursday after Hamm demanded an explanation.

At the state level, the focus of consumer agencies is usually on protection rather than on education. New legislation puts enforcement teeth into regulations.

Thirty Instant Muffler shops in the area have been taken to court by Attorney General William C. Brown on charges they violated state consumer laws while doing repair work on cars.

Brown filed a $700,000 lawsuit in Common Pleas Court yesterday, saying the shops charged customers for unnecessary repairs or services.

Problems handled by the attorney general's office include disputes involving credit agencies, most business establishments, lending institutions and mail-order companies.

Advocates see their function specifically as protecting the consumer, and most are vigorously committed to their cause. Almost an entire cottage industry has grown up around state and federal advocacy groups. And while their information may be regarded as "expert," the reporter must remember that they usually provide only one side of the story. They can be helpful, however, in broadening the reporter's knowledge of an issue.

WASHINGTON—Motorists spend about $3 billion more than they should on gasoline each year, mainly because of advertisements that make them think pricey, high-octane fuels are better, the consumer group Public Citizen said Wednesday.

"The ads suggest that high-octane grades are better for your car than regular gasoline," Public Citizen President Joan Claybrook said. "This is simply not true."

Many stories are produced through advocacy groups, such as the Center for Science in the Public Interest, the Committee on Children's Processed Foods, Consumer Federation of America and the National Association of Consumer Agency Administrators.

As always, the reporter should balance any news account with comments from trade associations that represent another side of the issue—the Grocery Manufacturers of America, for example, or the American Petroleum Institute, both of which represent business interests.

The 'Experts.'   Nearly everyone has an opinion, and the job of the reporter is to locate those who are really qualified. Experts at universities or government agencies usually can be considered impartial and unaligned sources in a dispute and add an extra dimension to a news story.

Physical education experts might help settle an argument over the usefulness of a new exercise product on the market that "guarantees" weight loss. A nutritionist or home economist often can provide sound information on a new foodstuff ingredient.

Analysis of economic trends usually falls to an expert in a university's business or economics department. Other areas in which expertise can be found include schools of pharmacology, accounting, health services, nursing, marketing or management, science, and even music.

The Reporter at Work

The consumer affairs reporter need not be a super-sleuth, lurking in back alleys for scandalous "scoops" that will shake the business community to the core. By simply contacting local experts, the reporter can produce "how to" stories that will touch a responsive chord in most readers or viewers. Some examples:

- How to cope with door-to-door sales representatives.
- How to get the most for your medical dollar.
- How to go to small claims court for relief.
- How to reduce your grocery bill while continuing to eat well.
- How to buy a used car with some assurance of safety.
- How to find mortgage money for a home.

These examples and their variations are basic "pocketbook" stories, but each offers the reporter an

```
┌─────────────────────────────────────────┐
│              BOX 15–2                     │
│          ─────────────                    │
│         Mission of the Reporter           │
│                                           │
│              ✳ ✳ ✳                        │
│                                           │
│  In 1926, a New York advertising agency   │
│  proclaimed:                              │
│      "We who have to bring in the busi-   │
│  ness must get out before the beloved     │
│  customer and shout, search, halloo,      │
│  promise, concede, coax, be funny,        │
│  thump, seek, knock, punch and GET the    │
│  order!"                                  │
│      That was the salesman's mission in   │
│  the 1920s. But nearly 70 years later,    │
│  the reporter's mission remains the       │
│  same: Put the "business" in perspec-     │
│  tive so that the shouts, halloos, knocks │
│  and promises can be more easily ana-     │
│  lyzed by the consumer.                   │
└─────────────────────────────────────────┘
```

opportunity to explore a specific area that often yields other information the reader or viewer can use.

While researching the small claims court story, for example, interviews with attorneys, court officials and litigants may uncover reasons *why* people go to court, as well as *how*.

In researching methods for getting the most out of the medical dollar, the reporter also may determine *why* medical care is so expensive and *who* actually determines how much people pay.

Ideas for consumer-related stories come from many sources. Not all wire service stories reach publication, and a telegraph editor should be encouraged to pass on discarded consumer affairs material. Many newspapers publish in-depth stories on specific issues, and exchange papers should be checked regularly for material that may be relevant to the community.

✳ ✳ ✳

A BUSINESS GLOSSARY

These terms are common to the economic community. Areas such as accounting, the stock exchanges and commodity markets require further refinement of the journalist's vocabulary.

AMORTIZATION: Gradual payoff of a long-term debt by several different methods.

ARTICLES OF INCORPORATION: The charter granted by a state authorizing a corporation to conduct business. It provides information on the incorporators, purpose, place of business and sometimes capitalization of the firm.

ASSETS: The published value of a company's resources, usually in terms of dollars.

AUDIT (INTERNAL): An audit conducted by employees to determine whether internal control procedures are working. **External audits** are conducted by outside accountants and government auditors.

BALANCE SHEET: A formal statement detailing the financial status of a company at a given time.

BANK RESERVE: The cash that a bank is required by law to maintain in proportion to its total deposits.

BANKRUPTCY: Abandonment of a business and assignment of its assets to its creditors, thereby discharging the operator from future liability. A petition for bankruptcy filed in the courts is voluntary when filed by the debtor and involuntary when filed by creditors.

BEAR: One who sells securities or commodities with the expectation of buying later at a lower price; the securities or commodity market is said to be a bear market when there is a downward trend in prices and the influence of bears predominates. See **Bull**.

BID AND ASKED PRICES: Prices offered by prospective buyers and prices asked by prospective sellers, the difference representing the spread in which sales are usually consummated.

BLUE SKY LAWS: Legislation regulating the sale of securities to protect the investing public.

BOND: A formal certificate of debt, usually long-term, with the borrower promising to pay the lender of funds a specified amount of interest at specified times; governments as well as private enterprises float bond issues for many different reasons; the bond markets are the source of interaction for these negotiations, usually in the form of bids for the bonds; bonds are rated by experts on the basis of their soundness, with interest rates varying on the basis of "prime," "high-grade," "sound," "medium-grade," etc.

BOOK VALUE: The probable value of a stock at liquidation. **Market value** represents the selling value of a stock at any given time, taking into consideration present and prospective income and dividend payments. **Par value** is the monetary value assigned to each share of stock in the charter of a corporation.

BROKER: A person dealing in purchase and sale of securities or commodities, with activities regulated by the Securities and Exchange Commission.

BULL: One who purchases securities or commodities in anticipation of a rise in their prices; a rising market is a bull market. See **Bear**.

CAPITALIZATION: The capital structure of a company; the sum of all of the securities it has issued, including the book value of its stocks and bonds and its surplus.

CASH FLOW: The aggregate of the depreciation taken by a firm (or the depletion in the extracting industries) and the retained earnings in a specified period. Cash flow enhances a firm's ability to expand operations or modernize without having to borrow money or increase its long-term debt.

CHARTER: Authorization through a written document to create and organize a corporation.

CLEARINGHOUSE: A central agency, usually voluntary, for collection, classification and distribution of information; banks maintain a local clearinghouse to facilitate daily exchange of checks, drafts and notes.

COMMERCIAL BANK: A bank that accepts deposits that are payable on demand and makes short-term loans to depositors and others; such a bank makes a commercial loan, usually repayable in less than a year. See **Savings bank**.

COMMERCIAL PAPER: Short-term negotiable instruments, such as notes and bills, handled by banks.

COMMODITY MARKET: Organized trading in specific commodities, such as agricultural products, precious metals and other articles of commerce; commodity exchanges and boards of trade in major cities around the world, deal in **Futures**—products that will be deliverable at later dates.

CONSOLIDATED STATEMENT: A financial statement itemizing the operations of a parent company and its subsidiaries.

CONSOLIDATION: The merger of two or more corporations.

CORPORATION: A body formed and authorized by law to act as a single entity, although composed of one or more people; it can engage only in activities specified by its charter or certificate of incorporation and is a legal entity, separate from the owners; a corporation makes possible accumulation of large amounts of capital, is highly permanent since its stock can be transferred and offers its owners limited liability for corporate debts. See **Partnership**.

DEBENTURE: A long-term bond secured only by the assets and general credit of a corporation rather than by a mortgage; repayment is sometimes contingent upon the profits of the firm.

DEBITS AND CREDITS: See **Double-entry accounting**.

DEFLATION: A period of generally declining prices. **Inflation** is a period of rising prices.

DEPLETION: Exhaustion of a wasting asset or natural resource, such as oil; the government offers **Depletion allowances** to encourage research for new sources and methods of extraction.

DEPRECIATION: Gradual reduction in the value of an asset due to physical wear, obsolescence or decline in the market value; the cost of an asset is **Amortized** over the period of its benefit.

DISCOUNT RATE: The interest rate used by banks to convert future payments to present values; the rate varies with conditions in the money market.

DIVIDEND: Distribution of the earnings of a corporation to its owners; earnings may be paid in the form of a cash dividend, a stock dividend, or with other securities, known as dividend in kind.

DOUBLE-ENTRY ACCOUNTING: The system of recording the transactions of a corporation that maintains the equality of the accounting equation; the **Debit**, or expense of doing business, is listed on the left-hand side of the account; the **Credit**, in the form of revenue or net worth, is listed on the right-hand side of the account, with the resulting totals equaling each other.

DUMPING: The sale of goods abroad at prices lower than those charged in the country in which they were produced.

EXCHANGE: A transaction between one entity and another, technically a reciprocal transfer; the term also refers to a market where transactions occur, such as the New York Stock Exchange.

EXCHANGE RATE: The price of one country's currency in relation to another country's currency.

EXCISE TAX: A tax on the manufacture, sale or consumption of goods produced.

FAIR MARKET PRICE OR VALUE: The price or value determined by a willing buyer and a willing seller, each acting in his or her own interest.

FAIR TRADE PRICE: A minimum sale price for a product, determined by agreement between manufacturer and seller or distributor; illegal in some states.

FIXED ASSETS: Assets of a relatively permanent nature, such as real estate or production machinery.

FIXED LIABILITIES: Long-term loans, such as bonds and debentures.

FLOAT: (v.) To sell on the market a new issue of securities.

FLOAT: (n.) The checks that are in transit between deposit in one bank and collection in a second.

FUTURES TRADING: Trading of various commodities, such as wheat, corn, beef and other products, and providing for delivery at some future date, usually one to eight months; also known as **Contract trading**.

HEDGE: The purchase or sale of one security or commodity in an effort to protect against possible loss in another transaction.

HOLDING COMPANY: A company that confines its activities to owning stock in other companies and supervising management of those firms; a **Conglomerate** operates dissimilar lines of business.

INCOME: The excess of revenues (and other gains) over expenses (and losses) for a specified period;

the earnings per share is usually shown on an income statement.

INDUSTRIALS: The market term used to designate securities of industrial corporations; the Dow Jones Industrial Average is the best-known market indicator.

INSOLVENCY: Inability to pay debts when they come due; a company may be insolvent even though assets exceed liabilities.

INSTALLMENT: Partial payment of a debt or the collection of a receivable, usually in fulfillment of a contract.

INTANGIBLE ASSET: A nonphysical asset such as a copyright, a patent, a trademark, goodwill, a lease or franchise, exploration permit, an import or export permit, or any other right that gives a company a preferred position in the marketplace. **Tangible assets** have a physical form.

INTEREST: The charge for using money, usually expressed in an annual rate.

INTERLOCKING DIRECTORATE: Individuals serving on the boards of directors of two or more corporations doing business with one another.

INVENTORY: Raw materials, supplies, work in progress and finished goods on hand that serve as a balance in an asset account.

INVESTMENT: An expenditure to acquire assets to produce revenue; when acquired, the investment becomes an asset.

INVESTMENT BANKER: One who assists in financing long-term capital improvements for business.

INVESTMENT TAX CREDIT: A reduction in tax liability granted by the federal government to firms that purchase new equipment.

INVESTMENT TRUST: A company whose income is derived solely from the holding of securities of other corporations.

INVOICE: A document detailing a sale or purchase transaction.

KITING: The illegal practice of taking advantage of the float, or the time that elapses between the deposit of a check in one bank and its collection in another.

LEASE: A contract calling for the user to pay the owner for use of an asset; a cancelable lease allows the lessee to cancel at any time.

LIABILITY: A legal obligation to pay a definite amount in return for a current benefit.

LIEN: The right of one person to satisfy a claim against another by holding the other's property as security.

LIQUID: Having a substantial but unspecified amount of working capital, which may be cash, current marketable securities or current receivables; a company closes its business by selling its assets and liquidating.

MERGER: The forming of a single economic entity from two or more corporations.

MORTGAGE: Conveyance of property as security for payment of a debt or a loan and becoming void upon payment or performance.

MUNICIPAL BOND: A bond issued by a city, county, state or other public body to raise money; interest on such bonds is usually exempt from federal income taxes and some state taxes; often referred to as "tax exempts."

MUTUAL FUND: An investment company, regulated by the federal government, that issues its own stock to the public and uses the proceeds to invest in securities of other companies.

NEGOTIABLE: Checks, notes and stocks that legally can be transferred by endorsement.

NET INCOME: The excess of all revenues and gains over all expenses and losses for a given period. **Net assets** are the owners' equity.

OFFERING: Putting a security or commodity up for sale.

OPERATING EXPENSES: Expenses incurred in the ordinary activities of a corporation, including selling, general and administrative expenses, and excluding costs of goods sold, interest and income tax expenses.

OPTION: A legal right to purchase something within a specified time at a specified price.

OUTSTANDING: Something that is unpaid or uncollected.

OVER-THE-COUNTER: Negotiated transactions of securities as opposed to the auction procedure used in organized exchanges.

PARTNERSHIP: A contractual agreement between two or more persons to do business as a legal entity, with each assuming responsibility for the liabilities and conduct of the business; in a **Proprietorship**, an individual takes responsibility for the business. See **Corporation**.

PATENT: An exclusive right granted by the federal government which excludes others from manufacturing, using or selling a claimed design, product or plan.

POINT: With reference to a stock, a point is $1; to a bond, a point is $10.

PRIME RATE: The rate for loans charged by commercial banks to their preferred customers, their best risks.

PROFIT AND LOSS STATEMENT: See **Income**.

PROXY: Written authorization given by one person to another so that the second can act for the first.

PURCHASE ORDER: Written authorization to a seller to deliver goods, with payment to be made later.

QUOTATION: The bid and asked prices of a stock at a given time; the **Closing quotation** is the final price for the trading period.

RECEIVABLE: In accounting, any collectible, whether or not it is due.

RECEIVERSHIP: Operation of a business by a court-appointed officer pending disposition of litigation affecting the firm.

REGISTRATION STATEMENT: A statement required by most corporations wishing to issue securities to the public; the Securities and Exchange Act requires the statement, which discloses financial data and other items of interest.

REORGANIZATION OR RECAPITALIZATION: A major change in the structure of a corporation that leads to changes in the rights, interests and implied ownership of the security holders; often approved by a court to forestall bankruptcy.

RESEARCH AND DEVELOPMENT: Part of the cost of doing business; research seeks new knowledge that will be useful in creating or improving a product, process or service; development translates the research findings into a new or improved product, process or service.

ROYALTY: Compensation for use of property, often copyrighted material, natural resources or a specially produced product.

SAVINGS BANK: A financial institution whose basic function is to gather savings and invest them in long-range investments; savings and loan associations are nonprofit mortgage banking institutions designed to promote home ownership. See **Commercial bank**.

SEVERENCE PAY: A monetary payment, usually based on years of service, to a worker whose employment is terminated.

SINKING FUND: Earnings earmarked for reduction of long-term debt.

SPECULATOR: An investor who seeks early and substantial returns, usually with an element of risk.

SPOT TRADING: Trading in the commodity market calling for immediate delivery; also called **Cash trading**.

STOCK: A holding in a corporation, attested to by issued certificates of ownership. **Preferred stock** is a claim on income or assets of a firm after bondholders have been satisfied but before common stock claims are satisfied; a **Stock dividend** is paid or distributed to existing shareholders; the right to purchase a specified number of shares of stock at a specified time is called a **Stock option**; a **Stock split** occurs when the number of common shares is increased without additional capital contributions by shareholders; the places in which organized security trading is conducted are called **Stock exchanges**.

SUBSIDIARY: A company owned by another that owns at least 50 percent of the voting stock.

TRADEMARK: Distinctive words or symbols that uniquely identify a corporation's product or service; the trademark right excludes others from making use of them.

TREASURY BOND: A bond issued by a corporation, then reacquired. **Treasury stock** is capital stock issued and then reacquired by the corporation, resulting in a reduction of stockholders' equity.

TREASURY CERTIFICATES, NOTES AND BILLS: The federal government borrows money for specified periods of time through issuance of these documents.

VOTING TRUST: Stockholders agree to deposit their shares with a trustee, giving the trustee voting rights for a specific length of time, but retaining other rights.

WORKING CAPITAL: The excess of a corporation's current assets over its total current liabilities.

***

SUGGESTED READINGS

Kirsch, Donald. *Financial and Economic Journalism*. New York: New York University Press, 1978.

Helpful chapters include Chapter 2, "Creation and Growth of a Corporation"; Chapter 3, "The 10 Key Stories"; Chapter 4, "The Interpretation and Meaning of Economic Indicators"; and Chapter 5, "The Interpretation and Meaning of Financial Indicators."

Merrill Lynch. *How to Read a Financial Report*.

A good primer for understanding a profit and loss statement and detailed financial reports.

Silk, Leonard. *Economics in Plain English*. New York: Simon & Schuster, 1979.

Chapter 16

Covering the Work Force

In an East Coast city, a ragged line of men carrying signs breaks up. Several scream obscenities at a television crew atop a truck as it cruises past the entrance to the food warehouse. The work stoppage has not been authorized by the union representing the workers, and nerves are raw on the disorganized picket line set up overnight.

The communications breakdown between the workers and the company is total. The TV reporter later tells her news director, "The feeling out there at the warehouse is just plain mean."

In a Midwest city, 14 men, distinguished only by the color and cut of their business suits, file into a conference room at a downtown hotel and take seats on either side of a long mahogany table. On one side are executives representing major trucking firms. On the other are representatives of union drivers seeking a new contract to replace the one about to expire.

The talks are in their final stages as negotiators hammer out an agreement that will satisfy the men in the suits—and those they represent.

Between these dissimilar scenarios lies the bulk of employer-employee activity that constitutes the "labor beat" for the mass media today. Coverage of union activity is only part of the work force story.

Issues with far-reaching implications include workplace safety and health, job security and automation in industry, pay scales, equal job opportunity, incentives and benefits, and the nature and ethic of the work force itself.

CHANGES IN THE WORKPLACE

The labor beat, an old-fashioned term, is in a state of flux today, creating new challenges for the press. On the one hand, some major segments of organized labor are falling apart: other segments are flexing their muscles and gathering power.

Organized labor, weakened by massive job losses in manufacturing, battered further by recessionary cutbacks in health care and virtually deprived of the power of the strike, is in trouble and knows it.

The *Journal of Commerce* cites shifts in production, the flow of manufacturing jobs to Mexico and other developing countries, and changes in U.S. labor laws as some of the reasons.

"Obviously you have to start with the loss of jobs to the global economy," said former Secretary of Labor William J. Usery. "The despondent thing is, so many jobs have been lost for good, or at least for a very long time."

But while there is attrition in this segment of the labor force, the power of the new public employee unions is changing the face of employer-employee relationships in many areas. Peter Schrag, an editor with *The Sacramento Bee* in California, wrote in 1992 about the increased power wielded by organized employee groups at the state and local levels.

Put most simply, California has entered a period of chronic struggle between a gridlocked and incompre-

hensible government and the power of the public employee unions and other interest groups that are rapidly replacing an alienated citizenry as the effective rulers of this state.

While Schrag's observations may seem overstated to some, there is no question about the power held by the public employee unions, and their effect on the layers of overlapping governments handling California's budget reforms.

The beneficiaries of this system are the groups with the power and expertise to replace the alienated citizenry: the California Teachers Association, the police and fire-fighters' unions, the prison guards' union, the trial lawyers, the insurance industry.

Regional problems such as this are creating new challenges for reporters. Other workplace changes are also affecting the way reporters approach their job.

The Decline of Organized Labor

Union membership has been dropping since 1945, when its share of the U.S. labor force was 35.5 percent. In 1990, union membership stood at 16,960,000, or 16.4 percent of the work force, according to the Department of Labor.

But despite the small numbers, organized labor plays a major role in enhancing the visibility of all the men and women in the workplace. Union pressure keeps the spotlight on safety, health, benefit and pension issues.

There are also enough unions scattered through various industries to maintain a formidable presence when negotiations begin on a new contract.

SPRING HILL, Tenn.—A national shortage of General Motors Corp.'s popular Saturn cars loomed Tuesday after workers struck at an Ohio factory that supplies parts. Saturn is losing 1,000 cars for each day of the United Auto Workers walkout in Lordstown, Ohio.

Effects of strikes such as these have a ripple effect through the major industries. Despite such visible reminders of former union strength, however, labor unions continue to lose organizing battles, particularly in the South.

LUGOFF, S.C.—The United Auto Workers union, which successfully organized workers two years ago at

Mack Trucks Inc. in Winnsboro, failed Thursday in its bid to organize one of Mack's principal suppliers. Employees at Dana Corp., which produces chassis for Mack, rejected UAW representation by more than 5–1.

Cheers and applause erupted outside Dana's employee entrance after the announcement.

"This is the best company there is and we don't need a union," said employee Karen Johnson. "We've got good pay, good benefits, good working conditions and good people."

The Rise of Public Employee Unions

DETROIT—School and union leaders reached a contract agreement Saturday to end a 27-day teachers' strike that has kept 168,000 students out of class.

The agreement was announced after four hours of negotiations between the school board and the Detroit Federation of Teachers, which represents 10,500 teachers.

Unionization of public employees has added a new dimension to the labor beat, complicating the traditional employer-employee relationship. Teachers, police officers, firefighters, postal workers, deputy

sheriffs and refuse removal workers, to name a few, have joined other organized wage earners in the private sector.

Some of these units refer to themselves as "associations," others as "action committees," and many prefer the traditional designation of "union." Through these groups, public employees bargain over wages, working conditions, benefits and other issues, and occasionally engage in work stoppages against the public that employs them.

Teachers have left the classrooms for the picket line, firefighters have stood by while houses and business establishments burned. Hospital workers have demonstrated and police have staged "sickouts," staying off the job and putting pressure on officials to settle contract disputes. The effect has been traumatic on those accustomed to traditional public employee loyalty.

Growth of Regulatory Agencies

Emerging protective and restrictive labor legislation at the federal and local levels affects virtually the entire U.S. work force. While unions enjoy legal status as a

Workers displaced by job cuts at a defense plant attend a career retraining course financed by a federal grant. A tight economy and widespread layoffs in some industries in the early 1990s forced many workers to relocate or change careers.
Photo by William Burrows, courtesy of The Day, New London, Conn.

BOX 16-1

Why Focus on Labor?

✳✳✳

Covering the business community is an all-encompassing effort. But while corporate actions regularly draw news coverage, it is equally important to focus on job holders themselves, both in the private and public sector.

Labor unions—groups of workers organized for the general benefit of their members—are the beginning point for a reporter covering the work force. But while unions constitute only a small proportion of the total work force, their activity and visibility as the voice of millions of salaried and hourly wage earners is unquestioned.

Furthermore, they are a formidable pressure group in this country. At nearly every political level, their action committees carry weight.

Joseph L. Powell, state president of the AFL-CIO, appeared before the Senate Finance Committee

yesterday to urge removal of food from the current 6 percent sales tax.

"It's a dollars and cents proposition with the workers," Powell warned. "Legislators are going to have to give them relief in this election year."

As a pressure group, organized labor wins as many battles as it loses. Moreover, its victories and defeats nearly always affect unorganized workers, as well.

Nationwide work stoppages have a direct, often disrupting effect on the consumer. A strike in western truck gardening centers, for example, hits as close to the average family as a lockout of workers by management of a trucking industry. Issues in contract disputes are recurring items in the news until their eventual resolution.

---

component of the private sector, similar to the corporations with which they deal, most of the American job force has only legislative protection.

While the proliferation of these agencies has been greatest at the federal level, state and local agencies now contribute to the weight of government involvement.

The president of the State Labor Council asked the Department of Labor yesterday to clarify new legislation mandating stronger safety measures in the construction industry.

The reporter must ask these questions: What's in the legislation? Who is affected and in what ways? How will standards change? What is the reaction of the construction industry and officials enforcing the legislation? How will the legislation affect timetables for completing current major projects?

It is important to note that while a representative of organized labor raised the questions, both organized and unorganized workers are affected by the legislation.

THE VOICE OF MILLIONS

The union organizer shook his head vigorously. "Look," he told his listeners at the plant entrance, "you're either with us or against us. There's no halfway."

Media coverage of labor affairs elicits a broad range of response from the public: bitterness over the issues dividing disputants, a deep pride in fellow workers' efforts to better themselves, chagrin over mounting labor costs and the need to provide a margin of profit, and the effects of those costs on prices paid by the consuming public.

Complicating the labor picture is the continuing attrition in manufacturing and fabricating jobs, lost when corporations decide to locate in foreign countries. Arguments over the benefits and drawbacks of the organized labor movement have been more than a century in the making, and even the experts disagree on its merits. The reporter accepts these conflicting viewpoints as an impartial observer.

Special Problems for the Reporter

The reporter must accept the proposition that in almost every labor dispute the parties will dig in at opposite ends of the spectrum creating unique challenges for the reporter:

- The parties gain bargaining advantage and appear to give up substantial ground during negotiations while actually only retreating to their true position. The reporter's efforts in such disputes should be to determine and report their "true" positions.

- Negotiators for both sides are always under pressure to produce agreements most beneficial to their clients—the union members or the company's stockholders. The reporter might hear threats like these from both sides: The general manager of the White Consolidated plant says he and the company's owner "have discussed the possibility of closing the plant permanently because of the prolonged strike." The union negotiator threatens to break off talks if management "does not recognize the reality of the situation."

Unions organize to obtain better contracts and conditions for workers, and the costs of higher wages and improved fringe benefits are passed along to the consumers. So the economic give and take between labor and management holds enormous implications for millions even though they are not directly touched by a specific negotiating issue.

The reporter faces these special problems in covering the work force, but they can be overcome.

Unpredictable Disputes

Like the political and business worlds, neither labor nor management will ever be completely satisfied with newspaper or broadcast accounts. Negotiators on both sides often complain of reportorial bias.

Further, nothing is predictable about most labor-management disputes. What an "expert" sees as early resolution of a difficult sticking point in a bargaining session may be nonnegotiable a day later.

For example, a local industry might agree to discuss formal inclusion of a new work and family provision in the contract under discussion. Union negotiators had argued that there is growing conflict in the workplace between a worker's role as an employee and as a family member.

However, after discussions dragged on for several weeks, negotiators for the firm suddenly announced they were tabling the issue, angering union officials who had believed agreement was imminent on a new program.

The issue of including work-family provisions in the contract quickly became the major issue in the negotiations. The reporter already had collected U.S. Department of Labor statistics showing the effect of a decade of social pressures at the bargaining tables.

Familiarity with new workplace issues makes it easier for labor reporters to discuss ongoing negotiations with both sides.

In attempts to influence public opinion or assess the reaction of the opposition, parties on both sides often float trial balloons through the media. Like their counterparts covering politics, labor reporters must appraise the validity of such material and the effect it may produce, weighing it against the needs of the reader or viewer.

A 'Private' Organization

The nature of organized labor as a private rather than a public enterprise poses another problem for the reporter, who has no more warrant to freely enter a union hall when a meeting is in progress than to enter a corporate boardroom when the directors are in session.

No legislation or freedom of the press decree opens labor meetings to scrutiny by the press.

In what was described as a "raucous meeting" last night, Carpenters Local #1376 voted to break off bargaining with three local prefabricated housing firms and strike at midnight Oct. 15.

Although reporters were barred from the union session and officials declined to comment, it was learned that the vote was very close.

The reporter is dependent upon his or her skill in gaining access to such meetings. Sometimes friendship with a union official or the perception that the reporter is owed a favor will do the trick. The argument that the reporter's attendance will promote accuracy and better coverage sometimes works. Short of actual access, the reporter must depend on trustworthy sources to supply information about the meeting.

The reporter is dependent upon his or her skill in gaining access to such meetings or at least obtaining reasonably accurate information afterward.

Problems are compounded during contract negotiations when cadres of government mediators join the disputants. Reporters nearly always cool their heels in anterooms, awaiting word of progress or stalemate. Each side finally appears to provide its version of developments, while the mediators remain silent. Such secondhand and often biased information makes the reporter's task more difficult.

Emotions Run High

Work stoppages, particularly those not authorized by the union leadership, can become highly emotional. Occasionally, more punches may be thrown than words out on the picket line.

> SALINAS, Calif.—Striking lettuce workers attacked harvesting crews in the Salinas Valley on Friday and two people were stabbed, authorities said.
>
> It was the first serious outbreak of violence in the two-month strike by the United Farm Workers union against six large lettuce growers.
>
> A spokesman for the Monterey County sheriff's office said several hundred strikers attacked crews in several fields. The two people who were stabbed were not seriously injured.

In this case, the reporter was not present, but often the story will be found at the center of such action, with its inherent dangers. Emotional complications extend beyond the strike experiences and are part of the labor-management relationship. On the one hand, workers trying to cope with rising prices and erosion of their earning power are negotiating to protect their interests and those of their families. On the other, management is seeking to keep its overhead to a minimum and profits at a maximum.

Perceptions Complicate Relationships

Working groups possess widely differing and sometimes quite negative perceptions of the role of journalists. The pipeline to the leadership often depends on how individuals perceive the press: friend or enemy.

The reporter's job also is made more difficult in cases where one side wants the exposure, while the other refuses to go public with the disagreement.

> A member of the committee negotiating settlement of the 11-day dock strike blamed the press for Tuesday's breakdown in negotiations.
>
> Grant Savage, president of the striking Longshoreman's Union, complained that the list of grievances submitted by the union should not have been publicized in the press.

In this case, the ability of the reporter to obtain information of legitimate interest to the public was seen by one side as inimical to its bargaining interests.

The Reporter as Economist

The reporter covering the work force should be familiar with the economic system and standard accounting procedures. The ability to understand and translate pay scales, complicated fringe benefits and Bureau of Statistics data is necessary if the issues are to be fully portrayed in disputes.

Frequently the pay scale itself is not the major factor in a labor dispute; job security, retirement benefits, working conditions and safety factors may be the big issues inhibiting the ability of disputants to reach agreement.

> With a strike deadline looming, a Pressman's Union spokesmen said today that only Mortello Publishing Co.'s insistence on eliminating 11 jobs separated the two sides from agreement.
>
> "Mortello wants a crew of 37 men to do the work that 48 have kept busy on in the past," said William Priest, business manager for the union.
>
> Company officials had said last week that the 11 jobs in question would be eliminated through retirements and other attrition.

The key question for the reporter: What are the similar staffing requirements elsewhere? For answers, the reporter might go to outside experts or seek information from comparable nondisputing firms. Government statistics could supply an answer.

Activities in the workplace are closely tied to an area's economy. For example, a major foundry is closing its plant, but the decision may be traced to government studies that show permanently lower demand for the firm's output.

Covering the Courts

The courts play a vital role in employer-employee relations, and a basic knowledge of how disputants use the system is necessary to good work force coverage.

While legislation may allow an industrial firm to seek a restraining order against its employees, the judiciary generally decides whether to grant or refuse such an order.

> Circuit Court Judge Will Robinson issued a back-to-work order Tuesday to striking employees of Vesco Engineering Co., directing them to resume bargaining in an effort to end the 15-day strike.
>
> The order was issued on the basis of a contract provision calling for a seven-day "cooling off" period between the parties, which Robinson ruled Engineering Local #627 did not observe.

The reporter must also be familiar with the relief afforded to the disputants through rules enforced by regulating agencies.

> Attorneys for Teamsters Union Local 71 filed objections with the National Labor Relations Board Wednesday, complaining of company tactics the union says cost it last week's election at the Fiber Industries plant.
>
> These were the major objections filed by the union, which lost the representation vote, 883 to 1,072:
>
> - Several days before the election, plant workers received a videotape dramatizing a Teamster strike riot.
> - Just before the vote, all plant workers were required to attend a company meeting at which armed county deputies were present.

Local governments regularly appeal to the courts to adjudicate workplace disputes. In a ruling that concluded 10 years of court argument, a federal judge in 1992 said the city of Birmingham's plan to hire more black firefighters did not violate the constitutional rights of whites. White firefighters had contended that the city's hiring plan denied them promotions and higher pay.

An automaker's decision to close a tool-and-die shop, eliminating 240 jobs, might violate an agreement that precludes subcontracting of work to nonunion contractors. Union officials would seek relief in the courts before taking more drastic action.

Another union might go to court over perceived conflicts of interest on the part of plant managers who maintain outside contracting services that supply the plant.

FROM AGRICULTURE TO INDUSTRY . . . AND BEYOND

The stereotypical union-busters, using tactics that would make a gangster blush, and their counterparts, the strong-armed labor organizers, exist today but in a somewhat different form. The tactics of 100 years ago in the labor movement have almost disappeared, replaced by somewhat tamer confrontation.

Although labor unions had appeared in the United States by 1800, fewer than a million workers held union membership in 1900. Spurred by labor legislation, the growth of unions was spectacular during the 1930s.

Three million workers were enrolled in 1933 alone, and the number had swelled to 14 million by 1945. Growth was steady to more than 19 million in 1980, but union membership then began a decline to its current total of about 17 million.

The union movement had paralleled the growth of a goods-oriented society in this country. In the 1800s, corporations began employing large numbers of people to handle tools and machinery under conditions over which the workers had little or no control. Recurring abuses led to large-scale organization of workers.

The American Federation of Labor was founded in 1886, marking the beginning of the organized labor movement. The AFL guaranteed "trade autonomy" to national unions that belonged to it, allowing the unions to make decisions for themselves. Membership also assured "exclusive jurisdiction" to those unions, giving them the authority to organize a specific occupation.

This craft union approach by the AFL was unchallenged until the 1930s, when the Committee for Industrial Organization emerged within the AFL to provide workers in one industry with a single organization. Such industrial unionism is characterized by membership in one industry, regardless of skill or occupation.

The group broke away from the AFL in 1938 to form the Congress of Industrial Organizations (CIO). The two organizations merged in 1955 to form the American Federation of Labor–Congress of Industrial Organizations (AFL–CIO), an umbrella group that includes 14.5 million members of many craft and industrial unions.

Economic trends have created an ebb and flow in union fortunes, with some experiencing spectacular growth and others an eroding membership. The Teamsters Union claimed 100,000 members in 1933, but that figure had soared to a million by 1951. Its 1990 membership was 1.6 million in 700 locals.

Meanwhile, the United Mine Workers, with the biggest membership in the country from 1898 to 1940, lost members to drastic shifts in energy production. UMW membership was 600,000 in 1951 and had dropped to 186,000 by 1990.

Reporters should not ignore other unions that have emerged because of the changing work force because they constitute the "frontier" of organized labor.

Teachers represent one such frontier, with dramatic growth in recent decades. Membership in teachers' unions stood at 165,000 in 1968, but had climbed to more than 2.8 million by 1990. One of the roles of the reporter covering labor is to reflect and explain these far-reaching changes.

More than 2 million state and local government employees are unionized. These workers are not bargaining with private corporations but with representatives of the public—mayors, county commissioners, city managers, fire and police chiefs, governors, and state agencies.

This can complicate the bargaining and reporting process. Does the official, who represents the public, have a different frame of reference than the negotiator for the city's biggest private industry? Or are the goals similar—getting the best "bargain" that the mayor or governor can in labor negotiations?

More than a year after city officials paved the way for contract negotiations, the Police Benevolent Association will present wage and benefits demands to the city tomorrow.

"We aim to get a binding contract down on paper," said Lt. Vincent Catola, PBA vice president.

The City Council formally recognized the PBA as bargaining agent for the police 13 months ago, and Catola blamed inertia on the part of the city as the reason for the lengthy delay.

All public officeholders must look over their shoulders on the issue of public unions, and the reporter on almost every public affairs beat will find employee-employer relations a major issue.

LABOR ORGANIZATION

The heart of union organization beats strongly at the local level, whether in the garment district of a metropolitan city, an industrial suburban community, or in a semirural area with only a few industrial plants spread over miles of countryside.

Popularly elected members administer the affairs of the locals, often with a business agent employed to direct the day-to-day financial affairs. Frequently a part-time salaried member will maintain the office and call meetings.

Meetings are scheduled regularly, with dues-paying members participating in the decision-making process. Akin to a fraternal organization, the local also provides an opportunity for socializing as well as attending to the business of protecting the rights of union members. Often the president, vice president or secretary takes on the bargaining function instead of the paid business agent.

Duties include pressing grievances of workers with management as disputes arise—although a shop steward chosen by fellow workers in a plant often assumes that responsibility.

The Art of Politics

Personalities and politics play an important part in union activity, with officeholders and would-be successors jockeying for positions of power. Old friendships and alliances are often important in success of union leaders, although empathy with the needs of rank-and-file members is a key element.

Effectiveness in negotiating contracts with management sometimes can be a springboard to more important positions. The reporter looks for success stories, as well as the failures, as signals of power changes within a union.

The candidate will find that support of the rank and file is necessary to maintain a power base within the union, but the leader who also has the confidence of the industrial community is generally more effective in leading the organization.

However, such confidence occasionally backfires in heated union election campaigns with opponents hurling charges that a candidate is "in the pocket of management and cannot be trusted." A labor leader will sometimes successfully combine a public demeanor of truculence with private expressions of willingness to cooperate with management. While these inside maneuvers are not always exposed publicly, the reporter close to the scene has a fuller picture of the workings of the system and can better communicate the overall effect on the public.

Confidence: A Key Element

The reporter needs the confidence of the union's leadership to function effectively at the local level. Even with such rapport, however, the reporter can expect to be forced frequently to accept press handouts in lieu of firsthand coverage.

This is a fact of life and the reporter should secure alternate news sources who can provide accurate information. These sources may be dissidents who want to keep affairs of the union public or merely union members who have no ax to grind and no compunction about telling the truth. Comparing information provided by the union leadership with such alternate sources assures a complete and balanced story.

Such problems of access become more pronounced during negotiation with management over new contracts or heated election campaigns.

Bakers Local #1600 voted 56–51 last night to demand a recount in the recent elections that brought a new slate of officers to power.

Reporters were barred from the union hall on Jefferson Street, and union officials provided only the results of the vote.

However, other sources said the dispute will be taken to circuit court this week. They added that last night's session was tumultuous, with constant banging of the gavel by new President Will Gammick.

Other benefits accrue from a good relationship with union leaders. A war of words may be part of the dispute, but tips leading to hard facts may put the issue in better focus. Or permission may be obtained to study disputed company documents possessed by the union. Even facts appearing in an advertisement can help illuminate an issue.

The president of the union representing 2,200 striking employees of the White-Westinghouse plant said the firm's chief officer was talking nonsense when he said a prolonged strike will jeopardize the future of the plant.

The strike at the plant on Phillipi Road is in its second week.

William Farley, president of Local 745 of the International Union of Electrical, Radio and Machine Workers, waved an advertisement clipped from Friday's edition of *The Wall Street Journal*.

The ad announced the seventh consecutive year of record sales and earnings for the company.

Being in the right place at the right time, persistence, good humor, and dogged pursuit of a story are sometimes perceived by union members as worthwhile qualities. The reporter is seen as a decent person who is only doing his or her job.

Links with Other Unions

Three public employee unions that have been engaged in a contract dispute with the State Department of Mental Health appear to have turned their guns on each other.

The unions—the American Federation of State, County and Municipal Employees, the Civil Service Employees Association and the Communications Workers of America—all have agreed to three-month contract extensions with the department in hopes of working out acceptable contracts.

But officials of all three unions scheduled press conferences Friday to "let off steam" at their counterparts, and to hint that efforts will begin to win over each other's workers.

Such power (and money) disputes are common among organized labor groups. At the same time, other unions are working together to unionize new plants and industries spawned by new technology and overseas markets. Often the target is major unorganized plants.

> GREER, S.C.—The new BMW auto plant will be at the center of a struggle between union organizers seeking inroads in a right-to-work state and nonunion groups wanting to keep intact what they see as a business attraction.
>
> Union representatives are putting together an offer for officials of the $250 million plant.

The reporter found that union officials also were targeting the 20 major suppliers that would move into the area to support the German automaker's operation.

> "There will certainly be organizing attempts," said state AFL-CIO President G.O. Smoak. "We'll try to do a coordinated effort among the unions."

BMW's German plants, which are unionized, pay about $22 an hour. Officials at the new U.S. plant say they plan an hourly wage rate of about $10. The unionization argument is almost certain to conclude in the courts.

Although local autonomy is traditional in the union movement, strength in numbers is essential for maximum influence in dealing with management and participating in the political process. Dramatic mergers are changing the face of organized labor. Two of the largest unions in the food industry, the Meatcutters and Retail Clerks, merged into what is now a 1.3-million-member United Food and Commercial Workers International Union.

Despite such mergers, frequent jurisdictional disputes can make news.

> The question of who should be first on the scene of a medical emergency has become the subject of a tense jurisdictional dispute between unions representing police and firefighters.
>
> At the center of the controversy is determination of who will assist residents who suffer heart attacks, near-drownings or other emergencies.

While most disputes may not be as dramatic, they form a regular pattern in many industries that depend upon workers who are members of several different unions.

An important function of councils, particularly at the state level, is to unify lobbying efforts to influence legislation. While state federations have little power in the internal operation of locals, they are effective as organized pressure groups.

> The State Federation of Unions yesterday called on legislators to ignore the right-to-work proposal introduced in the Senate on Monday.
>
> The proposal, backed by a group of seven senators from the southern end of the state, would drop the present requirement that an employee be a union member in good standing to be employed.

STATE GOVERNMENT INVOLVEMENT

The earliest labor legislation emerged at the state level, with legislation that assured the well-being, safety and health of workers. The current body of federal labor legislation did not begin to develop until the end of the 19th century.

The reporter should be familiar with state legislation affecting labor standards, especially because their enforcement becomes a major issue between unions and management. Regulations cover such disparate areas as shields on dangerous machinery, good ventilation, adequate washroom facilities and fire safety rules.

Extensive safety codes are common in all the states, but changes in legislation are often introduced in the interest of one group or another. Because so many workers are affected by statutory changes, the reporter focusing on the work force also should monitor the legislative process.

> A legislative committee has decided to study safety codes relating to the construction industry in the wake of the deaths of three workers who were killed in a machinery accident in Youngstown last month.

Protection of children in the labor force followed the early emphasis on safety, and legislation prohibiting employment of children under certain ages appeared.

As the growth of social legislation increased, states began adopting laws compensating workers for injuries sustained in employment. Workers' compensation legislation became common. In most states, employers support the program by paying the insurance premiums; the cost ultimately is passed on to the consumer.

A body of legislation also has grown up around fair employment practices, to prevent discrimination, especially against women, blacks, Hispanics and members of other minority groups. All the states also have enacted legislation to provide unemployment benefits to workers who lose their jobs.

Procedures for settling wage disputes also have been established, although the federal government tends to pre-empt this function when the national interest can be said to be affected. The two major approaches to such settlements, both at the state and federal levels, are through **mediation** and **arbitration**.

In mediation, designated individuals attempt to bring the disputing parties together, seeking to reach a voluntary settlement. The parties are encouraged to make concessions, but the mediator or mediation panel has no power to make binding decisions. They are merely using their "good offices" to help settle the dispute. Powers of mediators vary from state to state, with some having power of subpoena and other means to bring the parties together.

In arbitration, the parties to the labor dispute agree in advance to accept the arbitrator's decision. The arbitrator or a panel hears all sides of a labor question and returns a binding decision. Because it is a much stronger settlement procedure, arbitration is used less often than mediation.

Other state labor involvement includes operation of employment agencies, which are an excellent source of statistics on job markets and unemployment. States also regulate private employment agencies, including limiting fees and discouraging disreputable practices.

FEDERAL GOVERNMENT INVOLVEMENT

The federal government asserts itself in labor activities through the legislative process and through administrative rulings by agencies and boards.

The objective of these government units is to balance the rights of organized workers, nonunion employees

and the public. The reporter's access to information can be affected by the pressures on federal officials to avoid any show of partiality toward one group in dealing with labor matters.

The courts also constitute an important source of decision-making. Elected officials tend to be more sensitive to public opinion than the judicial branch of government, but the courts insert themselves into the process in many ways.

> Circuit Court Judge Robert Timmons yesterday refused to grant an injunction sought by management to halt a work stoppage at the Stone & Webster cement plant because of repeated acts of violence on the picket line.
>
> Instead, Timmons urged authorities to police the Wilson Road area 24 hours a day to assure protection to workers who want to cross the picket line.

Judicial interpretations of legislative action are vital to the extent and importance of labor legislation. Provisions of the Railway Labor Act of 1926, which dealt with the rights of workers to join unions, were contingent on the Supreme Court's action. The act was the first of its kind to pass the scrutiny of the court.

Federal involvement in labor affairs began with a Bureau of Labor created by the Congress in 1884. The agency became a separate Department of Labor in 1913, charged with "administering and enforcing statutes designed to advance the public interest by promoting the welfare of the wage earners of the United States, improving their working conditions and advancing their opportunities for profitable employment."

Since then, the department's scope has broadened to administer legislation and executive orders relating to labor union activities.

> WASHINGTON—A Labor Department investigation has uncovered "substantial" violations of federal overtime and child labor laws by the Food Lion supermarket chain, an agency official said Tuesday.
>
> Karen Keesling, chief of the department's Wage and Hour Division, said up to 250 instances of uncompensated overtime work are at the heart of the investigation.

Other sources for the story included officials of the food chain and the United Food and Commercial Workers Union, which filed the claims against the corporation. The reporter's check of court records also turned up pending lawsuits by the firm's workers, and countersuits by the company.

Federal involvement includes such areas as training (Employment and Training Administration), standards of employment (Office of Labor-Management Standards), labor statistics (Bureau of Labor Statistics), and safety and health (Occupational Safety and Health Administration).

OSHA, established by Congress in 1970 to develop safety and health standards, offers an example of federal jurisdiction and its implications for the reporter at the local level. When a scaffold being used in construction of a cooling tower for an Ohio River power plant collapsed, resulting in the death of 51 workers, OSHA was the federal agency that determined compliance with regulations.

The reporter covering the aftermath dealt with the regional office in Philadelphia. After an investigation, the agency charged a construction firm with committing "willful" safety rule violations that contributed to the deaths. The finding of "willful" by OSHA meant it could turn the matter over to the Justice Department for possible criminal prosecution.

New OSHA rules have become routine, but most are newsworthy because they affect so many workers in local communities.

WASHINGTON—The government issued new regulations Monday for protecting workers from HIV and other viruses, putting "full legal force" behind such standard precautions as wearing gloves, face masks and gowns.

Employers also would have to provide free hepatitis vaccinations to workers who might be exposed to that disease, the Occupational Safety and Health Administration said.

These regulations affect nearly 5 million health-care workers and another million people who routinely come into contact with blood or body fluids as part of their job. Included were law enforcement officers, fire and rescue squads, corrections facilities, the funeral industry and linen services.

A municipal police department, for instance, might train officers to wear gloves when breaking up a fist fight or handling bloodied evidence. Reporters on several beats might handle the story, including the medical reporter.

States have established their own occupational safety and health agencies, which deal with the federal agency.

Another office, the Pension and Welfare Benefits Administration, was created in 1984 to assure the prudent management of nearly a million private pension plans and more than 4 million health and welfare plans. Critics argue, however, that overwhelmed clerks in the agency are often unable to supply pertinent pension information.

DETROIT—General Motors, searching for a way to pare its $3.4 billion annual health-care costs, will force 190,000 white-collar employees and retirees to pay insurance premiums for the first time in the company's history.

The health-care cuts could save GM tens of millions of dollars a year. The world's largest automaker began a drastic plan late last year to downsize and cut costs after losing $4.45 billion, a record for any U.S. firm.

Delta Air Lines Inc., struggling with record losses in the early 1990s, is searching for ways to cut costs, including negotiations to force employees to pick up more of their benefit costs. The reporter covering the workplace will find such actions a major issue.

Labor Department statistics will constitute a major source for the reporter researching such stories.

Key Federal Legislative Actions

Among the legislative actions that shaped the course of labor-management relations in the United States, the National Labor Relations Act of 1935 (known as the Wagner Act) is considered by organized labor to be the most decisive. Quality coverage of union-management disputes is contingent upon a basic knowledge of its far-reaching provisions. The Wagner Act was designed to protect the rights of workers in practice as well as in theory.

Its three main provisions included forbidding employers from interfering with a worker's right to join a union, a new method of organizing by using a secret ballot election and establishment of a federal agency—the National Labor Relations Board—to administer and enforce the law.

The NLRB is an independent, quasi-judicial agency of the federal government, but it must seek enforcement of its decisions through the courts. Because board members are presidential appointees, NLRB actions often are the center of political controversy.

A second milestone in federal labor legislation was the Fair Labor Standards Act in 1938 establishing a minimum wage pattern, a basic workweek with provisions for overtime, and prohibition of child labor.

A third piece of legislation, the Labor Management Relations Act in 1947 (also known as the Taft-Hartley Act), modified and broadened the scope of the Wagner Act and outlawed the "closed shop," a company that hires only union members. The act was designed to balance regulations placed upon employer conduct in labor relations with new provisions regulating union conduct and setting up categories of unfair union practices. To facilitate the collective bargaining process, the act created a new independent agency, the Federal Mediation and Conciliation Service, whose duty is to prevent or minimize interruption of commerce growing out of employee-employer disputes. The service relies on persuasion to bring about agreement.

The most dramatic provision in the legislation was a process for settling disputes that might "imperil the national health or safety." The provision allows the president to appoint a board to determine the issues in such a dispute and ask for an 80-day "cooling-off" period in an effort to resolve the issues.

The Labor Management Reporting Act (the Landrum-Griffin Act) included a "bill of rights" for union members that assured them greater participation in union elections. Included is a provision requiring each labor organization to file annual financial reports with the Labor Department, detailing income and expenditures. These documents, which can point to conflict-of-interest transactions by union officials, are subject to public inspection and valuable to the reporter's research.

THE BREADTH OF WORKPLACE SOURCES

The story of a tragic fire in rural North Carolina Sept. 3, 1991, illustrates the variety of sources involved in workplace safety and health. They include police and firefighters, local and state agencies, state and federal legislatures and—even though the plant was not unionized—organized labor groups.

> HAMLET, N.C.—Fire engulfed a chicken-processing plant Tuesday, creating an inferno that killed 25 people and injured 40.
> Witnesses said panicked workers were trapped by blocked or locked doors.
> "They were screaming, 'Let me out!'" passerby Sam Breeden said. "They were beating on the door."

First reports of the fire came from local emergency agencies, but the list of sources spread quickly in ever-widening circles—to state and federal agencies, the state Legislature, the courts and unions. As residents buried their dead relatives, the state's labor commissioner said the factory had not been inspected during its 11 years of operation.

> The state has 16 health and safety inspectors, enough for a county, but "hardly supportive" for the state, Labor Commissioner John Brooks said.
> Because of the few inspectors, the Labor Department randomly chooses 1,000 or so plants a year to inspect, he said. The Hamlet plant had never been among them.

Another agency, the state Department of Insurance, had begun enforcing a statewide fire code three months before the fire, but had not inspected the plant. Neither had the county or town in which the plant was located.

In the midst of criticism of North Carolina's safety plan, U.S. Labor Secretary Lynn Martin threatened to strip the state of its worker safety enforcement powers if the state failed to correct deficiencies within three months. A review by the federal Occupational Safety and Health Administration had found numerous problems.

The issue spread quickly to the Legislature, which set up a committee to study ways to prevent tragedies like the Hamlet fire. At least 14 bills were filed for legislative action.

In the wake of the fire, the State Building Code Council mandated fire inspections at least once every three years by local fire officials.

The courts also became involved when the owner of the processing plant, his son and an employee were indicted on manslaughter charges in connection with the 25 deaths. After pleading guilty, the owner was sentenced to 20 years in prison. Charges against the son and employee were dropped. Civil actions also are making their way through the court system.

Within a year, legislation had reformed workplace safety in the state, with a new law adding 61 inspectors and giving North Carolina the second-largest state inspection staff in the nation. Before the Hamlet fire, the state had ranked last in the number of inspectors among 23 states operating their own inspection programs.

Organized labor was among the supporters of a stronger federal Occupational Safety and Health Act that would let employees report hazards without fear of losing their jobs.

> "The OSHA reform bill is something that's long overdue," said Michael Duffy, assistant director of the Service Employees International Union.
>
> The reform effort is partly a result of the fire at Imperial Products in Hamlet, which killed 25 workers Sept. 3. Workers at the plant said they would have been fired if they had reported unsafe conditions.

Although the plant has not reopened, state and local action continues to provide news copy on the tragedy.

STRIKE OR LOCKOUT?

No area of labor-management relations is more visible or newsworthy than the work stoppage. Machinery grinds to a halt or is kept in operation by shirt-sleeved management executives. The workers set up picket lines to try to stop the operation. There is shoving and shouting at the entrances to the plant; occasional violence is inflicted on machines as well as angry workers.

The middle ground in such disputes is occupied by the mediators and the press. The terms used to describe a work stoppage must be chosen with care.

Union spokespersons may object vigorously to use of the word "strike," arguing instead that workers have been "locked out" of their jobs by management. In turn, management may complain that the walkout is a "wildcat strike," unauthorized by the leadership of the union and in violation of written agreements between the two parties. Care must always be taken to differentiate between a work stoppage and an official strike called by the union.

Collective bargaining has brought about a more structured approach to labor disputes, but often mak-

Striking workers confront a company manager passing through their picket line. Labor strikes often provide dramatic moments, but reporters also should seek to explain divisive issues and the progress of negotiations.
Photo by Paula Bronstein, courtesy of The Hartford Courant.

ing them more difficult to cover because of the role played by the mediator. At one time, the reporter could deal with the union and company, each seeking to publicize its case through the press. Government involvement in the bargaining process has caused both sides to become more cautious about speaking to the press during disputes.

This approach, while still breached regularly by both sides as they try to rally public sentiment during negotiations, places greater responsibility upon the reporter to conduct preliminary spade work on the issues involved. Well before expiration of contracts, the reporter should identify the key issues that might be stumbling blocks when negotiations begin.

Is the percentage of wage increase the major point? Are fringe benefits, such as health insurance, an issue? Is a potential cut in standby staff the problem? What about staffing of the assembly lines?

The emotion-laden week that the contract expires is no time to try to identify the factors that created the crisis. If the issues have been reported before workers begin walking a picket line, the public will have a better perspective and the reporter will have an easier job.

After a work stoppage occurs, the reporter will have to monitor two key areas—the picket line and the negotiating table—to ascertain whether any of the issues have been resolved.

> Negotiators for the Food Processors Association and the union that represents workers in six plants emerged from their seventh bargaining session yesterday with agreement on an 8 percent across-the-board wage increase but with the other major issues unresolved.

Meanwhile, the parties in the dispute also are far apart in assessing effectiveness of a work stoppage. One side minimizes the effect of the strike, pointing out that "we're still operating at nearly full strength." The other side insists that the strike is "100 percent effective." The truth is somewhere in between.

In the aftermath of a dispute, the winners and losers may be difficult to identify. After a bitter five-month strike of Caterpillar in Aurora, Ill., in 1992, the United Auto Workers agreed to send its 12,600 strikers back to work in exchange for the company's promise not to hire permanent replacements while talks resumed

under federal mediation. Workers had to return under contract terms they once rejected.

The controversy continued as Caterpillar barred workers from plants in six Illinois cities, saying it would call back each worker individually. The company was vague on how many workers would be rehired. It had wanted to reduce its work force 15 percent.

> "Before the wounds even heal, they'll stab you again," George King, an assembly line worker, said bitterly.

The charged atmosphere on the picket line calls for low-pressure approaches. It may be a time to discard television equipment, note pads, coats and ties. The alternative may be an unwanted jostling by picket line participants.

At the point of a work stoppage, the reporter's relationships with union leaders and ability to deal evenly with them is vital. Earlier stories should have been reasoned and fair to all parties.

Work stoppages are often complicated by more than one union spokesperson in a labor dispute. A strike by the Fraternal Association of Steel Haulers incurred the wrath of the International Brotherhood of Teamsters, which refused to sanction the strike. In this case, the reporter had to deal with the Teamsters—a 1.6 million-member organization that included 10,000 truckers who haul steel products, FASH—an association of 20,000 truckers, and trucking companies that maintain close ties with both labor groups.

Reporting can be further complicated by the fact that one party may not have the right to bargain for its members as an "official" union recognized by management. Conflict often occurs, for instance, when an official labor organization attempts to become bargaining agent for law enforcement groups that traditionally have been represented by fraternal police organizations.

> A union seeking to represent the city's 98 patrol officers is seeking a temporary injunction to block contract discussions between city officials and the Fraternal Order of Police.
>
> Food Store Employees Union Local 325 filed the request in Circuit Court yesterday, claiming that the constitutional rights of the officers were violated by not allowing them to vote on whether the FOP or the union should represent police in bargaining talks.

Strikes are often round-the-clock situations, and reporters must often accept information secondhand. Care must be used to corroborate such information, especially reports that contain accusations of violence or wrongdoing, and to attribute it properly.

Because they are by definition unauthorized, wildcat strikes are particularly sensitive. Grievances will be more difficult to ascertain, and accurate information will be lacking. "Official" spokespersons won't be as readily available, and the reporter may have to follow them into the field.

> A three-day wildcat strike that has idled more than 7,000 coal miners in western Pennsylvania erupted into violence Thursday as state police scuffled with a group of 300 picketers near Blairsville.

Not all such disputes reach this stage, of course. As strike deadlines approach, many are settled at the bargaining table at the last minute.

Such workplace coverage is earthy and of interest to readers and viewers. The ability of the reporter to bridge the gap between corporate boardroom and union hall is essential when contract time nears. So is a knowledge of courtroom procedure and the ability to negotiate a picket line.

A meaningful gauge of the reporter's ability will occur when a labor issue has come full cycle. After covering contract negotiations, the tense strike watch, picket line encounters, the settlement by harried bargaining officials, and complex details of the final document, the reporter shakes hands with officials on both sides and hopes to find, not necessarily affection or friendship, but respect for a job competently handled.

***

A LABOR GLOSSARY

AGENCY SHOP: An arrangement that allows employees within the scope of a bargaining unit to remain nonmembers of the unit, but requires payment of a service fee.

AMERICAN ARBITRATION ASSOCIATION: A nonprofit organization that helps resolve labor disputes through arbitration, mediation and election.

ARBITRATION: A method of deciding a dispute in which the involved parties agree in advance to accept the decision of a third party.

BARGAINING UNIT: A group of public or private employees organized as a single unit to negotiate a contract with an employer. An employee is a member of the unit as long as he or she holds a position contained in the contract.

CHECK-OFF: Deduction of union dues from workers' paychecks, which is turned over to the union.

CLOSED SHOP: A place of employment which requires labor union membership as a condition for the employment. See **Open shop**.

COLLECTIVE BARGAINING: The process by which employees negotiate with an employer to produce a contract agreement that governs their relationship for a prescribed period.

COMPANY UNION: An organization of employees at a single corporate enterprise or plant, as distinguished from a labor union, which covers a wider area.

GRIEVANCE PROCEDURE: The policy (usually contained in a labor contract) that an employee follows in cases of alleged violations of the contract.

IMPASSE: The point at which union and employer believe further bargaining would be nonproductive without the assistance of mediators or arbitrators. An **Impasse panel** of representatives from both sides and an impartial third party seeks to settle the dispute.

JURISDICTIONAL DISPUTE: An argument between two (or more) unions over the right to perform certain work. Such disputes often lead to work stoppages.

MEDIATION: Assistance offered by private individuals or public officials, acting as third party, to bring the disputants together to settle differences.

NONREPRISAL CLAUSE: A statement assuring no punitive action against any participants for their participation or lack of participation in a dispute.

OPEN SHOP: A place of employment that does not require labor union membership as a condition for employment. Many states have passed such legislation. See **Closed shop**.

PREFERENTIAL BARGAINING: Preferential status is given by an employer to a single bargaining agent. In a preferential shop, an employer agrees to give preference to members of a particular union when hiring new employees.

RIGHT-TO-WORK LAW: A law that permits an employee to work without being forced to join a union.

SCAB: A derogatory term for a union employee who continues to work during a strike, or a nonunion worker who takes the job of a striking worker.

SECONDARY BOYCOTT: A party in a labor dispute that refuses to deal with a customer or supplier of an employer with whom the boycotters have a dispute.

SHOP STEWARD: An employee designated by the union to discuss grievances of fellow union employees with management.

WILDCAT STRIKE: A walkout by some or all of the employees of an industry or single plant that is not authorized by the union.

✳✳✳

SUGGESTED READINGS

Beale, Edwin F., and James P. Begin. *The Practice of Collective Bargaining.* 8th ed. Homewood, Ill.: Richard Irwin Inc., 1989.

A basic look at unions, collective bargaining and labor relations law.

U.S. Superintendent of Documents. *Monthly Labor Review.*

Deals with issues and trends in labor and the workplace, including legal decisions and expiring bargaining agreements.

Chapter 17

Reporting on Environmental Issues

Angry residents filled every seat of the hearing room, while people carrying children or placards lined the walls. At the front of the room, five members of the state Facilities Siting Commission sat at a long table listening to a man at the microphone.

"We don't want this waste dump," he bellowed as the crowd cheered. "You say it will be safe, but how can you be sure? Our kids go to school near there, and the town reservoir is only a half-mile away. We don't want it. Put it somewhere else."

The commission faced the unenviable task of deciding where to build a high-tech storage facility for the state's low-level radioactive waste. This was just one of a series of hearings around the state, and in each town, the reaction was the same. People worried that the waste would leak into the ground and eventually into the water supply. Several experts testified that the facility would be safe, but residents feared the worst.

The commission knew that wherever it decided to put the plant, local residents would be outraged.

Public hearings such as this are a familiar scene. The "NIMBY" reaction (Not In My Back Yard) is heard around the nation as citizens react fearfully to plans for new energy plants, waste-burning incinerators, and other facilities experts say are necessary to solve environmental problems.

For the reporter on the environmental beat, covering the emotion-charged public hearing is only part of the assignment. In the weeks before and after the commission's decision, the reporter should seek answers to many questions and write many stories.

- Is this facility necessary? Were other options considered?
- Will it be safe? For how long?
- Who will run it? Do they have experience managing such plants?
- How and why were these communities chosen?
- How do other states handle the problem?
- Have there been any long-term studies of the health risks if the waste seeps into the water?

Reporters seeking answers to these questions should obtain information from a wide range of sources, including scientists, health experts, environmental activists, political leaders, neighbors and government regulators. They should examine research studies, agency recommendations, and the operating firm's environmental record.

More difficult still, reporters should seek the truth that lies between the emotional protestations of residents and the routine assurances of officials. And they should strive to write stories that alert readers and viewers to real risks without alarming them about imaginary ones.

Stories involving such protests often are the local reporter's introduction to environmental reporting, along with stories about environmental accidents and new construction projects that threaten natural resources. But today's environmental beat spans a much broader range, including pollution control, health dangers from toxic wastes, global warming and the long-range effectiveness of environmental protection laws.

Local and global environmental issues both rank high among the public's concerns, and that interest is reflected in the news media's increased coverage of the environment. A 1990 survey of U.S. dailies with less than 50,000 circulation, conducted by the Scientists' Institute for Public Information, showed that 70 percent had increased environmental coverage of local issues during the previous two years. Nearly one in five of the papers had assigned at least one reporter to cover the environment either full-time or part-time. Local concerns were clearly at the root of the increased attention—stories about water quality and hazardous-waste facilities dominated the papers' environmental coverage.

THE NEED FOR SPECIAL SKILLS

Since the first wave of environmental reporting began three decades ago, the beat has evolved into a demanding and diverse reporting assignment. Few areas of public affairs reporting require the journalist to be knowledgeable in so many fields.

In a given week, reporters might write about a road project that will cut through a forest, new legislation intended to curb pollution, or a company's multimillion dollar plan to reduce dumping of toxic substances into a local river.

Or those stories may be postponed when a tractor-trailer carrying hazardous waste overturns on the highway near the local reservoir. With that story completed, the reporters' attention may turn to the safety of the water supply, state and federal laws for transporting hazardous substances, and the adequacy of local response and cleanup.

Traditional training for reporters has stressed a general background, and editors have liked to say that a good reporter can cover any story. But critics in and outside the profession complain that the generalist of the past is poorly equipped to write about complex environmental issues, often producing stories that are narrow, oversimplified, and even inaccurate. Reporters who are not at least marginally versed in science, economics, politics and law can find themselves adrift in a sea of technical jargon, conflicting expertise and hysterical claims.

A worker checks drums containing hazardous waste. Federal laws require manufacturers to document the safe storage and disposal of toxic waste. Many of those records are available to reporters under federal Right-to-Know laws.
Photo courtesy of Scientists' Institute for Public Information.

Environmental reporters operate in a field fraught with controversy and uncertainty. Government agencies are often overwhelmed by the task of monitoring and controlling pollution. Scientists, engineers and health experts offer conflicting assessments of the ecological and health dangers of environmental problems. Special-interest groups on all sides lobby heavily to sway public opinion and influence government action. Bombarded with information, the public is often left confused and frustrated about what the real problems are and whether the government's efforts to clean up the environment are working.

Making sense of the problems and proposed solutions is a challenging assignment. The successful reporter must combine the news judgment and deadline writing skills of the generalists with the economics understanding of a business writer, the savvy of the political writer, the technical understanding of the science writer, and the storytelling flair of the feature writer. Add to the mix a need for accuracy and clarity that will build credibility with news sources and readers and viewers.

The ideal environmental reporter combines traditional training in journalism and political science with a deep concern about environmental issues and a grounding in chemistry, biology, physics and economics. But in reality, few reporters who encounter environmental stories are so well-rounded.

Reporters covering local government, politics, business and other beats often face assignments with an environmental focus. These reporters need not be expert in every field but they need to recognize that environmental topics are seldom simple, and they must strive to produce stories that help readers and viewers sort through conflicting opinion and emotion-filled issues.

Many colleges and universities offer courses in politics, economics, history and science with an environmental focus. Students interested in these issues can obtain solid background from such courses.

A WIDE-RANGING BEAT

Today's environmental beat is like a big umbrella, stretching to cover what often seems like an infinite array of crises and issues. Following are several important categories of environmental stories:

- **Environmental accidents.**   Oil spills, chemical plant explosions, leaks of radioactive materials, and mishaps involving toxic-waste haulers that pose a danger to humans, animals and the environment.

- **Pollution.**   Legal and illegal discharges of toxic substances into the air and water from manufacturers, sewage systems, power plants and other polluters.

- **Enforcement.**   Governments' attempts to control environmental pollution through regulations, fines and criminal prosecution.

- **Health risks.**   Dangers to public health from potentially harmful substances in drinking water, food and the air from such sources as pollution, radiation and pesticides.
- **Waste disposal.**   Potential hazards from storage, transportation and treatment of toxic and dangerous materials.
- **Development and conservation.**   Environmental effects of new construction ranging from housing developments and golf courses to industrial parks and superhighways.
- **Siting facilities.**   How decisions are made for locating controversial facilities such as trash-burning plants and waste storage sites, along with the community reaction.
- **Scientific studies.**   Research on environmental problems and solutions conducted by government, business and environmental groups.
- **Conservation and natural resources.**   Threats to animal habitats and land, air and water resources from construction, mining, logging and oil drilling.
- **Economic effect.**   How environmental policies and pollution-control laws affect business growth, profitability and employment.

Few environmental stories fit neatly into a single category. A story about a chemical plant explosion, for example, might examine the effectiveness of existing safety regulations or scientific studies on the possible long-term dangers to neighbors.

Many stories can be reported from several perspectives—political, economic, scientific and regulatory—and the reporter's understanding of many fields is critical. A reporter who focuses on the political fighting over a proposed environmental law while glossing over assertions that it will improve the environment fails to answer the public's most pressing question: Will this new law do any good?

AN ENVIRONMENTAL HISTORY

What a difference a century can make. In the mid-1800s, towering factory chimneys spewing clouds of dense black smoke were portrayed as symbols of industrial progress and keys to economic prosperity.

By the mid-1960s, those same smokestacks had become symbols of a far different sort—evidence that society was recklessly fouling the air and perhaps choking the planet's future.

Society has a long and undistinguished record of using the air, water and land as a dumping ground for human waste and the byproducts of industrial growth. The first significant problem was air pollution, which resulted from the widespread burning of coal in homes and factories in the 1800s.

After the Civil War, the growth of industrial cities created new environmental and health problems. Waves of immigrants flocked to the United States to work in the rapidly expanding factories, steel plants and stockyards. They crammed into slum housing where the only place to dump garbage and human waste was in streets, courtyards and open cesspools. Later, sewer lines were installed, but they merely carried the waste to streams and lakes. Water from some wells and streams became undrinkable, and outbreaks of typhoid and other diseases reached epidemic proportions in some cities.

The problems were debated by government officials, physicians, engineers, industrialists and citizens groups, but health and sanitation concerns were usually "solved" by moving the pollution outside the city. Sewers carried industrial and human waste to rivers that transported it to downstream communities whose residents relied on the waterway for drinking water. Factory owners built taller smokestacks to push smoke pollution higher so winds could carry it away.

Pollution of air and water were viewed as local problems, and usually received a disjointed, ineffectual response from local government. Business interests often exerted strong political control, and efforts to stem pollution were perceived as anti-business. Except for small groups that advocated wilderness preservation, society didn't begin putting a premium on protecting the environment for its own sake until the 1960s. That decade brought widespread environmental awareness and the first coordinated national response.

The Modern Environmental Era

To properly cover environmental stories, reporters should understand the complex legal, political and economic history of environmental protection that has evolved over the past three decades.

The modern environmental era is often said to have started in 1962, with publication of *Silent Spring*, by Rachel Carson, a biologist who had worked for the U.S. Fish and Wildlife Service. *Silent Spring* alerted the nation to the dangers that widespread use of synthetic pesticides posed to drinking water and animals. It is often credited with helping to pass the federal Water Quality Act of 1965 and setting the stage for other anti-pollution laws.

Environmental awareness in the 1960s was fueled by glaring ecological problems: Rivers so dirty that fish could not survive; air in industrial cities so choked that it darkened the skies; pesticides and herbicides so poisonous that birds disappeared and farm animals fell sick and died.

Environmental Reporter Casey Bukro, who began covering environmental stories for the *Chicago Tribune* in the 1960s, says many early environmental problems were dramatically visible. The Cuyahoga River in Cleveland was once so heavily polluted with oil and grease, he recalls, that it burst into flames several times.

Throughout the 1960s, news accounts reported on disturbing environmental events. Pollution in New Jersey's Passaic River killed thousands of fish and threatened drinking water. In 1967, 30 miles of the Cape Cod National Seashore and 10 miles of the York River in Virginia were fouled by separate oil spills. The most notorious spill occurred in late 1969, when a leak on an offshore drilling platform released more than 250 million gallons of crude oil off the Santa Barbara Channel in California. The oil slick spread over more than 800 square miles of ocean; some made it to shore and covered the coastline with thick, black crude. Thousands of sea birds and several migrating gray whales were killed.

Environmental action erupted on many fronts in the 1960s. Massive river cleanups were launched. Citizens groups, once small and localized, flexed their muscles, while newly formed national organizations such as Friends of the Earth and the Environmental Defense Fund lobbied heavily for new laws and used the courts to force government action.

Congress, under increasing pressure from environmentalists and the public, began to strengthen envi-

ronmental laws. The year 1970 saw passage of the National Environmental Policy Act, creation of the U.S. Environmental Protection Agency, and celebration of the first Earth Day. The Air Quality Act of 1967 was strengthened and renamed the Clean Air Act.

Those years created the foundation and direction for today's environmental policies. Federal and state agencies set limits for discharging pollution into the air and water, industries were required to install expensive new anti-pollution equipment, and environmental groups became a potent political force.

It was about that time that several major newspapers, including *The New York Times* and *Chicago Tribune*, assigned reporters to cover the environment full time.

New Problems Surface

By the mid-1970s, new pollution laws and the vast network of federal and state environmental agencies lulled the nation into believing that the environment was no longer threatened. Throughout much of the decade, the public and the news media seemed to lose interest in the topic, as fears of oil shortages and an "energy crisis" pushed the environment off the front page. But new environmental problems surfaced by the end of the decade to recapture the public's attention.

Two stories that received enormous news coverage and triggered a second wave of environmental reporting were toxic contamination at Love Canal and a nuclear reactor accident at Three Mile Island.

Love Canal and Toxic Waste

In 1978, reporters flocked to a small town near Niagara Falls, N.Y., where local health officials had discovered abnormally high rates of birth defects, liver problems and miscarriages among residents. The Hooker Chemicals and Plastics Corp. had used the abandoned Love Canal as a disposal site for toxic waste in the 1940s. Later, it filled in the canal and sold it to the Niagara Falls Board of Education for one dollar. A school was built on the site and a neighborhood grew around it.

The Love Canal crisis prompted President Jimmy Carter to declare a national emergency, and during the next three years more than $30 million was spent by federal, state and local governments to relocate residents and clean up the site.

The fears raised by Love Canal reverberated throughout the country. For decades, industry had been quietly burying its hazardous byproducts or pouring them directly into the earth. After Love Canal, hundreds of buried and hidden toxic-waste dumps were discovered. Some had contaminated groundwater supplies. Local concerns were aroused when some scientists began to draw a link between human exposure to these chemicals and increased risk of cancer.

In 1980, Congress passed the Comprehensive Environmental Response, Compensation and Liability Act, commonly known as Superfund. The law authorized huge federal spending to clean up toxic-waste sites around the country. Reporters began writing about local abandoned waste dumps and landfills, the safety of nearby drinking supplies, and the costs and difficulties of cleaning up the sites.

Three Mile Island

On March 28, 1979, a nuclear reactor accident at the Three Mile Island plant near Harrisburg, Pa., caused the release of dangerous radiation that posed a risk to public health. Hundreds of reporters from around the world converged on the scene, turning the TMI incident into an international story. Later, investigators blamed the accident on human error and poor management, raising questions about plant safety at the more than 200 commercial reactors in the United States that were either operating, under construction or in the planning stages. Besides revealing weaknesses in the nation's nuclear power program, Three Mile Island showed that many journalists were unprepared to cover such a complex story.

Science writer Ann Marie Cunningham, who served on the staff of a presidential commission that studied the accident, noted that while a handful of experienced science and environmental writers were assigned to the story, most reporters lacked sufficient background. "Few ... who covered TMI had more than a rudimentary knowledge of nuclear power," she wrote in the book *Scientists and Journalists*. "Some, by their own admission, did not know how a pressurized

light water nuclear reactor worked or what a meltdown was. Few knew what questions to ask about radiation releases so that their reports could help the public evaluate health risks."

In the wake of Love Canal and Three Mile Island, the news media again rushed to report on the environment. Major newspapers assigned reporters to the beat full time, while national news magazines and television networks produced in-depth stories about toxic chemicals, nuclear plant safety and other environmental problems. For editors, the complexity of these topics underscored the need to assign reporters with a solid science background and a willingness to grapple with a story's technical aspects.

The Pendulum Swings

By the mid-1980s, the boom in environmental coverage went bust again, as the number of reporters assigned full time to the environment declined steadily. Many observers blamed the Reagan administration's hostility toward environmental regulation for declining public concern and press coverage.

Environmental issues regained their urgency in 1988 after *Time* magazine replaced its annual "Man of the Year" selection with "Planet of the Year"—Earth. The following year the world's attention focused on the Alaska coast when the Exxon Valdez spilled millions of gallons of oil. The spill required a large-scale, expensive cleanup, and led to federal prosecution of the oil company.

By the 20th anniversary of the first Earth Day in April 1990, the press was again treating the environment as a major story. The signs were everywhere. A survey of small U.S. daily newspapers proclaimed: "Environmental Reporting: The Beat is Back," and the first organization for reporters specializing in the environment, the Society of Environmental Journalists, was formed, attracting nearly 600 members in its first year.

But the pendulum began swinging again in the early 1990s when the nation slipped into a severe economic slump and many Americans began to reassess their enthusiasm for expanded environmental protection and regulation. During the 1992 presidential campaign, the environment took a back seat to the economy as an issue.

A FIELD WITH MANY PLAYERS

Reporters encounter many players on the environmental beat: government regulators, environmental activists, industry representatives, elected officials, scientists and public health agencies. These players may initiate stories with news releases, or their views might be sought for stories in progress. Reporters need to understand each player's role and purpose, and how they interact in environmental stories.

Regulatory agencies.   The U.S. Environmental Protection Agency is the nation's lead environmental agency, and most states have a counterpart that shares responsibility for enforcing federal laws and regulations. State agencies go by various names: Kentucky and Connecticut have a Department of Environmental Protection; Louisiana has the Department of Environmental Quality; California has a Department of Health Services.

Some large states are divided into county enforcement districts. In some states, peripheral matters are handled by other agencies: A state health department might monitor and test wells, while management of state parks may fall to a natural resources agency.

Regulatory agencies develop policies and regulations, issue permits for discharging pollution, conduct inspections and testing, maintain compliance and enforcement records, and impose penalties against violators. Within these agencies are separate divisions for regulating air and water pollution, drinking water supplies, use of pesticides and toxic substances, hazardous-waste storage and disposal, and solid waste (see Figure 17–1). Agency commissioners are usually political appointees, but divisions often are headed by career environmental specialists.

Although environmental enforcement usually occurs without much notice, state and federal agencies may issue a news release when a major polluter is fined for violating regulations.

> The federal Environmental Protection Agency has proposed that Dow Chemical be fined $75,819 for alleged improper handling of hazardous waste at its Allyn Point plant.
>
> The EPA said the company failed to document inspection of its hazardous-waste tank system, failed to keep a waste container closed and did not establish a contingency plan required by regulations. It was the first time the EPA has proposed fines for alleged violations at the local plant.

This story went on to report the company's response, the seriousness of the violation, and details of its overall environmental record. Enforcement stories do not end with a proposed fine. Companies frequently appeal and agencies may file lawsuits in federal court to force compliance.

> Chemtex Inc. paid a record $3.1 million water pollution penalty for discharges into the Delaware River, EPA officials said Wednesday.
>
> The U.S. District Court agreement came in a lawsuit over the company's discharges from a Weston plant in violation of pretreatment standards, the plant's wastewater permit and the Clean Water Act.
>
> The chemical company admitted no liability in agreeing to the settlement and said it was "unaware of any evidence that Chemtex's discharges caused any environmental harm or damage to aquatic life in the Delaware." The plant has since been sold and the processes blamed for the discharges have been halted.

Many environmental lawsuits end in such a compromise agreement where a company agrees to pay a fine and rectify problems, but admits no liability that could open it to civil claims.

Environmental groups.   Activism on behalf of the environment has grown into a potent political force. Environmental organizations can range from small grass-roots groups interested in local issues to large, well-staffed organizations with a national focus. Environmental activism can involve research, publicity, lobbying and lawsuits.

Environmentalists are often adept at attracting media attention with news conferences and demonstrations. Once small and poorly funded, national groups such as the Sierra Club, the Conservation Foundation and the Natural Resources Defense Fund have expanded their influence through effective fund-raising and are staffed with lawyers, scientists and full-time lobbyists. Their focus is usually on national problems, but many have chapters involved in local issues.

> Lawn mowers and chain saws add measurably to smog on a summer day, and the Edwardsville Sierra Club is threatening to file a lawsuit to do something about it.

"Lawn mowers and chain saws have all the pollution control equipment of a '57 Chevy without a muffler," said John Earle, president of the environmental group.

A chain saw operated for two hours emits as many hydrocarbons as a new car driven 3,000 miles, according to the California Air Resources Board.

Some environmental groups monitor the pollution records of companies and publicly single out major polluters. The Natural Resources Defense Council, for example, compiles a "Who's Who of American Toxic Air Polluters," listing some 1,500 companies by region. A separate network of Public Interest Research Groups, based at colleges and universities, often targets local polluters.

Almost half of the 121 companies with permits to discharge toxic chemicals into the state's waterways are guilty of repeated and serious violations, a private research group charged Monday.

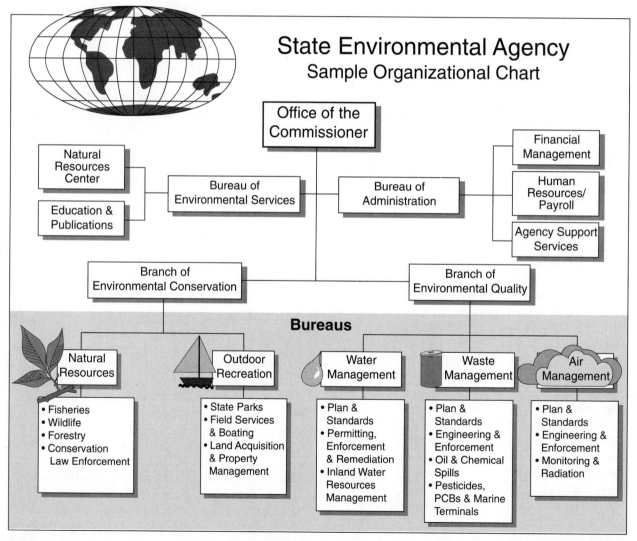

FIGURE 17–1
State agencies often are divided into two major divisions: environmental conservation and quality.

The state Public Interest Research Group cited 55 severe and chronic offenders for last year, including three local companies.

"We've got a serious problem with compliance with the Clean Water Act in this state," said James Leahy, the group's executive director. "It is an absolutely unacceptable situation."

Citizens groups sometimes form to battle specific projects or to serve as a local watchdog. These groups have successfully opposed new highways, pollution-producing factories, waste disposal facilities and recreation projects.

While many environmental groups provide useful and reliable information from studies and reports, some claims can be wildly exaggerated or scientifically flawed, especially those from small, less-professional organizations. Experienced reporters bring the same skepticism to their dealings with environmental groups that they do with business representatives. Reporters should check findings and health-risk claims carefully before echoing the alarm sounded by advocates.

Business and Industry.   There was a time when the typical industry response to environmental stories was "No comment." Company officials, often uncomfortable with interviews, refused to talk with reporters and prevented their representatives from releasing information. That changed during the 1980s, as many companies tried to reverse their image as villains in environmental controversies with aggressive public relations and strategic advertising campaigns.

Having lost many publicity battles to environmentalists, businesses now go on the offensive to get their side into news articles. Many companies employ "environmental communication specialists" to answer reporters' questions and publicize their efforts to reduce pollution and comply with environmental laws.

GROTON, Conn.—Pfizer Inc. plans to install a $40 million system that will significantly reduce the discharges into the Thames River of pollutants created during its drug and chemical manufacturing.

In announcing the plan yesterday, a company spokesman said the plant's discharge of waste, including toxic materials, will be reduced by 90 percent after the system is installed. The new system is expected to reduce annual discharges from 3 million pounds a year to less than 250,000 pounds.

The company initiated the cleanup program on its own and was not required by federal or state regulators to cut down on the pollution levels. Adrian Freund, of the state Department of Environmental Protection, called the project "a major environmental initiative" by the company that is welcomed by the DEP.

For this story, the reporter did not rely only on the company's optimistic projections, but interviewed state regulators and a scientist familiar with the river to assess the plan's potential effect.

Environmental policy expert Joseph M. Petulla notes that many companies have learned that "good environmental practice has become very good business," because it improves their public image and reduces financial liability for environmental accidents, cleanup and injuries. But he adds that some companies are still slow to comply with regulations, either because of weak state standards, poor agency enforcement or illegal activities such as unauthorized dumping in sewers or using unlicensed waste haulers.

Reporters have a responsibility to include the legitimate views and accomplishments of business in their stories, but they must be careful not to confuse easy access with candor. A company with an environmental program does not necessarily have a strong record of environmental performance. Industry claims of environmental progress need to be checked with other sources, including government regulators and impartial scientists, engineers and other experts.

Political Leaders.   Being an environmentalist is not only good business, it also can be good politics. The stakes are high: public image, votes, contributions and political endorsements.

Elected officials walk a fine line when it comes to the environment. Polls show the public wants a clean environment but it also wants jobs and prosperity. Politicians often seek to cultivate an image of supporting environmental action, while at the same time supporting a favorable climate for business growth. They may speak forcefully about the need to clean up the environment but oppose tougher environmental rules that industry says will hurt business and threaten jobs.

Confronted with an environmental controversy, governors, state legislators and city councilors may prefer to take a wait-and-see attitude "until all the evidence is in." They are more likely to take a stand on safe or nonspecific issues such as recycling and "a clean environment," especially when funding would come from outside sources.

> Millions of dollars in federal cleanup money could be coming to the St. Johns River if a 100-mile stretch nominated by Gov. Lawton Chiles becomes part of the National Estuary Program.
>
> "The St. Johns is a truly unique and irreplaceable economic resource," Chiles said. "It is our responsibility and obligation to do all within our power to protect and restore the river."
>
> The EPA plans to select up to three rivers this fall for inclusion in the program, which now has 17 waterways. If the agency agrees to include the St. Johns, it would provide up to $2 million a year in federal funds for three to five years.

Politicians often announce environmental initiatives with considerable fanfare, and reporters should follow up to determine if optimistic plans become reality. Similarly, elected officials may boast of having strong enforcement records. This story resulted from a prosecutor's speech to an environmental conference:

> In tough-edged remarks aimed at deterring pollution, state Attorney General Arthur Davidson said Monday a "tidal wave" of criminal environmental cases soon will be washing over the state and that violators "will almost certainly go to jail."
>
> Davidson said that fighting environmental crime has been among his highest priorities and that the results will be evident with cases being brought in federal and state courts. Davidson could not specify the number of cases pending but said they will send a strong message to industry that "intentional, willful violations of environmental laws will be prosecuted."

Reporters always should look beyond the rhetoric to see if it jibes with reality. This story also reported that 35 convictions had been obtained during the previous three years, but noted that recent enforcement had been hampered by a shortage of investigators. The reporter also might have interviewed environmental leaders to see if they shared the official's enthusiasm about his record, and examined prosecution statistics in other states. In the months ahead, the reporter should check the number of new cases prosecuted to see if the official's headline-making predictions come true.

An official's record on environmental issues also should be examined in light of political contributions and ties to the business community. Politicians may say they favor tough environmental standards, but their position on important legislation and funding for enforcement programs will speak volumes about their true allegiances.

Scientists.   To the public, it sometimes seems there are scientists on every side of an environmental issue, and often there are. Scientists who work for industry, government or advocacy groups typically support the views of their employer, and readers and viewers are often confused about which claims to believe.

> A preliminary report on pollution in the Charles River identifies Norris Industries, a local fertilizer manufacturer, as the source of much of the organic material causing low oxygen conditions that are harming the river's marine life.
>
> The study was conducted by Allied Science Laboratories for the Charles River Preservation Society, a local environmental group.
>
> Norris Industries disputed the report yesterday, saying it is incomplete and based on preliminary evidence. The company said a study it commissioned last year by an environmental consultant showed no effect from its discharges into the Charles.

Faced with conflicting scientific studies, the reporter turned to a third source to help assess the report's accuracy.

> Richard Barnard, head of the state's Water Quality Division, agreed that the recent study is far from conclusive. "The suggestion is premature and not supported by a verified mathematical model," he said.

Experienced reporters attempt to get objective viewpoints from scientists and other experts at universities or independent research centers who can evaluate the research and conclusions of scientists affiliated with a particular company or cause.

Public Health Agencies.   State and local health departments usually operate independently of regulatory agencies and can be a valuable source of health statistics, research findings and expert opinion. These agencies compile regional statistics on occupational injuries, death rates and incidences of serious diseases such as cancer.

Health agencies are often the first to detect pockets of environmentally related illness. Even before residents of Love Canal launched their citizens' crusade for government assistance, a New York State health officer had called attention to the high rates of health problems among people living there.

Most studies and statistical information compiled by health officials are public records. A reporter working on a story involving health dangers should ask state and local health departments for data that might shed light on the problem.

COVERING THE LOCAL BEAT

When 2,600 gallons of gasoline leaked from a service station's rusted underground storage tank in a small New England town, more than 31,000 people were put on water restrictions for several weeks because of threats to the municipal water supply. As reporters and TV cameras converged on the scene, state officials scheduled a press conference to announce they intended to take action against the gasoline station owner, a prominent businessman with a chain of stations.

After the immediate crisis was over, one reporter decided to take a closer look at the problem of leaky gasoline tanks and why this particular leak had gone undetected for so long.

A check of spill records at the state Department of Environmental Protection revealed that more than 50 gasoline and oil leaks had occurred at the owner's stations during the previous 10 years. Of the 50 spills, the records showed 16 involved leaky underground storage tanks, four of which polluted 11 private drinking wells. The reporter examined the DEP's regulations on gasoline storage tanks and learned that all underground tanks in the state that were more than 20 years old should have been replaced more than a year earlier. Why hadn't the tank at the site of the latest spill been replaced?

In checking the owner's permit file, the reporter found that the owner had applied for variances to extend the deadline for 12 of his stations, including the one where the most recent leak had occurred. The state had denied the variances. Still, the deadline had come and gone, and enforcement officials had neither

fined the owner nor made a serious attempt to determine if he had replaced his aging tanks.

Asked about the owner's poor compliance record, state officials called it "unacceptable" but conceded that he had not been fined or prosecuted for previous spills or for failing to meet tank replacement deadlines.

A closer look at spill records around the state revealed that the problem was far from isolated. Every year, hundreds of gasoline tanks leaked, contaminating soil and polluting drinking water. Many station owners failed to keep adequate inventory records that would reveal leaky tanks, and few met replacement deadlines. Despite this, only a handful of the most serious violations were prosecuted.

Enforcement officials defended their efforts and argued that they had neither the staff nor resources to adequately monitor the problem. They acknowledged that they usually relied on station owners to comply. Few owners did. It took a serious spill to get the state's attention.

The local newspaper published stories describing the station owner's record of violations, the state's poor enforcement system, and the potential hazards from other serious spills. After the stories appeared, the state attorney general announced the state was suing the station owner for $15 million in fines for the most recent spill.

Even as the state tried to give appearances that it was aggressively prosecuting polluters, facts uncovered by the reporter told a different story: Better enforcement probably would have prevented the accident in the first place.

Finding Local Stories

Federal, state and county environmental laws affect every community. By understanding how those laws are implemented and staying abreast of prevailing environmental issues, reporters can find many important local stories:

- Major polluters in an area can be identified and stories written about their efforts to reduce pollution and comply with laws.

- Federal and state enforcement of local pollution can be assessed.

- The effects of pollution and development on reservoirs, lakes, streams and recreation can be examined to see if their condition has worsened in recent years. The same can be done for local air quality.

- Industries that store, treat and transport hazardous substances can be identified and their procedures evaluated for compliance with existing laws. So can military installations involved in conventional and nuclear weapons production.

- Landfills and abandoned waste sites can be scrutinized to see if they are being properly monitored and made safe for other uses.

- Researchers studying local environmental problems can be reported on. Figure 17–2 shows U.S. newspapers' top environmental stories.

The condition of local rivers, lakes and other natural resources are a frequent focus of news coverage. Stories can examine attempts to reduce pollution, recent studies that evaluate environmental damage and efforts by elected officials to protect local resources.

> The state's congressional delegation has proposed a bill to create a special office for Long Island Sound within the U.S. EPA that would provide $3 million a year for grants on Sound-related research and management projects.
>
> The bill comes as scientists are concluding a five-year state and federal study to determine how the Sound's resources should be managed. Among the initial recommendations of the study are that sewage treatment plants along the shores of the Sound be required to reduce nitrogen levels in their effluent. Nitrogen promotes tremendous algae growth, which robs the water of oxygen and kills marine life.

The cost of environmental programs that target local problems is another story. Many federal programs provide funds to state and county governments for environmental cleanups, but often those governments are expected to share in the cost.

> The federal government will hit Lexington County with a $100,000 tab next year for studies it did preparing for a toxic-waste cleanup at an abandoned landfill south of Cayce, officials say.
>
> But that's just the start. By the time all the bills roll in during the next decade, the county could pay mil-

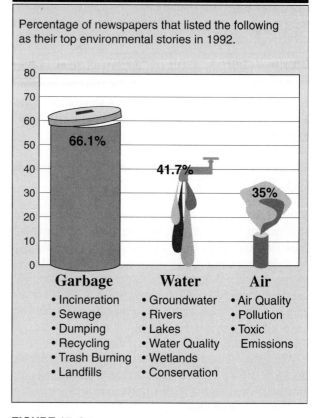

FIGURE 17–2
Source: *SIPIscope*, Fall 1992, p. 11. New York: Scientists' Institute for Public Information.

lions of dollars to eliminate contaminants that leaked into ground water near the site.

The story explained how local officials were trying to reduce costs and described health concerns that prompted the expensive cleanup.

> Preliminary studies show ground water at the landfill is tainted by unsatisfactory levels of arsenic, cadmium, mercury, selenium, chlorides and benzene. Those factors make cleanup vital, the EPA says, because there are 6,200 public and private wells within a 3-mile radius of the old landfill.

Development is a continuing local story in many parts of the country, as new housing, highway construction and other building projects transform open space. Protected wetlands, which provide sanctuaries for animal habitats and serve as a natural filter for water traveling to streams and lakes, are often at the center of development disputes.

Depending on the size of a project, various permits may be required to build near wetlands, and agencies at several levels of government may be involved. A small structure may require only a permit from the local planning agency, while a new road that would fill many acres of wetlands might need approvals from a state agency and the U.S. Army Corps of Engineers.

> The proposed Shady Greens Golf Course passed its first hurdle this week when the Middlefield Planning Board gave unanimous approval to the 140-acre project, over objections from a citizens' group.
>
> After a two-hour public hearing, the board sided with the developer, who insisted that the project would not harm animal nesting grounds or pollute the nearby Nautucket River.
>
> The project still needs separate permits from the state Division of Water Resources, which is concerned about possible river pollution from golf course fertilizers, and the U.S. Army Corps of Engineers, which is reviewing whether the project will increase the risk of flooding downriver. Both agencies are expected to decide later this year.

Since 1980, more than 100 million acres in the United States have been protected by federal and state laws, but Republican administrations have attempted to redefine wetlands in a way that would open many areas to new construction. One change proposed by the Bush administration would have cut the number of protected wetlands in the mid-Atlantic states from 106 to 28. The proposal eventually was withdrawn, but any future change in the definition of wetlands is sure to set off new development pressures, opposition from environmentalists and a flurry of news stories.

Preparing for the Beat

Unlike other beats such as the courts and municipal government, the environmental beat has few routines and no central location that must be checked every day. The beat is large and complex and requires an effective strategy for coverage. Preliminary steps can prepare the reporter and identify important issues and sources.

- Become familiar with the region's unique characteristics—its environmental problems, geography, natural resources and dominant industries, along with its system of highways and railways.
- Locate key agencies and individuals with responsibility over local environmental matters.
- Develop a varied list of sources, including regulators, industry representatives, business and environmental groups, and independent scientists.
- Learn what public records and reports are available for each environmental topic, including air and water pollution, solid waste management, hazardous-waste transportation, and drinking water safety.

The reporter who develops a reputation for accuracy, thoroughness and fairness on the beat will find sources on all sides of an issue willing to aid the monitoring process. Some government regulators or members of legislative committees consider themselves environmentalists and can offer valuable tips.

Reporters looking for the worst polluters in their region might begin by interviewing enforcement agents, who can identify serious offenders. Sometimes enforcement officers with a strong commitment to environmental protection can become frustrated by their agency's limited resources or what they see as political interference with their enforcement mandate. These sources can point out where the system is failing and how the environment may be suffering as a result. However, enforcement officials, no matter how cooperative, should be only one source of many. A familiarity with appropriate regulations and their intent also will help reporters recognize serious violations or enforcement lapses.

Industry workers also can become frustrated, especially if they believe their health is endangered on the job. Their information must be thoroughly checked but, at minimum, it can help reporters ask the right questions of people at the top.

A variety of public records, trade publications and government reports can assist the reporter in tracking important trends. It's often a matter of finding out what is available and where to look. Many state regulatory agencies publish annual reports to the governor or special reports for legislative committees. Most of these documents are available under state Freedom of Information laws. Enforcement staff and legislative aides often know what reports are being generated and can help reporters get copies.

Distances can be a limiting factor for reporters located far from state capitals. In large states, some agencies have county, regional or field offices; face-to-face contacts with sources there can pay off in tips and technical assistance. Local legislators serving on environmental committees also can help.

A source list is not complete without several independent scientists who can explain technical details and help the reporter find pertinent research studies. Chemists, biologists and natural-resource specialists are among the most useful. Universities are a good source of these experts, and the school's public relations office usually can help the reporter reach them quickly for deadline stories.

Reporters will get some help from news releases in identifying important stories but these should only be a launching point in news gathering. As on any beat, reporters who rely on releases and news conferences for their news open themselves to manipulation and their stories to distortion.

Unfortunately, even experienced environmental reporters on tight deadlines will sometimes rely on handouts for a story angle or important facts. Former EPA press officer Jim Sibbison described what he called "a principal occupational hazard in environmental reporting from Washington—relaying to readers self-serving statements by EPA officials as the truth."

Sibbison decried what he called "spoon-feeding" of the press and the lack of enterprise by reporters on the EPA beat. He described one favorite strategy used by the EPA when releasing air pollution figures: Stress only those statistics that will obtain a positive spin on the story. The strategy diverted "attention from the agency's failure to crack down on polluters and clean up the air," he said.

A healthy skepticism of optimistic claims, a reliable list of sources with whom to check those claims, and a willingness to dig will go a long way in avoiding "spoon-feeding."

Covering Environmental Accidents

Environmental accidents usually come without warning. When they do, any available reporter can wind up with the assignment, regardless of his or her experience with environmental stories.

Reporters usually hear about major accidents—chemical plant explosions, spills of oil or toxic waste—on the newsroom scanner, and may arrive at the scene within minutes of the first report, while emergency response personnel are still assessing the situation. In their enthusiasm to get the story, reporters may rush in before the full dangers have been evaluated.

At the top of its "Reporter's Checklist" for covering a hazardous-materials accident, the Environmental Health Center gives journalists this valuable, if obvious, warning: "Do not go into the hot zones. They present health risks to reporters no less than to other people. You don't have to endanger your health to cover the story."

At the scene, reporters should find the emergency response officials in charge or attempt to find someone designated to answer questions from the news media. The reporter needs to find out what chemical is involved and what type of hazard it poses. Here are some other important questions:

- Was anyone injured? What is the nature of their injuries?

- How and when was the chemical released? How much was released and does the quantity pose specific dangers?

- How is the accident affected by weather conditions, such as rain and wind? Will a sudden weather change increase or decrease the potential health dangers?

- Is the chemical unstable? Is there any risk that it will react dangerously with other chemicals at the site? How will it react with air and water?

- Is the chemical dangerous to human health? Are the effects long-term or short-term?

- Will the environment sustain long- or short-term damage?

- Are nearby neighborhoods, schools or public facilities endangered? Will residents need to be evacuated?

TABLE 17–1
Major toxic chemical laws administered by the EPA
Source: Environmental Protection Agency, *Environmental Progress and Challenges: EPA Update*, 1988.

Toxic Substances Control Act — Requires that EPA be notified of any new chemical before its manufacture and authorizes EPA to regulate production, use or disposal of a chemical.

Federal Insecticide, Fungicide and Rodenticide Act — Authorizes EPA to register all pesticides and specify the terms and conditions of their use, and to remove unreasonably hazardous pesticides from the marketplace.

Federal Food, Drug and Cosmetic Act — Authorizes EPA in cooperation with FDA to establish tolerance levels for pesticide residues on food and food products.

Resource Conservation and Recovery Act — Authorizes EPA to identify hazardous wastes and regulate their generation, transportation, treatment, storage, and disposal.

Comprehensive Environmental Response, Compensation and Liability Act — Requires EPA to designate hazardous substances that can present substantial danger and authorizes the cleanup of sites contaminated with such substances.

Clean Air Act — Authorizes EPA to set emission standards to limit the release of hazardous air pollutants.

Clean Water Act — Requires EPA to establish a list of toxic water pollutants and set standards.

Safe Drinking Water Act — Requires EPA to set drinking water standards to protect public health from hazardous substances.

Marine Protection Research and Sanctuaries Act — Regulates ocean dumping of toxic contaminants.

Asbestos School Hazards Act — Authorizes EPA to provide loans and grants to schools with financial need for abatement of severe asbestos hazards.

Asbestos Hazard Emergency Response Act — Requires EPA to establish a comprehensive regulatory framework for controlling asbestos hazards in schools.

Emergency Planning and Community Right-to-Know Act — Requires states to develop programs for responding to hazardous chemical releases and requires industries to report on the presence and release of certain hazardous substances.

Similar questions need to be asked for most environmental accidents, including oil spills and radioactive leaks from nuclear power plants. Reporters should interview outside experts, not only company officials, to evaluate possible harm to people and animals from accidental exposure to hazardous materials.

LAWS AND REGULATORY AGENCIES

Federal and state environmental protection constitutes the largest and most complex system of social regulation in the country. The Clean Air Act, Clean Water Act and the Superfund Act are just a few of the federal laws intended to address environmental problems (see Table 17–1). Each state can pass its own laws, and state environmental agencies adopt detailed regulations to enforce them.

Industry and other polluters face violation notices, compliance orders, fines and criminal prosecution for failing to adhere to pollution laws. States can adopt their own regulations to deal with local problems, but they must be at least as stringent as federal standards. For example, California has the nation's toughest emission standards for automobiles, which have been adopted by several other states.

Some government agencies are exempt from environmental laws. For example, municipal sewage treatment plants in some cities are among the worst polluters of rivers, but may not be required to meet the same standards as a manufacturing plant discharging into the same river.

A broad network of agencies is responsible for enforcing environmental laws. Although the U.S. EPA in Washington, D.C., is the nation's top environmental agency, more than 25 other federal agencies, ranging from the U.S. Coast Guard and Nuclear Regulatory Commission to the Food and Drug Administration and the National Parks Service are involved in environmental issues.

Divisions within the EPA have specific authority over air and water pollution, drinking water, pesticides and toxic substances, hazardous-waste storage and disposal, solid waste and emergency response programs. The agency also has an enforcement and compliance office, but serious offenders are turned over to the U.S. Justice Department for prosecution. Offices within the EPA also conduct research studies, training and education programs.

The EPA has 10 regional offices around the country that coordinate pollution-control programs with state and local agencies, industry and other public and private groups within their region (see Figure 17–3). Many enforcement and compliance records used by reporters are kept at regional offices.

Each state has its own counterpart to the EPA, with divisions similar to those noted above. In states authorized to enforce federal regulations, compliance reports are maintained by the state agency. Most state environmental agencies also oversee programs dealing with natural resources, parks, sewers and even swimming pools. Separate divisions or departments may exist to address local issues, such as agricultural pollution in farm areas or coastal development in shoreline states.

Using Environmental Records

Federal and state agencies that enforce environmental laws maintain a wide assortment of reports and records that can be a gold mine for reporters. Documentation is required for inspections and compliance by polluting industries, accidental releases of toxic chemicals, human injuries from chemical exposure and sites where hazardous chemicals are stored.

By checking the records of several agencies, reporters can identify major polluters in their areas, significant waste storage sites and closed dumps that may pose a threat to local drinking supplies.

Despite decades of enforcement, huge amounts of toxic substances continue to be discharged by industry, sewage treatment plants and power plants. Some pollution is released within limits set by federal and state laws, and specified on discharge permits. Some is dumped illegally, in violation of permit restrictions.

Enforcement agencies seldom have the staff to monitor every major polluter and instead rely on voluntary compliance. Several studies, including one conducted by the U.S. General Accounting Office, have found that polluters frequently violate discharge permits, with little follow-up by enforcement officials. By reviewing enforcement records, reporters can learn what local companies violate their permits and how aggressively officials pursue violators.

Reporters sometimes take a broad look at major polluters in a region to assess the total pollution being dumped into the local air and water. Robert Hamilton, environmental reporter for *The Day* in New London, Conn., reviewed dozens of documents, including discharge permits, spill reports, compliance records and company disclosure statements required under the Superfund Act to document that 67 chemicals considered toxic had been dumped into the Thames River over a 15-month period. While much of the dumping by individual companies occurred within permitted levels, Hamilton's story raised important questions about the pollution's cumulative, long-term effects:

Nearly 90 million gallons of effluent, laced with toxic chemicals and treated sewage, go into the Thames River each day from seven major industries and five sewage treatment plants on the river or its major tributaries.

Smaller industries, and numerous nonpoint sources—the waste oil dumped into a storm drain by a thoughtless backyard mechanic or the fertilizer running off agricultural fields—add to the river's burden.

Scientists say there has been no short-term damage to the river as a result of the effluent, but some are asking whether there will be long-term changes in the

EPA Regional Offices

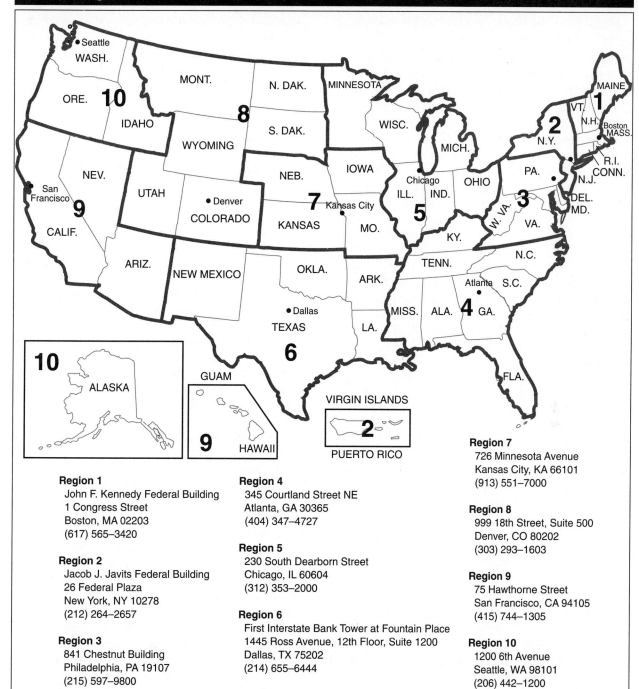

Region 1
John F. Kennedy Federal Building
1 Congress Street
Boston, MA 02203
(617) 565–3420

Region 2
Jacob J. Javits Federal Building
26 Federal Plaza
New York, NY 10278
(212) 264–2657

Region 3
841 Chestnut Building
Philadelphia, PA 19107
(215) 597–9800

Region 4
345 Courtland Street NE
Atlanta, GA 30365
(404) 347–4727

Region 5
230 South Dearborn Street
Chicago, IL 60604
(312) 353–2000

Region 6
First Interstate Bank Tower at Fountain Place
1445 Ross Avenue, 12th Floor, Suite 1200
Dallas, TX 75202
(214) 655–6444

Region 7
726 Minnesota Avenue
Kansas City, KA 66101
(913) 551–7000

Region 8
999 18th Street, Suite 500
Denver, CO 80202
(303) 293–1603

Region 9
75 Hawthorne Street
San Francisco, CA 94105
(415) 744–1305

Region 10
1200 6th Avenue
Seattle, WA 98101
(206) 442–1200

FIGURE 17–3

Source: U.S. Environmental Protection Agency.

aquatic life of the Thames as a result of the industrial brew now going into it.

The reporter described the chemicals considered most toxic, and interviewed several scientists to assess the possible dangers to fish and plant life in the river. In the process, the reporter discovered that the state's plan to study the cumulative effects of pollution had fallen far behind schedule.

Environmental violations can range in severity from the homeowner who fills in a small swamp in his yard without a permit to the manufacturing plant that routinely exceeds the discharge limits on its permit. Some violations are merely technical—a company may have accidently failed to file its monitoring reports—while others can reveal serious pollution problems.

Enforcement usually begins with a notice of violation, alerting the company to remedy the problem by a certain date. It can proceed to compliance orders, fines and, ultimately, criminal prosecution. Enforcement records can give the reporter an outline of the company's environmental performance and reveal how aggressively the agency has been seeking compliance. Companies often attempt to negotiate with enforcement officials for delays or variances. Records of those negotiations are public.

Water Pollution Reports

Several reports for individual companies required under the Clean Water Act are available to reporters, either from state agencies or regional EPA offices:

- **National Pollution Discharge Elimination System permits (NPDES).**   Files for individual companies contain permit information, violation details and copies of communications between the company and the enforcement agency.

- **Discharge monitor report.**   Companies must file periodic statements listing the amounts of toxic substances they discharge.

- **Violation warnings, notices and orders.**   Companies that violate their limits often are sent warning letters, followed by notices of violations. If the violations continue, the agency will issue a compliance order describing what steps are needed to correct the violations. Further action is referred to the

Justice Department or state prosecutors (see Figure 17–4a).

- **Quarterly Non-Compliance Reports.**   These reports show what companies have failed to comply, with listings by geographic area (see Figure 17–4b). Enforcement agencies often keep records of emissions of hazardous substances, listed by company, that exceed limits set by the EPA.

Toxic Release Inventories

Many reporters have used the federal Toxic Release Inventory (TRI), required under the Emergency Planning and Community Right-to-Know Act, to document how many different toxic and cancer-causing chemicals are released each year into the air, and in what quantities. Each company must file a TRI form indexing the volume and types of toxic chemicals it releases into the air, land and water.

In the early 1990s, newspapers around the country began publishing lengthy reports, based on TRI documents, describing the vast toxic threats in their states. Perhaps for the first time Americans began to get a sense of the immense volume of toxic pollution that is released into the environment.

The *Boston Herald* reported that in 1988, "A total of 6.1 million pounds of chemicals that the EPA believed causes cancer were released from Massachusetts plants—enough to fill Fenway Park 100 times with a gas mixture lethal enough to kill everyone in the stands."

The Macon Telegraph in Georgia reported that in the same year American industries had released an estimated 6 *billion* pounds of toxic and cancer-causing chemicals into the air (see Figure 17–5). The story explained how industries had at least 10 years to meet standards for many pollutants specified in the revised Clean Air Act of 1990.

A caution: The TRI forms can be imprecise and difficult to use. For one thing, the reported amounts are based on estimates calculated by the companies themselves, and the figures are usually six months old when they become available. Also, many newspapers that used TRI figures needed computers to analyze the data. The numbers alone may not tell the whole story; some chemicals are more toxic than others, and where a substance is discharged can mean the difference

DATE: 03/10/92 REGION 01 QUARTERLY NON-COMPLIANCE REPORT ** QNCR ** PAGE 1

MUNICIPALS ANY STATE FROM: 10/01/91 TO: 12/31/91

****

NAME LOCATION NPDES NUMBER GRANT LIMIT INSTANCE OF NONCOMPLIANCE		RNC	VIOLATION	VIOLATION DATE	ENFORCEMENT ACTION	ENFORCEMENT DATE	STATUS	STATUS DATE	COMMENTS
ACME MANUFACTURING		NON-COMPLIANT							
1000 MAIN STREET									
ANYTOWN									
0100048 $	***FINAL***								
SOLIDS, SUSPENDED	PERCENT RE	0011	EFF	12/31/91			NC	12/31/91	2C PERMIT EFFLUENT VIOLATION
SOLIDS, SUSPENDED	PERCENT RE	0011	EFF	11/30/91			NC	11/30/91	2C PERMIT EFFLUENT VIOLATION
SOLIDS, SUSPENDED	PERCENT RE	0011	EFF	10/31/91			NC	10/31/91	2C PERMIT EFFLUENT VIOLATION
COMPLETE PLANS & SPECS		DC	SCH	09/30/91			NC	12/29/91	3C COMPL SCHEDULE VIOLATION
SOLIDS, SUSPENDED	PERCENT RE	0011	EFF	09/30/91			NC	09/30/91	2C PERMIT EFFLUENT VIOLATION
SOLIDS, SUSPENDED	PERCENT RE	0011	TRC	08/31/91			NC	08/31/91	2C PERMIT EFFLUENT VIOLATION
SOLIDS, SETTLEABLE		0011	TRC	07/31/91			RE	10/31/91	2C PERMIT EFFLUENT VIOLATION
SOLIDS, SUSPENDED	PERCENT RE	0011	TRC	07/31/91			NC	07/31/91	2C PERMIT EFFLUENT VIOLATION
					********* SUMMARY SECTION ********				
ALL EFFLUENT					ADMINISTRATIVE ORDER (ST) DOCKET NUMBER: WC4943	05/21/90			DEP AO
ALL EFFLUENT					COMMENT (EPA)	12/11/89			DEP NEGOTIATING CONSENT ORDER WITH PERMITTEE FOR PAST EFFLUENT VIOLATIONS
SOLIDS, SETTLEABLE		0011	05/31/91 - 06/30/91				RE		RESOLVED
SOLIDS, SUSPENDED	PERCENT RE	0011	2/31/90 - 06/30/91				NC		CONTINUING NONCOMPLIANCE
SOLIDS, SUSPENDED	PERCENT RE	0011	04/30/89 - 04/30/90				RP		RESOLVED PENDING
IMPLEMENT WORK PLANS		DC	SCH	06/30/91			NC	09/28/91	3C COMPL SCHEDULE VIOLATION
SUB FINAL ENGINEERING RPT		DC	RPT	03/31/91			RP	07/31/91	3D REPORT OVERDUE
SUBMIT CORRECTIVE ACTION PLAN		DC	RPT	08/31/90			RP	12/31/90	3D REPORT OVERDUE
EMPLOY ENGINEER/CONSULTANT		DC	SCH	06/30/90			RP	10/31/90	3C COMPL SCHEDULE VIOLATION

FIGURE 17–4A
Environmental records help reporters track violators of pollution laws. Reporters routinely check Quarterly Non-compliance Reports (Figure 17–4a), which list each violator in the state and a record of violations. Next, the reporter examines Notice of Violations for the same company (Figure 17–4b), which detail infractions and outline a schedule for compliance.

FIGURE 17–4B

NOTICE OF VIOLATION
STATE DEPARTMENT OF ENVIRONMENTAL PROTECTION

TO: Acme Manufacturing, 1000 Main Street, Anytown.

The purpose of this notice is to inform you of violations which have been found at your facility/property. Be aware that DEP may take action in the future to collect penalties for the violations listed below, and that if these violations are not corrected, penalties will continue to accrue. In addition, this list is not necessarily all-inclusive. It is your responsibility to comply with all legal requirements whether or not the Department notifies you of a violation.

A.   The Division of Permitting, Enforcement, & Remediation, Bureau of Water Management, Department of Environmental Protection ("Department"), has found the following violations at your property at 1000 Main Street, Anytown:

    1.   Failure to submit a report describing proposed steps to eliminate toxicity as required by paragraph 10 (i) of permit No. 0100048 and section 22a-430-3 (j)(10)(C) of the Regulations of State Agencies.

    2.   Failure to submit the results of a second effluent toxicity test as required by paragraph 10 (h) of permit No. CT0100048 and section 22a-430-3(j)(10)(C) of the Regulations of State Agencies.

Additional Comments:

Violation 2 above, occurring after 5-30-91, constitutes four (4) permit violations.

Deadline for verifying to the Department that violation has been corrected:

Immediately correct violation 1, and within 30 days from the date of issuance of this notice submit a Compliance Statement on a form prescribed by the Department (copy enclosed) describing how the above violations have been corrected and enclosing supporting documentation therefore.

---

between a slight or serious health risk. Figure 17–6 shows a TRI form.

Despite their limitations, TRI regulations give reporters an inside look at many industries. The publicity alone about their toxic releases prompted some companies to step up plans to reduce pollution.

Right-to-Know Laws

Reporters are paying increased attention to the potential dangers from accidents at factories where hazardous chemicals are manufactured and stored.

In 1985, an EPA study of U.S. accidents that had released dangerous chemicals stunned many Americans living near facilities that used or produced

hazardous chemicals: During the previous five years, nearly 7,000 accidents had occurred, releasing 420 million pounds of toxic chemicals, killing 138 people, injuring 1,478 and forcing the evacuation of 217,000 residents. The study was done after the world's worst industrial accident in Bhopal, India, in 1984. More than 2,000 people were killed when the poison gas, methyl isocyanate, leaked from Union Carbide's pesticide manufacturing factory. A year later, toxic chemicals leaked from Union Carbide's plant in Institute, W.Va.

The Bhopal tragedy and concerns about possible chemical accidents in the United States prompted Congress in 1986 to pass the Emergency Planning and Community Right-to-Know Act. The act improved local emergency planning for responding to chemical

FIGURE 17–5
Reporters using Toxic Release Inventories in Georgia identified the state's worst polluters, the amounts of pollution released and changes in pollution releases.
Source: Georgia Environmental Protection Division and *The Macon Telegraph*, March 18, 1991. Copyright © by The Macon Telegraph Publishing Company.

Georgia's toxic top ten
Industries statewide with the greatest toxic releases in 1989:

Company	County	Toxics released (in pounds)	Change from 1988
1. Union Camp Corp.	Chatham	13,463,088	-17.6%
2. Macon Kraft Co.	Bibb	5,665,500	-1.4%
3. Georgia-Pacific, Brunswick	Glynn	5,039,025	-55.8%
4. Atlantic Steel Co.	Fulton	5,017,260	-7.3%
5. DSM Chemicals Augusta, Inc.	Richmond	3,719,240	+120.6%
6. Great Southern Paper Co.	Early	3,617,450	+5.4%
7. Chemical Products Corp.	Bartow	3,412,750	-21.1%
8. Atlantic Steel Co.	Bartow	3,092,093	-8.7%
9. PPG Industries	Fulton	2,727,892	+34.8%
10. Gilman Paper Co.	Camden	2,452,360	-8.2%
Total release from 'Toxic Ten'		48,206,658	-13.5%
Releases from 660 other industries statewide		73,075,135	-14.9%
Total toxic releases in Georgia		121,281,793	-14.4%

Note: Starting in 1989, industries no longer had to report two chemicals, sodium hydroxide solutions and non-fibrous aluminum oxide, because the EPA no longer considers them acutely toxic. Taking into account that 'delisting,' Georgia's actual reduction in toxic releases in 1989 was 12.1 percent.

SOURCE: Georgia Environmental Protection Division   RIC THORNTON / The Macon Telegraph

accidents, and provides the public and government agencies with detailed information about possible chemical hazards in their communities.

Reporters can get a quick profile of environmental hazards in a community by familiarizing themselves with the law and investigating whether local agencies and industry are making reasonable attempts to comply. Besides requirements for keeping Toxic Release Inventories, the act has three sections that generate public documentation that reporters can use to get a look inside private industry:

- **Emergency planning.**   State and local response agencies must develop plans to respond to chemical emergencies. Those plans are based on information industry supplies about chemical use, storage and manufacture.

- **Emergency release notification.**   State and local authorities must be notified when any one of more than 350 "extremely dangerous" chemicals is released into the environment. Notice also is required when chemicals listed under federal Superfund laws are accidentally released.

- **Hazardous chemical reporting.**   Any company using chemicals defined as "hazardous" must provide local fire departments and emergency planners with documentation on those substances.

Excessive releases of certain hazardous chemicals—more than 1,000 are listed—must be reported to State Emergency Response Commissions (SERCs) and Local Emergency Planning Committees (LEPCs) established under the law. A check of these reports can point to companies with poor control systems.

After any accident, the facilities coordinator is required to submit a written report to the local and state agencies that describes any emergency response and possible health risks to people exposed.

A reporter seeking background on potential hazards in a community also can turn to other documentary sources available under hazardous chemical reporting provisions of the law. Most useful of these are Material Safety Data Sheets (MSDS), which list chemicals being stored, their physical properties and possible health effects; and Annual Inventories, which list the amounts and general locations of hazardous chemicals being stored.

Some industrial accidents are so small that emergency agencies are not called in. However, by checking a company's emergency release notifications, a reporter may learn that the company has inadequate safety controls and has taken few steps to remedy recurring problems.

Compliance with the laws can be incomplete or nonexistent. Some communities, for instance, may be

FIGURE 17–6
The EPA's Toxic Chemical Release Inventory Reporting Form provides details of pollution discharges into the environment, including levels and types of toxins released.
Source: U.S. Environmental Protection Agency.

(Important: Type or print; read instructions before completing form.) Page 2 of 5

EPA — EPA FORM R
PART II. OFF-SITE LOCATIONS TO WHICH TOXIC CHEMICALS ARE TRANSFERRED IN WASTES

(This space for your optional use.)

1. PUBLICLY OWNED TREATMENT WORKS (POTWs)			
1.1 POTW name		1.2 POTW name	
Street Address		Street Address	
City	County	City	County
State	Zip	State	Zip

2. OTHER OFF-SITE LOCATIONS (DO NOT REPORT LOCATIONS TO WHICH WASTES ARE SENT ONLY FOR RECYCLING OR REUSE).			
2.1 Off-site location name		2.2 Off-site location name	
EPA Identification Number (RCRA ID. No.)		EPA Identification Number (RCRA ID. No.)	
Street Address		Street Address	
City	County	City	County
State	Zip	State	Zip
Is location under control of reporting facility or parent company? [ ] Yes [ ] No		Is location under control of reporting facility or parent company? [ ] Yes [ ] No	

2.3 Off-site location name		2.4 Off-site location name	
EPA Identification Number (RCRA ID. No.)		EPA Identification Number (RCRA ID. No.)	
Street Address		Street Address	
City	County	City	County
State	Zip	State	Zip
Is location under control of reporting facility or parent company? [ ] Yes [ ] No		Is location under control of reporting facility or parent company? [ ] Yes [ ] No	
2.5 Off-site location name		2.6 Off-site location name	
EPA Identification Number (RCRA ID. No.)		EPA Identification Number (RCRA ID. No.)	
Street Address		Street Address	
City	County	City	County
State	Zip	State	Zip
Is location under control of reporting facility or parent company? [ ] Yes [ ] No		Is location under control of reporting facility or parent company? [ ] Yes [ ] No	
[ ] Check if additional pages of Part II are attached. How many? ______			

EPA Form 9350-1(1-89) Revised—Do not use previous versions.

Environmental laws require careful labeling of hazardous waste containers.
Photo by Daniel G. Dunn.

The Shortcomings of Enforcement

The cost of environmental protection in the United States has grown steadily. By 1990, spending on pollution control by government, industry and other institutions totaled about $100 billion a year, nearly as much as the federal budget for education, health and veteran's benefits combined.

Yet many groups involved with environmental issues acknowledge that three decades of government regulation, large-scale public spending and scientific research have failed to solve environmental concerns. Old problems persist, new ones surface with disturbing frequency, and worldwide issues such as ozone depletion, global warming and ocean dumping are expanding the nation's view of environmental dangers.

In 1991, Walter Rosenbaum, an environmental policy expert at the University of Florida, observed in *Environmental Politics and Policy* that few people involved in environmental protection believe that the nation's regulatory approaches have been effective:

> A conviction is growing among major segments of the environmental movement both inside and outside the government that something is fundamentally wrong with many existing approaches to environmental regulation and that action must be taken quickly to change matters. There is ample evidence that many laws considered essential to federal environmental regulation are not working well, and some hardly work at all. Here environmentalists and their opponents often agree, although not about the remedies.

Rosenbaum's final point sets the background for environmental reporting of the future, as the various interest groups battle over which laws and policies to retain, which to discard or reform, and which new approaches to try.

The Clean Air Act offers an example of how regulation has fallen short of environmental goals. The 1970 act authorized the EPA to set emission standards to control the release of hazardous pollutants into the air from cars and industrial plants. The new limits on lead alone reduced the level of toxic emissions from each car by as much as 90 percent, but the number of cars and trucks on U.S. roads continued to grow. Despite two decades of air pollution control, the EPA reported in 1990 that 96 urban areas, home to 133 million

slow to create LEPCs and may not have the staff or money to assure that local industry is complying with the law.

Other useful documents are available under the Superfund program, which identifies more than 1,200 sites on its cleanup list, along with details about other abandoned waste sites around the country. The Centers for Disease Control's Agency for Toxic Substances and Disease Registry keeps records about serious diseases and deaths from exposure to hazardous substances, along with lists of areas closed or restricted because of toxic contamination.

Americans, still exceeded federal standards for ozone, the chief factor in the creation of smog and a health hazard to many people.

After nearly a decade of negotiation, the Clean Air Act was amended in 1990. The new act sets ambitious long-range goals for reducing air pollution, but some critics believe the new standards, like earlier ones, are unrealistic and unattainable.

A second criticism of environmental policy involves the way legislators deal with environmental crises. Rosenbaum noted that many laws and expensive programs are passed before potential dangers are thoroughly understood. "The congressional response to environmental problems is highly volatile," Rosenbaum said, "waxing and waning according to changing public moods, emerging environmental crises, economic circumstances or today's front-page ecological disaster."

The federal Superfund program offers a striking example of how a large government program was speedily passed by Congress to address an immediate crisis, only to be seriously questioned years later. By 1992, the EPA was budgeting $1.5 billion a year for the Superfund program, yet after 12 years, only 80 of 1,275 sites on the Superfund cleanup list had been restored.

Some critics began to question the actual health risks posed by the waste sites, as well as the program's management and priorities. The EPA predicted that 1,000 cancer cases a year resulted from exposure to dioxin and other chemicals at hazardous-waste sites, but some scientific studies questioned the EPA risk assessment figures.

Only history will tell whether the program is an appropriate remedy for a pressing health crisis or an expensive Band-aid for a relatively minor health danger. Meanwhile, attempts to implement the Superfund Act remain an important news story.

A third criticism of environmental policy is the ineffectiveness of government enforcement, which often is influenced by various political, technological and economic factors.

Rosenbaum noted that, "While practically every important environmental ill has been targeted by a major federal law, delay and difficulty in program implementation routinely impede enforcement. Implementation is frequently frustrated by decades of deficient agency staffing or budgets." For example, the entire U.S. EPA had only 45 people in 1988 involved in enforcing the Safe Drinking Water Act, whose provisions should be followed by more than 200,000 public water systems in the country.

Many state agencies also lack sufficient staff to enforce pollution laws. After an environmental group criticized one state's enforcement of the Clean Water Act, a reporter reviewed the agency's budget and staff levels.

> The state's Water Compliance Division has 11 fewer workers now than it did last year, and cuts in federal subsidies may eliminate another 38 workers from the unit during the next four years.
>
> The state's entire environmental protection budget was cut by 11 percent this year, the largest cut of any state agency, and the department is operating with 67 fewer employees than it did last year.
>
> The agency's commissioner is trying to restore 10 positions to the water compliance unit in next year's budget.

Public opinion, a slumping economy and the environmental priorities of a new administration also can influence a state's enforcement practices. Joseph Petulla's study of environmental protection described how enforcement became a low priority during the Reagan administration. From 1975 to 1985, Petulla noted, the enforcement workload at the EPA doubled with the passage of new laws to regulate hazardous wastes, pesticides and toxic substances. Yet the Reagan administration moved swiftly in 1981 to dismantle the agency's enforcement division and cut its operating budget by 35 percent.

Reporters should consider several other factors when writing about environmental enforcement:

- Some industries will do the minimum allowable to meet environmental regulations. Companies may deliberately stall, ignore notices and tie up regulators with lengthy appeals.

- Violators may decide it is cheaper to pay fines than to implement the required procedures or to install expensive equipment.

- Compliance deadlines specified in a law may be impractical. Industries often can obtain extensions by arguing that the deadline would cause an unreasonable financial burden. The claims may be legitimate, but they also can be a stalling tactic.

CONSTANTS OF THE BEAT

As the environmental beat evolves, it continues to be shaped by forces that for decades have defined issues and solutions, and influenced news coverage. The most dominant of these are economics, scientific uncertainty, emerging problems and, most recently, the NIMBY movement.

Scientific Uncertainty

Many environmental stories contain elements of scientific uncertainty, often dealing with health risks and safe limits for exposure to toxic substances, which complicate the reporter's efforts to supply accurate information. How safe is a proposed waste storage site? How will animal breeding grounds be affected by a new housing project? What level of contaminants in drinking water poses a cancer risk?

On these and other matters, scientists and other experts often disagree, and the reporter must weigh the preponderance of evidence on a subject and tell readers and viewers which claim has the most credence. The reporter must try to alert the public to real dangers while being careful not to trigger unwarranted fears.

The environmental reporter's task is further complicated by changes in regulatory standards and emerging new scientific information. Government regulators adopt standards to control the level of pollutants, but are those standards adequate? The standards may be criticized as too stringent by industry and too lax by environmentalists. A new study may cause the agency to revise the standard in one direction or the other, but in either case, the group adversely affected by the change will challenge the study and criticize the agency. The story of dioxin, long considered the most dangerous man-made carcinogen, is a case in point.

After the Love Canal crisis, the EPA adopted strict dioxin standards based on a 1978 study of 485 white rats whose food was laced with the chemical byproduct. A strong link to cancer was established when many of the rats developed tumors. The study concluded that even tiny amounts of dioxin exposure from water or soil contamination increased the risk of cancer in humans, and set an exposure limit of one part per billion.

The dioxin-cancer link led to federal requirements that many industries install expensive equipment to reduce dioxin emissions, and triggered lawsuits totaling billions of dollars against manufacturers whose emissions were alleged to have caused a variety of health problems.

By 1990, however, new techniques existed for detecting tumors, and several industries affected by dioxin regulations hired scientists to review the original study. Those scientists concluded that dioxin was less of a cancer danger than was earlier thought, and the companies pressured the EPA to re-evaluate—and possibly relax—federal standards. Although some scientists at the EPA disputed the companies' conclusions, agency director William K. Reilly ordered a formal reassessment of federal dioxin standards.

At the same time, other scientists, including several at the National Institute of Environmental Health Sciences, opposed lowering the standards. Some research had shown that dioxin might be more, not less, dangerous, and that it also could be harmful to human reproductive systems. Federal standards for other dangerous substances, including radon and asbestos, also came under assault from critics who said the agency's exposure limits were too strict.

The debate over dioxin and other substances illustrates issues common to environmental stories involving health risks. Reporters must remember the fluid state of scientific knowledge and avoid sweeping statements about scientific matters.

Reporters writing about risk issues may be tempted to gloss over technical aspects of a story or to generalize based on limited scientific information. For example, one environmental reporter described the dioxin debate this way:

> Scientists now say that evacuating Times Beach, Mo., in 1982 because of dioxin poisoning was a mistake because new studies indicate dioxin is not as serious a cancer threat as once thought.

That vague passage, with its reference to unidentified "scientists" and unspecified "new studies," gave readers and viewers a mistaken impression that the dioxin scare of the 1980s was unfounded, when in reality, scientific consensus was a long way off.

Economic Factors

In 1990, the environment was *the* dominant domestic issue. The 20th anniversary of the first Earth Day brought a flood of media coverage. But two years later, with the nation's economy in a severe slump, the environment was a minor issue in the presidential campaign. *Time* magazine described the shifting national mood this way:

> Who cares about a few spotted owls when loggers' jobs are at stake? Why worry about caribou when America needs more of Alaska's oil? Who can afford to think about the environment when the economy is the pits?
>
> When times get tough, the questions facing environmentalists get even tougher. And these days, economic anxieties and shifting political winds are threatening to produce a green-out effect that could make tree huggers feel as endangered as the California condor.

The relationship between environmental protection and the economy are inextricably linked, and environmental reporters follow such political developments closely. How will environmental policies affect the economy? Will they slow economic growth and business investment? Will companies be forced to close or move to other states or countries if regulations become too burdensome? Environmental regulation is costly for both industries and taxpayers, and in a tight economy new programs come in for increasing scrutiny.

> Scores of interest groups—including ranchers, miners, loggers, developers and manufacturers—have become allies in a "wise-use movement" to fight what they see as the extremism of those who put wilderness protection and the rights of endangered animals before the welfare of humans.
>
> "There seems to be a coalescing of different economic interests to fight the green devils," observes environmentalist Thomas Lovejoy of the Smithsonian Institution.
>
> The wise-users are pressuring Congress to weaken the Endangered Species Act and the Clean Water Act as a way to spur economic growth. Hoping to encourage a public and political backlash, the movement has

been adopting many of the tactics long-used by environmentalists—lobbying and lawsuits.

Similar scenarios are played out at the state and local level when economic interests feel threatened by environmental laws. Political and public support for environmental programs can rise and fall with the economy, and reporters must monitor these factors in covering environmental trends.

New Problems

Environmental stories such as air and water pollution, hazardous-waste disposal and conservation of natural resources continue to be an important part of the beat. But new concerns have arisen that also will shape environmental policies and politics—and environmental stories—in the coming years. Most recently, global issues such as ocean dumping, ozone depletion and destruction of rain forests have joined the environmental agenda.

One of the major environmental stories of 1987 was the U.S. Department of Energy's mishandling of nuclear weapons production at 14 plants around the country. News stories reported on serious leaks of radioactive materials, improper waste storage and handling, and deliberate concealment of information about possible health dangers. Nuclear reactors used in weapons production were shut down at military installations at Savannah River, S.C., and Hanford, Wash. As the story unfolded, reporters learned that evidence of serious accidents and breakdowns were concealed at some plants.

Rather than being a momentary crisis, the weapons production fiasco became a continuing story. Reporters followed government cleanup efforts and scrutinized plans to "decommission" nuclear reactors, a process that requires removing radioactive material and reducing residual contamination so the sites can be put to other uses.

Problems at the Savannah River Site, the nation's only facility for tritium production for nuclear weapons, became an ongoing story after the plant's main reactor was shut down in 1988. Frequent spills of radioactive tritium alarmed residents of communities that drew drinking water from the river. A spill of 150 gallons of contaminated water in December 1991 triggered a series of stories in *The State*, South Carolina's largest newspaper, that examined health risks, safety issues, damage costs and other concerns.

> The Beaufort-Jasper Water Authority stopped drawing water from the Savannah River Saturday, waiting until a plume of tritium-laced water clears its intake pipes. Officials said that could take as little as a few days or as long as two weeks.
>
> The contamination and shutdown has caused no interruption to the 50,000 people who get water from the authority. Several industries on the Georgia side also have stopped using water from the river.
>
> State Department of Health and Environmental Control technicians continued tests on the river Sunday. Meanwhile, plant officials said the levels of tritium released into the river were below Environmental Protection Agency safety standards.
>
> Although authorities said the leak presented little public health danger, the Department of Energy's ability to safely operate the nuclear weapons facility has been questioned since the leak.

In the aftermath, reporters also followed the government's efforts to calm public fears.

> Energy Secretary James Watkins Wednesday blamed "management insensitivity" and "human error" for last month's tritium spill at the Savannah River Site.
>
> Watkins and other officials concluded a two-day public relations blitz in South Carolina and Georgia. They admitted at each stop that poor management contributed to the spill and that poor communications unnecessarily frightened the public.
>
> "Any radioactive release from a reactor into the environment is a great concern to us," Watkins said. "The amount in this case, however, should not have raised fear and apprehension on the part of the public."

By probing below the surface of official statements, one reporter learned that the Energy Department had received sufficient warning to possibly prevent the accident.

> One month before the Christmas spill of radioactive tritium into the Savannah River, an Energy Department study warned that a leak from the reactor was possible and recommended "increased management attention to the problem."
>
> But those warnings weren't adequately heeded even though tritium leaks from the reactor have been frequent for more than a decade, according to congres-

sional sources. Those leaks also have been identified repeatedly as needing attention, with the latest call coming from Energy Secretary James Watkins nearly two months before the spill.

Finally, reporters tracked the story through the courts, where environmental groups had been trying to stop the DOE from reactivating the plant.

> Efforts to delay restarting the Savannah River Site's reactor until after a cooling tower is completed received new life Friday.
>
> The 4th Circuit Court of Appeals reinstated a lawsuit that attempts to block restart until the $90 million tower is finished. But the plaintiff's victory wasn't complete: The appeals court refused to grant an injunction prohibiting restart.
>
> The lawsuit was filed by the Energy Research Foundation of Columbia and the Natural Resources Defense Council.

Cost and safety issues surrounding these plants remain important local and national concerns, likely to generate news coverage for decades. New environmental concerns like these emerge both at the national and local level, and reporters must closely monitor regulatory agencies, courts and other sources where the problems may surface.

The NIMBY Movement

The scenario is familiar. Angry residents stage protests, give emotional testimony and file civil lawsuits to halt construction of a proposed facility in their neighborhoods. The proposal may be a new landfill, a trash-burning plant or a hazardous-waste disposal site.

Planners have dubbed this now-predictable pattern of local opposition the NIMBY (Not In My Back Yard) movement, and it is a pervasive element of much local environmental reporting.

The movement flourishes because state and federal laws give citizens groups considerable influence over implementation of environmental laws and policies. For example, several federal laws give citizens legal standing to sue federal agencies to force them to enforce regulations. Another law, the 1969 National Environmental Policy Act, requires that environmental impact reports be developed for large-scale projects or those involving federal funds. Citizens can challenge the reports in court, which can lead to costly delays or eventual abandonment of the proposal.

More than 20 states give citizens a role in writing, implementing and enforcing environmental laws. Some laws require public notice and hearings when new regulations are proposed or when permits are issued for pollution discharges or hazardous-waste sites.

These laws are often defended for giving the public a powerful voice in shaping environmental policies and opposing potentially dangerous facilities. However, critics argue that the movement has crippled legitimate efforts to build facilities that will, in fact, help the environment.

A recurring example involves the siting of new facilities to store and dispose of solid and hazardous wastes. While most Americans recognize and support the need to store toxic byproducts from manufacturing, few are willing to welcome disposal sites into their areas. Decisions about where to put controversial facilities can become intense political battles, pitting state against state, city against city, neighborhood against neighborhood. In recent years, siting boards have been criticized for locating controversial facilities in poor and minority neighborhoods whose residents lack the political clout of middle-class suburbanites to block them.

Controversies fueled by citizen opposition are a powerful magnet for reporters. Local activists are often well-organized and highly vocal, and frequently attract support from local officeholders.

> Nearly 10 months after a state panel picked three potential sites for a low-level radioactive-waste dump, key state lawmakers want the statewide search to start over again—but to avoid their districts.
>
> A group of legislators plans to introduce legislation next week that would require the state Hazardous Waste Management Service to develop a plan for choosing a temporary waste-storage site, and a new plan for a permanent disposal site. One of the main aims of several lawmakers is to eliminate their towns from consideration.
>
> Residents of those towns have argued that the sites are not suitable for dumps because they contain important drinking water sources and prime farmland.

While citizens often cite environmental concerns, critics of NIMBYism say opposition is often driven by

another concern—declining real estate values. Patrick G. Marshall, writing in *Congressional Quarterly*, noted the difficulty facing policy-makers—and reporters—in evaluating citizen opposition.

> The problem is distinguishing between legitimate protests and pure NIMBY actions. This can be difficult to do, however, because NIMBY activists sometimes cloak their self-interested concerns behind loftier goals. Residents may object to the siting of a landfill in their neighborhood on environmental grounds when their real concern is not environmental at all.

Reporters cannot ignore legitimate conflict in such stories, but there is a danger of focusing only on the heat generated by opponents without fully exploring other issues that may shed light on the issue. Reporters must attempt to place local protests in a broader context that examines elements such as the safety of the disposal technology being proposed, the need for such a facility and the site selection process.

SPECIAL RESOURCES

Interest in environmental issues has produced a growing array of resource guides and training programs to help reporters expand their knowledge and prepare to cover complex stories:

- One or two good general introductions to environmental science can help reporters new to the environment beat. A recommended book is *Living in the Environment*, by G. Tyler Miller.

- A quick reference source such as *Handbook of Toxic and Hazardous Chemicals*, by the Noyes Data Corp., or *Hawley's Condensed Chemical Dictionary* can be a valuable source for the many stories involving toxic chemicals the reporter can expect to write.

- Computerized data bases, including the federal government's Chemical Substances Information Network, allow reporters to conduct quick searches to learn about virtually every aspect of hazardous chemicals.

- The *EPA Journal*, published bi-monthly by the U.S. Environmental Protection Agency, focuses each issue on a specific topic, ranging from food safety and the greenhouse effect to the coastal environment and Superfund laws. The *EPA Journal* provides useful background and opinions from a range of sources and is available free to reporters.

- The Media Resource Service's computerized database contains the names of more than 25,000 experts in science, technology and medicine who are willing to answer reporter's questions. The toll-free number is 800-223-1730.

- Many universities, professional groups and government agencies offer short courses and seminars for reporters. Organizations such as the The Media Institute, The Environmental Health Center, Scientists' Institute for Public Information, and the Society of Environmental Journalists conduct workshops and other training programs, and publish newsletters and backgrounders on environmental issues.

  The Media Institute in Washington, D.C., for example, publishes a series of useful books for journalists on health and environmental issues. Two books, *Reporting on Risk*, and *Health Risks and the Press*, provide excellent practical advice for writing about the ambiguities of science and avoiding common errors in writing about complex and technical information.

  The Environmental Health Center, a branch of the National Safety Council, publishes the monthly *Environment Writer*, a free newsletter for reporters. It is filled with advice columns, feature articles on environmental writers, special interest news and reprints of selected articles. Its "Reading Rack" feature summarizes important recent stories from all media, while "Nose for News," alerts writers to important upcoming issues. Each issue profiles a chemical, listing its properties, health effects, industrial uses and laws regulating its production. The center also distributes journalists' guides to specific subjects, including *Reporting on Radon*, and an overview of municipal solid waste management.

***

AN ENVIRONMENTAL GLOSSARY

ABATEMENT: Elimination or reduction in the amount of pollution.

ACID RAIN: Precipitation in any form, including mist and dry deposits, with an acidity level higher than would be found naturally. Damages forests, vegetation and structures, and often is blamed for raising acidity in lakes and streams in the Northeast. Causes of acid rain include nitrogen oxides from motor vehicle emissions and sulphur dioxide from coal-fired power plants.

ACUTE EXPOSURE: Single exposure to a toxic substance that results in death or serious biological harm. Exposure of a day or less.

AGRICULTURAL POLLUTION: Liquid and solid waste from farming, including runoff and leaching of fertilizers and pesticides, animal manure and carcasses, erosion and crop residues.

AIR POLLUTION: Contaminants of polluting materials in the air that do not disperse, resulting in harmful effects to human health and the environment.

AIR QUALITY: The degree to which air is polluted. The lower the pollution level, the higher the air quality, based on aesthetic or medical criteria.

ALTERNATIVE ENERGY: Energy obtained from sources other than the burning of fossil fuels such as coal, petroleum or natural gas, or from nuclear reactors. Usually refers to solar power, wind power and hydroelectric (water-generated) power.

AMBIENT AIR STANDARD: A government standard for air quality in a region, defined in terms of pollution levels. Industries that discharge pollutants must limit emissions so as not to reduce air quality below the standard.

AQUIFER: A geological formation through which ground water can travel, supplying springs and wells. Aquifers that become contaminated can pollute wells and springs over a wide area.

ASBESTOS: A mineral fiber that causes cancer, asbestosis or other respiratory ailments when inhaled. The use of asbestos in construction and manufacturing is banned by the EPA.

BIODEGRADABLE: Any substance or material that can be broken down by microorganisms and bacterial action.

CARCINOGEN: A cancer-producing substance or one that contributes to the production of cancer.

CONTAMINANT: Any substance, physical, biological, chemical or radiological, that diminishes the quality of air, water or soil.

DEFORESTATION: The permanent removal of forest and undergrowth; considered to contribute to the greenhouse effect.

DIOXIN: A byproduct of herbicide and paper production. A known carcinogen, dioxin also is suspected of causing birth defects.

ECOSYSTEM: A community of interdependent organisms together with the environment they inhabit. An ecosystem is distinct from nearby environments.

EFFLUENT: Liquid waste produced by sewage treatment and industrial processes.

EMISSION: A substance, usually gas or liquid, released into the environment. Pollutants are often called **Toxic emissions**.

ENVIRONMENTAL IMPACT STATEMENT (EIS): A written report, based on studies, describing the environmental consequences of a specific action. State and federal laws require that many new projects undergo an EIS before approval.

ENVIRONMENTAL QUALITY STANDARDS: The maximum pollution level permitted in air, water and soil to protect human health and public welfare. Regulatory agencies set standards to control everything from toxic levels in industrial discharges to the amount of pesticide residue in food products.

FOSSIL FUEL: Fuel created by the incomplete decomposition of ancient organic materials. Includes crude oil, coal, natural gas and oil shale. When burned, they release carbon dioxide, a contributor to the greenhouse effect. Fossil fuels are considered "nonrenewable resources" because they are consumed faster than they are created.

GREENHOUSE EFFECT: Worldwide changes in weather and sea levels resulting from a warming of the atmosphere caused by release of carbon dioxide and other gases. The gases blanket the atmosphere, preventing heat from escaping. Major contributors to the greenhouse effect are burning of fossil fuels and the clearing of forests. Also, **Global warming**.

GROUND WATER: Water that fills pores and crevices in rock and soil below the Earth's surface, making up the bulk of the Earth's nonsaline supply. Ground water is an important source for public water supplies.

HABITAT: The dwelling place for a species of plant or animal, requiring specific environmental conditions.

HABITAT LOSS: The alteration or removal of environmental conditions, such as vegetation and water, resulting in the disappearance of plants and animals. Habitat loss often occurs from development for human use, including agriculture, roads and buildings.

HAZARDOUS WASTE: Any byproduct or refuse that contains substances harmful to life. Hazardous waste may be toxic, including pesticides and other poisonous substances; explosive or flammable; or corrosive, such as acids and alkalis.

HAZ-MAT: Short for hazardous materials, either toxic, flammable or corrosive.

HERBICIDE: A chemical used to kill weeds, used primarily in horticulture and agriculture.

INSECTICIDE: A chemical used to kill insects.

IONIZING RADIATION. Radiation capable of removing electrons from atoms and molecules, sometimes increasing chemical activity in an organism and damaging tissue. Excessive levels of ionizing radiation can produce effects on the body itself or genetic damage to chromosomes and genes. Sources of ionizing radiation include X-rays and gamma rays emitted by radioactive materials.

LANDFILL: A dumping site for domestic trash and garbage. The refuse is compacted and regularly covered with a layer of dirt to allow microorganisms to decompose organic portions. In the past, some landfills were used for illegal dumping of hazardous and industrial waste. Also, **Sanitary landfill**.

MELTDOWN: The overheating of the core of a nuclear reactor to the point that its fuel elements melt.

MORBIDITY RATE: The incidence of sickness or disease in a population.

MORTALITY RATE: The incidence of death in a population.

MUTAGEN: Any agent that causes biological mutation, including radioactive materials, ultraviolet light and certain chemicals.

MUNICIPAL WASTE: Materials discarded by households and businesses, but not including waste produced in manufacturing and industrial processes. Typically includes paper, garbage, plastics and metals.

NIMBY: Acronym for Not in My Back Yard. Local opposition to proposed developments stemming from a fear of reduced quality of life for residents and lower property values.

OZONE: A naturally occurring form of oxygen that, at high levels, can harm plants and irritate eyes and respiratory tissue. Ozone is a key component in the creation of smog.

OZONE LAYER: An atmospheric layer where oxygen molecules exposed to ultraviolet radiation from the sun produce ozone in levels greater than those found elsewhere in the atmosphere. The process of ozone creation absorbs energy from the radiation, keeping it from reaching the Earth's surface. Ozone depletion is an environmental concern because it allows more ultraviolet radiation to penetrate the atmosphere.

PESTICIDES: A generic term for chemical substances used to kill undesirable plants, animals, pests and disease-causing fungi. The term includes fungicides, herbicides and insecticides.

POLLUTION: The contamination of soil, water or air that creates a hazard or potential hazard to living species. Typically refers to discharges of noxious or dangerous substances, including industrial emissions and improper disposal of human domestic waste and sewage.

RADIOACTIVE WASTE: Waste that is contaminated with the unstable nucleus of an atom, called radionuclides. Radioactive waste must be isolated to avoid direct or indirect contact with humans, and disposed of by approved methods. Also called **Nuclear waste**, it is generally classified as low-level, intermediate-level or high-level.

RADON: A naturally occurring gas, odorless and colorless, that is present in most rocks, especially near ground level. Radon exposure at high levels is suspected of causing lung cancer, and the EPA sets recommended exposure limits inside buildings.

RECYCLING: The recovery and reuse of material from waste. Municipal recycling often requires separation of domestic refuse such as paper, plastics and used motor oil.

RIGHT-TO-KNOW: Short for the Emergency Planning and Community Right-to-Know Act, passed by Congress in 1986. The act requires local emergency planning for responding to chemical accidents and provides public access to information about possible chemical hazards in a community.

SEWER OUTFALL: A pipe that transports raw or treated sewage to a discharge point.

SMOG: A term originally used to describe a mixture of smoke and fog, it is often used to describe potentially dangerous air pollution produced when ozone and motor vehicle emissions undergo a photochemical action during exposure to sunlight.

SULPHUR DIOXIDE: One of several byproducts resulting from the use of fuels, including fuel oil and coal. Although it is not proven harmful to humans, sulphur dioxide is useful in measuring air pollution because its presence indicates levels of many other pollutants created in fuel consumption that are more difficult to measure. Sulphur dioxide is implicated as a contributor to acid rain.

TOXIC RELEASE INVENTORY (TRI):   Annual reports submitted by business and industry listing the types and quantities of toxic and cancer-causing chemicals released into the air. Mandated under the federal Emergency Planning and Community Right-to-Know Act of 1986.

TOXIC WASTE: A type of hazardous waste that is considered poisonous to plants and animals. Requires special disposal.

✳✳✳

SUGGESTED READINGS

Chemicals, the Press and the Public. Washington, D.C.: Environmental Health Center. 1989.

Practical handbook explaining the Emergency Planning and Community Right-to-Know Act of 1986 and how reporters use it. Provides advice on reporting chemical emergencies.

Citizen's Guide for Environmental Issues: A Handbook for Cultivating Dialogue. Washington, D.C.: National Institute of Chemical Studies, 1991.

"Covering the Environment." *Gannett Center Journal*. (Summer 1990).

Published by the Gannett Center for Media Studies, this issue contains a series of essays by journalists and others discussing national and international environmental issues.

Hodges, Laurent. *Environmental Pollution*. New York: Holt, Rinehart and Winston, 1984.

This excellent book provides detailed scientific discussions of environmental pollutants, their health effects and methods of control. It also provides a history of environmental action and legislation, as well as a discussion of current issues.

Klaidman, Stephen. *Health in the Headlines*. New York: Oxford University Press, 1991.

Chapter 1 is a critical look at health-risk assessments in news accounts. Chapters 2, 3, 4 and 5 discuss news coverage of EDB, radon, nuclear power and the greenhouse effect, respectively.

Logan, Robert A. *Environmental Issues for the '90s: A Handbook for Journalists*. Washington, D.C.: The Media Institute, 1992.

A comprehensive summary of environmental issues and resources for journalists, plus descriptions, addresses and telephone numbers of more than 75 government, trade and environmental organizations.

Miller, G. Tyler, Jr. *Living in the Environment: Introduction to Environmental Science*. 7th ed. Belmont, Calif.: Wadsworth Publishing Co., 1992.

A detailed introduction to environmental science and issues.

Petulla, Joseph M. *Environmental Protection in the United States*. San Francisco: San Francisco Study Center, 1987.

Chapters 2 and 7 contain useful discussions of the media's role and ethics in covering environmental stories.

Chapter 18

Science, Medicine and Health

In July 1985, Americans witnessed an explosion in media coverage about a devastating medical epidemic.

More than four years earlier, the U.S. Centers for Disease Control had published the first articles by researchers about young homosexual men in California and New York who had been diagnosed with rare and sometimes fatal medical conditions. Those conditions would soon become known as AIDS, acquired immune deficiency syndrome. News coverage at the time consisted of two brief articles by medical reporters for the *Los Angeles Times* and *The New York Times*.

By 1985, an estimated 12,000 people had been diagnosed with AIDS, and more than 6,000 had died. As the number of cases grew, top science and medical writers tracked the spread of AIDS and wrote about scientists' efforts to understand the mysterious disease.

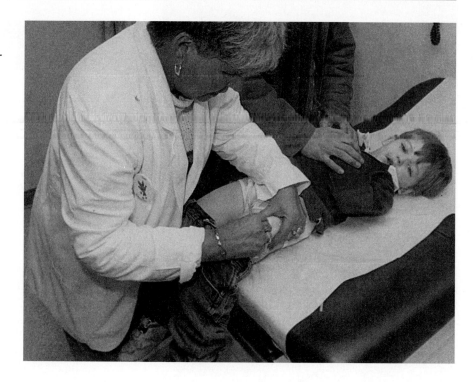

But even then, AIDS was not treated as a major story, nor was it portrayed in the press as a serious public health threat.

That changed in July 1985 when actor Rock Hudson disclosed that he was dying of AIDS. Almost overnight, four years of accumulated medical research, dire warnings and death statistics flooded onto news pages and into the airwaves. Both *Newsweek* and *Time* magazines published lengthy cover stories summarizing the current state of AIDS information. A month later, The Associated Press distributed to its clients a 35-story package about AIDS, totalling 28,000 words. In the six months between July and December 1985, NBC News carried three times as many stories about AIDS as it had during the previous four years.

More coverage did not always translate to better coverage, however. News reports, always a powerful shaper of public opinion, became the major information source about AIDS for most people, and critics had no trouble finding examples of sensationalized, inaccurate, even hysterical reporting. Yet, there also were examples of thoughtful, careful and accurate reporting, given the still-mysterious nature of the disease.

In his assessment of AIDS coverage in his book *Health in the Headlines*, author Stephen Klaidman concludes that the press did a credible job reporting the medical side of AIDS in the early years, but missed other important stories:

> The failure was not in the reporting of the medical science itself. It was that most journalists did not recognize, or at least were not reporting, two major non-science stories about AIDS: the toll the disease was taking in human suffering and the thoroughly inadequate Reagan administration response, which began to be evident as early as the fall of 1982.

James Kinsella, a newspaper reporter and editor who spent two years examining the media's coverage of AIDS, was often highly critical of the coverage.

> There are standouts in this (AIDS) epidemic, but pretty consistently we as journalists have missed the major stories. AIDS is often a confused story. Sometimes it's a story that gets the facts just dead wrong. I'm still scared about how we do our jobs and why we don't do them very well.

On the positive side, Kinsella said, the news media's experience covering AIDS taught it valuable lessons about covering complex science, medical and health issues.

More than any modern story, coverage of AIDS reflects the broad spectrum of issues, challenges and complexities facing journalists who write about science, medicine and health. Stories span the spectrum from scientific research and health risks to public health policy, rising medical costs, government funding, experimental treatments and medical insurance.

For many reporters, covering an AIDS story was their introduction to writing about science and medical issues. While some stories fell to the science and medical writers, beat and general assignment reporters with little science or medical background often were assigned to cover stories with AIDS angles in schools, prisons, hospitals and health agencies. For the first time, many reporters found themselves reviewing health statistics, questioning scientists and medical experts, and interviewing patients who were deathly ill.

In newsrooms large and small, the experience of covering AIDS triggered a new sensitivity to medical and health issues, and a recognition of their importance to people's lives and sense of well-being. Journalists also were reminded how easy it is, in the rush of daily journalism, to get facts wrong, and realized the difficulty of producing accurate and complete stories about medical and scientific topics.

Reporters who cover science, medicine and health must stay informed by reading both popular publications and scientific literature. They must gather background and understanding from many sources to help them know what issues to report and what information to emphasize. They must be able to clarify the conflicting views of experts, and to explain technical language and mind-numbing numbers. They must locate the right sources and question them intelligently. And finally, they must write clearly and accurately to capture the drama and mystery of a story without oversimplifying or sensationalizing.

WHY COVER SCIENCE, MEDICINE AND HEALTH?

For most adults, traditional science education ends with high school or college, but their interest in scientific, medical and health subjects continues after formal schooling ends. That's especially true when the information is relevant to their lives. For them, newspapers, magazines and television are modern science "teachers."

Public interest in scientific developments and technological innovations can be traced to development of the atomic bomb in the final years of World War II, followed by the United States' race for space with the Soviet Union beginning in the late 1950s. Medical advances such as the development of a polio vaccine in the 1950s, the first open-heart surgery in the 1960s and a series of dramatic organ transplants in the 1970s and 1980s further captured the public's attention.

The past 20 years have brought an explosion in the public's appetite for news about science, medicine and health. During the 1980s, national and local television news added regular medical and health reports, while dozens of newspapers launched their own special pages dedicated to news of science, technology and health. Surveys by The Scientists' Institute for Public Information have shown that the number of reporters whose primary assignment involves science and medical reporting has risen steadily since 1984.

Stories about subjects that affect people's health rank especially high in reader interest. Alerted by media stories, coffee drinkers wonder whether too much caffeine can lead to heart disease, sunbathers want to protect themselves from skin cancer, and people who live near nuclear plants worry about exposure to low-level radiation.

Increasingly, science and health stories have moved from inside pages to prominent display on front pages. The space program, environmental hazards and AIDS are only a few of the stories that have become part of the daily news flow. Today it's not unusual for a major metropolitan daily to carry as many as three science-related stories on a single day's front page.

One of the major medical developments of 1992 involved the safety of silicone gel breast implants received by an estimated 100,000 women a year. Although implant safety had been debated by medical experts for more than 25 years, the issue emerged as a major story after many women complained of medical complications and new studies suggested that the implants ruptured far more often than manufacturers and plastic surgeons believed. The Food and Drug Administration ultimately set limits on new implant surgery and ordered new studies on their safety.

> WASHINGTON—Silicone gel breast implants, one of the most popular cosmetic surgeries in the United States, will be available only to a limited number of women who will help test their safety, FDA commissioner David Kessler announced today.
>
> The implants will be available only to women willing to take part in controlled studies, transforming what was often an outpatient procedure in a plastic surgeon's office into an experimental procedure.
>
> Researchers are expected to closely study—for at least three years—all women implanted with the controversial silicone pouches. Women will be required to sign a detailed consent form outlining the risks, which include painful scar tissue around the implant, leaks and a possible hindrance of mammography to detect early breast cancers.

Stories about the implants examined medical complications among patients, the absence of earlier scientific studies to establish their safety, shortcomings in the FDA's procedures for approving medical devices and other aspects.

Supporters of increased media coverage of science and medicine argue that it helps create a more informed public that can play a key role in defining scientific and medical policies, as it did in the case of implants. Vast sums of public money go into scientific research, in fields as diverse as space exploration, medical research and military defense. Informed public input can help shape national priorities and government programs.

However, some scientists and policy experts believe the public is not sufficiently educated or informed to be allowed to influence scientific policy and spending decisions. They argue that media coverage of science is often superficial and sensationalized, creating controversy that places hurdles in the path of important research and policy decisions.

Few would dispute that the news media, especially television and daily newspapers, are an imperfect instrument for presenting science and medical information to the public. Still, responsible press coverage of science and medicine can help people understand its social and human consequences, and guarantee a strong public voice in decisions with long-term implications for society.

STORIES ON THE BEAT

On any given day, *The New York Times* may carry one or more stories on its front page involving some aspect of science, medicine, health and technology. But every Tuesday devoted fans of these topics go deeper into the paper to find *Science Times*, a weekly section of feature-length articles about trends in science, medicine, psychology and other fields involving important research.

In one issue, *Science Times* carried stories about an epidemic in wrist injuries among computer users, federal funding for a cross-country train that travels on an invisible magnetic cushion, counseling programs to help children reduce stress, and promising research to block transmission of AIDS from mothers to unborn children.

The diversity, depth and currency of the *Times'* coverage of science, medicine and health is mirrored in hundreds of newspapers and magazines around the country, and reflects the level to which the best reporting has risen. Some broad categories on the science and medical beats are stories about research studies, health effects, new technology and treatments, health-care delivery, occupational health, alternative medicine and legal and ethical issues.

Research Studies

It's no coincidence that many of the important medical stories reported in the nation's newspapers and newscasts appear on Thursdays. That's the day *The New England Journal of Medicine*, one of the leading medical publications and a premier source for the latest medical research, reaches subscribers. Knowledgeable watchers of medicine have come to expect interesting, important and sometimes offbeat medical stories in their local newspaper each Thursday, compliments of the *Journal*.

This wire service story, based on a *Journal* study, reported on a research study that discovered uneven vitamin levels in milk supplies. The story begins with a summary lead of the findings, followed by an explanation of their significance.

BOSTON—Most samples of milk from five eastern states contained either too much or too little vitamin D, researchers say. In one instance, the levels were dangerously high, causing medical problems for eight people.

In the study, published in Thursday's issue of *The New England Journal of Medicine*, doctors tested milk from supermarkets in Vermont, New Hampshire, Massachusetts, New Jersey and Virginia. They found that 62 percent contained substantially less vitamin D than listed.

The doctors say their work highlights the need for more stringent testing of milk to make sure it contains the proper amount of vitamins. In young people, a vitamin D deficiency causes rickets, which results in malformed bones, while among the elderly it leads to weak bones and fractures. Most of the nation's 500 milk-processing plants now add vitamin D to milk.

Reporters often use wire service reports of research studies to develop local stories. In this case, reporters could examine vitamin testing procedures in their states or counties, contacting the district office of the Food and Drug Administration, which sets national standards, the state health department, milk producers and local health agencies.

Around the country, in university laboratories, government research centers and private corporations, researchers conduct experiments designed to advance human knowledge in science, medicine and health. Each research field has its own journals that science and medical writers can follow to keep abreast of important findings and trends.

Much media coverage focuses on research that holds the promise of helping people improve their lives. While many stories require a direct, serious tone, writers sometimes take a lighter approach when the subject warrants.

Science has found an explanation for one of the obvious effects of drinking too much: the beer belly.

Swiss researchers report that when people drink alcohol, their bodies burn up fat much more slowly than usual. And any fat that is not burned is stored in the paunch, the thighs or other places where people put on weight.

The study was based on an experiment in which people were put on a diet that included about 3 ounces of pure alcohol a day, the equivalent of about six shots of whiskey or six beers. That much alcohol reduced their bodies' burning of fat by about one-third.

This writer used an essential technique—explaining scientific theories or procedures with familiar examples. Comparing 3 ounces of alcohol to six glasses of beer gave readers a simple and concrete image they could use to evaluate the study's relevance to their own drinking habits.

Typically, study results become public only when they are published in research journals, or after researchers present their findings at scientific conventions (see Figure 18–1). Most scientific journals will not publish a study until it has been reviewed by a panel of qualified researchers who evaluate the quality of the research procedures and the plausibility of the results, a process known as "peer review."

Occasionally, researchers take their findings directly to the public by issuing news releases or scheduling news conferences before the study is published in research journals. This practice is controversial in scientific circles because the results have not undergone peer review.

In 1988, Dr. William Masters and Virginia Johnson, the well-known researchers of sexual behavior, came under intense criticism from the scientific community when they released to the news media results of a controversial study that asserted that the AIDS epidemic was "running rampant in the heterosexual community." The researchers announced their findings—timed to coincide with release of their new book—at a news conference and in a cover story in *Newsweek* magazine, before they were reviewed by other scientists. Respected medical experts criticized Masters and Johnson for making an end run around the peer review process, and challenged both the findings and the study's research methods. While some news reports about the study carefully qualified the results with disclaimers from other researchers, many stories appeared with only the most sensational assertions, raising false fears in the public.

News conferences to announce research findings should be approached with caution. Reporters should ask whether the study has been accepted or published

FIGURE 18–1
Although the practice is controversial, some scientists issue news releases about their research before the results are published in professional journals. Reporters should be aware that such results have not been reviewed by other scientists, a process called "peer review."

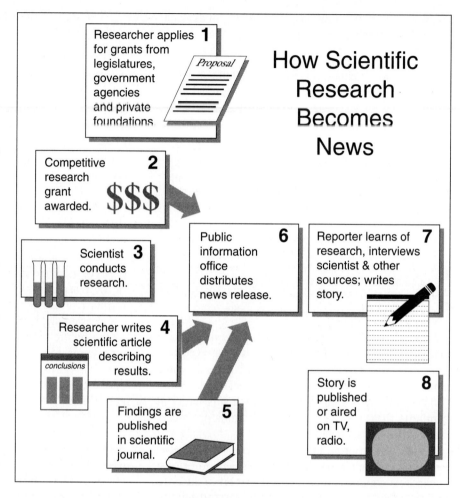

How Scientific Research Becomes News

1 Researcher applies for grants from legislatures, government agencies and private foundations. *Proposal*

2 Competitive research grant awarded. $$$

3 Scientist conducts research.

4 Researcher writes scientific article describing results. *conclusions*

5 Findings are published in scientific journal.

6 Public information office distributes news release.

7 Reporter learns of research, interviews scientist & other sources; writes story.

8 Story is published or aired on TV, radio.

in a professional journal or presented at a conference. The study and its result may be legitimate, but reporters should be aware that many scientists frown on news conferences as an unprofessional form of publicity seeking.

Some studies are worth reporting when they begin, especially if there is a local angle. Many national studies enlist research subjects from local physicians and hospitals.

During the next 10 months, heart attack patients at Memorial Hospital will have a chance to participate in a new international study aimed at determining the most effective drug therapy for saving lives.

Memorial is one of 1,300 hospitals worldwide and 600 in the United States to participate in the study,

which will compare the effectiveness of different clot-dissolving drugs in treating heart attack patients.

The study, being conducted by the University of Michigan and Duke University medical centers, will involve 40,000 patients who will be evaluated after treatment with a combination of three drugs, t-PA—or Activase, steptokinase and heparin. Local patients who are in the early stages of heart attacks will be recruited for the study when they arrive at the hospital's emergency room.

Reporters learn about interesting research studies through press releases, publications in journals and trade papers, and contacts at research institutions. When reporting research findings, experienced reporters should try to provide pertinent background about earlier studies in the field. The challenge of research stories is to make them accurate, complete, clear and readable.

Health Effects

The public is fascinated by stories about the positive or negative effects of eating certain foods or making certain lifestyle changes. Such stories can alert people to potentially dangerous habits and may suggest ways to improve their general health. Unless carefully reported and written, however, stories about health effects can sound false alarms and raise unnecessary fears. Stories that are oversimplified, that hype preliminary research findings without adding important qualifiers, only add to people's confusion about what is good and bad for them.

In the 1980s, several medical studies found a link between drinking coffee and heart disease, and many physicians subsequently recommended that patients with heart conditions reduce their coffee consumption. The findings were widely reported in the news media and many otherwise healthy people gave up regular coffee and turned to decaffeinated brands.

Some years later, more extensive studies came to a different conclusion: Drinking three or four cups of coffee a day was safe for virtually everyone, even people with heart disease. This wire service story reported the latest findings in an easy-to-read style that humanized the study results while adding enough explanation and detail so readers could judge whether to believe them.

BOSTON—Sit back and enjoy another cup of full-powered, extra-kick caffeinated coffee. A major study concludes that your morning brew is almost certainly harmless to your heart.

Contrary to the fears of many doctors and coffee lovers, coffee with a get-you-going jolt of caffeine seems to be perfectly safe as far as the heart is concerned.

"This study means that if there is a hazard with drinking caffeinated coffee, it's going to be very small and there may be none at all," said Dr. Walter Willett, who directed the study at the Harvard School of Public Health.

The story quoted researchers' explanations for different conclusions reached by earlier studies, then pro-

vided details about the latest study that showed it to be a major research effort.

Dr. Harvey Wolinky, of Mount Sinai Hospital in New York, said some previous research may have linked coffee and heart disease because heavy coffee drinkers are also more likely to smoke, which is clearly bad for the heart.

The latest research was based on a survey of the coffee-drinking habits of 45,589 men and was published in today's issue of *The New England Journal of Medicine*.

Public confusion about the potential dangers of drinking coffee points to an important fact about scientific research that is often missed by the public and not always clearly reported in news accounts: Few things in science are ever "proved" beyond a doubt and true medical "breakthroughs" are rare.

Medical experts often disagree about the dangers or benefits of certain eating and lifestyle habits, and researchers studying the same topic may reach different conclusions. Science is a gradual accumulation of knowledge about a problem, with each study building on earlier studies to shed a little more light on the road to scientific consensus. It may take years or even decades before the experts will agree on the effects of caffeine, as they do about the dangers of smoking.

While new research about the benefits of eating oat bran or taking vitamin C may spark media coverage and public interest, the best articles do not focus entirely on a single study. The skilled reporter is careful to report what other researchers have learned about the same subject and interview credible sources not connected with the study. The writer of the coffee story sought out such an expert.

Dr. Peter Wilson of the long-running Framingham Heart Study in suburban Boston said his group reached conclusions similar to the Harvard team's last year.

It is sometimes said that the public prefers an uncomplicated lie to the complicated truth, and that often applies to issues of health risks. The public may want simple answers, but health reporters must make clear the tentative nature of many research findings. In short, it's just as important to explain what is *not* known about a topic as it is to report what was most recently learned.

The Harvard study, for example, raised new concerns about decaffeinated coffee, but in this case, the researchers—and the reporter—were careful to underscore the tentative nature of those findings.

> The study found troubling hints that people who drink lots of decaffeinated coffee may increase somewhat their risk of heart trouble. However, the researchers cautioned that the link they found is statistically weak and that it is too soon to conclude that decaffeinated coffee is harmful.

New Treatments

Medical science is continually developing new treatments for illness and disease, everything from new medications and surgical procedures to diagnostic equipment that helps physicians detect medical problems.

New treatments for life-threatening conditions such as cancer and heart disease that touch large segments of the population receive wide attention. In the past two decades, for example, death from heart disease has been reduced through a series of treatments including open heart surgery, transplants, artery-clearing drugs and post-heart attack rehabilitation.

Also receiving wide coverage are advances in fetal monitoring, which allows doctors to check how a fetus is developing during pregnancy, and reproductive technology, such as in vitro fertilization, which makes it possible for infertile couples to have children.

New treatments become available first at large medical centers, but may be introduced at smaller hospitals within a few years. Local reporters should follow new treatments being offered in their areas. Technological advances in gynecological surgery, for example, have made it possible for women to be treated for a variety of conditions on an outpatient basis (not requiring an overnight hospital stay). One reporter examined how the availability of these treatments at a local hospital benefitted the region's women.

> A few years ago gynecological surgery meant spending several days in the hospital, and weeks at home recuperating, but these days a woman might check in on Friday, be home the same day and back at work Monday, thanks to advances in endoscopic procedures.

Jeffrey H. Hall, chief of obstetrics and gynecology at Central Community Hospital, said many conditions that in the past would have required a hysterectomy—major abdominal surgery—can now be done on an outpatient basis with basic endoscopy.

"We can offer a lot simpler surgery for patients who would have been having surgery anyway," said Hall. "And we can offer relief to a lot of women who previously chose to put up with symptoms they didn't like because they didn't want major surgery."

Reporters must provide simple explanations of complex procedures for lay people. This reporter also interviewed physicians about the medical aspects, and hospital administrators about the number of treatments performed, the cost of equipment and other improvements on the horizon.

> Endoscopy is a general term for a procedure that uses a small tube inserted through a body opening or a small incision. More specialized terms are laparoscopy, which is an endoscopic procedure in the abdomen, and hysteroscopy, an endoscopic procedure in the uterus.
>
> The growth in the number of endoscopic procedures has been incredibly fast at Central, said spokesman Anthony Kelly. In 1989, there were 267 laparoscopies performed, which increased to 322 in 1990 and nearly 400 in 1991.
>
> The equipment is expensive. The video equipment needed for physicians to monitor the progress of endoscopic tools, for instance, costs about $25,000. The hospital plans to replace its carbon dioxide laser next year at a cost of $100,000.

Extensive articles are not always warranted simply because a hospital or doctor's clinic acquires new equipment or offers a new type of surgery. In the past, before intense competition among medical providers, local newspapers routinely ran stories whenever a local hospital bought new equipment. Today, reporters exert tighter news judgment before writing such articles, checking medical publications or calling state health officials or experts at medical schools to learn how new the treatment really is and whether it is already available from other local providers.

New treatments are sometimes reported on while still in the experimental stage, called "clinical trials" by researchers. New drugs and cancer therapies, for example, undergo lengthy clinical trials at medical centers to show their effectiveness and safety before the FDA will approve them for the public. Once approved for patient use, many new treatments receive wide attention, especially those which have shown dramatically better results than earlier treatments.

One reporter followed a state mental hospital's plan to use patients in a clinical trial of a promising drug for treating schizophrenics.

> Nearly one third of the 420 patients at the Clairmont State Hospital could benefit from treatment with the experimental drug clozapine, which has produced dramatic results in treating schizophrenics.
>
> Hospital Superintendent Darryl Murphy said the state Legislature has provided $900,000 for an 18-month clinical trial of the drug at Clairmont. The funds were expected to pay for 100 patients for one year, but recent action by the U.S. Food and Drug Administration could bring down the drug's cost, making it possible to treat more patients, Murphy said.

Stories about new treatments should explain their success rates, plus any related dangers or side effects. Cost also can be a factor, especially when a new treatment is considerably more expensive than other therapies.

> A team of experts from the state Department of Mental Health is currently preparing a "protocol," a detailed plan for administering the drug and monitoring its effect on patients. "It has very significant prospects for a lot of our patients," Murphy said, "but we expect some very stringent review because this is a dangerous drug."
>
> Clozapine costs about $8,944 per patient per year, making it one of the more expensive drugs for schizophrenia on the market. By contrast, lithium costs about $500 a year, while prolixin costs about $780 a year.

The reporter also sought information from state mental health experts, spokespersons for the FDA and the drug company, and an independent advocate for mental health patients.

Health-Care Delivery

From the cradle to the grave, from neonatal clinics for newborns to nursing homes for the elderly, Americans spent $671 billion on health care in 1990, equal to 12.3 percent of the gross national product. That price tag supports a vast and complex network that includes physicians, hospitals, private labs, pharmacies and manufacturers of medical equipment. The health-care industry is a booming business, one of the few sectors of the economy to show growth in the first part of this decade (see Figure 18–2).

The pieces of this enormous and costly system are as diverse as the large university medical center that performs the latest organ transplants and the small rural health center that teaches young mothers about proper nutrition. It is also a system where some people get the finest, most advanced medical treatments available, but where an estimated 37 million people had no medical insurance in 1993.

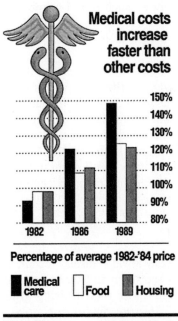

FIGURE 18–2

The cost of medical care in the United States has risen faster than the cost of other essential goods and services. Efforts to control costs were among the health-care reforms undertaken in the 1990s that received wide media attention.

Source: Milton Moore/*The Day*. Reprinted with permission of *The Day*, New London, CT.

The ways in which people receive medical care, the delivery system itself, continues to evolve. Today's hospitals advertise their services and compete for patients. Surgery that once required hospitalization for a week now is performed on an outpatient basis so people can go home the same day. State-of-the-art medical equipment keeps people alive who would otherwise die—but at tremendous cost.

Together, medical science and modern health care continue to extend the average life span for Americans. As people live longer, the cost per person for medical care continues to grow.

Every few years seems to bring renewed efforts to reform the medical delivery system, to cut costs and make it more efficient and equitable. The federal government, which finances the Medicare and Medicaid insurance programs, has instituted cost-control measures setting limits on how much it will reimburse physicians and hospitals for specific treatments. Many states have followed suit with their own cost-cutting measures.

Reporters can find stories in every corner of the health-care system. Some of the best stories look beyond costs and statistics to chronicle the human side of health care. In the hands of a skilled writer, moving accounts of personal tragedy and triumph can humanize the often byzantine workings of the health-care system. Reporters who dig deeply enough often uncover stories about waste, injustice, fraud, malpractice, profiteering.

Occupational Health

Secretaries who type all day at video display terminals complain of headaches, eye strain and sharp pains in their wrists. Steel workers lose their hearing after years of absorbing deafening on-the-job noise. Shipyard workers exposed to asbestos develop a host of lung diseases, including fatal lung cancer.

Few occupations are without some health hazard. Workers in a highly industrial society expect some on-the-job risks, but government and industry have both a legal and moral responsibility to minimize those risks and provide a safe working environment. Complaints about workplace safety and hazardous conditions are frequently reported by medical writers.

In 1970, the federal government established the Occupational Safety and Health Administration to monitor industry's compliance with safety regulations, and some states have similar agencies. Studies have shown that OSHA's enforcement of workplace safety has been sporadic, often relying on company reports for statistics on illness and accidents. Typically, OSHA figures only tell part of the story.

The *Occupational Health and Safety News Digest*, in a report critical of OSHA's death and injury statistics, observed that "only the most obvious problems tend to be counted, because trying to determine the origin of an illness can involve complicated medical judgments. The low total (provided by OSHA) for disease deaths suggests that employers are not including workers, even after court and compensation board judgments on the cause of death."

Despite federal and state laws to improve workplace safety, many hazards still exist and new ones continue to surface. Local reporters should identify industries in their region where workplace diseases and injuries might be a problem. OSHA reports can provide a starting point. Other useful sources include state worker compensation boards that handle complaints about debilitating injuries, and experts at state departments of health and labor who may compile statistics and conduct studies of local industries.

Some local hospitals run occupational health clinics to treat workers in high-risk industries, while university medical centers often study disease and injuries in those industries.

The state's first survey of occupational disease estimates that 250,000 residents—more than 10 percent—are at risk of developing illnesses related to their exposures at work.

In addition, an estimated 400 to 1,100 workers die each year in the state of work-related diseases from exposure to asbestos, crystaline silica, solvents, lead and noise, the report said.

The study was compiled over 18 months by a team of state officials, private health-care specialists and physicians at State University's Occupational Medicine Program.

Some attorneys specialize in occupational health cases, and court records will reveal when individuals and groups file lawsuits charging occupational injuries.

Labor unions may attempt to document injuries and negotiate better conditions. In 1991, three Connecticut police officers filed workers' compensation claims insisting that hand-held radar guns gave them cancer. Around the state, reporters followed the lawsuit's effect in their communities.

> Several local police departments have joined the state police and other departments in suspending the use of hand-held radar guns because of the possibility that they cause cancer.
>
> The state's two largest police unions have lobbied since April for departments to ban the use of hand-held radar guns, which are believed to be more dangerous than other models because they are held only inches from an officer's body.
>
> After suspending their use, several departments reinstated the radar guns in August after reviewing a study by the Institute of Police Technology and Management in Jacksonville, Fla., that concluded the devices are not dangerous if used properly.

Reporters should keep in mind that proving certain workplace conditions caused a medical ailment is extremely difficult. Workers who smoke for years, for example, have difficulty proving that exposure to asbestos caused their respiratory problems.

Reporters need to balance workers' claims by consulting independent medical experts and they should be careful before writing stories about individual cases unless lawsuits have been filed and medical documentation is provided.

Alternative Medicine

People frustrated with conventional medical treatments often turn to biofeedback, acupuncture, spinal manipulation, herbal medicines and other alternative treatments for relief of their ailments. These treatments can range from the generally accepted to the plausible to the patently bizarre.

Patients who claim to have benefited from such treatments may tell compelling stories of dramatic improvement and cures. Despite such claims, the medical establishment has not embraced these treatments. Many doctors view most of them as frauds, with no demonstrated medical value.

In the past, media coverage of alternative treatments tended to mirror the views of traditional medicine. But the media has begun to take a closer look at these treatments, acknowledging what proponents have long held: that traditional medicine, with its reliance on drugs and surgery, may not always have the best or right solutions for medical problems, especially chronic ailments such as headaches, back problems and hypertension.

The medical establishment itself has softened its position on a few alternative treatments. For example, back specialists had long dismissed as quackery a form of spinal manipulation practiced by chiropractors to relieve back pain. But in 1992, the American Association of Orthopedic Surgeons held its first symposium on back manipulation at its annual meeting. Nearly one third of the physicians in the audience said they had referred patients to a chiropractor.

Some physicians have suggested controlled scientific studies of Chinese medical practices such as acupuncture and herbal medicine to see whether they work. It is quite possible that the conventional thinking on these treatments may be revised in the years ahead.

Time magazine estimated that alternative medicine had grown into a $27 billion industry by the early 1990s. Any industry that stands to benefit from the public's pain, fears and frustrations is fertile ground for abuse. Reporters should bring along a healthy dose of skepticism when writing about alternative treatments and their practitioners.

Because so much is still not known about the effectiveness of alternative medicine, the reporter should be careful to balance health claims with comments from reliable medical professionals. At the same time, the reporter should remember that many medical doctors still consider these practitioners to be quacks no matter how compelling the evidence.

Legal and Ethical Issues

Residents of Oregon were faced with a troubling dilemma several years ago when a young boy died from leukemia after the bone marrow transplant that might have saved his life was disallowed by state Medicaid officials. The officials ruled that money set aside for prenatal care for poor children could not be used for the transplant. Since then, Oregon has adopted specific policies guiding which medical treatments it will finance with government funds.

Critics say Oregon's policies, often referred to as medical "rationing," run counter to the notion that society should provide the best health care for all citizens. In reality, however, many people receive inadequate health care while others get the very best. Oregon is not alone in having to grapple with the difficult question of setting priorities for medical treatment when public money is involved.

The Oregon case illustrates the complex legal and ethical issues that arise in science and medical reporting. Should family members have the right to order disconnection of life support systems for a brain-dead relative with no chance of regaining consciousness? Should doctors be allowed to harvest hearts, kidneys and other organs from anencephalic children—those born with almost no brain and who are expected to die soon—to help save other children? Is laboratory testing on animals for medical research acceptable, while animal testing for new cosmetics is not?

Journalists watch, listen and report as scientists, policy-makers and ethicists debate these and other questions. The public needs to be well-informed about such issues so it can intelligently influence medical and public policy. Reporters must strive to produce balanced, well-researched and carefully written stories that explore divergent viewpoints. Ethical issues are seldom easily resolved, and reporters should avoid taking sides in their stories.

Sometimes newspapers face their own ethical decisions in reporting—or not reporting—local medical stories. It is fairly common, for example, for the parents of a child who needs an expensive organ transplant not covered by insurance to request news coverage to help raise money for the operation. Editors naturally sympathize with a child who could die without the transplant or spend his or her life hooked to machines. But granting one request will surely bring others, and the newspaper may find itself in the unpleasant position of deciding which needy children merit an article and which do not.

The photogenic toddler who needs a heart transplant may make a touching human-interest story, but reporters and editors must ask if that child is more worthy of publicity than the high school dropout or the unemployed laborer who needs the same operation. Reporters considering such stories should research them carefully and realize that families who manage to raise substantial public donations may be able to have their child "bumped" ahead of the next person in line who cannot afford the surgery.

Reporters writing about legal and ethical matters can get help from several sources. Some hospitals have ethics committees to set guidelines and help decide difficult issues. Most medical schools have physicians who teach medical ethics, while law faculty may specialize in medical law. Some university philosophy professors may have experience in medical issues.

As with any "expert," reporters should inquire about sources' credentials before elevating them to expert status.

'Translating' Science

Beginning in the late 1980s, criminal prosecutors in many states began using a scientific process called "DNA typing" to link suspects to crimes such as murder and rape. Commonly called "genetic fingerprinting," DNA typing relies on each person's unique gene patterns as a method of positive identification. Not everyone agreed on its reliability—in part because of possible mishandling of samples in laboratories—but several states allowed DNA typing to be introduced in criminal cases.

Court reporters suddenly found themselves having to explain a complex scientific process in their trial stories. Here is how Kathryn Kranhold of *The Hartford Courant* wrote about it for a general audience.

> In DNA typing, scientists compare slices of deoxyribonucleic acid, the material that contains a person's genetic code. Some people have compared the slices with price bar codes in supermarkets because they contain a sequence of bars in varying lengths. Then the bar sequences are analyzed, either through visual examination by a scientist or a computer comparison. The sequence is supposed to be unique for each individual, except in identical twins.

After first explaining what DNA typing is, the reporter went on to describe how it is used in criminal cases.

Scientists can derive samples from saliva, white blood cells and hair roots. In a rape case, samples are taken from the victim's clothing and vagina. Then a sample is taken from the suspect. The two samples are compared to determine if the genetic code is alike.

Reporters in a variety of beats find themselves having to explain scientific terms and procedures in their storics. Hcrc, they face some of the same research and writing challenges as the science specialist. They must find reliable experts who can explain terminology and provide background, and they must translate technical language into explanations easily understood by the reader.

In the DNA example, the writer relied on several explanatory techniques common to science reporting—comparison, analogy and repetition. By comparing slices of DNA to supermarket bar codes, the writer gave readers a simple and familiar concept to help them visualize something complex. By repeating the phrase "bar sequence" in the next sentence, the writer reinforced the simplified image of DNA. Almost no technical language is used. The result is two easy-to-read paragraphs that help the reader understand how the technology works.

This example suggests another important point about science writing—dealing with unfounded or unscientific claims. Although most scientific experts agreed that DNA typing might not be foolproof, some prosecutors told judges and juries that it was virtually infallible. Prosecutors are not scientists, and the reporter went outside the trial proceedings to locate experts who could assess the reliability of DNA testing.

COVERING THE BEAT

Science writer Ronald Kotulak holds several distinctions in the *Chicago Tribune* newsroom. He's the person editors and reporters often turn to for guidance on science matters; he has unusual freedom to pick his own stories; and he gets more mail than anyone else. Kotulak described how something as simple as sorting through his weekly mail helps him cover his sprawling beat.

In a typical week I get about 300 pieces of mail, ranging from press releases to the latest editions of science and medical journals. I go through everything. The mail helps me keep up with what's going on, and it provides story ideas. . . . It offers a day-by-day slice of scientific life that tells you about things from the latest superconducting material to the newest skin-wrinkle remover. It helps a reporter to spot trends and to find the researchers who are doing work on the cutting edge.

But for Kotulak, reading his mail is just the beginning of a job that requires organizational skills, a deliberate nature and the ability to juggle many projects at once.

There are meetings and press conferences and briefings to go to, sometimes in town, sometimes in New York or Washington or Montreal. There are interviews to conduct, research labs to visit, newspapers, magazines and wire-service copy to read, radio and TV programs oriented toward science and technology to watch. It is not uncommon for reporters on any beat to have more to do than they can easily handle. But hacking one's way through the daily growth of information may be a particular challenge for science writers, in part because they have unusual freedom to generate most of their stories.

Most metropolitan newspapers and the major TV networks assign one or more reporters to the science beat full time. Some larger papers may have as many as a half-dozen reporters working in science areas, some covering general science news or health care, while others are assigned to a narrow field, such as space technology or AIDS research.

Some reporters come to the job with a strong background in science or medicine. Lawrence Altman, longtime medical writer for *The New York Times*, is a physician, while Robert Bazell, chief science correspondent who handled the early AIDS reporting for NBC, has extensive training in immunology.

More typically, science and medical writers emerge from the ranks of general assignment reporters. Many studied science in college or have taken courses in science writing. Armed with a good working understanding of science process and issues, these reporters grow into their beats, learning much of what they need on the job. However, the serious science writer's education never ends, and many continue their training at workshops and seminars, and through membership in professional organizations for science writers.

At many large and medium-size newspapers, the science-medical beat is handled by a single reporter who monitors scientific news, covers breaking stories and serves as the newsroom science expert. Unlike beats where the news flow is often dictated by scheduled events and political announcements, the science beat affords writers a great deal of autonomy.

Gathering Background

Research is a must for science and medical stories, as much as time allows. Reporters should do the kind of background research that will help assess whether an article is warranted, and supply background for the interview and important context for the story.

The newspaper's own library may contain useful clips on a topic, but that's just the start. Reporters should own a good medical dictionary, a layman's medical reference book and a glossary of scientific terms. Any reporter writing about science should routinely search a number of indexes, such as the *Reader's Guide to Periodicals* and *Social Sciences Index* for articles in both popular and academic publications. Databases such as InfoTrac or NEXIS can provide articles from newspapers and popular magazines. These articles may not provide useful specifics, but they often contain background and summaries of trends to give the reporter a solid foundation in the subject.

InfoTrac's Academic Index, available at most college and many public libraries, provides short summaries—called abstracts—of articles in professional and scientific journals. Index Medicus, a guide to medical literature available at hospitals and large public libraries, lists studies and articles on a range of subjects. For a fee, computer indexes such as Medline will search Index Medicus. Such research provides not only background for stories, but also the names of experts who can be contacted. One valuable source for trends in science and medicine is *Science News*, which is written in nontechnical language.

The Scientists' Institute for Public Information operates a toll-free referral service that provides reporters with the names of experts in most medical and scientific specialties.

Dealing with Sources

Few reporters are knowledgeable enough about the broad range of science topics that they can dash off at a minute's notice for an interview. Questioning scientists, medical experts and other specialists on the beat poses special problems that can best be solved with careful preparation and an understanding of the traditional reluctance many sources bring to an interview. Although an increasing number of these sources have been trained to be comfortable with reporters and may be seeking publicity, the reporter cannot assume this will be the case.

Sources often judge reporters as they would an expert in their field, and may want evidence of the reporter's knowledge and credibility to see if they are capable of understanding the material and reporting it accurately. The reporter may need to overcome a source's distrust of reporters from a previous experience. Some scientists and researchers may go so far as to request samples of the reporter's work before consenting to an interview.

A university or hospital's public relations staff can help lay the groundwork for a successful interview by supplying copies of research studies, background on the topic and previously published articles about the research. Some universities employ experienced science writers to work with reporters.

Paul Lowenberg, a public information officer (PIO) at the University of California who specializes in science, believes that "as scientific issues become more complex and, at the same time, more popularized, the PIO becomes an ideal early contact for a reporter researching a story. The PIO understands the reporter's needs as well as which scientists are good interviews, what recent findings have been made and where to look for more information. . . . They can help see that a reporter meets minimal resistance as he or she enters the ivory tower in search of a story."

Lowenberg often sees a scientist's apprehension magnified for television interviews.

Frequently the TV reporter sent to cover a science story is not a trained science journalist. The result of this sometimes-tense encounter is that the scientist is confronted with explaining monoclonal antibodies or quarks in 30 seconds and in language the average viewer can understand. A television news story can take an hour or two to film and result in 90 seconds on the evening news. The scientist, unfamiliar with the way television news works, then feels the reporter has trivialized his work.

Information specialists can provide genuine assistance to reporters, but they should not be allowed to control the tone or angle of a story. The science writer's best protection against one-dimensional reporting and manipulation by news sources is solid backgrounding. Writers who keep abreast of their fields and know how to research a story before conducting interviews are more likely to produce complete and balanced stories that serve the reader's needs rather than those of the news source.

Take the case of the reporter who receives a press release announcing that a medical center will open a new fertility clinic offering high-tech treatments such as in vitro fertilization (test-tube babies). By checking recent articles in major newspapers and medical journals, the reporter quickly learns that the procedure can be very expensive, has a relatively low success rate and often is not covered by medical insurance. Including such details in an article about the clinic might not please hospital administrators who are seeking publicity, but it would serve readers considering the procedure.

One Reporter's Lesson

One morning while scanning the newspaper, a reporter noticed an ad placed by a local dermatologist. The doctor was recruiting patients to take part in a national study to test the effectiveness of a commonly prescribed treatment for athlete's foot.

Thinking the study might make an interesting feature story, the reporter called the doctor and learned he was one of two dozen dermatologists across the country hired by the manufacturer to study the medication. The medication was actually a combination of two separate ointments with different properties. Although each ointment had been tested individually and approved by the U.S. Food and Drug

Administration, the combination medication had not, even though it had been on the market for three decades. The FDA had decided to re-evaluate all combination drugs and was requiring the manufacturer to study the anti-fungal medication. The reporter decided it was worth a feature story, because local residents were being recruited and being offered free treatment for using the medication.

During the interview, the doctor insisted that the drug was safe and that only its effectiveness was being tested. The reporter wrote a brief story, based almost entirely on what the doctor had told him and information supplied by the manufacturer. The story began with a light approach typical of many medical features:

> If you're just itching to get rid of that aggravating case of athlete's foot, a local dermatologist may have just the prescription for you.
>
> Dr. Thomas Golden is one of two dozen dermatologists recruited from around the country to study the effectiveness of a cream commonly prescribed for treatment of athlete's foot and other fungal infections. Golden has been advertising locally for people willing to be research subjects in the national experiment being conducted by the manufacturer of the medication. Several of his patients already have agreed to take part in the study.

A few days after the story appeared, the reporter received a wire service clipping in the mail that had appeared in another newspaper a few weeks earlier. That story explained that a consumer advocacy group, the Public Citizen's Health Research Group in Washington, D.C., had filed a petition with the FDA asking that the medication be taken off the market. The group linked the same medication with nerve and liver damage discovered in research animals by scientists at the University of Nebraska.

It remained unclear in the story whether the drug was actually dangerous to humans; FDA officials and other reputable scientists insisted there was no evidence the medication was harmful when used as prescribed. Still, the reporter realized the wire story contained information that he should have known. He might still have written about the doctor's effort to recruit patients, but the story would have contained added information important to prospective subjects.

The reporter decided to do a follow-up story and began his own research, calling the FDA and the scientists whose research had been cited in the petition to ban the drug. The reporter interviewed the dermatologist again, and asked why he wasn't telling patients about the FDA petition. The physician insisted that fears about the medication were unfounded and pressured the reporter not to mention the Nebraska research. The phone had been "ringing off the hook" with interested patients after the first article, the doctor said, and he feared they would back out if a second story ran.

The reporter then wrote a straightforward follow-up incorporating the new material and exploring medical claims on both sides.

> An anti-fungal cream being dispensed free by a city physician as part of a manufacturer's experiment is the target of a move to pull the drug off the market.
>
> But the Nebraska scientist whose research is the foundation of efforts to ban the drug says its use in the local study is probably safe as long as it is used only as directed. Meanwhile, a spokesman for the federal Food and Drug Administration said there have been no reports of serious side effects in humans from the drug and that the agency considers it safe.

The article explored both sides of the issue, presenting a more balanced and complete description of the experiment, including the consumer group's concerns about the medication.

The reporter learned a valuable lesson about the need to research medical topics carefully before launching on a story. Had he read other publications more carefully or even checked with the FDA, he probably would have learned about the petition. A computer search of newspaper articles might have turned up the wire story. A review of Index Medicus might have revealed the FDA's order that the medication be tested.

By relying on a single source—in this case a physician who was being paid by the drug company to take part in the study—the reporter had opened himself up to manipulation. The result was a superficial story that did not serve the readers' needs for reliable medical information. Instead of a promotional feature story, the facts suggested a straightforward news account about the study with enough medical background to

let readers form their own conclusions. Luckily the oversight was caught quickly and was corrected in the follow-up story.

'SELLING' SCIENCE

In recent years, the landscape in science reporting has taken on a new, often troubling dimension stemming from growing competition in the science and medical field. Individuals and institutions that once kept journalists at arm's length now welcome them with open arms to show off their research, services and programs.

Competition in all facets of science and medicine is stiff. Scientists and medical centers compete for research grants. Physicians compete for patients. Manufacturers of medical products compete for customers. Increasingly, some have sought to use the media to enhance their competitive positions.

Competition has led to some well-publicized abuses, such as premature release of tentative findings, exaggerated claims and hyped "breakthroughs." In 1984, just as public attention began focusing on AIDS, the Chiron Corp., a California biotechnology firm, announced that it had cloned the AIDS virus as "a major breakthrough" toward producing a test for AIDS and a possible immunizing vaccine. The next day, the company's stock shot up by 16 points.

Later, a biologist at the National Cancer Institute told a *Boston Globe* reporter that his center had accomplished the same cloning five months earlier but hadn't considered it significant enough to announce publicly. The scientist called the cloning a tentative step, and a long way from a possible vaccine.

The announcement of research results before they are published in scientific journals, especially by companies who stand to reap profits from the publicity, remains controversial and is deplored by most respected scientists. One of the beat's important challenges is recognizing legitimate science news amid the flood of public relations and promotion.

Universities see publicity as helping their image and their ability to get funding. Similarly, some scientists believe that the publicity from greater media exposure will enhance their reputations and help them get promotions and research grants.

The trend was noted with alarm by Jay Winsten while he was director of the Office of Health Policy Information at the Harvard School of Public Health. "In recent years," he wrote, "(an) increasingly prominent group has emerged from within science which has sought to exploit the press in pursuit of individual and institutional advancement."

Some medical centers, for example, no longer wait until the results of a research project are available before going after publicity. They schedule elaborate press conferences simply to announce receiving a research grant, even before work has begun. Like politicians and others who seek to use the media, these institutions have come to understand the natural competition among reporters. One former medical reporter described the experience to Winsten this way:

> "The institutions would use the journalists' competitiveness against journalism, and against, I thought, the public interest. And we would go up like lambs to slaughter, and do exactly what the PR people in the institutions would want. . . . All of these reporters, broadcast and print, would be at the press conference, and they would know that if they don't report the story today, they will be beaten by the guy sitting next to them. So everyone would rush to write the story."

Winsten warned that "the indiscriminate use of press conferences undermines the media's efforts to identify and report the most important and newsworthy research advances. What institutions seek to advertise often bears no relation to what is important in science."

A similar scenario can occur when a local hospital invites reporters to the unveiling of a new piece of equipment, or the announcement of a new type of treatment. A routine check by the reporter might find that another hospital nearby has the same equipment or already offers the "new" treatment. While the changing landscape has made many physicians and scientists more willing to be interviewed, this scientific equivalent of a photo opportunity has also opened the door to a certain degree of medical hype.

Science and medical writers are deluged with press releases, everything from information packets from drug companies to an announcement that a plastic surgeon has opened a local clinic. Some story suggestions are little more than requests for publicity.

Reporters must learn to distinguish stories with genuine news and human interest value from those that smack of promotion. It takes a confident, well-informed reporter—and a trusting editor—to resist the steady pressure for coverage.

A reporter should not make a habit of writing flattering or promotional stories, but granting requests for legitimate news or feature articles can smooth the way later when the reporter needs a source's cooperation on other stories.

COVERING LOCAL HEALTH CARE

Reporters for major newspapers may be free to pursue stories around the country, but those assigned to science and medicine at local papers usually are expected to develop most of their stories from within their own circulation area or state.

Reporters newly assigned to the beat need to identify the key individuals, organizations and institutions that are likely to generate important stories of local or regional interest. Valuable local sources are hospitals and the medical community; state regulatory agencies; universities and colleges; local corporations and government agencies that conduct research; government laboratories; and public health offices in both schools and government. These sources can provide reporters with a wide range of contacts and documents that will assist them in covering local issues.

Changing Focus

In the past, local reporting on health care focused almost exclusively on the area's community hospital. Coverage tended to be sporadic and low key, nothing like the aggressive, ongoing reporting that follows the city government, school system and other important local institutions. Typical stories dealt with routine news announcements such as the hiring of new administrators, the opening of a clinic or the kickoff of the annual fund-raiser.

At the other end of the story spectrum is what Carl Schramm, director of the Center for Hospital Finance and Management at Johns Hopkins Medical Institution in Baltimore, called "gee-whiz medicine."

Watch the local news. The nightly stories deal with the community's 15th new sports medicine clinic, or the local hospital's fleet of ambulances and its helicopter backup, the miracle of the latest CATscan to be installed and why the community needs two lithotriptors.

Never do viewers get any clues that all these technical features are not absolutely, critically necessary to the practice of medicine and to the maintenance of public health. There is never a suggestion of the down side. Nothing on unnecessary surgeries or variations in practice from hospital to hospital. The difficult stories on infant mortality rates among blacks or on child malnutrition never get covered.

The kind of issue-oriented coverage urged by Schramm can be found in the major media, but he accurately describes the superficiality found in much local coverage of medicine and hospitals.

Many journalists at smaller publications and news stations are taking a more critical look at how medical and health care is delivered in their communities. Medical coverage has taken on a less promotional tone as reporters focus on stories about nursing-home care, medical malpractice, competition among hospitals, emergency medical services, Medicare fraud and the quality of care available to the poor.

Community hospitals are usually nonprofit, private corporations whose function of serving the health needs of a region often rated them "sacred cow" status from the local media. But in reality, many hospitals are neither nonprofit nor private in the real sense. Community hospitals conduct extensive and lucrative fund-raising campaigns and seek donations from the public and businesses. On that basis, an argument can be made that hospitals should be accountable to the public for their decisions about services and expansion.

Many hospitals have "diversified" by opening profit-making businesses that help support the hospital. Surgical centers, laboratories and other services are "spun off" into separate but related companies. Some subsidiaries such as parking garages and real estate companies may have little to do with the medical field.

Reporters need to develop sources other than top administrators, doctors and public relations staff. Trusted sources throughout the medical community can help the reporter keep abreast of breaking news and provide tips that suggest investigative stories.

For example, one physician specializing in geriatric medicine told a reporter that he had treated several residents of a local nursing home for malnutrition. The reporter interviewed former employees, current residents and others and learned that the home routinely fed some elderly patients just once a day. The investigation also discovered instances of physical abuse, harassment and intimidation of residents. The resulting stories triggered a state investigation and led to criminal charges and substantial fines against the owners.

Reporters hoping to understand the inner workings of the local hospital and medical establishment should begin with the hospital's annual report, which can provide a profile of its structure, services and personnel. Annual reports contain limited statistics about admissions, surgery and services, along with financial summaries. These numbers, however, are just part of the hospital's total picture. Only by examining other records, such as audits and other public documents that must be filed with state regulators, can a reporter get a more complete profile of an institution.

Annual reports also contain the names and titles of key administrators and board members, and a list of the medical staff and members of important medical committees. Most physicians at community hospitals do not work for the institution; usually they have private practices and are extended surgical or treatment privileges at the hospital. Physicians are fiercely independent, and disputes can erupt between the administration and its medical staff over the hospital's policies and direction.

In some parts of the country, large hospital corporations have purchased local hospitals, changing their financial status from nonprofit to profit-making. Control shifts from a board of directors composed of prominent local citizens to a corporate board. The new owner's goals for maximizing profits may not always coincide with the community's health care needs. Reporters should find out exactly who owns and runs hospitals in their area.

The Medical Marketplace

Increasingly, hospitals are competing with one another for patients, offering new services they hope will help them keep up with—or surpass—other facilities in their region. A hospital may want to open a cancer treatment center or start offering open heart surgery to keep patients who otherwise would travel else-where. Large medical centers in the inner cities try to cope with a shrinking pool of patients by opening satellite centers in more affluent areas, often in com-petition with local hospitals.

> Open heart surgery has led to open warfare between a Rock Hill medical center and Columbia's Providence Hospital.
>
> Piedmont Medical Center has applied for permis-sion to do the procedure, but Providence Hospital has demanded a public hearing from the state health department in an attempt to stop approval.
>
> Providence Hospital, which does more open heart cases than any other facility, says approval of Piedmont's request will lead to higher health-care costs and, possibly, lower standards of care for state resi-dents.
>
> "We're trying to stop unnecessary duplication," Providence spokeswoman Dawn Catalano said. "And that's what this is."

News about expansion and new services should be treated not with wide-eyed enthusiasm, but with an understanding of the local health-care "marketplace" and competitiveness among providers. In that sense, medical and health reporting can be viewed as a type of consumer reporting, helping the public make sound decisions about which services to purchase and from whom.

In most states, a single state agency or appointed commission (see Figure 18–3) must approve all major expansion of medical services, including new bed space, outpatient clinics, advanced surgical procedures and purchases of expensive equipment. The reason: to control medical costs and prevent duplication of ser-vices. Hospitals must apply for a "certificate of need" with the state health department or hospital commis-sion to justify the new service or surgical procedure.

A regular check of regulatory agencies for new applications can help reporters monitor proposed changes in their region. Certificate-of-need applica-tions can be controversial and hotly contested by other hospitals. The medical reporter should understand the review and approval process in his or her state; often

public hearings are scheduled and opponents may file objections to the proposal.

Quality of Care

The quality of medical care at local hospitals is another legitimate subject for news coverage. A hospi-tal where post-surgical infections are higher than nor-mal or that fails to suspend operating privileges for a surgeon known to be incompetent does not serve the public interest by concealing these matters.

Hospital administrators and physicians accustomed to hands-off treatment from the local press may bristle at questions about medical care at their institution, but that should not deter a reporter who is raising reason-able issues. Hospitals may not like to discuss what they see as privileged internal matters, arguing that adverse publicity will harm their image and raise false fears in the public. But a public that supports the hospital with donations and patronage has a right to expect compe-tent, careful and compassionate medical treatment, and to be informed when that is not being provided.

Beginning in the mid-1980s, the federal Health Care Financing Administration (HCFA), which administers the federal Medicare program for the elderly and dis-abled, began contracting with local agencies called Peer Review Organizations (PROs) to compile records on individual hospital admissions as a cost-cut-ting measure. The statistics collected by PROs are public and can reveal problems at hospitals such as unnecessary admissions, high rates of post-operative infection and unusual deaths. Hospitals where certain surgical procedures are frequently performed—and where presumably surgeons are most skilled because of the level of practice they get—also are identified.

HCFA, which is in the U.S. Department of Health and Human Services, makes public annual mortality rates for hospitals treating Medicare patients. Reporters can use these to draw comparisons with state averages and hospitals in similar communities.

> The mortality rate for Medicare patients at Crestwood Medical Center was about 15 percent higher last year than the state average.
>
> The numbers show a dramatic rise from the previous two years, when the hospital's rate was well below the state average. A hospital spokesman said a number

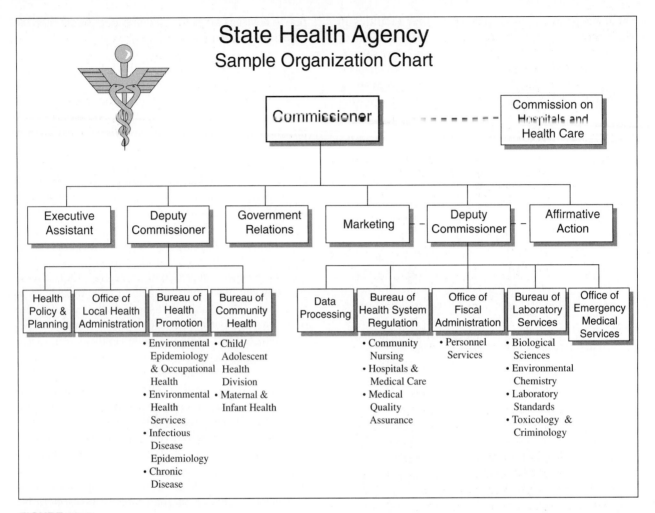

State Health Agency
Sample Organization Chart

FIGURE 18–3

Many states have separate agencies for health services and cost containment. In this sample chart, the agency's health commissioner directs health services and also sits on the state Commission on Hospitals and Health Care, which oversees new services and cost issues.

of factors, including a greater emphasis on outpatient care and sicker patients could explain the increase. "We're going to have to look at the specific categories for an explanation," he said.

The numbers cover the period between Oct. 1, 1992, and Sept. 30, 1993, and calculate mortality rates among elderly patients and those with disabilities for 30 days, 90 days and 180 days after admission.

Such records can be illuminating, but reporters must use them carefully and realize they also can be difficult to interpret. Some PROs have put together guidelines to help the public understand the figures. Be wary of drawing broad conclusions from raw numbers. It may be useful to consult with someone at the agency who can help identify actual problems or trends.

Regulation of Medical Providers

Licensing and regulation of hospitals, nursing homes and medical professionals usually is handled by the state. Agencies that regulate doctors, nurses, psychiatrists, dentists and other providers are usually part of the state or county health department and go by names such as "medical examining board" or "division of medical quality assurance."

These agencies receive and investigate complaints, and can suspend or revoke licenses, although such action is relatively rare. The licenses of an estimated 1,200 physicians a year are revoked by state boards; however, it sometimes can take years of court appeals before the order is upheld. Usually the problems must be serious and long-standing.

> The state Tuesday revoked the license of a Danielson physician who investigators say pocketed at least $1 million by billing insurance companies for medical services that were never performed.
>
> The state Medical Examining Board unanimously revoked the license of Dr. James S. Zupniak. In a consent order, Zupniak agreed never to seek to practice medicine in the state again and agreed to pay a $20,000 fine.
>
> The board based its action on the doctor's abuse of prescription drugs and phony billings to at least four insurance companies.

The reporter learned that the physician also was being investigated by the state's Department of Consumer Protection, the attorney general's office and the state insurance commission. On a tip, the reporter checked court records and learned that five patients had filed malpractice lawsuits against the physician. Documents in those cases provided details of the physician's operation.

> Five malpractice lawsuits filed by former patients of Danielson physician James S. Zupniak, whose license to practice medicine was revoked earlier this week, suggest a pattern of misdiagnoses and inappropriate prescriptions.
>
> Patients who went to Zupniak for relief from mild colds and sore throats found themselves in much poorer health as a result of his treatment, each lawsuit alleged.
>
> Court documents in the case support the pattern of mistreatment alleged in a monthlong investigation of Zupniak conducted by the attorney general's office.

Many health departments issue monthly or quarterly reports that summarize disciplinary action taken

against physicians and other medical professionals, along with child-care centers and nursing homes (see Figure 18–4). Reporters should review these periodically for local names and facilities—a notation on these reports often can point to larger problems.

Public access to a physician's disciplinary records varies by state; in some states the medical lobby has been able to keep files confidential unless formal action is taken against a physician or nurse. Even then, only the disciplinary action is made public and many details of the case may be sealed until appeals are exhausted. Reporters should check specific procedures and open-records laws in their state.

State and county medical associations also receive complaints about physicians, but they usually are handled internally. Like many trade groups, medical associations often are criticized for not taking more aggressive action against their members. Sources inside the association will sometimes alert reporters to serious problems in the local health-care field. These associations are valuable sources of background information on trends, and they often lobby on state legislation affecting their members.

Other health-care providers such as ambulance services, medical labs and providers of home health care also are regulated by state agencies that conduct inspections and review license applications. Records of these agencies are public in most states. Checking certification and inspection records can reveal problems with specific providers or may show lax inspections by the state (see Figure 18–5).

Universities and Medical Centers

Reporters should familiarize themselves with services provided by the large medical centers in their state or region. These institutions often are affiliated with medical schools, and combine teaching with medical research and advanced treatments. Centers may be renowned for their work in certain areas, such as heart surgery, treatment of Alzheimer's disease, organ transplants, cancer therapy or infertility.

Local patients who have not responded to standard treatments may be referred to a medical center by their doctor. When standard treatments have failed,

Regulatory Action Report
Summer 1992

Disciplinary Actions

Following is a listing of recent disciplinary actions taken regarding professionals licensed or regulated by the Department of Health Services.

CHIROPRACTORS

Ward, Henry, D.C./Lic. #123123/Mayfield
- Suspension stayed pending appeal – 19 May 1992
- Sexual offense

NURSES

Norse, Elizabeth, R.N./Lic. #231231/Wakefield
- Consent order – 9 April 1992
- 3-year probation with therapy, screens, employment restrictions
- Substance abuse/drug related

Vose, Sharon, R.N./Lic. #321456/Occum
- Memorandum of decision – 9 April 1992
- License revoked—effective 1 June 1992.
- Violation of probation

Hurd, Muriel, L.P.N./Lic. #496029/Pottsville
- Consent order – 12 May 1992
- Probation until Massachusetts program completed, Monson, MA. Participation in Massachusetts-based substance-abuse treatment through 1995.
- Substance abuse/drug related

Hughes, Regina, R.N./Lic. #293342/Mapleville
- Consent order – 12 May 1992
- Reprimand
- Incompetence/negligence

Norris, Annette, R.N./Lic. #004004/Chepachet
- Memorandum of decision – 18 June 1992
- License revoked – effective 1 August 1992
- Incompetence/negligence

Connetta, Suzanne, R.N./Lic. #354197/Smithville
- Summary suspension – 18 June 1992
- Hearing scheduled – 9 July 1992
- Violation of probation/substance abuse/drug related

Moreau, Lucille, L.P.N./Lic. #327676/Mendon
- Summary suspension – 18 June 1992
- Hearing scheduled – 9 July 1992
- Substance abuse/drug related

PHYSICIANS

Hutnak, David, M.D./Lic. #103123/Occum
- Modification of prelicensure consent order – 16 April 1992
- Allows him to perform insurance evaluations during the term of probation
- Incompetence/negligence

Hutnak, David, M.D./Lic. #103123/Occum
- Prelicensure consent order restrictions removed – 1 June 1992
- Incompetence/negligence

Bickford, Clifford, M.D./Lic. #301321/Kingstown
- Memorandum of decision–21 April 1992
- License revoked
- Substance abuse/drug related

Theodore, Neal, M.D./Lic. #323197/Wakefield
- Consent order – 21 April 1992
- One year probation, educational requirements, record review
- Incompetence/negligence

PODIATRISTS

Dresden, Patricia, D.P.M./Lic. #429121/Bradford
- Memorandum of decision and consent order – terms of probation completed
- Effective 1 May 1992
- Incompetence/negligence

Department Lists Civil Fines

The department's Hospital and Medical Care Division imposed the following civil fines during the state fiscal quarter ending June 30, 1992.

Shady Rest Convalescent Home
1564 Main Street
Norwich, NY 03212
- Class B Civil Fine, $300 – May 8, 1992 (related to excessive hot water temperatures)

Waterview Convalescent Home
139 Freeway Court
Oceanside, NY 03121
- Class B Civil Fine, $500 – April 28, 1992 (related to failure to protect a patient from an accident/incident)

FIGURE 18–4
This sample regulatory action report lists disciplinary actions taken against health professionals and facilities licensed by the state, along with fines imposed.

FIGURE 18–5
The results of complaint investigations of regulated agencies and health providers generally are available to reporters after the investigation is complete. They typically describe the allegation or complaint and include the investigators' observations, findings, conclusions and recommendations.

Sample Complaint Investigation
STATE OF CONNECTICUT
DEPARTMENT OF HEALTH SERVICES

Investigation of Complaint #92-9361
Shady Glen Nursing Home

An unannounced visit was made to the above facility on November 11, 1992 by a representative of the Hospital and Medical Care Division for the purpose of investigation of a complaint.

A portion of the complaint already has been investigated by the Department on Aging and a report of their findings is on file in their department.

Allegations:

1. *Medications failed to be given as prescribed on the 3 p.m. – 11 p.m. shift.*

2. *A nurse on the 7 – 3 shift is stealing controlled narcotics, e.g., Ativan, Buspar, and Xanax.*

Observations and Findings:

A. The Investigator *conducted Interviews with Facility Personnel* and the following was ascertained:

　　1. The *Director of Nurses* stated the following:

　　　　a. Non-controlled drugs that have been discontinued are kept for 30 days in a locked cabinet in the nursing office.

　　　　b. Controlled drugs are double-locked after being discontinued and immediately taken off the unit with the appropriate tracking count sheet.

A violation letter has been sent to the facility identifying the following violations of the State of Connecticut Public Health Code noted during the course of the visit:

1. A Schedule IV controlled substance was not stored in a locked permanently affixed container within another separately locked enclosure on November 4, 1992 (e.g., Ativan was stored in an unlocked refrigerator).

The above is a violation of the State of Connecticut Public Health Code *Section 19-13-D8V (b) Pharmaceutical Services (3)(C).*

---

patients may be asked to try one or more of the experimental procedures being tested at the hospital.

Research physicians at major medical centers may not be as accessible as local doctors. Many will not take calls directly from reporters and refer all requests for interviews to the public relations office. Taking the time to develop a working relationship with public relations staff, even by telephone, can pay dividends. When a big story breaks involving the institution, such

as a major research finding or a new type of surgery, the local reporter is less likely to be overlooked when television and the national media arrive.

When a major medical center performed its first heart transplant, a reporter for the home-town paper who was on a first-name basis with the public information director was allowed to watch the surgery along with a select group of doctors and medical students. The reporter also was able to get an interview with the surgeon and later with the patient in his hospital room.

Reporters should become familiar with the type of research conducted at nearby universities. Most universities have at least a few nationally known scientists, and their research may be worth a story. The school's public information office often compiles a list of ongoing research studies, and usually can provide reporters with an "experts directory" listing the names, telephone numbers and specialties of faculty members.

Reporters should look for scientific research with a local angle. Engineers, environmental scientists, zoologists and others often study local problems and conditions, and their research can make interesting reading for a local audience. One reporter learned that a scientist at the state university was studying the effects of acid rain on historic buildings in the Northeast. It turned out that several buildings in the study, including a public library, were in the reporter's city.

Local Corporations

Shortly before the FDA approved the drug AZT for treatment of AIDS patients, a medical reporter learned that a local pharmaceutical company was quietly shifting part of its manufacturing operation to produce large quantities of a compound needed in AZT production. At first the company refused to confirm the reporter's tip, but sources inside the company gave the reporter enough details about the operation to write a story.

The reporter contacted the company again and explained that she was prepared to run a story and wanted to give the firm another chance to comment. The company confirmed the details and provided its timetable for expanding the operation.

Depending on the region, reporters often can identify local companies that conduct scientific research on everything from fertilizers and pesticides to cosmetics and new drugs. Most private companies usually are reluctant to discuss their research while it is in progress. Unlike university and government researchers whose studies are in basic science, corporate research is typically in an applied field, meaning that the company is trying to develop a specific product that it can sell.

Some corporate reluctance stems from fear that a competitor may learn something in an article that would jeopardize the research firm's competitive edge. Corporations also are very careful, sometimes calculating, in timing their announcements for maximum exposure and effect.

A company may be conducting interesting research in the reporter's back yard, but its corporate headquarters won't let local officials talk about it. The headquarters is usually more interested in coverage by trade publications and major newspapers in New York or Washington, and may see no benefit in granting a local reporter an interview. A combination of persistence and a good track record for accuracy and fairness can be the reporter's best wedge in prying open the corporate doors.

WRITING ABOUT RESEARCH

Writing research stories might seem a simple matter of reporting what scientists have found but there are several important questions whose answers are essential to a complete story.

- What exactly has been learned? Are the findings really a new development? How do they compare with what other scientists have found?

- What were the underlying assumptions of the study? What hypothesis was being tested?

- Has the study been published in a scientific journal or presented at a conference?

- What testing or research methods were used? How many human or animal subjects were studied? For how long?

- Could other factors have been responsible for the same results?

- If animal tests were done, how do the findings relate to humans?

- Who funded the study, a government agency or private company? Does the sponsor stand to benefit from the result?

- What areas of future study do the results suggest?

The answers to these questions give the story depth that can help readers decide how much weight to give the study and whether it might affect them.

This story about a medical study, written by Associated Press Science Editor Paul Raeburn, combined new information with background and an explanation of the study's value:

> One of the oldest and most widely used heart drugs significantly increased the risk of extremely sudden death in people who had survived a heart attack, a study shows.
>
> Researchers found that a surprisingly high number of heart attack survivors—about one in three—later died of extremely sudden heart rhythm disorders within 60 seconds.
>
> One million Americans survive heart attacks each year and about 25 percent of them are treated with the drug digitalis, said Dr. Arthur Moss of the University of Rochester Medical Center. The study, presented at the annual meeting of the American Heart Association, found that digitalis increased the risk of the sudden heart rhythm disorders.

The story then provided readers with background about earlier studies, who was studied and how the findings may be applied to medical treatment.

> Previous studies of digitalis have suggested that it could pose some risk, but this is the first to link it strongly to these sudden deaths, Moss said.
>
> The findings came from a study of 2,400 heart attack survivors, 229 of whom died over a two-year period. The study is part of an effort to determine which people with heart disease are most likely to die suddenly and unexpectedly.

Finally, the story adds qualifications and cautions for the reader, noting the tentative nature of the research and the need for further study before patients stop taking the drug.

> Moss did not say that patients who use digitalis should be taken off the drug. He said further study is needed to identify which patients faced the risk of sudden death from the drug. The National Heart, Lung and Blood Institute is now designing a study to further explore the risks and benefits of digitalis.

The press is often criticized for hyping research studies and announcing breakthroughs where none have occurred. The word *breakthrough* itself is loaded and should be used with great caution. For decades, the public has been tantalized with headlines about breakthroughs in the search for a cancer cure. What the story usually means is that a scientist has learned something at the cellular level that brings medical science one small step closer toward possibly finding a cure.

Careful attribution and choice of wording is essential to keep stories about research from creating false hopes and fears.

Handling Complex Information

When the Three Mile Island nuclear reactor in Pennsylvania was shut down suddenly after a major leak of radioactivity, a wire service story carried this quote from a company representative to explain the cause:

> The core geometry in the upper regions of the core, especially near the center, is believed to be severely distorted due to the loss of fuel cladding integrity.

It's hard to imagine that the writer or readers had any idea what that convoluted, jargon-filled phrase meant. But the reporter must have thought that an unintelligible explanation was better than none and simply put quotation marks around the statement.

Science and medical writers must never forget that their job is to explain, clarify and simplify for the reader. Following a few guidelines can keep technical explanations and statistics from overwhelming the reader:

Avoid jargon.   Scientific terms are precise but they can intimidate and confuse readers. Try to translate terms and processes into everyday language. If a term is essential and will be used often, define it clearly the first time it's used. The reader can always refer to the earlier explanation if necessary. But don't let the definition become too technical.

In the language of researchers and bureaucrats, poor people become "indigent populations," and people who answer questionnaires become "survey respondents." Science writing for the public should try to humanize, not sanitize, stories.

Give it background.   Deciding how much background to include in a story is a matter of judgment and audience. Writers should try to assess how much background knowledge the average reader has. Is the story for the front page or the science section? Has the issue been in the news before or is this new ground? More is better than not enough, and background can always be trimmed as space allows. Avoid basic background that should be general knowledge.

Make it familiar.   Analogies and examples go a long way in helping readers visualize relationships or processes. One writer trying to describe molecular structure called it "a latticework of molecules." The phrase suggested a crisscrossing framework that one might see on a door or in a garden, the kind of image that stays with a reader throughout the story. If needed, the familiar phrases can be repeated instead of technical ones.

One article about air pollution sought to explain why clouds containing droplets of diluted sulfuric acid are brighter than normal clouds, which contain larger water droplets. The writer compared the effect to sugar and explained it this way: "A bowl of powdered sugar with its tiny particles is a brighter white than a bowl of ordinary granular sugar." Simple, concrete and effective.

Because the mind learns more effectively going from the specific to the general, it is often helpful to give examples first, then provide explanation, referring to the example as needed.

Use numbers.   Statistics and other numbers are useful when they lend credibility to the central idea of a story. Numbers should be checked carefully, with the original study or source when possible. Do the percentages in a survey story total 100? Are these the latest numbers? When were they compiled?

When numbers reach mind-numbing proportions, simplifying them can heighten the effect. For example, if 100,000 Americans are killed each year in car accidents, it might be more effective to say 274 every day, or nearly 12 people every hour.

The Reluctant Scientist

Scientists and journalists are different breeds, by training and by the nature of their work. Scientists train in an exact specialty. They speak and write in a precise

scientific language often understood only by other scientists. They work slowly and deliberately, spending years or even decades on the same project.

In contrast, most journalists begin as generalists. They are trained to work quickly, to write in clear, simple language, and to move quickly from one story to the next. While it is difficult to generalize about the relationship between all scientists and all journalists, it is true that they traditionally have viewed each other with wariness, skepticism and distrust.

Reporters often see scientists as aloof and arrogant, incapable of explaining their research in plain language that reporters and their readers or viewers can understand. Many scientists consider reporters untrained civilians with a tendency to oversimplify, misrepresent or, worse, sensationalize their research.

Although more scientists are cooperating with the press, for decades many scientists saw no benefit to themselves or their research in talking with reporters or taking the time to explain complex scientific data. The scientific culture frowned upon scientists who tried to "popularize" their research through newspaper articles. The reluctant scientist who did talk to reporters was usually more concerned with how colleagues would perceive a story than whether the public could understand it.

Reports of scientific studies contain complex technical details about the researchers' scientific hypotheses and the methods they used. Studies are typically written in carefully qualified language, and findings are stated within precise limits of what was studied and learned. Some scientists think such information should be included in news stories so readers will understand the true scientific merit of their research. But most news stories give only brief, if any, mention of a study's methodology and other arcane details.

Journalists try to highlight key information, adding only enough background to give the story context for the lay reader. When reporters try to translate technical jargon into everyday language, scientists often think something important has been lost in translation.

Dorothy Nelkin, a Cornell University sociologist who has written extensively about the uneasy relationship between scientists and journalists, believes many scientists have an incomplete or self-serving view of the press' role.

Scientists often talk about the press as a conduit responsible for converting science into a form that can be conveyed to the public. They want journalists to convey a positive image that will promote scientific interests. Many science writers, snowed by technical complexities, accept this view, and are reluctant to question or challenge their sources. As a result, the public's need to know about science—its problems as well as its promises—is often poorly served.

Nelkin adds that the difficulties facing science reporters are often intensified by the specific demands of journalism and by reporters' lack of scientific training:

> The character of science journalism reflects, in part, the practices of a profession constrained by deadlines, competitive pressures and the need to attract a broad range of lay readers. It also reflects the background and personal predilections of the individual writers, many of whom are in awe of science, insufficiently trained to exercise judgment about scientists and inclined to accept the words of scientists as consistently neutral and objective. The complexities and uncertainties characteristic of many scientific issues encourage their (reporters') often uncritical reliance on scientific sources.

Reporters often afford physicians, psychiatrists and other medical practitioners the same reverential treatment. While reporters shun this type of dependence on news sources in most reporting fields, it remains all too common in science and medical writing.

Leaders in both fields have tried to bridge the often cavernous gap between science and journalism. Both sides acknowledge the need to improve the quality of science writing while expanding access to science information. Increasingly, reporters assigned full time to medical and science beats are better trained. Editors who understand the complexities of science writing give reporters more time to prepare stories and more space in which to tell them. At the same time, most universities and medical centers help scientists publicize their research, and provide training and written guidelines so they can better communicate science information to the public.

In addition, professional groups offer workshops, short courses and resource material for science and medical writers. Among them are the Council for the Advancement of Science Writing, National Association of Science Writers, American Association for the Advancement of Science, and Scientists' Institute for Public Information.

SPECIALIZED DICTIONARIES

Several specialized dictionaries are available to reporters in science, behavioral science, health, medicine and health care. While some are aimed at a more technical audience, those marked with an asterisk (*) are considered most useful to journalists.

Health Care

(*)*The Facts on File Dictionary of Health Care Management*, by Joseph C. Rhea, et al. New York: Facts on File Publications, 1988.

Medicine and Health

(*)*The Encyclopedia and Dictionary of Medicine, Nursing and Allied Health*, ed. by Benjamin F. Miller, et al. Philadelphia: W.B. Saunders, 1983.

Dictionary of Abbreviations in Medicine and the Health Sciences, by Harold K. Hughes. Lexington, Mass.: Lexington Books, 1977.

(*)*Dorland's Illustrated Medical Dictionary*. Philadelphia: Saunders, 1984.

Mosby's Medical, Nursing and Allied Health Dictionary, ed. by Walter D. Glanze, et al. St. Louis: Mosby, 1990.

(*)*Stedman's Medical Dictionary*, by Thomas L. Stedman. Baltimore: Williams and Wilkins, 1990.

Science

(*)*Dictionary of Behavioral Science*, ed. by Benjamin B. Wolman. San Diego: Academic Press, 1989.

(*)*The Encyclopedic Dictionary of Science*, ed. by Candida Hunt. New York: Facts on File Publications, 1988.

(*)*The Facts on File Dictionary of Science*, by E.B. Uvarov and Alan Isaacs. New York: Facts on File, 1986.

The Penguin Dictionary of Science, by E.B. Uvarov and Alan Isaacs. Harmondsworth, Middlesex, England; New York: Penguin, 1986.

***

SUGGESTED READINGS

Burkett, Warren. *News Reporting: Science, Medicine and High Technology*. Ames, Iowa: The Iowa State University Press, 1986.

Cohn, Victor. *Reporting on Risk: Getting it Right in an Age of Risk*. Washington, D.C.: The Media Institute, 1990.

Useful explanation of how scientists assess risk and tips for reporters writing about risk assessments.

Friedman, Sharon M., Sharon Dunwoody, and Carol L. Rogers. *Scientists and Journalists: Reporting Science as News*. New York: The Free Press, 1986.

Goodfield, June. *Reflections on Science and the Media*. Washington, D.C.: American Association for the Advancement of Science, 1981.

Jarmul, David, ed. *Headline News, Science Views*. Washington, D.C.: National Academy Press, 1991.

Series of essays about a wide range of health and science topics.

Klaidman, Stephen. *Health in the Headlines*. New York: Oxford University Press, 1991.

Chapter 1 is a useful overview of assessing health risks in news accounts. Chapters 6, 7 and 8 discuss news coverage of AIDS, cholesterol and the dangers of smoking, respectively.

Moore, Mike, ed. *Health Risks and the Press*. Washington, D.C.: The Media Institute, 1989.

Nelkin, Dorothy. *Selling Science*. New York: W.H. Freeman and Co., 1987.

Part Five

Special Problems and Solutions

Chapter 19

The Press as Watchdog

"There is an ideal relationship for government officials and journalists everywhere," wrote journalism scholar William L. Rivers, "and the relationship should be that of adversaries."

Rivers' prescription for the media's watchdog role advocated neither a single-minded hostility nor a fawning servility from reporters. Instead he urged journalists to give government and other institutions room to do their jobs, yet to aggressively report when they do not. Every public affairs reporter must strive to strike a balance.

This chapter discusses the inherent conflicts between government and media, with suggestions for reporters seeking the right balance between toughness and compliance. It also examines a formidable obstacle confronting the reporter in the watchdog role—the continual barrage of public relations and opinion-shaping techniques that influence news coverage. Finally, the chapter includes a discussion of one of the reporter's most valuable tools for reporting government's inner workings—federal and state Freedom of Information laws.

GOVERNMENT AND MEDIA IN CONFLICT

Nowhere is the public affairs reporter's role more complex than in relationships with public officials, all of whom possess what they believe to be the most efficacious programs and priorities, not the least of which is survival in public service. A seemingly straightforward reportorial account of the issues surrounding a controversy will be construed as hostility by one party and as cronyism by another, depending upon the circumstances.

Many journalists see a healthy adversary relationship as a service to the public. However, to establish a legitimate operating range, several questions must be asked:

1. Of what should the adversary relationship between press and government consist, if indeed there is to be such a relationship at all?

2. How much confrontation is too much?

3. To what extent should the press cooperate or collaborate with government without compromising its principles?

One reporter suggests that the adversary relationship is simple—responsibility for achieving different goals. A working press seeks to know; a bureaucrat seeks to preserve the status quo and is reluctant to tell. The bureaucrat wants to work without interference and without the press making waves and complicating his or her job.

Another reporter sees the adversary relationship as skepticism of public policy, with the press holding the institution of government to account for all its actions.

Still another sees the relationship as not unfriendly but rather as the reporter exerting constant pressure to obtain information in the public interest. Respect for each other's position is the benchmark in the relationship between reporter and official.

However, the official definition of adversary places it at the more hostile end of the spectrum. Says *Webster*'s:

adversary (adj.): having or involving antagonistic parties or interests.

adversary (n.): one that contends with, opposes or resists; antagonist, enemy or foe; an opponent in a game.

These enemy-focused definitions must be tempered by the reportorial necessity for fairness and balance, but the frequently antagonistic nature of press-government relations makes it more difficult.

Complicating this are the perceptions among the public that the press is either too cozy with or too antagonistic toward officials trying to do their job. Furthermore, what one reporter sees as an acceptable relationship, another may find unacceptable.

These examples place seemingly innocent acts along the spectrum between cronyism and hostility:

- An officeholder invites a reporter to lunch to discuss pending actions under his jurisdiction, and refuses to let the reporter pick up a share of the check.

- The official gives the reporter a ride to a legislative hearing in a distant city. They talk politics, and the official reminisces about his days as a struggling young lawyer trying to support a family.

- At a later date, the official offers the reporter what he describes as the "inside story" on a dispute over construction of a new power plant and asks the reporter to write about it.

- The reporter knows the official is meeting informally with associates to settle sticky issues before they are aired in public, but does not pursue the matter.

- Another reporter knows about such meetings, and arranges to be outside the door when the group breaks up, badgering individuals for their stands on issues.

- The second reporter contacts critics of the official to get their opinion about the propriety of the private meetings.

Each of these scenarios can be placed along the spectrum and seen as acceptable or unacceptable, depending on many variables.

The relationships between reporters and public officials are shaped by the length of time they have dealt with one another, mutual admiration and the possible friendships that have resulted. Superiors also play a part, either by pressuring the reporter to resist all blandishments or to succumb to those that promise newsworthy results.

A last variable—the reporter's own experience, education and subconscious prejudices and biases—also plays a role in determining what constitutes an adversary relationship.

A Natural Tension

A natural tension exists between a government that exercises power and the press that reports, explains and criticizes the use of that power. Political scientist Ithiel de Sola Pool sees the tension stemming from the difficult position in which the journalist is placed:

> To do his job he must grow close to politicians and win their trust, but his job is also to publicly expose them. To do his job, he must develop confidential relations with sources and protect those sources, but his job is also to strip the veil of privacy from everyone else's business.

The relationship creates conflict and tension within a shared system, Pool contends. "The whole relationship of reporter and politician resembles a bad marriage. They cannot live without each other, nor can they live without hostility."

Rivers argues that too many reporters take on the role of "sweetheart," not only with federal officials but with state and local public figures as well. Rivers lauds reporters who challenge what he calls "officialdom":

> The necessity for a challenging journalism does not spring primarily from the fact that officials lie. They do. But far more often, the public is misled because well-meaning, high-minded officials really believe in their policies and programs. They would not be likely to serve well if they did not believe. But believing as devoutly as many of them do, they approach the public interest through a narrow channel and from a narrow perspective. Such men cannot be expected to really

serve the public interest because their perspectives are so narrow—unless they are called to account by an independent press. These facts have led me to the conclusion that the proper role of the political reporter is that of adversary.

A different viewpoint is expressed by Irving Kristol, who sees the adversary relationship as a concept inappropriate to journalism:

> You cannot have an adversary procedure that works only one way. So, if media is an adversary to government, should the government be an adversary to media? I think it is as idiotic for the government to be an adversary to the media as for the media to be an adversary to the government.

These two dissimilar views point up the broad range of philosophies regarding the role of the press and raise further questions: Is there a limit to the pugnacity that a reporter should display in dealing with public officials? Is there a point on the spectrum of tension beyond which a journalist should not venture?

The adversary relationship, if it should exist at all, becomes a delicate balance of tact and antagonism, of cooperation and conflict. Not much is required to disrupt that balance.

Is Some Hostility Beneficial?

Those supporting the adversary theory hold that some element of hostility is helpful to the system, since it serves to prevent political alliances that might leave the public unprotected. The question remains, however: What degree of hostility is necessary? Does it become inimical to the public interest at some point, undercutting a reasonable expectation that legitimate goals can be achieved?

Reporter Jules Witcover sees three basic responsibilities for the press in reporting affairs of government:

1. Report what the government says.
2. Find out whether it is true.
3. Determine whether the policy will work, or whether it did or did not work.

This seems a simple and cogent formula; yet political scientist Pool raises the question that a further function of the press might be to create a consensus behind national policy, enabling the diverse elements in a nation of more than 250 million people to assure that such a policy is carried out.

Can the press be an agent of cohesion and at the same time a source of criticism? Press support of non-divisive issues can help create a national consensus, but opponents argue the line separating divisive issues from nondivisive ones is narrow.

Press coverage of the Vietnam War offers an example. In 1968, the administration of President Johnson was referring to the Tet offensive in Vietnam as a "major allied victory" that left the enemy, the Viet Cong, "crippled and ineffective after an obvious suicide mission." Government officials bitterly criticized the press for insisting that the Tet offensive was actually a defeat for American military forces. Years later, after publication of the now-famous Pentagon Papers, which detailed U.S. involvement in the Indochina war, the press and public learned what U.S. military leaders were saying privately:

> To a large extent, the Viet Cong controls the countryside. His determination appears to be unshaken. His recovery is likely to be rapid, his supplies adequate. He has the will and capability to continue the war.

While the Vietnam conflict was an example of government insistence that a war effort was supportive of peace, decency and freedom, millions of Americans believed otherwise. This genuine division of opinion was merely being reported by the media. This may be regarded as an easily definable "divisive" issue, but others are not so clear-cut:

- To help reduce the sale of illegal drugs, police officials urge citizens to report anyone they suspect of drug-related activity. The press editorializes in favor of citizen reporting.

- To reduce auto fatalities, the government urges people to fasten their seat belts and observe speed limits.

- To protect the environment, the government and the press urge recycling of cans and paper.

- Bond drives to improve education facilities, library resources and other worthy causes are supported by the press.

Whether these are "divisive" depends upon the perception of the public. Almost any bond drive whose approval will increase taxes on the property owner is bound to be controversial, and the long-distance highway hauler will argue that the 55 mph speed limit for trucks may save a few lives but is unrealistic and costs consumers money. Despite the laudatory goal of halting drug dealing, anonymous complaints against citizens that lead to police investigations are viewed by some as a violation of civil rights.

So while it is clear that the press is a major instrument of communication in the policy-making process, its role as an agent of "cohesion" is open to question. Merely because an issue appears to be nondivisive is no reason for the press to support it. Sharp divisions over the handling of the wars in Vietnam and the Persian Gulf remain, and the argument over whether the press should be adversary or partner continues unabated.

Other Reasons for Disagreement

In seeking limits, however broad, to the adversary relationship, journalists and public officials find little ground for agreement. Political scientist Irving Kristol believes journalists lack specialized expertise (many appointed and elected public officials are similarly deficient) that would enable them to master analytic writing about highly technical government problems. "They turn instead to procedural matters that they can understand: who took what stand against whom in congressional debate, the course of an issue through the courts, who sides with whom on an issue." Because of this, Kristol suggests, the adversary stance replaces the "craft of getting the facts straight."

However, editor Harold Liston argues that the adversary role of the press does not target government but, rather, those who staff the government—the policy-makers and administrators. Liston adds an important ingredient:

> I have no love for the careless use of "adversary" to describe the press' role in dealing with government. But surely it does not mean hostility toward American institutions. However, something more than good-humored skepticism must be among the tools of a free press.

Many factors intrude to create an adversary relationship. Even the manner in which a news story is written, the way in which it is edited and the play it receives in publication are open to question. A straightforward wire service story received wide front-page display with this lead:

WASHINGTON—The Federal Trade Commission slapped price-fixing and other charges against the dental profession Friday, an action aimed at allowing Americans to shop around for tooth care.

The dictionary definition of "slap" suggests "putting, placing or throwing with careless haste or force" or "to assail verbally." Accordingly, some newspapers recast the lead to the story, placing the material in different perspective:

The Federal Trade Commission accused the American Dental Association Friday of illegally restraining competition among dentists by prohibiting its members from advertising their services and engaging in price competition.

To impute some deep-seated hostility to the wire service reporter would be unfair, and most journalists pass off the incident as an effort to create readability. The lesson to be learned is that attempts to punch up a lead can result in unintentional but unacceptable bias.

The 'Secrets' of Government

At what point does the intrusion of the press in government become unwarranted and thus an unacceptable adversary relationship? The lines are often blurred depending on the legitimacy of the government's claim that certain information should remain secret for the public security or welfare.

Columnist Jack Anderson was awarded a Pulitzer Prize in 1970 for reporting the confidential details of meetings of the National Security Council in Washington. While the administration of President Nixon professed to be neutral in the sensitive dispute between India and Pakistan, Secretary of State Henry A. Kissinger privately directed the State Department to "tilt" toward Pakistan. Anderson was criticized for breaching national security in publishing the material.

Government at all levels tries to keep certain information from public view. The reporter who is able to obtain such information is faced with a difficult decision: Is withholding the information truly in the public interest, as the officials contend, or is the public best served by reporting the story?

Nowhere is this better illustrated than at the local level when a community attempts to improve the economic climate of the area. Several cities may be bidding for location of a major new industry, which promises to employ up to 2,500 people and dramatically improve living and working conditions in the city in which it locates. The race is on among several cities to acquire the industrial plum.

Public officials argue that premature publication of the sensitive negotiations could jeopardize acquisition of the industry, and the press agrees to keep the "secret," awaiting the moment when officials are ready to make the announcement.

But a nearby city has apparently lost out in the bidding, and the newspaper in that community, under no such constraints, identifies the communities that remain in the running for the acquisition. The "secret" is no longer a "secret," despite local officials' contention that publication would continue to endanger acquisition.

Other factors complicate this hypothetical negotiation. The 2,500 jobs envisioned for the facility might turn out to be only 200 because of automation. The effect on the economic climate might be minimal, and prime industrial land might be put to better use. The disadvantages of acquisition might then outweigh the advantages, but because of the secrecy, there has been no public debate.

The reporter who sits on the story risks the loss of credibility, and should ask: Did lack of open debate on the issue affect the public interest?

Allowing Administrative Convenience

The City Hall reporter for a medium-size newspaper learns that an important administrative position has opened. The mayor wants to appoint a political ally but needs assurance that the person will accept. The mayor doesn't want the embarrassment of later having to offer the job to someone who will realize that he or she is second choice. The mayor prefers to make the offer and obtain a rejection—if one is forthcoming—in secret.

In allowing such administrative convenience to the mayor by withholding speculation on the nominee, is the reporter acting in the public interest? Is it important to the public to learn the identity of a potential administrator and his or her qualifications before the mayor plans to announce it?

Other questions arise: How much energy should the reporter devote to prying out information that public officials will produce in the normal course of events? When he or she decides to identify candidates before officials are ready to do so, does it constitute an unnecessary adversary posture?

Some indication of the wide range of response comes from two editors of the *New York Times*, Max Frankel and James Reston. Frankel offers this observation on administrative convenience and its effect on the adversary relationship:

> Scotty Reston and I sometimes differed because when I was diplomatic correspondent, he thought one of the great things to do for the prestige of the newspaper was to report who would be the new ambassador to Moscow three days before it was announced. I used to say, "Scotty, I can find that out. It's easy. It's going to take me two days. In those two days I might learn something far more substantial, which we would never learn if I didn't invest the two days. But the ambassador to Moscow we will find out by the announcement." Is it important?
>
> He regarded me as insufficiently zealous for feeling that it isn't. Always want to be first, he argued, because vigilance resides in that instinct. He feels that if you get into the habit of waiting for government to tell you when it wants to tell you, you're going to lapse on more serious matters.

How Far Is Too Far?

The reporter has engaged the mayor in a freewheeling television conversation, touching on such noncontroversial subjects as progress on the new sewage disposal plant, new snow removal policies, and purchase of riverfront property for recreation expansion.

Now the reporter takes a different tack. Councilman Svoboda had resigned suddenly the previous week, citing the press of business and family problems. "Mr. Mayor," the reporter asks, "could you give us your thinking on the effect of the Svoboda resignation and a vote on the proposed city income tax?"

The mayor stiffens perceptibly. It is a politically sensitive subject. He responds carefully.

"That's something the Council will have to work out, Bob. But I'd rather not get into it at this point, if you don't mind."

The reporter leaves the politically sensitive issue behind and turns to other subjects. But the question remains: At what point does the adversary relationship, seemingly nonexistent at this stage of questioning, become an unjustified burden in the mechanics of governing?

What if the reporter had persisted by repeating the question and prefacing it with the comment, "The people have a right to know, Mr. Mayor." Or asked it a third time, adding, "I'm afraid we'll have to insist on a response, sir."

An amicable exchange holds the potential for turning ugly if the reporter wills it. What if the reporter had turned to the television audience and said, "You are looking at a public official who refuses to answer what the press sees as a question in the public interest." Then he turned to the mayor and asked, "Are you going to answer or not, Mr. Mayor?"

Long before reaching this point, the reporter left the politically sensitive question hanging, but pursuing it later could be interpreted as being unfair to the public official.

In this case, the reporter, to assure a continuing and amicable relationship with the mayor, stopped short of fulfilling his mission to his audience—to provide additional information on the resignation and its effects. He could have pursued the issue, but at risk to the relationship.

The adversary relationship thus becomes a delicate balance of tact and antagonism, of cooperation and outright hostility.

When *The New York Times* obtained a copy of the Defense Department study detailing U.S. involvement in Vietnam in 1971, the newspaper began publishing the hundreds of pages of top-secret material, so classified for reasons of national security. The government sought and obtained an injunction temporarily barring

The Times from further publication, on grounds that publication of the material compromised national security.

In this case, the government believed the press had exceeded its bounds and had to be restrained, even though the study was years old by that time.

Although the Supreme Court ultimately upheld the right of the press to publish the Pentagon Papers, and *The Times* resumed publication, the issue remains: How far is too far in the adversary relationship?

The Dangers of Cronyism

The reporter's raison d'etre is to communicate the business of government to the public, and in that daily employment deals with powerful and well-known personalities at the local and national level.

Through this process, friendships between journalists and public officials develop, with reporters often engaging in tacit bargaining with those they cover. The process is subtle. By withholding from the public some of what they know (sometimes embarrassing information), reporters assure continued amiable contact and keep sources in their debt. Exposing a public official, or sometimes merely irritating him or her, endangers that channel of information.

The effect of these close relationships makes the reporter a part of the system, with a continuing danger that he or she will feel a greater stake in supporting the system than by exposing abuses in it. The seduction is subtle, and good journalists take steps to minimize the danger. In the *Aspen Notebook*, Washington correspondent James McCartney warns that a loss of independence leads to even more serious problems:

> Some reporters are so enthralled by authority that in the extreme form reporters become spokesmen for their news sources rather than dispassionate observers. They become sloppy about recognizing that alternative views may exist, and about digging out and including alternative views in their stories. Over a period of time, some may be press agents for those they are covering and, indeed, sometimes perform that role, or something very close to it.

Herbert J. Gans, in *The Levittowners*, sees a system of mutual obligation between reporter and decision-

maker, which incorporates the journalist into the process by inviting him or her backstage, but with the requirement that the journalist subtly limit coverage of the actual government.

> The reporter learns all (or almost all), but cannot tell; the decision-maker tells all (or as much as he has to), but knows he will not learn about it in next morning's newspaper. The relationship is perhaps less a system than a tug-of-war, for the decision-maker is always trying to reveal as little as possible, and the reporter attempts to publish as much as he can without alienating his source.

The danger is always present that the journalist who is on a first-name basis with the public official will accept thinly disguised propaganda in the form of press releases, publishing it with little or no reference to origin and with little or no editing. The journalist's most effective defense against cronyism lies in awareness of its dangers and refusal to allow any fragment of it to influence his or her judgment.

Booster or Watchdog?

In sharp contrast to the image of aggressive watchdog, some journalists and political scientists ascribe another function to reporters, especially on local beats: that of collaborator or cooperator in the public interest, sometimes serving as booster in the community to promote what the press perceives as the public welfare.

However, the term "booster" suggests an overly supportive enthusiast who views the community only through rose-colored glasses, ignoring its imperfections. A more appropriate designation might be "community builder" or "responsible citizen."

Whatever the designation, its intent is that the press identify with the community, encouraging its prosperity because the future of the press is inextricably tied to it. Unfortunately, this function does not always neatly jibe with other accepted functions.

In researching Levittown, N.Y., several years ago, Gans found that its citizens wanted a performance by the press that would give the outside world an idealized picture of the community. If an event reflected negatively on Levittown, many citizens preferred to have it hushed up.

Disruptive incidents that force the reporter and editor to make difficult decisions are always present. The choice often is to fulfill one function or the other: watchdog to the community or "responsible citizen." This is one example:

> The reporter covering the County Health Board is knowledgeable about its operation, and the public is receiving good coverage of the agency. The members of the board are concerned citizens intent upon assuring the community that the agency offers good service, mainly diagnostic. A private audit determines that one of the agency's department heads has been quietly misusing some of the funds with which she has been entrusted.
>
> Before details become public, the employee, who has served with distinction for 20 years, decides to reimburse the agency nearly $2,000, and take "early retirement." The board decides to accept this approach, choosing only to adopt safeguards to protect against future incidents. It declines to discuss the matter with the press, preferring to drop the matter.
>
> The reporter is left with the choice of insisting upon pursuit and publication of the story or allowing it to quietly fade away, justifying the decision by arguing that no purpose would be served by detailing the imperfections of the employee and agency.
>
> Most journalists, of course, will insist upon a public accounting, arguing that the public has a right to know how its business is being handled. Others will take the approach that the money has been returned and that no prosecution was initiated; thus the matter is best left unpublished.

"The reporter begins to identify with the community," Gans wrote, "omitting uncomplimentary items, and helping people and causes he thinks deserve publicity." Gans cited one editor who provided extra space to a local organization and kept out stories of its internal conflicts because the organization provided a worthy community service.

Other editors, however, insist on a more thorough accounting of local events. In Chicago, a much bigger city, a cultural affairs reporter published the disruptive internal conflicts in the nationally acclaimed orchestra.

"If you are not a combination watchdog and booster, over a period of time you will disassociate yourself from your readership, alienate yourself and have no impact at all," said a Midwestern editor.

Another warned that undue emphasis on the newspaper as "community builder" would reap adverse dividends:

> If "booster" means running a story in the spring saying Mannington is a nice place in the spring, I see nothing wrong with that. But if it means covering up or ignoring a serious housing problem in the city for fear it might frighten away industry, that's absolutely out.

While pure "boosterism" has no place among the reporter's functions, the journalist should develop an affinity for where he or she lives and works. No cut-and-dried formula exists for achieving this goal, but development of a philosophy that assesses the community and its people with some sensitivity is desirable.

PUBLIC RELATIONS: HELP OR HINDRANCE?

> Whatever these men and women may choose to call themselves—public relations counsel, publicity advisers, special assistants to the president, good will ambassadors, molders of the mass mind, shepherds of the herd reactions, mouthpieces, advocates at the court of public opinion, front men or spacegrabbers—they seek approximately the same thing. They are paid for using their ability and ingenuity to the end that the interests they represent, whether it be a transit corporation or a visiting magician, appear before the public in a light which is favorable and pleasant, or at least in a guise as friendly as the circumstances will permit.—*Stanley Walker*

The editors of Stanley Walker's day saw the press agent as a counsel for special interests. Walker, a New York editor when he penned those words in 1934, represented one side of the equation. The press agents of the early 20th century represented the other—often richly deserving the epithets hurled at them by men like Walker.

Although press agents first appeared as early as 1830, the seeds of modern public relations were planted in the corporate world at the turn of the century to stave off government regulation and counter public dissatisfaction with large monopoly corporations such as railroads and utility companies. The early public relations agents were usually former journalists hired to present the companies' views to government officials, stockholders, customers, workers and the public.

In the 1960s, diverse segments of American society—consumers, minority groups, environmentalists, universities—began adopting public relations techniques, joining with expanded government and corporate public relations to create a potent opinion-shaping industry.

While the role and techniques of today's public relations are more sophisticated than in Walker's day, the function remains basically the same: to inform various segments of the public about an organization's positions and policies by distributing information, and to assess and influence public opinion.

Today, public relations specialists are employed by political organizations, government agencies, business and industry, nonprofit advocacy groups, the entertainment industry and education institutions. A 1990 estimate placed the number of public relations specialists in the United States at more than 150,000, higher than the 130,000 full-time journalists.

Public relations efforts range from one-person offices to national organizations, and their functions run the gamut from advertising, promotion and community relations to producing in-house publications and legislative lobbying. But regardless of their purpose or size, virtually all public relations departments direct some effort to communicating information about their operations to the news media, which controls access to a mass audience.

Public relations has flourished in the United States because of the direct way the American political system and business world respond to public opinion. Politicians monitor opinion polls before announcing policies. Companies base their advertising campaigns on market research. Government agencies tailor their announcements for positive press coverage. Despite its sometimes tarnished image, public relations has prospered largely because it is so effective.

Author Doug Newsom notes this definition from the First World Assembly of Public Relations Associations, in 1978, as a reflection of the contemporary goals of institutional public relations:

The art and social science of analyzing trends, predicting their consequences, counseling organizational leaders and implementing planned programs of action which will serve both the organization and the public interest.

Critics of public relations and some journalists question whether this expressed dedication to the public interest is, in fact, mere public relations. Many argue that the goals of some organizations are often at odds with the public interest and usually dominate public relations activities.

This definition from the *American Heritage* dictionary adds another dimension to the goal of public relations: "The methods and activities employed by an individual, organization, corporation, or government to promote a favorable relationship with the public." Dispensing complete, timely and accurate information to the news media may not always be consistent with that goal.

It is worth noting that people who specialize in creating positive images for others have been unable to accomplish the same for themselves. Public relations has been called "a tool used by the untrustworthy to deceive the unwitting," and public opinion polls consistently show the public's distrust of PR practitioners. Public relations historian Alan R. Aucher observed:

> For many people "public relations" has continued to mean the opposite of truthfulness and genuine substance; a "public relations ploy" stands for the disingenuous and manipulated effort. Some critics have obviously feared that skillful propagandists would hold too great a sway over public opinion at the expense of substance and rational discourse.

Such suspicions are shared by many journalists. A 1991 survey of more than 2,000 journalists, conducted by a public relations firm, found that two-thirds did not trust public relations people. At the same time, four out of five acknowledged that they depend on them.

Conflict and Cooperation

The relationships between public relations agents and the news media are a curious mixture of friendships and animosities, cooperation and conflict.

Cooperation often stems from their shared backgrounds, interests and contacts.

- Many public relations practitioners are former journalists. Many organizations today continue to seek applicants for public relations jobs who have experience as reporters.
- Many public relations professionals have attended journalism schools and taken many of the same courses as journalists.
- Astute public relations people follow the news as closely as do most reporters and are familiar with current events. They travel in the same world as journalists, often attending the same professional meetings. News gatherers are comfortable with those who have these common threads of interest and awareness. Journalists at the management level often mingle with public relations counterparts at civic functions.
- The journalist's world, like that of the public relations person, includes relationships based on mutual need. This give-and-take behavior, "you do this for me and I'll do that for you," is common in the world of communications and depends on a delicate balance that serves both parties.

More to the point in explaining the relationship is the dissimilarity in roles. While both journalists and

Companies often stage elaborate presentations to explain their side of a story. Here, the manager of a pharmaceutical company tells reporters about plans to reduce the plant's toxic emissions.
Photo by William Burrows, courtesy of The Day, New London, Conn.

public relations agents are communicators, one represents a client or employer and the other sees his or her role as representing the public. So the reporter's perception of what is news may differ sharply from that of the public relations person.

Public relations specialists have grown increasingly sophisticated in achieving their goals. They understand the needs and weaknesses of the news business, and what reporters and editors consider newsworthy. They understand deadlines and the media's attraction to articulate spokesmen and spokeswomen, and they continually look for ways to present information or story ideas in an attractive and usable form.

They also are keenly aware that many reporters view them with suspicion or hostility. The most successful public relations specialists generally take a low-key approach, having learned that the most effective way to deal with reporters is to be available, knowledgeable and credible.

The facility with which a skilled public relations agent can supply useful information can be an attractive trap for the lazy or complacent reporter. The tendency to "go easy" on a valuable source or to succumb to subtle manipulation that allows the agent to shape a story or diffuse negative information is always a danger.

The public relations agent will seldom lie in response to a reporter's questions, but may not always volunteer the truth. If a reporter learns about information that was not disclosed by the public relations agent, the response may be "you didn't ask me."

Recognizing these problems, the reporter should set clear ground rules in an effort to maintain open lines of communication. Public information officers often can be helpful, if care is taken to avoid cluttering the news pages with unnecessary trivia that crowds out important stories.

Care also should be taken to avoid distortion through unchecked use of prepared materials such as news releases, taped interviews and photographs. Most packaged press material is prepared from the client's point of view rather than that of the journalist or the public.

The reporter should remember that public relations people serve two functions: to cultivate a positive image for their organization and to be a source of information. Within limits, this second function can assist the journalist, with pertinent questions answered, interviews arranged with key sources within the organization and much time saved in the process.

The Specter of Manipulation

Businesses, politicians and special-interest groups always have tried to get favorable publicity and diffuse negative stories. Press conferences, staged "pseudo events" passing as news and selective leaks to favored reporters are but a few of the tactics used to influence news coverage and public opinion.

Officials often inundate reporters with press handouts, hoping to keep them so busy they won't have time to dig up potentially damaging stories. All too often, some reporters are content to let these handouts meet their editor's demand for daily stories.

During the 1980s, the Reagan administration came under frequent criticism for its attempts to manipulate the press. Mark Hertsgaard, author of *On Bended Knee: The Press and the Reagan Presidency*, concluded that the news media frequently allowed the Reagan White House to shape the content of news stories, especially on television.

"Manipulating TV news coverage was a high priority for the Reagan public relations apparatus," Hertsgaard told *The New York Times*. "One of the distinguishing approaches to the Reagan strategy toward TV (was) manipulation by inundation. The Nixon people decided to keep information from the press but the Reagan people came to the opposite conclusion, that the networks would take what they fed them. Their attitude was that if you hand the networks a premasticated story each day, they'll go away."

News management continued in the Bush administration. In 1990, The Reporters Committee for Freedom of the Press, a Washington-based watchdog group, cited nearly 100 cases of "news orchestration, press restrictions and disinformation" by the Bush administration. One public relations gimmick backfired. During a 1989 television address to kick off his "War on Drugs," the president held up a bag of crack cocaine and asserted that it had been seized in a drug raid near the White House. The intended message was clear: If drugs were being sold so close to the president's home, no place in America was safe. Reporters soon discovered—and reported—that the White House had arranged the drug purchase to provide a prop for the president's speech.

The influence of public relations in news gathering is cause for concern among journalists. One frequently cited figure estimates that 40 percent of all news content originates with public relations specialists. In a survey of 2,432 journalists conducted in 1991 by a public relations firm, 38 percent said they receive half of their stories from public relations offices. The numbers were even higher in specialized areas such as entertainment (75 percent) and health (90 percent).

Wherever it exists, manipulation is a two-way street. If public relations efforts are able to obtain favorable publicity and slant news coverage, it is often because reporters gain something in the exchange. *Time* magazine described the relationship this way: "It is difficult to find heroes and villains. The journalistic world is not like some slave market, in which the roles of exploiter and exploited are clear-cut. It is more like a chaotic bazaar, filled with news peddlers trying to get public exposure and journalists seeking dramatic stories, quotes or facts."

Reporters must recognize and guard against manipulative tactics, and not relinquish news judgment to advocates for a cause or organization.

Packaging the News

The continued growth and influence of public relations escalated, not coincidentally, at a time when the size of news staffs was being reduced. The economic recession that began in the late 1980s saw cutbacks in the news operations of large and small outlets. Many of these operations began using more prepackaged public relations material in their stories, including news conferences and one-dimensional press announcements.

Scott Cutlip, a retired public relations teacher and journalism dean at the University of Georgia, argues that much packaged news content "goes through American journalism unfiltered" because "the news media are outnumbered and outgunned by the public relations industry in many forms." He notes that The Associated Press can afford to assign only one

reporter to the Pentagon, while the Department of Defense spends $50 million a year on public affairs and employs nearly 1,000 public information officers.

New technologies have created new opportunities for news packaging, such as high-tech video news releases (VNRs). These professionally prepared video clips created a stir in journalistic circles when they first appeared in the mid-1980s. Made to look and sound like news reports, they are produced entirely by public relations departments.

The *Columbia Journalism Review* noted the growing use of video news releases by many local television stations hit by newsroom cutbacks. When Northwest Airlines announced a ban on in-flight smoking, its public relations firm beamed its own VNR of the news conference around the country by satellite. According to the company's spokesman, more than 100 stations nationwide used some or all of the packaged story.

Most troubling about the video news releases was that many stations did not identify the source of the material, instead leaving the impression that the segments were prepared by news departments.

Video news releases soon spread to the government sector. Congressional press offices began producing their own VNRs and sending them to local stations back home that otherwise might not cover Congress. The press secretary for a North Carolina congressman, for example, explained that he used the video releases "to cut off bad publicity—to put our own spin on things." Some stations canceled their contracts with Washington-based news services and began using the video handouts instead.

These high-tech news releases succeed as a public relations device for the same reasons a well-prepared written release does: They meet the press' needs, are packaged in an easily used form, and are delivered—in this case by satellite—to satisfy tight news deadlines.

On the print side, the one-page news release is often supplanted by elaborate press kits containing background material, photographs, results from surveys and studies, and the names of sources to be interviewed. Some even contain story suggestions, sample questions and canned quotes from members of the organization.

Whether representing a hospital, corporation or special-interest group, most well-financed public relations departments produce these press kits. One pharmaceutical company supplies hefty "writer's guides" on topics such as arthritis, cancer, jet lag and panic disorders. The packets contain story suggestions, illustrations and detailed "backgrounders" written in news form. These backgrounders typically quote several scientists, including one or more from the company.

The potential problem with these modern publicity devices lies in the way the press uses them. Journalistic training stresses the need to use packaged information carefully, to avoid blatant promotion, to check information with outside sources, in short, to force the information through a sieve of independent judgment that serves the reader or viewer rather than the source of the information. Yet the temptation to use prepackaged information without exercising such judgment can be great when a deadline looms, the subject is technical or other sources are unavailable.

Public relations can provide a useful service. Reporters learn about interesting people and programs worthy of coverage, and viewpoints that might otherwise be missed are included in the dialogue on public issues. But when public relations attempts to manage or distort news content, the reporter must reject such efforts in the interest of readers and viewers.

Techniques of Manipulation

Young journalists must realize the potential for public relations efforts, both obvious and subtle, to influence what they report and write. While their jobs require that they develop professional relationships with these practitioners, reporters must be sufficiently informed and enterprising not to be unduly swayed by story ideas and news angles provided to them.

Understanding the strategies public relations people use to shape news coverage can help reporters guard against manipulation. While not all deceptive, these techniques have proved to be effective in influencing news coverage:

Spin Control.   An old idea, this attempt to influence the angle or lead of a story received a new name during the 1988 presidential campaign. After each campaign event, public relations specialists, nicknamed "spin doctors," rushed to supply reporters with an interpretation that reflected favorably on their candidate. Spokespersons representing a range of interests now attempt to put their own "spin" on a story, and negative stories are interpreted with a positive "spin" to neutralize their effect. To a spin doctor, the glass is never half empty, but half full.

Damage Control.   Public relations people prefer to call it "crisis management," taking steps to minimize adverse publicity from a negative event or development. Organizations confronted with an adverse story have learned that a "no comment" often hurts their credibility and image. A mayor facing a scandal in his administration or a manufacturer ordered to recall an unsafe product will take the initiative, often staging a dramatic announcement to diffuse negative publicity. The mayor may call for an internal investigation at a news conference. The product manufacturer may offer to replace the faulty product with a better model. Both are trying to create the impression they are taking effective and reasonable steps to solve the problem. Thorough reporting can place damage control tactics in their proper light and help assess if the announced actions are more show than substance.

Pre-empting Bad News.   A common public relations strategy is to head off negative publicity before it hits. A school system whose students score lowest in the state in reading skills may announce the hiring of reading specialists before test scores are released publicly. The effect of the low scores on public opinion may be dulled if it appears administrators recognize and are trying to correct the problem. The real question for a reporter, however, is when did administrators learn of the scores and why weren't steps taken sooner?

Controlled Timing.   Timing of news releases gets careful consideration. Sources may issue routine news releases on slow news days, knowing they will get better play. Positive news is released immediately, while negative information may be held until it is no longer newsworthy or its effect is dulled. A source also might issue a release just before a deadline, knowing that the reporter won't have time to confirm facts or call other sources.

Coaching Interviewees.   Just as lawyers coach their witnesses before testimony, media specialists instruct clients how to handle themselves during press interviews. Scientists, business executives and other experts are taught to relax and speak in plain language. Often the client wants a particular angle or theme to appear in a story and is shown how to promote that theme no matter what the line of questioning. The theory is that if a theme is pushed hard enough, a reporter will think it must be important or use it in the interest of fairness.

Exclusives and Leaks.   Reporters, especially those for influential news media, may be offered news tips or exclusive interviews with the unspoken understanding that a particular angle will be stressed in their story. If the angle doesn't appear, the flow of tips may stop. Such a system of rewards and punishments exists in many reporter-source relationships. The reporter who lets the lure of exclusives cloud his or her news judgment will soon lose the respect of peers and credibility with informed readers and viewers.

Staging and Pseudo-events.   Press conferences, speeches and protest rallies are often mere "pseudo-events," staged to provide an attractive visual setting for television and news photographers or to create an event that can be reported. A local officeholder disliked by environmentalists tours a scenic park on Earth Day, or a beleaguered school superintendent greets first-graders on the first day of school. While the news value may be negligible, reporters who have invested time and editors who expect the competition to report the story have difficulty ignoring these events. Reporters should scrutinize pseudo events for actual news value, and publish or air only material that meets the test.

Exercising Sound Judgment

On most public affairs beats, reporters face a steady stream of news releases, announcements and story ideas from public relations offices. A few guidelines can help the reporter exercise sound news judgment:

- Do background research to evaluate handouts for news content and distortion.
- Determine what is new in the information. If nothing is new, it is probably not newsworthy.

- Always rework prepared handouts to serve the reader or viewer's needs, not the source's.
- Check facts and statistics with other reliable sources.
- Avoid canned quotes; they are often created by the public relations person. If you need quotes, interview sources yourself.
- Avoid single-source stories. Seek outside comment from others to support and balance a story.
- Avoid pseudo-events and publicity stunts. Insist on knowing in advance what will be said or done.
- Don't rely on a small circle of public relations sources.
- Do your own legwork whenever possible and dig below the surface.
- Attempt to understand the source's motives in supplying the material or pushing a particular angle.
- Resist pressure to report incomplete stories or unverified information.
- Be cautious, relying on a healthy skepticism rather than cynicism.

Building Relationships

The best relationships between reporters and public relations agents are built on trust, respect and mutual need. These suggestions can help reporters develop an appropriate affiliation.

- Set the ground rules for the relationship early, recognizing that misunderstandings can lead to animosity. Always use an even-handed approach, avoiding threats or intimidation to obtain information.
- Determine how much authority your public relations source has to supply important information, then try to develop sources beyond that point, if necessary.
- Do not promise a public relations person something you might not be able to deliver, such as agreeing to place the emphasis in a sensitive story on certain points.
- Do not accept gifts in any form from public relations people, including such items as lunch or din-

ner. Pay your own way, or encourage your editor or publisher to pay it for you.

- Remember that public relations people can be helpful in cutting through red tape and supplying important information at deadline time. A "thank you" never hurts.

- You don't want your source to lie to you, so don't lie to him or her.

- Try to explain why you did not use information provided to you that created special problems for your source. Acknowledge receipt of special material, even though you may not be able to use it.

- Avoid violating confidences with public relations people and try to observe release dates, if the public interest will not be hurt. You should be the final judge.

ACCESS TO RECORDS AND MEETINGS

A reporter goes to jail. Police records and other important documents are locked away in government file drawers. Cameras and tape recorders aren't treated as equal to pens and pencils in the courts' eye. "Public servants" make critical decisions in private that affect thousands of lives. Sounds like a Freedom of Information report 20 years ago. It's not.

In the early 1990s, Frank Gibson, president of the Society of Professional Journalists, was sounding the alarm about growing threats to freedom of information and access to public records. Gibson, whose group publishes an annual update on Freedom of Information issues, pointed to a disturbing trend that threatened to reverse many of the gains achieved by journalists and others in opening the activities of public agencies to closer scrutiny.

The press, arguing that the public has a "right to know" about the operation of the government and its agents, has long advocated greater access to government information and legal protections for journalists gathering that information.

In the early 1970s, those efforts were bolstered by mounting public concern over government secrecy and corruption, triggered in part by disclosures involving the Vietnam War and the Watergate scandal. The federal Freedom of Information Act, enacted by Congress in 1966, was strengthened, and many states adopted their own versions of "sunshine laws" that provided unprecedented access to meetings of government bodies and files kept by public agencies.

The consequences of two decades of greater press access can be seen in the media every day: more personal information appearing about public officials and private citizens, everything from criminal records and tax information to the details of public figures' private lives. By the early 1990s, many journalists and advocates for greater access feared the pendulum of public opinion had begun to swing in the other direction, propelled by growing concern about such issues as privacy and victims rights.

Some public officials have seized upon public dissatisfaction with the press to argue for less, not more, public access. They have been successful in some cases, as press efforts to strengthen state and federal access laws have met stiff resistance. Although the battle over public access continues in the judicial system, state legislatures and the court of public opinion, Freedom of Information laws remain a powerful reporting tool.

Freedom of Information Laws at Work

Across the country, tucked away in government filing cabinets and computers, public records await the enterprising reporter who will tell their important and dramatic stories. These four news leads illustrate how reporters have used public records effectively:

The Department of Energy and its contractors virtually ignored warnings for six years that substandard bolts riddled its $7.5 billion nuclear weapons production complex, an internal investigation shows.

***

The Army says its soldiers committed at least 34 sex crimes in the Persian Gulf during Operations Desert Storm and Desert Shield, including rape and indecent assault against fellow U.S. soldiers.

***

Federal inspections are so sloppy that top-of-the-line "USDA Prime" and "USDA Choice" labels turn up in grocery meat cases on everything from cheaper cuts of beef to pig ears, feet and tails, a report shows.

***

The state is investigating black eyes, bruises and "other major injuries of unknown origin" inflicted on mentally retarded residents of a state hospital, apparently by workers.

Each story was based on a public document obtained through federal or state Freedom of Information laws. Although not every report holds such dramatic findings, the reporter who knows where to look and how to ask for public records will find a wealth of material.

Studies show that commercial users, public-interest groups, scholars and prisoners often outpace journalists in filing Freedom of Information requests. Journalists often debate the value of state and federal open-records laws in news gathering, and some argue that long delays and bureaucratic resistance often make using the laws impractical for daily reporting.

Still, the very existence of Freedom of Information laws has forced much previously hidden information into the public domain. And despite the time-consuming correspondence and expense involved, FOI laws have proved essential to reporters trying to monitor the inner workings of government.

Whether it is to support conclusions or identify important trends, reporters frequently use government statistics, court records and other public documents on daily stories and long-term projects.

FOI Laws and Breaking News

After the arrest of Los Angeles police officers in the 1991 beating of motorist Rodney King, U.S. Attorney General Dick Thornburgh announced a nationwide review of police brutality cases by the U.S. Department of Justice. Within a few days, *The Dallas Morning News* had obtained investigative data under the federal FOIA showing that from 1984 to 1989, the Justice Department had investigated 2,015 reported cases of police brutality in Texas, the highest in the country.

The report was picked up by other news media, who quickly examined the figures to produce stories with a local angle. Rhode Island, for example, had just 230

brutality investigations, but that number amounted to nearly 25 for each 100,000 residents, giving it the second highest rate in the country. With their own news hook, reporters interviewed police officials, the local U.S. Attorney and the American Civil Liberties Union to add context to the raw figures.

> In a letter to the U.S. Attorney General, ACLU Director Steven Brown said, "The public has a right to know why the number of complaints of police abuse in this state are so high and why the prosecution rate for such misconduct remains so low."
>
> U.S. Attorney Lincoln C. Almond said, however, that the public should not jump to conclusions.
>
> "It's very difficult to make anything of them," Almond said. "It's very easy to make a complaint in Rhode Island. It's a small state. In some states you have to drive three or four hours to get to the nearest FBI office to file a complaint."

Loopholes and Exemptions

Every Freedom of Information law exempts some records. Most laws specify that all records should be open unless specifically exempted. However, many categories of exempt files are broadly worded and often open to different interpretations by journalists and officials who control their release. Key categories of exemption:

- Personal information about individuals, such as confidential medical files, tax returns or other records whose release might invade someone's privacy.

- Interagency communications, but not internal and external policies.

- Active law enforcement investigations.

- Records of pending claims and litigation. (Some records may be available to reporters from court files.)

Reporters should become familiar with the wording of FOI laws in their states to understand specific exemptions.

FOI laws often give officials wide latitude to edit reports and black out names of individuals before making them public. Although there is a legitimate need in some cases to protect the privacy of individuals, some officials use the provisions to censor material

that should be public. The released version may effectively sanitize the report, eliminating newsworthy
information or diffusing accountability. Some officials
edit liberally, either content to let the courts decide a
legal challenge or confident that reporters won't file a
lawsuit.

Three months after *The Providence Journal-Bulletin*
requested a report about alleged abuses by National
Guard officers, the report was released—but heavily
censored.

> The Army has investigated allegations that senior
> National Guard officers engaged in sexual harassment,
> falsified travel records and wore unauthorized medals,
> according to a report Monday.
>   An edited version of the report showed the investi-
> gation looked into allegations of sexual harassment of a
> female soldier while under the influence of alcohol; fal-
> sifying travel records, including the personal use of
> Frequent Flyer miles accumulated on military business;
> and using an alias when traveling.

The story then reported the many unanswered questions raised by the edited version.

> It was unclear whether the investigation found any of
> the allegations to be true. The version had the names
> of those investigated blacked out, along with the rec-
> ommendations and conclusions of the investigation.
>   The Army general counsel's office refused to release
> the unedited version, saying the Freedom of
> Information Act allows the Army to withhold informa-
> tion that would invade the privacy of Army personnel.

Not satisfied with the edited version, the newspaper
filed a lawsuit under the federal FOI act to force the
Army to release more details.

Agencies will sometimes go to elaborate lengths to
avoid releasing material. Information about applicants
for top government jobs from police chiefs to school
superintendents often is withheld with the argument
that people would be discouraged from applying if
their names and qualifications became public.
Journalists make the counterargument that the public
is closed out of the process and only learns of candidates' qualifications after a decision.

In South Carolina, school boards used a different
twist to dodge FOI requests about candidates for

superintendent. They hired the South Carolina School
Boards Association, a trade group, to conduct
searches and retain all files. The schools insisted that
the association is not a government agency and not
bound by the state's FOI law. *The Sun News* in Myrtle
Beach filed a lawsuit to obtain the records and prevent
future violations, arguing that the association was subject to the open-records law because it received and
spent public funds. As the lawsuit moved slowly
through the court system in 1993, school boards
around the state continued to conduct hiring searches
through the association and private consultants.

Court challenges of this type are sometimes necessary to clarify the law and to establish whether a particular organization is subject to it. Cases decided in
favor of the press also serve to keep others from trying
similar tactics.

The Federal Act

The federal FOIA outlines procedures for requesting
material, appeal routes and costs for searching and
duplicating. Federal agencies take differing paths in
implementing the act. Some, such as the Justice
Department and Securities and Exchange
Commission, have set up specific departments to
locate requested information and to decide whether to
release it. Other agencies maintain traditional procedures, leaving press offices to respond to requests.

A telephone call or visit to the agency is the first
step. Many federal records are kept at regional offices,
and the reporter must be able to describe the information well enough that a clerk can identify the material.
Sometimes an official will reject a telephone request
and order that it be made in writing. Calling first may
provide some idea of how long and expensive the
search will be.

Each agency is allowed to assess "reasonable standard charges" for document searches and duplication.
To save time and money, some reporters inspect documents in person. Many agencies provide space where
reporters can work, and sometimes they will duplicate
a small amount of material for free.

The act specifically exempts some information, such
as executive orders classified as secret "in the interest

of national defense or foreign policy." However, the act specifies that the courts will decide whether such a claim is justified.

Other exempt documents include those related solely to internal personnel rules and practices of an agency, trade secrets of private industry, personnel and medical files, and those specifically exempt from disclosure by statutes other than the Freedom of Information Act, such as Internal Revenue Service regulations.

FIGURE 19–1

Sample State FOI Request Letter

Date

Name of Agency or Official
Title
Name of Agency
Address
City, State, Zip

Dear _____:

Under the provisions of the (name of state) Freedom of Information Act, I am requesting access to *(identify the records as clearly and specifically as possible).*

Optional: I am requesting this information because *(state the reason for your request if you think it will assist you in obtaining the information).*

If there are any fees for searching for, or copying, the records I have requested, please inform me before you fill the request. (*Or . . .* please supply the records without informing me if the fees do not exceed $_____.)

As you know, the Act permits you to reduce or waive the fees when the release of the information is considered as "primarily benefiting the public." I believe that this request fits that category and I therefore ask that you waive any fees.

If all or part of this request is denied, please cite the specific exemption(s) that you think justifies your refusal to release the information and inform me of your agency's administrative appeal procedures available to me under the law.

I would appreciate your handling this request as quickly as possible, and I look forward to hearing from you within *(number of)* working days, as the law stipulates.

Sincerely,

(Signature)
Name
Address
City, State, Zip

Also exempt are records of investigations by law enforcement agencies, to the extent that their release would interfere with one in progress or deprive a person of a fair trial. However, the burden is on the government to prove that the documents were compiled for law enforcement purposes.

Details of the Freedom of Information Act, along with specific government agencies which deal with it,

FIGURE 19–2

Sample State FOI Appeal Letter

Date

Name of Agency or Official
Title
Name of Agency
Address
City, State, Zip

Dear _____:

This is to appeal the denial of my request for information pursuant to the (name of state) Freedom of Information Act.

(Select one)

   A. On *(date)*, I received a letter from *(individual's name)* of your agency denying my request for access to *(description of the information sought)*. I am enclosing a copy of this denial along with a copy of my original request. I trust that upon examination of these communications you will conclude that the information I am seeking should be disclosed.

   B. On *(date)* I submitted a request for access to *(description of the information sought)*. Since your agency has not responded within the *(number of days)* deadline stipulated in the state law, I am considering the request denied. I trust that upon examination of these communications you will conclude that the information I am seeking should be disclosed.

   As provided for in the Act, I will expect to receive a reply within *(number of)* working days, as the law stipulates.

Optional: If you decide not to release the requested information, I plan to take this matter to court *(or appropriate state commission)*.

Optional: It is sometimes helpful to set out some of your legal arguments in your administrative appeal. Otherwise, all that the appeal authority has is the denial authority as argument.

Sincerely,

(Signature)
Name
Address
City, State, Zip

are published widely, including in the U.S. Government Manual.

How to File an FOIA Request

These suggestions were adapted from a user's guide to filing an FOIA request produced by the Freedom of Information Clearinghouse in Washington, D.C. Although it is designed for using the federal FOIA, its suggestions can be adapted for filing requests with most state agencies in charge of releasing public records (see Figure 19–1).

Getting Started.   The first step is to determine what you want, because the law requires that your request "reasonably describe" the records you seek. You must request records describing a particular subject in sufficient detail that a government employee can find the records.

The next step is to determine which agency has the information and the address of the office that processes Freedom of Information Act requests.

- Your request should state it is being made pursuant to the Freedom of Information Act (5 U.S.C, Sec. 552).
- You should write "Freedom of Information Request" on the envelope and on the letter.
- You should follow up your request with a phone call.

Under the FOIA, an agency may deny your request only if the documents are specifically covered by one of the act's exemptions. Moreover, agencies may release records even though they are covered by an exemption.

Getting Computer Data.   The law makes no provision for access to electronic records. If you want records in a form other than paper, specify your wishes as precisely as possible. Practices differ for each agency. (Details about gaining access to state and federal computer records are outlined in Chapter 3.)

How to Appeal.   If your request is partially or entirely denied, you have the right to appeal. The denial form should inform you of appeal procedures. Your appeal

letter should include a description of your request, a copy of your request and a statement indicating that you are appealing the agency's decision (see Figure 19–2).

Time Deadlines.   The law sets specific deadlines for replying to FOIA requests: 10 working days on the initial request and 20 working days on an appeal. Delay is common but if an agency fails to respond on time, you may consider the request denied and appeal or sue.

Costs.   Fees depend upon who is requesting the information. Commercial users pay standard search and copy charges, but educational or noncommercial scientific institutions and the media may only be charged for reasonable duplication costs. To save money, you may ask to see the documents themselves instead of having copies made.

You may be entitled to a waiver or reduction of fees if "disclosure of the information is in the public interest because it is likely to contribute significantly to public understanding of the operations or activities of the government and is not primarily in the commercial interests of the requester."

Going to Court.   If your appeal is denied, you may sue in U.S. District Court. If the government can't prove the documents are exempt, the court will order the agency to surrender them.

Open Meeting Laws

The scope and limits of open-meeting laws vary greatly from one state to another, but generally their intent is to ensure that public bodies discuss and decide most matters during an open session. Laws broadly define what constitutes a meeting and a public body, and specify how notice of meetings is to be posted.

State legislatures, city councils and zoning commissions are clearly public bodies, while political party caucuses and administrative staff meetings are not. However, there are many gray areas. The law is often vague about whether meetings of quasi-government agencies such as bridge authorities and fire districts or publicly funded community service groups are public, and journalists sometimes must take the question to court.

A meeting is generally defined as a gathering of more than half a body's members to discuss a matter over which it has authority. Agencies are usually required to post notice of regular meetings in a public place, and some must make an agenda available to the public 24 hours in advance. Emergency meetings are exempt from such requirements.

Before the passage of open-meeting laws, some officials made a practice of convening secret or informal meetings, gathering at a local tavern or a member's home to discuss matters before a regularly scheduled session.

Today, such gatherings violate the spirit and sometimes the letter of the law, and are less frequent than they once were. However, officials intent on conducting business in secret will find ways to do so. A board chairman may poll individual members by telephone or small groups of members may meet privately, with representatives of each group gathering later, again in private, to hammer out details. A court challenge may be necessary to halt such practices. Another solution is to write about them. A reporter who documents efforts to circumvent open-meeting laws may find adverse publicity is enough to curtail them.

Most laws allow boards to close their meetings for specific reasons but they must publicly vote to do so and state the reason. Many reporters avoid using the bureaucratic euphemism "executive session" to describe portions of meetings that exclude the public, calling them simply "closed meetings."

The most common reasons given by officials for closing meetings are to discuss "personnel matters," "negotiation" and "litigation." Each category has a legitimate application under the law, but some officials interpret them broadly to cover any potentially sensitive matter. A closed meeting with a school teacher whose classroom antics have prompted complaints from parents may be acceptable for a school board, but private discussions of a superintendent's job evaluation might not be. Courts considering such distinctions tend to weigh the privacy concerns against the legitimate public interest in the information.

Some states require that agencies be specific about litigation or negotiations—purchase of land for a new school, for example, or a discrimination lawsuit against the city—so the public and press can ascertain if the session is being closed legally.

Reporters should become familiar with specific wording about exemptions in their states and understand how the law has previously been applied to these broad terms. A reporter who thinks a meeting is being closed illegally can make a formal protest and ask that it be noted in the meeting's minutes. Then if a lawsuit is filed, the board will have difficulty proving it had no idea it was acting illegally.

Many statutes specify that a written record of a closed session be kept, usually a general description of what matters were discussed. Those records are usually exempt from disclosure, at least until the matter is no longer sensitive.

Appealing possible violations of open-meeting laws can be time-consuming, frustrating and expensive. A few states have commissions that arbitrate disputes and can fine public bodies for violations. Elsewhere, written complaints can be filed with an attorney general authorized under the law to sue an offending agency. In most states, however, news outlets and private citizens must file their own lawsuits. While suing won't produce information for an immediate story, it may, if successful, deter the board from future illegal closures and set a precedent for other cases.

Sources of FOIA Information

Several national organizations and most state press groups are useful sources of information about FOI laws and recent revisions.

The Society of Professional Journalists' "Annual FOI Report" gives a summary of open-records and open-meeting laws by state, along with names and telephone numbers of contact people. The Reporters Committee for Freedom of the Press publishes *Tapping Official's Secrets*, a comprehensive, state-by-state compendium of FOI laws. The committee also has a toll-free hotline, 800-FFOI-AID. The University of Missouri's Freedom of Information Center operates its own hotline at 314-882-4856.

The Freedom of Information Clearinghouse, P.O. Box 19367, Washington, D.C. 20036, is another good source of current information.

A 22-page booklet called "Access to Campus Crime Reports" is published by the Student Press Law Center, 1735 Eye Street NW, Suite 504, Washington, D.C.

***
SUGGESTED READINGS

Blyskal, Jeff, and Marie Blyskal. *PR: How the Public Relations Industry Writes the News*. New York: William Morrow and Co., 1986.

This book is highly critical of the public relations industry's ability to control and manipulate news media coverage. Focuses on well-publicized cases and interviews with journalists and practitioners.

Dorsen, Norman, and Stephen Gillers, eds. *None of Your Business*. New York: Viking, 1974.

Recommended is "The Secrets of Local Government," by M.L. Stein.

Dunn, Delmar D. *Public Officials and the Press*. Reading, Mass.: Addison-Wesley, 1969.

Chapter 5, "Public Officials' Views of the Press."

Newsom, Doug, Alan Scott, and Judy Vanslyke Turk. *This is PR: The Realities of Public Relations*. Belmont, Calif.: Wadsworth Publishing Co., 1989.

Chapter 2 offers a useful history of public relations, while Chapter 10 focuses on techniques for understanding and working with the news media. A useful text for understanding the role and practice of public relations.

Ott, Richard. *Creating Demand*. Richmond, Va.: Business One, 1991.

Intended for a business audience, this book describes how businesses can prevent negative publicity and obtain positive news coverage. Useful background for reporters.

Safire, William. *Before the Fall*. Garden City, N.Y.: Doubleday, 1975.

Chapter 5, "The Press is the Enemy."

Ullmann, John, and Jan Colbert, eds. *The Reporter's Handbook*. New York: St. Martin's Press, 1991.

A publication of Investigative Reporters and Editors. Chapter 4 focuses on using Freedom of Information laws.

Chapter 20

Privacy and the Media

- A family bereaved by the loss of a child in a street murder is photographed at a private funeral. The pictures are published in the next day's newspaper.

- A reporter joins angry tenants in eavesdropping on a landlord they have charged with violating housing agreements, and airs a news story based on the resulting information.

- The mayor's two teen-age sons are arrested and charged with using marijuana. Two young friends with them also are arrested. The newspaper and the local TV stations use the names of all four juveniles.

Decisions on stories like these are made daily, indicating the thin line between the press' right to speak (or the public's right to know), as defined by the U.S. Constitution, and the individual's right to privacy.

When is the legitimate right to be left alone compromised by the public's equally legitimate right to know the facts? The journalist may argue that a congressman forfeits his right to privacy when he runs for public office. A similar argument could be made for the spouse of an influential public figure.

An editor might contend that politicians should be held to an exacting standard because they are inclined to preach morality, such as "family values," in one form or another. Therefore, the editor says, their morality becomes the public's business.

A civil rights advocate might argue that the right to privacy exists despite that fact, and many of the congressman's constituents will contend he has the same right to privacy that they do. The courts increasingly are being asked to determine these issues.

Beyond the courts, however, lie important ethical considerations. Journalistic codes adopted by some news organizations mention the need to respect the rights of people involved in the news and to observe common standards of decency.

But the subject of an "expose" might argue with equal fervor that the press traditionally has failed to observe these standards in pursuit of "hot" stories.

THE 'PUBLIC FIGURE'

Resolution of some of these questions lies in the definition of *public figure*. The U.S. Supreme Court has ruled that the determination of a public figure is always factual and limited to two types:

1. People who occupy positions of such pervasive power and influence that they are deemed public figures for all purposes, or people who are "intimately involved in the resolution of important public questions."
2. Otherwise private individuals who have voluntarily entered a significant public controversy to influence the resolution of the issues involved.

The bereaved family, the landlord who was bugged, and the jailed juveniles cannot be cast in either of these molds, the courts have agreed. Nevertheless, their actions, conversations and records are in the public domain.

The child's funeral, although private, has become a "public" event because of the circumstances surround-

ing the death. Each newspaper and television station will use or not use its photos based on its guidelines for newsworthiness.

Similar guidelines will apply to the landlord whose privacy has been breached, and to the jailed juveniles. If the stories are sufficiently important, they will be used. But in all three cases, editors will discuss the ethical guidelines they might have in place to further evaluate use of the material.

The journalist actually confronts two problems in this sensitive area of privacy:

1. How and when should the press report on legitimate public figures? Does a legislator who is prone to indulge in extramarital flings have a right to privacy if the practice does not affect his handling of the job? Does the relative of a public figure have a right to privacy, if only out of common decency? Are the hours that a celebrity spends outside the public eye his or her own business?
2. How much should the press report on people who may not be legitimate public figures and who may have a greater right to privacy? A person on a public payroll or a person caught up in a newsworthy event may not always be a public figure.

Two Sets of Limits

Compounding these two problems are two sets of "limits" with which the reporter must constantly grapple:

1. The legal limits, as defined by common law and statute, of a person's right to privacy.
2. The ethical limits to those rights, as defined by the public's perception of the limits and by the journalist's obligation to be fair and understanding, while observing the common standards of decency.

Some of the answers are to be found in the press' perception of its right to probe for confidential information and publish it. Other answers hinge on government, which in this country reflects the public will. Still other answers depend on the public itself, which often speaks up when privacy crosses the line into secrecy. And some answers, of course, depend upon the judicial process, which is subject to constantly shifting opinions.

LEGAL LIMITS

It is easier to distinguish these constitutional guarantees through the legal process. While it is too simplistic to argue that the public's right to know extends to anything that the press cannot be sued for, this approach tends to represent the practical application of privacy rights as they exist today.

If a reporter or editor believes that information lies in the public domain and is in the public interest to reveal, it is published. Then begins the process of determining through the courts whether the right to privacy actually exists in a specific area.

A newspaper publisher filed a lawsuit against a magazine writer, charging defamation of character in an article published in a national magazine. However, the publisher withdrew his action when the court ruled that he was a public figure. The effect of that ruling was to generally place newspaper publishers in the role of public figures, and future actions will be decided on that premise.

In some cases, the journalist can successfully argue that some people become public figures unwillingly, through events that are thrust upon them. So members of the bereaved family, whatever the standards of common decency, become public figures through an act of providence. Such figures cannot rely on the legal process to protect them; rather, they must rely on the standards of decency and good taste.

Public figures are saddled with a heavier burden of proof than are private individuals. Any official on a public payroll must claim this heavier burden. So must a private contractor who does consulting work for a public agency. An official for a private agency such as the United Way or the Better Business Bureau loses some of his or her privacy by dealing with the public. There is no question that the director of a local health agency qualifies as a public figure, but the status of her subordinates is more questionable—depending on their visibility and the news being generated.

The grief of people touched by tragedy provides drama to news accounts, but journalists must balance the public's interest against an individual's right to privacy. Here, a clergyman consoles a young woman waiting to learn if a loved one was among those killed when a building under construction collapsed in Bridgeport, Conn.

Photo by Robert Patterson, courtesy of The Day, New London, Conn.

But it must be remembered that in cases of public and private persons, while truth is a solid defense for journalists against libel actions, this is not necessarily so in a lawsuit for invasion of privacy.

Growth of Privacy Claims

During the past 30 years, journalists have watched the U.S. Supreme Court grapple with the shifting laws of privacy, in an effort to reconcile them with the rights of the press. Communication lawyers warned in the 1980s that increasing demands for privacy legislation would lead to a growing number of civil claims against the press. Since that time, dozens of courts throughout the United States have been confronted with claims, some for the first time.

The growth of sophisticated communications has led to new interpretations of the right to privacy. In his book *The Assault on Privacy,* Arthur R. Miller discusses the natural limitations on privacy invasion before the turn of the century:

> Snooping in the days before mass circulation newspapers, radio, television, computers, or even telephones, was inhibited by the natural limitations of the human eye, ear, voice and memory.

But the picture was changing dramatically:

> As larger amounts of information began to be gathered and circulated to wider audiences, the chances that those receiving it would have direct knowledge about the subject or be able to test the truth of what they heard or read decreased, while the likelihood that the printed or spoken word would be accepted as truth increased.

It is not surprising, Miller noted, that the law began to entertain second thoughts about recognizing a right to resort to the courts to protect individual privacy.

Development of Privacy Rights

Ironically, what was perceived as excess by the press before 1900 led to the idea that individuals have an interest in privacy, which the courts have some obligation to protect. In Boston at the time, newspapers vividly described parties given by socially prominent citizens of the city. Two young law partners, Samuel D.

Warren and Louis D. Brandeis, who was later to become a justice of the Supreme Court, produced an article in the *Harvard Law Review* in 1890 complaining that the press had served "idle and prurient curiosity" in its accounts, overstepping the bounds of propriety and decency.

Warren and Brandeis argued that recognition of a right to privacy was essential to protect individuals from "mental pain and distress far greater than could be inflicted by mere bodily injury." They warned that recent innovations, particularly photography and mass-circulation newspapers, presented grave new threats to personal privacy:

> Gossip is no longer the resource of the idle and of the vicious, but has become a trade, which is pursued with industry as well as effrontery.

There was widespread support for the writers' contentions, but its acceptance through the statutory process was slow. Now, a century later, some states have adopted legislation specifically protecting individuals, although nearly all the states recognize the right as common law. While the dimensions of protection vary from state to state, the law has become fairly standardized within clear boundaries.

The Common Law of Privacy

Invasion of privacy, and the growth of protection for individuals who consider themselves wronged, can be separated into four basic areas: disclosure of truthful but embarrassing facts, placing a person in a false light, intrusion, and misappropriation. Some are more important to the reporter than others, but all are relevant to the press.

To many, the vast collections of records maintained on individuals are cause for serious concern, one that spills over into the area of mass communication. In a comment on this country's diminishing right to privacy, California Judge Leonard M. Friedman noted:

> Our nation's current social developments harbor insidious evolutionary forces which propel us toward a collective, Orwellian society. One of the features of that society is the utter destruction of all privacy, the individual's complete exposure to the all-seeing, all-powerful state. Government agencies, civilian and military,

federal, state, and local, have acquired miles and acres of files, enclosing revelations of the personal affairs and conditions of millions of private individuals. Credit agencies and other business enterprises assemble similar collections. Microfilm and electronic tape facilitate the storage of private facts on an enormous scale. Computers permit automated retrieval and dissemination. These vast repositories of personal information may easily be assembled into millions of dossiers characteristic of a police state. Our age is one of shriveled privacy.

Collection of private facts is a touchy area for the media. A misstep on the part of a reporter or photographer, whether unintentional or deliberate, can result in judicial action with expensive consequences. So long as the action is perceived as an invasion of privacy, there is danger of retaliation in the form of a lawsuit. The journalist should remain abreast of developments in this area of the law.

Disclosure of Truthful but Embarrassing Private Facts

Michael Virgil, a well-known sports figure, told a reporter for *Sports Illustrated* magazine about his hobbies—putting out lighted cigarettes in his mouth, eating spiders and diving down flights of stairs to impress women. He later decided, however, that he did not want the information made public. The magazine went ahead and published an article about Virgil, and he sued for invasion of privacy.

In ruling against the surfer in 1975, the U.S. Court of Appeals said a publication cannot be found liable for publishing a truthful description of private facts about a person in the news because such facts are "newsworthy." However, the court warned, "the line is to be drawn when the publicity ceases to be the giving of information to which the public is entitled and becomes a morbid and sensational prying into private lives for its own sake, with which a reasonable member of the public, with decent standards, would say that he had no concern."

To win an invasion of privacy lawsuit, a person must prove that the published material:

1. Would be highly offensive to a reasonable person, that is, embarrassing to that person;

2. Is not of legitimate concern to the public, that is, not newsworthy; and

3. Was published without the person's consent.

Many courts have specified that public figures also must prove actual malice.

For the reporter, then, the problem is determining whether the material can be construed as being of legitimate public interest. Fortunately for the press, the courts have generally deferred to the media view of what constitutes newsworthy material or is in the public interest to disseminate.

And while truth is not a defense in a privacy issue, the existence of a public record usually prevents recovery for invasion of privacy. If a matter is public record, such as a birth or marriage date, or an official court record, its publication usually escapes successful lawsuits against the publication.

Embarrassing facts about a public official, for example, might be defended on the basis that the official's place on the public payroll entitles the public to some information which might not be similarly considered if the individual were in the private sector.

While college athletes have been ruled public figures, privacy laws prevent officials and teachers from disclosing academic grades to reporters. If such records are leaked to reporters, the reporters will use them, and that use has been upheld in privacy cases. The now-defunct *Washington Star* and the University of Maryland student newspaper were sued for $72 million for invasion of privacy because of articles the two papers published about basketball players' academic problems. The private facts claim was dismissed by the court.

The question often hinges on whether a person is considered a public figure. Merely being on the public payroll as mentioned earlier does not automatically place an individual in the public domain. That person must put himself or herself into the public limelight.

For example, a public schoolteacher might lead a quiet private life but is suddenly thrust into the public eye when he has a sex change operation. A reasonably anonymous college professor might mount a soap box in defense of free choice. The distinction quickly becomes clear in these cases, but others are not so easy to categorize.

The key for the journalist is care. The protection of newsworthiness tends to evaporate if carelessness or deliberate misrepresentation can be proven.

False Light

Making individuals appear to be something they are not, even if it is not defamatory, is considered "putting the plaintiff in a false position in the public eye" and has proven costly to some publications.

Identifying a person at a rally as a supporter of the political figure present, when the person had merely stopped at the rally out of curiosity, puts the person in a false light and creates a climate for court action.

For a basic false light claim to be pursued, these factors must be present:

1. The material in question is false;

2. The material has been published without the complainant's consent;

3. In cases involving public figures, there was actual malice or reckless disregard for the truth.

False light is often confused with libel, but the two are distinguishable. Libel implies damage to a person's reputation, while false light does not. As in the case of the bystander at the political rally, an individual may be cast in a false light without being defamed.

A photograph of a woman taken in an Alabama funhouse with her skirt blown up over her head was accurate, but she charged it placed her moral character in question. Even the photographer who snaps an innocuous picture of a young woman jumping over a rain puddle on a downtown street runs the risk of court action if it is an awkward or revealing pose.

Intrusion

A third area of invasion of privacy is intrusion, which has generally been defined as "physical" invasion of an individual's privacy. There must be some kind of trespass without consent, but the area is a sensitive one for the journalist. If the reporter or photographer has successfully obtained someone's consent, or even the clear implication of consent, there should be no problem. The act of intrusion, rather than publication of the material, is the basis for this privacy claim,

although some courts have not always made the distinction.

Modern technology has expanded the scope of such lawsuits in recent years. Peeking into windows and hiding behind doors are only traditional examples of intrusion. Use of sophisticated long-range telephoto lenses on cameras and electronic recording devices that can be carried in a pocket have brought intrusion claims. So has unauthorized use of private documents.

The courts have generally ruled that it is not an invasion of privacy to take a picture in a public place, but private property is another matter. Climbing a telephone pole to peer into a private window has been ruled an invasion of a person's privacy.

Taking microphones or other wiretapping equipment into a person's house without his or her consent also is considered intrusion. Furthermore, state and federal statutes prohibit wiretapping.

The courts have ruled that the press is protected when it publishes information obtained from someone else who invaded an individual's privacy, but the reporter who encourages or helps another to invade a private area without consent also may be held liable. The issue of trespass has been clouded by the reporter's physical presence on the scene.

A staffer employed by U.S. Sen. Thomas Dodd provided copies of private documents to the late columnist Drew Pearson, and the material was subsequently published. Even though Pearson knew the documents were stolen, the publication of the material did not constitute an action for trespass, because the journalist did not participate in the unlawful reproduction of the documents.

Despite the 1974 federal privacy act's protection of the confidential records of students, the lawsuit against the *Star* and the University of Maryland student newspaper for intrusion was dismissed on the ground that the material was gratuitously obtained from an unidentified source. The reporters had not inspected, solicited or authorized inspection of confidential files.

There is no unanimity on what is considered a "public place," where trespassing cannot be claimed, and jurisdictions have ruled differently. Neither is there unanimity on what constitutes a "private place." Some courts have given reporters protection when covering police raids on private property and in reporting fires and other disasters.

This issue was placed in somewhat clearer focus in 1977, when the Florida Supreme Court ruled in favor of a photographer who had been invited to join police officials in a tour of a burned house in which a young girl had died. While in the house, the photographer took several pictures, including one of a silhouette remaining on the floor after the body had been removed. The girl's mother sued for trespass after the picture was published, charging invasion of privacy and intentional infliction of emotional distress.

The defendant, the Florida Publishing Co., claimed that its photographer was acting in accordance with press custom in covering a newsworthy event. While the court ruled in favor of the press, it noted that the customary right of entry vanishes when one is informed "not to enter at that time by the owner or possessor or by their direction." Left unanswered was the liability had the reporter and photographer been specifically directed by the distraught family not to enter the house.

In another trespassing lawsuit, a New York state judge ruled against a television news crew after the crew, without permission, entered a New York City restaurant that had been charged with city code violations. The judge ruled that "the right to publish does not include the right to break and enter, or the right to invade or otherwise to enter upon and trespass upon the property of these plaintiffs (the restaurant)."

The courts also have distinguished between private and public officials when surreptitious surveillance has been involved.

A man accused of practicing medicine without a license was secretly photographed by a couple posing as a patient and her husband. The couple also carried a hidden transmitter so police nearby could record the conversation. The material was published in *Life* magazine, and the action was ruled an intrusion of privacy.

In a 1971 decision, an appeals court agreed the story was newsworthy, but that the eavesdropping constituted an invasion of privacy.

However, a television reporter's secret filming of a police officer's undercover investigation of a massage parlor did not constitute intrusion in view of the public interest in the officer's conduct. The court carefully distinguished the police officer's role as a public official.

Misappropriation

Anyone who appropriates the name or likeness of another for his or her own benefit is subject to a lawsuit for invasion of privacy. A variety of court cases in recent years suggests that the cause for action has moved substantially beyond the mere application of a person's name or likeness.

The four factors necessary for a successful appropriation claim are publication, identification, commercial gain and lack of consent. While advertisements using a person's name or picture without permission have been the most common basis for claims, news operations also are targets.

The U.S. Supreme Court has ruled that the First Amendment to the Constitution does not protect the press from liability for broadcasting a performer's act as a news report.

On the other hand, an actress' claim that her photo on the cover of a magazine which contained a story about her invaded her privacy was dismissed. Another claim, that a private individual viewing a public parade as a spectator was entitled to damages because written consent was not obtained, was denied by the courts.

Privacy Legislation

During recent years, many of the states have enacted statutes protecting people from invasion of privacy. Thirty-eight states recognize as actionable the disclosure of truthful but embarrassing facts. Thirty-one states recognize false light claims, and thirty-nine recognize claims for intrusion. Thirty-eight states recognize the right to protect one's name or likeness against misappropriation by others.

One of the major statutory directions of individual rights has come at the federal level, mainly in the Privacy Act of 1974 and accompanying amendments designed to protect the privacy of students and parents in public schools.

The legislation was enacted by Congress to counter harm to individual privacy from the increasing use of computers and sophisticated information technology.

The law gives individuals the right to inspect records maintained on them by most federal agencies through establishment of a code of fair information practices for use of government records.

Most federal agencies must now obtain written permission before releasing an individual's records for anything but routine use or to anyone other than law enforcement officials. Federal employees are subject to criminal penalties for releasing personal information or records without permission from the person in question. The act also placed limitations on the use of Social Security numbers as personal identifiers.

Congress later enacted the Family Educational Rights and Privacy Act, which protects the privacy of parents and schoolchildren. The act generally ensures access to school records by parents and students but denies such access to others. Written permission must be obtained from the student or the parents to obtain access to information. There are exceptions—school officials of the institution where the records are maintained and those considering a student's application for financial aid.

Consent is not required to disclose information to groups conducting educational studies if the student will not be identified in the reports or conclusions. If it is necessary to protect the health and safety of the student or others, however, identifying information may be disclosed. And student "directory information" may be provided to the press and public, unless the student or parent requests that it be withheld. This information includes the student's name, address, telephone number, date and place of birth, major field of study, participation in officially recognized activities, height and weight if an athlete, dates of attendance and awards received, and the most recent school attended.

But while the legislation protects the privacy of individuals, it also has the effect of limiting access of the press to educational information. An athlete with academic problems, for example, may be threatened with suspension from a team; yet little or none of this kind of information may be officially supplied.

Another changing statutory area deals with information that journalists traditionally have considered public—police and court records of adults. Most states have enacted statutes providing that public records of arrests and convictions can be sealed or expunged under some circumstances. The laws generally cover persons with long-ago convictions who are considered rehabilitated, and those who were arrested but never convicted.

Many journalists see such statutes as restrictions on freedom of the press. Should they be denied the right to inform the public that a candidate for public office once was convicted of embezzlement? Or that a candidate for a day-care center directorship once was arrested on a charge of child molestation, but never taken to court?

Sealed records also can hinder a reporter who is assessing the performance of police, judges and prosecutors. Some state courts have ruled that arrest records, including a police department's daily arrest log or "blotter," continues to be public record. But some courts have ruled that a court clerk does not have to make it easier for a reporter to see alphabetically filed case files containing arrest and disposition records.

DEFENSES AGAINST PRIVACY CHARGES

The best defense in invasion of privacy cases continues to be the concept of newsworthiness. Two other useful defenses have emerged for the press:

1. Convincing the judiciary that a person is a legitimate public figure and thus newsworthy in his or her own right.

2. Consent by a person to have his or her privacy invaded.

Newsworthiness

No two journalists agree on the definition of newsworthiness, and the courts are equally divided. One court has defined news as "that indefinable quality of information which arouses public attention." Journalists have often insisted that news is whatever interests people. Within this loosely drawn concept, the courts have tended to accept journalists' definitions of news.

People who seek public office or any kind of celebrity status, willingly placing themselves in the public limelight, have generally been found by the courts to have given up to some extent their right to be left alone. Such people—actors, politicians, athletes or explorers—have made themselves newsworthy and have given up their privacy.

Some, however, are caught up in the news as unwilling participants, when they would prefer the anonymity of private citizens. But in such cases, the courts generally have ruled that such people cannot recover damages in cases of public interest and in which the accounts of the event have been accurate.

The courts also have ruled that persons who are essentially private figures lose their right to anonymity when they seek redress through the courts. Substantially accurate accounts taken from the public record have been ruled in the public domain as well as pertinent photographic coverage and other details of the case.

The privilege of newsworthiness occasionally has been attacked on the basis that passage of time has eliminated the news element. While the event may have constituted legitimate news when it occurred years before, it is now out of the public limelight and thus is a private affair. Used by itself, however, the time lapse argument has generally failed to stand up to the basic argument of newsworthiness.

Recent decisions of the Supreme Court have narrowed the definition of a public figure who has been out of the public eye for a long time. The court ruled in 1979 that a reclusive plaintiff who had been convicted of contempt of court in 1958 was not a public figure for purposes of a 1974 court action. Some justices relied on the passage of time, finding that the plaintiff had acquired public figure status in 1958 but had lost it by 1974.

The courts have generally relied upon Time Inc. vs. Hill (in 1967) as a standard for the defense of newsworthiness. The case stemmed from a *Life* magazine article about a play based on a book about a family held hostage in its home by escaped convicts. The article said the novel was inspired by the true-to-life ordeal of the James Hill family in 1955.

Hill sued under New York State privacy statutes, alleging that the article was intended to give the impression that the play mirrored the Hill family's experiences. The magazine knew this was false, Hill argued, but still referred to the play as a re-enactment of the Hill family ordeal.

Hill won the lawsuit, but the magazine successfully appealed to the U.S. Supreme Court. The court ruled that the Constitution prevented applying the New York privacy statute in matters of public interest "in the absence of proof that the defendant published the report with knowledge of its falsity or in reckless disregard for the truth." However, the protection of newsworthiness can suddenly disappear if carelessness can be proved.

Consent of Parties Involved

For the defense of consent by the party involved to stand up in court, the consent must be proved by the defendant in an action, and the consent must be as broad as the invasion of privacy. A young man had consented to have his picture taken, ostensibly for a story about the World Series. *Front Page Detective* magazine used the photograph, however, to illustrate an article titled "Gang Boy." Courts allowed the photographed person to recover damages, ruling that consent to one thing is not necessarily consent to another.

The best course is to obtain a signed release, something that many subjects are not always willing to provide to a reporter. Good intentions are not necessarily a good defense, and a reporter may honestly believe that he or she had implicit consent from a person to invade that person's privacy. Without clear and specified consent, however, the danger will always be present. The reporter should remember that the burden of proof will be on him or her to show just what the plaintiff in an action consented to.

Journalists should not take excessive comfort in the defenses of either newsworthiness or consent. Both remain subject to the perception of judge and jury.

ETHICAL LIMITS

The legal limits to privacy are constantly changing, and the ethical limits, which are more subjective, are even more difficult to pin down. Often the limits depend on the reporter's perception of what is news, but more often social fabric of a community helps to determine those limits.

Ethics, the discipline dealing with the ideas of "good," "bad" and "moral duty," puts a special responsibility on the journalist. The community plays an important part in setting the ground rules concerning privacy. The reporter must think not only about the legal limitations in pursuing a sensitive story, but also about the ethical ramifications when making decisions to print or broadcast material that invades a person's privacy.

It is basically accepted that people do have a right to privacy and that the public does have a right to be informed about issues that concern it. The basic questions then become: What do people have a right to know? When do they have a right to know it and in what form should it be presented? How much do they have a right to know before it becomes merely a prurient interest in the affairs of others?

To draw from an example, a mayor is considered a public figure, yet many people believe he is entitled to some privacy. While his public duties are subject to constant scrutiny, his private life usually remains private. However, one night, the mayor becomes involved in an altercation at a tavern. Police are called but no charges are filed. While no one will discuss the incident "for the record," a persistent reporter uncovers the details. Does this public official still have the right to privacy in this instance?

A motorcyclist is struck and critically injured by a piece of concrete thrown from an overpass. A 15-year-old boy is arrested and charged with felonious assault. While the charge is considered public record, many newspapers will withhold the juvenile's name. In this case, however, the local newspaper decided to identify the boy, using the seriousness of the charge as a guide.

Newspaper policy traditionally has been to withhold the name of a person who has been criminally assaulted, even though police and court documents place them in the public domain. The trial of boxer Mike Tyson offers one of the most visible examples of this policy.

INDIANAPOLIS—Mike Tyson testified in his rape trial Friday that he and a teen-age beauty contestant made love in his hotel room. He insisted that he didn't force her, and said she never protested.

"I didn't violate her in any way," Tyson said. "She never told me to stop, or I was hurting her, nothing."

In accordance with generally accepted policy, the press chose not to identify the rape victim. Only after Tyson's conviction did the victim step forward and identify herself.

In another celebrated case, most newspapers maintained the anonymity of the woman who had charged William Kennedy Smith with rape in West Palm Beach in 1991. There were some exceptions, including a supermarket tabloid, *The Globe*, which identified the woman. The tabloid was prosecuted under a Florida law barring the news media from identifying sex crime victims, but a judge ruled the law was unconstitutional. Only after Smith was acquitted by a jury did the woman identify herself to the press.

After the tabloid published the woman's name, *The New York Times* and NBC television news identified her. Most other newspapers did not follow suit, and the controversy over publication of a plaintiff's identity in rape cases continues.

Editors and news directors are divided over the issue, calling it a matter of judgment. The prevailing view has been that there is a stigma in being a rape victim that makes it incumbent on news organizations to respect the victim's privacy. However, that view may be changing.

The emergence of AIDS (acquired immune deficiency syndrome) as a worldwide medical problem has posed special problems for the media in the area of privacy. The disease has been associated with sexual practices among homosexual men and sharing of contaminated syringes by intravenous drug users. It also is spread in other ways—by dentists who acquired the disease, and through medical procedures.

Black tennis star and author Arthur Ashe lived privately with the AIDS virus for four years before being forced to go public in 1992. Ashe feared his privacy would be lost forever, afraid that he would be branded a "leper of the '90s."

A reporter for *USA Today* called Ashe to confirm he had AIDS, and Ashe chose to call a news conference to announce it himself. Despite the announcement, the press was criticized for invading Ashe's privacy. One editor argued that the former tennis star had become a "private man," despite the books he had written and his frequent appearances in public life.

But for a figure as public as Ashe, the media rules are reasonably clear: No matter that he had contracted AIDS through surgery; his privacy was gone forever. Most major newspapers played the Ashe story prominently, with comments about the likelihood of contracting the virus through blood transfusions. In this way, the health issue became a major part of the story.

Said one editor: "Probably the interest was heightened because the disease was AIDS. But even if Arthur Ashe had bone cancer, I think we would have covered it."

Newspapers and broadcast outlets also grapple with the AIDS issue on the local level.

- How to handle with sensitivity a story about a teenager who has contracted the virus through sexual contact and wants to go public with it?

- How much to publish about a victim of AIDS who has died a violent and public death or for that matter, someone who simply was well-known?

- How to protect the privacy of AIDS victims who are about to testify in court against a person who has deliberately infected them with the virus.

- What focus to take when a leading composer, diagnosed with AIDS two years ago, contracts to sing in a fund-raiser for AIDS victims, but prefers to focus on the performance rather than the ravages of the disease.

Most editors and news directors wrestle with privacy decisions every day, and believe that each one has to be judged on its merits. While no blanket policy is possible, guidelines can help in making difficult decisions:

1. The journalist has a duty to tell the truth, yet maintain concern for the consequences of disclosure. Consideration should be given to possible good and possible harm.

2. Is this something that affects the public? If so, it should be reported, albeit with sensitivity. If legitimate news value is involved, the issue becomes simpler.

3. When there is danger that privacy becomes secrecy, the decision to publish becomes clearer.

Reporters should be sure they are seriously appraising each case, rather than adhering rigidly to simplistic rules that excuse them from giving any thought to the ethical value of the argument.

When citing "the public's right to know," journalists must not confuse information that serves the public interest with details that the public is merely curious about.

Legitimate Public Figures

It is always easier to make privacy decisions about public figures, those who occupy the positions of pervasive power and influence or those who thrust themselves into the public eye.

The press, however, has been ambivalent in its coverage of the purely personal affairs of such public figures. Until recent years, the press has overlooked many of their foibles. One powerful congressman's problems with alcoholism, for example, were well-known for years but went unpublicized until after his death. Another congressman's well-known alliance with a nightclub entertainer was the subject of much talk in the nation's capital, but it did not break into print until a minor traffic infraction created news coverage that ultimately resulted in the official's resignation from office. The late President Kennedy's personal friendships with a number of women were not unknown to many reporters, yet they went unreported until long after his death in 1963.

No consensus exists for covering political figures today, especially those running for office. Close scrutiny of character is common, but the propriety of exploring a politician's sexual habits remains a subject of intense debate. In 1988, presidential candidate Gary Hart engaged in a risky liaison with a woman not his wife, prompting questions about his judgment. Newspapers, including an investigative team from *The Miami Herald*, produced extensive stories about the liaison, and Hart was forced out of the race. There was considerable soul-searching in 1992, mostly after the fact, about handling Gennifer Flowers' charges that she had a 12-year affair with presidential candidate Bill Clinton. Clinton denied it, but admitted his marriage has had troubled periods.

Sen. Brock Adams (D-Wash.) was accused of sexually harassing and physically molesting female employees over two decades. The women, fearful of the public spotlight, all spoke to *The Seattle Times* on condition their names not be used, but agreed to sign statements attesting to the truth of their stories. The disclosures followed public statements of one woman, who identified herself.

Adams called the news accounts "the worst kind of journalism, anonymous vilification," but they ended his bid for re-election.

One way to lessen the effect of such a story with "prurient" overtones is to explain to readers or viewers that invading the person's privacy in this case served the legitimate public interest in the personal conduct of a candidate for high office. An expert often can be found to help make the point. Another useful device to balance the effect of privacy invasion is a sidebar story or occasional column explaining how such stories are serving the public interest.

The reporter may find it easier to make a case for publicizing an illness or a liaison that offers potential conflict of interest for an officeholder, but the difficult cases remain. Who is qualified to decide whether a messy divorce, late-night partying, a child's misstep or psychiatric treatment in a private hospital facility affects a public official's fulfillment of his or her duties.

Questionable Public Figures

An official hired to administer a county office may qualify as a public figure because he or she is on the public payroll, yet maintain a certain right to privacy because there is no effort to seek the limelight. The spouse and child of a public official may not seek the public eye, and may not even campaign for the candidate, yet are considered to be public figures. However, they too have a right to a degree of privacy.

Other public positions also are difficult to categorize:

- A certified public accountant volunteered to perform accounting work for a political committee in 1971. An erroneous report that the accountant's firm was a "laundering agency" for political money resulted in a libel lawsuit. However, the court granted the defendant's request to drop the case, deciding that no malice was involved and that the

accountant had thrust himself into the public eye by volunteering to assist the political committee.

- The noted Firestone case has narrowed the court's protection of the press in the area of privacy:

  Mrs. Russel Firestone, wife of the heir to the tire fortune, had filed a lawsuit against *Time* magazine after the publication reported in 1967 that she had been divorced "on grounds of extreme cruelty and adultery." The magazine also noted, "According to certain testimony in behalf of Mr. Firestone, extramarital escapades of Mrs. Firestone were bizarre and of an amatory nature that would have made Dr. Freud's hair curl."

  After losing a Florida court decision to Mrs. Firestone, *Time* appealed to the U.S. Supreme Court, contending that she was a public figure, which would obligate Mrs. Firestone to prove that the magazine was guilty of "actual malice" as well as inaccuracy. *Time* contended that Mrs. Firestone had conducted press conferences during the divorce proceedings and subscribed to a press clipping service, further enhancing her status as a public figure.

  The court, however, decided for Mrs. Firestone, ruling that she had a right to sue *Time* because she had merely exercised her privilege as a private person of going to court for a divorce. The Firestone case indicates the murkiness of the privacy waters for reporters trying to draw a line on legitimate privacy.

Purely private figures such as business owners often can be construed as affecting the public interest in their roles. The industrialist who operates a huge plant in a city may become a subject of public debate when his actions in closing part of the operation affect the tax structure of the community. How far is the reporter justified in personally pursuing the industrialist to complete the story? The press often can make a good case for pursuit of people operating in the private sector because of the involvement in the business, financial or industrial structure of the city.

David Shaw, media writer for the *Los Angeles Times*, has raised pointed questions about public figures:

Is it a legitimate news story when Doris Day's son files for divorce? Or when (former Vice President) Spiro Agnew's son is arrested on charges of voyeurism? What about when Los Angeles Mayor Tom Bradley's daughter and Jerry Lewis' son are arrested on relatively minor drug charges?

Many respected newspapers all across America printed these stories—because the stories involved the offspring of celebrities. Stories about divorce, suicide, voyeurism and routine drug cases rarely are published if they involve the children of truck drivers, waitresses or bank tellers.

Many editors, Shaw wrote, wonder whether such celebrity stories constitute an unwarranted invasion of privacy for both parent and child, but there are no rules to go by. Almost every case, an ethics committee convened by the American Society of Newspaper Editors decided, had to be judged on its own merits. There was no broad consensus.

Danger Zones

Some areas of reporting pose more problems than others. Here are a few that require extra thought as well as sensitivity:

- **Divorce and custody cases.** A husband charges that his wife took their children and deserted him after he suffered permanent disability in an accident. The mother of a missing child accuses her ex-husband of kidnapping their children. Custody cases are often bitterly contested in the courts, and the reporter must be sensitive in dealing with those that are newsworthy.

- **Illness and death.** Health problems can create privacy problems for people otherwise deemed private citizens. A mother's dating habits causes a son's suicide, and the reporter must decide how much information to provide. After a father is charged with sexually abusing his child, the reporter will effectively identify the alleged victim by publishing the father's name.

- **Resurrecting old stories and facts.** A rehabilitated convict is entitled to some measure of privacy. But the problem goes beyond the courts. An embarrassing incident that occurred years ago and is resurrected can cause new pain for someone who only wants to forget it. Old photos also should be used with care.

- **Police statements.** Invasion of privacy only intensifies grief, and the police beat is one example of a sensitive and changing area. A woman was accosted by a gunman who climbed into her car, drove her miles away and freed her. He left with the car and her purse. The incident was listed on the police report, but the woman's husband asked editors to keep her name and address out of the news story. In this case, the editors complied and decided to review their guidelines on use of such information.

Some editors believe all such facts should be printed, while others avoid publishing the names of crime victims. Still others are struggling with the murky line that is drawn when the victim is the spouse of a prominent citizen.

Police actions often create a climate in which privacy is inadvertently invaded. The reporter believes, and usually rightly so, that identification should be made when an official charge is brought against someone. But sometimes the need for withholding a person's identification overrides the need for the public to know.

The Journalist's Responsibility

In the end, the responsibility for making such decisions rests with the reporter and editor, who must exercise good taste, judgment and restraint.

The statement of principles adopted by the American Society of Newspaper Editors places on newspaper people a "particular responsibility":

> Journalism demands of its practitioners not only industry and knowledge, but also the pursuit of a standard of integrity proportionate to the journalist's singular obligation.

Under a section on fair play, the statement places this additional responsibility on the reporter:

> Journalists should respect the rights of people involved in the news, observe the common standards of decency and stand accountable to the public for the fairness and accuracy of their news reports.

While these principles are general, their use as guidelines is unquestioned. Such a yardstick can help the public affairs reporter resolve an ethical question and do the right thing.

✳✳✳

SUGGESTED READINGS

Miller, Arthur. *The Assault on Privacy*. Ann Arbor, Mich.: University of Michigan Press, 1971.

Shaw, David. *Journalism Today*. New York: Harper, 1977.

Chapter 1, "Public Figures, Private Lives."

Practising Law Institute. *Communications Law*.

A reference manual produced annually. Special sections on development of privacy law.

Citations

Where appropriate, bibliographic entries include notations in parentheses citing specific chapters where material was used.

Books

Aspen Notebook on Government and The Media, ed. by William L. Rivers and Michael J. Nyhan. New York: Praeger, 1973. (Chapter 19).

Biagi, Shirley. *Interviews that Work*. Belmont, Calif.: Wadsworth Publishing Co., 1992. (Chapter 2).

Blyskal, Jeff, and Marie Blyskal. *PR: How the Public Relations Industry Writes the News*. New York: William Morrow and Co., 1986. (Chapter 19).

Bollens, John C. *Special District Governments in the United States*. Westport, Conn.: Greenwood Press, 1978. (Chapter 7).

Chase, Stuart, and F.J. Schlink. *Your Money's Worth: A Study in the Waste of the Consumer's Dollar*. New York: The Macmillan Co., 1927. (Chapter 15).

Chemicals, The Press and the Public, ed. by Bud Ward. Washington, D.C.: Environmental Health Center, 1989. (Chapter 17).

Cohn, Victor. *Reporting on Risk: Getting It Right in an Age of Risk*. Washington, D.C.: The Media Institute, 1990. (Chapter 18).

Covering the Environment, Gannett Center Journal, ed. by Everette E. Dennis and Craig L. LaMay. New York: Gannett Center for Media Studies, Summer 1990. (Chapter 17).

Federal Regulatory Directory. Washington, D.C.: Congressional Quarterly, 1990. (Chapter 8).

Gallup, George Jr., et al. *Politics and the Press*, ed. by Richard L. Lee. Washington, D.C.: Acropolis Books, 1970. (Chapter 14).

Gans, Herbert J. *Deciding What's News*. New York: Pantheon Books, 1974. (Chapter 19).

Gans, Herbert J. *The Levittowners: Ways of Life and Politics in a New Suburban Community*. New York: Pantheon Books, 1967. (Chapter 19).

Ghiglione, Loren. *The American Journalist, Paradox of the Press*. Washington, D.C.: The Library of Congress, 1990. (Chapters 1, 2).

Gilbertson, H.S. *The County: The "Dark Continent" of American Politics*. New York: National Short Ballot Organization, 1917. (Chapter 7).

Gulick, Luther H. *The Metropolitan Problem and American Ideas*. New York: Knopf, 1962. (Chapter 7).

Hage, George, et al. *New Strategies for Public Affairs Reporting*. Englewood Cliffs, N.J.: Prentice Hall, 1983. (Chapter 1).

Herbers, John. *No Thank You, Mr. President*. New York: Norton, 1976. (Chapter 8).

Investigative Reporters and Editors. *The Reporter's Handbook*, ed. by John Ullmann and Jan Colbert. New York: St. Martin's Press, 1991. (Chapters 2, 3, 8).

Jaspin, Elliot G. *Out with the Paper Chase, In with the Database*. Gannett Center for Media Studies, 1989. (Chapter 3).

Kessler, Lauren, and Duncan McDonald. *The Search: Information Gathering for the Mass Media*. Belmont, Calif.: Wadsworth, 1992.

Killenberg, George M., and Rob Anderson. *Before the Story*. New York: St. Martin's Press, 1989.

Klaidman, Stephen. *Health in the Headlines*. New York: Oxford University Press, 1991. (Chapter 18).

Kotulak, Ronald. "Sorting Through the Chaff." *Health Risks and the Press*, ed. by Mike Moore. Washington, D.C.: The Media Institute, 1989. (Chapter 18).

MacDougall, Curtis D. *Interpretative Reporting*. New York: Macmillan Publishing Co., 1977.

Mencher, Melvin. *News Reporting and Writing*. Dubuque, Iowa: Wm. C. Brown Publishers, 1991.

Mencken, H.L. *A Carnival of Buncombe*. Baltimore, Md.: The Johns Hopkins Press, 1956. (Chapter 14).

Meyer, Philip. *The New Precision Journalism*. Bloomington: Indiana University Press, 1991. (Chapter 3).

Nader, Ralph. *Unsafe at any Speed: The Designed-in Dangers of the American Automobile*. New York: Grossman, 1965. (Chapter 15).

Newsom, Doug, Alan Scott, and Judy Vanslyke Turk. *This is PR: The Realities of Public Relations*. Belmont, Calif.: Wadsworth Publishing Co. 1989. (Chapter 19).

Peters, Charles. *How Washington Really Works*. Reading, Mass.: Addison Wesley Publishing Co., 1992. (Chapter 8).

Petulla, Joseph M. *Environmental Protection in the United States*. San Francisco: San Francisco Study Center, 1987. (Chapter 17).

Rivers, William L. *The Adversaries*. Boston: Beacon Press, 1970. (Chapter 19).

Rosenbaum, Walter A. *Environmental Politics and Policy*. Washington, D.C.: CQ Press, 1991. (Chapter 17).

Scientists and Journalists: Reporting Science as News, ed. by Sharon M. Friedman, Sharon Dunwoody and Carol L. Rogers. New York: The Free Press, 1986. (Chapter 18).

Shaw, David. *Journalism Today: A Changing Press for a Changing America*. New York: Harper's College Press, 1977. (Chapter 20).

Sigal, Leon V. *Reporters and Officials: The Organization and Politics of Newsmaking*. Lexington, Mass.: D.C. Heath, 1973. (Chapter 19).

Sinclair, Upton. *The Jungle*. New York: New American Library, 1960. (Chapter 15).

Smith, Charles W. *Public Opinion in a Democracy*. New York: Prentice Hall, 1942. (Chapter 14).

Smith, Robert G. *Public Authorities, Special Districts and Local Government*. Washington, D.C.: National Association of Counties Research Foundation, 1964. (Chapter 7).

A Treasury of Great Reporting, ed. by Louis L. Snyder and Richard B. Morris, New York: Simon and Schuster, 1949. (Chapter 1).

Walker, Stanley. *City Editor*. New York: Blue Ribbon Books, 1938. (Chapter 19).

Weaver, David H., and G. Cleveland Wilhoit. *Newsroom Guide to Polls and Surveys*. Bloomington: Indiana University Press, 1990. (Chapter 3).

Journals and Periodicals

Access. The University of Connecticut, January 1992. (Chapter 3).

"AIDS Coverage in the 1990s: The Second Decade." Freedom Forum Media Studies Center, Special Report, July 4, 1991. (Chapter 18).

AP Log. The Associated Press, Sept. 16, 1985. (Chapter 18).

Bailey, Jeff. "How Two Industries Created a Fresh Spin on the Dioxin Debate." *The Wall Street Journal*, February 20, 1992. (Chapter 17).

"Big Cities Lag in Clean Air, U.S. says." The Associated Press, Aug. 17, 1990. (Chapter 17).

Bland, Dorothy. "Computers Can Turn Ordinary Reporters into Super Sleuths." *ASNE Bulletin*, January–February 1991. (Chapter 3).

Bukro, Casey, and Stevenson Swanson. "Ecology Special Report, 1991." *Chicago Tribune*, Nov. 17, 1991. (Chapter 17).

Casey, Mike. "Lives on the Line: Analyzing OSHA's Database." *IRE Journal*, January–February 1992. (Chapter 3).

Chatters, Carl H. "Another Point of View—A Comment on the Foregoing Paper." *The American City*, February 1955. (Chapter 7).

Collins, Mary. "News of the Congress, By the Congress." *Washington Journalism Review*, June 1990. (Chapter 19).

Cose, Ellis. "Shopping in the News Bazaar." *Time*, March 26, 1990. (Chapter 19).

"Covering AIDS: It's Not Just Another Story." *SIPIScope*, Winter 1988. (Chapter 18).

Cutlip, Scott M. "Public Relations: The Manufacture of Opinion." *Gannett Center Journal*, Winter 1990. (Chapter 19).

"Downgrading the 'Authorities'," (editorial). *The American City*, November 1956. (Chapter 7).

Findlay, Steven, and Joanne Silberner. "What the Press Release Left Out." *U.S. News and World Report*, March 21, 1988. (Chapter 9).

Gibson, Frank. *Annual FOI Report*. The Society of Professional Journalists, 1990–1991. (Chapter 19).

Gulick, Luther. "Developments in Public Administration." *Public Administration Review*, 1961. (Chapter 7).

Hampson, Rick. "PR-Journalists Survey." The Associated Press, Sept. 2, 1991. (Chapter 19).

Hilts, Philip J. "U.S. Aides Retreat on Wetlands Rules." *The New York Times*, Nov. 23, 1991. (Chapter 17).

Hunter, Margaret. "Writers Score with Databases." *Folio*, May 1989. (Chapter 3).

Jaspin, Elliot G. "Just do it!" *ANSE Bulletin*, December 1991. (Chapter 3).

Johnson, J.T. "The Unconscious Fraud of Journalism Education." *The Quill*, June 1992. (Chapter 3).

Kettleborough, Charles. *The American Political Science Review*, November 1914. (Chapter 7).

Kranhold, Kathryn. "National Panel Presses for Standards in 'DNA Typing,' but Backs Court Use." *The Hartford Courant*, April 15, 1992. (Chapter 18).

Kristol, Irving. "The 'Adversary' Role." *Editor and Publisher*, March 5, 1977. (Chapter 19).

Krumenaker, Lawrence. "Get A Clue." *The Quill*, June 1992. (Chapter 3).

Leonard, Teresa. "Databases in the Newsroom." *Online*, May 1992. (Chapter 3).

Lowenberg, Paul. "The Research University: A Rich but Tricky Resource." *The Journalist*, Fall 1985. (Chapter 18).

Miller, Tim. "The Data-base Revolution." *Columbia Journalism Review*, September-October 1988. (Chapter 3).

Montez, Abel. "Computer Age Poses New Obstacles, New Options." *Annual FOI Report*, The Society of Professional Journalists, 1989–1990. (Chapter 3).

National Municipal Review, November 1933. (Chapter 7).

Nelkin, Dorothy. "Science and the Media: Uneasy Relationship." *The Boston Globe*, May 14, 1984. (Chapter 18).

Newfield, Jack. "The Abuse of Authority." *Village Voice*, March 29, 1983. (Chapter 7).

Ott, Richard. "Both Sides of the Media." *Nation's Business*, May 1992. (Chapter 19).

Pfretzchner, Paul. *The American City*, August 1957. (Chapter 7).

"Private Governments," *Forbes*, Oct. 2, 1978. (Chapter 7).

Raeburn, Paul. "Widely Used Heart Drug is Linked to Sudden Death." The Associated Press, Nov. 13, 1991. (Chapter 18).

Raucher, Alan R. "Public Relations in Business: A Business of Public Relations." *Public Relations Review*, Fall 1990. (Chapter 19).

Regan, Mary Beth. "EPA Has Given Up on Some Toxic-Waste Sites." *Orlando Sentinel*, July 23, 1992. (Chapter 17).

"Reporting on AIDS." *ASNE Bulletin*, April 1986. (Chapter 18).

Ripley, Jim. "In Dayton, Ohio, Reporters in the Newsroom Can Access County Records with a Few Keystrokes." *ASNE Bulletin*, December 1991. (Chapter 3).

Rosenau, Neal. "After the Cutbacks: What's the Damage to Local TV News?" *Columbia Journalism Review*, September–October 1988. (Chapter 19).

Schramm, Carl. "A Regulatory Approach to Health Care Costs." *The Journalist*, Fall 1985. (Chapter 18).

Schulte, Fred. "Tracking Bad Cops." *IRE Journal*, November–December 1991. (Chapter 3).

Shaw, David. "Coloring the News." *The Quill*, May 1991. (Chapter 1).

Sibbison, Jim. "Dead Fish and Red Herrings: How the EPA Pollutes the News." *Columbia Journalism Review*, November–December 1988. (Chapter 17).

Siegel, David. "No News Isn't Good News: Effective Public Relations." *NASSP Bulletin*, January 1989. (Chapter 19).

Smith, Sylvia. "Bradlee Speaks." *ASNE Bulletin*, September 1991. (Chapter 2).

"20 Years on the Beat." *SIPIscope*, Spring 1990. (Chapter 17).

"250-Plus Registrants Mark First SEJ National Conference." *Environment Writer*, October 1991. (Chapter 17).

Ullmann, John. "Tapping the Electronic Library." *IRE Journal*, Summer 1983. (Chapter 3).

Weintraub, Tina. "The 'Authority' in Pennsylvania, Pro and Con." *Bureau of Municipal Research*, 1949. (Chapter 7).

Whisnant, Elizabeth. Four-part series, *News and Tech*, April–July 1991. (Chapter 3).

"White House and News." *The New York Times*, Aug. 25, 1988. (Chapter 19).

Winsten, Jay A. "Science and the Media: The Boundaries of Truth." *Health Affairs*, Spring 1985. (Chapter 18).

Index

ISBN 0-02-408042-X

90000>

9 780024 080424